COMPUTER GRAPHICS DICTIONARY

COMPUTER GRAPHICS DICTIONARY

edited by

Roger T. Stevens

CHARLES RIVER MEDIA, INC.
Hingham, Massachusetts

Publisher: David F. Pallai
Production: Publishers' Design & Production Services, Inc.
Cover Design: The Printed Image

CHARLES RIVER MEDIA, INC.
20 Downer Avenue, Suite 3
Hingham, Massachusetts 02043
781-740-0400
781-740-8816 (FAX)
info@charlesriver.com
www.charlesriver.com

This book is printed on acid-free paper.

Roger Stevens. *Computer Graphics Dictionary*.
ISBN: 1-58450-019-0

Library of Congress Cataloging-in-Publication Data

Stevens, Roger T., 1927-
   Computer graphics dictionary / Roger T. Stevens.— 1st ed.
     p.   cm.
   ISBN 1-58450-019-0
   1. Computer graphics—Dictionaries.   I. Title.
   T385 .S772 2001
   006.6'03—dc21

                            2001005473

Printed in the United States of America
02 7 6 5 4 3 2 First Edition

INTRODUCTION

The popularity of special effects movies and the video game industry has introduced thousands of new terms, techniques, and software applications to both the computing professional and the general user. Unfortunately, these graphics creations represent a convergence of expertise from several different subject areas, resulting in a lack of familiarity with many terms. This unique dictionary includes over 4,000 definitions and illustrations from the computer graphics world, including the following subjects:

- Animation
- Mathematics
- Artificial Intelligence
- Game Programming
- Game Design
- Fractals
- Wireless Communication
- Networking
- Video/Filmmaking
- Digital Photography
- 3D Lighting
- Facial Animation
- Modeling
- Photorealism

SELECTED APPLICATIONS

Just as many terms are specific to a particular subject area, some terms are specific to certain software applications and are therefore usually neglected in general computer science dictionaries. The refined focus of this dictionary on the world of computer graphics allows for detailed coverage of terms and features that relate to the following applications:

- Poser
- Universe
- Game Creation System
- LightWave
- trueSpace
- form•Z
- Adobe Acrobat
- Bryce
- The Games Factory
- Final Cut Pro
- Photoshop
- Carrara
- Java
- 3ds max
- Cinema 4D XL

Software applications are identified in the text with italics and are alphabetized by product name rather than company name. In many cases, cross-references have been included at the company name, especially when the company name is actually part of the formal name of the product. For example, the definition for **Adobe Photoshop** appears at **Photoshop**, by which it is more commonly known. A cross-reference for the term (See *Photoshop*) appears at **Adobe Photoshop.**

FORMAT OF ENTRIES

Entries are presented in a consistent format throughout the dictionary. First, the term is provided (in boldface), followed by any abbreviation of the term (in parentheses, also in boldface), when appropriate. The term is followed by its definition (in plain text) and ends with any cross-references (in italics) to other terms that may provide more information on the topic. In some cases, a cross-reference substitutes for a definition, directing the reader to another entry that defines the term.

Figures appear close to the term to which they apply, usually on the same page. Each figure has a caption that identifies the term to which it corresponds.

Many terms have additional material or full color versions of figures on the companion CD-ROM. These terms feature a CD icon 💿 at the end of the entry.

ORDER OF PRESENTATION

Entries are presented in alphabetical order, letter-by-letter, ignoring spaces and all other characters that are neither letters nor numbers. For example, *analogous colors* falls between *analog digitizers* and *analog RGB monitor*, and *active-surface table* falls between *active subtree* and *active values*.

Terms that begin with numbers or symbols are grouped in the "#" section at the beginning of the book and are listed in ascending ASCII order. Terms that begin with a letter, but contain a number, are first listed alphabetically, then according to ascending ASCII order when a number is encountered.

As a rule, acronyms are defined where the term is spelled out, with cross-references at the acronym itself. Some exceptions have been made for terms that are known almost solely by their acronyms. In these cases, the spelled-out terms and definitions are provided at their respective acronyms.

ABOUT THE CD-ROM

The companion CD-ROM contains over a thousand items that supplement the illustrations and definitions in the text. These items include graphics, source code, animations, additional figures, and full color versions of the figures that appear in the text.

A CD icon ⬤ in the text indicates a CD file or folder that corresponds with a specific entry. The folder or file name on the CD is identical to the term to which it corresponds. CD entries are organized similar to their textual counterparts, grouped alphabetically within folders for A-Z and #.

SYSTEM REQUIREMENTS

Certain files on the CD-ROM may only run on their intended platrforms (e.g., Macintosh or Windows), and/or their intended application may be needed to run the files (e.g., Bryce, Universe, etc.). You must "unzip" the applications folders to view all of the files. Files must be saved to a folder on your desktop before being opened. Some items may rely upon other files (found in the same folder in which the items appear) in order to open. We recommend saving the entire contents of each folder to a new folder on your desktop before opening them.

WINDOWS: Windows 95 or higher, Pentium System, 32MB RAM, 200mHZ or faster, Web browser (Internet Explorer 4 or later, or Netscape Navigator 4.0 or later), full color monitor, CD-ROM drive, mouse or compatible pointing device.

MACINTOSH: PowerMac G3 or better running system 8.0 or higher, 32MB RAM, Web browser (Internet Explorer 4 or later, or Netscape Navigator 4.0 or later), full color monitor, CD-ROM drive, mouse or compatible pointing device.

The files on the companion CD-ROM are saved in a wide variety of formats. Files should be opened from within appropriate applications. Viewing some files will require additional applications not included on the CD.

ABOUT THE EDITOR

Roger T. Stevens is a veteran graphics programmer and author of several books, including *Graphics Programming with Java, 2/E*. He holds a Ph.D. in electrical engineering and resides in New Mexico.

ABOUT THE TECHNICAL EDITOR

Shamms Mortier has written a number of successful books, including *3ds max: Building Complex Models*, *The Bryce 3D Handbook*, and *The Poser 4 Handbook*.

FUTURE EDITIONS

If you find any errors in this dictionary, or if you have suggestions for entries that should be added, expanded, or modified in future printings or editions, please contact us at the following address: Computer Graphics Dictionary Editor, Charles River Media, 20 Downer Avenue, Suite 3, Hingham, MA 02043.

SOURCES

The majority of the entries in this dictionary, including items on the companion CD-ROM, have been adapted from the following sources.

Stevens, Roger. *Quick Reference to Computer Graphic Terms*. Boston: Academic Press Professional. 1993.

Long, Ben, Sonja Schenk. *Digital Filmmaking Handbook*. Hingham: Charles River Media. 2000.

Lyn, Craig, Ben Long. *Macintosh 3D Handbook 3/E*. Hingham: Charles River Media. 1998.

Robalik, Nick. *True Space F/X Creations*. Hingham: Charles River Media. 2000.

Stevens, Roger. *Graphics Programming with Java, Second Edition*. Hingham: Charles River Media. 1999.

DeLoura, Mark. *Game Programming Gems*. Hingham: Charles River Media. 2000.

Rindner, David. *form • Z Modeling for Digital Visual Effects and Animation*. Hingham: Charles River Media, 1999.

Mortier, Shamms. *Poser 4 Handbook*. Hingham: Charles River Media. 2000.

Fleming, William. *Animating Facial Features and Expressions*. Hingham: Charles River Media. 1999.

Pearrow, Mark. *Web Site Usability Handbook*. Hingham: Charles River Media. 2000.

Mortier, Shamms. *Creating 3D Comix*. Hingham: Charles River Media. 2000.

Paries, Jeff. *Animation Master 2000 Handbook*. Hingham: Charles River Media. 2000.

Gallardo, Arnold. *3D Lighting: History, Concepts, & Techniques*. Hingham: Charles River Media. 2000.

Dobbs, Darris and William Fleming. *trueSpace 3 & 4 Creature Creations*. Hingham: Charles River Media. 1998.

Ahearn, Luke. *Awesome Game Creation: No Programming Required*. Hingham: Charles River Media. 2000.

Ng, Kian Bee. *Digital Effects Animation Using Maya*. Hingham: Charles River Media. 1999.

Fleming, William and Richard Schrand. *3D Creature Workshop, Second Edition*. Hingham: Charles River Media. 2001.

Byrne, John. *Java for Cobol Programmers*. Hingham: Charles River Media. 2000.

Watkins, Christopher. *Stereograms*. Hingham: Charles River Media. 1995.

Lecky- Thompson, Guy. *Infinite Game Universe: Mathematical Techniques*. Hingham: Charles River Media. 2001.

Mortier, Shamms. *3D Graphics Tutorial Collection*. Hingham: Charles River Media. 2001.

Mortier, Shamms. *3ds max: Building Complex Models*. Hingham: Charles River Media. 2000.

Ahearn, Luke. *Designing 3D Games That Sell*, Hingham: Charles River Media. 2001.

Mortier, Shamms. *Advanced Bryce Creations: Photorealistic 3D Worlds*. Hingham: Charles River Media. 2001.

Freire, Eunice and Kelly Valqui. *Web Design & Development*. Hingham: Charles River Media. 2001.

Watkins, Adam. *3D Animation: From Models to Movies*. Hingham: Charles River Media. 2000.

Paull, David. *Programming Dynamic Character Animation*. Hingham: Charles River Media. 2002.

Schrand, Richard. *Macromedia Web Design Handbook*. Hingham: Charles River Media. 2001.

Sledd, John. *Electric Image Handbook*. Hingham: Charles River Media. 1998.

Mortier, Shamms. *Bryce 3D Handbook*. Hingham: Charles River Media. 1998.

Sledd, John. *Ray Dream Handbook Second Edition*. Hingham: Charles River Media. 1998.

Campesato, Oswald. *Java Graphics Programming Library: Concepts to Source Code*. Hingham: Charles River Media. 2002.

Lengyel, Eric. *Mathematics for 3D Game Programming and Computer Graphics*. Hingham: Charles River Media. 2001.

Beck, Patrik. *The LightWave 6.5/7.0 Project Handbook*. Hingham: Charles River Media. 2001.

Moore, John. *The Flash Webisode Production Handbook*. Hingham: Charles River Media. 2001.

Monroe, J. Brook and Erica Sadun. *JavaScript CD Cookbook, Third Edition*. Hingham: Charles River Media. 2000.

Sadun, Erica and Kelly Valqui. *HTML TemplateMaster, Third Edition.* Hingham: Charles River Media. 2000.

Pfaffenberger, Bryan. *HTML/CSS Developer's Resource Guide.* Hingham: Charles River Media. 1999.

Long, Ben. *Complete Digital Photography.* Hingham: Charles River Media. 2001

Hartman, Annesa. *Producing Interactive Television.* Hingham: Charles River Media. 2001.

# #

16-bit color mode A computer color mode in which each color is represented by a 16-bit number. This allows 65,535 different colors, which is sufficient for an adequate reproduction of a colored image.

1D hinge joint A means of linking sections of an object in *trueSpace*.

24-bit color mode A computer color mode in which each color is represented by a 24-bit number. This allows 16 million different colors, which is more than can be distinguished by the human eye.

2D art assets Two-dimensional images that are used in game creation. They include *menu screens, credit screens, logos, user interfaces*, and *in-game assets*. Menu screens include the toolbar in word processors, browsers, or even favorite games. Credit screens often contain art such as logos, images, and even "fonts" or special letters from the product, people, and companies they represent. Logos for companies, products, and services can be simple letters, 2D or fully rendered 3D scenes. User interfaces are broken down into background images, buttons, cursors, and other art objects a user must click on or interact with. In-game assets are images used within a game. In the game, the sights are the textures on the walls, the floors, and the characters. Even the 3D models and objects have 2D art applied to them.

2D graphic A graphics image in which all objects are two dimensional and coplanar.

2-manifold A boundary where every point has an arbitrarily small neighborhood of points around it that are topologically the same as a disk in the plane.

2-pop The last two events in a countdown leader. After the "2" (counting down "5, 4, 3, 2") there is a short pop that occurs instead of a "1." This *2-pop* is used for syncing audio and video when shooting non-sync sound.

32-bit color mode A computer color mode in which each color is represented by a 32-bit number. This allows over 4.29 billion different colors and is the highest color resolution ever used in a computer system.

3:2 pulldown A method for transferring 24fps film to 29.97 fps NTSC video. The film is slowed down by .1% and the first film frame is recorded on the first two fields of video, the second frame is recorded on the next three fields of video, and so on.

3/4 lighting See *Rembrandt lighting*.

3/4" U-matic A video tape format developed in the 1960s that makes use of analog ¾ inch tape. It is still widely used in government, educational, and industrial productions. It provides much lower quality than any DV format.

3D accelerator card A card that speeds up the operation of the video display. 3D accelerators are now usually incorporated into the video display card.

3D digitizer A hardware device used to digitize real world models or objects into the computer. The user inputs X,Y, Z coordinates and creates a mesh surface which represents the surface of the actual object. There are four major types of 3D digitizers available: *mechanical arm, ultrasonic, magnetic resonance*, and *laser*.

3D Energy A plug-in for *trueSpace* that consists of three modules: Lightning, Electro-Glow, and StarLite. Lightning creates mesh objects in the shape of lightning, with adjustable shape and branches. Electro-Glow is a postproduction unit for adding a glow effect to lightning or any other object. StarLite is another postproduction unit for adding highlight flares (stars) with adjustable brightness, color, spikes, style, etc. Parameters can be animated.

3D graphics A graphics system in which a three-dimensional data set is converted to two dimensions for viewing.

3D hologram Holography is a useful technology for 3D. A 3D hologram system consists of a liquid crystal device and a holographic screen formed of holographic optical elements. This display can construct animated 3D images in real-time by updating LCD pixels.

3DMF format The 3D MetaFile format, created by Apple Computer as a part of their QuickDraw 3D package. The 3DMF format handles high-end geometry such as NURBS, texture mapping information, animation characteristics, lighting, and hierarchy.

3D modeling process A process that is accomplished in the following three phases: sketches and source material analysis; geometry generation; and customizing geometry organization for animation and mapping.

3D RAD A 3D game development tool from BitPlane.

3DS file format The 3D object format written by *3ds max*, for export to other 3D applications. 3DS format is seamlessly read by *Cinema 4D XL*, including lights and cameras. *Cinema 4D XL* is able to read and write 3DS format on both Mac OS and Windows platforms. In *form•Z*, 3DS export/import capability is available only in the Windows version. Because of *Cinema 4D XL*'s seamless ability to read and write 3DS files, all guidelines for 3DS export for *3ds max* apply to *Cinema 4D XL*. 3DS is a good exchange format to use when on the Windows platform. Windows requires that no objects exceed the 65K triangle count, and that object names do not exceed eight characters.

3ds max A popular modeling and animation environment package, formerly known as *3D Studio Max*.

4:2:2 A method of encoding pixel color information where 8 bits are allowed for each pixel, with 4 bits used for luminance, 2 bits for the *I* color component, and 2 bits for the *Q* color component.

60 Hz tone See *sixty-cycle tone*.

8-bit color mode A computer mode in which 8 bits are used to define each color in the display. This allows for 256 different colors. Often this is not enough to make the colors in an image look photorealistic.

A

α (Greek "alpha") Angle between the normalized direction of reflection vector and the normalized viewpoint direction vector in the Phong illumination model.

A* algorithm (pronounced "A star") An algorithm that searches in a state space for the least costly path from a start state to a goal state by examining the neighboring or adjacent states of particular states. In essence, the A* algorithm repeatedly examines the most promising unexplored location it has seen. When a location is explored, the algorithm is finished if that location is the goal; otherwise, it makes note of all that location's neighbors for further exploration.

A* algorithm, aesthetic optimizations Paths calculated by A* weave and bob their way efficiently to the goal, although in an unorthodox fashion. This is a serious problem that undermines the believability of any game's AI. An improvement in the aesthetics of a path can be achieved by promoting straight paths through careful cost weighting within the A* algorithm.

A* algorithm, master node list and priority queue open list implementation A technique for reducing the time required to execute the A* algorithm. It involves storing all of the nodes that have already been explored in a *master node list*. In addition, all nodes that could be searched are stored in an *open list* that can be sorted as a *priority queue*. This can be implemented as a binary heap. The A* algorithm can then often find the next node required in the master node list or the priority queue open list (whichever is faster) without having to perform a complete new search procedure.

Aaton timecode An electronic timecode for film developed by the camera manufacturer Aaton. Electronic pulses are stored on the film itself and can be added to telecine transfers as window burn timecode.

AB and ABC channel mixing *Bryce* offers the user two ways to combine more than one channel to create composite-mixed materials. Each of these is unique to *Bryce*. Because the four channels are referred to as ABCD, these techniques are named according to the channels they address: AB and ABC. In general, AB mixing allows a blend of the A and B channels so that the information in each is composited on the selected object in an altitude-sensitive manner. The data in the A channel are written to the bottom half of the object, while the B channel data are written to the top half. ABC mixes are a little different. The data are written so that there is a mix of the data from A and B, mixed through the alpha channel data of C.

abend An abbreviation of "abnormal end." The end of a program in other than the desired manner. Some types of programming or hardware errors permit the program to stop and report an error message that may give clues as to what went wrong. Other types of errors cause a *system crash*, in which the system locks up and must be manually reset, often causing loss of data.

ABI See *applications binary interface.*

A/B input switching Most pro monitors allow for more than one input source, and the user can switch from the "A" source, usually the NLE, to the "B" source, usually the primary VTR. (Note: This doesn't work for DV-format editing systems, since all video will be coming through the VTR.) This can be useful when outputting a project to tape and comparing what the computer is sending out to what the video deck is actually recording.

A/B rolling See *checkerboard.*

ablate To remove. Optical disks are written by ablating material from the disk surface with a laser beam, forming pits that can be read.

abort command A command that allows the user to prematurely terminate a command that is still being performed and restore the computer system to the exact state that it was in prior to the command being issued.

abscissa The horizontal or *x* component of a two-dimensional coordinate system. The vertical or *y* component is the *ordinate.*

absolute 1. In geometry, specified with respect to a fixed origin. For example, when a set of coordinates is given with respect to the origin of the coordinate system rather than with respect to the previous point specified. 2. In algebra,

the numerical part of a number, irrespective of sign. For example, *–3* and *+3* both have an absolute value of *3.*

absolute address In computing, the address of the memory location where a datum is stored, referenced to the beginning of memory (address 0). Compare with *relative address.*

absolute coordinates A coordinate system for defining the positions of objects in a scene to be rendered that is independent of the display screen or the objects within the scene. In contrast, the position of an object may be defined relative to the observer, the display screen, or some other object for convenience during the rendering process.

absolute pseudoprime A number defined by $N|(b^{N-1} - 1)$ for all **(b,N) = 1.** The smallest absolute pseudoprime is $561 = 3 \times 11 \times 17$. Also known as a *Carmichael number.*

absolute temperature scale A temperature scale that uses *absolute zero* as its lowest measurement. See *Kelvin scale* and *absolute zero.*

absolute value In algebra, the numerical part of a number, irrespective of sign. For example *–3* and *+3* both have an absolute value of *3.*

absolute zero The temperature at which all molecular activity ceases. This is 0 K on the Kelvin scale, or –273° Celsius. See *Kelvin scale* and *absolute temperature scale.*

absorption 1. Act or process of being taken in. Particularly of concern in graphic renditions because certain light frequencies can be absorbed by certain otherwise transparent materials, thereby causing the light color to change. 2. The non-conductance or retention of light by matter or media that does not result in either a reflectance or transmission.

absorption coefficient The fraction of incident intensity of light absorbed by a material per unit of thickness for small thicknesses.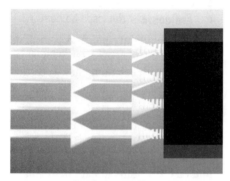

absorption coefficient.

abstract concrete Proposed fractal structure of concrete suggested by David Jones, in which proper arrangement of particles sized from coarse gravel to the finest dust can be used to reduce the needed binder to an arbitrarily small amount, thereby reducing cost.

Abstract Window Toolkit (AWT) A package of Java classes that permit the user to create window-like displays, operate on them, and produce graphics such as lines, rectangles, circles, ellipses, etc. Java 2 has a set of classes called Java Swing components that have more advanced capabilities for performing these functions.

a-buffer algorithm A variation of the *z-buffering* technique that facilitates *antialiasing*. Given a number of three-dimensional objects that are to compose a picture, the z-buffer algorithm ends with a frame buffer that is an array of pixels having the x (horizontal) and y (vertical) dimensions of the final image with each pixel location containing the color of the nearest three-dimensional object and a z-buffer that is an x-y array that contains z, the distance from the image plane of the nearest object at that x-y location (the maximum number represents an object at the image plane and 0 represents an object at maximum distance from the plane). Initially, all members of the frame buffer are set to the background color and all members of the z-buffer are set to 0. Then for each pixel location, the appropriate member of the z-buffer is tested against all objects that intersect that location. If the object's z value is greater than that in the z-buffer, the value in the z-buffer is replaced by the object's z value and the color in the corresponding member of the frame buffer is replaced by the object's color. The *a-buffer* uses the same type of array as the z-buffer, but instead of each element containing a distance from the image plane, height, it contains a pointer to a stack of data that not only defines the current pixel but also surrounding ones, so that the proper color value for antialiasing may be computed.

acceleration 1. The rate of change of velocity of a body that is increasing in speed, direction, or both. In graphics, often used to refer to hardware or software techniques used to speed up graphics operations. 2. A control in *The Games Factory* that allows the user to set the rate at which an object will reach its maximum speed.

accelerator board 1. A plug-in board for a computer that speeds up operations by using a more powerful microprocessor or some similar means. 2. A plug-in board specifically designed to speed up video operations, either by improving the speed of memory access or by providing a special processor that performs primitive operations such as line or shape drawing faster than could be done by the computer's microprocessor.

accelerator cards Custom hardware that can accelerate certain features such as 3D rendering, rendering of plug-in filters, or display of complex video.

accelerator keys Commands that speed up interaction with a computer. For example, selecting an action by hitting a single keyboard key rather than by using a mouse.

accelerator port In a graphics accelerator card, the I/O port that receives data for processing by the card, as opposed to the *direct frame buffer port*, which permits bypassing the accelerator card and passing video data directly to the display memory.

accent light A light used to highlight or draw attention to a specific part of a scene. Usually a spotlight or point light source is used.

acceptance test procedure A formal document describing a series of tests that a system or software package must pass in order to be accepted (and paid for) by the customer.

Accept button A control in *Game Creation System (GCS)* that enables the user to set up a new game. When the user clicks the Accept button, *GCS* then creates a directory on the hard drive containing the files that the 3D game

engine needs for the 3D world the user is about to detail. This directory will have the same name as the project name.

accessibility The ability of a computer to access a Web site using a standard browser. Most Web sites should be capable of being accessed by Microsoft Internet Explorer and Netscape Navigator.

accessible boundary point A point p on the boundary of an open set W for which there is a path beginning in W such that p is the first point not in W that the path hits.

access method The manner in which data are stored and retrieved. This is highly dependent upon the media used. Tape units usually store all data in a sequential stream. Disk drives are divided into sectors (often of 512 bytes), any one of which may be accessed by the computer. This gives a lot of flexibility but has a drawback: over time a file may be broken up into a lot of individual sectors spread across the disk, resulting in what is known as *fragmenting*, which slows disk access considerably. Any one of multiple files stored on a CD-ROM may be accessed almost instantaneously. Any byte of RAM can be accessed directly. The speed with which a particular datum can be accessed may be critical in such applications as transferring data to the display screen fast enough to produce satisfactory moving pictures.

accessories Additional devices added to a computer to improve digital filmmaking, such as a coprocessor to accelerate rendering, or professional audio editing hardware.

accommodation 1. The automatic adjustment of the eye to permit focusing at different distances. 2. The range of distances over which the eye can focus.

accumulation Process in plants where the increase or decrease in certain cell components is measured to determine when flowering will begin. This is one method of modeling plant growth to determine when to begin constructing blossoms.

accumulation point A starting point in the complex plane for an iterated equation to which the solution of the equation returns periodically during the iteration process.

accutance The perceived edge sharpness or definition of a recording media such as film. It is also the ability to distinguish minute changes in contrast and definition.

ACE A Color Expert. An expert system for selecting user-interface colors.

acetate-base film Photographic film in which the emulsion has been laid down on an acetate substrate. Acetate is one of the substrate materials that meets ANSI safety standards (particularly because it does not burn rapidly).

a-channel Channel containing ambient-reflection values for all objects in a picture. Since ambient light impinges equally on all surfaces, regardless of direction, the intensity of ambient reflection is the same for every point on an object, so only one value per object need be stored.

achromatic 1. Colorless, thus comprised only of black, white, and shades of gray. Also referred to as *monochrome*. This is the light used in a black and white television set, where only various intensities of light are used to make up the

display. 2. The ability of a lens to focus two or more different colors at the same point.

acknowledgment A computer output indicating that a particular piece of information has been successfully received.

ACM See *Association for Computing Machinery*.

acoustic tablet A device for detecting the position of a stylus on a tablet and converting it to a pair of (x,y) coordinate electrical signals. Strip microphones are used on the horizontal and vertical edges of the tablet to detect sound emitted by the stylus. The time of travel of the sound to each microphone is measured to determine the stylus position. This technique is particularly adaptable to three-dimensional space measurements. By adding a third strip microphone at right angles to the other two (z coordinate), the position of the stylus in a cube of space can be determined.

Acousto-Optic (A-O) Method of using sound waves passing through a transparent medium to deflect a beam of laser light.

actinic A chemical change, particularly in a light-sensitive photographic emulsion, produced by the shorter wavelengths such as violet or ultraviolet rays.

action 1. A change that takes place over the course of the frames that make up an animation sequence. 2. The middle section of a three-act feature film structure. The film structure consists of *set-up, action*, and *pay-off*.

action attribute The action attribute instructs the Web browser where to send form data. Data may be mailed to the address yourname@yourdomain.com.

7

Form data can also be sent to special programs written in C, Perl, or Java, in which case the action attribute should point to that program's URL, for example, <FORM METHOD="post" ACTION= http://www.charlesriver.com/cgi-bin/formail.pl. There are browsers that do not support the "mailto" (Internet Explorer and Netscape Navigator support the mailto action); it is recommended to use the "mailto" action only if no other option is available.

action, overlapping The world does not operate on a sequential timetable; everything starts and stops at different intervals. Try to overlap the motion so the action looks more natural. Take a walking character for example. As its foot starts to travel forward, the calf and then the thigh start to rise. Finally the hip swings forward as well. When a character prepares to jump, notice how several things are happening at once. The character crouches down, its arms move down and back, and its eyes close. Although this is done in a cartoonish way, the resulting animation is more realistic than if the character had crouched first, then moved its arms, then closed its eyes.

action phase A phase of a game in which the user may cause direct or indirect changes to the total game environment.

action point The point at which items like bullets and missles are fired from objects. If, for example, there were a large spaceship with a gun mounted aboard, the action point would be set at the end of the barrel of the gun, where the bullet would first appear.

action routines Routines that the user activates to change the current state of the computer transition network by placing events in the event queue or by changing one or more of the state variables.

action safe The area of an image that will most likely be visible on any video monitor. Essential action should be kept within the action-safe area, as action that falls outside this area may be lost due to overscan.

active array A group of loudspeakers, radio antennas, radar antennas, or television antennas whose characteristics of beam width and direction can be controlled by proper phasing of the drive to the individual units.

active bank In early PCs, normally 64KB (65536) of computer memory addresses were allowed for display memory. Super VGA cards often had more memory than would fit in this addressing space (even using the 4 bank EGA/VGA memory configuration). Consequently, the super VGA display memory was divided into 64K banks, only one of which was mapped to the computer addressing space at any given time. This bank was known as the *active bank*. Reading and writing could be done only to the active bank, thus slowing graphics operations. Modern PCs do not have these memory restrictions. Many current graphics adapter cards have 4 megabytes or more of graphic memory without bank restrictions.

active character sets The PC may have a number of character sets resident in its Basic Input/Output System (BIOS). These are stored in read-only memory (ROM) in the computer. At any one time, two of these character sets may be selected for display. The selected character sets are known as the *active character sets*.

active data base In flight simulators, the portion of the graphics database that is kept in random access memory (RAM) so as to be quickly accessible to the graphics display.

active display area That portion of the display screen upon which pixels can be changed in color and intensity to produce a desired display. Most computer monitors have areas around the edges of the screen that cannot be accessed and therefore are not part of the active display. In addition, a border around the active display area is colored with a selected background color and cannot otherwise be modified.

active edge list A list used in scan conversion techniques. As the scan line scrolls in the y direction, the active edge list contains x values for each line that straddles the active scan line.

active-edge table The scan-line algorithm that determines how to fill a polygon stores all of the set of edges it intersects and the intersection points in an array called the *active-edge table*.

active matrix LCD An LCD display in which each monochrome pixel or each red, green, and blue dot making up a color pixel is controlled by a discrete transistor (these transistors are all incorporated in an integrated circuit). This technique, while using more transistors than a standard LCD display, permits sharper contrast and increased writing and screen access speeds, and eliminates loss of cursor (submarining).

active objects Active objects are used mostly as the main characters of computer games. These are the characters and objects used to assign behavior and controls to. This is done by either allowing the player to use the mouse or keyboard, or the computer controls the objects.

active page The display memory for the PC EGA or VGA card may be configured to have from 1 to 8 pages of full screen graphics, depending upon the display mode and the amount of memory on the card. Only one page at a time may be selected for display. The selected page is called the *active page*.

active server pages (ASP) Web pages that are acted out upon a server. Typically, ASP pages are used for accessing databases. However, the user can use them to run different functions with JavaScript or VBScript. One of the problems of using scripting languages such as JavaScript on Web pages is Webbrowser compatibility. ASP pages can solve this problem. The script is executed on the server when called upon, and the results are then displayed in the user's Web browser.

active subtree In ray-tracing constructive solid geometry (CSG) images, the part of the CSG tree that contributes to the image for each scan line.

active-surface table The scan-line algorithm that, in two dimensions, creates an active-edge table can be extended to three-dimensional objects, in which case the array that holds the intersections is called the *active-surface table*.

active values In a user-interface management system (UIMS), the parameters used to propagate changes among interdependent objects and from these objects to their visual representations.

active window The window that is at the front of the screen when several programs are being run simultaneously in the Windows environment. All input from the keyboard will be directed to this window. A window is made *active* by placing the mouse cursor on any part of it and clicking.

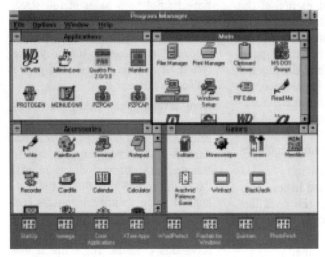

active window.

active zone In constructive solid geometry (CSG) where simple primitives are combined to represent a complex object using Boolean set operators, the active zone of a CSG node is the part of the node that, when changed, affects the final solid.

activity network A chart used in project planning that utilizes boxes containing summaries of tasks, and lines connecting the boxes to show the order in which the tasks must be performed.

actors 1. An actor is a small subroutine that is called once per frame to determine the characteristics of an object in an animation. 2. Another term for the foreground of a *Bryce* animation.

actuator Mechanical device that moves an object, such as the voice coil or stepping switch that positions the read/write head of a disk drive.

Adams-Bashforth method A technique for solving differential equations, used to graph the Verhulst attractor fractal.

adaptation The ability of the brain to vary the size of the pupil of the eye and to chemically vary the sensitivity of the retina to adjust the eye's sensitivity to light over a wide range of light intensities.

adapter, video A printed circuit card that plugs into a PC to provide the interface to a video monitor. The earliest video adapters were the Monochrome Display Adapter (MDA), which displayed monochrome text only, with no graphics, at a resolution of 720 × 350 pixels; the Color Graphics Array (CGA), which displayed 4-color graphics at 320 × 200 pixels and higher resolution text; the Enhanced Graphics Array (EGA), which displayed 16-color graphics at a resolution of 640 × 350 pixels and also lower resolution and text modes; and the Video Graphics Adapter (VGA), which displayed 16 colors at 640 × 480 pixels, 256 colors at 320 × 200 pixels, as well as all the EGA modes. Most PCs now use much more sophisticated video adapters that have much higher resolutions as well as the capability to display any of many million shades of color. Motherboards may now include the video adapter circuitry as a built-in feature.

adaptive compression A data compression technique that continually analyzes the data content and modifies the compression algorithm to achieve near-optimum compression ratios. The Lempel Ziv Welch technique used in creating GIF graphics files is an example of this.

adaptive division graph A technique used in ray tracing in which the space to be ray traced is subdivided using an octree containing voxels (elements of volume) of varying size based on distribution of objects in the space. Then each voxel has attached to it a quadtree for the neighbor of each face.

adaptive forward differencing (AFD) A technique for rendering images on curved surfaces that uses the surface, viewpoint, and display resolution information to determine the amount of detail needed for the image; then it adjusts the number of points to minimize the necessary computer computations.

adaptive meshing Technique for breaking a picture up into patches whose size is inversely proportional to intensity variations when generating a picture using the radiosity method.

adaptive sampling Method of sampling in which the sampling density of a parameter is controlled by use of a quality estimate.

adaptive subdivision A technique for adjusting the sizes of polygons that make up a mesh representing a curved surface, the size of each polygon being determined by its projected size or by the local curvature of the curved surface or both.

adaptive supersampling A technique used in ray tracing that begins by tracing five rays through the center and four corners of a pixel. If they are found to be of about the same color, the pixel is colored that color; if they differ significantly in color, the pixel is subdivided into smaller regions and the process is repeated.

adaptive tree-depth control A technique which causes a ray tracing system to stop tracing a ray when its contributions to the color of the ultimate eye ray fall below some selected threshold.

ADB See *Apple Desktop Bus*.

A/D converter See *analog-to-digital converter*.

Add CV tool A tool in *Universe* that allows the user to create more control and reshape an object in any way desired.

adding an alpha channel into a clip The alpha channel is used to store the transparency information that the user will need to lay different layers on top of one another. Like a sophisticated matte or stencil, the alpha channel determines what will be seen in a particular layer. The Apple Macintosh mostly uses the PICT graphics format, which is something of a platform standard. A PICT file can be written as a 32-bit image with 8 bits of information reserved for each of the red, green, and blue channels. The last 8 bits of information are reserved for the alpha channel, which is an 8-bit channel that can be used to control the transparency of the image. alpha channels are also vital when compositing graphics and animations in applications like Adobe *After Effects* and Discreet *Combustion*. All professional 2D paint applications allow the user to configure alpha channel data in any file format that can contain that data.

adding/deleting and importing/exporting materials Operations that can be performed within all professional 3D applications. When performing these operations, the following should be noted. Instead of deleting a material preset, the user is advised to consider exporting it out to a separate folder for later use. Export similar presets to the same folder for later import. Then the user can safely delete the item in the library.

When adding material creations, don't save them automatically to a library; instead, try to fit them in one of the other preset categories. When saving an object with a customized material wrapped on it in *Bryce* and many other 3D applications, there may be no need to save the material separately. Remember that objects are saved with materials attached, so importing the model imports the material, too. A group of objects with similar materials can be saved together, perhaps a group of wine glasses with materials customized for each. Loading that object to the scene would then allow the material to be copied and pasted on other needed objects. It might be easier to classify materials according to the object class they belong to, especially if that object class is not represented in the Material Presets library (like lizard skins, fabrics, or other material classifications). With an extra hard drive, the user can dedicate its use to texture and material libraries. That way, textures (procedural and image based) will be at instant disposal for complex projects.

adding special effects Although effects such as particles and lens flares are available in most 3D applications, it's often better to add such effects to rendered scenes during postproduction. In addition to saving hours of 3D rendering time, postproduction effects are isolated from the other elements in the composition and are easy to change and edit later.

additional figures library list A library of hand models for *Poser*. Among other models, there are two hand models, left and right, contained here. They are very important because they are disembodied hands, so that they can be added to a scene as standalone items.

addition, Boolean A process in which two or more three-dimensional objects are combined into a single object whose shell goes around the entire group of objects.

additive color primaries Primary colors of light that can be added together to produce any desired color. The most commonly used system consists of red, green, and blue. Note that the results are not the same as would result if pigments of these colors were added together.

additive color synthesis Combining light of the primary colors red, green, and blue to produce light of a desired color, as opposed to subtractive color synthesis in which white light is absorbed by pigments of crimson, yellow, and light blue, leaving the unabsorbed component as the apparent color of the object.

Add Keyframe command or action A command in all 3D applications that creates a keyframe for every single animation channel in a group.

Add Operator A function of *Carrara* that allows the user to modify the shading of an object.

address 1. A number that identifies a particular location of a memory storage device, such as random access memory (RAM) or disk. 2. v. To select a specified memory location. 3. A frame of video as identified by timecode information. 4. An Internet location—either a personal, company, or institution's contact address, or a Uniform Resource Locator (URL) target address.

addressability 1. The ability to place information at a certain location in memory. Most modern PCs can address such large amounts of memory space that there is plenty of room for directly addressing every pixel of a display in adjacent memory locations, even if each pixel requires several bytes of memory to define its color. Early PCs had very limited addressability, so that several memory planes or many memory pages were needed to define graphics information, making extracting of graphics information more difficult. 2. The number of individual dots per inch that can be created on a display. This number may be different on the horizontal and vertical axes.

addressable capacity The total number of memory locations that a computer can access. For personal computers, each location usually contains one byte (eight bits) of information. When addressing display memory, 16-color EGA/VGA display modes contain information for the color of eight pixels at one memory address. The four bits that represent one of sixteen colors are one bit in each of four display memory planes that are at the same computer address, the four planes being accessed internally by the display card. For 256-color VGA modes, a memory address contains the data for the color of one pixel. For higher color capabilities, several adjacent memory bytes are used to define the color of each pixel.

addressing modes Ways of addressing computer memory. When using assembly language, the three basic addressing modes are *immediate addressing*, which refers to the exact memory location; *indirect addressing*, which refers to a register that contains a pointer to a memory location; and *indexed addressing*, which allows the programmer to add an offset to the indirect address.

address track timecode A method of converting the odd frame rate of NTSC video (29.97 frames per second) to a whole number. There are several standards of timecode, and a deck or camera can read only timecode that it has been designed to understand. SMPTE timecode is the professional industry standard set up by the Society of Motion Picture and Television Engineers (SMPTE). All professional equipment can read SMPTE timecode. DV timecode is the format developed for the DV format. For those who plan on using only DV-format equipment, DVTC will be an acceptable alternative to SMPTE timecode. As the popularity of the DV formats increase, DVTC is becoming more integrated into the realm of professional video-editing equipment. RCTC (Rewriteable Consumer Time Code) is a format Sony developed for use with consumer Hi8 equipment.

Add Rib tool A tool in the UberNurbs Palette section of *Universe* that can be used to draw lines across a cage to create ribs.

adjacency table A table used in generating words for names in games. The table indicates whether letters can be adjacent to each other to create a reasonable English word.

	A	B	C	D	E	...	X	Y	Z
A									
B									
C									
D									
E									
.									
.									
.									
X									
Y									
Z									

The gray squares in the 26 × 26 grid will be filled with a number, which indicates whether one letter may be followed by another. In simplest form, if there is a 1 in the gray square referenced by the letter D along the x-axis, and R on the y-axis, then the combination DR is allowed.

adjacent facets Two facets of a polygonal solid that have a common edge.

adjoint matrices If A_{ij} is the cofactor of the determinant $|a|$ of a square matrix $[a_{ij}]$, the matrix $[A_{ji}]$ is the adjoint of $[a_{ij}]$. The adjoint matrix has some special properties; for example, multiplication of it by the original matrix is commutative, which is not generally true of matrix multiplication. As an example, the adjoint of the matrix

$$[a_{ij}] = \begin{vmatrix} 2 & 0 & 7 \\ -1 & 4 & 5 \\ 3 & 1 & 2 \end{vmatrix}$$

is the matrix

$$[Aji] = \begin{bmatrix} 3 & 7 & -28 \\ 17 & -17 & -17 \\ -13 & -2 & 8 \end{bmatrix}$$

To see how the elements of this second matrix are obtained, we note, for example, that the cofactor of a_{11} (2) is

$$\begin{bmatrix} 4 & 5 \\ 1 & 2 \end{bmatrix}$$

which evaluates to $(4 \times 2) - (1 \times 5) = 3$, which is thus the value for the first element of A_{ji}.

Adjust Heights At Intervals A contour evaluation method used in *form•Z*. In topographical terms it is called "height interval" or "contour interval." When using this option, *form•Z* assumes that the height offset is constant between each contour line. Thus, with this mode, the steepness of the terrain is controlled by projected proximity of contour lines to one another and a defined contour height interval. When viewed from an orthographic projection view, usually the top view, the distance between contour lines defines the steepness, or rate of elevation change, of the terrain. For example, if three contour lines are positioned to be 200 meters apart, when viewed from the top, with 10 meter contour intervals, then this particular region of terrain will gently rise 20 meters along its 400 meter length. The main rule to remember is that the closer the contour lines, the steeper the terrain. If the same three contour lines were moved to be only 1 meter apart with the same 10 meter contour intervals, then the terrain would rise 20 meters while traversing only 2 meters in the horizontal.

ADO See *Ampex Digital Optics*.

Adobe *After Effects* See *After Effects*.

Adobe *Illustrator* See *Illustrator*.

Adobe *Pagemaker* See *Pagemaker*.

Adobe *Photoshop* See *Photoshop*.

Adobe *Premiere* See *Premiere*.

Adobe *Type Manager* See *Type Manager*.

ADR See *automatic dialog replacement*.

ADSTAR Automatic Document Storage And Retrieval. A system that can select and display electronically stored images that meet some user-specified criteria.

advanced media management The treatment of special files used in digital filmmaking such as proprietary file formats for *shot logs*, and Flexfiles for *film telecine logs*; text files used as shot logs.

Advanced Motion Lab A special editing screen in *Bryce*. It customizes animations from the Materials Lab and the Terrain Editor to address materials and terrain objects. The Advanced Motion Lab has animation controls for every aspect of the *Bryce* world, so materials as well as objects can be animated.

Advanced Television Systems Committee (ATSC) An organization established to set the technical standards for DTV, including HDTV.

adventure game In an adventure game, the player walks around endlessly and tries to fulfill a quest or unravel a mystery. Information and items are collected. *Zork, Hitchhiker's Guide to the Galaxy,* and *King's Quest* are examples of adventure games.

advertising on the Web, rates for Banner ad rates vary depending upon the site one chooses. The advertiser can expect to spend anywhere from $5 to $45 per thousand impressions (CPM). Most Web sites post rate card information on their site (usually indicated by a link called "Advertise"). Typical CPM charges as of this writing are as follows (these rates are constantly being revised):

City Guides: $50 to $60
Top 100 Web Sites: $25 to $100
Search Engines: $20 to $50
Small Targeted Content Web Sites: $10 to $80
Sponsored Content: $45 to $85

aerial perspective The perception of depth due to light scattering, caused by the atmosphere, making distant objects "bluish" as well as making them fuzzy and out of focus. We always perceive distant objects as soft and slightly blurry as

aerial perspective.

well as having a more bluish hue the farther away they are. Atmospheric haze and fog are also examples of this kind of depth perception, even if these phenomena are closer to the observer than pure atmospheric scattering. 3D applications like *3ds max, LightWave, Carrara, Universe, Bryce, MojoWorld,* and other higher end 3D software contain tools for applying depth, distance, and fog/haze effects. The new tools coming into play in compositing systems (like Adobe *After Effects*) are starting to address these same aerial illusions through special 2D effects and plug-ins.

AES/EBU An abbreviation for the Audio Engineering Society and the European Broadcaster's Union; also a standard for professional digital audio that specifies the transmission of audio data in a stream that encodes stereo audio signals along with optional information.

AFD See *adaptive forward differencing.*

affine capabilities in Java A set of affine transformation capabilities in Java 2 allows a Graphics2D object to be translated, scaled, rotated, or skewed by any desired amount. For example, without this capability, to draw a square that is rotated 45 degrees, one would have to calculate the coordinates of each of the four corners of the rotated square and then draw lines between adjacent corners. Any arithmetic mistake would result in a grotesque figure. With Java 2, it is possible to simply specify a square with one corner at the origin and sides along the x and y axes and then use the affine capabilities to rotate and translate the square in two simple operations.

affine combination. Given points P and Q in an affine space and the real number t, the affine combination is a point that is a fraction t of the way from P to Q. This affine combination is called a *convex combination* if t is in the range from 0 to 1. Performing the mathematics, the affine combination of P and Q by t is

$$P + t(Q - P)$$

Note that in this form of mathematics it is not possible to regroup the terms, since multiplication of a point by a scalar is not permitted.

affine map An array of information defining transformations that consist only of translations, rotations, scalings, and shears. Also known as an *affine matrix.*

affine space A set in which geometric operations make sense, but which has no distinguished point (such as the origin).

affine transformation A transformation that consists only of translations, rotations, scalings, and shears. The array of information that defines the affine transformation is usually stored in an *affine matrix.* This type of transformation is particularly important in creating fractal representations of pictures using iterated function systems.

affricative phonemes An affricative is a plosive immediately followed by a fricative in the same place of articulation. In the word jump, "J" is an affricative made by combining a plosive "D" immediately followed by a fricative "Z." The two affricatives in the English language are "CH" and "J." Affricative phonemes are strong sounds, therefore it is recommended to use a visual phoneme for them. These are consonant phonemes that cannot be dropped from lip synch since they are so prominent.

AFP See *AppleTalk Filing Protocol.*

After Effects Software from Adobe Systems, Inc., used to create sophisticated effects for film, multimedia, and the Web. A dedicated compositing program that provides more compositing power by allowing the user to stack many layers of video and stills. In addition, *After Effects* allows the user to nest one composition inside another to ease project management. *After Effects* also allows the user to animate the properties of layers to create sophisticated, 3D animated effects. *After Effects'* interface is very similar to a 3D animation program with a keyframe-based, linear time line. In addition to simply compositing one layer on top of another, any property of a layer—its position, rotation, scale, opacity, distance on the Z or depth axis—can be animated independently. Special effects filters such as color changes, warps, ripples, and many others can be applied and animated over time with a high degree of control.

afternoon light Understanding this subject is an important factor when creating scenes in scenery generation applications like *Bryce, MojoWorld, World Construction Set, Natural Scene Animator,* and similar applications that focus upon environmental renderings. The angle of the sun relative to the ground during the morning hours is identical to the angle it forms in the afternoon. However, the atmosphere is warmer in the afternoon due to being heated all day, which makes the air expand and scatter more light. When the sun sets, the blue spectra get scattered more and the atmosphere passes more reds and yellows; hence we see a colorful sunset. Blue is scattered more because it has a shorter wavelength than red and yellow. The atmosphere acts as a giant prism, and its molecules scatter short wavelengths (Rayleigh scattering) instead of letting them pass through. Particles, water vapor, and dust near the horizon scatter the longer wavelengths (Mie scattering) and pass through the shorter wavelengths, which results in the horizon appearing white or light blue. The atmosphere scatters blue light about four times as much as red light; that is the reason the sky appears blue.

aggregate object An object defined by a collection of primitives such as facets, parallelograms, circles, etc.

AG_Shaders A program by Agrapha Productions that provides a set of building blocks that can be used in programming shaders.

AI See *Artificial Intelligence.*

Aida Gate-level simulation accelerator software used for the simulation of LSI logic gate-array designs. A product of Teredyne, Inc.

AIIM See *Association for Information and Image Management.*

aiming symbol A symbol, such as a circle, that appears on a display to serve as a tracking point for a light pen.

airbrush A tool in 2D and 3D applications that paints the image in a manner similar to that of a real-world airbrush. A controls palette allows the user to change settings such as density, opacity, flow rate, and sometimes even the shape that is being sprayed. An example of a high end airbrush tool is the Image Hose in Corel *Painter* and *Painter 3D.*

air f/x Air f/x includes everything that is necessary to customize or effect the look of the sky in *Bryce* and similar applications. This includes haze and fog effects, since the sky is not just something "up there," but includes an array of atmospheric parameters.

air resistance 1. Opposition to a moving body imposed by the earth's atmosphere. An important factor in modeling and animating aircraft and missile trajectories. 2. A setting in many 3D applications (*Universe* is one example) that determines the amount of environmental force fragments will encounter when a shockwave comes barreling through.

AIX A version of the UNIX operating system developed by IBM.

albedo effect The color of sky light is due to light scattering and transmission through the atmosphere and also to the *albedo effect*: the reflection of light from the ground back to the sky. The color of sky light changes in accordance with the height of the sun above the horizon, the cloud/atmospheric conditions, the perspective of the viewer, and the reflection of the ground onto the sky. The best way to analyze the placement and simulation of sky light is to follow the way the direct illumination spreads and reflects around a scene, with emphasis on the objects surrounding the subject. Sunlight first hits the atmosphere; some of the light passes through while the rest is scattered and absorbed. The sunlight that does not get scattered that much becomes the directional light that casts shadows on the objects in the scene. The scattered and transmitted light becomes the sky light; since there is light dispersion, the light's color shifts to blue.

Albers' equal-area conic map projection Method of projecting a portion of a sphere or ellipsoid onto a two-dimensional map in a way that minimizes distortion. The method intersects a cone with a hemisphere so that there are two circles of intersection, each at a constant latitude. The hemisphere is then projected onto the cone and the cone unrolled to produce a map.

Alchemy Mindworks A company that produces programs for use in graphics applications. One is a general graphics program called *Graphics Workshop*. The other is used to create multiframe GIF files for animation purposes. It is called *GIF Construction Set for Windows*.

algebraic behavior Behavior of a function that can be characterized by two simple power laws with exponents 1 and 1! respectively.

algebraic irrational numbers The set of algebraic numbers that cannot be expressed as the ratio of two integers.

algebraic numbers The set of all positive and negative numbers.

algebraic surface A surface that is the locus of points defined when a given algebraic function is set equal to a constant (frequently zero).

algorithm A rule or procedure for solving a problem. It consists of a series of steps, usually in the form of a set of mathematical equations, for accomplishing a logical or mathematical process in an unambiguous manner. A particular instance may be implemented by software or specialized hardware.

algorithm, Cohen-Sutherland Algorithm used for clipping lines that extend beyond the bounds of a specified window. The algorithm defines the world into nine regions, one being the specified window and the others above, below, to the right, and to the left of the window and combinations of these. Each region is assigned a unique four-bit number, which is used in processing the line endpoints.

alias 1. A name that can be used to replace another name. In C programming, the *#define* statement can be used to create aliases. For example, *#define T TEST* would allow the programmer to use

T instead of *TEST* anywhere in the program. 2. Electronic mail distribution list of addresses for a particular topic. 3. An icon placed on the desktop as a "shortcut" for opening an application.

Alias A company that is known for its high-end 3D software applications, including *Maya*.

aliased line A line shaped like stair steps as the result of attempting to draw a slanting line as an aggregate of points from a grid of limited resolution.

aliasing The visual artifact that results from producing an image by sampling a function at a sample frequency lower than the highest spatial frequencies contained in the function. This occurs when a real scene is reduced to the number of samples dictated by the available pixels on a display screen. The effects include stairstepping of surface edges, breakup of thin lines into dots, and moiré patterns in finely detailed areas.

aliasing, in scan converting conics A form of aliasing sometimes occurs when scan converting conics. This occurs when the conic contains frequencies too high to be resolved at our sampling rate, causing the resulting image to jump to the opposite side of the conic and then to drift away from the conic altogether.

aliasing in sliver polygons A sliver polygon is a polygon whose area is so thin that its interior does not contain a distinct span for each scan line. In other words, instead of each scan line having a beginning and an ending pixel, each of which defines one side of the polygon, each scan line has only one pixel that may be the beginning or ending pixel. The result is a particularly objectionable form of aliasing in which an irregular line is produced, rather than two sides of the polygon.

aliasing, temporal Temporal aliasing occurs when the frame rate of an animated display is too slow to properly record changes that take place in objects that make up the images. An example that frequently occurs in motion pictures is when the wheels of a wagon appear to go backward when the wagon speeds up.

AlienSkin Software A developer of 2D plug-in effects volumes for *Photoshop* and compatibles, as well as for *After Effects*. Volumes include *EyeCandy* and *Xeono Effects*.

alien storm *Bryce* offers the capacity to animate sky planes by manipulating the light and patterns and create animations that use completely different skies on separate keyframes. The result is that one sky type gradually washes over another. The Randomize buttons at the upper right of the Sky&Fog toolbar allow the user to march through a series of unexpected sky parameters and patterns. Adding these two capacities together, the ability to keyframe different skies and the ability to generate random skies results in strange animations that show one unique sky morphing into another.

alignment 1. The arrangement of objects in a straight line. 2. The adjustment of a device or its parts so that the proper conditions exist for optimum operation. 3. For color cathode-ray tubes, the positioning of the electron beams from the red, blue, and green electron guns of the tube so that a group of red, green, and blue phosphor dots are activated to produce light at exactly the same place on the screen. 4. A steering behavior of swarms or herds, in which a member steers toward the average heading of local flockmates.

alignment error An error in positioning of the electron beams of the red, green, and blue electron guns of a color cathode-ray tube. It is measured as the mean distance between centers of color spot pairs (R-G, R-B, and G-B). Also known as *misconvergence*.

Alignment palette A command in *Carrara* that allows the user, once an object is placed in the proper position, to position other objects relative to it.

align tool A tool used in 3D applications to position objects relative to each other.

Align to Path *Align to Path* or *Auto Rotate* among the most common commands available in most 3D applications. For example, to script an animation of an airplane flying through the sky, weaving among the clouds and gently banking while it turns, first the user must create a motion path for the airplane, which is as simple as moving the time line forward and then moving the airplane in space. The problem is that the airplane will be continually facing forward, no matter where it is on the motion path. Manually aligning the body of the airplane in the direction in which it's traveling is very difficult. However, using an automated *Align to Path* tool, the computer automatically aligns the body of the model in the direction it is traveling.

all-1s problem A classical problem that can be expressed in the language of cellular automata. Each square on an $n \times n$ chessboard is equipped with a light and a switch that reverses the state (on or

off) of the neighboring (the square itself and its four edge-adjacent neighbors) lights. The problem is to start with a completely dark chessboard and find which switches must be activated to light up all of the bulbs.

Allegro Software for printed circuit board layout developed by Valid Logic, Inc.

all-inclusive package A software package that will handle the entire modeling, rendering, and animation process.

allocate To reserve amounts of a resource, such as memory or disk space, that are required for a particular application.

allometry The property of a tree that expresses a relationship between the length of a point on a branch measured from the base of the tree and the diameter of the branch at that point. For many trees, when this length changes by r, the branch diameter changes by $r^{3/2}$.

all points addressable (APA) An array in which every cell can be individually addressed.

Alpha-1 A modeling system used for creating *sweeps*. A sweep is a new object created by sweeping an object along a trajectory through space.

Alpha Attribute Thumbnail This button in the *Bryce*CAB channels provides a thumbnail view of the alpha attribute of a texture. This is the information that is accessed when manipulating the value controls for that channel.

alpha-beta pruning The concept that the tree of game decisions can be pruned wherever it is clear that further investigation of a part of the game tree is fruitless. This occurs whenever it is obvious that the opposing player can get a better outcome elsewhere, so the board position being investigated will never be made available by that player.

alpha blending 1. Use of information in an alpha buffer to modify the color information of an image. 2. Varying the alpha or transparency coefficient of pixels to achieve a realistic appearance for surfaces of lakes, oceans, etc.

alpha buffer A plane that contains image information, whether or not it is physically located in the same frame buffer that holds the color information for the image. Also known as a *depth buffer*.

alpha channel 1. The memory used to store the value or occlusion mask representing the fractional coverage of a pixel. Can be used along with color video information to ease the composing of video images. 2. An 8-bit color channel (see *channel)* which is used to specify the transparency of each pixel in an image. An alpha channel works like a sophisticated stencil and is the digital equivalent of a matte (see *matte*). Alpha channel data can be applied to any channel in a material mix to create a range of effects. Applied to the specular channel, alpha channel data can result in a realistic look of wear and tear.

alpha compositing operator An operator used in an alpha buffer to modify image color information. Assuming two color vectors, A and B, that are modified by alpha compositing operators F_A and F_B, if both operators are 0, the result is completely transparent; if F_A is 1 and F_B is 0, the new color is A only; if F_A is 0 and F_B is 1 the new color is B only; and for other combinations of the operators various mixtures of the two colors occur.

alphageometric Drawn with graphics primitives rather than by using character symbols.

alpha map A map created to designate the geometry of transparency and/or other object effects in an object. Also called *genlocking*.

alphamosaic Formed with character symbols rather than drawn with graphics primitives.

alphanumeric 1. A character that is either a letter of the alphabet or a number. 2. A character that is neither a control character (such as form feed, carriage return, line feed, etc.) nor part of a control sequence. May be a letter, a number, or a punctuation mark.

alphanumeric COM A computer output format that is limited to letters of the alphabet, numbers, and punctuation marks. Not capable of handling raster or vector graphics.

alphanumeric display A computer display that can show only alphanumeric characters.

alpha test A test of a new product, particularly software, at a point when obvious problems have been fixed, but there hasn't been adequate debugging to make the product robust enough for public distribution. An *internal alpha test* is performed by users within the developing organization; an *external alpha test* allows selected users outside the organization to try the product. See also *beta test*.

alternate color maps Fractal pictures, such as Mandelbrot sets, are usually created by assigning sequential colors (within the limits of color capability of the display system) to represent the number of times the base equation is iterated before it reaches some limit. However, other ways of assigning the colors give strikingly different pictures that give new insights into the fractal nature and structure. Each different way of assigning colors to create a fractal is known as an *alternate color map*.

alternate color option A capability offered by the *FRACTINT* fractal generating program, which permits two variations of a fractal to be generated using shades of red for one and shades of blue for the other, so as to permit three-dimensional viewing using a special set of glasses.

alternate complementary colors Alternate complementary colors are composed of a triad color plus a complementary to one of the hues.

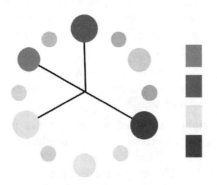

alternate complementary colors.

alternate data rates When streaming QuickTime files from a Web site, it is possible to specify several copies of the same movie, each optimized for a different data rate. The server will then decide which movie is best for the speed of the user's connection.

altitude adjusting A way of adjusting the altitude of selected objects in the *Game Creation System*. The elevation adjustment tool operates on selected ob-

jects. The user can raise a whole cluster of objects by a certain amount, or move them all to the same new elevation.

altitude maps Data arrays that describe terrain in *Bryce*. The user can create altitude maps in the Terrain Editor with the paint tools provided, or create them in a separate paint application, and import them into the Terrain Editor afterward.

altitude maps, external painting *Bryce* can translate 24-bit, 256-color, or black-and-white bitmap art into altitude maps. Since the final operation uses a 256-color palette or smaller, it's better to work in index color modes of 256 or fewer colors in a paint application to produce the altitude map art. *Bryce* assumes the art will be saved as a BMP (Windows) or PICT (Mac) for import.

altitude maps, generating from photos In addition to creating altitude map images by painting them, images can be produced as altitude-map data for any 3D applications that allow the inclusion of altitude-map (also called *height-map*) data. With digital photography, a digital photograph is produced by any photographic method that results in data that can be read into the computer. The grayscale data can then be imported into the 3D application as an altitude map for terrain object creation.

altitude maps, plug-in filters Plug-in filters can be used to enhance the capabilities of altitude maps. There are hundreds of plug-in filters available for paint applications, each one offering new image enhancement and modification capabilities for the creation of altitude maps. A blur is usually applied to the altitude map design to decrease the slope between the resulting lower and higher elevations.

altitude maps, preparing photos Using a paint application, there are several things the user can do to make photos more suitable for translation into 3D altitude map-based objects in 3D applications, especially if the 3D application is *Bryce's* Terrain Editor. The user can use a blur filter several times on the image. This tones down the areas that are prone to be translated as 3D spikes. Another possibility is to enhance the contrast of the image. This will make altitude data more contrasted and obvious. 24-bit color can be changed into grayscale. This allows visualization of what the translation might look like in 3D. Finally, unwanted data can be deleted. This can be very important. If the user needs to translate facial information to 3D, for instance, there is no need for the background. For translation in the *Bryce* Terrain Editor, make the unwanted data pure black. For translation in the *Materials Lab*, make the deleted parts of the photo white. If both translations are needed, create two images, one with a white backdrop and one with black. This allows precise mapping of colored image data on a 3D object later on. Image data is usually mapped perpendicular to the height data.

altitude maps, scanning real-world objects It is possible to scan more than 2D images on a scanner. A variety of 3D objects can be placed on the scanning platen (as long as the user is careful not to scratch the glass). Exploring and experimenting may allow the user to wind up with a graphic that translates into an interesting altitude map.

always event An event in a game created with *The Games Factory* that always oc-curs when that point in the game is reached.

amacrine cells Cells in the retina of the human eye that help collect and integrate adjacent photoreceptor signals.

Amapi A 3D application for creating and customizing props for a wide range of other 3D applications. *Amapi* is available for both the Mac and Windows. *Amapi* is a full-fledged 3D design system in its own right, allowing creation of models from scratch. Amapi can also be used as a 3D file translator, an intermediate step in getting the user's favorite models into other 3D applications. *Amapi* can import *Amapi*, 3DS, 3DMF, Art•lantis *Render*, DXF, IGES, *Illustrator* 3, PICT, and VRML 1 files. It can export *Amapi*, 3DS, 3DGF, 3DMF, Art•lantis *Render*, *Bryce* 2, Clipboard, DXF, FACT, HPGL, IGES, *Illustrator*, *LightWave*, PICT, *POV-Ray*, *Carrara*, *RenderMan*, STL, Strata *Studio*, *trueSpace*, and VRML 1 formats.

ambience value In *Bryce*, the amount of the ambience component that should be applied to the material. If the ambience element is based upon either a color palette assignment or a texture in one or more of the ABCD texture channels, the Ambience Value slider will determine how strong its presence will be in the material. To avoid having the texture appear washed out, be sure not to set the ambience value too high. An exception might be a material that suddenly suffers a blast effect from a cosmic or nuclear device.

ambient color 1. The color of the material when it is in shadow. 2. A color control in *Bryce*. Ambient color is the trickiest to apply, because it can easily throw the color in a scene off balance. In other applications, this is called a "glow" color. It sets the color of an object to be displayed no matter what, in light or in darkness. If used consciously, it can create effects like streetlights and lit windows. If used haphazardly, it can destroy the ability of an object to receive the right shadowing and throw off the balance of a scene, giving the object a washed-out, overexposed appearance.

Ambient Glow A setting for glass or plastic in the Material Generator in the *pluS-pack1* for *trueSpace*. It controls the brightness of the object regardless of light sources.

ambient light Nondirectional light that illuminates objects in a scene as a result of scattered reflection. In an outdoor scene, this light comes from the hemisphere of blue sky and is approximately 20% of the intensity of direct sunlight. In modeling scenes with a computer, an ambient light term is usually applied to every object rendered.

ambient light.

ambient reflection coefficient The ambient reflection coefficient (k), which ranges from 0 to 1, is the amount of ambient light that is reflected from an object's surface.

ambient value A brightness control for a material's shaded regions. The ambient value of a material determines the amount of ambient light that a material will reflect. Higher ambient values result in less contrast between the ambient and diffuse colors of an object because the ambient areas are reflecting more. If the ambient value of a material is lower, the area of a material that is in shadow will be closer to black.

ambiguity function In radar, a function of range and range rate that vanishes everywhere except at one sharp function, thereby eliminating ambiguous radar signals that might be confused with the real target.

American National Standards Institute (ANSI) A nongovernmental organization that develops and publishes industry-wide standards for voluntary use throughout the United States. See *ANSI Standards*.

America Online (AOL) A popular online service that offers Internet connection and e-mail services. One of the main reasons AOL gained its popularity is its implementation of an easy-to-use interface for new computer users.

amicable number One of a pair of numbers for which the sum of the divisors of one of a pair of amicable numbers equals the other amicable number, and vice versa.

ammonia A common chemical used in the processing of diazo film. It alkalizes the acidic elements of an exposed diazo coating, leaving the image on the paper. Xerography has largely replaced diazo processing except for very large drawings.

A-mode EDL An *EDL* sorted in order of master record in timecode.

Amorphium Pro A 3D application from Electric Image that offers a technique for creating and texturing organic models. More akin to real-world sculpting than normal 3D modeling, *Amorphium* lets the user create 3D shapes by painting on amorphous blobs. As the user strokes the object, the brush either pushes or pulls the surface of the blob, or creates a wide range of additional 3D effects.

amorphous solid A solid whose atoms are randomly distributed.

amp Short for *ampere*, a unit that measures electrical current.

Ampex Digital Optics **(ADO)** A machine using multipass transformations for video production.

anaglyph 3D drawing A drawing using red and green pixels to produce a picture that appears three-dimensional when viewed through special eye wear, in which one lens is red and the other green. A number of developers market automatic anaglyph plug-ins for the major 2D compositing applications.

analog The representation of data or physical quantities by a continuous signal whose instantaneous amplitude is a function of the value of the data or physical quantity that the signal represents. For example, the instantaneous amplitude of the voltage produced by a sensor to represent the speed of rotation of a shaft would be considered an *analog* signal. Contrast to *digital*, which represents data or physical quantities by binary numbers. In the example given above, the *digital* representation would be in terms of a series of numbers representing the value at various sampling points.

analog camera A traditional camcorder that stores video and audio on tape as analog waves.

analog color Color movies stored in analog form. There are three types of analog video connections, and each treats color differently. In ascending order of quality, they are: *composite video*, *Y/C video*, and *component video*. Composite video bundles all of the luminance and chrominance information into a single signal (i.e., a composite signal). It typically connects to a deck or monitor through an RCA connector or a single BNC connector. In Y/C video (also known as *S-Video*), the video signal is broken down into two parts: luminance and chrominance. This results in better signal quality than composite video, but not as high a quality as component video. Y/C video connects using a proprietary connector. Component video divides the video signal into four different parts: YRGB, where Y = luminance; R = red; G = green; and B = blue. This results in a higher-quality signal than composite or Y/C video. Component video typically connects using four separate BNC connectors, one for each video signal.

analog computer A computer in which variables used to represent data are continuous rather than discrete. An analog computer can, for example, use electric voltages and currents to represent quantities that vary continuously. Components of an analog computer consist of circuits that perform simple mathematical functions on the analog signals, such as summation, multiplication, division, differentiation, or integration. These components are connected in series as needed to apply a desired mathematical equation to the incoming data. Analog computers are limited in accuracy by the precision of the parts used in the circuits; by changes in part characteristics caused by temperature, humidity, pressure, or aging; and by variations in the supply voltages.

analog consumer format Formats developed for home video such as VHS, S-VHS, Betamax, 8mm, and Hi8.

analog digitizers A device (such as the *Targa 2000, Canopus Rex, Media 100,* and some Avid products) that takes an analog signal from a camcorder or deck and digitizes it using a video card installed in the computer. After digitizing, this same video card compresses the video signal for storage on the hard drive.

analogous colors Any combination of colors adjacent to each other on the color-wheel.

analog RGB monitor A color computer monitor that accepts and displays red, green, and blue signals of any amplitude from zero to some maximum level. This permits creation of an unlimited number of different colors, whereas a digital monitor, which accepts just a few levels of each color, is severely limited in the number of colors it can produce. On the

other hand, producing signals from a digital computer to drive an analog monitor is much more complicated than producing driving signals for a digital monitor. EGA monitors are digital monitors. VGA monitors (and television sets) are analog monitors.

analog-to-digital (A/D) converter A device for converting a voltage level into a digital number consisting of a series of bits that represents the level. A digital voltmeter, for example, accepts a voltage level input, passes it through an analog-to-digital converter, and displays a number representing the voltage. A voltage of 412 volts would be converted to the binary number 110011100, which is equivalent to the decimal number 412.

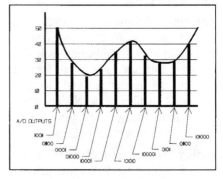

analog-to-digital converter.

analysis of light Lighting analysis is the evaluation of the way a specific luminaire (a light fixture) affects an environment as well as the analysis of mixed-lighting situations, including daylight. It can be a direct visual display of computed luminance values on the scene's surface or a graphic representation of those values. Either way, it shows how a specific scene handles both artificial and natural light. With the advent of IES files, (Illuminating Engineering Soci-

analogous colors.

ety) lighting analysis is more accurate, because the visualization program is directly using the manufacturer's measured light distribution data. Lighting analysis could fall under the category of *design visualization*, but this term normally refers to architectural and interior design analysis, which primarily is concerned with mass, form, shape, and material property selections on a scene.

anamorphic image 1. An image that is unequally scaled in the horizontal and vertical dimensions. 2. A distorted image frequently used in movie formats (such as Panavision) where the width field of a wide-angle picture is compressed into a 35-mm frame and the process is optically reversed on projection to give a wide-screen display.

anamorphic lenses Special lenses that shoot a wide-screen image, but optically compress the image to a normal 4:3 aspect ratio. The wide-screen image can be uncompressed by a projector fitted with a similar anamorphic lens, or by software that knows the image should be stretched.

anastomosis Branch reconnection that may take place between the veins of a leaf. Important in modeling plant structures.

anchored sprites In the *Game Creation System*, objects or symmetrical objects are things like trees, floor lamps, and chairs. Unlike walls, which are stationary and can be viewed from various angles, symmetrical objects always look the same. The viewing direction does not matter because they always rotate to face the player. These stand-up objects are also called *anchored sprites* and will always turn to face the player.

anchor of pattern The relation of the area of a pattern to that of a primitive so as to permit determining which pixel in the pattern corresponds to the current pixel of the primitive.

AND 1. A logic function whose output contains a one in every bit position where both of two inputs contained a one. Normally written in all capital letters, although not an acronym, to distinguish that it is a logic function. 2. To perform the AND function.

Anderson localization A lack of diffusion in certain disordered systems, which can be solved exactly through the use of the Bethe lattice.

Anderson Report, The A monthly newsletter on computer graphics, specializing in graphics industry business actions and new graphics products.

Andrew A window-management system.

Andromeda F/X A number of volumes of plug-ins for 2D graphics applications, each offering unique painting and texturing tools that can help the user create texture maps and backgrounds for artwork. These include *Screens, LensDoc, Perspective, CutLines,* and *S-Multi*. Andromeda specializes in creating filters that make digital work resemble traditional artwork in many cases.

anechoic environment A volume in which no reflections of waves exist.

Anfy Java A set of 40 animated Java applets that can be used to enhance Java programs or Web pages.

angle increment In turtle geometry, the angle through which the turtle is turned in response to a + or - command.

angle of incidence The acute angle between a ray that is incident to the surface of an object and the surface normal at the point of intersection with the surface.

angle of reflection The acute angle between a ray that is reflected from the surface of an object at the point where an incident ray intersects the surface and the surface normal at the point of intersection.

angle of refraction The acute angle between a ray transmitted through an object from the surface and the surface normal at the point of origin of the ray.

Angle of Revolution A setting in *Universe* that determines the angle through which a profile is revolved to create an image using the Revolve tool.

angular deflection The displacement of points in rotational transformation in which each point at a specified distance from the origin is deflected by a specified angle.

angular distortion The variation in appearance of an object as the viewing distance is changed, due to the characteristics of the human eye. Too large a viewing distance makes the object appear flat. Too small a viewing distance makes the object appear distorted and overly angular.

angular momentum The momentum of a mass m moving with a speed v in a circle of radius r. The angular momentum is mvr. Angular momentum is an important factor in creating animated displays of particle or planet orbits. When a body is moving relative to a point of reference and its motion is not directly toward or away from that point, it is said to have angular momentum with respect to that point. The angular momentum vector, L, is defined as the cross product of the position vector r and the linear momentum vector p. The vector L is therefore orthogonal to both r and p. When a force acts to change angular momentum, it is said to cause a torque. The time derivative of the angular momentum is equal to the net torque on the body.

angular velocity The speed at which a body is rotating, usually expressed in revolutions per some time unit, such as revolutions per second or revolutions per minute. An important factor in creating animated displays of particle or planet orbits.

animal models, assigning human characteristic An alternate approach in *Poser* for posing animals is to apply the *Poser* controls that are normally used to pose humans. The resulting animations make animals behave more like humans, which may sometimes be desired.

animal models, natural posing In *Poser*, animal models have a number of parameter controls such as Mouth, Waist Bend, Neck Bend, Shoulders, Tail, etc. (depending upon the model) that may be used to simulate natural positions of the animal. These can be used to represent animal positions that are associated with such animal actions as wildness, begging, stretching, jumping, etc.

animals and Walk Designer The Walk Designer in *Poser* addresses one of the most complex tasks that an animator faces: how to create a realistic walk pattern for a targeted character. In *Poser*, the targeted character is usually bipedal. The Zygote Chimpanzee and the Raptor are animals that work well with Walk Designer. ⬬

animatable objects hierarchy Animatable objects hierarchy refers to the organization of geometry within separate animatable objects. Subobjects within the model may need to be animated separately, and should be designed as separate objects. A model of a robot cannot be effectively walk-animated if the legs are one single object. A decision on how effectively a model is structured for animation must be made within the context of a shot. A model may be suitable for one shot but not for another. ☞

animated ambient light In all 3D applications, ambient light can be animated. Animating ambient light in conjunction with other lighting is a way to create fade-ins and fade-outs.

animated GIF images A collection of sequential images placed into a single file. The GIF format is especially suited for Web animations.

animated hand A hand can be manually animated in *Poser* as follows. First, move any of the elements that need to be posed. Then go to the Animation Controller and move to another frame. Pose the hand elements again. Repeat this process until the elements at the last frame have been posed. Then, preview the results, edit where necessary, and save to disk. ☞

animated map A map that is applied to the surface of an object to create an animated texture, i.e. the texture changes during the display period.

animated reflections, *Poser* An animated reflection can be created with *Poser* by recording an animated figure against a light blue background, rotating the figure 180 degrees around the y axis, and then flipping the figure horizontally. The flipped animation can then be added to the original animation and

moved and enlarged slightly so that both figures can be seen. ☞

animatics Moving animated storyboards. Animatics and volumetrics are 3D models that are geometrically simplified versions of complex (existing or planned) 3D models. Animatics are used as temporary stand-ins for complex geometry inside the animation environment to speed up the animation work flow. Because they have only a fraction of the polygons of final models, animatics can be manipulated quickly. Often the animation environment can manipulate animatic and volumetric models in real time, even with low-cost 3D acceleration hardware, or on systems using only software-based 3D acceleration. Both volumetric and animatic models are used in the same fashion; the only difference is that animatics have slightly more geometric detail than volumetrics. Ideally, both volumetrics and animatic geometry should have similar topological arrangements as the final shot models. That is, inside the animation environment, animatic and volumetric models have the same parent/child relationships, the same link/pivot points, and the same inverse kinematics constraints as the complex geometry for which they are substituted.

animating appendages To animate appendages in any 3D application, insert appendage controls between all child and parent objects that make up a linked hierarchy for sets of body parts. ☞

animating deformers Deformers give animations a lifelike elasticity. Without deformers, a character might seem rigid and dry. Clever use of the stretch deformer "springs" an animation to life so that the body stretches during takeoff, and then squashes upon landing.

animating facial expressions There are three simple rules that help create realistic facial expressions: First is to keep the head moving. One common mistake made in character animation is to keep the head still. In reality the head moves quite frequently. It is not always a dramatic movement but there is plenty of subtle movement. Incorporating this movement into animations will add depth to the character, making it appear more believable. When the head moves frequently throughout the entire animation, the motion serves two purposes. It brings the figure to life and it keeps the viewer interested in watching the figure. The second rule is to move the eyes. Steady eyes are boring, not to mention eerie. The character shouldn't stare at the viewer. People's eyes are always looking about for something interesting to focus on. The movement doesn't have to be dramatic, but it should be frequent and there must be times when the movement is severe, meaning they look to the side or even up and down. In order for an animation to be realistic, this eye movement needs to be incorporated. The eyes should move frequently during conversation. This breaks the monotony of the animation. Also notice that the head is leading the eyes when a figure turns his head. There is a common misconception that the eyes lead the head. While the eyes may pick up on items in their peripheral vision, the head initiates the move before the eyes lock onto the target. The third rule is to move the mouth. This is a critical technique of effective facial animation. It's obvious the head moves for lip-synch, but what

about the times when the character isn't speaking? Subtle mouth movements are very natural in humans, particularly when they think. They will quite often bite their tongues, lick their lips, roll their lips inward, press hard on them, and even chew on them. These are all common nervous habits; they may be undesirable nervous ticks, but they make realistic animations. Also, don't forget about saliva. We are constantly swallowing saliva but a 3D character seldom does it. In a good animation the figure may tighten his lips and his throat will move upward. This demonstrates the act of "swallowing." The character should also "chew," as older people tend to do, and lick the lips. These subtle touches make a great impact on the animation.

animation 1. Literally, to bring to life. 2. A graphic method that creates the illusion of motion by rapid viewing of individual frames in a sequence. Each frame has differences from the previous one in terms of position, shape, color, transparency, structure, or texture of an object, so as to give the appearance when viewed of a real-life changing scene. Because not all parts of a frame change from one frame in the sequence to the next, the amount of memory required can be much less than would be required for the same number of independent pictures. 3. The use of computer graphics to prepare sequences of frames for simulating motion. 4. A codec for saving or storing an animation. See *animation compressor.*

animation, basic rules Rules that have been developed for producing animated displays. They include *squash and* *stretch*, in which, for example, a bouncing ball elongates as it nears the floor, squashes when it hits the floor, and then elongates again as it rebounds; *slow-in and slow-out* to smooth interpolation and avoid distracting jerky motions; and *staging action properly*, which includes selecting a view that supplies the most action about an event and isolating events so that there is only one event occupying the viewer's attention at any time.

animation, cartoon-character Animation began with the creation of cartoon characters in the early 1900s. Many of the foundations of animation were established at that time and are still being used.

animation compressor A lossless Quick-Time codec that can handle 32-bit depths. This means that it can preserve Alpha channel information as the user moves files between applications. Because this codec is not fast enough to handle most playback situations, it should be used only as an intermediate or archiving codec.

animation, conventional Animation produced by manually preparing each frame of the animation sequence. Usually a *storyboard*, a display that shows the structure and ideas of the animation, is laid out first. Then *key frames* are produced for critical parts of the sequence. Finally, in a process called *in-betweening*, the intermediate frames are filled in.

animation, creating Given a set of animation frames, they can be combined into a multiframe file in several formats (QuickTime, AVI, FLASH, GIF, etc.) and displayed on a computer monitor with the right viewer. Using an application called *GIF Construction Set for Windows*, one can view animated GIF files. See *Alchemy Mindworks*.

animation, double-framed order A technique for recording an animation by recording each even-numbered frame twice and dropping the odd-numbered frames. When displayed, the resulting animation makes animation errors more obvious.

Animation Editor A feature of *The Game Factory (TGF)* that makes animation of objects easy. There are two methods to edit or create an animated object using *TGF*. The user can go to the Level Editor and open a library of objects from the pull-down bar in the menu, and then pick an object from the Object Shelf on the left of the Level Editor. Alternatively, a new active object can be created using the New Object icon on the toolbar at the top of the screen. Only active objects can be animated from the Animation Editor.

animation, explicit control Control of animation by providing a description of everything that occurs in the animation, either by fully specifying changes such as scaling, translation, and rotation, or by defining key frames and specifying the interpolation methods to be used between them.

animation, flip book A traditional form of previewing an animation in which successive frames are printed on successive pages and the appearance of motion is achieved by flipping through the pages of the resulting book.

animation GIF files GIF files that contain a sequence of animation frames so that when properly viewed an animated picture appears on the computer display. These files are especially suited to Web publishing.

animation, graphical languages Computer languages that describe the changes that take place in a computer-generated animation in a visual, rather than a textual, manner.

animation, key frame One of a number of important frames that are used initially to delineate the "key" actions in an animation sequence. The intermediate frames are then filled in (called *in-betweening*) to complete the animation.

animation, linear-list notations A language for describing animation by listing the beginning frame and ending frame and the action that is to take place (the event) for each action in the animation.

animation, look-up table (lut) Use of a double-buffering scheme to improve animation when computation of color information requires so much time that display time would be marginal. One frame buffer is loaded with the current object colors, then the next set of color calculations is placed in a second frame buffer, then the next set of color calculations is placed in the first buffer again and so forth. Since one buffer always has a completed set of color combinations, the display can switch back and forth to display good data all the time, independent of the required calculation time.

animation, loop interpolation/quaternion interpolation Methods of interpolating between keyframes when using *Poser*. Quaternion interpolation is a special mathematical interpolation technique that produces in-between motions

that are more predictable between poses, but can cause strange-looking discontinuities in the graphs of individual rotation parameters. The interpolation happens by using all three rotation channels at once, instead of simply interpolating each one individually (which is the default). It is useful only for animators who are really getting into the fine details of working out animations, and are experiencing difficulty. Loop interpolation allows for easier creation of cycling animations. If the user has a 30-frame sequence, puts keyframes only at frames 1 and 15 (introducing some change at 15), and turns on loop interpolation, the user will see that the animation smoothly blends through frame 30 back to frame 1. If the user puts keyframes near the end that are not similar to frame 1, he may get some very unexpected and strange in-betweens in the frames just before these, because the last frame is essentially the frame before the first frame.

animation, Make Movie A button in *Poser* that prepares the final recording. There are three separate steps, each with its own dialog: Movie Parameter Settings, Compression Settings, and the Save Path dialog.

animation, Mute Sound/Clear Sound Controls used in *Poser* to control sound from an audio file when one is loaded as part of the animation.

animation, on fields With conventional television video, a complete frame is created by two full passes across the screen called *fields*; the first reproduces the odd numbered scan lines and the second reproduces the even scan lines. The entire process is repeated each 1/30th of a second. This is known as *interlacing*. For animation on fields, the pixel colors are computed as for a television display, but the entire frame data is displayed for each $\frac{1}{60}$th second scan. The result is a better display than the usual television display, but not as good as if all pixels were calculated for each field.

Animation palette.

animation, on-twos Animation that is produced with a temporal resolution that is on half the display's refresh rate so that each animation frame is shown for two display refresh cycles. The result is jerkier animation or a more blurred display.

animation painting A class of post-production applications that allows one to add painting effects to animation frames. Important applications to consider for animation painting include: Adobe *After Effects*, Corel *Painter*, NewTek *Aura*, Discreet's *Combustion*, and Ulead's *Media Studio Pro*.

Animation palette A set of controls for editing *Poser* animation. At the bottom of the palette is a green line with an arrow on each end. This represents the play range of the animation. The user can move the right arrow to the right until it reaches the last frame in the sequence, and to the left to any frame before that. The user can move the left arrow to the right to any frame before the right arrow, and to the left as far as the first frame. Limiting the play range allows the user to preview a sequence of

any length, which is very useful for catching and correcting unwanted glitches.

animation, physically based Animation in which the movements of objects in the image sequence are simulations of the physical movements that occur with real-life physical objects. Most animation is of this nature.

animation, play movie file A control that allows the user to play AVI or QuickTime movies inside of any 3D application, though the term may have somewhat different wording. This is useful in previewing an animation that could be used for a background or in previewing an animation that has just been created but not yet saved in its final resolution.

animation, procedural control Control of animation by causing the various elements of a model as a command interface in order to determine the animation's properties.

animation retiming A command that permits retiming an animation sequence from one length to another without reconfiguring all the keyframes. *Poser* is a 3D application that includes animation retiming, while a similar feature is also offered in Adobe *After Effects* for 2D-composited animations.

animation script A rough draft of how an animation should be set up, usually preceeding a storyboard.

animation sequencer A graphic linear time line sequencer for plotting the sequencing of an animation film.

animation setup dialog A window or panel with settings for animation. The first and most important item to configure is the FPS (frames per second) input; numbers less than 10 or more than 30 are not used. The most common FPS rates are 15, 24, 29.97 (and other SMPTE rates), and 30. Some applications do not offer interleaved 60 FPS field rendering, commonly used in broadcast video productions. 30 FPS is the best video choice for NTSC (25 FPS for PAL), except for SMPTE work (called "drop frame"), which involves the capacity to add and edit synchronized audio with specific hardware. Three additional options that have an important effect on animations may be available: Once, Repeat, and Pendulum (sometimes called "Ping-Pong"). These options affect how the animated objects in the scene will be displayed when previewed, and also how they will act in a rendered animation if the sequence is long enough. Play Once is the default, allowing the animation to move from start to finish as expected. Repeat plays the animation from start to finish over and over again until the stop button is hit. Pendulum plays the animation from start to finish and then finish to start, continuously, until the stop button is hit. These preview options are important because some multimedia and Web designers need their animations to play in a looping manner, and this allows a preview of those motions.

Animation Shop A full-featured tool for creating animated GIFs that has been included with *Paint Shop Pro*. Note that GIF animations have a 256 color palette.

animation, staging of Arranging animation so that it is most easily viewed. This includes selecting a viewpoint that supplies the viewer with the most information possible about the events taking place and arranging the timing of events so that only a single event at a time occupies the viewer's attention.

Animation tab 1. A feature of *trueSpace* that allows the user to define the animation length (in frames), and decide how often to set keyframes. 2. A tab in the *DynaWave* plug-in for *trueSpace* that provides access to all of the plug-ins' basic features, including wave setting and object effectors. 3. A tab present on the interfaces of most animation applications, giving access to the animation controls.

animation techniques, linked material shells Just as clouds can be mapped to an outer sphere that revolves around a planet object, any object can also have its own outer shell. Shells can also be used for clothing on a human figure for more esoteric results. It is possible, for instance, to wrap a shell on a human, animal, or robotic figure and map it with a fuzzy light, giving the figure a perceptible aura as it moves in the scene.

animation techniques, null objects A null object is any object in a scene that has power over other objects or facets of an animation without itself having to be rendered. Null objects are usually invisible and vital for certain animation actions and effects. There can be an infinite array of null object types. Five important uses are: appendage controls, gravity wells, negative and intersecting Booleans, camera targets, and propagation engines for creating object arrays.

animation techniques, propagation The Propagation toggles in *Bryce* are the four options under the Linking member name in the Animation tab of the object's Attributes dialog. They appear when the user sets the linked parent's name. They are Distance, Offset, Rotation, and Size. They take any or all of these attributes from what the user does to the parent. If the user activates Rotation, for instance, the linked child will rotate when the parent of that child is rotated.

animation tools Tools that are used to produce and modify animations. They include the following: spline-based motion paths, point-at and align-to-path functions, velocity controls, inverse kinematics for character animation, and more.

animation, tracking live action Enacting a scene with live actors who have sensors at critical parts of their bodies, and recording the information gathered to use in drawing animation frames. The same technique is used to create BVH motion files that many 3D applications can apply to various animatable characters for extremely-real motion sequences.

animation, weighted morphing The ability to morph a base or anchor model into two or more target models simultaneously. The user can select the percentage of the base model that is to be morphed into each target model and thereby create a precisely-determined new figure.

animism The primal view that everything in the world, from rocks and trees to all of the animals, is conscious and alive. Animism is a motivating principle for animation, especially the animation of non-human and non-organic objects that seem to evidence a personality.

anisotropic materials Materials for which the refractive index depends on the direction in which the light travels. The term *anisotropic materials* commonly refers to a reflection or transmission that changes relative to the rotation on the surface's normal. It means that the reflection or the transmission depends on the viewer's angle. It is a kind of directional reflection that depends on the viewer's perspective and angle.

anisotropic reflection A variation in the index of refraction in birefringent crystals with direction of an impinging light beam, produced by the orderly arrangement of the atoms in the crystalline lattice.

anisotropic transformation A mapping that does not preserve the original ratio of the x (horizontal) and y (vertical) components, thereby transforming squares to rectangles and circles to ovals. This often occurs unintentionally when using computer graphics displays that don't use square pixels. It is then necessary to provide correction so that pictures will be accurate representations.

anisotropy The exhibiting of properties with different values when measured along axes in different directions, such as those produced when light impinges on the orderly array of atoms in a crystalline lattice.

annotation The attachment of alphanumeric or other data to a graphics image in a computer.

annotation text Text that is always displayed in a predetermined size and orientation. See *structure text*.

anomalous dimension A dimension between normal integer dimensions. For example, a line that wanders around to fill almost all of space intuitively appears to have a dimension greater than 1 (which is the normal dimension of a straight line) and less than 2 (which is the normal dimension of a plane). See *Hausdorff dimension* for an example of how an anomalous dimension is found mathematically.

ANSI See *American National Standards Institute*.

ANSI standards Standards developed and published by the *American National Standards Institute*.

answer expression An expression that provides the viewer with a visual answer to a question posed. Common answer expressions include the following: crying, surprise, laughter, phony smile, exertion, phony laughter, pain, smiling, terror, facial shrug, repulsion, disgust, and disdain. Answer expressions quite often follow *question expressions*. For example, the question expression "afraid" suggests that the person is concerned about some impending doom. When creating animations, or even a still, the faces of the characters should communicate the story. A facial animation is a success when the sound can be turned off and the viewers can still understand the intended message.

answer print The final print of a film after color-timing.

Antialias Document A menu option in *Poser* that antialiases the Document Window contents.

antialiased brushes A technique for drawing antialiased curves on a digital picture. The brush is a square array of pixels that has a resolution 16 times as high in each coordinate direction as final bitmap. The path along which the brush is dragged is also stored in high resolution. The resulting curve is filtered to eliminate the high-resolution components, resulting in a low-resolution bitmap without aliasing.

antialiasing 1. The act of taking special precautions to limit or eliminate aliasing artifacts. Also known as *anti-aliasing*. 2. In image generation, any technique that is used to remove the artifacts (such as staircasing and line breakup) that are caused when producing an image by sampling a picture that has higher spatial frequencies than the sampling frequency. When applied to individual primitives rather than the whole image, other artifacts may be introduced. Techniques that are applied before sampling actually prevent aliasing rather than remove it. There are several commonly used filters for antialiasing. The *box filter* simply picks the closest values for interpolation. The *Gaussian filter* makes use of the Gaussian function for weighting. The Gaussian function is:

$$\text{Gaussian} = \frac{1}{\sqrt{n}} = (x)2^{-nx^2}$$

The most commonly used values of n are 2 and 4. The *Lanczos2 sinc filter* uses the Lanczos2 sinc function for weighting. This function is:

$$\text{Lanczos2}(x) = \frac{\sin(\pi x)}{\pi x} \frac{\sin(\frac{\pi x}{2})}{\frac{\pi x}{2}}, \quad |x| < 2$$

$$0, \quad |x| \geq 2$$

antialiasing.

antialiasing, 2-bit A method for antialiasing on a computer display with a very limited number of color shades (by representing the color by two bits per pixel). In this case, a simple area-sampling technique will provide adequate antialiasing.

antialiasing, analytic The use of mathematical techniques to determine directly the exact solutions needed to perform antialiasing (within the limits of computer precision).

antialiasing, circles and conics Because of the continuous and varying curvature, antialiasing of circles and conics is more difficult than antialiasing lines. One way to antialias a circle of unit thickness is to define a decision variable $S(x, y)$ that is proportional to signed distance of a point from the circle. This number can be used as an index to a Gupta-Sproull look-up table, just as in the case of lines. Usually, the nearest point to the circle is determined by choosing between the east and northeast pixels when principally stepping horizontally and between the north and northeast pixels when principally stepping vertically. For circles or conics, as the direction changes and a different technique is required, a notch is left if the curve is wider than unit width. Hagen uses a clever technique for antialiasing that widens sometimes vertically, sometimes horizontally, and sometimes diagonally. This works well for circles and conics.

antialiasing, Gupta-Sproull The Gupta-Sproull scan-conversion algorithm makes use of a precomputed table of values of a filter function that determines the color and brightness of a pixel as a function of the distance between the line and the pixel's center. The algorithm chooses the next point to be displayed and then uses the table to determine its intensity and that of its two vertical neighbors.

antialiasing, numerical Use of numerical techniques to obtain estimates for the information needed to perform antialiasing.

antialiasing, polygons and rectangles Line antialiasing techniques work well for rectangles and polygons except at the points where two sides join together. Gupta and Sproull have a method that handles these cases. It uses two numbers, the distances from the pixel to the two adjoining sides to provide the entry point to the Gupta-Sproull table.

antialiasing, temporal Any technique for reducing the aliasing artifacts caused by the rate of frame sampling in an animated sequence being too low in frequency to capture all of the changes caused by the motion of objects.

antialiasing, text Text cannot be satisfactorily scan-converted on a stroke by stroke basis because the geometry of the characters in a type font is highly interrelated, with size, thickness, and shape of individual characters critical. Therefore, fonts are usually represented by sequences of spline curves giving the outline of each character. These can be used to generate characters on a display that do not have aliasing artifacts, but the cost is that storing the splines requires a large amount of memory.

antialiasing, Wu An antialiasing technique developed by Xiaolin Wu that moves along the major axis of a line a pixel at a time, but instead of using a decision function to determine whether to paint the pixel that is above or below the line, it paints both the pixels but uses the decision function to determine the color and intensity to be used to paint each one.

anticipation The few movements that lead up to the primary action. If something is being shot out of a cannon, for example, it would be boring to see a cannon sitting there and then a puff of smoke emerging from it. In terms of cartoons, the cannon usually swells first and then spits out a cannonball as it returns to its regular shape. The same principle is true of a character. If someone is going to jump into the air, he crouches down first before springing away.

anti-halation backing A coating on the back surface of a film that absorbs light and thereby prevents reflection back to the film emulsion, which would cause a *halo* or glowing effect that reduces resolution.

antihelix An element of the ear that is two-thirds the height of the ear and extends from the top of the earlobe to just under the helix.

antipersistence The quality of not having independent increments.

A-O See *Acousto-Optic*.

AOL See *America Online*.

APA See *all points addressable*.

aperiodicity Irregularly occurring; not having a defined term, limit, or period.

aperiodic orbit An orbit in which the same value never occurs twice.

aperiodic tiling Filling of a plane by two different tiles.

aperture In any type of camera, light is focused by the lens, through an aperture and onto the focal plane. The size of the aperture controls how much light passes through to the focal plane. The size is controlled by a ring of metal leaves called a diaphragm. In addition to controlling the brightness of the exposure, the aperture controls the depth of field in the image. By balancing the size of the aperture (as measured in f-stops) with the shutter speed, the photographer can trade off between varying depth of field and/or the ability to better resolve fast motion. Aperture is the size of the opening of the lens diaphragm. Changing the aperture affects the exposure of the film. The aperture controls the amount of light flow. It is primarily a controller of intensity or brightness of light. Enlarging the aperture opening allows more light to pass through the lens; inversely, decreasing the aperture opening diminishes the light flowing through the opening. *F-stops* in still photography and *t-stops* in motion photography indicate the size of the aperture opening. F-stop is short for focal stop; t-stop is short for transmission stop. The difference between an f-stop and a t-stop is that t-stops are more accurate; they are based on the actual light transmission of a particular lens. F-stops, in contrast, are based on the ratio of the lens focal length with the iris. ⌒

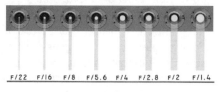

F/22 F/16 F/8 F/5.6 F/4 F/2.8 F/2 F/1.4

aperture.

apex maximal One type of cross-section in *form•Z* is a standard key cross-section. A key cross-section is a user-defined 2D shape, usually a planar closed curve that defines the shape of the 3D form at the location along the loft trajectory where it is placed. A key cross-section is placed along the loft trajectory

and is aligned to both profile shapes. With respect to profile shapes, a key cross-section is placed at apex points of maximal curvature for each of the profiles. The position at which a key cross-section is placed is called an *apex maximal*, and it is a point on a curve where the degree of curvature is the greatest. The simplest example of an apex maximal point is the widest portion of an egg, when viewed in profile. Using a lifting body aircraft design as an example, there is a point at which the blended airfoil surfaces begin. That point is the apex maximal and that is where a key cross-section is placed.

Apfelmannchen German for *apple mannikin*. A name applied to the Mandelbrot set in many German publications. The set is a plot representing the result of iterating the equation:

$$z_{n+1} = z_n^2 + c$$

where z and c are both complex numbers. For a picture of this set, see *Mandelbrot set.*

API See *application programmer's interface.*

Apollonian packing of circles A fractal produced by drawing three circles tan-

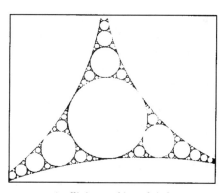

Apollinian packing of circles.

gent to one another, then filling the circular triangle created by the three circles with the largest circle tangent to all three, which creates three smaller circular triangles, each of which is filled with the largest circle tangent to the three bounding circles, and continuing the process forever. The resulting figure is also known as the *Apollonian gasket* or *Apollonian net*.

apostlib An international unit of luminance. An apostlib is equal to 0.1 millilambert. Also known as a *blondel*.

apparent length To an observer, the length an object appears to have, as opposed to its true length.

appendage control An object, most commonly a sphere, inserted between the moving child object in a linked hierarchy and its parent.

Apple Computer Apple Computer Co. was founded in 1976 by Steve Jobs and Steve Wozniak, who designed the Apple 1, a simple personal computer based on the 6502 microprocessor chip. Apple has grown to be one of the largest personal computer companies. Its current Macintosh and G4 models are well known for their desktop publishing and graphics capabilities.

Apple Desktop Bus (ADB) Vintage plug-in port on the Apple Macintosh computer for connection of the keyboard, mouse, trackball, etc. See also *USB* and *Firewire*.

Apple DV A codec built into QuickTime that clamps luminance. There is no option to make it do otherwise. In addition, the QuickTime codec performs a slight adjustment to the midtones (or gamma) to darken DV images so that they will be improved on the computer screen. The user can undo Apple's automatic gamma correction by applying a levels filter to the footage. Use a gamma setting of about 1.2. To undo this correction, apply a levels filter with a gamma of around .84.

AppleScript A script created with the Mac AppleScript editor to establish a configuration that is needed for a particular application.

applet A small, self-contained Java program that is embedded inside HTML files so it can be downloaded from the World Wide Web into a Java-enabled browser. A Java applet includes several methods used by the runtime system to determine how to handle the applet, such as when a user looks at a page, or clicks an applet icon.

AppleTalk Filing Protocol (AFP) A protocol used by non-Apple networks to access data from an AppleTalk server.

appletviewer A feature of the Java language that allows the viewing of applets.

application-dependent data Stored data from which, with minor modifications, many different images may be drawn. For example, a list of polygons could be stored that describe a head-on view of a human face and then many different faces could be drawn by adding a slight amount of information that specifies changes in the position of some of the polygons for a particular face.

application program A software program designed to accomplish some particular set of tasks unrelated to computer systems operation, as opposed to a *system program* whose primary purpose is to improve computer operations.

application programmer's interface (API) Those portions of a program that create the look and feel of a program interface and determine how it is used.

Application Specific Integrated Circuit (ASIC) A proprietary integrated circuit design produced through standardized methods of modifying standard integrated circuit cell assemblies or gate arrays.

applications binary interface (ABI) Low-level interface specifications for a graphics or software system.

approximating fraction When a continued fraction is used to represent the true value of a fraction, an *approximating fraction* is created by breaking off the continued fraction at any point. The more terms included in the approximating fraction, the closer the approximation approaches the true value.

approximating function A continued fraction used to approximate a function.

approximation A simplified expression that gives an estimate of the true value of a function.

APT See *automatically programmed tool.*

arbitration A protocol used to determine which of competing modules requesting use of a computer bus shall be given control.

Arboretum Ionizer A noise reduction plug-in for sound editing that permits adding of special effects and cleaning field recordings and telephone interviews.

arc 1. A portion of a circle or ellipse. 2. In typeface design, a curved stroke that is a part of a character not enclosing an area.

arc.

Arc2D A Java method that defines, draws, and fills an arc.

Archimedean solids, semi-regular A solid whose faces are regular n-gons with more than one n in symmetric arrangement.

Archimedean spiral A spiral curve generated by the following equations:

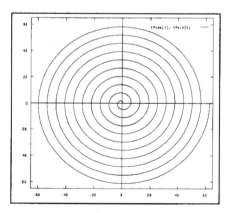

Archimedean spiral.

41

$$x = r_x \theta \cos(\theta)$$

$$y = r_y \theta \sin(\theta)$$

Archimedes cup A solid constructed by expanding a parabola into the third dimension by dividing it into successively smaller triangular shapes and applying a negative midpoint displacement in altitude to each side of each triangular shape.

architecture 1. The style of computer system design at the functional module level which is used to create a machine that is simple and logical. 2. The style of the microprocessor chip used as the basis for a computer such as 80386 architecture or 6880 architecture.

archiving Storing a backup copy of digital data for future reference, particularly for the purpose of restoring the data in the event that the working copy is somehow destroyed. With DOS it is possible to mark working files as having been archived so that a subsequent back-up needs to consider only those files that are new or have been changed.

arc light A bright and powerful type of lamp that emits light by passing electricity through two electrodes.

arc, movement and A 3D application will set "in-between" frames between keyframes that define where the object should be at every point in the animation. Although often the computer's interpolation is in a rounded path, it tends to choose the shortest path between two keyframes. For example, when animating a head turning from side to side, the user sets one keyframe at the point where the head is looking in one direction, and another keyframe when the head is looking in the other direction.

Though the computer's guess of interpolation is a direct curve, organic motion is rarely in a straight path. Almost always, human motion takes place in arcs or curved paths. Thus a more normal head turning operation involves a dip, which typically needs to be considered in organic 3D animation. Keep in mind that although the 3D application is fairly good at making curved paths, these curved paths are often inaccurate for portraying good movement. Although keyframe economy is good (do not insert more than are needed), one should not cheat the movement by not giving enough keyframes to define good, believable movement.

arcsine law The arcsine law says that the probability $p_{2n}(2k)$ that a random walking particle will spend $2k$ time units in a positive region in the time interval from 0 to $2n$ is given by the equation:

$$p_{2n}(2k) = \binom{2k}{k}\binom{2n-2k}{n-k}2^{-2n}$$

area block One of a number of equally-sized regions of terrain features that comprise a terrain database for flight-simulation graphics.

area filling Any method for filling a closed two-dimensional figure with a given color. Many graphics programs have built-in software for filling circles, arcs, and polygons. Another form of filling is *flood-filling*, where a seed point is selected within a bounded surface and color fill proceeds in all directions from this point until the boundaries are encountered.

area-filling curve An infinitely long curve that will completely fill a plane.

area-length relation for river basins
Relationship between the length of a river and the area of its drainage basin, which demonstrates the fractal nature of a river's curve. The relationship is expressed by the equation:

$$K = \frac{(river\ G - length)^{0.6}}{(basin\ G - area)}$$

where *river G-length* is the river's length measured with a ruler of length *G* and *basin G-area* is the area of the river basin measured with the same *G* ruler.

area light A type of light that lights a region of space with soft and diffuse illumination. These are really a group of point source lights arranged in an array.

area-number relation for islands An empirical law that gives the number of islands of a region that are above a given area. The expression is:

$$Nr(A\rangle a) = F'a^{-B}$$

where *Nr(A>a)* is the number of islands whose area is greater than *a,* and *F* and *B* are positive constants, with *B* being less than 2.

area rendering A capability of *trueSpace*. It makes it possible to render only a portion of the screen to file. The button that allows this is in the Render pop-up. Simply select this option and use the mouse to select a rectangular area of the screen. The area inside the rectangle will render immediately.

area sampling A method of antialiasing in which each pixel that is intersected by a line of specified width is painted with an intensity that is proportional to the amount of the pixel that is intersected by the line. In *unweighted area sampling,* equal areas contribute equally in determining the intensity. In *weighted area sampling,* areas close to the pixel's center have more influence on the intensity computation than areas farther away.

area subdivision algorithm A method for visual surface determination. It involves developing decision logic that determines which polygons are visible in an area of the projected image. If this logic is applied to an area and it determines which polygons are visible, they are displayed. If no decision can be reached, the area is divided into smaller areas and the decision logic is applied to them. This process is applied recursively until everything has been displayed.

area subdivision algorithm, Warnock The Warnock area subdivision algorithm divides the display area into four equal squares. For each square, if there are no polygons intersecting the square, it is painted with the background color. If there is only one polygon that intersects the square and it surrounds the square, the square is painted with the polygon color. If there is only one polygon intersecting the square, the square is painted with the background color and then the part intersected by the polygon is painted with the polygon color. If there are several polygons that intersect the square but the nearest one is a surrounding polygon, the square is painted with this polygon's color. For all other cases, the square is divided into four smaller squares and the process is repeated recursively.

arithmetic instruction An assembly language instruction that causes the processor to perform an arithmetic operation (such as add, subtract, compare, increment, or negate).

arithmetic mean A number that is inserted between two other numbers in an arithmetic progression having a value such that the formula $l = a + (n - 1)d$ (where a is the first term, l is the nth term, n is the number of terms, and d is the common difference) is preserved.

Arnold's cat map A two-dimensional map for the description of Hamiltonian nonlinear systems based on the following equations:

$$x_{n+1} = x_n + y_n \bmod 1$$
$$y_{n+1} = x_n + 2y_n \bmod 1$$

The expression *mod 1* means that only fractions in the half-open unit interval [0, 1] are considered.

Arnold's cat map.

Arnold tongues Frequency-locked regions of a Cantor set fractal.

ARPANET Advanced Research Project Agency Network. A pioneering computer network that linked computers of colleges, universities, government agencies, nonprofit laboratories, and

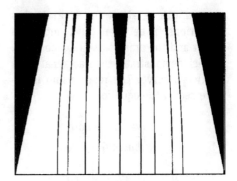

Arnold tongues.

industry. Developed and managed by the Advanced Research Project Agency of the U.S. Department of Defense, *ARPANET* developed into the currently-used Internet.

array 1. A collection of pieces of related data. 2. In Java, an object of a fixed size. 3. Two or more hard drives that have been striped using RAID level 0. An array acts as one volume, with information written in an alternating fashion across both devices. Arrays are generally used for digital video applications that require a high data transfer rate. See *redundant array of inexpensive or independent disks*.

Array, Compiled Vertex (CVA) An array that stores vertex information that won't be changed by the application. This allows the driver to optimize the data range once, and re-use the optimized version until the application unlocks the data.

Array it! A plug-in for *trueSpace* from the Mages of the Blue Circle, Inc. It makes it possible for the user to create multiple copies of an existing object at constant and/or regularly increasing or decreasing intervals, and rotations from the original object or a specified center point. One option will also allow the user to glue all objects as siblings.

array modeling, multiple replication
With this *Bryce* tool, the user can create many clones of an object. The user can determine how each object in the array is separated from other objects by offset on the XYZ axes, as well as rotation and sizing. Each object in the array will continue the progression of offsets, resizing, and rotations. All of the members of the array can be grouped as one object, or acted upon separately.

ArrayProxy class A proxy class that represents a single row of an array.

arrays, 3D complex light, box A box 3D light array is composed of five lights arranged in a lattice. The main central light with the highest intensity is centered on the cube/lattice of four peripheral lights occupying the corners of the 3D box light array.

arrays, 3D complex light, combination
The combination 3D light array is a composite of all possible 3D light arrays. It can be a ring array, with each outer ring having its own peripheral light, or a blending of the box array with the diamond array. This type is used mostly to solve complex lighting situations. Three-dimensional light arrays do not always need to have a central main light. It is possible for a combination array to be composed only of peripheral lights arranged in form or shape. The purpose of the main central light is to be the central hot core of direct illumination that dominates the scene; the peripherals serve as an edge illumination colorant. It exists to give a subtle coloration to the direct illumination without the use of fill lights. The use of

peripheral lights does not mean fill lights are no longer necessary. They are still necessary, especially for light modeling and form. The peripheral lights are there only to give the direct illumination some edge coloration, a kind of "wrap-around illumination." The array's peripheral lights need not be of the same color or intensity, although setting all the peripherals to one intensity makes it easier to predict the illumination and shadowing behavior of the 3D light array. The use of several lights (as one) enhances the subject through its subtle coloration and intensity changes across its surface, especially in the areas around the highlights and middle tones.

arrays, 3D complex light, diamond A diamond-shaped 3D light array is composed of seven lights. There is a main central light, complemented by six peripheral lights. The main central light generally has the highest intensity of all the lights; it gives the 3D light array its dominant color. The six peripheral lights are arranged in a diamond shape that frequently differs in color from the main light. The peripheral lights can be either shadow casting or non-shadow casting.

arrays, 3D complex light, dome A dome is commonly composed of 8 to 16 lights arranged in a hemispherical shape. This is really a variation on the pyramid 3D light array. The 3D dome array can also be inverted causing it to behave just as the inverted pyramid light array.

arrays, 3D complex light, pyramid This type of 3D light array is composed of six lights arranged in pyramidal form. The main central light is in the center axis of the pyramid, above the base. Four lights compose the base, and a single light forms the apex. The pyramid could also be inverted so the brighter main central light is lower and the base array of light is above.

arrays, 3D complex light, ring A ring is generally composed of 12 to 16 lights arranged in a circular shape around a central main light. The ring arrangement can be horizontal, vertical, or even oblique. Each half of the ring can even have its own color.

arrays, 3D complex light, tubular The tubular type of 3D light array can be composed of lights as few as 9 and as many as 25 or more. The main central light or lights are situated on the invisible central axis of the light cylinder, with the peripherals on the sides arranged in a ring.

arrays, 3D dual light The dual light array is generally composed of two lights, one of which is non-shadow casting. The purpose of the non-shadow casting light is to fill in the shadows of the scene without the need for an actual fill light. This is, in a way, a kind of localized ambient light setting, because it makes the visible object's shadow lighter. It is important that the second light in this kind of setup be non-shadow casting because it would function as another light only if it is not a non-shadow casting light.

arrays, 3D light Three-dimensional light arrays are relatively easy to create in *trueSpace* because the user can simply create one light, set the correct color temperature and intensity, and copy the light to create more instances. Normally, the main, central light is created first; it serves as the most dominant light in the array. This light has the most intensity

and determines the color of the diffuse and specular reflections on the objects. The peripheral lights are then created with $3/4$, $1/2$, or sometimes even less of the main light's intensity. This is to ensure that the peripheral lights do not overpower the influence of the main light. The peripheral light is easier to obtain by cloning (duplicating) the main light, then changing its color temperature and its intensity. It is then displaced from the center of the main light to create one instance. This light is then copied and displaced around the main light to create different 3D light arrays.

arrow A control in the *Displacedatplace* plug-in from the *pluSpack* for *trueSpace*. It determines whether the white value in the image is considered high or low.

arrowhead Another name for the Sierpinski fractal triangle. This curve can be created by starting with a filled-in equilateral triangle and removing the triangle created by connecting the midpoints of the sides. This leaves four filled-in equilateral triangles for which the same process is repeated, and the procedure then continues for as long as desired. The curve is interesting because it turns out that if the proper parameters are inserted in many different fractal generating methods, the result is a Sierpinski triangle. See *Sierpinski triangle* for a picture of this fractal.

Arrow tool A tool in *Paint Shop Pro* that enables the user to activate specific images. This is useful when several images are open at the same time. It also is used to scroll around images that are too large to fit on the window.

ArtBeats REELs CD-ROM collections of animated sequences of clouds, water, fire, explosions, and other environmental effects.

art director The person in charge of the execution of the production designer's vision, managing set construction, set dressing, props, and scenic painting.

Art Director A plug-in for *trueSpace* that allows viewing of material libraries in a scrolling grid view. It also allows the user to view all libraries at once or organize them into library pages.

arthropods Arthropods are by definition animals with a segmented body and jointed limbs, covered with a rigid exoskeleton. In other words, nature has constructed them of various solid pieces that are joined together. It is easy to emulate nature and construct them in the same way with any 3D application that features links and hierarchies.

articulated figure A computer representation, usually of the human figure, in which the arms, legs, etc., are capable of being moved with respect to one another.

articulated object A computer graphics construction with various parts that move with respect to one another.

articulation, manner of The way in which air is obstructed in pronouncing a phoneme.

articulation, point of The point where the airstream is obstructed in pronouncing a phoneme. In general, the point of articulation is simply that place on the palate where the tongue is placed to block the stream of air. After the air has left the larynx, it passes into the vocal tract. The constriction of airflow determines whether the phoneme is a vowel or consonant. If the air, once out of the

glottis, is allowed to pass freely through the resonators, the sound is a vowel. If the air, once out of the glottis, is obstructed in one or more places, partially or totally, the sound is a consonant. There are a number of places where these obstructions can take place. These places are known as the articulators, several of which are indicated in the following list: lips (labial), teeth (dental), hard palate (palatal), soft palate (velar), and back of throat (uvula/glottis).

artifact A visible difference between a computer image and the real visual image, usually due to limitations of the computer graphics rather than software mistakes.

artifacts, dithering Unwanted patterns that are superimposed on an image as a result of dithering.

artificial intelligence (AI) The representation of human thinking activities by machines. The goal is a computer program that reasons in a way similar to that of human beings, but, while computers are better than humans at storing and remembering data, there still are many intuitive mechanisms in human reasoning that we currently cannot understand and cannot reproduce. Artificial intelligence has many uses in the development of computer games, especially related to programming the moves of an opponent.

artificial intelligence (AI), engine design The design of software that controls functions for replicating human intelligence by a computer. Among other things, it should easily allow communication between objects, offer a general and readable solution to implementing

AI behavior, and facilitate keeping debug records of every event.

artificial intelligence (AI) engine, event driven An artificial intelligence engine in which objects wait to receive news of an event.

artificial intelligence (AI) engine, message objects An object that has five fields: a descriptive name, the name of the sender, the name of the receiver, the time at which it should be delivered, and any relevant data. If handed a message, the user should have all the information necessary to pass it to the correct game object at the right time. The receiver of the message gets the message along with all of the information inside it, such as who sent it and any extra data. Following is an example of a message:

name:damaged, from:dragon, to:knight, deliver_at_time:245.34, data:10 (amount of damage)

In effect, messages become an electronic paper trail of what is happening in a game. This is a powerful concept that provides many benefits. One of the uses of this concept is that every message that is sent can be recorded and dumped into a file. That way, if there is a bug, the file can be examined to determine what triggered certain actions. This ability becomes invaluable when the problem involves the interactions of tens of game objects over a fraction of a second. Another use of this concept is that any game object can "listen" to any other game object's messages. Since messages have the intended receiver built in, the intended recipient of the message is easy to determine.

artificial intelligence (AI) engine, polling An artificial intelligence engine in which objects actively watch the world and react to changes in other objects.

artificial intelligence (AI), finite-state machine (FSM) A simple machine that consists of a finite number of states or conditions. For instance, consider a door; its states can be open or closed and locked or unlocked. An FSM has an input, which affects a state transition from one state to another. An FSM can have a simple (or complex) state transition function that determines what state will become the current state. The new current state is called the *output state* of the state transition of the FSM, or the state to which the FSM has transitioned based on the input. For example, when a door is in a closed and locked state, the input of user key may cause the door to transition to the unlocked state (the output state of the state transition and the new current state of the door). Then the input of user hand will cause the door to transition to the open state. When the door is in the open state, the input of user hand will transition the door back to the closed state, etc. In sum, an FSM is a machine that has a finite number of states, one of which is a current state. The FSM can accept input that will result in a state transition from the current state to an output state, based on some state transition function, and the output state then becomes the new current state.

artificial intelligence (AI), neural nets and See *neural net*.

artificial intelligence (AI), scripting behavior outside code A poor coding practice that complicates design and debugging. Normally, logic should be inside the code and data should be outside.

artificial lighting Lights other than natural sunlight that are used to illuminate a scene. The closest of all of the artificial lights to natural sunlight is the halogen light. Halogen lights have bright whites that tend to be very warm. When recreating a halogen light in 3D, it is important to use a very focused light source such as a spotlight. Using a point light might overexpose the scene and ruin the illusion. The falloff of a halogen light is fairly long, which is why they make excellent headlights or flashlights. Light bulbs are the warmest type of light source.

artificial lights, The *3ds max* image painting program has an extensive set of options for lights, including exclusion lists, so it offers numerous ways to simulate artificial lighting. The most important aspect of simulating artificial light is to establish the presence of the key dominant light before any other lights are added to the scene. In *3ds max,* it is not easy for the lights to function cumulatively, so the user has to compensate by tweaking the existing lights whenever adding new lights. However, without the exclusion list, ambient term, and attenuation parameters for each light, lighting in *3ds max* would be harder since the user would have only distance and intensity to work with. This is how real-world light behaves, so it is important to learn about lighting using realistic light behavior.

artificial object A member of the catalog of graphics objects in a flight simulation environment that is used for convenience of computer operations but is not actually displayed.

artificial reality 1. A computer simulation of the world that provides video and audio inputs and permits the user to manually interact with the display so that the simulation seems to be the same as actuality. See *virtual reality*. 2. A technique for three-dimensional viewing. Two tiny displays, one for each image, can be mounted on a headset, and mirrors used to present the images to each eye. This is the technique normally used in virtual reality systems.

ArtMatic A fractal graphics and animation creation utility that translates images into sound, and saves out audio data graphic files for selected applications. Its control variables make it possible to create myriad images and animated sequences that can be used as 2D/3D backdrops or as textures for models.

Arzela-Ascoli theorem A theorem of rational mapping that states that a family F is normal on D if and only if it is equicontinuous there.

ASAS A computer language built on top of LISP, which includes constructs for concisely creating animated displays. These include vectors, polygons, colors, three-dimensional solids, points of view, and light sources.

ascent line A horizontal line corresponding to the maximum height of any character in a type font.

ASCII American Standard Code for Information Interchange. A standard for encoding alphanumerics and control characters into 7-bit or 8-bit binary code.

ASCII sort Sorting of a list of data according to the ASCII code.

ASIC See *Application Specific Integrated Circuit.*

ASP See *active server pages.*

aspect 1. A property of a graphics primitive (color, for example) that does not affect its geometry. 2. In a polygonal mesh model, any two segments sharing a point have a particular aspect to each other. *Aspect* is the angle between the two segments. When a mesh is transformed, the aspect angle remains constant.

aspect ratio The ratio of width to height of a graphics entity such as a pixel, a character block, or the entire graphics display. Computer monitors and television sets have an aspect ratio of 4:3. Wide-screen video has an aspect ratio of 16:9. For 640×480, 800×600, and 1024×768 pixel computer displays, the aspect ratio of the pixels is 1:1, meaning that the pixels are perfectly square.

assemble edit An edit onto a videotape that records over the entire tape, including the video track, the audio tracks, and the control track.

assert To set the level of an electronic control signal to the state in which the control action is initiated.

assert macro A programming device that allows checking while the program is running. By giving the assert macro a condition to evaluate, the user is asserting that this condition should be TRUE. If the condition evaluates to FALSE, assert brings up a dialog box indicating that a problem has occurred. The user can then choose to ignore the assert and continue executing the code, abort the program, or break directly into the code where the assert failed. The assert macro lets the user program defensively. If the user knows a pointer should be NULL, the user should assert that it is NULL. The use of assert in code allows for catching of mistakes before they can do much damage.

assert macro, copy-and-paste A technique whereby the assert macro not only brings up a dialog box when it fails but also allows copying of any debugging information to the Windows clipboard.

assert macro, customizing Creation of an *assert* macro that embodies the user's specialized requirements.

assert macro, embedding The inclusion of additional troubleshooting information in the assert macro to make clearer the nature of the failure that occurred.

assert macro, "Ignore Always" option The addition within the assert macro of code that causes the assert failure to be displayed only once and then ignored thereafter. It's particularly useful when an assert is failing every frame, but the user will still want to run the game without clicking through a million asserts. To implement this feature, each assert keeps track of whether it should be ignored and purposely suppresses itself should it fail in the future.

assert macro, superassert implementation A technique whereby stack information is included within the assert macro so that the user can trace the path up to *assert* failure. This has been called a *superassert*.

assistant camera (AC) An assistant to the camera operator. The first AC is responsible for loading the film camera, setting up the lenses and filters for each shot, and making sure the shot is in focus. The second AC is responsible for keeping camera reports, slating each shot, and sometimes loading film into the magazine.

association The mapping of one space into another. The use of a neural net as a memory that can produce a response by processing input that is incomplete or "noisy." If the response is the input itself, the process is called *autoassociation*. If the response is different from the input, the process is called *heteroassociation*.

Association for Computing Machinery (ACM) Society for those involved professionally with computer hardware or software.

Association for Information and Image Management (AIIM) A professional society for those involved with micrographics, optical disks, and electronic image management.

association, Hopfield nets for See *Hopfield nets*.

association, neural nets for The use of neural nets for either autoassociation (the mapping of an input with itself) or heteroassociation (the mapping of an input with something else).

asymptotic self-similarity A sequence that is only self-similar as the number of recursions approaches infinity. As an example, consider the following equation based on the infinite product for $2/\pi$:

$$s_n = \prod_{k=1}^{n} f_k - \frac{2}{\pi}$$

which has the recursion

$$f_{k+1} = \left(\frac{1+f_k}{2}\right)^{\frac{1}{2}} \qquad f_0 = 0$$

For n = *1, 2, 3, 4,* ... the solutions to the equation are:

$s_1 = 0.070482$

$s_2 = 0.016620$

$s_3 = 0.004109$

$s_4 = 0.0001024$

These terms approach a constant scaling factor of 4.0, so that the expression is self-similar only in the limit as $n \rightarrow 8$. Thus the expression is *asymptotically self-similar*.

asymptotic value The value of a line that is associated with a curve such that as a point moves along an infinite branch of the curve, the slope of the curve approaches the slope of the line, and the distance between the point on the curve and the nearest point on the line approaches zero.

AT Advanced Technology. A model of the IBM Personal Computer using an Intel 80286 microprocessor and a 16-bit I/O bus. Often applied to similar IBM-compatible 80286 computers.

ATA A type of hard drive interface. Not as fast as SCSI, but fast enough for DV.

atmosphere Computer graphics modeling of visual effects produced by the earth's atmosphere such as fog, clouds, haze, smog, and light attenuation.

atmospheric attenuation The changes of color and reduction of intensity caused by increasing amounts of intervening atmosphere as objects are farther and farther away from the viewing plane. These effects can be modeled to increase the realism of the resulting graphics image.

atmospheric conditions The conditions of the atmosphere through which a scene is viewed, such as sunlight, moonlight, fog, snow, sleet, hail, rain, smog or pollution, underwater, or artificial lighting.

atmospheric effects, aerial perspective See *aerial perspective*.

atmospheric effects, foreground planes In a picture or an animation, the way target subjects are framed by other elements often becomes the major part of a composition. For example, a black silhouetted foreground often acts as a frame for color targets in a picture. Framing components can be introduced into projects as follows. In a paint application, set the palette to work in two colors, black and white. Paint a silhouetted scene with black, allowing the dropout color to be white. One of the most common subjects of a foreground painting like this is a jungle scene, a silhouetted image of a group of trees, vines, and associated elements. Save the image to disk in a format that a 3D application can read. Then, import the image. The alpha channel should not need to have anything done to it since the white areas will be set for dropout automatically. If not, invert them. Next, map this picture to a picture plane that covers the screen. Make sure there are no lights in back of the scene, including sunlight, so the foreground picture remains totally black except for the transparent cutouts. Place 3D elements in the scene in back of this picture plane. The final rendering should show the 3D world as framed by this 2D graphic. If the graphic is large enough, panning the camera will allow different parts of the 3D scene to become visible.

atom 1. The smallest particle of a chemical element. 2. The smallest amount of work that must be processed by a computer without interruption.

atomic 1. Compact software module containing all necessary elements for a particular task. 2. Computer processor state that can be updated by a single (uninterruptible) instruction.

atomic unit of length A measure of length corresponding to the radius of a hydrogen atom. It is 5.3×10^{-11} meters.

ATSC See *Advanced Television Systems Committee*.

attached scripts Scripts that are used by loading Python code into a *trueSpace* object using the Script Manager. Once this is done, the script becomes an internal part of that object. The script will remain attached until it is removed from the object, or another script is assigned to that object. There can be only one script attached to a *trueSpace* object at any given time. If a *trueSpace* object is saved as a .COB file, the script is saved along with it. Attached scripts can be assigned to any *trueSpace* object, including meshes, lights, cameras, and even the scenes themselves.

attack accuracy property When inserting an enemy in the *Game Creation System*, this property controls how often the enemy will hit a pursuer with his weapon.

attack strength property When inserting an enemy in the *Game Creation System*, this property controls how much damage is inflicted on the player when the enemy strikes or fires upon the player.

attenuation 1. Decrease of wave energy due to absorption by the medium of propagation, such as sound or light falloff with travel through the atmosphere. 2. Decrease of wave intensity over distance.

attenuation of light The rate at which a light decreases in intensity at a greater distance. The attenuation of light is the square of the distance traveled. An object twice as far away from a light receives a quarter of the illumination.

attenuation maps Maps that are used to store light attenuation data in the form of a texture map.

attenuator A circuit that lowers the strength of an electronic signal.

AT&T Pixel Machine A special-purpose computer designed to perform fast ray tracing.

attraction, basin of The area of a strange attractor that includes all points that, upon iteration of the attractor's iterated equation, approach a particular point. Also known as *domain of attraction*.

attractive cycle A cycle of period n is an *attractive cycle* of f if it contains an attractive periodic point of f having the period n.

attractive periodic orbit A periodic orbit for which the absolute value of its eigenvalue is greater than zero and less than one.

attractor A set of points to which a number of nearby orbits converge upon repeated iteration.

attractor, Henon The attractor produced by the recursive formulas:

$$x_{n+1} = y_n - a * x_n^2 + 1$$

$$y_{n+1} = b * x_n$$

attractor, Lorenz The attractor produced as the solution to the dynamical set of equations:

$$x' = -(y + z)$$
$$y' = b * x - y - x * z$$
$$z' = x * z - c * z$$

attractor, parabola The attractor produced by repeated iteration of the recursive formula:

$$p_{n+1} = p_n + k * p_n * (1 - p_n)$$

attractor, Rossler The attractor produced by repeated iteration of the recursive formulas:

$$x' = -(y + z)$$

$$y' = x + \left(\frac{y}{5}\right)$$

$$z' = \frac{1}{5} + z * (x - 5.7)$$

attractor, strange A set of values on which many orbits of a dynamical set of equations tend to land.

attractor, Verhulst The attractor produced by repeated iteration of the formula:

$$p_{n+1} =$$
$$p_n + \frac{1}{2} * k * (3 * p_n * (1 - p_n)) - p_{n-1} * (1 - p_{n-1})$$

attribute A property of a graphics primitive not directly associated with its underlying geometry. Some typical properties are color shade and intensity, line width, and area pattern.

attribute bundle, PHIGS A collection of attribute values for a primitive that is stored during initialization of standard PHIGS (Programmer's Hierarchical Interactive Graphics System).

attribute controller Registers in a VGA card that contribute to the translation of 4-bit codes from display memory into 6-bit color register assignments.

attribute, cosmetic An attribute of a primitive that cannot be described by geometric expressions attached to the primitive.

attribute, geometric An attribute of a primitive that can be described by geometric expressions attached to the primitive.

attribute, inheritance An attribute of a parent primitive that is passed as a parameter to one or more child primitives. This makes it possible to create child primitives with a full set of attributes already specified and yet change one or more of these attributes locally without affecting the parents.

attributes box A pop up menu for *trueSpace* that allows the user to set attributes.

attributes of objects In the *Game Creation System*, each wall in a level has various attributes. These attributes alter the way the wall is drawn by the 3D game engine and how the wall interacts with both the player and enemies.

attributes, SPHIGS Attribute values for primitives in the SPHIGS (Simple Programmer's Hierarchical Interactive Graphics System).

attributes, SRGP Attribute values for primitives in the SRGP (Simple Raster Graphics Package).

audio 1. The range of frequencies that can be perceived by the human ear (between about 20 Hz and 20,000 Hz). 2. Describes anything related to sound, such as an *audio compressor, audio guide track*, or *audio mixer*.

audio compressor A filter (or piece of hardware) that reduces the dynamic range of a sound to accommodate loud peaks.

audio guide track A mixed audio track from the off-line final cut that is placed onto one of the audio tracks of the on-line master to serve as a guide during the on-line editing session.

audio mixer A piece of hardware that takes several audio signals and mixes them together, allowing for the mixing of different sources. Mixers usually include some sort of equalization control.

audio sampling rate The number of samples per second that are used to digitize a particular sound. Most DV cameras can record at several audio sampling rates. Higher rates yield better results. Measured in kilohertz (kHz). 44.1 kHz is considered audio CD quality and 48 kHz is considered DAT quality.

Aura A Windows application from NewTek that was created to add animated 2D painting effects to movies, originally for *LightWave* and *Inspire* 3D frames. It can also be used various animated effects. *Aura* is useful for planning the animation of *Poser* figures in *LightWave*.

Aural Exciter A device, developed by DigiDesign, that increases the intelligibility of voices in audio tracks and brings muddled sounds into the foreground.

Aurora Borealis with shimmer An effect that can be created with *Bryce*. It should be composited against a dark sky. An example follows. Create a scene with a few mountains and a dark blue sky. Then, place a 2D vertical plane in the scene in back of the mountains. Make it large enough so that edges are not visible when viewed from the camera. With the 2D Plane selected, open the Materials Lab. Load the Waves2 texture from the list into channel A. Activate Diffuse, Specular, Specular Halo, and Transparent Colors; Diffusion (100), Ambience (82), and Specularity (53) Values; Transparency Optics (22). Leave the Specular button in the color palette mode, because this allows alteration of the color of the Aurora over time to see that color against a dark sky. Create a 120-frame animation at 30 FPS. At random places on the time line, alter the specular color and the size of the Aurora. Render and save to disk.

auto balance An advanced posing feature of *Poser*. When activated, it attempts to realign the figure according to the calculated weight of each of the body parts for maximizing realism.

Auto-IK A capability of *Universe* that constrains a child on a chain so that it stays in position as one of its parents moves.

AutoCAD **(Computer Aided Design)** A computer program for creating complex mechanical drawings. Available from Autodesk Retail Products.

autocompletion, command A method of speeding up typed commands. A list of all possible commands is stored and as soon as the user types in enough letters of the command for an unambiguous match with one of the words in the list, the computer automatically completes the word.

autoconfiguration A software technique that enables a computer to identify the configuration of a hardware system and adjust its operations accordingly.

autocorrelation function The mathematical function:

$$c(\tau) = \int u(t)u*(t + \tau)dt$$

which is the correlation of a signal with its delayed self. A waveform needs to be designed so that its *autocorrelation function* has values as near zero as possible

except when $\tau = 0$ if resolution of data is needed. Applying the *autocorrelation function* can then reduce noise effects and extract signals otherwise buried in noise.

autodimensioning A feature of CAD and drafting programs that automatically computes the (scaled) distance between two points, draws dimension lines, and inserts the proper numerical value.

Autofact A conference sponsored by the Society of Manufacturing Engineers, which is concerned with design tools applied to the automobile industry. Currently, many of these tools are graphics oriented.

automatic dialog replacement (ADR) Used to replace badly recorded sound, fix a muffed line, or insert dialog that could not be recorded on location. If a dialog was not recorded during the shoot, ADR is where the film will be "dubbed." In a professional ADR facility, a projector or deck shows the scene to be re-recorded, then immediately rewinds and plays the scene again (without audio) and the new dialog is recorded. Sometimes, a continuous "loop" of the scene is shown; hence the term "looping." The actor is usually cued with a series of regular beeps that count down to the start of recording. The actor's goal is to match his vocal performance to what he just saw on-screen.

automatic display detection A feature of some VGA cards, in which the card automatically detects the type of monitor connected to it and reconfigures itself for proper interface.

automatic keyframing In creating an animation, *automatic keyframing* allows the user to simply move the current time marker to a point in time, alter the model, and the 3D application will automatically place keyframes to all altered objects.

automatic size adjustment A feature of some VGA cards in which signals to the monitor are automatically adjusted so that displays of different resolutions and numbers of pixels all fill the entire display screen.

automatically programmed tool (APT) A programming language for describing the motions of tools required to perform particular machining operations using digitally-controlled machining equipment.

autonomous agents Individuals that take part in group behavior, such as flocks of birds, schools of fish, or swarms of bees. Also called *boids*.

autosense A capability built into some display adapter cards that have the ability to use either an 8- or 16-bit bus interface. *Autosense* detects whether the interface bus is 8 or 16 bits and automatically selects the proper hardware and software configuration to work with the detected bus.

AutoShade A program for drawing realistic pictures using a personal computer.

autosizing Capability of a display adapter to adjust size automatically so that displays of different resolutions and numbers of pixels fill the entire screen.

autostereogram A technique for viewing three-dimensional images. One technique is to overlap the left and right images, and indeed to overlap multiple copies of each. The result is called an *autostereogram*. The left and right images can use random dots or any arbitrary

pattern for displaying the depth, with no coloring information (making a random dot stereogram or single image stereogram), or they can be in full shaded color (resulting in a wallpaper stereogram). Another technique is to combine the shaded color at each pixel 50/50 with a random value, giving a sort of speckled autostereogram. This combines the proper color shading of the wallpaper stereogram with the depth precision of the random dot technique.

A/UX A variation of the UNIX operating system designed to be run on Apple Macintosh computers.

auxiliary video extension A connector on an EGA or VGA card that provides video signals for an unspecified purpose. These connectors still exist on many cards, but are seldom used.

average contractivity condition A case in which repetition of a set of affine transformations always results in convergence.

AV hard drive A high-speed, high-capacity hard drive capable of sustaining an increased data transfer rate. AV drives usually do not experience thermal recalibration, which causes an interruption in the data stream.

avi files Video/audio clip files that have the extension .avi. avi files are common on Windows platforms.

avoidance One of the rules of flocking, which states that the flock should steer to avoid running into local obstacles or enemies.

AVR Avid Video Resolution. A series of low and high-resolution codecs included with the Avid family of editing systems. AVR77 has the highest 2-field compressed resolution available, although some Avid products offer uncompressed resolutions as well.

AVS Application visualization system. A high-level graphic software interface developed by Stellar Computer, Inc.

Awave Audio A dedicated audio file format batch converter. It performs conversions from the approximately 60 audio file formats that it can read into any of the 30 or so audio file formats that it writes.

A without B A function that is similar to the Boolean subtraction function. When one uses a regular Boolean subtraction, the computer fills in the negative shape of the subtracted object. In *A without B*, the 3D application chops out the subtracted shape but does not fill in its negative space, leaving a hole in the remaining shape that exposes the empty shell.

AWT See *Abstract Window Toolkit*.

axes, object An important concept to remember is that objects have their own axes. When objects are first created, this object axis is usually at the same point as the world axis (0,0,0). However, as soon as an object is moved, two axis keys will become apparent. One represents (0,0,0) for the digital world's coordinate system, and the other represents the axis for the object. This becomes more important when performing such functions as rotation and rescaling.

axes, object rotation and Besides being able to move objects around digital space, objects can also be rotated around their axes. This varies from program to program, but the premise is the same. Each object has its own axis around which it rotates. For many programs, it

is through the symbol for this axis that rotation of the object can be performed. Like object movement, 3D applications allow for the unconstrained free rotation of objects, or a constrained rotation for certain situations, e.g., where the user wants a car to be facing north instead of east, but without it sitting on only two tires. An important part of the rotation process is the ability to move the object's axis and thus effectively change the axis of rotation.

axes, realignment of It is often easier to position and rotate objects if their axes are realigned. For example, the easiest way to model a wineglass is with it lying on its side. To make it stand up, the user would then have to rotate it 90 degrees on the X axis. Realigning the axes would let all the rotation values be zero when the wineglass was standing up, making it much easier to work with the wineglass while positioning it within the scene.

axial ray The ray that is the center of a bundle of rays.

axial resizing The resizing of a model's elements on any selected axis in *Poser*. Either the Resize tool or the Parameter dials can be used to do this. It is easier with the Parameter dials, because the user has more control over each dimension. In standard computer graphics terms, this operation is called a "stretch."

axiom In mathematics, a statement of self-evident truth.

axis 1. Any lengthwise central line around which parts of a body are centrally arranged. 2. One of the three mutually perpendicular lines (x, y, and z) which make up the Cartesian coordinate system. The location of any point in Cartesian three-dimensional space is referenced to these axes.

axis indicators Three axis lines that can be shown on a *Carrara* display. When using the Transform tab of the Properties palette to rotate objects, axis indicators make it much easier to determine which axis needs to be rotated and by how much. They are color coded to match the orientation axes in the Numerical Properties dialog box. To turn the axis indicators on, select Preferences from the File menu to open the Preferences dialog box. Select Perspective from the popup menu in the upper left, click on Show Axis Information at the lower left, then click on OK.

axis link An axis link allows the child to be rotated around the parent object on one of the three axes. Both the slider and axis links allow the user to limit movement to a specified range. One can also specify custom combinations of the slider and axis links.

axis of symmetry A real or imaginary center line around which parts of a body are symmetrically arranged.

axonometric view A method of looking at a scene in 3D modeling that is completely without perspective. Also known as an *orthographic view*.

azimuthal equal-area projection A mapping of a sphere onto a plane that employs a simple scale change to account for the area contributions as the radius changes incrementally from the chart center.

azimuthal equidistant projection A mapping of a sphere onto a plane that gives simultaneous bearing and radial distance for great-circle travel away from the chart center.

B

b The angle between the vector **N** normal to a hypothetical specular reflecting surface and the halfway vector **H**. The halfway vector is a vector halfway between the direction of the light source and the viewer.

B 1. The value of radiosity, the rate at which light energy leaves a surface, which is the sum of the rate at which the surface emits light energy and the rate at which the surface reflects light energy. 2. Back distance. The distance from the view plane to the back clipping plane.

backbone 1. The part of a communications network that carries the heaviest traffic. 2. The part of a network that joins local area networks (LANs) together.

back clipping plane A plane perpendicular to the line of sight, beyond which all objects are clipped (removed from the image). Also called the *yon* plane.

backdrop 1. A painted, photographed, or printed background used in portraits, set windows, and doors. 2. The setting against which the action of a game takes place. Once created, it remains static for the duration of its lifetime. The backdrop is usually seen as a collection of objects that have a variety of properties that are initialized at the start of their lives and do not change. Traditionally, the backdrop has been stored on the distribution media, in *expanded form*.

Games that rely on this are generally action games or ladder- and level-style games such as *Doom, Manic Miner, Repton,* and *Quake*. Note that some 3D applications treat and define backdrop differently: *Carrara, LightWave,* and *3ds max* are three examples.

backdrop object Backdrop objects are normally used in *The Game Factory* to "set the scene" in games. They provide backdrops for players to move over, or even to interact with. Backdrop objects cannot be moved or changed in appearance when the game is playing, as with active objects. But it is possible to change their positions on the screen, as well as their sizes, shapes, and colors, using the Level Editor.

backface culling The process of testing faces of a convex polygon object and eliminating those that are not visible (as identified by the fact that the normal to the face is pointed away from the screen) so that they do not have to be processed for display.

backfacing polygon A polygon in an image being rendered that has its normal pointing away from the current observer viewpoint. A backfacing polygon is not included in the image view and therefore can be eliminated from further processing.

background The basic color or image for parts of a picture not occupied by objects. Most 3D rendering systems allow a 2D image to be used as a background when the scene is rendered. When choosing a background, the following should be taken into consideration. White is the best choice for work that is to be printed, since that saves on ink used for the background color. Select black for work to be transferred to tape, since it pops out the images better for video and multimedia, and also lends a better 3D look to the composition. Note that some 3D applications treat and define background differently. *Carrara* and *3ds max* are some examples.

background, animated The illusion of motion can be achieved through the movement of elements that would normally stay still during an animation. The user can give the illusion of forward motion to the character in a scene by moving the scenery around it. This allows the camera and the character to remain stationary while the foreground and background elements do all of the work. Most professional 3D applications allow the user to use QuickTime or AVI media files or a series of sequenced frames as background content.

background blurring Backgrounds appear to be more blurred than the objects in front of them that have our visual attention. This is probably due both to the limited focusing depth of field of the ocular lens, and to the reduced resolution available outside of the ½ degree field of the fovea centralis, as well as the effects of mist and dust in the intervening atmosphere. The effect has been widely used by painters, photographers, and cinematographers to give a 3D feel to their images. LOD (Level Of Detail) is used in many 3D applications to force

the camera to blur content farther from the camera.

back light A light positioned behind the subject used to separate the subject from the background. This separation lends a sense of depth to the image and helps make the subject "stand out" better. Sometimes the back light is a different color from the *key* and *fill* lights mainly bluish or orange. The back light is placed behind the model to cast a halo or rim of light around the object. A back light defines the edges of a model from the background. The back light, like the fill light, should start out with an intensity of 25%, which should be increased only if necessary. If the model blends too much into the background, increase the intensity of the back light, or move it slightly to one side. Also known as the *kicker*.

backlighting The positioning of the key light either above and behind or completely behind the subject. The intense highlight glow outlines the subject and, because of the contrast that occurs, backlighting creates volume and depth. Backlighting visually separates the foreground object from the background. A backlit object has a large, dark shadow area with a small, strong highlight around it.

backlit Describes a display screen that has a light source behind the image to enhance viewing under low ambient-light conditions. A cathode-ray tube screen does not need to be backlit, since the data are fluorescent and therefore are lighted when there is no ambient light at all. However, LCD displays cannot be seen at all unless they are backlit or there is good ambient lighting.

backplane A circuit board providing power and communications wiring and connectors for daughter circuit boards.

back porch The portion of a composite television signal that includes the part of the blanking pulse that contains the color burst signal.

back sides of walls In the *Game Creation System*, each wall has a front and a back side. This is useful when making a room within a room, where the viewer wants to see both sides of the wall.

back up To make a copy of a program or data set for use in case the primary program or data set fails.

backup geometry Backup files that are made with a 3D modeling program at various steps in the modeling process. These files can be used to create new objects that diverge to produce different-looking models.

Backus-Naur form (BNF) A method of defining sequencing and defining user interface with a computer.

backwards ray tracing The generation of a scene by tracing rays of light from the observer viewpoint to each pixel on the viewing screen and thence to objects in the scene that are intercepted by the ray. From the first object encountered, rays are traced according to how they are reflected or refracted by the object.

bad sector A defective segment of a floppy disk or hard disk. Bad sectors are often present from the beginning as a result of disk manufacturing defects. Such sectors are automatically locked out by the disk-formatting program.

balance The appearance of a scene that is pleasing to the eye and does not appear random or helter-skelter, yet does not have excessive symmetry.

balanced audio A type of microphone connector that provides extra resistance to interference by using the extra shielding of balanced cables and connectors. Sometimes needed if for microphone cable lengths of 25 feet or longer.

balancing filters Filters used to correct for tungsten or daylight, or to tint an image or strengthen particular colors.

balancing light sources In a lighting setup with several different light sources, the process of making the color temperature of all the lights the same, either to match daylight or tungsten light. Usually this is done with CTO or CTB lighting gels.

ballistic gain A feature of some trackballs and mice that makes the cursor move faster when the user moves the mouse or trackball faster.

banding An artifact of using normal coding to store image information. It manifests itself as bands of color across a single colored object.

bandwidth The frequency range over which a bus, interface, or device is capable of transferring digital information.

bandwidth limiting Removing the high frequencies from a signal so that it can be represented by sampling at a lower rate. This reduces the amount of storage required for the signal, but blurs the detail of a video image because this detail is contained in the higher frequencies. Also known as *low-pass filtering*.

bank and zoom Just under and to either side of the XZ Cross Control in *Bryce* are two small buttons that are important to animation work. The one on the left is a banking control, while the one on the right controls the camera zoom. Banking and zooming are possible in all professional 3D applications.

banking on curves When animating flying things, it is necessary to pay very close attention to banking. When we see a jet fighter take a sharp turn, it doesn't turn on the Z axis (yaw) and go in the other direction, as a car would. It must bank—change angles in both pitch and roll—to make all of the forces of physics compatible, so that they will oblige in the request for a direction change.

banner ad An advertisement displayed on someone else's Web page. A banner needs to work quickly to be effective, so it is one of the first things a viewer sees as the Web page downloads into his browser. Its file size should generally be no larger than 10KB to 20KB. The ad needs to fit exactly to the standards of the Web page where it is to be displayed. Two groups are playing a role in the standardization of banner ads: the IAB (Internet Advertising Bureau) and the CASIE (Coalition for Advertising Supported Information and Entertainment). Both organizations promote a voluntary standard for banner advertisements. These standards were created in response to an industry-wide concern about the creation of types and sizes of banners most commonly used on the Web today. Using these standards is strictly voluntary; however, more and more advertising agencies are conforming to these standards, as are advertisers. The Standards and Practices Committee of the IAB with input from CASIE identifies the following as the most commonly accepted banner sizes:

Size (pixels):	Type of banner:
468 × 60	Full Banner
392 × 72	Full Banner with Vertical Navigation Bar
234 × 60	Half Banner
125 × 125	Square Button
120 × 90	Button #1
120 × 60	Button #2
88 × 31	Micro Button
120 × 240	Vertical Banner

bar chart A graph in which data values are represented by the lengths of rectangles or the relative sizes of graphic symbols.

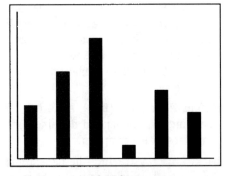

bar chart.

bar code A system of vertical lines of variable width that are converted to alphanumeric data by a scanning device. The *UPC* code used for supermarket pricing is an example.

bare winding number The frequency ratio of a circle map.

barn doors 1. A set of hinged door-like flaps that attach to the front of a light and serve to control where the light falls. 2. A transitional effect between two video clips created by a function in a post-production compositing application.

barrel distortion A defect of display systems in which sides of a rectangle bulge outward to look like the outline of a barrel.

bars and tone A combination of color bars and 60 Hz audio reference tone, usually recorded onto the beginning of each videotape. Used for calibrating video and audio levels.

base alignment The arrangement of columns of text so that the text is aligned across the entire page regardless of the size of elements in each of the columns.

base font The typeface that is used by default when no other typeface is specified.

baseline An imaginary line upon which characters of a type font appear to rest. Individual characters may have descenders that drop below the baseline.

BaseResource class A "C" language class that is able to automatically load, discard, and reload data based on usage patterns. It includes a manager to coordinate the available resources and control access to the resource objects through the use of handles, which are essentially unique identification numbers. When an application is expected to use more data than can be held in memory at one time, but the additional data is available in a medium from which it can be dynamically loaded while the application is running uninterrupted (such as a hard drive, CD, or DVD), this class can perform the necessary management for data transfer.

basic camera movements See *camera movements, basic.*

basic cinematography See *cinematography, basic.*

basic lighting See *color theory, basic.*

basic light kit See *light kit, basic.*

basic matrix See *matrix, basic.*

basic object memory manager See *object memory manager, basic.*

basin boundary metamorphoses A sudden jump in the boundary of a basin of attraction as a parameter is changed.

basin of attraction The area of a strange attractor that includes all points that upon iteration of the attractor's iterated equation approach a particular point. Also known as *domain of attraction.*

basis, of a vector space A set of vectors defining the span of a vector space where any smaller set of vectors has a smaller span.

basis matrix A 4×4 matrix used in describing a parametric cubic curve. The curve is defined by $Q(t) = T \times C$. The coefficient matrix can be rewritten as $C = M \times G$, where M is the basis matrix and G is a four element column vector of geometric parameters called the *geometry vector.*

basis spline See *B-spline.*

basis, standard The standard basis for three-dimensional space is the set of vectors e_1, e_2, e_3, where

$$e_1 = \begin{bmatrix} 1 \\ 0 \\ 0 \end{bmatrix}, \quad e2 = \begin{bmatrix} 0 \\ 1 \\ 0 \end{bmatrix}, \quad e3 = \begin{bmatrix} 0 \\ 0 \\ 1 \end{bmatrix}$$

basis weight A measurement of the weight (and therefore quality) of paper. This is given as the weight of 500 sheets (one ream) of 24 inch $\times$ 36 inch sheets. Common letterhead paper weights are in the range of 20 to 24 pounds.

batch capturing The capability to log an entire tape and then capture all logged clips in one unattended operation.

batch processing The processing of a group of computer programs in a single operation.

batch rendering queue The batch rendering queue is one of *Carrara's* most valuable features. The Batch Queue (accessible under the Render menu) allows the user to set up several files to render, and takes care of opening each file, rendering it, and saving it. This means the user can render several files while away from his computer.

batch, screen updates A method used with the SPHIGS graphics package in which efficiency is improved by not doing any screen updates during editing of a structure until the structure is closed.

baud rate Rate of serial data transmission (from J. E. Baudot, inventor of serial code for telegraphy). The *baud rate* is the reciprocal of the duration in seconds of the shortest signal element. In normal computer serial data transfer, this corresponds to the transmission rate in bits per second.

Bayer dithering A method of dithering in which each 8×8 block of pixels in a source image is compared with a fixed 8×8. Pixels larger than the corresponding pattern pixel are colored white. The remaining pixels are colored black.

BBN Butterfly A shared-memory multiprocessor that can be used for raytracing. Contention for shared memory prevents this processor from achieving maximum speed in this application.

BCC See *Block Check Character*.

beam current The amount of current in the electronic beam that is generated by the heated cathode of a cathode ray tube. It is controlled in amplitude by the control grid, is focused, deflected, and finally impinges on the phosphor to create the light image on the CRT face.

beam penetration display A type of color cathode ray tube in which layers of red and green phosphors are applied to the interior of the faceplate in such a way that the color of the display depends upon the amount that the electron beam penetrates the phosphor layers, which in turn depends upon the voltage of the electron beam. It provides simpler and higher resolution displays than colormask tubes, but cannot produce shades of blue. Also known as a *penetron*.

beam recording A method of recording directly on film using a laser or electron beam.

beam tracing 1. A method of ray tracing in which intersection computations are made for a polygonal cone of rays rather than a single ray, in order to minimize computations due to the coherence of adjacent rays. 2. A method of drawing an image that traces pyramidal beams instead of tracing the path of each individual ray of light, as with *ray tracing*.

bed of nails A fixture having many pin-type probes that impinge on various points of a printed circuit board to permit internal testing of the board.

benchmark A set of computer software applications that exercises a wide variety of computer parameter functions. A benchmark is used to test various computers and computer configurations and obtain comparisons of time and performance characteristics.

bend 1. A modifier used in all professional 3D applications that is used to bend a selected mesh or other modeling type. 2. A modifier available in Primitive Itch's *Mesh Forge* plug-in for *trueSpace*. It adds curvature to the mesh. The user can control the amount of curve, the direction of curve, the radius of the circle around which the mesh bends, and the axis.

Bend Body Parts A choice in the Display menu of *Poser*. It should normally be left on; otherwise figures will show ugly separations between their elements.

bending and bones Bones deform objects in different ways and with different effects. For instance, some objects need to bend like a piece of macaroni, while others need to bend like a finger. The methods to control the power or strength of each bone vary greatly from program to program. However, most 3D applications do allow for the definition of how the joints actually bend. Similarly, different 3D applications allow for different methods of bone influence, or the number of polygons the bone actually has pull over, and nearly all allow this sort of control. Some especially effective methods include selection sets, vertex mapping, and weight maps.

BER See *bit error rate*.

Bernoulli box A hard disk storage system with removable disks that uses the Bernoulli principle of fluid dynamics discovered by the 18th-century Swiss scientist Daniel Bernoulli. This technique makes use of the high-speed revolution of the hard disk to create an air cushion that keeps the read/write head at the desired distance from the disk's surface, thereby avoiding any frictional wear effects between the disk and the head.

Bernstein basis function A polynomial used to compute a Bezier curve. Also known as a *Bernstein polynomial*.

best boy The first assistant to the gaffer (head electrician). The person who manages the other electricians in setting up lights, etc.

Betacam SP (BetaSP) A video tape recording format developed by Sony in 1980. It is widely used for broadcast television.

Betacam SX A digital video tape recording format aimed primarily at SNG (satellite news gathering) and ENG applications.

beta spline A method of curve drawing used for graphics modeling. The beta spline is a derivation of the generalized uniform cubic *B-spline*.

beta test Testing of a new software product by actual users prior to its release as a commercial product. Extensive beta testing uncovers many problems that are not discovered during testing by the software manufacturer and thus produces a more robust final product.

Bethe lattice A graph without loops in which each node has the same number of branches. Also known as a *Cayley tree*.

bevel A tool that lets the user apply a softened or beveled edge to an object.

beveling Filling in to permit joining of two wide lines whose end center points are coincident.

bevels In *form•Z*, adding bevels to edges is especially critical when modeling surfaces that are perfectly mated to each other. If two adjacent and mated objects, such as panels, do not have their edges beveled at the seam, they will shade as a single surface, or at best there will a hairline seam. For the panels to render realistically, the edges at the seams should have a bevel. The two bevels, one on each edge, will form a V-groove that will catch a shadow at the bottom of the trough and the bevels will generate small subtle highlights. The combination of a bevel highlight and groove shadow creates a subtle yet realistic effect.

bezel The metal or plastic frame that surrounds a display or dial.

Bezier curve A type of curve that is defined as the function-weighted sum of four or more control points, two at the ends of the curve and two at other points. A *Bezier curve* always lies within the convex hull of its control points.

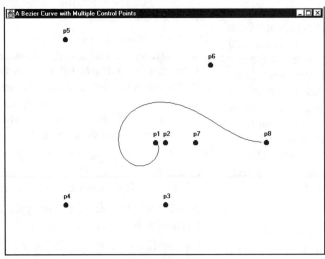

Bezier curve.

Bezier patch A type of bicubic patch formed by using Bezier curves.

Bezier points, converting to B-Spline control points If extra smoothness is desired, it is possible to change Bezier curves to equivalent B-spline curves, as

long as there are four control points. There is a direct conversion that can be applied to the Bezier control point values to obtain the B-spline control points that will yield the same curve. It is given by the following equation:

$$
\begin{bmatrix} p_1 \\ p_2 \\ p_3 \\ p_4 \end{bmatrix} = \begin{bmatrix} 6 & -7 & 2 & 0 \\ 0 & 2 & -1 & 0 \\ 0 & -1 & 2 & 0 \\ 0 & 2 & -7 & 6 \end{bmatrix} \begin{bmatrix} q_1 \\ q_2 \\ q_3 \\ q_4 \end{bmatrix}
$$

where the qs are Bezier control points and the ps are B-Spline control points.

Bezier simplices Surfaces such as triangles, tetrahedra, etc., whose sides are Bezier curves.

Bezier Tweener A feature of *Carrara* that permits smooth transitions between frames.

BFT See *binary file transmission*.

Bias parameter, B-spline Either of two additional parameters that are added to the representation of a B-spline curve to give additional control over its shape.

bicubic patch A small piece used to define part of an arbitrary surface. It is defined by three polynomials of third degree with respect to parameters s and t.

bidirectional printing A technique for increasing a printer's speed by printing a line from left to right, the next line from right to left, the next line from left to right, etc., in contrast to unidirectional printing in which every line is printed from left to right.

bidirectional reflectance A function applied over a small solid angle to relate incoming light intensity in a given direction to outgoing light intensity in another direction.

bidirectional reflectivity (r) The ratio of the reflected radiance from an object (intensity) to the incident irradiance (flux density) that causes it (when both directions are different). It is composed of specular and diffuse components.

bifurcate To divide in two.

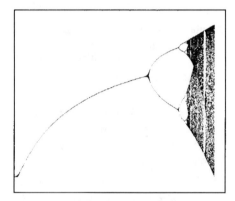

bifurcation diagram.

bifurcation diagram A fractal picture that shows where an iterated equation splits into two or more solutions and where areas of chaos occur.

bilevel A monochrome display technique in which each pixel is assigned one of two levels, either black or white.

bilevel display A display that is capable of showing only black or white.

bilinear filtering An option available with the *Game Creation System* that per-

forms a smoothing operation on the pixels in the screen's image.

bilinear interpolation Interpolation to obtain the value of a point located within a triangle or quadrilateral by a series of linear interpolations between the vertices of the triangle or quadrilateral.

bilinear patch A quadrilateral in three-dimensional space defined by four vertices that need not be coplanar. Intermediate points on the patch are determined by linear interpolation from the vertices.

bin A film-editing term that refers to the place where the shots for a scene are stored. In software editing systems, bins can also be referred to as *folders*, *galleries*, or *libraries*.

binary A system for encoded digital information using two components: 0 and 1.

binary decomposition A method of creating fractal curves of Julia sets.

binary file transmission (BFT) A standard for transmitting facsimile data between two fax boards that is faster than conventional fax transmission techniques.

binary order, animation recording A method of recording animation frames in which the animation is double-framed halfway through the recording process, quadruple-framed one-quarter through the process, octuple-framed one-eighth through the process, and so forth. This permits animation errors to be detected earlier than they would if sequential recording were used.

binary recursive subdivision A technique for determining the intersection between a ray and a triangle.

binary search method A technique for searching that depends upon representing the datum searched for as a binary number. The data to be searched are divided into two bins, those whose most significant binary digit is one and those whose most significant binary digit is zero. The bin containing the desired datum is then divided again based on the next most significant binary digit, and this process is repeated until only the desired datum remains.

binary space partition tree (BSP tree) A technique for subdividing three-dimensional space with planes so that each resulting partition contains the same number of primitive objects. Reduces the number of computations required for intersection computation or hidden surface removal.

binary tree See *bintree*.

binocular disparity The difference in perspective between the views from the two eyes of an observer due to the fact that each eye is located at a different position.

bintree A mathematical tree structure in which each branch of the tree can divide into two branches. Used in creating signal representations with wavelets. A bintree is a tree-like subdivision of three-dimensional space created by recursively subdividing a cube into equal halves about a single axis, cycling through a new axis at each. For any particular subdivision it is possible to stop the subdivision process without going further. Thus a bintree could be created where subdivision stopped when each subdivided cube contained precisely one primitive graphics object. The *bintree* often has more nodes than the *quadtree* or *octree* for the same object, but often

enables simpler processing. Also known as a *binary tree*.

BioVision data A format that allows the user to export scripted animations from supporting 3D applications (*Poser* or *Life Forms,* for example) and apply these motions to models in any 3D package that supports motion capture features.

BioVision Motion Capture files A capability to capture motion from human models and transfer it to digital models that is available in *Poser, LightWave, 3ds max,* and other professional 3D applications.

biped Literally, the term refers to two-legged creatures. In *3ds max*, it also refers to a specific skeletal arrangement that can be addressed by the *Character Studio* plugin.

bipolar cells Cells in the retina of the eye that act as an amplifier for the photoreceptors as well as an inhibitor, depending upon the signals they receive from the photoreceptors.

bird's eye view A view taken from above the scene, looking down on it. Some 3D applications distinguish bird's eye view from top view.

bis Term used by CCITT to designate the second in a family of related standards. The term *ter* designates the third in the family.

bisection, Sturm sequences A method used to isolate any real root of $f(x) = 0$. It starts with an interval

$$b \rangle a; s(a) - s(\infty) \geq k; s(b) - s(\infty) \langle k$$

Repeated bisection of the interval will isolate the root to any desired accuracy.

bit Contraction of *binary digit*. The smallest unit of data, a bit may have either of two conditions: on or off, or 1 or 0.

bit array An array of bools (or 1s and 0s) in C++ or another language. Typical examples are a one-dimensional array of bits, a two-dimensional array of bits (a location is identified by two indices), or a two bit array, where each member consists of two bits and can therefore represent values from 0 to 3.

BitArray2D class A two-dimensional analog of *BitArray class*.

BitArray class An array of bits stored in a buffer of longs in an endian-independent manner. It is similar to a regular C++ array with the added benefit of dynamic bounds and additional operators.

bitblt Bit block transfer. A technique for fast movement of a (usually rectangular) collection of bits to/from or in display memory. Used to display moving objects.

bit depth The number of colors in an image is measured in terms of *bit depth*. An 8-bit image has 256 colors, a 16-bit image thousands of colors, and a 24-bit image millions of colors. A 32-bit image is a 24-bit image with an 8-bit Alpha channel.

bit error rate (BER) A measurement of the average number of errors that occur during data transmission.

bitmap A representation of characters or graphics in a display by individual pixels usually arranged in order of a row of pixels horizontally and then additional similar rows to make up all the rows in the display. Monochrome data can be represented by one bit per pixel. Color displays may require up to 32 bits per pixel, which may be sequential or a separate *bitmap* may be generated for each bit of the color representation.

bitmap labels, adding to projects Labels can be added to an object as follows. First, develop a graphic of the label-to-be in a paint application and make an alpha map of it. Save it to disk in a format that the 3D application can import. Then, import a suitable object to wrap the label on, a bottle or can for example. Use any materials desired on it, and give the material a transparency if needed. Next, create a cylinder that fits around the middle of the object, which will act as the label object. Make the cylinder about 2% larger than the object in circumference as seen from the top view (that is, enlarge the label object's X and Z scale). With the label object selected, open the materials module for the software. Set the channel parameters. Then, load the label art and the alpha map of the label. The result window should show the label in full color. Use object front or cylindrical mapping to wrap the label to the object. Alpha-transparent areas of the label will be invisible. Render the object, and save it to disk.

bit-mapped font A set of bit patterns that represents all of the characters of a type font of a particular size.

bit-mapped graphics Images that are drawn on a display by a raster scan that scans from left to right in rows and then from top to bottom, with each dot that is to make up the image illuminated at the proper point in the scan.

bit-mapped texture The basic idea of a bit-mapped texture is that the user can use any created or altered bit-mapped image (including photographs) in any bitmap application (like *Photoshop*), and project or place it on the surface of polygons. Some 3D applications also allow bitmap images/animations to be used as volumetric textures that are applied at every depth of the object. Also known as a *texture map*.

69

bit-mapped texture.

bit-mapped texture channels The real power of bit-mapped textures is the ability to control different channels. Texture channels are synonymous with texture characteristics. That is, there is a channel for a texture's color, another for its reflectivity, another for its glow, transparency, bump, geometry, etc. In each channel of a given texture, an image (called a "map") can be placed that tells the 3D application how that texture will appear.

Bitmap Picture Editor A *Bryce* capability for editing bitmap pictures. Bitmap pictures are configured in the Picture Editor, which is switched on from the Edit button in one of the ABCD channels. *Bryce* allows *Photoshop* filters to be applied to the image.

Bitmap Picture toggle The four component textures in the *Bryce* CAB channels can be either procedurally or bitmap based. This button selects the bitmap option. This means that editing of the texture is done in the Picture Editor.

Clicking on the Bitmap Picture toggle and then on the Procedural Texture button randomizes the texture for that channel.

bitmap rotator A routine that rotates a bitmap using table look-up.

bit plane A memory buffer that holds one bit which is a partial definition of pixel color. Thus, to define 16 colors, one might use four bit planes. Combining the bit values from each of the four planes for the same pixel address at each plane would yield the 4-bit color information for the addressed pixel.

bit plane encoding Application of run-length encoding to each bit plane separately to compress and store an image.

BitProxy class A class that represents a single bit of the *BitArray* class.

bit specifications The number of colors or gray levels that may be displayed at one time. This depends upon the characteristics of the graphics controller card and the amount of memory it contains. The EGA can display 4-bit color, for a total of 16 colors. The VGA can display 8-bit color for a total of 256 colors. Super VGA cards may have 16-bit color (65,536 total colors) or 24-bit color (16.8 million colors).

bits per inch (bpi) The number of bits stored per linear inch on a magnetic tape.

bits per second (bps) The number of bits transferred in a data communications system in one second.

bitwise operations Mathematical operations that can be performed on arrays of bits. These may be described by English language or by Boolean operators.

black and coded tape A "blank" videotape that has been striped with a combination of a black video signal and timecode.

black body An ideal body that absorbs and emits light. A black body can be approximated using an opaque hollow sphere in an oven with a tiny opening through which spectral measurements are taken. However, there are no perfect black bodies in the real world. It is only a way to show that the temperature of an object can be known by looking at its spectral emission (light).

black burst A composite video signal with a totally black picture. Used to synchronize professional video equipment. Black burst supplies video equipment with vertical sync, horizontal sync, and chroma burst timing.

black burst generator A piece of video hardware that generates a black composite video signal, or *black burst*, used to sync professional video equipment and to black and code tapes.

black level The voltage level of the displayable part of a video signal that corresponds to a completely black video input.

black lights A feature available on some graphics programs that allows the use of light sources with a negative intensity value. This makes the light source absorb rather than emit light. In a scene where there are multiple light sources and the image appears overexposed or plagued with hotspots, a black light can be configured to absorb the excess. In many programs, negative lights not only remove diffuse and specular light but color as well.

black line A positive image consisting of black lines on a white background.

black matrix A picture tube in which each group of color phosphor dots is surrounded by black for increased contrast and clarity.

black noise Noise that has a power spectrum proportional to f^β where $\beta > 2$.

black wrap A heavy-duty aluminum foil with a matte black coating on one side used to block light. A black wrap can also be wrapped around light sources to make them more directional.

blanking The process of shutting off the electron beam of a cathode-ray tube between sweeps so that nothing is shown on the screen while the deflection circuits reposition themselves for the next horizontal or vertical sweep.

blanking level The voltage level of a video signal that totally suppresses the electron beam of the cathode-ray tube during blanking. Also knows as *pedestal level*.

bleed In publishing, the positioning of a picture on a page in such a way that it extends beyond the margin to the very edge of the page. Normally such a picture extends slightly beyond the finished dimension of the page, with the excess trimmed off during binding.

bleeding 1. In a cathode-ray tube display, a phenomena in which the color of one pixel affects the color of neighboring pixels. 2. The appearance of colored light on a surface that is produced by diffuse reflection from another surface. This makes the surface appear to be different from its true color. For example, a blue carpet can bleed a light blue tinge to nearby white walls. Also known as *bounce light*.

bleeding white A defect in display systems that results in white areas appearing to flow into black areas.

blending The smooth transitioning of one line, surface, or color into another without an observable joining edge.

blending functions The weights that are applied to two curves to assure continuity without an observable junction. They are usually in the form of cubic polynomials.

blend surface A surface added to provide continuous transition between two intersecting surfaces in a graphics model. See *surface blending*.

blink A capability of *Poser* to allow eye movement. A blink works on both eyes at the same time, while a wink works on only one eye. Use the Left and Right Blink parameter dials to animate either. Using a negative value opens the eye very wide, and can be useful for emotional responses like surprise or shock.

blinking Changing the intensity or color of a particular graphics area in order to highlight it.

blinking text A capability that is available in most programs for creating Web sites, but is now considered unprofessional. Furthermore, blinking text can provoke a seizure in viewers who suffer from epilepsy.

Blinn shading The computer graphics application of the Torrance-Sparrow-Cook shading model, based on realistic specular-to-diffuse reflections. The Torrance-Sparrow-Cook illumination model assumes that the surface of an object is made up of microscopic facets that are specular and capable of self-shadowing. It also accounts for the edge specularity on certain materials when viewed from certain angles. It is a physically based shading model. The Torrance-Sparrow-Cook reflection model was first applied to computer graphics by James Blinn; thus the term *Blinn shading*.

Blinn shading.

blip 1. A target signal on a radar screen. 2. A timing or counting mark placed on microfilm.

blitting functions Functions that move a rectangular block of pixels from one part of display memory to another.

blob An algebraic surface that can be defined by a quadratic equation. A number of blobs can be combined to approximate an irregular surface in a way that simplifies ray tracing.

blobby The term used to identify metaball objects.

block Quantity of data recorded on a disk or magnetic tape in a single continuous operation. Blocks are identified by track and sector addresses and are separated by physical gaps.

Block Check Character (BCC) A control character appended to a block of data which is used to determine whether the received block contains errors. See *cyclical redundancy checking*.

blocking Choreographing the movement of the actors for the camera when photographing a motion picture scene.

blockquote A capability of the HTML language that indents a block of text framed by the statements <BLOCKQUOTE> and </BLOCKQUOTE>.

blondel A unit of luminance equal to 0.1 millilambert.

blooming A condition in a video display or video camera in which excessive brightness causes white areas to expand and cover up darker areas.

blown dust and dirt An effect created in *trueSpace* by creating pyramid particles with *Primal Particles* and then shading them with *wfmm glow* and *wfmm motrails* from *CoolPowers*.

blown dust and dirt.

blue noise A set of samples having a frequency distribution that is close to that of a Poisson distribution.

blueprints Working drawings for constructing an object. They can often be scanned into a computer to be used as a template for the cross sections of an object.

blue-screen A special screen, usually composed of blue cloth or backdrops painted with special blue paint, which is placed behind a foreground element. Blue-screen shots are later composited with other elements through the use of a chroma key function. Green is used more often than blue these days (green-screen) because most living animals have few naturally-occurring green colors.

blue spill A bluish light that is cast onto the back of a foreground subject due to a reflection from a blue-screen.

blurring Intentional reduction of image sharpness. This is automatically achieved by using film rather than electronic recording, though blur filters are common in most 2D and 3D applications.

BMP file A windows file format for storing graphics data without using any form of compression. It makes use of a header consisting of up to 54 bytes of data followed by graphics pixel data stored by horizontal line, with 4, 8, or 24 bits per pixel, depending upon the number of bits per pixel specified in the header and a number of pixels per line and number of lines for the graphic as specified in the header.

BMP files and Java A BMP file cannot be directly transferred to Java since BMP files do not treat integers in the same way that Java does. Therefore some conversion is necessary before Java can handle the file.

BNC Connector A connector used to carry composite video, component video, timecode, and AES/EBU audio signals.

BNF See *Backus-Naur form*.

boards Spreadsheets showing cast member names and important elements of scene information.

body color model Software that models the absorption of light through a translucent media.

BodyPaint3D An application from MAXON Computer that offers high-end 3D painting and texturing, with the capability to save in most professional 3D modeling formats.

Bohm algorithm A method for determining new control points when subdividing non-uniform B-spline curves.

boids See *autonomous agents*.

boilerplate Text material that is used repeatedly, without change, in different documents.

Bolanzo-Weierstrass theorem A theorem that states that every infinite sequence x^n, where n is an integer between 1 and infinity, of S contains a subsequence that is a Cauchy sequence.

boldface One of a set of terms used to describe the weight or thickness of a type font. The most commonly used weight of a type font is known as *medium* or is not specified at all. The next greater weight or thickness is called *bold* or *boldface*. An even thicker type font is called *extra bold*. There can also be a smaller than normal width thickness called *light*.

bones, bending See *bending and bones*.

Bones Pro MAX A plug-in that is useful in creating animated sequences involving human and animal objects. It works with *Character Studio*.

Boolean algebra An algebraic system developed by English logician George Boole. It is usually applied to operations with sets or to operations in logic. Boolean operations with sets are useful in combining polygons to create more complicated figures for creation of graphics displays.

Boolean functions In 3D modeling, Boolean functions enable the user to add or subtract two intersecting volumes. The four major types of Boolean functions are union, difference, split, and intersection.

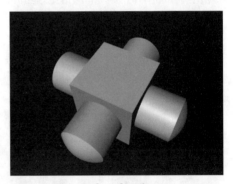

Boolean functions.

Boolean intersection The Boolean operation A*B. This takes two (or more) in-

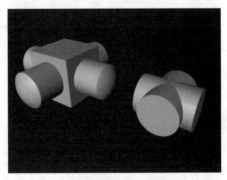

Boolean intersection.

tersecting shapes and gets rid of all the polygons that are not in direct contact with the polygons of another shape.

Boolean operations The three standard Boolean operations addressed by a 3D application are Add, Subtract, and Intersect. Boolean oprations are used to perform any of these three options on two or more objects in a scene.

Boolean operations on polygons, regularized When ordinary Boolean operations are applied to three-dimensional figures, it is possible that the resulting more complicated figures may not be three-dimensional. Consequently, a set of regularized Boolean operators has been developed whose application always results in three-dimensional objects.

Boolean Subtract tool A tool in *Universe* that allows the user to perform a Boolean subtraction of selected objects.

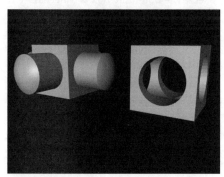

Boolean Subtract tool.

boom A long (sometimes up to 100′ long) pole with a microphone at the end. Technically, a boom is a large, sometimes hydraulically controlled device, as opposed to a *fishpole*, a smaller, handheld pole. Increasingly, the term *boom* is used to refer to any stick with a mic on the end.

boom operator One who operates the boom. This is very demanding work since the mic at the end of the boom is very directional and thus must be positioned very carefully.

boot To start a computer. Usually, permanently built-in software causes the computer to read a designated sector or sectors from a disk. These sectors, in turn, give instructions from which the computer loads the entire operating system.

border The width of the border of an image is specified in pixels. The default color of a border is black; however, if the image is a hyperlink, the border will render blue.

border layout in Java A procedure that allows Java programmers to create a window with a border that contains text at each of the four sides, as well as the center. (*see Figure next page*)

Borel field If *(X, d)* is a metric space and *B* is the σ-field generated by the open subsets of *X*, then *B* is called the *Borel field* associated with the metric space. Any element of *B* is called a *Borel subset* of *X*.

Boris FX A high-end series of filter volumes used in *After Effects, Combustion, Premier*, and other effects-compositing applications. The volumes include *Boris FX, Boris FX AE*, and *Boris Graffiti*.

bottlenecking The problem in transformations where the rotation is 90 or 270 degrees, resulting in the cosine of the rotation angle being undefined. As the transformation approaches these critical angles, the cosine blows up to the point where the new pixels are poor in quality. The problem may be avoided by breaking the transformation into two separate

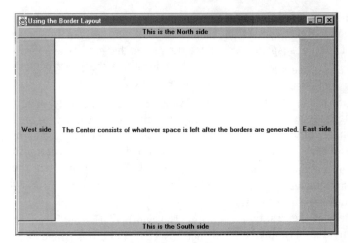

border layout in Java.

transformations, neither of which approaches the critical angles.

bounce cards Often pieces of white foam core board, bounce cards are used to create soft, indirect lighting, as opposed to reflectors (shiny boards) that are used to re-direct lighting from a bright light source, such as the sun.

bounce light See *bleeding*.

Bounce Randomizer An option in *The Games Factory* that makes "bounces" more random in their direction when this control is set high.

Bouncing Ball Movement A menu in *The Games Factory* that allows the user to set up an object to behave like a bouncing ball and control such characteristics as speed, deceleration, and bounce angles.

boundary fill algorithm An algorithm for filling an area with color where the largest region of pixels whose value is not some given boundary value is filled with the desired color.

boundary representation (b-rep) Specifying the surface boundaries of an object in order to model it, as contrasted to

defining an object by the intersection of primitive solids as in constructive solid geometry. The surface boundaries include vertices, edges, and faces.

boundary scanning method A method of generating fractal curves from Julia sets.

bounding box A rectangular polyhedron that encompasses one or more primitive objects. Used to simplify ray tracing. If a ray doesn't intersect the bounding box, one knows that it doesn't intersect the enclosed primitive objects, so no more testing is required. Only if the ray intersects the bounding box is it necessary to perform more complex tests to see if the ray intersects one of the enclosed objects. This reduces the amount of computer time required for intersect testing.

bounding sphere Similar to a bounding box, except that the bounding solid is a sphere.

bounding sphere collision detection Determination of whether two bounding spheres collide. Calculating bounding spheres is very simple; all that is needed is to find the center of the object, then to compute the maximum distance between the center and a vertex in the object. By storing the radius of each bounding sphere, bounding sphere collision detection can be performed by adding the radii of the two objects, then taking the distance between the two center vertices. If the distance is greater than the sum of the radii, the spheres are certainly not colliding.

bounding volume Similar to a bounding box, except that instead of a rectangular polyhedron, any shaped solid that permits easy intersect testing may be used.

bounding volume for torus A volume that consists of a sphere cut by two planes, which encloses a torus. It is the most efficient bounding volume for determining intersection of a ray with a torus.

bounding volume, octrees and When an octree is being designed, each node of the octree must include a bounding cube that defines the space that the node encloses.

box filter A method for modifying the color value of a pixel by averaging it with the color values of those pixels surrounding it. Used in anti-aliasing.

Box Image Mode In *The Games Factory*, a Box Image Mode imports a series of images from a disk using a single operation. Box Image Mode is ideal for creating animation sequences.

box layout A procedure that is part of the Java Swing components that allows the programmer to create a box containing text.

bpi See *bits per inch*.

bps See *bits per second*.

bracket A device on which a camcorder, lights, and microphones can be mounted to provide additional steadiness while photographing.

branch One of two or more lines, curves, or solid objects that meet at a node.

break action 1. A set of predetermined instructions that directs a COM system about where to place the next block of data after a break condition. 2. Indication of the end of a recorded frame of data in a COM system.

breakdown The art of listening to a pre-recorded track of dialogue and figuring out the timing. Also known as *track analysis*.

break-out box A box that has connectors and ports for attaching video and audio peripherals. Usually provided with complex video digitizing systems.

breath mist See *cold breath mist, creating*.

Brent's method A technique for inversion of monotonic functions in a single variable.

b-rep See *boundary representation*.

Bresenham's algorithm A mathematical algorithm for determining which pixels should be illuminated for the most accurate representation of a straight line, given a specified pixel resolution.

Bresenham's circle algorithm A variation of *Bresenham's algorithm* that draws a circle rather than a straight line.

Brewster angle The angle of incidence at which incident light impinging on a dielectric is completely polarized when reflected or is not reflected at all if it is inappropriately polarized.

bricks Bricks tend to be laid in some sort of alternating or offset manner that goes beyond a simple uniform grid, and provides an interesting pattern. There is a way to achieve a similar effect in *Carrara* without having to resort to using a texture map in the bump channel. The secret to this technique is a carefully orchestrated mix that combines the wires and checkers functions. Although it takes a little experimentation to get the hang of it, the basic concept behind it is that there are a number of ways to get a variety of Shader effects.

brick wall icon A control in the *Game Creation System* that allows the user to add walls to game levels.

brightness 1. The average light intensity of an image. 2. The perceived amount of light as determined by the luminance and chrominance of the source. Brightness is based upon the perception of the human eye, which varies with frequency, so that brightness is not proportional to physical energy emitted. 3. An option in the *Game Creation System*. If the monitor is too dark to see walls and textures very well, the user can use this option as a last resort. It will increase the brightness, but at price, since colors will become washed out.

brightness.

brightness, apparent An object's perceived brightness as attenuated by distance.

brightness, intrinsic Brightness related to a light's own energy emission per second, which is called *luminosity.*

brilliant Having both a high color value and a high degree of color saturation.

BRIM A system for storing general attributes of image objects in a database.

broad A light that has wide area coverage; used as a fill light.

broadcast colors A computer monitor can display many more colors than can NTSC video. Broadcast colors are those colors that are safe—that is, they will display

properly for use in broadcast video. Many programs, such as Adobe *Photoshop* and Adobe *After Effects*, include special filters that will convert the colors in an image to their nearest broadcast-safe equivalent. See also *NTSC legal*.

broadcast colors filter A filter that will convert the colors in an image to their nearest broadcast safe equivalent. See also *NTSC legal*.

broadcast quality The minimum quality considered acceptable for broadcast television. Until the 1980s, ³/₄" Umatic tape was considered broadcast quality. Then Betacam SP was introduced and became the standard for broadcast quality. Today, Hi8 and MiniDV is often considered broadcast quality due to the fact that the final master is usually on Digital Betacam.

brow lifting muscle See *frontalis*.

Brownian motion A path that is defined as the integral of white noise.

brown noise Noise that has a power spectrum proportional to f^2.

brow ridge The brow ridge is the midpoint of the face. A common technique for determining the size of the brow ridge is to use eye lengths. The head width along the brow ridge is five eye lengths wide. The brow itself is four eye lengths wide. Another thing to note when creating the brow ridge is to dip the center of the brow where it lies over the glabella, just above the nasion. Quite often a 3D model's brow runs straight across the forehead, which tends to make the character look like a troglodyte.

browser A program that communicates with Web sites and displays Web pages. The two most widely-used browsers are

Microsoft Internet Explorer and *Netscape Navigator.*

browser specific extensions Netscape and Microsoft have developed HTML extensions which often contradict the current HTML standard. These extensions are designed to control the design and layout of Web pages.

brush An electronic replication of the brush used by an artist to draw wide lines to form an electronic image. The representation is often rectangular or circular. More complex algorithms take into account the effects of slanting the brush and the beginning and ending of lines.

Bryce An innovative 3D graphics application from Corel that allows users to design, render, and animate photorealistic scenes, including natural and fantasy 3D worlds and abstract 3D sculptures. The controls in *Bryce* let users create a variety of objects to populate landscapes and environments they create. The animation tools let users add the dimension of time to landscapes and environments.

B-spline Basis spline. A method of specifying control points to determine the shape of a curve that is very similar to the Bezier curve, but permits additional control of shape and continuity. A cubic B-spline has four control points. The following equation is applied to each element of the control points to build the B-spline curve:

$$B - spline = \begin{bmatrix} -1 & 3 & -3 & 1 \\ 3 & -6 & 0 & 4 \\ -3 & 3 & 3 & 1 \\ 1 & 0 & 0 & 0 \end{bmatrix} \frac{1}{6}$$

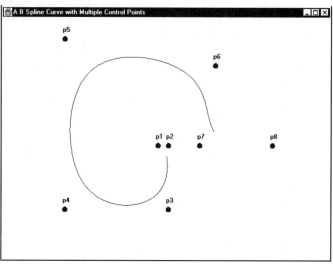

B-spline.

B-spline patch A bicubic patch formed using B-spline curves.

BSP tree See *binary space partition tree.*

BT. 601 A document that defines the specifications for professional, interlaced video standards as the following: 720 × 480 (59.94 Hz), 960 × 480 (59.94 Hz), 720 × 576 (50 Hz), and 960 × 576 (50 Hz) 4:2:2 YCbCr. Also called *CCIR 601* and *ITU-R 601.*

bubble A technique for recording data on optical disks in which a laser beam strikes nonimage areas, causing bubbles to form, while the image area remains clear to reflect the light of the reading laser.

bubble sort A technique for sorting lists of words into alphabetical or numerical order. The bubble sort scans a list until it finds a number or letter that is lower than the first number or letter in the list and then exchanges the two. It then picks up where it left off on the list and continues making comparisons with the first number. When the list has been completely scanned, the process is repeated, starting and comparing with the second number or letter, and so forth until finally everything is compared with the next to last number. At that point, the list is completely sorted.

bubble test A form of clipping in which a computed sphere surrounding a portion of a three-dimensional graphics volume is used as the clipping boundary.

buffer Memory space designed for temporary storage. Usually used when data arrive from a transmitting device at a rate faster than they can be accepted by the receiving device.

bug A defect in computer hardware or software.

bug list A list of known defects in a particular version of a piece of computer software together with suggestions for getting around the problems until a new edition of the software is released.

building rough cut Creating the first cut of a scene. Usually done by *drag and drop editing*, in which the scenes are sorted by scene number, shot number, and take number, and then the good takes are dropped into the timeline of the NLE.

building set Providing a synthetic location for filming when the right natural location is difficult to find. Whether building a set on a stage or at a location, it is necessary to spend some extra effort to make it look real. Sets are usually built out of *flats*, which are large, hollow wooden walls that are held up from the rear with supports.

Bump Attribute Thumbnail This button in the *Bryce* CAB channels gives the user a thumbnail view of the Bump attribute of the texture. This is the information that is accessed when the Bump Height controls for that channel are manipulated.

bump channel This channel allows for virtual bumps across the surface of an object. It does not actually change the geometry of polygons at all. Instead, the 3D application understands that the user wants it to render shadows within the object as if there were the geometry present to define raised and lowered areas of the surface. This tool can save hours of modeling little bumps and divots in a shape by simply defining it with a bump map. Since a bump map can depict complex surfaces without adding extra polygons, it can save a lot of time when it comes time to render the objects. Beware, however; since bump maps do not actually alter the geometry of a given shape, the profiles of bump-mapped shapes are not accurate. If the profiles will actually be seen, consider using the displacement channel.

Bump Height Value A control for bump mapping in *Bryce*. Bump mapping applies what looks like height values to parts of a material, even though no real distortion of the underlying geometry of the object ever occurs. Bump mapping usually looks best when applied with the object in mind. Mountains look good close up with bump-mapped materials, while mountains in the distance need no bump maps. The Bump Mapping Value slider is one that has both positive and negative settings, ranging from –100 to +100. Negative values reverse the look of the bump map, so what looks raised with a positive setting will look depressed with a negative one. Bizarre animation effects can be generated by reversing the two over time.

bumping up The process of transferring a videotape from a lower quality format to a higher quality format, i.e, bumping up miniDV tapes to DVCPro.

bump map An 8-bit grayscale image that is used to simulate surface texture in the rendering process by manipulating surface normals. A bump map creates the illusion of texture, but does not alter the surface geometry of an object.

bump map, animating Animating the bump channel can be used to create a wide variety of effects, from rippling water to spontaneously-emerging text. *Carrara* provides many ways to animate the bump channel.

bump map, lighting Lighting plays a crucial role in achieving and controlling

the look of a *bump map*. In photography, to accentuate surface texture, lower the light source(s) and "strafe" it across the object.

bump mapping Producing the appearance of a nonsmooth surface on an object by randomly perturbing the direction of the surface normal prior to computing the shading for each pixel.

bump mapping.

bump shader A shader used with *true-Space* to produce bumpy surfaces. Good duplication of ocean waves can be created using the *layered bump* shader, the *Crumple* shader, and the *Perlin Noise* shader (*see Figure next page*).

bundle table A table of workstation-dependent aspects for a particular primitive in the GKS or PHIGS graphics standards.

buoyancy, simulating Objects float on water because their overall density is less than that of the surrounding water. The force of buoyancy on an object is

81

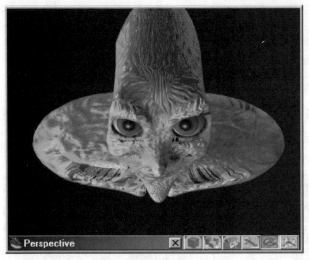

bump shader.

equal to the weight of the water displaced by that object. This force is actually in the direction of the pressure gradient, but in most cases, the direction normal to the water surface is appropriate. If the shape of the hull is approximated as a set of discrete points, normals, and area patches, the force of buoyancy can be calculated by performing a volume integral over the submerged portion. The volume of water displaced by a section of the hull is:

$$\Delta V_k = \Delta A_k \left(z_{water} - p_{k,z} \right) n_{k,z}$$

where z_{water} is the bilinearly-interpolated water height at p_k. Bilinear interpolation is recommended, since other methods might produce primary or first order discontinuities. The buoyant force at this position is:

$$F_k = \rho \Delta V_k n$$

and the torque is simply:

$$N_k = r_k \times F_k$$

where r_k is the vector from the center of mass to p_k. The total force and torque are calculated by summing the contributions from each hull vertex. Remember also that only the submerged portions contribute to the buoyancy.

Burkes error diffusion filter A dithering technique in which the error between the color of a pixel and its representation by black or white is partially added to the two pixels on the right of the current pixel as well as the five pixels surrounding the current pixel location on the line below.

burst See *color burst*.

bus A set of lines on which signals are entered for use by many connected devices.

bus mouse A mouse that is connected to a computer through an expansion card slot rather than through a serial port.

butterfly effect The image generated by plotting the solutions of the Lorenz strange attractor equations. See *attractor, Lorenz*.

butterfly lighting A key light that is positioned above and slightly in front of the subject. In portraiture, butterfly lighting forms a "butterfly shadow" under the nose. This type of top lighting is used mostly in glamour and fashion shots. Hollywood portrait photographers such as George Hurrell popularized this type of glamour lighting. Butterfly lighting minimizes the imperfections on the subject's face or surface, and accents the cheekbones and the neckline in portraits. It also elongates the bridge of the nose, lengthening it in some subjects. Even though butterfly lighting is flattering for many subjects, it should never be used with broad-faced or round-shaped subjects, because it will widen the appearance of the subjects' faces.

button 1. A mechanical switch-like device, such as on a mouse, which provides an input to a computer. 2. An image on a display that gives the appearance of a mechanical button. It is activated by using a mouse to position the cursor on the button image and then activating the mouse's mechanical button.

button mask, locator The area within which the cursor must be located in order for a press of the mouse button to trigger some specific event.

button state A visual version of a *button*. For example, during clicking, the button is in its *down state*; when dormant, it is in its *up state*. When the mouse is hovered over the button (during a "mouseover"), the button is in its *over state*.

Butz's algorithm An algorithm for generating an *n*-dimensional Peano curve.

BVH Motion Capture An ability of *Poser* to import BVH Motion Files, and to target them to any selected bipedal figure. It opens up a number of handshaking possibilities with other applications that create these file formats. This also allows the user to collect volumes of BVH Motion File data found in various independently marketed CD volumes.

byte A unit of computer data consisting of eight *bits*.

C

C A computer language used to write the UNIX operating system. C provides considerable flexibility at the price of not including very many safeguards against programmer misuse of the language. C is one of the most widely-used languages for the development of professional programs.

C++ An extension of the C language, designed by Bjarne Stroustrup to include object-oriented programming techniques and the overriding of mathematical operators.

C0 See *continuity, positional.*

C1 See *continuity, tangential.*

C2 See *continuity, curvature.*

C3 or C^3 Military command, control, and communications systems.

CAB (Color, Alpha, Bump) channels *Bryce* has four CAB channels that enable the user to create the component textures that are ingredients for a material. The settings that can be adjusted using a CAB channel include transformation options, edit button, texture name, texture lists, color, alpha, and bump attribute thumbnails, procedure texture toggle, bitmap picture toggle, mapping type name, and mapping type list.

cabinet projection A projection in which the direction of projection makes an angle that has the arctan value 2 (63.4 degree angle) with the projection plane. Distances parallel with the x and y axes are projected at actual length, while lines perpendicular to the projection plane are projected at half their actual length.

cable Wires within a sheath used to carry a signal between electrical units.

cache (pronounced "käsh") A portion of high-speed memory used to store frequently-used disk data to reduce the retrieval time when the data are required. The success of caching schemes depends upon how well the associated software can determine which data should be included in the cache at any given time.

cache coherency Keeping data values in a cache consistent with the data in the larger memory that the cache mirrors.

CAD See *computer-aided (or -assisted) design (or drafting).*

CAD lighting Lighting needed by a CAD program so that the user can determine such things as the orientation of a house or the placement of windows to optimize the use of natural light. Some CAD programs can replicate the natural light of any season of the year.

CAE See *computer-aided engineering.*

CAV See *constant angular velocity.*

cage modeling A modeling process that begins with a cube or rectangular solid, draws out portions of it to approximate the desired shape, and then rounds it off.

CAI See *computer-aided instruction.*

calculation of size The determination of the size of a map that is to be placed on the surface of an object. The map size is dependent upon the physical size of the final rendering.

calderas, inverting Real-world volcanoes, especially active volcanoes, have very distinctive mountain tops. After flow stops, the lava at the top of the volcano cools and recedes back into the Earth, creating a familiar bowl-shaped region at the top called a *caldera*. A caldera for a particle mountain can be created by inverting the height field values above a certain altitude about the horizontal plane defined by that altitude.

calibrating The process of adjusting a monitor to produce standard colors.

callback procedures Computer subroutines called by the *dispatcher* or *notifier* to respond to user actions by specified actions.

calligraphic display A type of cathode-ray tube display in which lines and characters are drawn by directly moving the electron beam to trace out the desired shape rather than scanning the beam in a raster and illuminating the appropriate points in the raster scan. Also known as a *stroke display* or *stroker.*

CAM See *computer-aided (or -assisted) manufacturing.*

camera angle The positioning of the camera with respect to the principle characters in the scene being photographed.

camera animated reflections A technique for showing a person moving in front of a mirror in *Poser.*

camera, conical The standard camera model used in creating a digital scene. It views a scene as a person would—with perspective. Distant objects appear smaller, and parallel lines converge toward an invisible vanishing point on the horizon. While this results in a natural-looking image, it also makes it difficult to position objects accurately in a scene.

camera control, level of detail Objects and characters are represented in computer graphics as geometric models. Models can be created at different *levels of detail* (LODs), with more polygons and larger textures for the more detailed models, and fewer polygons and smaller textures for the less detailed models. Selecting the proper LOD can improve rendering performance and visual quality. Drawing fewer polygons when objects are far away from the camera reduces the polygon count of the scene, and so speeds up rendering. Having a more detailed model for use when an object is close to the camera improves visual quality. If only a single model is used, then there is always a tradeoff between performance and quality—multiple levels of detail help to achieve both. To implement LOD rendering, multiple models are created at different levels of detail, and the model to be rendered is chosen, with each frame based on distance from the camera. As a rough rule of thumb, each level of detail should have about twice the number of polygons as the preceding level. The models are created to reduce "popping" as much as possible—when the character or object switches from one level of detail to another, the visible change in geometry (especially at the silhouette edge) and texturing must be minimized. The artist's job is to create models that change as little as possible when rendered at the scale where the transition will occur. The programmer's job is to determine when to change LODs to achieve the desired performance and quality while minimizing the number of LOD transitions.

camera controls, advanced Advanced camera controls used in professional 3D applications. The camera controls allow the user to tweak a camera's position, origin, banking, focal length, pan x or y, and zoom x or y.

camera controls *Poser* has a number of controls for a simulated camera. These include: The Rotation Trackball, which allows the user to rotate the camera left/right and up/down. It has no effect in an orthogonal camera view. The button to the upper left controls the camera zoom. Below that is a button that controls the camera's focal length setting. To the upper right is a button that allows the camera to bank left and right. The crossed arms control camera movements left/right and in/out of the screen. Instantly alter the camera view by clicking and dragging left or right over the Central icon in this group. The Hand icons allow the user to move the camera on either the ZY or the XY planes. The Key icon is a switch that turns animation on or off, and the Looping Arrow icon switches on the Fly Around feature, so the user can preview a scene from all sides. Clicking activates either the left or right Hand camera views, or the Head camera. Always use the Head camera when posing a face.

camera control techniques, B-spline Use of a B-spline curve to determine the path of a camera. The curve provides the position of the camera, but we also need a target and an up vector. For multiple curves, each control point should be associated with a target position. Hence, the camera will continue to focus on the target as it moves along the curve. Once it encounters a new target position, the camera control logic can simply interpolate between the points to get the desired effect. A more complex but flexible solution would be to use two B-Spline curves, one for camera position and the other for target position.

camera control techniques, look at Basic first-person camera models rely on "look-at" utilities such as OpenGL's gluLookAt(). Given a camera position, view direction, and up vector, this function returns an orientation view matrix. The view matrix is then placed on the OpenGL MODELVIEW matrix stack and concatenated with orientation matrices for each object in the scene as they are rendered.

camera control techniques, scripted Scripted cameras are a crucial part of many games, from cinematic scenes in role-playing games to helicopter fly-throughs of a golf course. Most games that use this camera technique use an animation package to script the camera, then import the animation into their game engines. This is an excellent solution for a static path, but it is harder to implement for dynamic paths.

camera control, use of quaternions Specifying the position of a camera in terms of Euler angles can result in singularities at certain critical angles that cause undesired jumps in camera position. These can be avoided by specifying the camera position in quaternions, which state position without any singularities. See *quaternions*.

camera damping Damping is the key to making camera controls look and feel right. The following function will return a vector that approaches the target vector such that as it reaches the target, it begins to slow down.

```
vector3 dampType1(vector3 currX,
    vector3 targetX) {
        return currX + ((targetX -
    currX) / 16.0F);}
```

However, there is a major problem with this solution; it is frame-rate dependent. As the frame rate increases, the damping effect decreases. Using physics is one possible solution for damping. Applying accelerations and friction to the camera's position will produce the desired result, and physics equations are frame-rate independent. But physics is more appropriate for an interactive solution. It doesn't easily offer a current and target position interface, which would be more useful in situations where the camera is scripted or affected by fixed animations. Springs are the perfect solution. The following spring equation can be applied to achieve the desired damping:

$$F = ma = -k_s x - k_d v$$

camera interpolation Interpolating the orientation of a camera into an animated scene. The lack of a good technique for interpolating complex camera motion limits most animations to fixed- or extremely limited-camera motion.

camera, isometric A type of camera provided by *Carrara* and other 3D applications. Viewed through an isometric camera, same-sized objects appear the same size no matter how far away from the camera they are, and parallel lines remain parallel as they move away from the camera. This makes it easy to properly position objects.

camera, lens flare simulation Lens flare is an optical effect created by inter-reflection between elements of a lens when the camera is pointed toward a bright light. The result is a shifting pattern of translucent shapes and colors emanating from the light source. The effect is often seen in TV broadcasts when the sun enters the video camera's field of view. In real life, lens flare is considered a defect, and camera manufacturers go to great lengths to eliminate it through special lens coatings. Video games, however, like to emphasize and exaggerate all the fantastic aspects of reality, and lens flare is definitely fantastic. Real lens flare is due to complex interactions of light with surfaces in the optical system of a camera. Video game lens flare is all about appearances. An attractive lens flare effect can be achieved using only a small amount of code and artwork, without needing to know anything at all about physical optics.

camera light A light source that is similar to attaching a radial light to the top of the camera. Everywhere the camera goes, the light follows. This is especially useful for exploration-type effects where the point of an animation is to take the viewer through an old castle, cavern, tunnel, or some other place that needs discovering. The light is linked to the camera.

camera movements, basic There are three basic camera movements that are used in animation: *zoom in*, *object fly-by*, and *dolly*. To"zoom in," position the camera away from the subject and then gently zoom in on the object. Once satisfied with the speed of the zoom, rotate the camera slowly around the object while zooming in. This is the most basic camera movement. Another technique is an *object fly-by* with the camera in a stationary position. Place the camera fairly close to the motion path of the moving object. As an example, set the camera near the center of the length of the distance that the object will be traveling. Depending on the speed of the object and the distance from the camera, the viewer will be able to see the object grow larger, then fly by, and then grow smaller. The overall feeling of the shot is that the action flows smoothly and evenly. Another object fly-by technique sets the camera toward the beginning of the motion path of the object. In this setup the action starts abruptly with the object flying past fairly early in the action. This will grab the viewer's attention immediately. Put an interesting background or model for the object to fly toward in the later part of the animation to shift the viewer's attention toward the background model. A shot like this makes a good transition to a clip featuring a close-up of the background model. A third object fly-by technique places the camera near the end of the motion path, which gradually draws the viewer's attention toward the subject of the animation. This is a good way to introduce a model into a scene. With the model slowly growing in size and separating itself from the background, the viewer is gradually brought into the action. An alternative to the fly-by is the *dolly*. In movie production, a camera has to be fairly steady and level when it is tracking a moving object, especially when the camera itself is moving. In 3D

it is useful to recreate the same results as a dolly. The first type of dolly movement has the camera moving alongside the model as the model travels along. In a second dolly method the camera has a higher speed than the model, and eventually passes the subject. This type of shot shows the viewer more of the front end of the model. In a third dolly method, the camera moves more slowly than the object, eventually falling behind. This type of camera footage is good for showing the back end of the model.

camera negative After film stock is exposed in the camera and processed, the result is the *negative*, also called the *camera negative*, which is usually transferred to video using a telecine process and then, after editing, used to strike the final print.

camera obscura A darkened room with a single small opening, the *camera obscura* was the forerunner of the modern photographic camera. Light coming through the opening projected an inverted image of a brightly-lit exterior object onto the opposite wall of the darkened room. The camera obscura was originally used to view eclipses. Later, artists used it to trace reflected images. By the 19th century, lenses and mirrors had been added to the camera obscura to eliminate the inversion of the image and to make it convenient to project the image onto a piece of paper. J. N. Niepce was the first to use the camera obscura to project an image onto light-sensitive paper, creating the first photographic prints.

camera, panoramic vistas Vistas in *Bryce* and other 3D applications that support panorama images can be translated to

Web panoramas for use on home pages with the display help of Apple's Quick-Time VR technology or other applications. Visitors can stand in the center of the scene and turn the camera around to appreciate the view. QuickTime allows the camera to move to see what is above or below as well.

camera shake The amount that the camera shakes during the filming of a scene. Normally, the camera should be held as steadily as possible. This can be achieved by buying a camera that has built-in optical image stabilization or by using a tripod for all shots. However, some effects, such as explosions or car crashes, are enhanced by deliberately adding shakiness. This can be done after the fact by using such a program as Adobe *After Effects* and adding a *jitter*.

camera shake setup A dramatic effect created in *trueSpace* produced by using the *Shakadelic* or *Shakadelic Pro* plug-in.

camera space A coordinate system that has its origin at the observer (or camera) viewpoint and its positive *z* axis pointed along the direction of view.

camera, trackball A camera option that may be chosen in the Director's View mode of *Bryce*. This is the item to choose to create an animation that is similar to the Flyaround option. It locates the camera so that it is focused on the global center of the scene, allowing the user to orbit the scene by using the trackball. Set this option while in the Director's View and set the keyframes. After setting each keyframe, select Camera >> Director's, then set the next keyframe in the Director's View.

camera, vector A generalized form of the matrix-based camera found in many tra-ditional graphics engines. Matrices are often difficult to read due to the fact that they typically hold several operations concatenated together. The vector camera uses only simple vectors to describe its orientation, position, field of view, and aspect ratio. This format allows for some interesting optimizations to the overall graphics pipeline. The vector camera uses the same information found in matrix-based cameras. The world-to-camera matrix (view matrix) is broken down into four vectors. Three vectors represent the three axes that define the camera's orientation, and one vector represents the camera's position in the world coordinate space. In total, this provides six degrees of freedom. The main advantage of the vector camera is that it can operate in both local and world coordinate space. The camera's orientation and position vectors are stored in world space; however, they can be inversely transformed into local space using the inverse of the model's local-to-world matrix. The camera and the object won't move in relation to each other; rather, the camera's new orientation and position are relative to the local space object. These are the only transformations required to render the object. Now that the vector camera is in local space, it can project the local space coordinates, and no further transformations are required. After doing almost no work, the vector camera can now cycle through each of the local space vertices in the model, and project them into 2D screen coordinates. If the model is static, like a mountain, the model data can be stored in world space. This allows for an even faster code path. With both the object and the camera in world space, no inverse matrix needs to be calculated, and no transformations are required at all.

camera view Selecting how the camera is used to view the scene. Available cameras in *Poser*, for instance, include the Main, Posing, Head, Hand, and Dolly cameras.

camera, viewing A method of viewing a scene in which a camera position (the center of projection) and a center of attention are specified together with a view plane that is perpendicular to the vector connecting the camera position and center of attention.

Camera view window A display in *Universe* that provides a list of all cameras and shadow-casting lights.

camera, virtual Most 3D applications allow the user to place a virtual camera that can be moved around within the digital space. Cameras are the views from which 3D projects are usually finally rendered and presented. Because of this, most cameras present perspective views. One of the most popular ways to view digital space for modeling and positioning objects is to have three orthographic views open (front, side, and top), and another view or camera view that is using perspective projection.

cancel command A user command that allows the system to revert to its state just previous to the latest user command.

candela A unit of luminous intensity. One candela is the amount of light per unit solid angle from a point source. It is expressed as the luminance of a particular light in candelas per square meter. It is equal to one lumen per steradian.

candidate list In ray tracing, a list of primitive graphics objects that need to be tested for intersection by a given ray.

candlelight Candlelight burns at a much lower color temperature than incandescent light, at about 2,300–2,500K. At this color temperature, the perceived color is drastically shifted toward the yellows, if not the reds. Since we have affection for this type of illumination, it is advantageous to be able to evoke that feeling in computer graphics; that is a sense of warmth and intimacy when using candlelight. When scenes are lit with candles, they seem inviting and sensual; the use of candlelight in cinema is always a conscious decision to evoke these emotions. Candlelight simulation in computer graphics might seem deceptively easy: just make the light yellow-orange, or even make it slightly white-tangerine. However, solving the problem this way tends to make the rendering flat and uninteresting, because the candlelight wraps around the object and has subtle tonal gradations, even if there is only one light. The surfaces closest to the candlelight are lighter than the surfaces far from it, and the obstructed surfaces are very dark. Candlelit middle tones tend to be desaturated and colorless, which means they become gray instead of shifting their color to gray. The key to a successful candlelight simulation lies in the control of the middle tones and highlights more than the shadows. Actually, this rule is true for most local lights. The color of the highlights and the middle tones suggests the kind and type of light source that is present in the scene.

Canoma A program designed by MetaCreations (now owned by Adobe) for architectural modeling. *Canoma* takes the power of camera mapping and places it in an interactive 3D interface.

canonical fill algorithm An algorithm for filling a closed polygon with a selected color by starting at a seed point within the polygon and expanding in all directions until the polygon is filled. The canonical fill algorithm was developed by Smith in 1979.

Can't Bump Into Object attribute (Collision Detection off) An object attribute in the *Game Creation System*. By setting this attribute, the user allows the player to pass through the object as if it were a ghost or hologram.

Cantor set A set of numbers that has measure zero. The basis of a number of interesting fractals.

canvas A complex icon or menu stored in bitmap or pixmap form in off-screen memory, from which it can be recalled to the screen display when desired.

Canvas A 2D bitmap and vector application.

capstan A driven cylinder that drives a magnetic tape at the proper speed. The capstan is usually affixed to a flywheel, which eliminates speed variations of the driving motor. The capstan has a large area in contact with the tape surface, which assures that the tape moves smoothly.

capsule An object that resembles a cylinder with rounded ends.

capture utility A utility that is part of many editing packages that permits loading video from video input hardware into a computer.

capturing The process of moving video data from a DV camera into a computer. Because the camera has already digitized the data, the computer does not have to perform any digitizing.

CAR See *computer-assisted retrieval.*

car camera mounts Special vacuum suction devices that attach a camera to the body of a car. These are essential to get good footage inside a moving car.

Cardano's formula A formula for finding the roots of a cubic equation.

cardinal splines Curves composed of segments that are curved with intermediate control vertices.

cardioid The roughly heart-shaped pattern of the area from which a cardioid microphone can "hear."

card layout A procedure that is part of the Java Swing Components that allows the user to produce a display that has the appearance of a card file. Along the top of the display are a number of file tabs that the user can fill with headings. When one of these headings is selected, the remainder of the window will be filled with the text associated with that heading.

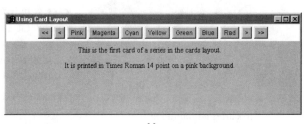

card layout.

caricature The creation of a human or animal model or image, whose features have been exaggerated. This can be accomplished in the original modeling or painting process, or through 2D or 3D morphing.

Carrara *Carrara*, from Eovia supersedes both *RayDream Studio* and *Infini-D* from MetaCreations. *Carrara* also folds in most of RayDream's capabilities and tools. *Carrara* can be used to develop modeled figures for *Poser*, and also to craft morph target data, since it does read and write the WaveFront files *Poser* demands.

carrier 1. In communication, the radio-frequency signal upon which data are modulated. 2. In electrostatic printing, a substance that moves and disperses toner without actually toning an image.

carrier sense multiple access (CSMA) A technique for preventing two stations on a network from attempting to access the same device at the same time.

Cartesian coordinates The common rectangular coordinate system, consisting of three mutually-perpendicular axes (x, y, and z), from which all points in a volume are referenced.

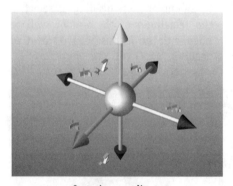

Cartesian coordinates.

Cartesian product Representation of the color of a pixel as a number that combines the three coordinates of a point in three-dimensional space, using scaling to give optimum representation of all colors.

cartography The mapping of a sphere onto a plane.

Cascading Style Sheets (CSS) Also known as *style sheets*, Cascading Style Sheets allow a Web-page designer to assign several properties at once to all of the components on Web pages by adding additional components to HTML tags. Originally, HTML was not intended to provide layout control when it came to creating Web pages. In late 1996, the first version of the style sheet standard (CSS1) was finalized, and the support in Web browsers became available. The second version of style sheet specification (CSS2) was standardized in 1998. Using style sheets formatting can be accomplished by simply typing in a few lines of syntax on the top of a Web page or in an external document. Style sheets are also easy to change. The designer can change the format of paragraphs, headings, links and other elements simply by editing one or two lines of syntax using style sheets versus going through a complete HTML document and changing every single tag.

CASE See *computer-aided software engineering*.

case sensitive Capable of differentiating between capital and lowercase letters. To a case-sensitive device, *example* and *EXAMPLE* are two different and totally unrelated words.

cassette A magnetic tape storage device that includes take-up and supply reels as well as a length of tape. The most commonly used cassettes are the VHS, 8-mm, and Beta video units and the 3-inch audio unit.

Cassini's divisions The divisions in the rings of Saturn.

casting call In animation, the analysis of a storyboard to determine all models that need to be created and how detailed each needs to be.

catalog A listing of files and/or directories that are stored in computer memory or on a disk or tape.

catenary The curve formed by a sagging cable suspended at each end.

cathode-ray tube (CRT) A display device used in computer monitors and television sets. The cathode-ray tube consists of an electron gun that projects a beam onto a phosphorescent screen. These are enclosed in a glass envelope, the interior of which is evacuated. The electron beam is focused at the desired spot on the screen by electromagnetic coils mounted external to the tube. The electron beam then excites the phosphor at that point, causing it to emit light.

Catmull-Rom patch A bicubic patch that is generated using *Catmull-Rom splines*.

Catmull-Rom spline A type of spline used in generating graphics curves, in which the curve passes through all of the control points.

Catmull subpixel area-subdivision algorithm A technique for antialiasing that determines the amount of each pixel covered by the visible parts of each polygon and computes a weighted sum of the visible parts' colors to determine the color of the pixel.

CAT (Computed Axial Tomography) scan The production of a display by computed tomography in which each point on a 2D display has a brightness corresponding to the density of a corresponding point in a 3D human or animal tissue object.

Cauchy sequence If x_n is a sequence of points in a metric space (X, d) and this sequence converges to a point x that is within X, then the sequence is a *Cauchy sequence*.

caustic In optics, light focused by reflection from or refraction through a curved object. Caustics are generated when a beam of light hits a reflective surface and bounces spots of light onto another surface. Caustics are also generated when light passes through a transparent surface such as glass or water. The refractive properties of a transparent object bends the light, causing the rays to focus or spread, depending on the curve of the object. *LightWave* is capable of rendering interesting caustics.

CAV See *constant angular velocity*.

cavalier projection A projection in which the direction of projection makes a 45 degree angle with the projection plane. All distances are projected at actual length, so that there is no foreshortening.

Cayley tree A graph without loops in which each node has the same number of branches. Also known as a *Bethe lattice*.

Cboid class A class used in modeling the behavior of flocks or herds. This class handles all aspects of a specific agent's motion and existence: how it moves, how it senses its environment, and how it prioritizes its actions.

Cbox class A class used in modeling the behavior of flocks or herds. This class defines the world in which our boids can move.

CBT See *computer-based training*.

CCD See *charge-coupled device*.

CCIR 601 See *BT. 601*.

CCITT See *Comité Consultatif Internationale de Télégraphique et Téléphonique*.

C-curve A curve used in *form•Z* to represent a curved shape. C-curve editing controls are available to establish the shape of the curvature.

CD Compact disc. A $4^3/_4$-inch disk upon which digital data are recorded for playback by a laser reader. CDs provide a high-quality method of storing music since the digital recording technique is immune to noise generated with most other recording techniques. CDs have the capability to store large amounts of computer data (650-700 MB). MiniCDs also exist, holding about 150 MB of data. MiniCDs are used in the latest Sony cameras.

C/D ratio See *control to display ratio*.

CD-R Compact Disc-Recordable. A special type of compact disc that can be recorded by the end user using a special drive. Capacity is 650 to 700 MB. Standard audio or data formats are supported by most recording programs, along with Video CD, a special format that can store 70 minutes of full-screen, full-motion MPEG1-compressed video. MiniCDRs also exist for storing image data from a camera.

CD-ROM Compact Disc Read-Only Memory. A storage system for digital computer data using CDs as the storage medium. A CD-ROM holds about 650 to 700 megabytes of data.

CD-RW Compact Disc-ReWriteable. A blank compact disc that can be recorded and also rewritten many times by a suitable recorder. Capacity is 650 to 700 MB. Suitable for making copies of large amounts of computer data when it is desirable to be able to re-write and reuse the disk many times. MiniCD-RWs also exist, and are used to store data from a selection of Sony cameras.

cel 1. An animation technique in which an image is drawn on transparent material so that successive images may be overlaid to produce a composite picture. 2. A pattern consisting of color and transparency values that is mapped as a texture onto a computer graphics scene. A cel is particularly useful for clouds, smoke and haze, and tree foliage. 3. A single frame of animation. A cel, or *celluloid*, is a transparent piece of film that is used by a traditional 2D animator as a canvas.

cell The color of a rectangular picture element as defined for GKS and PHIGS graphics standards.

cell array An array of cells in the GKS graphics standard that defines the color of a patch of an image.

cell decomposition The decomposition of a solid into a set of primitive adjoining nonintersecting solids or cells, thereby permitting the representation of a complex solid by a number of simpler ones.

cellular automata A technique for modeling growth. Cellular automata are made up of mathematical cells in an array. Each cell changes its value or state according to some specified set of algorithms. The state of each cell is affected by the states of neighboring cells.

celluloid film Celluloid was the first synthetic plastic, a highly flammable cellulose nitrate with camphor and alcohol. In 1890, Darragh de Lancey developed a way to coat celluloid with a continuous emulsion. Hannibal Goodwin invented the modern roll film that does not need a paper backing for support, which made handling the film easier. In 1885, Eastman Dry Plate and Film Company introduced a transparent substrate coated with emulsion, the form of film used today.

Center Edge Snapping tool A tool in *Universe* that allows positioning of the edges of an object to grid lines.

center of gravity The point in a body about which all points of the body balance each other. For a triangle, this is the intersection of the medians.

center of interest An object or space on the screen to which the viewer's eye is naturally drawn. The remainder of the composition should be balanced around this focal point. To assure that the viewer's attention remains on the center of interest, the object should be well-lit within the scene, and nothing else should be larger than the object for an extended period of time.

center of projection (COP) A point from which rays are projected to every point in an object. At some point in their trajectory they pass through a *projection plane*. These intersections form the projection of the object's image.

center of rotation The point in a three-dimensional object about which all rotation occurs. *Universe* has a tool that allows the user to select this point.

center of window (COW) In projection, the center of the portion of the view plane that contains the image.

central processing unit (CPU) The box that contains the motherboard, peripheral cards, and some storage drives for a computer. Also used to refer to the main processing chip that the system uses.

central projection A projection of a sphere onto a plane where the projection is accomplished through rays that begin at the center of the sphere. Also known as *gnomonic projection*.

Central Structure Storage (CSS) A special-purpose database used by PHIGS to store graphics information.

Centronics interface The standard 36-pin parallel interface that is used to connect printers and other parallel devices to a computer. Normally this 36-pin connector is at the printer end of the cable and a standard 25-pin RMA connector is at the other end. Named for the Centronics Corp., which used them in the first parallel printers.

CEPS See *color electronics prepress system*.

Cesaro curve A self-similar fractal curve produced by starting with a line segment, replacing it with two lines that with the original would make a right isoceles triangle, and then repeating this for every newly created line segment as many times as desired.

Cflock class A class used in modeling the behavior of flocks or herds. This class represents a basic flock of boids and serves mostly as an organizational tool rather than a strict representation of each flock per se. Its various functions are fairly simple and deal primarily with the "bookkeeping" that one might desire when handling flocks.

CG See *character generator*.

CGA See *Color Graphics Adapter*.

CGI See *computer generated imagery, Computer Graphics Interface,* or *Common Gateway Interface*.

CGM See *Computer Graphics Metafile*.

chain The hierarchy of bones within a modeled figure.

change matrix A matrix that specifies the direction and amount of change to a transformation matrix.

changes in tone Changes in audio quality from one scene or edit to another.

channel 1. A layer of information in a frame buffer. Also known as a *plane*. 2. The color in an RGB image is divided into *channels*, one each for the red, green, and blue information in the image. When these channels are combined, a full-color image results. Certain effects are easier to achieve by manipulating individual color channels. Additional alpha channels can also be added for specifying transparency and selections See *alpha channel*.

channels, texture The real power of bit-mapped textures is the ability to control different channels. *Texture channels* are synonymous with texture characteristics. That is, there is a channel for a texture's color, another for its reflectivity, another for its glow, transparency, bump, geometry, etc. In each channel of a given texture, an image (called a "map") can be placed that tells the 3D application how that texture will appear.

chaos The field of mathematics that studies disorderly behavior of equations and physical phenomena.

chaos band Regions of chaotic behavior between which a function behaves in a normal orderly manner.

chaos game The application of integrated function systems (IFS) to create fractal images.

character A letter of the alphabet, a number, or a punctuation mark. If the ASCII code is used, as with PCs, a character is represented by one byte.

character-based user interface (CUI) A computer system in which user-typed characters are used to control computer operations.

character, boldface A character whose lines are wider than those of a character in the normal font.

character cell A matrix of dots assigned for the display of a character. Typical character cell sizes for the PC are 8 H 8, 8 H 14, and 8 H 16. Each character to be displayed is represented by a unique combination of lighted and dark dots in the character cell.

character descender The part of some characters that descends below the normal character baseline.

character device A printer or other output device that receives data from the computer on a character-by-character basis rather than in blocks of data.

character field The rectangular region that marks the bounds within which a character may be displayed.

character generator (CG) A special machine for creating titles and other text characters for inclusion in a video. Most editing packages include CG features.

character graphics A set of predefined characters designed to create simple graphics images. Typically it includes single and double vertical lines and various types of intersections of single and double lines.

character, italic A character that is slanted rather than straight up and down as is a normal font character.

character lights The character's form and presence in the scene always dictate the addition of character lights. The ambient scene lights and tonality also dictate it. The new lights should not violate the property and quality of a scene's lights. They should enhance only the character's form and shape. This does not mean that the character's lighting is secondary to the scene lighting. It means that the direction and placement should be the same. If the scene's warm key light is coming from the right side, the character's key light should also come from the right side and be warm as well. The new lights should not alter the scene light's property and quality because it will make the scene look unnatural and contrived.

character pitch The number of characters per inch in printed or displayed text. The most common pitches are 10 for *pica* typewriter type and 12 for *elite* typewriter type. Strictly speaking, *character pitch* refers only to the width of the character, but normally, the height of characters of a given pitch is adjusted to produce a pleasing typeface.

character recognition The use of a computer program to recognize written or printed characters and convert them to their computer equivalents for storage in memory. A typical program that does this is *OmniPage*.

character, roman A normal character from a font, as contrasted to *boldface* or *italic*.

character set Those symbols that are available with a particular type font. In English, the *character set* always includes uppercase and lowercase alphabetical characters, numbers, and some punctuation marks. Other special characters may be available, the exact variety of special characters being dependent upon which type font is selected.

character, single-mesh A character created from one large polygon through Hyper-NURBS patches. With a single-mesh character, there is no hierarchy available since the entire character is one object. However, the character can be animated through the use of bones.

characters per inch (cpi) The density of characters per inch on paper or tape. For characters on tape, this is the same as *character pitch*.

Character Studio A professional-level bone deformation and muscle animation plug-in available from Discreet.

character terminal A terminal that can display text only, not graphics.

character typeface The style with which characters in a font are drawn, including line widths, handling of curves, use of serifs, etc.

character width In most fonts, each character has its own specified width, with the lower case *i* usually being the narrowest character and *m* and/or *w* being the widest character. The overall height is fixed for every character of a particular sized font, whereas the width may differ for every character. A few fonts, based upon typewriter type, use the same width for every character.

charge-coupled device (CCD) An array of light-sensing semiconductors upon which a lens image is focused to convert the image to electrical impulses. The array provides a high-resolution image on a microchip.

cheat keys A feature of the *Game Creation System*. This system has five cheat functions the user can invoke during a game, using the following codes: Kill All, which kills all enemies on a level; Invincible, which turns on God mode; Magic Heal, which brings the player to 100% health; Open Doors, which opens all doors on the level for a few seconds; and Teleport n, which teleports the user to entry point #n. To use a cheat code, hold down the left Shift key and press the C key. Enter the cheat code at the prompt and press Enter.

check bits Additional data bits that are inserted into a data transmission to permit determining whether any transmission errors have occurred. The simplest use of check bits is to assign a check bit to a block of n data bits, with the check bit a one if the sum of bits that are one in the block is odd, and a zero if the sum of the bits that are one in the block is even.

checkbox 1. A type of display, often used in Java, in which a small box is displayed with a number of labeled buttons or icons, which can be clicked on in various combinations to set up the characteristics of some attributes of the current programs. 2. A command in HTML that creates a box on the display that can be checked by the user.

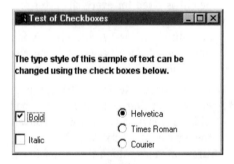

checkbox.

checkerboard A way to arrange each piece of sound across a group of audio tracks so that no piece of sound is directly "touching" any other piece of sound, resulting in a checkerboard-like appearance. Also called *A/B rolling*.

checksum A set of bits that gives the sum of bits that are one in a block of transmitted data. When compared with the sum of the received block, the checksum should be identical if no transmission errors have occurred.

cheekbones When modeling the head, the cheekbone is a vital part of the facial structure. It gives the head personality and character. Its placement is crucial for proper facial animation since the cheek muscles play a major role in facial expression. The baseline of the cheekbone lines up with the base of the nose. The cheekbone starts at the top of the nasal bone and runs 30 degrees diagonally from the corner of the eye socket to the angle of the jaw. The depression of the cheekbone is at the midpoint of this diagonal line. The last element of the cheekbone is the arch, or top, of the cheekbone. This starts at the infraorbital margin and lines up with the termination of the nasal bone, or midpoint of the nose, and ends roughly in the middle of the ear.

Cheek Puff Target Morph A *Poser* technique for using morphing to puff the cheeks of a modeled face.

chiaroscuro A method for applying value to a two-dimensional piece of artwork to create the illusion of a three-dimensional solid form. This way of working was devised during the Italian Renaissance and was used by artists such as Leonardo daVinci and Raphael. In this system, if light is coming in from one predetermined direction, then light and shadow will conform to a set of rules. A highlight will mark the point where the light is being reflected most directly. This is usually bright white. As one's eyes move away from this highlight, light hits the object less directly and therefore registers a darker value of gray. Some indirect light is available because the dark side does not turn solid black. This is the result of reflected and refracted light that naturally occurs. The extreme edge of the form will be markedly lighter than the shadowed area of the object. Light in the environment is illuminating the back edge. The cast shadows are usually divided up into separate values as well. The area closest to the object is usually the darkest area that is being portrayed. Then, as more light becomes available, the same cast shadow lightens in increments until it reaches the shadow's edge. Often, a drawing does not have this exact transition of grays. One can control and manipulate this formula to create interesting moods and character in a piece of work. *A high key drawing* is one that has mostly light values, probably with no value of more than 60% at the darkest points. A *low key drawing* would be one that has mostly dark values. In both low and high key pieces, this system of chiaroscuro can be used to create the illusion of three-dimensional space in a drawing.

child 1. A subset of data that is dependent upon another data set. 2. A node in a hierarchy that is below another node.

child program A second program that is executed by a currently running program without user intervention.

chin When modeling the head, the chin comprises one-third of the mass below the nose. At its widest point, it aligns with the sides of the mouth.

Chin Jut Target Morph A *Poser* technique for using morphing to jut the chin of a modeled face. In this Target Morph, the chin can either jut out or in.

choice box A small box display used in Java that shows only a currently selected item. When an arrow to the right of the box is clicked a sublist of possible choices is displayed. When one of these is clicked, it becomes the selected item that is shown in the choice box and which determines a computer action.

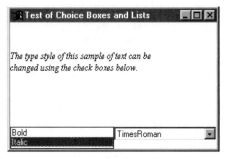

choice box.

choice device In the GKS graphics specification, a logical input consisting of a number that indicates the choice of a predetermined set of alternatives.

choice logical device An input device that permits an operator to select from a set of possible actions or choices.

choice set A set of computer tasks from which the user may select one for execution.

chord fill A term used in Java to denote a method of filling an arc with color. Since an arc is not a closed figure, some assumption has to be made as to how it will be filled. If a *chord fill* is used, Java actually draws a chord between the ends of the arc and then fills the resulting closed figure with color.

chord, locator button state An array that shows actions selected by the user pressing buttons, where it is possible to select two or more buttons simultaneously.

99

choroid The dark brown vascular membrane within the inner eye. It is the middle layer between the *sclera* and the *retina*. As with the sclera, it is thicker in the back than in the front. Since most of the vascular system in the eye originates from the back, the choroid is interrupted at the back by the optic nerve, and its inner system is attached to the retina. The choroid is pigmented to prevent unwanted light from striking the retina and confusing the visual system. It also absorbs light after it has passed through the retina.

chroma 1. The hue and saturation components of a color, not including its brightness. 2. The part of a video signal that contains the color information.

chroma control A control on a monitor that adjusts color saturation.

chroma key A special key function that will render a specific color in a layer transparent. For example, if someone is filmed in front of an evenly-lit blue screen, a chroma key function can be used to render the blue completely transparent, thus revealing underlying video layers.

chroma keying The process in post production of replacing a specific color in a clip with another image or piece of footage.

chromatic aberration A characteristic of glass in lenses that causes rays of different colors to be bent by different amounts, thereby focusing them at different points.

chromaticity, color Three standard primary colors, X, Y, and Z, which can be combined to specify any given color. These were developed by the Commission International de l'Èclairage to replace the red, green, and blue (RGB) primaries, since all visible colors can be created by positive mixtures of X, Y, and Z , whereas some colors require negative amounts of R, G, or B and therefore cannot be represented in that system.

chromaticity coordinates The three standard primary colors (coordinates) of the chromaticity system, X, Y, and Z.

chromaticity diagram A plot of the (X,Y) portion of the *CIE color space*.

chrome text effect Chrome text provides a nice effect to text images. It gives a look similar to real chrome.

chrominance The part of a composite color video signal that comprises the hue and saturation information. See also *YIQ color model*.

Chyron A title, identifying a speaker in a documentary, that runs along the bottom of the screen, so-called after the Chyron character-generator popular in many post-production facilities. These I.D. titles are also known as *lower thirds*.

CIE See *Commission International de l'Èclairage*.

CIE chromaticity diagram See *chromaticity diagram*.

CIE color space An internationally defined device-independent color space supported by Java. It is capable of very precise color definition, but the complexity of the color transforms needed to translate colors to the device-dependent color spaces such as those for monitors or color printers is burdensome. Furthermore, the only way to be sure that the color relationships are maintained exactly is to attach a profile of the input color space to a transmitted image and compare it with the output.

This substantially increases the size of the file being transmitted. The primary colors of the CIE color space, represented by X, Y, and Z, are *superred, supergreen,* and *superblue,* respectively. They are not physically possible because they would require negative intensities, but they are useful in specifying the components of realizable colors. Also known as *CIE XYZ.*

CIE LAB A standardized color space which provides equal steps of perceived color change (by the eye) for equal changes in the coordinate values. The space is defined in cylindrical coordinates. *CIELAB* is the acronym for the *Commission International de l'Èclairage* plus *lightness* plus $a*$ and $b*$ axis labels.

CIE LUV uniform color space A color space in which two colors that are equally distant from two original colors are perceived by the viewer as being equally distant. This is typically not true of the X, Y, Z chromaticity space because the distance that is just noticeable to the human eye varies throughout the spectrum.

CIE XYZ See *CIE color space.*

ciliary body The thickened, protruding part of the *choroid,* from which the lens is connected and suspended. The elastic fibrous part of the ciliary body is called *zonule fibers* and is responsible for eyes' ability to compensate for near and far vision. In short, the zonule fibers are there for sight *accommodation.* Accommodation is the ability of the eyes to focus and adjust near-vision distance by changing the shape of the lens. When the ciliary muscles are relaxed, the zonule fibers exert tension on the lens, and the lens flattens, making distant vi-

sion possible. When the ciliary muscle does contract, the zonule fibers remove the tension on the lens, which makes the lens revert back to its rounder, more natural shape. The natural shape of the lens allows close vision.

CineHair A plug-in for *Cinema 4D XL* that can be used to grow geometric hair-like fibers from any model, including those originating in *form•Z.*

Cinema 4D XL A high-end 3D application from MAXON Computer that includes a wide array of tools and effects, as well as fast rendering.

Cinematographer See *Director of Photography.*

cinematography, basic The use of a camera to actually film an animation. It is important to have enough frames in the animation to keep the action slow so that the user can grasp what is happening.

cine-mode Method of recording data on a filmstrip so that it can be read when the strip is held vertically.

cinepak A QuickTime codec that is very lossy but ideal for delivery media with low data rates such as CD-ROM or the Web.

circle 1. The locus of all points at a given distance from a center point. 2. An option in *Bryce.* In an object's Animation tab in the Attributes dialog, one more option that has an effect on the way the object moves along its path: Make Circular. This command creates a closed loop, so that the first frame of the animated object on its path will equal the last frame as far as position is concerned.

circle of confusion The circle on a projected image produced by a lens transmitting a point of light. For a perfect lens, this circle should be a point. The larger the circle, the poorer the quality of the lens.

circle, wide line A circle with a line that is wider than one pixel. Java enables one to draw such figures by defining a basic stroke width.

circular addressing See *circular buffering*.

circular arc A portion of the circumference of a circle.

Circular Arrow option In the *Game Creation System*, an editing icon for rotating groups of objects by 90 degree increments.

circular buffering A memory addressing technique in which pointers are stored indicating the beginning and end of the data sequence. Additional data are added to the end and the end pointer is changed accordingly. When data are removed, the start pointer is changed to reflect the new beginning of active data. When the end of the buffer area is reached additional data are inserted at the beginning of the buffer area. An error occurs if an attempt is made to store too much data so that data overlap in the buffer.

circumcenter A point within a triangle that is equidistant from all three vertices.

circumference The perimeter of a circle.

circumradius The distance from the circumcenter of a triangle to any of the vertices.

CIT See *composite interaction task*.

clamp light A light attached to a clamp that can be attached to any convenient place such as a door, window frame, or chair and positioned so that the light is pointed in the desired position for illuminating a scene.

classification A ray tracing technique in which rays are grouped according to direction, origin, or some other characteristic to reduce the number of required computations.

Clay Studio/Clay Studio Pro Metaball modeling plugins for *3ds max* from Digimation.

clearing frame and natural wipes An easy way to create a smooth transition between two scenes is to cut out of a shot (as the actor clears the frame) and cut into the next shot as the actor enters the frame in another location. This method can become repetitive very quickly if it is overused. When a large object passes through the frame, such as a passing car, a person in the foreground, and so on, it can be used as a natural "wipe," to easily transition to the next scene. In *Rope*, Alfred Hitchcock concealed his few edits in the film by hiding them under natural wipes.

clenching muscle (masseter) The jaw muscles actually include one major muscle and several smaller supporting muscles. The main muscle is the *masseter*, which is used to clench the teeth and raise the jaw. The masseter is located at the base of the jaw. This muscle plays a major role in any movement in which the lower jaw is dropped wide open. Two of the expressions created by the masseter muscle are fear and yawning. In both of these expressions the masseter muscle is used to raise the jaw to the neutral position. The masseter muscle is also used to clench the teeth together in a chewing action. It's used heavily when one eats food, particularly when it's something that requires a lot of grinding.

click and drag interaction A method of moving a selected symbol from one position to another using the cursor. Holding down the mouse button selects the symbol to be moved; it then follows the cursor motion until the mouse button is released, which freezes the symbol in the new position.

click() method A method used in Java to simulate a click without the user's input.

click-through When a visitor to a Web site actually clicks on a banner. This is one way to pay for an advertisement. The number of actual click-throughs a banner receives will determine the cost of the advertisement.

client A program that is built on top of a windows system and makes use of its services.

clip art A collection of digital images from which a user may select pictures for use in his own publications, in either bitmap or vector formats. Clip art also exists for 3D formats.

clipboard The temporary memory cache in a computer.

clip boundary The definition of a region outside of which graphics objects are eliminated in producing an image.

clip mapping A feature of professional 3D applications that, unlike transparency mapping, creates holes that will let light through, so the non-clipped areas will cast shadows.

clip path A two-dimensional boundary outside of which graphics objects are eliminated in producing an image.

clipping 1. The process of eliminating those portions of graphics primitives that extend beyond a predetermined region, so that they do not appear in a reproduced image. In Java, when the dimensions of a window are established, the language automatically takes care of clipping anything outside the window. 2. Setting limits to the maximum white and minimum black signals of a composite video signal and eliminating portions of the signal that exceed these limits. 3. In digital media, an electronic limit that is imposed on the audio and/or video portion of the signal in order to avoid audio that is too loud and video that is too bright, too saturated or too dark. *Clipped blacks* are any blacks in an image that are darker than the set black level, or 7.5 IRE. *Clipped whites* are any whites that are brighter than the set white level, or 100 IRE. *Clipped audio* is any sound that goes into the red area on a VU meter. *Clipped media* is indicated by a flat line in a waveform view of the signal.

clipping, Cohen-Sutherland line algorithm A technique for minimizing the computer operations required to clip lines. First each end of the line is examined for trivial acceptance. If the

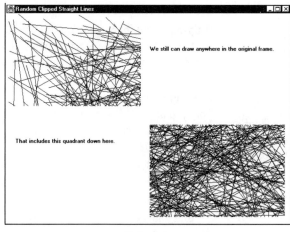

clip boundary.

line cannot be trivially accepted, each endpoint is assigned a four bit code which indicates which region it is in when we extend the boundaries of the clipping rectangle to form nine separate regions. If we logically AND the four bit codes for the two line ends and the result is not zero, the line can be trivially rejected. Otherwise, we find the intersection of the line with one of the clipping boundaries and divide the line into two line segments at this point. One of these segments should be capable of being trivially rejected. We then perform the same process with the other segment, which is computed and used as the line ends for the clipped line.

clipping, Cyrus-Beck algorithm An improvement on the *Cohen-Sutherland line algorithm*. This algorithm uses a parametric approach in which the parametric representation of the line segment being tested is found at its intersection with each of four lines that are infinite extensions of the four sides of the clipping rectangle. A series of comparisons determines whether any of the four values found represents an actual intersection of the line segment with the clipping rectangle. Finally, if there is an actual intersection, the x and y coordinates are calculated. This algorithm is faster and requires simpler calculations than the Cohen-Sutherland algorithm.

clipping, endpoints Clipping an individual point is quite simple. If the x coordinate of a point is between the minimum and maximum values of the clipping rectangle x coordinate and the y coordinate of the point is between the minimum and maximum values of the clipping rectangle y coordinate, the point is kept; otherwise it is discarded.

clipping, Liang-Barsky line algorithm An improvement on the *Cyrus-Beck line algorithm* in which each of the parameter values is examined when it is first generated. This often makes it possible to reject a line segment before all four of the parameter values are calculated. Also known as the *Cyrus-Beck-Liang-Barsky algorithm*.

clipping, Liang-Barsky polygon algorithm An extension of the *Liang-Barsky line algorithm* that permits removing of parts of a polygon that are outside a clipping window.

clipping, Nicholl-Lee-Nicholl (NLN) line algorithm A clipping algorithm in which a line segment PQ is first examined to determine which region P is in (when we extend the boundaries of the clipping rectangle to form nine separate regions). Then finding the position of Q relative to lines from P to each of the four corners of the clipping rectangle determines which edges of the clip rectangle PQ intersects.

clipping plane A plane in three-dimensional space that is parallel to the image plane and which marks the boundary between objects that are to be rendered and those that are not.

clipping plane, back (yon) The clipping plane at the back of a three-dimensional scene, beyond which no objects are rendered.

clipping plane, front (hither) The clipping plane at the front of a three-dimensional scene, in front of which no objects are rendered.

clipping, polygon An algorithm to clip a polygon. If it clips a concave polygon, the result may be two polygons.

clipping, Sutherland-Hodgman polygon-clipping algorithm A technique for clipping a polygon to within a rectangular clipping window by clipping the polygon against each of the four lines that make up the clipping rectangle successively.

clipping, three-dimensional Clipping of a solid against a clipping cube. The *Cohen-Sutherland line algorithm*, the *Cyrus-Beck line algorithm*, and the *Liang-Barsky line algorithm* can all easily be extended to handle three-dimensional cases.

clipping, trivial acceptance, trivial rejection The determination that a line should be totally included in an image because it is entirely within the clipping rectangle or totally rejected because it is totally outside the clipping boundary, with no further computer tests needed.

clipping, Weiler polygon algorithm A method of clipping one polygon to another arbitrary polygon. Drawing the clipping polygon *A* and the polygon to be clipped *B* results in a number of disjoint regions, each of which is entirely in *A*, entirely in *B*, entirely contained in both, or contained in neither. The clipped polygon consists of all the regions that are contained in both *A* and *B*.

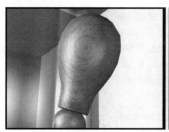

clip rectangle A rectangular boundary outside of which graphics objects are eliminated in producing an image.

clip region In a window system, the portions of the display outside the selected window, from which output is removed by clipping.

clip test Any quick test for determining whether a pixel is outside the clip boundary and therefore should not be reproduced.

clone An exact copy of digital video data. There will be no losses in this copy.

Clone Brush tool A tool in *Paint Shop Pro* that enables the user to copy portions of an image to either the same image or to a new image. Additionally, this tool can be used to cut certain parts out of an image.

closed object An object whose surfaces can be seen only from one side, the other side being hidden inside the opaque object.

close-up A shot where the subject fills the majority of the frame. If the subject is a person, the shot will consist primarily of his head and shoulders. This intimate shot has been standardized by television. It is so standard, in fact, that we as an audience expect to be close

close-up.

enough to see the intricacies of the scar on the villain's twitching face or the lack of blemishes on the placid skin of the heroine. The most important part of the close-up is the intimacy it gives us with a character's eyes. ⊂⊃

closure 1. The accuracy with which lines that are supposed to meet at a point actually do meet. In mapping, due to surveying, measurement, and scaling errors, there is always an *error of closure,* where two measurements of the same point via different methods give results. In a final map, these errors are manipulated so that the map appears perfectly accurate. 2. A principle of good visual design in which stimuli that almost enclose an area or seem to enclose an area are arranged so that the viewer sees that area.

Cloud Cover A control in *Bryce.* A setting of zero creates a blank sky, showing only the color set for the middle color slot in the Sky Modes/Custom palette (as long as the frequency and amplitude of the clouds is flattened). Altering the color in the palette attached to the Cloud Cover will colorize the clouds and have no effect on the coloring of the rest of the user's world. Altering Cloud Cover produces interesting animation effects. ◯

Cloud Frequency and Amplitude A control in *Bryce.* This tool is completely intuitive, allowing the user to "read" what the clouds in a sky will look like. When flattened, clouds are set to zero. Altering Cloud Frequency and Amplitude produces interesting animation effects.

clouds 1. Clouds, fog, and haze can be modeled stochastically and composited into textured ellipsoids (by Gardner) or by use of fractals (by Voss). 2. Creating a clouds shader is an excellent example of how to use *Carrara's* shader functions to create effects that go beyond what one might think the functions are capable of. ◯

cluster 1. A group of computers, terminals, or workstations connected in a single system. 2. A group of convex graphics objects that are linearly separable from other such groups so that a

plane may be established between two clusters without intersecting either. See *Schumacher algorithm.*

clustered-dot dither A technique for creating dot patterns similar to those in halftones to permit printing of a photographic image.

CLV See *constant linear velocity.*

C-Mesh A tool available in *form•Z* to create and smooth surfaces.

C-M interface The body of information that permits construction of a mathematical model from a conceptual model and the transfer of data between them.

C-Mode EDL An EDL sorted non-sequentially by source tape number and ascending source timecode.

CMTM See *composite modeling transformation matrix.*

CMX A hardware-based linear on-line editing system. CMX-format EDLs are often the default for other editing systems.

CMY A color space that means cyan, magenta, and yellow. ◯

CMYK Cyan, magenta, yellow, and key (for black). The four subtractive colors used in color printing. All colors in a picture are comprised of these four basic colors. Color printing is accomplished by four passes through the printing press, each pass using ink of one of these basic colors. ◯

coax Coaxial cable. A cable consisting of an inner conductor surrounded by an insulator and then a sheath of shielding braid. Coaxial cable is designed to have a characteristic impedance so that it can be matched to prevent unwanted signal reflections. It has a wide bandwidth and thus can carry transmissions that simultaneously pass a great deal of information.

codec Coder-decoder. A pair of devices for compressing data by encoding it and for decoding the compressed data to obtain the original information. Normally used for reducing the bandwidth required to transmit information. Codecs can be either software-based or hardware-based.

coding information The use of a color or symbol to represent a piece of information. To avoid confusion the selected color or symbol should always have the same meaning.

coding, redundant The use of two or more different types of code to represent the same information. For example, color or shading, width of the border line, and shape of a geometric figure could all represent a particular user action, so that by noting that the icon has any one of these characteristics corresponding to a desired user action, the user can click on the proper icon.

coding, visual The creating of visual distinctions between several different types of objects so that the user can select the desired object to click to initiate a particular user action.

cofactor The *cofactor* of an element of a matrix is the matrix that is formed when the row and column containing the element are removed. For example, the cofactor of the element $a11$ in the matrix:

$$\begin{bmatrix} 4 & -5 & 6 \\ 12 & 23 & -8 \\ 2 & 9 & 16 \end{bmatrix}$$

is

$$\begin{bmatrix} 23 & -8 \\ 9 & 16 \end{bmatrix}$$

Cohen-Sutherland line-clipping algorithm See *clipping, Cohen-Sutherland line algorithm.*

coherence 1. The quality of portions of an image having a common relationship. 2. The tendency of adjacent pixels, adjacent scan lines, or successive frames of an animation sequence to have similar color or relative motion. This tendency can be used to develop algorithms that reduce the number of computations required to produce images and thereby speed up the image-generating process.

cohesion A rule for steering in defining flocking behavior. The rule states that each flock member should steer to move toward the average position of local flockmates.

cold breath mist, creating Producing the effect of a person breathing in a cold atmosphere using *trueSpace* with a combination of the *Primal Particles* plug-in, the *wfmm glow* shader, and the *wfmm motrails* shader.

cold breath mist, creating.

colinear The fact that two or more points lie on the same line.

collage theorem A theorem that is central to generating fractal pictures using *iterated function systems (IFS)*. The theorem says that it is possible to find a set

107

of transformations (contraction mappings) whose IFS will approach a particular image to any desired degree of accuracy.

collimate To generate an image that is optically focused so that it appears to be at infinity. This is the image that is easiest for the eye to observe, since the eye muscles are fully relaxed when focusing at infinity.

collision detection In a game, the determination of when objects collide so that realistic results of the collision can be programmed into the system.

collision detection, bounding sphere Determining collisions by the use of bounding spheres. Calculating bounding spheres is very simple; all that is needed is to find the center of the object, then to compute the maximum distance between the center and a vertex in the object. By storing the radius of each bounding sphere, one can perform bounding sphere collision detection by adding the radii of the two objects, then taking the distance between the two center vertices. If the distance is greater than the sum of the radii, the spheres are not colliding.

collision detection, line-plane intersection A technique used to determine whether two triangles collide. First the plane containing the first triangle is determined. Then a line is drawn between two vertices of the second triangle. The main idea is that given two vertices of the second triangle, we take the line defined by these vertices and determine at what point that line collides with the first triangle's plane. If the collision point is between the two vertices, the second triangle is colliding with the first

triangle's plane; if it isn't between the two vertices, we iterate through the other two lines of the second triangle to see if there are collision points between those points.

color The frequency of emitted light. The human eye records a wide variety of beauty in color, but actually all that is being perceived is differences in the frequency of the observed light. With the exception of brightly colored spotlights, the color of the lighting in a scene is something that a lot of people never think about. Yet color plays a dominant role in defining mood. A soft, warm light (a light that moves toward the reds, yellows, and browns of the color wheel) usually invokes feelings of heat, calm, and ease. Cool light (light that moves toward the blues and greens of the color wheel), on the other hand, is more apt to invoke a feeling of cold, unease, and harshness. Contrasting colors (those that appear opposite each other on the color wheel) can create a sense of tension, while complementary colors (those that appear close to each other) tend to create a sense of harmony. Also known as *hue*.

color, achromatic A color that is devoid of hue, such as white, black, or gray. *Achromatic* color can be described only in terms of intensity and luminance, which are light properties. Objects with hue are called *chromatic*. It is better to use the word *hue* in place of *color* since the latter term can also mean black, white, or gray, and these are not hues.

Color Attribute Thumbnail A button in the *Bryce* CAB channels that provides a thumbnail view of the Color attribute of a texture.

color bars A test pattern used to check whether a video system is calibrated correctly.

color bleeding Color can *bleed* from one object to another. For example, the color of a table can bleed onto a different colored ball that is resting upon it.

color blind Affected with partial or total inability to distinguish one or more chromatic colors, such as green or red.

color burst A short set of cycles of the chrominance subcarrier in a color television signal. It is used to synchronize the color oscillator frequency in the display system.

color cast A perceptible dominance of one color in all the colors of a scene or photograph.

color channel Color maps are perhaps the most descriptive of the channels, as they instantly let us know if we are looking at a slice of tofu or cheddar cheese. A color map tells the 3D application which color to place where. Sometimes, color maps are simple flat colors, while at other times, color maps are actual figures or photographs.

color constancy The ability to perceive and retain a particular object's color property under different lighting conditions. Sometimes when we go from one lighting situation to another, we tend not to notice the color that each light source "casts" on our perception of color. A paper that looks white outdoors would still look white indoors in fluorescent light as well as under incandescent lights if our eyes were given enough time to acclimatize. This means that initially, under incandescent lighting, the paper would look orange-yellow; however, once our visual system got used to the warmth of the incandescent light, the paper would then look white. This ability to perceive an object the same way under different lighting conditions is called color constancy. Color constancy is the ability to ignore or negate the color of the illuminant under different lighting conditions. This means that our visual system knows and recognizes the object reflecting the dominant light and "guesses" at the "right" color.

color controls A set of controls in *Poser*. The color controls provide the user with instant access to global color settings for the Background, Foreground, Shadows, and Ground Plane.

color correction 1. The modification of colors in an image to a more desirable set of values. For example, if a photograph is taken on film balanced for daylight colors using artificial illumination, the colors will be different from the actual colors and will be displeasing. *Color correction* can be applied to this image to bring the colors back to the original ones observed in the scene. 2. A postproduction process to correct the overall color of a videotape master in order to get the best quality image, with an emphasis on enhancing skin tones. 3. The changing of color hues either to correct for errors in recording the original image or for artistic effect. Most editors are capable of performing such changes.

color cycling Changing of colors in a video display in such a way as to simulate motion or strobing.

color depth The number of colors that on a given video system can be displayed. The greater the number of bits-per-pixel that are used to store color, the higher the color depth.

color descriptor table A table that describes a limited number of discrete colors in terms of their red, green, and blue components.

color dithering Simulation of colors not directly available to a display or printer by the use of varying patterns and sizes of dots of the available colors.

color edging A line of incorrect color which occurs at the boundary of two colors in a video image. Also called *fringing*.

color electronics prepress system (CEPS) A system for electronic pagination and imaging for color printing that is computer controlled, using the Neugebauer equations to calculate color values.

color gamuts Color ranges that show the effect of adding colors together.

color gradient An area that is colored by specifying two points, each having a different color, smoothly varying between the two colors along a line drawn between the two points, and assigning the color for a particular point as the color where the above line is intersected by a line perpendicular to it through the particular point.

Color Graphics Adapter (CGA) A graphics adapter card that interfaces PCs to a color monitor using a low resolution color graphics standard.

color, hardware oriented models Hardware-oriented color models are geared toward their use with hardware, such as computer monitors, printing presses, etc. The red, green, blue (RGB) color model is used in monitors. The color gamut is projected on a cube, with blue, cyan, magenta, red, green, yellow, black, and white positioned on the cube's corners. The black and the white are on the opposing edge and quadrant. The cyan, magenta, yellow (CMY) color model is the model used for dealing with printed copies. The CMY model is also projected on a cube. The CMYK model is related to the CMY model and is used in the four-color printing process. Black (K) is added instead of equal amounts of C, M, and Y to generate contrast and tones.

color harmony The use of a selection of colors that are pleasing to the eye when used together. One way to do this is to select colors by traversing a smooth path in a color model rather than selecting them at random. Another restriction is to use colors having the same lightness or value. Finally, colors are best spaced at equal perceptual distances.

colorimetry The study of the human perception of colors, including attempts to relate human color perception to quantitative measurements.

colorizing 1. Assigning pseudocolors to an image. 2. Converting a black and white motion picture to color through artistic and/or computerized techniques.

color keying Filming of a picture on a solid color background (usually blue) so that it can be superimposed upon another image to produce a composite picture.

color map A color image that is used to color or cover the surface of a 3D object.

color mapping The assignment of colors to represent some quality of the data being displayed.

color mixing Color can be perceived as either coming from a luminous object or reflected from pigments. Color mixture in pigments is different from luminous color mixing, which occurs in a TV, computer monitor, or projector. When the three primary colors of red, green, and blue are projected, the resulting color is white. With pigments, however, mixing red, green, and blue results in a muddy dark brown. Actually, it is supposed to produce black, but since there are impurities in the "colorant," muddy color results. Colored light produces white because it is an additive approach. It is called *additive* because by adding light, a new spectrum is added into the mix, and since a mixture of all colors produces white, it is an "additive" process. Additive color is made up of three primary colors: red, green, and blue (RGB). Other colors are obtained by mixing these three colors.

color model The systematic arrangement of available color of an object or system in a 3D coordinate system. See *CMYK, HSB, PMS,* and *RGB.*

color models, perceptually oriented Perceptually oriented color models are based on artistic sensibilities about color. These are commonly found in 3D applications and image-editing software. The hue, saturation, and value (HSV) color model is projected on an inverted hexcone (a six-sided pyramid) with black at the bottom and white on the middle of the flat face, and the colors cyan, green, yellow, red, magenta, and blue on the six corners. The hue, lightness, and saturation (HLS) color model is projected in a double hexcone (a diamond) with black and white on both apexes. The edges of the double hexcone are the colors red, yellow, green, cyan, blue, and magenta, assigned in a counterclockwise manner. The hue, value, and chroma (HVC) color model is projected onto a distorted double hexcone

to account for the uniform distribution of the color space.

color, output to video and If an animation is to be broadcast or played on a TV, there are some color issues. Just as the RGB color palette used by television screens and monitors has a larger range than the CMYK palette used for color printing, a multiscan computer monitor's color range is much broader than an NTSC TV monitor's color range. With postproduction software, one can render with the full 24-bit color palette and then convert an animation to an NTSC-safe palette before committing it to tape, but color loss may occur.

color, perception of Based on Newton's theories, white light is composed of a mixture of all the colors. This means that objects themselves do not carry the color information within themselves; rather, objects reflect and absorb certain colors. In other words, a red hat is not actually red, it only absorbs all the other colors and reflects red. A white object reflects all the colors falling on it, so it is perceived as white. A black object absorbs all the colors falling on it, so it does not reflect any color, therefore appearing black. Black also can be generated through the absence of illumination. The sky really should be black, since there is nothing there but space; however, due to light scattering (Rayleigh scattering), the blue spectra are passed through, "coloring" the sky. The retina's photoreceptors receive and interpret the most dominant wavelength reflecting off an object and analyze its color.

Color Picker An Apple program that permits the hue of a color to be input in a numeric field ranging from 0° to 360° or

111

by simply dragging the cursor to the desired hue.

color, pigment mixture characteristics Although the terms *hue, saturation,* and *value* can be used to describe a color, when dealing with pigments we use different but related descriptions. Value changes are called *tint, shade,* and *tone.* Tint primarily results from the addition of white to a pure hue. The consequence of adding white to a pure color is decreased saturation. Shade is the opposite of tint. A shade is created by the introduction of black to a pure hue. The addition of black decreases the object's lightness. Tone results from the addition of black and white to a pure color, so tone is really hue plus gray.

color quantization The reduction of a large number of colors to a limited number of discrete colors by determining which sets of the original colors can be assigned to common colors in the reduced color space.

color reference frame The specification of the chromaticity of three primary colors as a standard for a color television system.

Color Replacer tool A tool in *Paint Shop Pro* that allows the user to change one color into another color throughout the entire image.

color sampling ratio In component digital video, the ratio of luminance (Y) to each color difference component (Cb and Cr). 4:2:2 means that for every four samples of luminance, there are two samples of chroma minus blue and chroma minus red. 4:2:2:4 indicates an additional four samples of the alpha channel or keying information.

color, saturation A hue can be pure depending on its mixture with gray. This property is called saturation. A saturation scale ranges from gray to the pure color. In other words, saturation is the vividness or dullness of a hue. It is also a perception of a hue's purity. Saturation is, in effect, the perceived intensity of a hue. Saturated colors are perceived to have a no white color component. An example of a saturated color is fire-engine red; the unsaturated version of red is flamingo pink. Commission Internationale de l'Eclairage (CIE, the International Commission on Illumination) defines saturation as "the colorfulness of an area judged in proportion to its brightness."

color separation The process of separating color images into individual primary color components. When applied to a cathode-ray tube display system, the primary color components are the additive colors red, green, and blue. When applied to color printing, the primary color components are the subtractive colors cyan, magenta, and yellow, with black often used also.

color space Any three-dimensional space used to represent the range and qualities of possible colors.

color spectrum The range of visible light, which extends from violet to red.

color table A look-up table used to translate color index codes into red, green, and blue color components.

color temperature The perceived quality of a light source as denoted in numerical scale by comparing it to a perfect energy radiator. It uses the absolute Kelvin scale (K). A warm candlelight would have a color temperature of 2300K, while the sun would have 5500K. ⊙

color temperature blue (CTB) A special color of lighting gel or camera lens filter that changes tungsten light to daylight.

color temperature orange (CTO) A special color of lighting gel or camera lens filter that changes daylight to the color of tungsten light.

color theory, basic Unlike mixing pigments, mixing light is an additive process. The more colors that are added to a pool of light, the whiter the resulting hue. In most Macintosh programs the user has a choice of using the RGB (red, green, blue), CMYK (cyan, magenta, yellow, black), or HSL (hue, saturation, luminance or lightness) color models. The CMYK color model is primarily used in print-based applications, while people working in video, multimedia, or 3D usually use the RGB or HSL color models.

color theory, opponent Ewald Hering, a German physiologist/psychologist (1834–1918), found that people who are blind to green are also blind to red. This is also true for yellow and blue. Color afterimages also show these pairings. For example, if one stares at a green circle for 20 seconds and then looks away and then stares at a white area, he sees a red after-image. If one stares at a yellow circle, it creates a blue after-image. Because of the inability of the Helmholtz-Young theory to account for color blindness and such after-images, Hering proposed the *opponent color theory*. Hering believed that four basic colors exist as opposing pairs: red paired against green and blue against yellow. The color information can only be sent only

through these two channels. A channel takes input from at least two of the pairs, and the signal sensation is either allowed or blocked. This theory has a third channel for black and white that sums up all the other sensory inputs.

color theory, trichromatic Since color is more varied than light, it is impossible for the eyes to have a receptor for all possible colors. In 1807 Thomas Young proposed a color theory that tried to explain it in perceptual terms. He proposed that there are three types of receptors that function as a filtration system in the eyes. The signal on each receptor produces a single sensation of the three possible colors: red, green, and violet. Since the wavelength response of each receptor is continuous, the wavelength responses overlap the sensitivity of the other receptors. Each receptor is tuned to a specific wavelength, but the color sensation is not singular. Hermann von Helmholtz (1821–1894) improved on Young's theory with the *trichromatic theory*. Helmholtz found that some receptors in the eyes are most sensitive to short wavelengths, whereas others are sensitive to long wavelengths. Helmholtz was also able to derive a sensitivity distribution curve that shows to which colors our eyes are most sensitive. This theory explains the changes of the response of each receptor as the wavelength varies.

color timing The process of setting the red, green, and blue lights when creating a film print. Usually the color settings are timed to change with each significant scene or lighting change in the film.

color wheel The color wheel is an elegant and simple way to present colors and show their relationships. The wheel is a polar coordinate plotting of colors in which the colors are arranged in quadrants, as follows: Primary colors are fundamental colors that when mixed create secondary colors. These hues are said to be pure colors, including red, blue, and yellow. Secondary colors are the colors that result when the primary colors are mixed. These colors are green, violet, and orange. Tertiary colors result from the mixture of the adjacent secondary colors. These three main groups of color can be further categorized as follows. *Triad colors* are any three colors that are balanced and equidistant from each other on the color wheel. *Complementary colors* are hues that are opposite each other on the color wheel, such as yellow

color wheel.

against violet or blue against orange. *Split complementary colors* use three colors of any hue and the two colors adjacent to its complementary color, such as yellow, lavender and magenta or red, apple-green and cyan. *Analogous colors* are any combination of colors adjacent to each other on the color wheel. These colors are said to have a common hue among them. *Double-complement colors* are made up of a pair of complement col-

ors, such as yellow and violet or blue and orange. *Tetrad colors* are a cross of four hues composed of a primary color and secondary and a tertiary color. *Alternate complementary colors* are composed of a triad color plus a complementary color to one of the hues.

column-preserving transformation A transformation of an image in which rows are changed but columns are not. A column preserving transformation followed by a row preserving transformation corresponds to a rotation of the image.

COM See *computer output microfilm.*

comb function A filter function which when used to multiply a signal in the spatial domain produces the same result as sampling a signal in the frequency domain.

combination light arrays See *arrays, 3D complex light, combination.*

comic-mode A method of recording data on a film strip so that it can be read when the strip is held horizontally.

Comité Consultatif Internationale de Télégraphique et Téléphonique (CCITT) An international group that develops standards for telephone and telegraph communications.

Commission International de l'Èclairage (CIE) An international organization devoted to dissemination and cooperation on artistic, cultural, scientific, and technical issues on illumination, lighting, and color. It is responsible for developing specifications for color matching systems.

Common Gateway Interface (CGI) A standard which lets programs operating outside of World Wide Web environments interact with forms produced by Web browsers. CGI programs serve information. They produce documents that Web browsers can read. CGI programs can be connected to databases, image-generation programs, electronic mail, and almost any other program that runs on a computer. A *CGI-bin* is a repository of CGI programs.

Commotion A program, by Puffin Designs, that permits opening a QuickTime movie for rotoscoping with a full assortment of painting tools. *Commotion* allows the user to use spline masks to composite content layers. *Commotion* allows the user to apply filters, both its own and QuickTime's, over the entire animation, as well as allowing onion skinning and other professional animation effects and processes.

commutativity, matrix operations In general, the matrix operations required for scaling and rotation are not commutative. However, if we take an object that we wish to rotate and/or scale and move it to the origin, then commutativity holds and we can rotate and/or scale as desired. The object can then be returned to its original position.

Compact Disc See *CD*.

Compact Disc Read-Only Memory See *CD-ROM*.

Compact Disc-Recordable See *CD-R*.

Compact Disc-ReWritable See *CD-RW*.

compaction algorithm An algorithm that permits compression of data so that it can be stored in less space.

comparison of holograms A vital step in the production of finished holograms is making a visual comparison between the photoresist and the screen output. All

the pixels are inspected for brightness and quality as well.

Compiled Vertex Arrays (CVA) A capability of *OpenGL* which allows building an array of vertex data for vertices that will not be changed during use of an application.

complementary colors 1. Color hues that are opposite each other on the color wheel, such as yellow against violet or blue against orange, etc. These are the colors that, when combined, create a harmony and balance. 2. Cyan, magenta, and yellow. The colors derived when the primary colors (red, green, and blue) are extracted. ☜

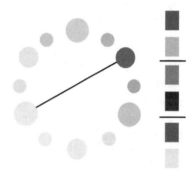

complementary colors.

complete candidate list A list of graphics objects that is guaranteed to contain the nearest object intersected by a given ray (if one exists).

complex colored The use of multicolored gels to create interesting shadows.

complicated motion sandwiches A technique of *Bryce* used to cooperatively alter the movements of animated objects, camera, and/or lights. This method involves the Animation Setup dialog, the Animation tab settings from the Attributes dialog, and the Advanced

Motion Lab. All three of these setup areas can work together to influence how selected objects move in a *Bryce* world. The order is vital: First is the length of animation setting in the Animation Setup dialog; second is the Animation tab of the object's Attributes dialog; third is the Return to Length of Animation setting in the Animation Setup dialog; and fourth are the Advanced Motion Lab settings.

component 1. In Java, a part of a display. A *container* encompasses several components. 2. In Java, a procedure that is one of the Java Swing Components.

component video A video signal consisting of three separate color signals (or *components*), usually RGB (red, green, blue), YCbCr (Luminance, Chroma minus Blue, and Chroma minus Red), or Y, R-Y, B-Y (Luminance, Red minus Luminance, Blue minus Luminance).

composite architecture A way of speeding up frame rendering by storing partial images in parallel frame buffers and then scanning the buffers in parallel to produce a final image.

composited figures Figures in *Poser* that can be created by combining one or several parts from *Poser* figures into one amalgamated whole, or by replacing elements of a figure with other figure elements, drawn from inside *Poser*. This is especially useful in creating cross-species composites, replacing elements of a figure with other elements (drawn from outside of *Poser* and imported), modifying elements of a figure with morphed elements (used mostly for heads, but possible for their body parts as well), or completely replacing all of a figure's parts with either internal props or externally created imported objects.

composite interaction task (CIT) Combinations of *basic interaction tasks* integrated into single units. Typical types are *dialogue boxes*, which specify several units of information; *construction*, which creates objects that need to have several positions specified; and *manipulation*, which reshapes existing geometric objects.

composite modeling transformation matrix (CMTM) A combination of local matrices used to transform primitives.

composite solid A complex solid object composed from primitive solids using constructive solid geometry.

composite transformation The translation, rotation, and/or scaling of a vector through the application of a *composite matrix*.

composite video A video signal that contains all the luminance, chroma, and timing (or synch) information in one composite signal.

Composite Wizard A program by Puffin Designs that includes filters for improving composites. In addition to helping the user remove fringes around foreground elements, *Composite Wizard* can automatically match the overall color tones of the foreground and background. *Composite Wizard* can also add light to the edges of the foreground to make it look like the foreground element is affected by the lighting in the background plate.

compositing The process of layering media on top of each other to create collages or special effects.

compositing, a-channel A method for determining the color of pixels of a picture composed of two or more different colored images, where the color of each pixel is given an *a* value representing the coverage of the pixel by that color.

compositing, camera shake setup See *camera shake setup.*

compositing, exploding pillar setup See *exploding pillar setup.*

compositing, fire effect setup See *fire effect setup.*

compositing, image The process of combining images to create new images.

composition 1. The arrangement of elements within a photograph so as to be pleasing to the eye. 2. See *layering.*

composition of matrices The combining of matrices, each representing a rotation, translation, or scaling, into a single matrix. Applying this *composite matrix* has the same effect upon the original vector as applying each of the original matrices in turn.

compound blends Blends that blend three or more surfaces.

compound document A file that contains more than one type of data (such as text, graphics, voice, and video).

compression Any software or hardware technique that reduces the storage space required for a set of data.

compression, image Reducing the size of an image file by changing the representation method and/or eliminating data that does not contribute significantly to the picture. See *wavelets.*

compression ratio The size of a block of original data divided by the size of the data after compression.

computed tomography The computation of the density of human or animal tissue at each point on a three-dimensional grid.

computer-aided (or -assisted) design (or drafting) (CAD) Software used to assist a designer or draftsman in creating a design and the drawing for it. The output of a CAD program can produce a drawing on a printer or plotter.

computer-aided engineering (CAE) Computer software that simulates hardware designs to permit a device to be analyzed without actually building it.

computer-aided instruction (CAI) Computer software used to facilitate teaching through interactive text, questions, and responses of the computer to correct or incorrect answers.

computer-aided (or -assisted) manufacturing (CAM) A system which can take the output of a CAD program and use it to directly operate machinery to fabricate the part described in the CAD output.

computer-aided software engineering (CASE) A computer program that permits the computer to generate the details of program code when basic relations are entered into the program.

computer-assisted retrieval (CAR) A computer system that locates documents stored on paper, microfilm, or microfiche. Such a system usually has complex cross-referencing and search capabilities that permit identification of a particular document when a minimum of information is available.

computer-based training (CBT) An interactive program which enables the computer to teach a subject. Also referred to as *courseware.*

computer-generated holograms Computer-generated holography has succeeded in many of its goals. Holographic programs provide simple computer-generated holography to a global audience, with all calculations done on a workstation. There are several possible uses for a holographic program. First and foremost is a rapid visualization tool for interference. The program is capable of providing beautiful examples of interference in a short amount of time. Hologram programs may be used as a design tool for people creating holograms of two-dimensional images. Hologram programs are not limited to the domain of light—they can design holograms for any media that follows wave physics. This includes water, sound, radio waves, etc. Hologram programs can certainly generate enough detail to handle longer wavelength media.

computer-generated imagery (CGI) Images generated by a computer for display on a computer monitor. Used to refer to any effect that is created digitally, be it a composite, or a fully digital image such as a walking dinosaur. CGI is often used as a singular noun, such as in "we'll fill that spot with some CGI of a duck."

Computer Graphics Interface (CGI) An ANSI/ISO standard currently under development that will be used to establish formats for direct communication of graphics primitives from computers to display devices, printers, and plotters. Also known as *virtual device metafile*.

Computer Graphics Magazine Magazine published by the Special Interest Group for Graphics of the Association for Computer Machinery (SIGGRAPH).

Computer Graphics Metafile (CGM) A computer graphics standard that permits interchange of vector and bit-mapped graphics between widely differing computers.

computer hop In animation, an unrealistic sequence in which an object jumps, crests, and lands all in the same fluid motion at the same speed.

computer imaging The creation of a picture through the use of computer techniques to generate each pixel of a display image.

computer output microfilm (COM) A computer peripheral device that produces computer output directly on microfilm.

computer readable Data in a format and/or on a medium that can be read directly into a computer.

concave polygon A polygon in which the sum of the interior angles is greater that 360 degrees. For a *concave polygon* a line can be drawn that will intersect more than two edges.

conceptual design Definition of the principal application concepts that must be mastered by the user in order to use a computer program. The conceptual design of a user interface may be in the form of an analogy to some device that is familiar to the user, such as a typewriter or drafting table. Also known as *user's model*.

conceptual model A description of the properties, features, characteristics, etc., of the thing being modeled.

condenser A type of microphone that records sounds through a "capacitance" mechanism. Condenser microphones require a power supply (usually in the form of a small battery). Because of the nature of their pickup mechanism, condenser microphones can be made very small.

conductor A medium that conducts light.

cone A quadric surface that is created by sweeping a line segment around an axis when one end of the line segment is on the axis.

cone filter A weighting function for sampling a primitive in which the most weight is given to the intensity of the area at the pixel center, with the weight decreasing proportionally to distance. The graph of the function is a cone, because of rotational symmetry.

cone plus cosine An antialiasing filter which uses the sum of a cone and a cosine as the weighting function.

cones One of the two types of photosensitive receptor cells in the eye. These cells function only when enough light is available. Cones are centrally located in the retina, directly in the light pathway from the eye's lens. Cones are responsible for acutely detailed color vision. Cones make it possible to see the warm hues of a sunset, the rich greens of the forest, and the cool blues of the ocean. There are also red, green, and blue cones in the retina that detect the millions of hues we see. The other type of photosensitive receptor cells are *rods*.

cone tracing A ray tracing technique that uses conical regions rather than individual rays of light in order to reduce the total number of computations required to generate an image.

conformal modeling A set of procedures ensuring the construction of 3D geometric entities that conform to the curvature of another 3D object or a group of objects in all three axes. Conformal modeling can also be thought of as a style of modeling where groups of objects are curved along the same lines of force. One of the simplest examples of conformal modeling is a case of two circles, with the circles having different radii

and coresident centers. If one takes an arc segment of both circles and examines the shape of the two arcs he will find that the larger arc is more shallow but is conformal to the smaller arc.

conforming The process of meticulously recreating an off-line edit, usually using higher quality footage with the aid of an EDL or cut list.

Conform To A *Poser* command that permits substitution of other clothing for that presently worn by a figure.

conglomerate object Any object or model made up of a mix of parts, either from separate models, or from object primitives and imported components. Because there are an infinite number of ways that conglomerate objects can be stitched together, there are many problems that can crop up when the object is animated.

conics Curves that can be generated by intersecting a cone with a plane. Examples include ellipses, circles, parabolas, and hyperbolas.

connectivity of regions A *region* consists of a collection of pixels. It may be either *4-connected*, if every 2 pixels in the region can be joined by a sequence of pixels using right, left, up or down moves; or *8-connected* if in addition up-and-left, up-and-right, down-and-left, and down-and-right moves are required.

consistency, user interface The design of a user interface so that all actions can be performed in a uniform manner, following a few simple rules, with no exceptions or special conditions.

consistency, visual Organization of a complex graphic image by a consistent combination of primitives.

console game system A rudimentary computer designed especially to play games.

console game system, data loading The loading of data from a CD-ROM into a console game station. Since game systems are often designed to load a sector at a time, care must be taken to avoid overwriting necessary data in the system.

console game system, debugging Debugging a game that runs in a console game station is much more difficult than debugging a game that runs in a computer because of the lack of flexibility in the game station. A program called *Stats* has been designed to help with this process.

constancy, color See *color constancy*.

constant A value that is normally unchanged during the running of a program. Constants used in games should not be hard coded, but instead should be put in a data files so that they can be easily changed if necessary.

constant angular velocity (CAV) A method of data recording in which the same amount of data is recorded for each revolution of a disk, even though it would be possible to record more data at the outer edge of the disk than at the inner edge of the disk.

constant linear velocity (CLV) A method of disk drive design in which the disk speed is varied with head position so that the linear amount of disk surface passing under the head in a given time is the same for large outer tracks as it is for smaller inner tracks. This permits more data to be stored on the outer tracks.

Constant Radius/Offset A setting used by the Rounding tool in *Universe* to determine how much rounding is to be applied to edges of an object.

constant shading The assignment of one color to an entire object. It is really the computation of one "shade" with the absence of shading. The 3D objects are not really given any dimension. This is the most primitive of all the shading models.

constant shading.

constraint A limitation placed upon 3D movement to help aid in exact object placement when depth relationships are uncertain. Constraints include gridding, gravity, or use of such devices as trackballs or joysticks that are designed to move most easily along the principal axes.

constraint, in line drawing A limitation on how a line is drawn in response to cursor movement. For example, a horizontal constraint would result in drawing a horizontal line from the beginning cursor position, even if the cursor was moved diagonally instead of horizontally.

constraints on movement Limitations on the amount or direction of an object or part of an object.

constraints on scaling Limitations on the amount of change in size of an object allowed by a program.

constraint to object See *Auto-IK*.

constructive planar geometry A technique for modeling complex two-dimensional figures by using Boolean combinations of primitive polygons.

constructive solid geometry (CSG) A solid modeling technique that uses a Boolean combination of primitive solid objects to construct more complex solid objects.

constructor In Java, a structure that determines how an object that is an instance of a class will be initialized when it is created.

contact copy counterfeit technique Contact copying is the simplest way to optically copy a hologram. In this case, the holographic emulsion is brought into direct contact with the hologram. The appropriate wavelength of laser light is directed though the plate to expose the emulsion. This type of counterfeit hologram is relatively easy to create with little equipment and training necessary. The primary advantage to the counterfeiter is that the contact-copied hologram can be produced within a day. The disadvantage to counterfeit holograms made with the contact copy technique is that the hologram produced is not as bright as the original and contains more optical noise. A trained eye can easily tell the original from a fake when compared side by side. An untrained eye will be fooled almost all of the time by a contact copy.

container 1. A class containing a collection of data. A number of types of containers have been standardized for the C++ language as part of the *Standard Template Library (STL)*. 2. In Java, either a frame (a whole window) or a panel which contains one or more components.

container, adapter A higher level abstraction container such as *stack, queue,* and *priority_queue*. They describe a container's behavior but allow for different types of underlying implementations. For example, a queue might be implemented internally using a vector, list, or deque.

container, associative A data array in which the inserted data is ordered based upon certain sorting criteria.

container, map The most complex basic container. The map is essentially a value-pairing container. Two arbitrary types of data are paired as a key/value structure and inserted into the container. Looking up the value via the key can then occur in O(log n) time. Although not quite as efficient as a *hash table*, the difference is often negligible and has the advantage of sorting the data during insertion. This process allows iteration of completely sorted data, which is a beneficial consequence of the method of storage (a balanced binary tree, otherwise known as a red-black tree).

container tags Used to delineate the extent of an operation in HTML. Container tags require an "<>" open tag and a "</>" closing tag. In other words, one tag will turn the HTML command "on," while the closing tag will turn it "off." This will tell the browser when to begin the command and when to end it. Container tags are more common because HTML formats elements as a whole. For instance, if the designer wants to align an image to the center of the Web page, he will need to tell the Web browser where to begin the center alignment and where to end the alignment.

containment The case where one object is contained as a member of another object. Also known as *layering, composition,* or *embedding.*

containment tree A structure for storing disjoint contours, created by Boolean operations, that is used to combine primitive polygons.

contention The attempt by two or more computer devices to access another device. If there is a possibility that *contention* may take place, some *collision avoidance* technique must be used to assure that only one of the contending devices obtains access at a given time.

context, *Postscript* A description of a *Postscript* environment which is saved on a stack and can be used to restore the environment when desired.

context-sensitivity, user interface The limitation of useable user commands to those which are valid in the current mode or context.

context switching The switching of a graphics system from an application running in one window to an application running in another window.

contextual search The process of searching files for a particular word or phrase rather than looking for a particular file name.

contiguous Items that are adjoining.

contiguous partitioning A method of dividing pixels into contiguous blocks in such a way that only pixels that will be visible need to be processed.

continuity 1. The property of a curve such that the magnitude and direction of the derivatives of curve segments at

the join point are equal. If this is true for the first n derivatives, the curve is called C_n *continuous.* 2. During a shoot, the process of keeping track of dialogue changes, actors' positions, wardrobe, and props so that the footage from shot to shot, and day to day, will cut together. Usually the person in charge of continuity makes notes on a copy of the script and takes photographs of the set.

continuity, curvature (C2) A means of blending of surfaces. The C2 continuous blend surface is the most desirable and most difficult to achieve of the three types of continuity. It has the softest curvature that is evenly distributed across the blend surface. The $1/3$ of the surface nearest a blend edge has the same curvature as the base surface at a, the last $1/3$ of the surface at b has the same curvature as surface b at its blend edge. The intermediate $1/3$ of the blend surface gradually transitions the curvature at a to curvature at b. Even though the C2 blend surface has the "softest" curvature and is the prettiest of the three surfaces, it is very subjective. The kind of blend that is needed is dictated by the demands of the project. It is quite possible to mix the curvature types on the same blend surface for custom effects.

continuity, positional (C0) A means of blending of surfaces. With C0 continuity, the blend surface has no curvature at the blend edge. Many times it is just a straight line ruled-surface bridge between the two surfaces. It is called *positional continuity* because the blend edges of the blend surface are coresident with the blend edges of the two surfaces.

continuity, tangential (C1) A means of blending surfaces. C1 continuity exists between two blended surfaces when the coresident blend edges have identical tangents. C1 blend surfaces have moderate "softness." The curvature of the C1 blend surfaces is most pronounced at the blend edges. The intermediate area has relatively shallow curvature. Think of this as curvature density. In Tangential blend surfaces, the curvature is "concentrated" mostly at or near the blend edges.

continuous image An image that is defined over a continuous domain, as compared to a *discrete image*, which is defined only for the discrete points within an array of pixels.

continuous potential method A method for generating the fractal curves of Mandelbrot or Julia sets.

continuous tone An image, such as a photograph, that may contain all values of gray or color.

contour A curve which is the locus of points having a value equal to a given constant. The most common example is the contour lines on a map, each of which represents an equal elevation of terrain.

contouring, intensity The development of pixel patterns for halftoning that minimize pattern differences for successive intensity levels, thereby minimizing contour effects.

contractive transformation An affine transformation which decreases the distances between all pairs of points.

contrast The difference between light and dark areas of a visual image. It is the ratio between the amount of light striking the film compared to the amount of light passing through it.

CONTRAST

contrast.

contrast enhancement transform A transform that alters the slope of a transform to change the contrast of an image.

contrast of film One of the basic, perceptible properties of film. Contrast is the tonal difference between the highlights and shadow areas of the subject. The contrast of the film is dependent on the amount of exposure on the shadows as well as the amount of development of the film. Contrast is the tonal ratio of shadows to highlights. The differences in the density of the film determine its contrast.

contrast threshold function (CTF) The minimum perceptible contrast for a specific display observer, as a function of spatial frequency.

contribution factor The percentage contribution of a given ray to the eye ray.

control grid of CRT The element of a cathode ray tube which uses an applied voltage to control the intensity of the electron beam (and consequently the intensity of the light emitted by the phosphor when the beam impinges on it).

control hull A graphics construct created by connecting the control points for a bicubic patch that encloses the patch.

control points Points that are used to determine the parameters of an equation that is used to define the geometry of a spline, Bezier curve, or patch.

control strips A series of color bars and percent tints that are placed just outside the actual image area to be used in adjusting ink color to achieve consistent color in color printing.

control to display ratio (C/D ratio) The ratio between the movement of a control device such as a mouse and the resulting movement of the cursor on the display.

control track A part of the video signal that contains the timing, or synchronization, information, used to regulate the motion of the tape itself as it plays through a VTR.

control vertex (CV) A point along a NURBS cage that controls the position and strength of the NURBS curve when modeling a surface.

convergence Color cathode-ray tubes have a phosphor that consists of many clumps of three dots: one red, one green, and one blue. When the three electron guns that illuminate the three different color dots are properly aligned, the dots will *converge* at the face of the tube, resulting in a dot that is apparently white. The process of adjusting each gun focus to achieve this effect is called *convergence*.

conversion between color models The CIE standard is the world-wide standard for modeling color space. There are a number of other color models: RGB (red, green, blue), used with color monitors; YIQ, used for color TV broadcasting; CMY (cyan, magenta, yellow), used for color-printing, etc. Each of these models requires a method of conversion to at least one of the other systems. These are usually matrix transformations.

converting the hierarchy See *hierarchy*.

Convert Polyline to NURBS tool A tool in *Universe* that enables the user to convert a curve to a NURBS curve.

Convert to Single Spline tool A tool in *Universe* that converts a Bezier curve into a NURBS curve.

convex In geometry, the property that any two points within a geometric figure may be connected by a straight line that lies entirely within the figure.

convex decompositions A technique for dividing an arbitrary polygon into more elementary convex figures, such as trapezoids or triangles.

convex hull The smallest convex shape that contains a given set of points or objects.

convex polygon A polygon whose interior angles sum to 360 degrees.

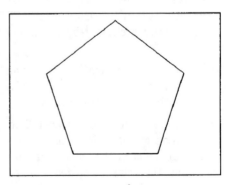

convex polygon.

convolution Application of an integral to a set of data so as to replace each input data item with an output data item that is a weighted sum of neighboring input data values. This usually helps to reduce the noise content of a noisy signal.

convolution kernel A matrix of weighting values for neighboring pixels to be used in computing a new value for a central pixel.

cookie An irregularly patterned object placed in front of a light source to cast discernible shadows on a wall to break up uniformity. Also called *cucaloris*.

Cooley-Tuckey algorithm The original fast Fourier transform algorithm, used for computing the frequency components of a digitally sampled signal with the minimum amount of computation.

CoolPowers A set of plug-ins and shaders that can help achieve movie-quality special effects in *trueSpace*.

CoolPowers wfmm plug-ins Two plug-ins that can be used with *trueSpace* to create such effects as water spewing from a fountain, or blood spatter. The first of the plug-ins, *wfmm Null*, is used to emit the null object as particles. The second plug-in, *wfmm Swappo* is used to replace the particles with metaballs.

CoolPowers, wfmm shaders A set of shaders for use with *trueSpace*. They include the following. *wfmm bloom* is a shader that can be used to create realistic blooming effects on objects. *wfmm bloom* creates a glow around a hotspot on an object, or an area that is very reflective and bright. *wfmm catcher* is a reflectance shader that allows the user to create "dummy objects" in the rough shape of objects on the background image that appear invisible when rendered, but receive shadows from the 3D objects. This helps the user to better integrate the 3D objects into real-world scenery, allowing the user to create the illusion that the CG objects actually belong in the scene. *wfmm glow* can create simple glows, flames licking the side of a building, zero-G explosions, and more, all by changing a few simple settings. Combine the *wfmm glow* shader with the *wfmm motrails* shader to get cool trailing effects without the need for applying motion blur, which would be a much more processor-intensive and time-consuming render. The *wfmm overlay* shader was created to let the user complete all of his compositing directly inside *trueSpace*. This comes in handy when adding 3D objects to a real-world photograph or animation. *wfmm postgame* is a post-process shader that allows the user to alter the image at render time, changing image hue, saturation, value (contrast), and brightness. After the first frame in an animation is rendered, a window pops up that allows the user to alter the image settings. The post shader will then apply these changes to every image in the sequence automatically. *wfmm postgame* helps cut down the time needed in post-production on the animation, which is useful when dealing with a long animation where the camera angle or scene changes, and a consistent look is needed.

Coons patch A surface that is fitted to four arbitrary boundary curves.

coordinate rotation digital computer (CORDIC) An iterative fixed-point technique used to compute coordinate rotation, discrete Fourier transforms, exponential, logarithmic, forward and inverse circular, and hyperbolic functions.

125

coordinate system A set of references used to locate a position in space. For example, in two-dimensional space, the Cartesian coordinate system locates positions with respect to two orthogonal axes, the horizontal x axis and the vertical y axis. In the polar coordinate system, a position is located by specifying its angle θ with respect to the x axis and its distance r from the origin. In three dimensional space a third axis, the z axis, is added orthogonal to the x and y axes.

COP See *center of projection*.

coplanar Two or more points or lines that lie within the same plane.

co-processors Extra processors that are used to speed up a computer or to perform special functions. See *accelerator cards*.

copy A duplicate of a disk or tape. If the data are digital, copies of copies may be made with no degradation from the original. If the data are analog, each copy of a copy will be degraded from the one the copy is made from, due to accumulation of noise.

copy/paste function 1. A standard function in all 2D and 3D applications that allows for the copying and pasting of data. 2. A function in *Poser* that permits selection of the choreography of any body part on any model and application of it to any body part on any other model, even across both gender and species lines if desired. This leads to exacting symmetry, which in some cases can be very humorous.

copy picture, *Poser* A *Poser* command that copies the image content in the Document Window to the system buffer.

It is useful when the user wants a quick image to customize in a 2D bitmap application.

copyPixel A command used by the *SRGP* graphics system to copy data for a group of pixels from a specified source to a destination. Also known as *bitblt* (bit block transfer) or *pixBlt* (pixel Blt).

CORDIC See *coordinate rotation digital computer*.

Core Graphics System An early device-independent graphics system developed by ACM SIGGRAPH in 1977.

Corel *Draw* See *Draw*.

Corel *Lumiere Suite* See *Lumiere Suite*.

Corel *Photo-Paint* See *Photo-Paint*.

Cork A shader provided with *Carrara* which gives a realistic representation of a cork surface.

cornea The hemispherical, transparent protrusion in the front of the eyes. The cornea can be considered part of the sclera that becomes transparent to let light in as well as bend it. The cornea is sometimes wider than it is tall. The cornea controls most light bending since the light bends more when it goes from the air to another medium.

corotron An electrostatic charging device used in electrostatic copying machines or printers.

correction See *color correction*.

cosine fractal A fractal curve produced by iterating the equation

$$z_n = cos(z_{n-1}) + c$$

with $z_0 = 0 + i0$ and c varied over the complex plane.

cosine shading See *Lambertian shading*.

cost, arrival A term used in the A* algorithm to calculate the cost required to cross from a cell to each neighboring cell.

cost, heuristic A term used in the A* algorithm to denote the estimate of the true cost from a particular node to the goal. If the heuristic estimate happens to overestimate the true cost, the heuristic becomes "inadmissible," and the algorithm might not find the optimal path (and might find a terrible path). The way to guarantee that the cost is never overestimated is by calculating the geometric distance between the node and the goal. When coding A* for the first time, this is the best thing to do until it's time to optimize. Since the cost will never be more than this distance, the optimal path will always be found.

cost, path function The cost function for the path between two locations represents whatever it is the path is supposed to minimize—typically, distance traveled, time of traversal, movement points expended, or fuel consumed. However, other factors can be added into this function, such as penalties for passing through undesirable areas, bonuses for passing through desirable areas, and aesthetic considerations (for example, making diagonal moves more costly than orthogonal moves, even if they aren't, to make the resultant path look more direct).

COUSIN A program that automatically generates menus and dialogue boxes from inputs consisting of commands, parameters, and parameter data types.

coverage Shooting all of the footage that will be needed to properly cover an event or scene.

coverage chart A chart that shows the directional pattern of a microphone.

COW See *center of window*.

CP See *current position*.

cpi See *characters per inch*.

CPU See *central processing unit*.

cracking The creation of unintended gaps between polygons that are intended to share edges, caused by lack of sufficient mathematical accuracy.

Cramer's rule A method for finding an adjoint matrix.

crawling A result of aliasing in which an edge appears to move discretely from one scan line to the next, rather than moving smoothly.

CRC See *cyclical redundancy checking*.

Create Full Body Morph A *Poser* command for performing morphing of an entire figure.

Create Magnet A Magnet is one of the two Deformation tools in *Poser*. Depending on the size and position of the Magnet's Zone of Influence, all or part of a targeted object or figure is distorted in accordance with the Magnet's position and rotation.

Create New NURBS Curve from CVs A tool in *Universe* and other 3D applications that allows converting a group of control vertices into a NURBS curve.

Create New Object An icon in *The Games Factory* that allows the user to place or create a new object on the screen at certain times or due to certain events.

Create toolbar A set of tools in *Bryce* that enables the user to obtain "canned" objects or scenes. Objects that can be created include water, skies, ground planes, terrains, rock mirrored terrains,

Create Toolbar.

spheres, elongated spheres, tori, cylinders, cubics, tetrahedrons, cones, flat planes, and lights.

Create Walk Path A command in *Poser* to activate the Walk Designer, which produces lifelike walking of bipedal figures.

CreateWave The Wave is the second *Poser* Deformer. It attaches itself to any object or figure element selected in the scene, and renders it as a *wavy* object.

credit roll Text at the end of a motion picture which lists participants in the filming and other pertinent information.

Credo Interactive's Life Forms A motion scripting/choreography application that provides an interface for scripting the motion of one or more human characters. The resulting motion data can be exported to a 3D animation package and applied to models.

crisp set A set for which a given element either belongs to the set or doesn't. For example, define a crisp set called M, which consists of all real numbers between 5 and 10:

$$M = [5, 10]$$

This is a crisp set because any given number in our universe is either in set M or not in set M—that is, either the number is between 5 and 10, in which case our function returns one, or it isn't, in which case it returns zero.

critical angle The maximum angle at which light passing from one medium is refracted to another. For angles equal to or larger than the critical angle, the light is totally internally reflected.

critical fusion frequency The display refresh rate at which flicker is no longer visible to the human eye. The value is affected by display angular size, display brightness, ambient lighting, and the particular human observer.

cropping Selecting a portion of an image for use and discarding the rest.

crop tool A tool in *Paint Shop Pro* and other applications that enables the user to crop an image. It allows a specific part of an image to be cut out.

cross-hairs A type of graphics cursor consisting of horizontal and vertical lines whose intersection is the selected point.

cross-hatch To fill a region with a pattern composed of uniformly spaced horizontal lines intersected by uniformly spaced vertical lines.

cross-platform Programs or hardware available in different versions for different platforms. Ideally, the program's interface and features are identical from one platform to the next.

cross polarized images A technique for three-dimensional viewing. Two normal displays are used and their images are polarized at right angles to each other, and then combined with a half silvered mirror.

cross-product The cross-product of two vectors **a** and **b** is written **a x b**. It is defined as:

$$a \ x \ b = \begin{vmatrix} i & j & k \\ \alpha_x & \alpha_y & \alpha_z \\ b_x & b_y & b_z \end{vmatrix}$$

Also known as the *vector product* or *outer product*.

cross-species composites Strange beasts created in *Poser* by combining parts of different animals.

crosstalk The overlapping of input values in a neural net so that some inputs are not as distinct as they could be. This results from the limitation that the input space can no longer keep everything partitioned into a finite number of dimensions.

crossview A technique for three-dimensional viewing. The images are placed side by side, left on the right and right on the left. This is commonly called the *crossview* or *transverse view*. To view such images, the viewer must keep the eyes crossed, as if looking at something closer than the screen, while focusing on the screen. The images are now no longer restricted in their spacing as with the freeview technique, and can be of arbitrary width. However, again, only half the area of the display can be used for each image, effectively halving the display resolution.

CRT See *cathode-ray tube*.

CRT monitor A computer monitor. CRT is short for *cathode-ray tube*.

Crumple shader A shader that allows creation of rocky mountains using *trueSpace*.

CSG See *constructive solid geometry*.

CSMA See *carrier sense multiple access*.

CSO See *currently selected object*.

CSS See *Central Structure Storage* or *Cascading Style Sheets*.

C-stand (Century stand) A rolling metal stand designed to hold lighting accessories, such as flags and nets.

CTB See *color temperature blue*.

CTF See *contrast threshold function*.

CTO See *color temperature orange*.

CTP Pro A PC-compatible computer program specifically designed for broadcast-quality animated series production.

cube architecture A special hardware system for accessing a row of voxels corresponding to a single pixel in parallel.

cuberille Of or related to a model used for visualization of three-dimensional data. It divides space into equal-sized parallelopiped volumes and uses data values to construct polygonal faces on selected volumes to render the image.

cubic curve The curve resulting from graphing a cubic polynomial.

cubic mapping A method of applying either a color or texture map to an object. Cubic mapping applies a map in a cubic fashion. Another way of visualizing this is that a map is applied to the six faces of an imaginary cube around an object.

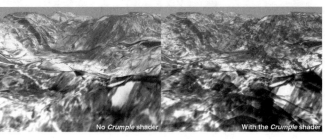

Crumple shader.

This method works very well for objects that are squarish in shape, but doesn't work so well for round objects, as it makes the seams where one projector's image ends and the next one begins too obvious.

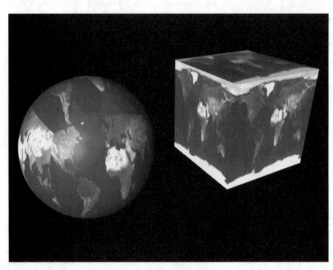

cubic mapping.

cubic texture mapping A feature of *true-Space*. This is a manner of UV projection that causes a texture to be mapped on every face of a cube. This differs from planar mapping in that planar mapping applies the texture to one side of an object flatly and the texture then penetrates through the object in the same direction. Using cubic mapping, the texture is mapped from the front, back, left, right, top, and bottom. This is useful for much more than cubic objects. In fact, whenever the user has an object to which it seems impossible to apply the texture without smearing or stretching, he should try applying it as a cubic map.

cuboctahedron An Archimedean solid having fourteen faces that consist of squares or triangles. Also known as a *nolid*.

cucaloris See *cookie*.

cue list A list showing the exact pieces of music that are needed to accompany a motion picture and any specific timings that are needed.

CUI See *character-based user interface*.

culling Eliminating data from graphics processing by using relatively simple tests to isolate objects that will be invisible in the finished image.

culling, backface The process of testing faces of a convex polygonal object and eliminating those that are not visible (as identified by the fact that the normal to the face is pointed away from the screen) so that they do not have to be processed for display.

culling, field of view Assume the field of view is the area in 3D space visible from the current point of view of the camera. This area is typically described using front and back clip planes and the viewing angle. The culling process uses the bounding sphere (in world space) of each object's mesh, and tests if it falls inside the field of view. To perform this test, transform the bounding sphere center point into view space (relative to the camera) and check the new Z value against the near and far clip planes. One can then test the center point against the left, right, top, and bottom clip planes. The clip planes for the field of view can be pre-calculated at the start of the render loop. Because these clip planes are in view space, we can simplify the clipping test. The front and back clip planes will be perpendicular to the Z-axis, so a simple comparison against the Z value can quickly decide if the mesh is in front of or behind the camera.

culling, occlusion Occlusions are normally four-sided flat or planar polygons, but they can use more or fewer sides, providing the polygon is planar. We can pre-calculate the occlusion's clip planes in the same way as for field of view culling, except we need only a front plane and four edge planes. The occlusion area differs from the viewing frustum in that it describes a hole. If any mesh lies inside this hole, it won't be rendered. The front plane of the occlusion won't always be perpendicular with the front clip plane, so we will have to use all four coefficients of the plane equation.

culling, octree construction for At the highest level, an octree is simply a tree (an acyclic directed graph) with a maximum of eight children at every node. It turns out that this is an ideal structure for representing a three-dimensional world enclosed by cubes. The root node of an octree contains a cube that encloses all the geometry in the world. The children at each node are the eight cubes of equal size that subdivide the parent into octants.

Cult Effects **(Cycore Computers)** A *Paint* plug-in that lets the user paint directly onto frames in *After Effects*, thus providing a convenient rotoscoping environment. *Cult Effects* also includes other filters, such as a lightning filter, and a number of seemingly abstract filters that can be used to create real-world effects such as flowing lava and mud-slides.

currently selected object (CSO) The object presently being operated upon by the graphics system.

current position (CP) The coordinates of the pixel currently being operated upon by the graphics system.

current state The present state of a finite state machine.

current time marker This is represented differently in specific programs, but most 3D applications have a symbol that shows where in time the user is. If animation has been done within a scene, when moving the current time marker, the 3D application will redraw the editor window to show the state of the objects at that point in time. With the current time marker, one can jump forward or backward to any point in time within the animation.

cursor A symbol (usually blinking) displayed on the computer screen which indicates where an input will have effect.

curved surfaces A surface that is curved in three dimensions. One way of defining such a curve is to take a parametric cubic curve and move it through the third dimension along the path of another parametric cubic curve.

curve, parametric cubic A curve where a parameter t is used in the definition of the functions x and y.

curve segment A portion of a curve that lies between two specified points.

Custom Global Shaders panel A panel in *trueSpace* that provides access to advanced shaders such as *CoolPowers* and *Pyrocluster*.

CUT The file extension used to designate a bit-mapped image file in the format specified for the *Dr. Halo* paint program.

cutaway A shot of something other than the main action or dialogue in a scene that is used to build the story and smooth rough edits.

Cut/Copy/Paste Standard commands available in many text and graphics editing applications, such as *Poser*. When a user invokes the Cut command, the item is placed in the system buffer. Copy/Paste operations allow a user to copy all of the parameters from any human or animal model and paste them to any other. This is a quick way to get symmetrical figure choreography elements.

cut list A list of each edit by fill roll and keycode numbers. The equivalent for film of an edit decision list (EDL) for video tape.

CV See *control vertex*.

CVA See *Compiled Vertex Arrays*.

cyan A bluish-green color which is one of the primary colors used in subtractive color imaging processes.

cyan, magenta, yellow, and black (CMYK) The four subtractive colors used in color printing. All colors in a picture are composed of these four basic colors. Color printing is accomplished by four passes through the printing press, each pass using ink of one of these basic colors.

cyanotype The use of salts in paper sensitization resulted in the invention of cyanotypes by Sir John Herschel. These are iron-based salts, basically ferric ammonium citrate/dichromate and potassium ferricyanide, coated and dried in the dark. The paper was then contact printed with a negative and exposed to the sun. The paper was then washed in water. The iron oxide formation gave it its name, which means "blue-colored paper process." Photosensitive paper that does not require development is called *a print-out process*. It is the oxidation and exposure to the sun that causes the image to come out.

CyberMesh A plug-in for Adobe *Photoshop* from Puffin Designs that permits converting images to geometry. Although it exists in a 2D world, it creates DXF, 3DS, and OBJ object formats that can be used in *Poser* as replacement body parts or as props. *CyberMesh* transforms grayscale art into height data, so that a flat bitmap painting becomes a 3D object. The lighter the bitmap, the "higher" the object is at that point. One can use *CyberMesh* to wrap 3D data around a sphere or cylinder, and then save it out as a true 3D object. The most important use for *CyberMesh* for *Poser* users is that facial portraits can be translated into 3D objects, making all sorts of new heads or facial masks for *Poser* figures.

cyclical redundancy checking (CRC) An error checking technique in which a checksum is computed for a data block by dividing by some convenient number (usually a power of 2) and taking the remainder. The CRC is saved. When doing error checking, the block CRC is computed again. It must be the same as the saved value if no errors have occurred.

cyclic overlap An arrangement of a set of graphics objects such that they cannot be placed in a priority order so that higher-priority objects always cover lower-priority objects.

cycolor A photographic printing process that makes use of a special film having embedded microcapsules containing colored dyes to permit full color and full tonal reproduction of continuous tone colored images.

cylinder A quadric surface that is created by sweeping a line segment around an axis when the line segment is parallel to the axis.

cylinder-frustrum interaction test Before attempting to render a complex object, many games first determine whether a geometrically simple volume (bounding that object) is visible. Due to their computational efficiency, spheres and boxes are commonly used as bounding volumes, but it is sometimes the case that objects are naturally suited to be bounded by a *cylinder*. An algorithm for determining whether an arbitrary cylinder potentially intersects the view frustum (and thus whether the object is visible) is almost as fast as a sphere or box test. The efficiency of the algorithm relies on the fact that we can reduce the problem to that of determining whether a line segment intersects a properly-modified view frustum. Given a cylinder described by a radius and two points in space representing the centers of the end faces, we individually move each of the six planes of the view frustum outward by the cylinder's effective radius with respect to that plane. The effective radius depends on the cylinder's orientation, and ranges from zero (when the cylinder is perpendicular to the plane) to the actual radius (when the cylinder is parallel to the plane).

cylinder, generalized A technique used to determine obstacle avoidance. The space between neighboring obstacles can be considered a 2D cylinder, the shape of which changes as it goes along. Between each pair of neighboring obstacles (including the walls or boundaries of the map), calculate a central axis. The intersections of these lines provide the locations for the search.

cylinder primitive A graphics primitive that is used to represent the bonds between atoms in molecular modeling.

cylindrical equal area A method of projecting a sphere onto a plane in which a unit cylinder is wrapped around a unit sphere and parallels of latitude are projected directly outward along planes normal to the polar axis.

cylindrical equirectangular map A method of projecting a sphere onto a plane in which the sphere is projected onto an encasing vertical cylinder.

cylindrical mapping A method of applying either a color or texture map to an object by wrapping the texture around an object in one direction. This technique works very well with bottles or cans, but does not work as well with most complex forms, because of lack of texturing on the tops and bottoms.

cylindrical mapping.

D

D-1 Recording format introduced by Sony in the mid-1980s. D-1 was the first practical digital video format. With its high image quality, it is mostly used for mastering and broadcast graphics, compositing, and animation production.

D-2 Recording format developed by Ampex in the mid-1980s. D-2 is a composite digital tape format that has recently been superseded by Digital Betacam as the most popular mastering format for American broadcast television.

D-3, D-5 Very high-quality digital studio mastering formats developed by Panasonic.

D-5 HD A high-definition version of D-5. D-5 HD allows for the 1.2 gb/sec data rate and 1080 line interlaced (1080i) or 720 line progressive scan (720p) video of the American HDTV video standard.

D-9 Recording format developed by JVC as a digital upgrade of S-VHS. D-9 offers high, 4:2:2 image quality and a cheaper price tag than Digital Betacam.

D-9HD The high-definition version of JVC's D-9 format.

D/A converter Digital-to-analog converter. Converts a set of digital pulses representing a number into an analog voltage whose amplitude is proportional to the digital number. The device must be tailored for a digital pulse train of a particular length, pulse characteristic, and pulse repetition rate.

DAD Digital audio disk. See *compact disc.*

daguerreotype A photographic method that forms a positive image on the metal plate by fusing it with iodide crystals and then exposing a plate to bright light for 15–20 minutes. The metal plate is then developed using heated mercury. The mercury blends with the exposed silver to form a hard amalgam. The areas that are not exposed are washed away using "hypo" (sodium thiosulphate). *Daguerreotypes,* as these images became known, are renowned for their exquisite detail and fidelity. They were the first types of photograph to be widely disseminated and commercialized. With all their success, however, daguerreotypes have one major drawback: their inability to be reproduced.

daisy chain A group of devices (such as printers, storage devices, etc.) that have been chained together so that each can be accessed independently.

DAL See *data access language* and *DAT auto loader.*

damping A counter force that causes motion to be slowly reduced to zero.

dark adaptation See *rods* and *cones.*

dark line image A conventional printed image having dark type on a light background. Also known as a *positive image.*

DarkTree Textures A standalone program for producing procedural textures, exportable to *3ds max* and *LightWave.*

DASD See *direct access storage device.*

DAT See *digital audio tape.*

data A group of facts or pieces of information, stored in a format that can be accessed and understood by a computer.

data access language (DAL) Apple software that converts databases from other than Apple computers to a form readable by the Macintosh.

database A collection of data arranged in an orderly fashion to permit quick access to any desired datum.

data communications The movement of data from one isolated system to another. In contrast, *data transfer* refers to movement of data within a single system.

data compression Any technique for reducing the amount of space required for a particular data set by various means of encoding. Usually used before a data set is stored in order to reduce storage requirements. A compressed data set must be decompressed before use.

data driven design A technique of program design in which the data used in the program is decoupled from the logic (program code) so that significant details can be easily changed without having to modify the basic program structure.

data header A heading for a data set that contains an identifying title and often format information in some standardized format.

data, loading quickly When a program requires frequent loading of data, speed can be increased by making sure that the data is stored in the form needed by the program, so that no data conversions are needed.

data set A collection of related data, usually stored in a single file.

data structure The way in which a set of data is arranged in a file.

data transfer Movement of data within a single computer.

DAT auto loader A device which contains a magazine of several DAT tapes, any one of which can be read when desired.

daVinci 1. A modeling plug-in for *3ds max* from Digimation. *daVinci* uses a unique modeling process that in many ways resembles metaballs. 2. A professional digital color correction system.

dawn light The moment the sun casts its first light in the sky, even if the sun itself is still below the horizon, it changes the lighting of the environment. Since very few rays reach the atmosphere, the light gets scattered and reflected, bathing the eastern sky with a blue tint that gradually lightens. As the sun slowly rises, the sky's color shifts from low-intensity white to an orange-yellow glow to yellow as the morning goes on. Finally, it becomes yellowish-white four hours before midday. This gradual color shift occurs because in the morning, when the sun is hitting the atmosphere at an angle, it scatters more blue, so it lets the reds and the yellows pass through, and that's what we see. In computer graphics, to simulate the morning sky we need to mimic this behavior of the sun as its light gets scattered and filtered through the atmosphere. The angle of the sun from dawn to morning changes from a grazing angle (0) to around 38 degrees, although this range varies depending on the location (latitude and longitude).

daylight 1. The combination of sunlight and skylight. 2. The time of day when the sun is out and visible. 3. The contribution of the atmosphere in global illumination calculations.

DBm See *decibel milliwatt*.

DBSPL See *decibel sound pressure loudness*.

DCR-PC1 A tiny video camera made by Sony.

DCR-PC100 A tiny DV camera made by Sony. It sports an upright design that makes it ideal for run-and-gun shooting.

DCT See *discrete cosine transform*.

DDA See *digital differential analyzer*.

DDS See *digital data storage*.

deallocate To release a reserved block of memory for use by other applications.

Debabelizer A software package that can translate images from one format to another, as well as create new image content.

deblock To extract a single data record from a large block of recorded data.

debounce Circuitry to read only one input when a switch closure occurs and ignore secondary opens and closures that occur as the switch contacts settle down to their new position.

debugging The process of finding errors in a computer program. This may including temporarily inserting lines

of code that perform analysis or print out messages at critical points in the computer's operation.

decal An image that is mapped to a surface to specify its texture. Also known as a *texture map*.

de Casteljau evaluation algorithm An algorithm for generating a *Bezier curve*. It begins with a quadrilateral consisting of the four control points *a1, a2, a3,* and *a4* that are used to define a Bezier curve. The midpoints of the first three sides of the box, *t1, t2,* and *t3* are then found. Then three more midpoints are found: *t4*, which is the midpoint between *t1* and *t2*; *t5*, which is the midpoint between *t2* and *t3*; and *t6*, which is the midpoint between *t4* and *t5*. Next, two new quadrilaterals are created, one by connecting *a1, t1, t4,* and *t6*; and the other by connecting *t6, t5, t3,* and *a4*. The subdivision process is repeated recursively with the new sets of quadrilaterals for as many iterations as desired to give a smooth curve.

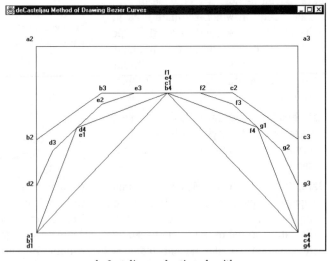

de Casteljau evaluation algorithm.

decibel The standard unit for measuring sound. The decibel scale measures relative loudness. One decibel equals one increment of "loudness."

decibel milliwatt (DBm) A unit for measuring sound as electrical power.

decibel sound pressure loudness (DBSPL) A measure of the acoustic power of a sound.

decimation 1. The process of changing a sampling rate to represent a signal with fewer samples than were originally used. 2. The process by which a polygonal model's polygon count is reduced. All professional 3D applications contain a tool that does this, some more effectively than others.

Decimator A dedicated polygon-reduction application from Raindrop GEOMAGIC Corp. Its primary purpose is to convert high-polygon meshes with low-resolution ones. *Decimator*'s utility lies in its ability to retain the smoothness and clean rendering of the original mesh and apply it to the decimated version.

decoder Device or software that converts data in a coded (and usually compressed) form back to the original data state.

decompress To reverse the procedure used to compress a block of data so as to restore it to its original form for use by a computer.

dedicated human body and tree modelers Modeling programs that enable the computer to automatically create models of the human body or of trees. *Tree Professional*, from Onyx, and *Xfrog*, from GreenWorks, allow the user to model trees and all sorts of shrubs.

dedicated terrain modelers Programs for modeling terrain. A typical terrain modeler is Corel's *Bryce*, which offers sophisticated terrain generation and realistic texturing of land, water, and atmosphere. Another example is *MojoWorld* from Pandromeda Software.

deep Having high color saturation and low color value, thereby producing a pure dark color.

DeepPaint 3D Software from Right Hemisphere that comes as both a 3D application that handshakes with *3ds max* and *LightWave*, and as a plug-in for *Photoshop*. As a 3D application, one can use *DeepPaint* to interactively paint on 3D objects.

Deep Sky Editing An air f/x process in *Bryce*. The same Deep Texture Editing process that allows the user to get to the very roots of texture generation when it comes to customizing materials is also available for creating sky textures.

Deep Texture Editor An editor in *Bryce* that gives the user control over creating texture components.

defect management Any technique used to compensate for defects in a recording medium. With hard disks, the first defect management technique is usually to scan the unrecorded disk, locate defective tracks, and lock them out, prohibiting their use for recording. In addition, once the disk is recorded, various checksum methods can be used to restore a few missing or defective bits.

Defogger An air f/x tool in *Bryce*. Using fog settings, the user can generate animations that reveal things that were previously hidden in a progressive manner.

deformation 1. An operation that transforms simple shapes to more complex shapes by deforming the space in which the simple shape is embedded. Some uniform sorts of distortions such as bending and twisting are included in many 3D packages. These allow for easy alterations of shapes using structured techniques. Typically, this is a *nondestructive* form of altering an object. Nondestructive forms of modeling are those that allow the user to go back to the original unaltered shape. 2. In *form•Z*, any animated change in geometric shape but not topology of the mesh. Bend, Twist, Wave, Taper, Shear, Skew, Conform To Spline, and Bulge are all examples of standard geometric deformations found in most 3D animation applications. Nonuniform (NU) Scale is also a deformation, as it has the effect of stretching a model along specified axes. In some applications NU Scale is actually a stretch tool. Deformation occurs in a model whenever a region of its topological entities is transforming at a different rate from others, and the result is that the elements change their relative positions to one another.

deformer A tool in any 3D application that allows the user to bend and/or twist objects to give them a new shape. See *deformation*.

defragmenting a drive When using a hard drive (or partition) regularly, it can become fragmented; that is, its contents can be distributed throughout all of the sectors on the drive. Even individual files—such as a clip of video—can become fragmented across an entire drive. This can slow down throughput, as the computer will have to spend extra time moving the read/write head around to locate the next collection of data. "Defragmenting" or "optimizing the drive" will reorder the contents of a drive so that the computer can read as quickly as possible.

defuzzification The conversion of a concept in fuzzy logic to a numerical value that can be used for precise computations.

degauss To completely erase all the information on a magnetic video or audio tape, using a demagnetizing device.

de-interlacing De-interlacing will throw out one field of television video, and duplicate the remaining field to fill in the missing lines. This means that every pair of fields (that is, every 60th of a second of displayed video) is identical, effectively reducing the frame rate to 30 fps. This will immediately give the video a more film-like motion. Unfortunately, it will also lower the detail in the image and can worsen any existing aliasing troubles.

delaration See *style sheet, syntax of*.

Delete Edge tool A tool in *Universe* that allows the user to delete edges of an UberNurbs cage.

delimiter See *field separator*.

Delirium A collection of plug-ins for rotoscoping a video tape and adding animated effects, developed by DigiEffects. Providing fire and smoke filters, along with rain, snow, and fairy dust filters, *Delirium* offers a balance of practical effects.

delivery medium The medium through which a video is displayed, such as web/multimedia, home video, broadcast television, projection, or digital projection.

DeMoivre's theorem For any real number x representing a radian angle of measure, the following identity exists:

$$e^{ix} = \cos x + i \sin x$$

This equation can be used to derive a multitude of trigonometric identities. The formula can be verified by expanding the function e^{ix} into its power series and collecting real and imaginary terms. Also known as the *DeMoivre formula*.

Demo Marker This tool is meant for production houses, where a creative team may be working on a *Bryce* project. The marker leaves a bright red trail, useful to production managers and art directors for calling attention to needed details in a *Bryce* scene. It works on any part of the *Bryce* interface, so it can be used to call attention to tools as well as elements in a scene.

ent image and 0 for one that passes no light whatsoever. *Opacity (O)* is the reciprocal of *transmission*. It is 1 for a completely transparent image and infinity for one that passes no light. *Density (D)* is the logarithm (to the base 10) of *opacity.*

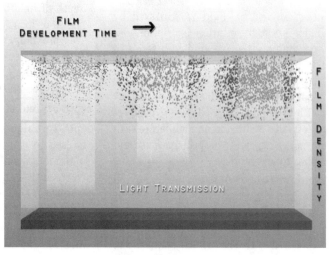

density.

dendrite A branching tree-like figure.

densitometer A device that measures the transmission characteristics of images, thereby making it possible to obtain a large number of uniformly colored prints.

density A measurement of the transmission characteristics of an image on film. Density is the difference between the amount of light striking the film and the amount of light that actually passes through the film. In other words, density is a measurement of how much transmitted light passes through the film. *Transmission (T)* is the amount of incident light passed through the image. It is 1 for a completely transpar-

depressor labii inferioris (lower lip curl muscle) A facial muscle that pulls the lower lip down and out. It is located around the upper and lower lips and attaches to the mandible. This muscle is not one of the more frequently used, but it is a crucial muscle for creating expressions like "surprise." In this expression the depressor labii inferioris muscle is used to curl the lower lip out and down.

depth buffer A plane that contains image information, whether or not it is physically located in the same frame buffer that holds the color information for the image. Also known as an *alpha buffer*.

Depth Cued A *Poser* command in the Display Menu that causes objects farther from the camera to look more faded.

depth cueing Reducing an object's color and intensity as a function of its distance from the observer.

depth cues, fog for This recreates a natural phenomenon called *aerial perspective*. In reality, light is scattered by moisture and pollution in the air. Depending on the time of day, it tends to scatter the blue light while letting other light pass through. Thus we see misty blue mountains in the distance instead of bright green. In Hollywood visual effects, this is simulated in miniature with a misty fog, and the principle also applies to 3D graphics.

depth of field (DOF) The minimum and maximum distances from a camera lens at which the focused image is acceptably sharp. The *depth of field* should not be confused with the *critical plane focus*. The critical plane is where the actual "focus" of the lens falls (which is the actual focus that the user selects, either by turning the focusing ring on a manual camera or by setting the autofocus on an automatic camera selector). The

depth of field.

depth of field lies before and after the critical plane focus. The depth of field functions as a regional sharpness compressor and expander as dictated by the aperture opening. These far and near planes of focus change with the aperture. Wide apertures (smaller f-stop numbers $f/1$–$f/5.6$) have a very narrow depth of field because the far and near planes of focus are closer to each other. This proximity throws the background and the foreground beyond the two planes into a blur because the light is not focused on those areas.

depth of field effect See *focal length*.

depth-sort algorithm An algorithm that is used to paint polygons into a frame buffer in order of their distance from the viewpoint, beginning with the shortest distance. Also known as the *Newell-Newell-Sancha algorithm*.

depth value of a vertex The depth specified for one part of a polygon in rendering a scene. When vertices of two polygons are projected onto the image screen, they must have the same depth value, otherwise strange artifacts are produced. Thus a function must be used which can offset a polygon's depth in a scene without changing its projected screen coordinates or altering its texture-mapping perspective.

deque (pronounced "deck") A double-ended queue, implemented in a manner that allows amortized constant time insertion or deletion of elements at either end of a randomly accessible array-type structure. Deques are also known as sequence containers because they store ordered sets of data, meaning that the order in which the data are inserted affects the order in which they are stored.

derivative object In *form•Z*, any object that is created using existing geometry. A vector line that is created by snapping its points to the edge points of an existing surface is a derivative. A boundary edge curve of an existing mesh is also a derivative.

descender In typography, the portion of a lowercase character that falls below the main part of a letter. The lower-case letters that have descenders are g, j, p, q, and y.

descending sort Sorting data backwards, beginning with *z* and ending with *a*.

descriptor A key word used to characterize the contents of a document so as to permit its retrieval by an automatic sort.

desktop publishing (DTP) The creation of quality printed documents using a personal computer. The material to be published is created and stored on the computer and either printed directly on a desktop laser (or similar quality) printer or stored on disk for reproduction by a commercial printing process.

destination monitor The monitor or window that displays an edited sequence as it plays, as opposed to the source monitor, which plays unedited source footage. Also called the *record monitor*.

destructive editing Any form of editing (either video or audio) that physically alters the original source material.

detail, level of See *level of detail*.

deterministic In generating a series of pseudorandom numbers, a sequence of numbers that is entirely predictable in nature without prior knowledge.

developing agent The chemical in a photographic developer solution that converts exposed portions of the silver halide emulsion to black metallic silver.

device control The ability of a piece of hardware, such as an edit controller or a CPU, to control a peripheral device, such as a VTR, via a remote control cable.

device coordinates A graphics coordinate system that is an integral part of a device such as a digitizing tablet.

device dependent A quality (such as the number of available colors) that is characteristic of a particular device and may change if a different device is used.

device driver A small computer program that conducts communication between the computer and a peripheral device such as a disk drive, a modem, or a printer.

devil's staircase A stair-like fractal, having steps of different sizes and heights, derived from the Cantor sets.

Dewdney's algorithm An algorithm for generating a set of random numbers. The equation follows:

$$n \rightarrow (n \times m) + k$$
$$n \rightarrow n \; MOD \; p$$
$$n \; is \; the \; random \; number$$
$$Repeat \; with \; n$$

This yields random numbers that are less than p-1. The values of n, m, k, and p are chosen before execution. The numbers m, k, and p remain the same for all random numbers generated. The choice of these numbers is critical, since not all sets of numbers yield a good set of random numbers. Dewdney notes, "Unless m, k, and p are carefully chosen, the pseudorandom numbers fail to pass even the most primitive tests of randomness."

DHTML See *Dynamic Hypertext Markup Language.*

diagonalizing Diagonalization of a matrix involves changing to a basis in which all the off-diagonal elements become zero. This basis is unique and consists of the eigenvectors of the matrix. The diagonal elements with respect to this basis are called the eigenvalues of the matrix.

diagram A plan for shooting a scene, which includes positions of the backdrop, scenery, camera, actors, and lights.

Diagrammatic Animation Language (DIAL) A computer language used to design animated sequences.

DIAL See *Diagrammatic Animation Language.*

dialogue Contrast between objects in a scene, such as a rose growing up on a rusty iron fence or a dove flying over war-torn land. Called *dialogue,* the elements have a relationship to each other that speaks to the viewer.

dialogue box A type of menu that remains visible until it is dismissed by the user. This is suitable for use when the user wishes to specify several related characteristics, such as the style, size, and attributes of a type font. When these are all satisfactory, the user can then dismiss the dialogue box with an explicit command.

dialogue editing The process of organizing dialog so that it can be easily adjusted and corrected, and preparing it for the final mix.

dialogue, music and effects (DM&E) A four-channel, split audio mix that allows for easy remixing in case the audio needs to be dubbed to a foreign language.

diamond square algorithm A midpoint displacement technique in two dimensions. Rectangles are a bit more complicated than line segments, since not one but five midpoints must be calculated for each rectangle. That is, the midpoint of the rectangle itself must be calculated, as well as the midpoints of each of the four line segments that make up the sides of the rectangle. In the diamond-square algorithm, the calculation of the rectangle's midpoint is called the *diamond step*, and the calculation of the side midpoints is called the *square step*.

diazo process A photographic process that produces positive copies (dark areas reproduced dark, white areas reproduced white) using exposure under ultraviolet light and development with either liquid or gaseous ammonia.

dichotomous branching The process whereby a tree divides into branches.

dicing The rendering of an object by dividing it into small *micropolygons* which are constant shaded quadrilaterals whose size is approximately half a pixel along each side.

die cutting A process used in producing holograms. Metalized paper is die cut or guillotined like plain paper and board. A die cutter should address and help solve in an efficient manner the problem of high volume, high speed, precision die cutting of embossed holography.

dielectric A non-conducting surface.

diffeomorphism A mapping in which both the mapping and its inverse are Cantor sets.

differential pulse code modulation (DPCM) A set of image data compression techniques that makes use of an algorithm for predicting successive data from past data and encoding the differences between the predicted data and the actual data.

diffraction A deviation from normal propagation of light that occurs when a light wave intersects an object whose features have a size on the order of the wavelength of visible light. Diffraction produces alternating bands or patterns of light and dark.

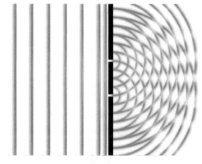

diffraction.

diffraction specific holograms The diffraction-specific approach breaks from the traditional simulation of optical holographic interference by working backwards from the 3D image. The fringe is treated as being subsampled spatially (into functional holographic elements or *hogels*) and spectrally (into an array of *hogel vectors*).

diffuse The even omnidirectional reflection of light from a surface. It also refers to scattered non-direction soft illumination.

diffuse color The color of the light that emanates from the material from all directions. Assigning a basic blue color as

the material, for example, would show a bright blue when the diffuse color slider is moved to higher percentages, and black if the diffuse color slider is set to zero. If a texture is set to be the place the diffuse color is being taken from instead of a palette color, then the overall color of the texture would be brightest when the diffuse color slider was set to 100% or more, and very dark when the diffuse color slider was set to zero. The diffuse color of an object is the color seen when an object is completely illuminated. Diffuse color is often referred to as the actual color of an object.

diffuse light Light from a soft, undirected source, such as a typical household bulb.

diffuse maps Maps used to control the location and amount of diffuse light reflected off of the surface of a model.

diffuser A light modifier accessory that changes the light quality. It could be placed either in front of the light source or directly in front of the lens.

diffuse reflection A situation in which a light ray incident on an object's surface is absorbed and re-radiated after passing through the object. The re-radiated light is distributed uniformly. It has its intensity reduced proportionally to the distance it travels through the object. Its color is a combination of the color of the original light and the absorption spectrum of the object's surface.

Diffuse tab A control in *Universe* that is part of the Material Info Window. It allows the user to set the diffused color of an object.

diffusion The even scattering of light by reflection from a surface. Diffusion also refers to the transmission of light through a translucent material.

diffusion.

diffusion channel Diffusion deals with irregularities in surface color. For instance, if the user is dealing with a metallic surface that has subtle changes over the face of the surface, he can map these changes out with a diffusion map.

diffusion gel A semi-transparent piece of white plastic used to make a light softer.

diffusion-limited aggregation A method of drawing fractal planar trees.

DigiBeta See *Digital Betacam*.

Digimarc A *Photoshop* filter that allows embedding of a personal watermark in an image.

Digimation Developer of dozens of plug-ins for *3ds max*.

DigiEffects Developer of an array of effects plug-ins for *After Effects*.

digital The storing of data in the form of coded pulses, as opposed to *analog*, which is the storing of data as voltage levels.

digital audio equipment Equipment that records audio in digital form, such as DAT or MiniDisc. Note that equipment for playing these formats does not always produce output in digital form.

digital audio tape (DAT) A high-quality audio tape format developed by Sony that records and plays audio in a digital form using a sampling rate of 48 kHz and is capable of recording SMPTE time-code information.

Digital Betacam (DigiBeta) A recording format introduced by Sony in 1993 as a digital upgrade of Betacam SP. Many high-budget digital films, such as *The Buena Vista Social Club*, are shot on Digital Beta. Digital Betacam decks can also play (but not record) analog Betacam SP tapes.

digital camera A camera that records an image by first projecting it onto an array of photocells and then storing the information from each cell in the array in digital form.

digital certificate A digital certificate enables SSL (Secure Socket Layer encryption) on the Web server. SSL protects communications with a server so credit card orders may be taken securely, and ensures that hackers cannot access clients' information. Also known as an *SSL Server Certificate*

digital data storage (DDS) A format for storing data sequentially on tape. Usually used for backing up a complete hard disk, since access to a particular file can be obtained only by scanning all the way from the beginning of the tape.

digital differential analyzer (DDA) An algorithm used to rasterize a line or curve by recursively using the line slope formula to compute a point on the line in one direction for a unit step in the orthogonal direction and then rounding off to the nearest pixel.

digital dissolve effect A method of dissolving one image into another when both images are available only in digital form. One such method is to randomly write the pixels of the second image over the first.

digital filtering Improving the appearance of an image by replacing a pixel by some function of that pixel and its neighbors. Also known as *discrete convolution*.

digital holography A method of displaying true three-dimensional images by digitally computing the laser-interference patterns that would be produced if an image were to be illuminated by laser light.

digital image stabilization Circuitry to correct for the effects of camera shape or movement when using a small video camera. There are two kinds of image stabilization: *electronic* and *optical*. *Electronic image stabilization* (sometimes called *digital image stabilization*) requires a CCD with a larger imaging size than the actual image size that is displayed. Electronic digital stabilization works by detecting camera motion, analyzing it to see if it's intentional or not, and then digitally moving the image to compensate for unwanted motion. Because the camera is overscanning the actual field of view, there are enough extra pixels around the edges to allow for this kind of movement. Since the camera is constantly moving the image about the screen to compensate for shake, electronic stabilization can often result in softer, slightly blurred images.

digital projection A system that converts digitally-recorded data directly to an image that is projected on a screen. It is predicted that these may ultimately replace film projectors. They are especially sensitive to narrow depths of field and special effects compositing.

digital signal processing A branch of engineering that deals with the relationship between analog signals and their digitally-sampled counterparts, together with methods for analyzing and processing the digital signals.

digital television (DTV) A format for transmitting television signals in digital form. "DTV" includes ATV (Advanced Television), a transmission system for broadcast; HDTV (High Definition Television), a subset of DTV; and SDTV (Standard Definition Television), a digital broadcast standard for existing analog video. The FCC has required that all broadcasters switch from NTSC to DTV by 2006. Most stations will use HDTV which has a resolution of 1920 × 1080 pixels with a 16:9 aspect ratio and either 24 or 30 progressive scan frames per second.

Digital Terrain Elevation Data (DTED) Highly-accurate terrain data for the United States topology, available from the United States Geological Survey (USGS).

Digital Terrain Map (DTM) Map available from the United States Geological Survey (USGS) that provides terrain elevation data.

digital-to-analog conversion The conversion of a digital number to the analog signal level that it represents.

digital typography The specialized field of designing type faces that can be represented by pixels without unpleasant artifacts or variations of thickness.

digital video (DV) A video signal encoded as a sequence of binary numbers. See *D1* or *D2*, which are two standard formats for digital video.

digital video deck A device for playing digitally-recorded video tapes.

digital video disc See *DVD*

digital video effects (DVE) Special effects that are added to a digital video. The term originally referred to the XYZ rotation of a plane that produced "spinning logos." Digital video effects are now used widely in professional linear video editing and apply to what has become a fairly standard set of effects: wipes, dissolves, picture-in-picture, barn doors, and split screen, etc.

digital video interactive (DVI) A technology for the compression and reconstruction of video images that are stored digitally.

digital video timecode (DVTC) A timecode format developed for the DV format. DVTC is an acceptable alternative to SMPTE timecode if only DV format equipment is used. As the popularity of the DV formats increases, DVTC is becoming more integrated into professional video editing equipment.

digital zoom A "fake" zoom that creates a zooming effect by enlarging the image on-the-fly. Unfortunately, when enlarging, the image is severely degraded.

digitize The process of converting a signal or image into a collection of digital data. The information to be converted is usually scanned in an orderly fashion and the data stored sequentially.

digraph In typography, two vowels that are joined together to form a single character. Also known as a *diphthong*.

Dijkstra's algorithm An algorithm used in game programming to compute the shortest path between two points. Dijkstra's algorithm computes the shortest path from a given node of a network (called the *root* node) to every other node in the network.

dimension, fractal A dimension assigned to a curve that accounts for its space-filling capabilities. For example, an ordinary straight line has a Euclidian dimension of one and a fractal dimension of one. A line that has many convoluted curves so that it entirely fills a plane still has a Euclidian dimension of one, but its fractal dimension is two, indicating that it fills all of two-dimensional space. Also known as the *Hausdorff-Besicovitch dimension*.

dingbat In typography, a non-alphanumeric symbol that has the same size as a letter or number such as a "smiling face." Type fonts consisting entirely of *dingbats* are available. Using such a font, each letter or number of a standard keyboard will cause an associated *dingbat* to be printed. Also known as a *pi character*, or *wingdings* (Microsoft Word).

DINR The *Digidesign Intelligent Noise Reduction* plug-in for *TDM* or *AudioSuite* systems. It can be used for removing any kind of noise from a recording. Tape hiss, rumbling air conditioners, or annoying hums can all be automatically eliminated. If an intrusive noise artifact has muffled some or all of the sound, *DINR* may be able to save the footage, or prevent an expensive ADR session.

diophantine A number α is *diophantine* if there exist $c > 0$ and $v > 0$ such that

$$\left| a - \frac{p}{q} \right| > \frac{c}{q^v}.$$

diopter An adjustment on the eyepiece of a camera that allows the user to correct the focus of the eyepiece to match his vision.

diphthong In typography, two vowels that are joined together to form a single character. Also known as a *digraph*.

direct access The capability to access a desired data set directly rather than by means of some indexing scheme.

direct access storage device (DASD) An on-line, directly addressable storage device, such as a floppy or hard disk drive or a CD-ROM or tape player.

direct derivative See *virgin object*.

direct image film A film that produces an image of the same polarity as the image being copied, i.e., a negative image produces a negative copy or a positive image produces a positive copy.

direction One of the controls in the *Material Generator* plug-in for the *trueSpace pluSpack*. It controls the direction that the vein runs through the texture when using the marble setting.

directional light A light source that radiates nonuniformly in space, as, for example, a spotlight.

direction cube A method of subdividing space that is used in ray tracing algorithms. A cube is centered at the origin of the rectangular coordinate system, with the coordinate axes passing through the center of the faces of the cube. The faces are then subdivided into small rectangles.

direction of projection (DOP) A vector from the center of projection to the projection plane.

direction of reflection (DOR) The direction in which a ray of light that impinges on a surface is reflected from the surface.

Direction tab A tab in *Wave Generator* that lets the user visually or numerically define the hotspot (or starting point) for the Circular and Ripple wave types. Used in conjunction with the preview feature,

one could create wave vertex animation from a stone skipping across a pond, for example, and visually place the location of the ripple wave it would create.

direct manipulation In *Carrara*, a way to tell which way a camera is pointing and what the field of view is. Direct manipulation allows the user to edit its parameters with the same visual representations.

directories See *search engine*.

Director of Photography (D.P.) The film, lighting and camera specialist responsible for the look of the photography and in charge of the camera and lighting crews.

direct port A hardware device that bypasses graphics accelerators to permit direct reading and writing into the graphics frame buffer.

direct user A graphics system user who accesses graphics devices directly through the lowest level graphics language in order to obtain maximum speed and efficiency.

direct-view storage tube (DVST) A cathode ray tube that stores an image by writing it once on a storage mesh having an embedded phosphor, using a slow-moving electron beam. The image need not be refreshed until a data change occurs.

DirectX A Microsoft Windows capability for speeding graphics. DirectX results in a slight increase in rendering speed, especially for complicated objects, and the background bitmap will be stored in video memory if possible. DirectX supports the use of "sprites" when rendering. Whenever a scene contains slow rendering objects, the renderer will switch to "sprite" mode. All nonselected objects are drawn to the background and the renderer will refresh only the selected object. The speed of the 3D card will determine the "switching" time. Additionally, in scenes that contain a lot of textures, when the video memory is full, textures are cached to system memory. Cache memory will be cleared whenever a new D3D window is created and video memory is low or the window is resized. *trueSpace* supports the import and export of Microsoft *DirectX* objects. This will be of benefit primarily for those who are developing games and interactive 3D content as they will no longer have to purchase separate modules for this purpose. Both binary and ASCII files are supported, including motion data.

discontinuities, visual The most common problem associated with triangulated geometry is the formation of visual discontinuities. Radiosity shows the computed solution by shading interpolation across the polygon and in areas where the polygon is bisected into triangles; the boundary shows up as a line. This is especially true since the eye emphasizes the edge boundary between light and dark areas. This result is known as *mach bands*. This is purely a perceptual issue. Mach bands can sometimes be eliminated by creating a denser mesh. The subdivision of an irregular polygon normally results in the creation of triangles. Triangles with acute angles are sometimes intensified through a limb or edge darkening caused by discontinuities in the shading. The only way to avoid interpolation artifacts is to minimize the use of triangles or the eventual subdivision of quadrilateral surfaces into triangles by bisecting irregular polygons

manually into quadrilaterals. Some triangles, however, such as equilateral triangles, are suited for radiosity because the use of interpolation shading with it does not emphasize an edge or a quadrant.

discrete An electronic component that is a single circuit element such as a resistor, capacitor, inductor, or transistor, as opposed to an integrated circuit that contains a number of these devices on a single chip.

discrete convolution Improving the appearance of an image by replacing a pixel by some function of that pixel and its neighbors. Also known as *digital filtering*.

discrete cosine transform (DCT) A mathematical technique for image compression in which blocks of pixels are represented by spatial frequencies. The process removes frequencies that have small coefficients. It is used in image compression with the JPEG algorithm.

discrete Fourier transform Fourier analysis uses a set of sine waves to represent a complex waveform. The *discrete Fourier transform* determines the coefficients of the Fourier transform using a digital technique that is easily adapted to computers.

discretely shaped B-splines B-spline curves that associate distinct values of b_1 and b_2 with each control point, thereby providing local control of the curve shape.

discretization The subdivision of all the visible surfaces in a scene into a uniform mesh. This process sets up the patches and the elements in a radiosity scene. The process of discretization collapses geometry hierarchy (geometry parentage and gluing are removed) and partitions it in an ordered fashion. This partitioning is always a precursor to every radiosity processing action. Geometry collapsing makes all the visible objects in the scene known. Each of the discretization's patches is stored in memory. Moreover, this process makes it possible to dissipate the energy into the environment.

disk array A combination of multiple disk drives together with software that produces redundant storage so that in the event of failure of a single disk drive, no data are lost. See *redundant array of inexpensive or independent disks*.

diskless workstation A computer with processing capability but no disk storage device of its own. It must be connected to a local area network that permits it to share the disk storage facility of a server station.

dispersed-dot ordered dither A method of assigning individual dots to represent shades in an image on a CRT. This technique cannot be used on a printer, since it cannot reproduce the individual dots.

dispersion The separation of light into different wavelengths due to passing through different media that have different refraction indices from each other. This is the common "prism effect" or "grating effect." Dispersion requires the presence of two different media to work. It is the change in the index of refraction as a function of the wavelength in a transparent medium. ⌭

displacedatplace A plug-in that is part of the *pluSpack* for *trueSpace*. It is used to create a *displacement map* object from an image file.

displacement map A grayscale image that is used to alter the surface of an object. Like a *bump map*, a displacement map assigns an altitude based on the lightness or darkness of a corresponding pixel. Unlike bump maps, though, which affect only the shading of an object, therefore simulating an irregular surface, a displacement map actually alters the geometry.

Displace tool Displace is a terrain and irregular-surface modeling tool within *form•Z* that uses grayscale images created in external image-editing applications to create meshes based on the luminosity values of the pixels within an image. As in texture mapping, the Displace tool uses the projection of the grayscale map around the displaced object to determine the offset of individual points in 3D space.

display buffer Memory for storing the data that comprise an image to be displayed.

display device The component of a display system that converts signals into a visual image, such as a cathode-ray tube or an array of liquid crystal display devices.

display element A primitive graphics shape that is to be displayed, such as a line, a circle, a sphere, etc.

dispersion.

Display Extents A feature of *Universe*. When turned on, it shows straight lines around the edges of an object and a center line.

display file Data that can be used to display an image, stored as a single file.

display holography Display holography includes *point of purchase, trade show* and *corporate display*. Point of purchase displays can use all types of holograms from decorative foils to eye-catching stereograms showing products or fashion models. Trade show and corporate display applications usually involve large-format holograms for their dramatic effect. Commissioned artistic holograms have been used effectively in corporate headquarters, adding a special high tech statement.

display list A list of display data and commands sufficient to build and display a particular image.

Display Modes A control in *Bryce* that allows the user to select the display mode as Wireframe, Wireframe/Render composite, or Render. It allows the user to work as he would in the edit screen with wireframe proxies of objects, except that the user sees the wireframes against the last-rendered picture. This is a very useful technique when placing objects in relation to others.

Display Paths A feature of *Universe*. When turned on, it draws the animation path across the display.

display traversal The traversal that is used to compute a new view of a model.

dissolve To change from one image to another by superimposing a minimum-intensity version of the second image on top of the first and then increasing the intensity of the second image and decreasing the intensity of the first image over time until only the second image is displayed.

distance and scale of lighting Distance and scale are very important when considering the lighting of a scene. Scale is determined by many different factors, lighting being one of them. As a light recedes into the distance, it will get smaller and dimmer. Emissions become less pronounced and shadows less defined. *Universe* offers direct visual feedback over the size of lights.

distance from point to line The minimum of all distances from a point to points on the line.

distance, relative object size and A small object paired with a large object is seen as farther in the distance, as long as the objects are identical. Furthermore, with two objects of identical size, if one of the objects is shrunk, it appears to recede into the distance.

distance, shadow sharpness and Real-world lights cast very sharp shadows when we are close to them, and then get softer as we move farther away. Most shadows in computer graphics do not behave this way; they are either sharp all the way to the back (ray traced shadows) or they are soft from the moment they leave the light source (shadow maps). The solution is to either combine these two types of shadows or create multiple instances of ray traced shadows to suggest a soft light source.

distance, simulating dominant light quality Dominant lights, whether simulated as a single light or in an array, give noticeable light quality. Light quality is primarily dependent on its distance from the object and light source, and if the light source is diffused or filtered through another object between the light source and the object. Light quality is dependent on distance physically—large light sources that are 10 feet long behave like point-source lights if they are placed 100 feet from the object, and point-source lights behave like a large light source if they are very close to the object they are illuminating. This is the way lights behave in the real world. However, getting a single point-source light in computer graphics to behave like a diffused light is not possible due to the built-in assumptions of how this type of light should illuminate a computer graphics object.

distance, texture gradient and Texture gradient is the so-called "impressionism" effect, the perception of depth based on the merging of small details as they are repeated on both the foreground and the background. The repetition of the pattern as it approaches the horizon is perceived as receding into the background. This concept is very easy to visualize if we think of a field of grain or grass that extends to the horizon. Texture gradient cues are also related to another monocular depth cue, the spatial summation cue.

distant light A light source that covers a wide area that has parallel rays. It is also called *infinite light* because of the way it extends and influences the scene.

distributed frame buffer An arrangement of pixel data in a buffer that permits parallel processing for faster operation.

distributed ray tracing A multidimensional form of *stochastic ray tracing*.

distributed rendering A feature of rendering applications that distributes the burden of rendering an animation over several computers.

dithering Simulating gray tones by the use of varying patterns and sizes of black background dots.

dither matrix An array of numbers that represents a dithering pattern. This pattern is usually repeated in blocks over the entire screen.

dividers HTML rules used to create separations in Web pages for the purpose of making them more attractive. These dividers, also known as *horizontal rules*, use the <HR> tag. The horizontal rule is a straight line that goes from the current indentation to the right side of the screen.

DLT An optical tape back-up system. DLT tapes typically hold about 20GB of media.

D-max The highest density (darkest image) obtainable for a particular photographic medium.

DM&E See *dialogue, music and effec*ts.

D-min The lowest density (lightest image) obtainable for a particular photographic medium.

Document Setup Screen Configuring the options listed in the setup screen (Document Setup in the File menu, or the downward-pointing arrow at the bottom of the left-hand toolbar) is a necessary first step when entering the *Bryce* environment. The most important decision in the Document Setup Screen dialog is how the user configures the document resolution and the associated aspect ratio. The document resolution sets up the *Bryce* scene as it appears on the monitor. If the monitor cannot display this resolution because of its own limitations, the setting will not take place on the *Bryce* screen.

dodecahedron A solid having twelve plane faces. The *regular dodecahedron* has faces that consist of pentagons. The *rhombic dodecahedron* has sides that consist of rhombuses.

dolly A type of wheeled platform on which the camera and operator can be stationed so that they can be gradually moved throughout the filming of a scene.

dolly grip Extravagant movie productions have special grips who are employed to operate cranes, dollies, and other heavy equipment.

domain of attraction The area of a strange attractor which includes all points which, upon iteration of the attractor's iterated equation, approach a particular point. Also known as *basin of attraction*.

domain, frequency The defining of a signal as the sum of a set of sine waves, each having its phase shift, frequency, and amplitude specified.

dominant wavelength 1. The wavelength of monochromatic light that can be mixed with white light to match a given color. The *dominant wavelength* does not have to be a component of the given color. 2. The wavelength of the color seen by the human eye when viewing light.

doming Outward change in the shape of the shadow mask of a cathode-ray tube caused by heating by the electron beam. The result is errors in color purity as different colored dots that are supposed to superimpose on the screen surface no longer do so. This limits the maximum luminance that can be produced on a region of the display unless sophisticated corrective measures are employed.

Doom A classic computer game in the "first person shooter" genre.

door icon An icon in the *Game Creation System*. If the user selects a wall and uses this icon, it will assign the properties of a door to that wall.

DOP See *direction of projection*.

dope sheets Forms used in animation to map the motion planned to the sound planned over the frames needed.

Dore A graphics system designed to provide increased flexibility to the programmer.

dot 1. A display of one pixel. 2. A circular marker of selectable size on an image.

dot cloud A set of dots used in molecular modeling to represent transparent surfaces.

dot leaders A series of dots that fill the space between two items on the same line, as between a table of contents descriptive item and the corresponding page number.

dot matrix A printer whose printing mechanism is a column of solenoid-actuated pins that produce dots on the paper. By actuating the proper combination of solenoids for each column, characters or graphics may be produced.

dot matrix hologram Dot matrix technology allows the hologram to reflect extremely bright colors viewed from many angles. An example of exposure time would be approximately 48 hours for a 6" × 6" hologram which includes almost 360,000 exposures. Each individual pixel is exposed.

dot pitch The distance between two phosphor dots of the same color on adjacent lines on a cathode-ray tube screen.

dot product Also known as the *scalar* product or *inner* product. The dot product of two vectors **a** and **b** is the scalar given by

$$a \cdot b = ab \cos w$$

where w is the angle between the two vectors.

dot size The diameter of a single dot on the output of a printer or display tube.

dots per inch (dpi) A measure of the quality and resolution of a display or printer. This is the number of horizontal or vertical dots that can be displayed or printed in a linear inch. A typical computer monitor displays 75 to 90 dpi. A printed image usually needs to be 300 dpi or more if it is to look acceptable in print.

Douady rabbit The Julia set for *c = −0.12256 + i0.74486.*

double buffer In graphics, an arrangement of memory such that one portion of memory can be used to store an image that is currently being displayed while a new image is being constructed in another portion of memory. When the new image is complete, switching occurs so that the new image is displayed and another image is constructed in the part of memory that was initially being used for display.

double ended queue See *deque.*

double-hexcone HLS color model A color model defined in the double-hexcone subset of cylindrical space.

double scan A technique used to allow the VGA to produce low-resolution images in a format designed for the CGA. Each hori-zontal line of data for a 200-line image is drawn twice to give a 400-line image.

do what I mean (DWIM) A technique for spelling correction when the word typed in by the user does not match any of the names stored in a list in the computer. The user is presented with the nearest matches so that he can select one of them.

downloads, font Web users can download new fonts if a designer embeds them into a Web page. The font, however, must be in a special format; for example, Microsoft Internet Explorer requires the font to be in .eot format. The user can convert installed fonts to the .eot format by using a special program called WEFT.

D.P. See *Director of Photography.*

DPCM See *differential pulse code modulation.*

dpi See *dots per inch.*

dpsVelocity A Windows-based, Pentium turnkey editing system capable of capturing and outputting uncompressed, D1 quality video. *dpsVelocity* offers real-time, dualstream playback and effects in the Video for Windows AVI format. The editing interface is similar to that of *Media 100* and has everything a user needs to edit long-format, complex projects: unlimited video and audio tracks, full-featured audio equalization and mixing, and multiple levels of undo.

drag-and-drop editing A two-step editing method where the user selects a shot and "drags" it from one position and "drops" it in another position. Examples include dragging a shot from a bin to drop it in the timeline, or from one position in the timeline to another.

dragging A feature of graphics software that enables the user to position a cursor on the desired object using a mouse or trackball and then to press a button to cause the graphics object to follow a path directed by the mouse to a new location.

dragon curve A fractal curve that is a plot of the set representing the result of iterating the equation:

$$e^{ix} = \cos x + i \sin x$$

DRAM See *dynamic random access memory*.

dramatic lighting Lighting that brings a sense of drama or urgency to the image. Contrast and drama may be suggested by creative use of dramatic lighting. Consider a stage performance, for example, and the critical role lighting plays in real-world theater. Strategically placed and illuminated spotlights key in on certain cast members as they perform. So it is in animation projects. While there will be many times that a project will not call for dramatic lighting (if it were used all the time it would not be dramatic), selective use brings a sense of isolation and importance to an object in space.

Draw A dedicated drawing program by Corel.

drawing complex curves with Java A useful technique for drawing a complex curve is to break it into a large number of very short straight line segments and draw each separately. Rather than having to specify a large number of line draw operations, Java 2D allows one to specify all of the coordinates first and then draw the curve in one operation. This requires use of the *Java.awt.geom. GeneralPath* package.

Drawing eXchange Format (DXF) The *de facto* 3D file format on the MacIntosh, created by AutoDesk, Inc. Most 3D programs support one new form or another of DXF.

drawing octants Eight sections of a circle or ellipse, into which the figure is separated to increase the speed and efficiency of drawing.

Draw tool 1. A tool in *Paint Shop Pro* that enables the user to draw lines on images. The user can adjust the size of the lines through the Control Palette or change from normal lines to Bezier curves. 2. Tools included in the *Game Creation System Paint* program. They include Undo, Pen, Fill Bucket, and solid and outlined forms and shapes.

DreamWeaver A popular Web-editor program.

dressing The addition of props to an empty set to complete the desired set appearance.

drift When an object is stared at for a long time, the bright source appears to move off center and wander off. This phenomenon is called *drift*.

drifting smoke effect An effect created with *trueSpace* using *Primal Particles*, *wfmm sphereglo*, and two of the post shaders that come with *CoolPowers*: *wfmm glow* and *wfmm motrails*. This effect could be used to simulate smoke coming up from a sewer grate in a large, urban city, or cigarette smoke flowing up from a cigarette (*see Figure next page*).

Droop Target Morph This target morph in *Poser* selects points on the front of the face from the nose to just below the lips, so the face can move up or down, stretching other skin along with it.

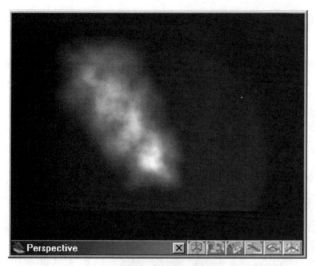

drifting smoke effect.

to grab any color on the image to use as a background. This technique makes it easy to match colors exactly and eliminates color guessing.

drop shadow A shadow cast by an object on a surface. *Photoshop* has the capability to create drop shadows from defined image areas.

Drop to Floor A command in the Figure Menu of *Poser*. Dropping a figure to the "floor" is especially useful when shadows are on, so the shadows seem more realistic. For maximum effect, the Ground Plane should also be visible.

drop frame timecode Because the frame rate of NTSC video is an odd 29.97 frames per second, drop frame timecode was developed to help round off the fractional frames to less awkward whole numbers. With drop frame timecode, the frame itself is not dropped, just the number in the counter. In other words, the frame rate is still 29.97 fps, but the counter is counting at 30 fps.

drop out 1. A weak portion of the video signal which results in a problem in playback. Hits are small drop-outs that are only one or two horizontal lines in size, glitches are larger, where 5% or more of the image drops out. Large analog drop-outs can result in a few rolling video frames and large digital drop-outs can result in random "holes" across the screen. 2. A defective section of magnetic media on which data cannot be recorded.

Dropper tool A tool in *Paint Shop Pro* that allows the user to grab a color from an image. For example, this allows the user

dry processing A technique for developing a latent photographic image without chemical treatment.

dry silver film A nongelatin silver film emulsion which is processed by heat rather than chemicals.

DS Fractal Noise A special three-color fractal shader that allows the user to map the fractal based on an object's UV coordinates. With this shader, the user can create swirling nebulas and wormholes, clouds, camouflage, and many other different surfaces (*see Figure next page*).

DTED See *Digital Terrain Elevation Data*.

DTM See *Digital Terrain Map*.

DTP See *Desktop Publishing*.

DTV See *digital television*.

dual state In *Bryce*, single objects represented as a blend of two diverse materi-

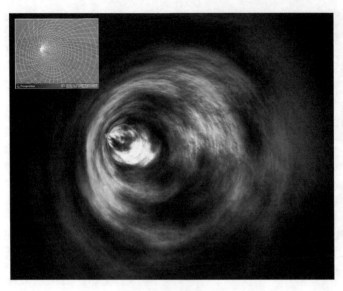

DS Fractal Noise.

in a program rather than using subroutines or global definitions so that the set needs to be coded only once. This makes programs large and inefficient and so should be avoided whenever possible.

duplication To assist in adding control over where new copies of objects appear, most programs offer duplication or replication tools. Duplicating/replicating functions allow the user to determine how many copies of an object will be created, and if these new copies will be moved, scaled, or rotated. With a little planning, these duplicating/replicating functions can make for a large variety of shapes on complex patterns that would be very laborious to maneuver by hand. Even more powerful is the ability in many programs to make duplicates that are mirror images of the original. This cuts the modeling time in half for many objects like the human body that are essentially symmetrical in composition. *Carrara's* duplication features allow the user to repeat a series of position, orientation and resize operations when creating objects. For example, to generate a wheel, one spoke can be created and then used as a master object. The Duplicate command can then be used to create a new instance of the spoke, and the new spoke rotated into position. With the new spoke still se-

als, remaining that way over time. For example, an object that is a blend of wood and glass can be created without blending the materials in the Materials Lab Mode.

dual stream-processing The ability to handle up to two video signals at a time.

dub A copy of a videotape, also known as a *dupe*.

dubbed audio Audio added after filming is complete, rather than being recorded live during the recording of the video.

Duff's formulation A method of curve interpolation using control points.

Dufus option An option for setting enemy artificial intelligence in the *Game Creation System*. It is used to ensure a "lethargic" opponent.

dump A printout of raw data contained in a file.

duplicate data syndrome The repetition of a set of in- structions in many places

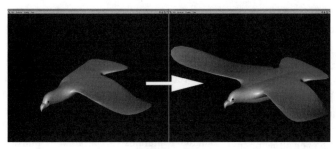

duplication.

lected, the Duplicate command can then be used 12 more times to create and position each of the other 12 spokes automatically. The same technique can be used for the bolt heads.

duvetine A black felt-like cloth used to block out unwanted light sources, such as windows.

DV See *digital video*.

DVCAM A recording format by Sony which offers higher tape speed than DV, but not quite as high as DVCPro. It uses the same metal tapes as DV.

DVC Pro A recording format with a faster tape speed than DV and DVCAM.

DVD Digital video disc or digital versatile disc. An optical storage medium that is the same physical size as a compact disc. There are several different DVD standards and formats ranging from DVD-RAM (a rewritable format), DVD-ROM (a read-only format) and DVD-video (the format that is used for video releases).

DVE See *digital video effects*.

DVI See *digital video interactive*.

Dvorak keyboard A keyboard layout invented by August Dvorak that arranges the letters and characters for fastest and easiest typing. The standard QWERTY keyboard was deliberately designed to slow up typing speed so as not to exceed the capabilities of original typewriter mechanisms.

DVST See *direct-view storage tube*.

DVTC See *digital video timecode*.

DXF See *Drawing eXchange Format*.

dyadic Of the form $p2^{-k}$.

dye polymer recording An optical storage technology which uses a laser beam to record data on layers of dyed plastic.

DynaCloth A near real-time cloth simulation plug-in, developed by Mentemagica for *trueSpace*. With *DynaCloth*, one can create fully-clothed realistic characters without the need for a super high-end machine. *DynaCloth* lets the user define the stiffness of the cloth on a per-vertex basis, so the user can have realistic seams or something like shoulder pads in a suit, where the cloth on the pads wouldn't be as loose as on the arms. One can link vertices to another object, so the user can achieve a waving flag, or even a matador swinging his cape in front of a bull.

dynamic A microphone that derives its power from the pressure of the sound that it picks up which moves a coil through a magnetic field. Handheld microphones are usually dynamic.

dynamic beam focusing A means of modifying the focusing current applied to the electron beam of a cathode-ray tube so as to compensate for beam length differences as the beam traverses the screen, so as to have the beam always in focus at the screen surface regardless of distance changes.

Dynamic Hypertext Markup Language (DHTML) DHTML uses scripting languages to create its dynamic effects. HTML leaves a Web page static. DHTML takes static HTML and a scripting language such as JavaScript, combines the two, and then displays a dynamic Web page allowing interactivity with a viewer.

dynamic random access memory (DRAM) Integrated circuit memory that uses the charge in a capacitor as the memory storage medium. This simplifies the memory elements so that high storage density at low cost can be achieved. However, since the charge on the capacitor slowly leaks off, it must be refreshed periodically in order to preserve the stored information.

dynamic range 1. The ratio of the maximum level of a signal to the minimum level. 2. The dynamic range that an electronic circuit is capable of handling. 3. The ratio between the maximum and minimum intensities that can be displayed on a cathode ray tube. 4. The ability of a system or object to exist or generate in different states. It is a measurement of how much a system can handle changes in the amount and extent of data input or output.

dynamics Changes that spread across a sequence of pictures, such as changes of position, size, lighting, and material properties.

DynaWave Designed by Mentemagica, the first true dynamic liquid simulation plug-in available for *trueSpace*.

***DynaWave*, Animation tab** See *Animation tab*.

***DynaWave*, Effectors tab** See *Effectors tab*.

E

ear, human The vertical placement of the ear lies between the eyebrow and the base of the nose. The horizontal placement of the ear is roughly in the middle of the head. Actually, the curved edge of the tragus is lined up with the vertical centerline of the head. One common mistake made in 3D heads is to place the ear along a vertical line on the head. In reality, the rear is rotated back 15 degrees. The ear's angle is usually in alignment with the angle of the lower jaw.

ear target morph A Target Morph in *Poser* that pulls the ears outward and upward. The results range from Spock ears to "velociraptor" head wings.

EBCDIC See *extended binary coded decimal interchange code.*

ECC See *error correction code.*

echo The return of a command to the user by video or audio for the purpose of informing the user that the computer received and is responding to the command.

Echo Time A control in *Universe* that uses the Echo Time setting to offset several copies of an image, effectively stretching it out behind an animated object when the echo time is negative, and moving it in front of the animated object when the value is positive.

EDAC See *error detection and correction.*

edge The curve that marks the intersection of two surface primitives or that marks where a surface primitive ends.

edge choice functions Functions that are used to determine the least significant edge in a progressive mesh so as to collapse that edge. Generally, once there is an edge choice system in place that gives fairly acceptable results, there is little to be gained in trying complex evaluation functions.

edge coherence The fact that many edges that are intersected by a scan line are also intersected by the next scan line. This provides the basis for various techniques that reduce scanning computations by using existing information.

edge collapse A technique used to simplify a progressive mesh. The basic principle can be simply described as taking a mesh, repeatedly deciding which is its least significant edge, and removing this edge by making the two vertex positions at its ends equal. This edge collapse operation typically makes two triangles sharing the edge redundant. Detail is put back into the mesh by reversing these collapses through vertex splits.

edge density A rendering feature that controls the density or opacity of an object's outer or inner regions.

edge detector A first derivative filter used to sharpen digitized images.

edge enhancement The changing of the intensity or color of the edge of an object to make it stand out in an image.

edge merging The process of filling in the gaps caused by *cracking*, resulting in an image without objectionable gaps.

edge roll A blended edge surface that simulates rolling or bending the edges on a surface. This is very common when dealing with simulating sheet metal surfaces. In real life, a metal break would be used to roll the edges. In computer graphics, rolled edges add a significant amount of realism to the model. The decision whether or not to stitch the edge roll surface with base surface depends on texture mapping and material applications considerations.

edges, difficult Banning some special case edges simplifies the algorithm used in progressive meshing. These cases stem from triangles sharing the same point in 3D space, but not sharing some other vertex data, such as vertex normals, texture type, or texture coordinates. It is an extra complication to have triangles pointing to shared texture coordinates and shared vertex positions. To avoid this, and to be friendlier toward current graphics hardware, vertices can contain all texture coordinates, normal and position information. This way, the mesh will contain multiple vertices in the same position but with different material information.

Edge Snapping A tool in *Universe* that is used for attaching lines tangent to existing parts of an object. Edge Snapping is a tool for modeling objects that have been designed at an angle. Note that similar functions can be accomplished in other 3D applications, although tool names may differ.

edges, rounded All edges have some depth to them; they have some degree of curvature no matter how small. For this reason, "imperfect" rounded edges can make a big difference between realistic models and ones that look computer-generated. Even a tiny amount of curvature on an edge will add subtle highlights and other visual clues that give it a "real-world" look.

edge table A table that contains the set of edges that a scan line intersects and the intersection points.

EDIF See *electronic data interchange format*.

editable PostScript PostScript language commands translated into a text file that can be edited without reference to the software which originally generated the PostScript file.

Edit Cage tool A tool in *Universe* that is used to edit the control vertices of a NURBS curve.

Edit Decision List (EDL) A list of all the edits in a project, identified by a chronological event number, source name, source in-point, source out-point, master in-point, and master-out point.

EditDV software A Macintosh or Windows standalone editing package for DV-based projects.

editing, animation workflow Most TV programs or movies usually entail a large amount of cuts from one camera angle to another. Rapid and numerous cuts are the norm in the cinematographic experience. The process of a final animation project almost always includes serious editing time in a nonlinear digital video editor (NLDV).

editing, close-up See *close-up*.

editing, long shot See *long shot*.

editing, medium shot See *medium shot*.

editing menu A menu used in controlling editing options in all 2D and 3D applications.

editing, NLDV See *non-linear digital video*.

editing tool A tool that writes and manages text files in a game program. It is usually known as a *game editor*. Such a tool doesn't change the data-driven methodology; it merely makes it more robust and efficient.

edit lights A dialog box in *Bryce* that allows the user to edit the characteristics of lights and light intensity. Other 3D applications also allow this action, although the name of the command may differ.

Edit Menu 1. A menu of options present in all 3D and 2D applications. 2. A menu in *Bryce* that allows the user to change the characteristics of a scene. Remember that copying and pasting materials can create scenes with cohesive elements much faster. It is possible to load in a few terrains, followed by a number of rocks and a ground plane, and assign the same material to each element in this fashion. 3. A menu in *Universe* used for changing the characteristics of objects.

Edit Sky&Fog A command in the Atmospheric Effects section of *Bryce*. Edit Sky&Fog brings up a three-tabbed Environmental Attributes dialog. The tabs are named Sun & Moon, Cloud Cover, and Atmosphere.

EDL See *Edit Decision List*.

edutainment games Games whose purpose is both to educate and to entertain, for example, *Where in the World is Carmen Sandiego* and *Jeopardy*.

EEPROM See *electrically erasable programmable read-only memory*.

effectors 1. A powerful inverse kinematics technique. Effectors are often either very small bones at the end of a chain or null objects that have no geometry at all. These effectors can be easily moved as the childmost object, and the parent objects will move to match. 2. In *Universe*, a form of null parent. A null parent is simply a set of X, Y, and Z coordinates that has no geometry associated with it. When it comes time to render a scene, nulls do not appear in the final image. Applications such as *Universe* let the user define the way that a null or Effector appears on screen, displaying the Effector as a cube, cross, or joint. Nulls or Effectors are most commonly used in applications that support Inverse Kinematics.

Effectors tab A tab in the *DynaWave* plug-in for *trueSpace* that provides a list of all object and wind effectors that are present in the scene. It also shows which objects the effectors are linked to, if any, by displaying the object name with the checkbox unchecked, as the object cannot actually act as an effector.

effects Additions to improve a video. They include transition effects to create a bridge from one shot to another, image enhancement effects to improve poorly shot video, motion effects to freeze, slow down, or speed up a shot, compositing effects for titling, collage, etc., and 3D effects to move a video layer in true 3D space.

effects lighting Effects lighting is important for directing and moving the viewer's eye by calling attention to certain areas of the scene. A soft-edged spotlight on a single object with low ambient-light settings, for example, isolates that object and directs the viewer's attention to it. One can control the viewer's eye this way and lead him around the scene. Effects lighting also encompasses a variety of special effects that can be added to a scene, from light passing through a stained glass window to simulated neon glows, laser effects and explosions.

Effects Rollup A menu in the *Primal Particles* plug-in for *trueSpace* that lets the user define the particle rotation, gravitation/wind, and the initial/final size (the expansion settings) of the particles using a percentage from 100% to 1000%.

EGA See *Enhanced Graphics Adapter*.

egg crate A sectioned metal frame that attaches to soft light sources to make them more directional.

E$_i$ (incident irradiance) The flux density of the light reflected from an object.

EIASTree, Tree Storm Two versions of *Tree Pro* made by Onyx to be used with Electric Image *Universe*. *EIASTree* is a plug-in that lets the user create trees directly in *Universe*. This saves the trouble of going to a separate application to create trees, making it simple to adjust the parametric values of trees without having to re-export and import tree models into Universe. *Tree Storm* is a Universe plug-in that creates blowing, waving trees. With full control over wind speed and gustiness, *Tree Storm* is a tool for creating realistic tree animations in all sorts of weather conditions. *TreePro* and *Tree Storm* also address other 3D applications.

EIDE A type of hard drive interface. Not as fast as SCSI, but fast enough for DV.

eigenvalue If **v** is an eigenvector and **T** the associated transformation, then if **T(v) = lv**, l is known as the *eigenvalue*. Also known as *characteristic value*.

eigenvector The *eigenvector* of a transformation **T** is a vector **v**, where **T(v)** is a scalar multiple of **v**. Also known as the *characteristic vector*.

EIS See *electronic image stabilization*.

EISA slots A type of expansion slot used in Windows-based computers.

elasticity The ability of a material to stretch and deform without permanent damage.

Elastic Reality The first truly professional level 2D morphic application.

EL display See *electroluminescent display*.

electret condensor An inexpensive, lower-quality version of the condensor microphone.

electrically erasable programmable read-only memory (EEPROM) A memory chip that is designed so that it can be programmed with data which remain until erased, regardless of whether the chip is powered.

Electric Image *Universe* See *Universe*.

electroforming holograms Electroforming is used to produce a copy, an exact negative, of the master hologram. This copy is called a shim. Electroforming involves the electro-deposition of a metal onto a model, capable of conducting electrical current.

Electro-Glow See *3D Energy*.

electroluminescent (EL) display A display consisting of a grid-like structure which contains a layer of electroluminescent material between two panels. When a voltage is placed on one horizontal and one vertical grid line, the point at the line intersection glows.

electromagnetic deflection A method of positioning the beam of a cathode-ray tube by using the magnetic field produced by orthogonal coils of wire (the deflection yoke) positioned around the neck of the cathode-ray tube.

electromagnetic energy Energy of various frequencies that is radiated through the universe in accordance with physical laws. Energy having wavelengths of 400 to 700 nm. can be perceived by the human eye as light.

electromagnetic spectrum The wide range of radiation that extends from the short gamma and x-rays to the long wavelength radio waves. It also includes the visible part which we perceive as light and color.

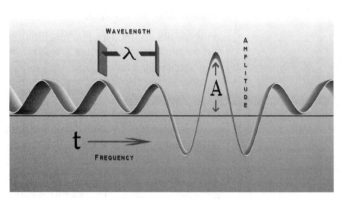

electromagnetic spectrum.

electron gun The device in a cathode-ray tube which generates a stream of electrons that impinges upon and thereby activates the phosphors that make up the screen, thus causing them to emit light.

electronically programmable logic device (EPLG) A memory chip in which the

memory cells, when programmed electronically, hold the data continuously, regardless of whether the device is powered, until the data are erased by exposure to intense ultraviolet light through a window on top of the chip package.

electronic data interchange format (EDIF) A standard format for exchanging CADDS data defined in *Electronic Design Interchange Format.*

electronic forms Graphics that are merged with data to form a single display.

electronic image stabilization (EIS) Special circuitry in a camera that attempts to compensate for shaking and vibrating by electronically shifting the image to compensate for camera movement. Electronic image stabilization frequently results in a slightly blurred image.

electronic publishing The process of producing and providing documents in a digital form.

electronic zoom Electronic controls that are used to zoom the lens in and out. These are the only zoom controls found on most prosumer camcorders.

electrophoretic display A display that consists of positively charged colored particles that are suspended in a solution of a contrasting color and sealed between closely-spaced parallel plates.

electrophotographic printing A printing technology in which light projected on an electrically-charged drum removes the charge from selected areas of the drum. Toner is applied to the drum, where it sticks only to the non-charged portions. Paper is then pressed against the drum, causing the toner to transfer to the paper. The paper is then heated to permanently set the toner. Used in copying machines and laser printers.

element, structure network An element in the PHIGS graphics system is a primitive, appearance attribute, transformation matrix, or invocation of a subordinate structure. A *structure* is a sequence of elements.

Elite A complex computer game developed by David Braben and Ian Bell in 1980. It has been ported to many home computer formats and is still widely played. Although designed for limited computer resources, it still boasts an impressive depth of play.

ellipse An oval two-dimensional figure defined by the equation:

$$\frac{x^2}{R_x^2} + \frac{y^2}{R_y^2} = 1.$$

ellipse.

ellipsoid An egg-shaped solid defined by the equation:

$$\frac{x^2}{a^2} + \frac{y^2}{b^2} + \frac{z^2}{c^2} = 1.$$

elliptical torus The solid generated by sweeping an ellipse about a given axis.

elliptical weighted-average filter An algorithm for pattern mapping onto polygons which makes use of both the Feibush-Levoy-Cook technique (for accuracy) and the MIP (*multum in parvo*—many things in a small place) technique (for efficiency).

em In typography, a square space that is a space having the same width as the height of the type font. In traditional typefaces, this is the width of a capital *M*, but this is not necessarily true for all modern typefaces.

embedding See *layering*.

embedding plane The plane containing a polygon that one wishes to test for intersection by a ray.

emboss To raise in relief from a surface.

embossed hologram A white-light transmission hologram that has been backed with a mirror (metalized mylar), so that it appears similar to a reflection hologram. The Polaroid *Mirage* film is an embossed hologram. It is easy to see in most light. Embossed holograms are geared to low-cost mass production. Direct mail pieces, catalogs, brochures and packaging, as well as security and anti-counterfeiting applications, have all used this format.

embossing A printing technique in which text is raised above the surface of the paper.

emission styles See *Particlz*.

emittance Pertaining to light emitted by a surface.

empty tags Empty tags in HTML do not require a closing tag. An empty tag executes an HTML command that embeds an element all on its own. For instance, the <HR> tag embeds a horizontal rule on the Web page. Once the user types the tag to execute a specific HTML command, the browser will read the command and execute it. The three most common empty tags that are used extensively are: <HR> (Horizontal Rule),
 (Line Break), and <P> (Paragraph). <HR> executes a line across the page. This is common when creating a break between text and separate sections.
 inserts a line break in a specific place. This is commonly used when writing paragraphs. <P> inserts a paragraph. It is also used as a container. The <P> tag is better used as a container tag (<P></P>) because it makes it easier to identify where the tag begins and ends. Using the paragraph tag as a container is considered more proper than using it as an empty tag.

emulsion A light-sensitive photographic coating over film or paper. Most emulsions consist of light-sensitive silver salts suspended in gelatin.

en In typography, a space that is half the width of an *em*. In traditional typefaces, this is the width of a capital *N*, but this is not necessarily true for all modern typefaces.

Enable commands Commands in *Universe* that permit the user to perform the following: "Enable Animation" creates an animation sequence; "Enable Illumination" controls the illumination from a light source; "Enable Limits" activates preset rotation limits; and "Enable Reverse Movement" gives the user the ability to go backwards. With Enable Reverse Movement turned off, only forward movement is possible.

encapsulated PostScript (EPS) A file that includes the complete description of graphics and text in the PostScript language. Such a file contains all of the information that is needed for a PostScript printer to print the graphics and text data.

encapsulated PostScript image A PostScript language file that contains, in self-standing form, all of the information needed to produce an image. Such images are compatible with almost any hardware or software capable of understanding the PostScript language.

enclosure A surface that surrounds another surface.

encoder 1. An electronic device that takes separate red, green, and blue signals produced by a color television camera and combines them into a composite video signal for television transmission. 2. A software package that converts statements in a computer language into assembly language commands that can be processed by hardware. 3. A device for compressing data.

encryption The coding of data so that it cannot be read by a casual browser. Most encryption schemes assume that a trusted sender and a trusted recipient want to communicate over a channel that is not secure.

ENCTYPE An attribute of the FORM tag in HTML. The ENCTYPE attribute selects the data format. There are three choices: application/x-www-form-urlencoded; multipart/formdata; and text/plain. application/x-www-form-urlencoded, the default, results in a conversion of spaces to the "+" sign and non-alphanumeric characters to their encoded equivalent "%" followed by a hexadecimal code. While this type of string is fairly easy to decode, it's tough to read. multipart/formdata is supported by Netscape and should be used when the form is set to accept. text/plain sends the form as plain text, using carriage returns rather than "&" to separate different fields.

end of file (EOF) A special character that indicates the end of a file.

energy distribution See *spectral energy distribution*.

engine, physics A real-time physics engine is central to creating a 3D gaming environment where the player can easily suspend his disbelief. Instead of just realistic pictures, the physics engine provides realistic interactions between objects in the pictures. These interactions provide the player with a basis for reality. In other words, the player can better understand and navigate in a world where things act as they do in real life. The first, and arguably most important step in setting up a real-time physics simulation is having accurate collision detection; once collisions are detected, the simulation can react accordingly.

engine, scripting A means of supporting communication in game programs. Scripting engines must be able to interface with the game's functionality in a type-safe, efficient, and convenient way.

Enhanced Graphics Adapter (EGA) A display interface for PCs, developed by IBM. The EGA is capable of displaying 16 colors at a resolution of 640 by 350 pixels.

environment The volume of space enclosing a scene that is to be ray traced and the collection of graphics objects contained therein.

environmental bound A simple convex volume that surrounds the ray tracing environment. When a ray passes through the *environmental bound* it can never again enter the environment, so that further intersection testing is unnecessary.

environment channel This channel allows creation of a faux reflection. It actually paints an environment (defined by the map the user gives it) on the face of the texture as if the object were actually sitting in the environment depicted in the map.

environment lighting Environment lighting is important for setting the general mood of a scene and, properly used, will help stimulate specific emotions in the viewer. For example, soft, warm environment lighting can elicit a sense of calm, comfort, and serenity. Cool, harsh lighting, on the other hand, will elicit a sense of apprehension, sterility, and unease. The user can even mix the two to create a feeling of confusion and anxiety. This most basic form of lighting will have a significant effect on a scene.

environment map An image, often computed as a projection on a cube, used to reduce computation in rendering of reflecting surfaces. It is produced by first computing each point of an image as a function of the direction from the center point of the object and then referencing the image to the directions of reflected rays from the surface of the object.

environment saucers A method used to create a convincing background image. An environmental sphere is scaled along its Y axis so that it becomes more saucer shaped than spherical. By placing a 2D square or rectangle in the center of the saucer, a ground plane can be created.

EOF See *end of file.*

eot format A special file format for storing fonts within an HTML program. See *downloads, fonts.*

EPLG See *electronically programmable logic device.*

EPS See *encapsulated PostScript.*

EPS Invigorator A program, developed by ZaxWerks, that can be used for creating title sequences and simple 3D effects. A full 3D extrusion and rendering tool, *EPS Invigorator* puts a tremendous amount of 3D power directly into *After Effects*. A version of *Invigorator* is also distributed as a plug-in for *Universe.*

EQ See *equalization.*

equalization (EQ) The process of adjusting the volume of individual frequency ranges within a sound. Equalization can be used to correct problems in a sound, or to "sweeten" or enhance the sound to bring out particular qualities.

equalizer A device that enables the user to control the loudness of different parts of the sound spectrum.

equalizing pulses Pulses that are a part of the vertical retrace portion of a television signal. They are used with the signal for an interlaced display to enable odd frames to start at the beginning of a horizontal scan line and even frames to start at the midpoint of a horizontal scan line.

equicontinuous A family $F = \{f_\alpha\}$ of continuous functions is *equicontinuous* if, for any $\xi > 0$, there is $\delta = \delta(\xi, z)$, such that $|f_\alpha - f(_\alpha(\omega)$, when $|z - \omega| < \delta$.

equipollent forces Two or more forces that result in the same net force and torque.

equipotential A closed curve representing points of equal potential.

Erase A function of *trueSpace* that gives the user the capability to weld and/or delete selected vertices. Erase can be found in the Point-editing tools. This is especially useful when making minute adjustments at the point level, and can aid in keeping the polygon count low.

Eraser tool 1. A tool in 2D graphics applications that allows the user to erase portions of an image. It is useful for correcting mistakes. It is also a good way to change a color by painting over the original color. 2. An editing tool in the *Game Creation System* that enables the user to remove objects.

ergonomics The science of designing and arranging things with regard to the characteristics of people so that people and things will interact most effectively and safely. Also known as *human engineering.*

erosion, terrain The wearing down (and thus smoothing) of terrain by the actions of wind, rain, snow, and running water. This makes terrain-generation techniques, such as fractal fault formation, produce unrealistic terrain models because of the sharp edges produced. To simulate realistically the results of erosion, pass the above terrain simulation through a low-pass filter.

error correction code (ECC) A coding technique that permits recovering a block (2048 bytes) of data read incorrectly from a CD-ROM.

error detection and correction (EDAC) A technique for assuring that data are correctly written to a storage device. It requires writing a prearranged extra block of data after each block of regular data. The prearranged block is then read. If it is correct, the regular data block is also assumed to be correct. If not, an error is assumed and the regular data block and prearranged block are rewritten.

error diffusion dithering A dithering technique in which the error in approximating a given pixel is used to bias the values of nearby pixels so as to balance out the error. Also known as *error propagation dithering*.

error measure The measure of the distance of the pixels that make up a displayed line or curve from the true position of the line or curve.

error rate The number of user errors per interaction with the system.

establishing shots Initial shots that announce that a new scene is about to start, help orient the audience, and serve to set the location.

Euclidean Geometry model A model for real space. The Euclidean geometry model depicts x as horizontal, y as vertical, and z as depth. These values can be positive or negative, depending on their relative position to the center of the digital universe where all values of x, y, and z are 0.

Euler angles The angles of rotation of a rigid body around the principal axes of the coordinate system. Orientation in three-dimensional space can be represented with three Euler angles: yaw, pitch, and roll (also known as azimuth, elevation, and roll). Yaw, pitch, and roll account for the rotation in the Y-axis, X-axis, and Z-axis, respectively.

Euler angles, gimbal lock with With a Euler three-angle (roll, pitch, yaw) system, there are always certain orientations in which there is no simple change to the three values to represent a simple local rotation. It is possible to see this rotation "pitched up" 90 degrees when one is trying to specify a local yaw left or right. *Quaternions*, although more complex, do not suffer from gimbal lock and are considered a better solution in many cases.

Euler operators A set of operators that may be used to operate on objects that satisfy *Euler's formula* to transform the objects into new objects that also satisfy the formula by adding or removing vertices, edges, or faces.

Euler method A technique of integration used in solving differential equations. The *explicit Euler method* is easy to implement but suffers from instability in which errors build exponentially and the solution quickly becomes infinite. The *implicit Euler method* is an efficient and highly-stable integrator.

Euler's formula A formula that expresses the invariant relationship between the number of vertices, edges, and faces of a simple polyhedron. This formula is:

$$V - E + F = 2$$

where V is the number of vertices, E is the number of edges, and F is the number of faces.

even-odd rule If a line which is drawn from some specified point to a point distant from a polygon intersects the edges of the polygon an odd number of times, the specified point is within the polygon; if it intersects the edges of the polygon an even number of times, the specified point is outside the polygon. This rule is useful in determining which points should be used to fill a polygon with color.

event The activation of a device by the user, causing the computer to take certain specified actions.

event listener A procedure in Java that waits for some specific action by the user then initiates the performance of some computer actions in response.

event routing dispatcher A routine that accepts events and routes them to the appropriate event-handling routines. Also known as a *notifier*.

Exabyte A digital, optical tape-based storage system, used for backing up projects with large amounts of data. Exabyte tapes typically hold many gigabytes per tape.

Executive Producer, The A program for logging data.

excitation purity, color The saturation of the color.

exhaustive testing The testing of a ray for intersection with every graphics object in a scene. Also known as *exhaustive ray tracing*.

expanded form In animation, a way of storing objects in which the entire collection of objects is stored, along with their properties, and all that is required is to read them into memory at the appropriate time.

expert system A computer program that tailors its menus to fit the needs of a new user by changing in accordance with the commands that the user most often selects.

explicit functions Functions that are expressed directly in terms of the defined variables of a system, without the need of intermediate parameters.

explicit surface A surface on which each point is defined by evaluation of a set of parametric equations.

exploding head A special effect in which a person's head is shown shattering into a million pieces after an over-strenuous sneeze.

exploding head.

exploding pillar setup An extension of the *cracking pillar* setup to cause the pillar to appear to explode. This is accomplished in *trueSpace* by using the *Primal Particles* plug-in.

explosions Effects in digital image creation. The following effects are available in most 3D packages:

Explode/shatter is essentially an animation function that takes the polygons of a shape, splits them apart into their own constituent shapes, and then flings them about (explode) or collapses them (shatter). The specifics vary from program to program, but low poly-count objects may render quickly and explode quickly, but the resultant explosion often looks like numerous triangles floating around aimlessly. Higher poly-counts mean heavier models and longer rendering times, but they produce finer clusters of polygons and thus more effective explosions. Even with a high poly-count, it is often easy to see the telltale square or triangular segments of the source shape. To hide this, try add-ing a texture to the object that glows as it explodes. The resultant glow of the shards can hide the shape of the shards.

Morphing is the smooth transition between shapes. There are many different reincarnations of this effect, from shatter morphs to endomorphs (used heavily in facial animation). In special effects, this usually refers to the unworldly changing of recognized shapes to unforeseen forms. Not all applications have this restriction, but many 3D applications morph best between NURBS, and more specifically, morph most effectively between shapes with the same number of control points or rendered polygons. If possible, create all morph targets by altering copies of the original shape.

Particle emitters are construction shapes that spew forth objects according to the settings the user defines. Often, particle emitters allow for a variety of speeds and sizes of the particles emitted. Some programs (like *Cinema4D XL*) allow the user to place any desired shape as the particle to be emitted. One obvious use of particle emitters is water fountains; however, they can also work very well for the creation of a variety of special effects, from smoke to the spurting of blood. One post-production application used to generate explosions and other pyrotechnic effects is *Illusion* from Impulse, Inc.

explosions F/X A simulated explosion created in *trueSpace* using the *Primal Particles* plug-in. The Decompose feature is used to explode a dense, triangulated sphere in all directions to simulate a huge explosion of a gas tanker or possibly a meteor striking the earth. The *wfmm glow* and *wfmm motrails* shaders are used to obtain the proper coloring (*see Figure next page*).

exportation layer An exportation layer in *form•Z* equals an object within the animation environment. This system allows the user to have an object with any amount of geometric surface detail, and

explosions.

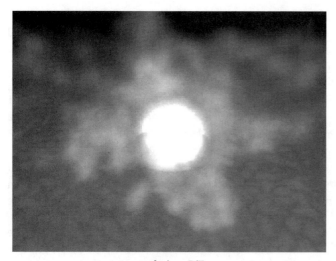

explosions F/X.

provides a very tight and straightforward way of controlling how geometry is exported.

export geometry In *form•Z*, this is the geometry, completed and arranged, ready to be exported to the animation application. The arrangement of the export geometry depends on the target animation package, intended type of animation, and texture-mapping strategy.

export transformation In *form•Z*, export transformation is used to modify the local space of the exported geometry in order to make it more compatible with the target animation package or with a preexisting project within that package. Export transformation is especially useful when importing geometry into an existing project with models from other modelers.

exposure The process of allowing light to enter the camera, exposing the film, which results in a recorded image.

extended binary coded decimal interchange code (EBCDIC) An 8-bit code used for alphanumerics and characters. Developed by IBM for use in large mainframe computers.

Extended Graphics Adapter (XGA) An IBM standard graphics adapter that supports resolutions of up to 1024 pixels by 768 pixels.

extended light source A source of illumination in the description of a scene to be rendered as a graphics image, in which the light is emitted from a finite surface rather than from a point.

extensibility The capability in a computer language to define new terms as combinations of existing terms.

Extensible Hypertext Markup Language See *XHTML*.

Extensis A developer of multiple effects plug-ins for *Photoshop, Illustrator,* and *Quark*.

extent The minimum and maximum values of a graphics object in each of the coordinate directions.

extent test A test of whether a ray intersects an extent. If it does, further testing is necessary to determine whether the ray intersects the graphics objects within the extent; if it does not, there is no intersection and no further testing is necessary.

external form In *Poser*, any 3D element created in any non-*Poser* application. Since *Poser* can import *3D Studio, Wave-*

front, *DXF*, *QuickDraw 3D*, and *Carrara* formatted objects, one can use almost any 3D application to construct *Poser* figure elements and/or Props. All 3D applications save out data in one or more of the formats that *Poser* can import.

external style sheets External style sheets are ideal for giving Web pages (within a Web site) a common look. Instead of applying style sheets or other HTML formatting to individual pages, a designer can set each of the Web pages to consult an external source. The style sheet code is actually written in a separate document, saved as text with the .css extension and then linked within the <HEAD> commands using the <LINK> tag of the respective HTML documents. When all of the documents are referenced to the external style sheet, the designer can then make changes to the styles of all of the Web site pages in one location—the external style sheet.

extinction coefficient A measure of absorption of light passing through a translucent medium.

extrapolation A technique for creating objects by exaggeration of those features that set two objects apart and using these differences to create a new object.

Extra Primitives tSX A plug-in for *true-Space* by Black Knight Productions. This plug-in offers an extended set of new primitives and the ability to add primitives of custom design. The primitives include hemisphere, rounded cylinder, pyramid, tube, and diamond. The plug-in is in tabbed form with a tab for each category of primitive such as cubical, spherical, etc.

extrude A modeling feature that allows the user to create a 3D object out of a 2D shape. The extrude modeling feature is most like a real-world "pasta machine," pushing a 2D shape along a straight line.

extrude on path A modeling feature that lets the user create a 3D object out of a 2D shape by pushing a 2D shape along a line, path, or curve.

extrusions Pulling a two-dimensional shape into a third dimension. One can also add a bevel to extrusions to give them a different sense of depth. The extrusion profile refers to the path the source two-dimensional shape takes as it extends into three-dimensional space. Therefore, if the extrusion profile is straight, the shape goes straight back; if it is curved, then the object will be beveled. Different applications have different ways of referring to these bevels.

extrusion texture A texture that is generated by a texture function that is constant along certain parallel lines in the volume being textured.

eyeball topographer Developed for use in laser-assisted keratectomy. A scanning resolution set of projected lines provides near-real-time depth data on the surface of the eyeball.

Eyebrow dials Settings in *Poser* that allow control of the eyebrows in a face. There are three Eyebrow settings types for the Left and Right brows separately. They are Left/Right Brow Down, Left/Right Brow Up, and Left/Right Worry. The dials can be turned in both negative and positive directions, and the settings can be applied to each brow separately.

Eyecandy A plug-in, by AlienSkin Software, that provides a number of improvements over *After Effects'* built-in filters, including a Gaussian Blur filter that can extend beyond the boundaries of a layer, and an HSB Noise filter. *Eye-candy* also provides filters for beveling, chiseling, and carving shapes out of a layer, as well as a filter for making a layer glow.

eye-hand coordination The ability of the user to observe a cursor location with the eye and use the hand to move a mouse or similar device until the cursor reaches the position where he wants it.

eye-level view The viewing angle from the perspective of a human observer. This is the way we are used to seeing things and is probably the most common way of presenting a scene, due to its familiarity.

eye light An effect light that enhances the actor's eyes and creates "eye sparkle." The eye lights are used to open up the subject's eyes and make them come alive by creating a visible specular.

eye muscles, corrugator The *corrugator*, or frown muscle, compresses the skin between the eyebrows, creating a frown. It is located directly between the eyes. The corrugator muscle is used to create expressions such as intense concentration and disgust. In these expressions the

Intense Concentration   **Disgust**

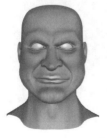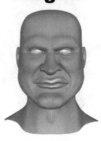

eye muscles, corrugator.

corrugator muscle is used to compress the skin between the eyebrows, making the character appear angered.

eye muscles, orbicularis oculi The *orbicularis oculi*, or squinting muscle, is used to close the eyes and make the character wink or squint. Common expressions using the orbicularis oculi muscle would be of sleep or of being drowsy/tired. In these expressions, the orbicularis oculi

Asleep   **Tired**

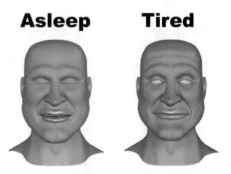

eye muscles, orbiscularis oculi.

muscle is used to compress the eyelids and even close them. This is probably the most relevant muscle in facial animation. It doesn't play a major role in expressions, but it does add that hint of realism by making the character blink occasionally.

eye point The viewpoint. Also known as the *eyepoint*.

eye ray A ray that begins at the eye point and passes through the display screen.

eye-readable Images recorded on microfilm that can be read without magnification. These are usually in the form of headings that enable the user to determine whether he or she has the right microfilm reel before inserting it into the microfilm reader.

Eyes Parameters in *Poser* that permit control of the shape, position, and size of eyes in a face.

eyes, human The eye socket, or ocular cavity, extends halfway down the length of the nose, terminating at the top of the cheekbone (zygomatic bone). The eye itself is roughly one and a quarter inches in diameter and nearly perfectly round, with the exception of the conjunctiva and cornea, which form the bulge in front of the iris. The shape of the eye mass is very important since it's the center of focus when viewing the face. Poorly-modeled eyes are a common problem found in 3D human head models. They suffer from many problems, such as exposed upper eyelids. It is nearly impossible to have clearly visible eyelids on a human head because the supraorbital margin hangs over the upper eye. The proper formation of the upper eyelid has the tissue under the supraorbital margin covering the upper eyelid. Another commonly overlooked aspect of the eye is the shape of the eye opening. Most 3D models tend to have an oval eye opening, which is close, but there are subtle nuances in the shape of the eyelids that make the eye more detailed and interesting. The eye opening is not a symmetrical oval, but rather oblique.

The high point of the upper eyelid is close to the inside of the eye while the low point of the lower eyelid is close to the outside of the eye. The iris is the major feature of the eye and its placement is essential for proper facial expression. It appears to hang from the upper eyelid, hovering just above the lower eyelid, allowing a sliver of the eye white to be visible between the bottom of the iris and the lower eyelid. The last detail of the eye is the size of the iris. This is an important measurement since a poorly-sized iris will make the eye appear unnatural. The pupil is roughly one-half the width of the eye opening. In the scope of head modeling one should focus the majority of time on the eyes, because they will be the most critically judged by the viewer.

Eye Stretch Target Morph A target morph for *Poser* that stretches the eyes very subtly, addressing just a few poly-

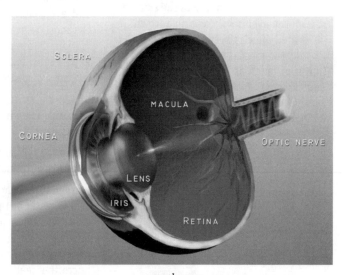

eyes, human.

gons. The results can create radical deformations.

eye tracker A device that can be attached to the head to track the direction in which the eye is pointing, thereby allowing the user to move the cursor around the screen by movements of the eye alone.

Eye Zoom A plug-in for *trueSpace* that allows the user to zoom in and out using a selection area, instead of scrolling with a mouse.

F

F_1 See *Fresnel term*.

façade pattern This pattern is generally used as a "manager class." This is a class that provides a single interface to a large collection of related classes, usually some sort of subsystem. These classes are often designed as singletons because it usually makes sense to have only one manager object per type of subsystem. For example, only a single object is needed to manage access to audio or graphical user interface subsystems. A façade or manager is necessary in order to keep interdependencies between classes (known as *coupling*) to a minimum. The maximum number of interdependencies between classes can be described as $(n - 1)^2$, where n is the number of classes in a project.

face A polygon that is part of a three-dimensional graphics object.

face boundary The edge of a face polygon that is shared with an edge of another face polygon.

face curve The intersection of an implicit surface with a proximate interval's face.

face normal A vector that is perpendicular to the surface of a face. It usually is normalized (the vector is set to have a length of 1).

Face Pull Target Morph A process available in *Poser*. This target morph pushes the face backward or pulls it forward, for interesting animation keyframes or character development.

Faces A police identification software application for creating faces. It contains a library of thousands of face parts, all based upon photographic data. Using the photographic facial elements in the *Faces* libraries, the user can create a whole population of diverse faces and ethnic types.

faces, encoding Determining points based on a set of faces, which connect lines, which in turn allow a rendering of a photograph of the face in line fashion. Encoding these lines merely requires storing pairs of x,y coordinates that determine the start and end points of the lines that make up the face. This technique has been used by a variety of researchers in averaging together the encoded faces of a large population of female faces in order to arrive at the perfectly average face. The technique can be used for a variety of objects, from teapots to bananas, and provides us with a second way to encode generic objects. Another approach that is used by artificial intelligence experts is to encode the object as a series of cells in two dimensions, which depict the shadow of the object. This is specifically tailored to applications where the object is viewed in two dimensions.

FaceShifter An extension from Autonomous Effects Inc. that morphs between a set of templates using sliders on a control panel to select the desired proportion of each template shape. It can animate separate sections of the same mesh independently of each other. To use *FaceShifter*, build shapes from the initial reference shape, assemble all the shapes in a common group, and decorate them with various controls.

faces, polygon modeling of The modeling of a face as a connected network of polygons whose positions are determined by muscular action.

facet One of a number of flat surfaces that together make up a solid object.

faceting The irregular appearance of a three-dimensional object when it actually has a smooth surface, but for simplicity is represented by a number of facets.

facial characteristics, animating Faces can be animated in *Poser* by manipulating some of the facial features. There are two main approaches to animating faces. One is to animate the distortions of the face caused by altering tapers and sizes. The second is to animate the mouth, eye, and eyebrow features. A third option, morphing, can also be used. Using tapers and resizing, as well as animating features (because distortions are involved) can be considered internal morphing. All of these methods can be used singularly or in combination.

facsimile (fax) A technology that converts the images and text on a paper document to digital data which it transmits to a remote device (usually via phone lines), and prints a d uplicate of the images and/or text on paper at the remote fax system.

FACT A native model file format developed by Electric Image for *Universe*. It is a Mac OS native format. This file format automatically organizes objects on a layer basis when the grouping method is set to By Layer. To use FACT files with *Cinema 4D XL* one must download the *FACT* plug-in for *Cinema* from MAXON Computer.

factorial polynomials Polynomials defined in a form that permits discrete analogs of *Taylor's formula*.

factoring of user interface commands The reduction of commands until the parameters that need to be specified by the user are minimized. For example, a *Draw_line* command might require the user to enter two parameters for starting and ending points. By factoring into three commands, *Set_beginning_point*, *Set_ending_point*, and *Draw_line*, the user would enter one parameter for the first command, one for the second and none for the third. This often simplifies the use of the system.

factory pattern A pattern that deals with organization in the creation of objects. A form of the pattern is defined as a method for allowing abstract interface classes to specify when to create concrete, derived implementation classes. This method is often required in application frameworks and other similar class hierarchies. However, game programmers often deal with a specific subset of the factory pattern—namely, the use of factory objects with enumerated object creation located in a central class, usually via a single-member function. This means that a single object is responsible for creating a wide variety of other objects, usually related by a common base class. This class often takes the form of a class with a single method that accepts some sort of class ID and returns an allocated object. The advantages of clustering object allocation into a single location are especially noteworthy for game developers. Dynamic memory allocation is expensive, so it is necessary to carefully monitor allocations. Allocating all objects in a central area makes it easier to monitor these allocations. Often, common initialization or creation methods must be called for all objects within a class hierarchy. If all object allocation is put into a central area, it becomes easy to perform any common operations (such as inserting them into a resource manager) on all objects. A factory allows extensibility by allowing new objects to be derived from the existing factory. By passing in a new class ID (which can easily be obtained from data instead of code), a developer can provide run-time extensibility of new classes without changing the existing base code. The final point stresses extensibility as a benefit of using the factory pattern. For this reason, creating simple functions or static classes should be avoided, since new classes cannot be derived from them.

fade in and fade out 1. A standard fading effect used in post-production applications. 2. Fading audio signals. 3. See *animated ambient light*.

Fade Lights with Distance An option in the Extra Features Editor of the *Game Creation System*. The Fade Lights with Distance option lets the user choose whether or not to have lighting effects diminish with distance.

fade operator An operator that causes a pixel to become more transparent while maintaining its color.

fade out A dissolve from full video to black video or from audio to silence.

Fade Start Distance An option in the Extra Features Editor of the *Game Creation System*. The user can have the walls and floors fade to black as they recede from the viewport. The walls will be shown at maximum brightness until they reach a distance from the observer equal to the Fade Start Distance. This is in regular GCS units, where one typical wall section is 400 units. Total Darkness Distance is the distance where the brightness has faded all the way to zero. No wall sections will be drawn at that point. For example, if the Fade Start Distance is set to 1,000 units, a wall will be drawn at full brightness if the player is close to the wall. As he backs away, it will stay at full brightness until he is 1,000 units away; at that point it will start to darken as the player moves even farther away.

fading A technique for simulating the appearance of atmospheric haze in images. Each pixel of the image is mixed with a color that is exponentially weighted according to the distance of the object from the observer. The color is usually white for daylight scenes and black for night scenes.

falloff The decrease in intensity of light from a spotlight as a function of the angle from the beam center. See also *attenuation of light*.

false coloring 1. The assignment of frequencies outside the visual spectrum to frequencies within the visual spectrum. 2. Assignment of colors other than the natural object colors to objects in an image. Usually accomplished through the use of a color table. 3. Producing unavailable colors by dithering of colors that are available.

false contours Changes in color intensity or hue that are caused by quantization errors, but appear to the observer to be contour lines.

false laser lights *Bryce* contains an object for laser beam creation. For example, in the Imported Objects folder of the Objects library is a screw. Its threads act to give a light object just the right touch of variance and randomness. When stretched out, the user can no longer tell what the object is, because the threads are stretched into flowing curves. A screw object can be used as the beam. The beam can be textured with the Volumetric Red Laser Beam on the Volume side of the Materials Lab. Flat, Additive Shading with a Volume Altitude Blend can be used. The sliders can be set to 100 for Diffusion and 17 for Ambient Value, a Base Density of 17, an Edge Softness of 50, a Fuzzy Factor of 142, and Quality/Speed at 5.

false spherical lights In *Bryce*, objects that can be used effectively as suns and mapped with plain color or more evocative materials for use as background planets. Used for this purpose, they are not usually transparent, but just fuzzy around the edges. If they are made transparent, they can be used as ghostly lights that can be placed anywhere in the scene.

F Animator A plug-in for *trueSpace* that allows the user to create animation using mathematical formulae and input data.

Farey tree A tree structure of numbers that includes each rational number between 0 and 1 exactly once.

fast anamorphic image scaling A technique for remapping an image by stretching, rotation, skewing, or rescaling.

fast Fourier transform An algorithm for computing the frequency components of a digitally sampled signal with the minimum amount of computation. The original algorithm for this purpose is known as the *Cooley-Tuckey algorithm*.

fast Phong A simplified technique for Phong shading that reduces the amount of computation required by evaluating the Phong shading at vertices, and then interpolating to obtain a value for a particular point on a face.

fast triple A *LightWave* modeling plug-in that transforms selected polygons into triple-sided polygons.

FAT See *file allocation table*.

fat fractal A fractal derived from the Cantor sets that has nonzero measure for certain projection directions.

Fatou set The complementary set to the *Julia set* using complex numbers.

fault line generation Fault line landscape generation works by choosing two points at random and drawing a line at a given height between them. Next, two more points are chosen, and again, a line is drawn between them. This is repeated until there are a predetermined number of lines on the screen. The next step is simply to apply a subdivision technique to smooth the differences between the points. This renders a series of "islands."

F Creator A plug-in for *trueSpace* that allows the user to create, modify, and animate objects by mathematical formula.

FDDI See *fiber distributed data interface*.

FDM See *frequency division multiplexing*.

feature extraction An optical character recognition technique in which unique features of each character are stored in a table so that the optical scanner can compare a scanned character with the stored features and thereby identify it.

Federal Communications Commission (FCC) The United States government agency responsible for establishing wireless transmission specifications, assigning frequencies for transmission, and establishing limits on spurious transmissions by electronic equipment.

feedback 1. In electronic circuits, the application of a portion of the output signal back to the input with 180 degree phase shift to improve stability and reduce distortion. 2. The application of cues in a display to indicate the actions taken by the user and that the program is responding properly to them. If the computer is taking a long time to process a command, it is important to have some means of displaying the fact that the computer is still working on the command and has not "frozen." 3. A process used in creating game objects in which the result of the previous iteration provides input to the next one. Pseudorandom-number generators are examples of feedback systems. Feedback happens only when the exact value arrived at by a portion of an algorithm is fed into the next iteration.

feedforward Whereas a *feedback* system takes the result of an algorithm and uses it to provide input to the next iteration, a *feedforward* system can insert data arrived at during the execution of an algorithm and pass it to the next stage within that algorithm. Self-seeding, pseudorandom number generators are examples of this. In these cases, they provide information for the next iteration, but some of the information arrived at during the calculation process is also fed into either the next stage or, in some cases, the next iteration. Feedforward can also have a role in passing information between two processes that are not otherwise related.

feet, for game objects If the user makes map squares smaller than some game objects, then there is a danger that objects' interactions are not detected because they are far enough apart in map squares to ever check each other—although physically they do touch. The user can solve this by giving each object "feet." As a result, objects do not sit in the map directly (unless they are small enough); instead, small "helper" objects sit in the map squares that the object touches.

Feibush-Levoy-Cook algorithm An algorithm for transforming images that is especially effective for mapping textures onto surfaces.

Feigenbaum constant A number equal to 3.678573510..., which often marks the boundaries of chaotic behavior.

Fermat primes Prime numbers found by the formula:

$$p = 2^{2^n} + 1$$

ferric chrome A layer of mixed ferric oxide and chromium dioxide particles that makes up the recording medium for a tape or disk.

ferric oxide A layer of particles that makes up the recording medium for a tape or disk.

Feshner's law The basic scientific law regarding perceived response. It states that the perceived response to a sensory stimulus is proportional to the logarithm of the intensity of the stimulus.

fiber distributed data interface (FDDI) An interface to a wide-bandwidth fiber-optic digital data network.

fiberoptic cable A cable consisting of thin strands of glass through which data are transmitted in the form of light. The bandwidth of a fiber optic cable is orders of magnitude larger than for wires or coaxial cables, thereby allowing simultaneous transmission of many more simultaneous sets of data than for a wire or coaxial cable or bundle of the same size.

Fibonacci number system A set of numbers developed from the recursion relationship:

$$F_{n+2} = F_{n+1} + F_n$$

The sequence begins 0, 1, 1, 2, 3, 5, 8, 13, 21, 34, 55....

fiche Short for *microfiche*.

field 1. In a database, a space reserved for an individual item of information, such as name, address, etc. A set of fields make up a data record. 2. The data that make up one vertical scan of a cathode-ray tube.

field dominance Hardware and software that play the field of video containing the odd-numbered scan lines first are known as field one dominant. Those that play the field of video containing the even-numbered scan lines first are known as *field two dominant*. Field one dominance is the norm.

field frequency The number of video fields that are displayed in one second.

field monitor A portable monitor that can be used to view video recording as it is being made.

field of view The number of degrees used to describe the amount of the surroundings visible from the front of a camera lens.

field of view culling A technique for culling parts of an image that are not visible. The *field of view* is the area in 3D space visible from the current point of view of the camera. This area is typically described using front and back clip planes and the viewing angle. The culling process uses the bounding sphere (in world space) of each object's mesh, and tests if it falls inside the field of view. To perform this test, transform the bounding sphere center point into view space (relative to the camera) and check the new Z value against the near and far clip planes.

field rendering The rendering on a display of the scan lines that make up only one field of an interlaced display.

field separator A code or character used to separate the fields of a record. The most common field separator is the comma. Also known as a *delimiter*.

FIELDSET tags The <FIELDSET> tag in HTML allows the designer to group together data fields that relate to each other to help organize a form. By grouping related form controls, HTML authors can divide a form into smaller, more manageable parts improving usability by confronting users with fewer form controls. The <FIELDSET> tag creates a box around a portion of a form. The content of a <FIELDSET> element must begin with a <LEGEND> tag to provide a caption for the group of controls. Consider the following example:

```
<FORM>
<FIELDSET>
```

181

```
<LEGEND>Credit Card Info</LEGEND>
<P>
<INPUT TYPE=radio NAME=card VALUE=visa> Visa
<INPUT TYPE=radio NAME=card VALUE=mc> MasterCard
<BR>
Number: <INPUT TYPE=text NAME=number>
<BR>
Expires: <INPUT TYPE=text NAME=expiry>
</P>
</FIELDSET>
</FORM>
```

fields, video Each frame of interlaced video consists of two fields: one field contains the odd-numbered scan lines and the other field contains the even-numbered scan lines. In NTSC video, each field has 262.5 horizontal lines.

FIFO See *first in, first out.*

fight choreographer A person who plans the moves of actors in a fight scene so that they will appear realistic.

Figure Circle A command in the *Poser* Display menu which toggles the reference circle on and off.

figure developers See *Poser Props Modeler's Guild* and *Zygote Media Group.*

figure ground A technique used to judge the composition of an image. The scene is rendered in silhouette so the viewer's eye is not distracted by color or content.

Figure Height A command in the *Poser* Figure menu that allows the user to select figure height. Simply select an option, and watch the figure assume that specific physique. Some options are Baby, Toddler, Child, Juvenile, Ideal Adult, Fashion Model, and Heroic Model.

figures as props In *Poser*, one can pose a figure and then use it as a prop. Typical examples are placing a figure on a pedestal to create a statue, using legs of a figure as table legs, using a hand to create a hand chair, or using arms to make a doorway.

figures, rendering The computer process of taking the three-dimensional model with its accompanying textures and lights, and turning that into a two-dimensional image composed of an array of pixel colors is called rendering. In simplest terms, to tell a computer to "render" is telling the computer to paint all the information thus far created.

file A set of related data, stored in a computer or a storage medium such as a disk or tape, and referenced by a single file name.

file allocation table (FAT) An area on a disk which shows the tracks and clusters assigned to each recorded file.

file extension The characters following the period in a file name. In MS/DOS, file names may consist of up to eight characters and a file extension of up to three additional characters.

file extensions for Web page files In order for a Web browser to recognize and correctly display an HTML document as a Web page, the appropriate file extensions must be given. Web browsers recognize the .htm or .html extensions. PCs running on Windows 3.x, only recognize three-digit extensions, so only the .htm extension may be used. Windows 95 and higher use the .html and .htm extension, and Macintosh systems use the .html extension.

file format The manner in which data are arranged within a file.

file transfer protocol (FTP) The Internet standard for transferring and uploading files. There are FTP programs that make the process of uploading files very easy and user-friendly. Later versions of Internet Explorer use FTP directly from the Web site. Some other Internet browsers do not support FTP.

file structures Organizing files is necessary when linking to other related files within a site to avoid the possibility of broken links due to a non-systematic linking system. The most common ways that Web developers organize their Web sites are *hierarchical, linear,* and *webbed*. Although all three formats are equally useful, the decision on which one to use depends on how large the Web site will be. Some Web sites are simple enough so that one file will hold everything. On the other hand, some Web sites may be so complex that the files may need to be broken down into subfolders. A hierarchical structure is organized with all the pages branching off of the main page. In other words, subpages and so forth follow multiple main pages. This is the structure most commonly used by Web developers. Linear structure organizes folders in a particular order.

fill To apply color to the interior of a closed figure in a graphics image.

fill algorithm A mathematical technique for filling a closed geometric figure with color.

fill, boundary A fill algorithm that fills regions that are boundary-defined where a *boundary-defined* region is the largest connected region of pixels whose value is not some given boundary value.

filled-in Julia set The set, J_c, of initial values z_0 for which the values of z_n in the Mandelbrot equation are bounded for a given parameter c. The Julia set proper consists of the boundary points of J_c.

filled rectangle tool See *rectangle and filled rectangle tools*.

fill, flood An algorithm that fills regions that are interior defined. An *interior-defined* region is a region where (starting with a pixel P) the value of all points is the same as that of P.

filling circle The method used for filling a circle with color. A circle is a special case of the ellipse.

filling ellipse The method used for filling an ellipse with color. The figure is scanned one horizontal line at a time. Since each line intersects the ellipse only twice, only the beginning and ending points need to be calculated for each line, after which the space between them is filled with color.

filling, pattern The process of filling a geometric figure with a pattern rather than a solid color. This is accomplished by adding an additional control to the filling algorithm that picks up the proper color to write to each pixel from a pixmap pattern.

filling polygon The procedure for filling a concave polygon is the same as that for filling a rectangle. For convex polygons, a scan line may have more than two intersections with the polygon. To properly fill the figure, each scan line must fill the sections between odd-numbered intersections and even numbered intersections, but not fill the sections between even-numbered intersections and odd-numbered intersections (*see Figure next page*).

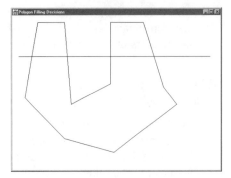

filling polygon.

filling rectangle To fill a rectangle with a solid color, one sets each pixel lying on a scan line running from the left edge of the rectangle to the right edge of the rectangle with the color. Each scan line has only two intersections with the rectangle. This is repeated for each scan line that intersects the rectangle.

fill light A second light, dimmer than the key light, which is used to fill in the strong shadows caused by the *key light*. It is not necessary to delete the shadows, but to achieve a pleasing ratio between the lights and shadows on the subject.

fill, seed A fill algorithm that starts with a pixel that is within the region. Both *boundary fill* and *flood fill* are *seed fill* algorithms.

fill, soft A fill algorithm in which the criteria for ending a region is something more subtle than detecting a change of color.

fill, tint A fill algorithm that determines the end of a region as the point at which the original color has faded to zero, rather than as the point where another color is detected.

Fill tool A tool available in *The Games Factory* used to fill an area with a solid block of color. The area to be filled should be completely enclosed. If there is a gap of even one pixel, the color will "leak" out into other areas of the frame.

FilmLogic Program to perform film matchback.

film matchback The process of generating a *cut list*. See *cut list*.

film output resolution Film output is typically measured in pixels instead of inches, with a number of dots per inch. Before making an animation to be reproduced on film, consult with the output service provider for specifics on the film resolution and, if it is animation, the frames per second. Actual resolutions vary depending on the film recorder. Typically, an output service may want images which are at least 3,000 to 4,000 pixels wide for 4 × 5 transparencies and 1,500 to 2,000 pixels wide for 35mm slides.

film plane See *focal plane*.

film recorder A device that takes the images from a cathode ray tube and records them on film.

film recordist The person responsible for transferring (or recording) video to film.

filter 1. To electronically change a signal by changing the relative amplitudes of its component frequencies. 2. To select certain specified types of data from a file.

filtering The process of removing part of the spectrum from a signal. Removing the high frequency part of the spectrum is called *low-pass filtering*. Removing the low frequency part of the spectrum is called *high-pass filtering*. Removing both ends of the spectrum is called *band-pass filtering*.

filter 1. A glass attachment that can be added to a camera lens to change the optical properties of the lens. 2. A plug-in that can be added to a host application to perform special image processing functions.

Filter tab A tab in *Bryce* that allows the user to customize and explore further a model in the Terrain Editor. Filters are preset modification operations that apply general reshaping processes to the Terrain model. The shape of the filter curve compares to a silhouette of the intended effect, but exactly how it reshapes the terrain depends upon the existing shape of the terrain.

final audio mix Setting the level of each piece of sound in a video project and then combining the tracks into a final mix.

Final Cut Pro A complete, high-end, professional editing/compositing system by Apple. Packing a full collection of high-end editing tools wrapped up in an interface with mouse and keyboard support, *Final Cut* also includes a fully keyframable compositing module integrated directly into the program.

Final Draft A script editing program, developed by BC Software, that formats scripts in standard screenplay format as they are written. In addition to formatting, *Final Draft* provides automation. Character names can be entered by typing the first few letters of a name, and the program can anticipate what the next character's name will be, making it simple to type back-and-forth dialog. *Final Draft* provides other utilities, including a scene navigator that lets the user see scenes as a series of index cards that can be easily rearranged.

fine-cut The final editing of a video project.

finite element modeling To divide a mechanical object into small, cubic sections, so that each section can be analyzed separately.

finite state machine (FSM) 1. A C++ language class that is designed to have certain characteristics useful for artificial intelligence. 2. A machine that has a finite number of states, one of which is a current state. The FSM can accept input that will result in a state transition from the current state to an output state, based on some state transition function, and the output state then becomes the new current state.

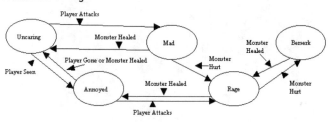

finite state machine.

fire effect setup Creation of a torch's fire in *trueSpace* by using the Pi Flame shader in *ShaderLab*.

fire F/X using *Primal Particles* Creating an animated texture of fire using the *Primal Particles* plug-in with *trueSpace*. The source of the fire is created by choosing a sphere and applying the *Wave Generator, 3D Wave,* and *2D Wave* types to it (*see Figure next page*).

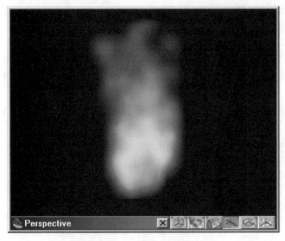

fire F/X using Primal Particles.

fire F/X using *PyroCluster*. A simple technique for creating fire F/X by using the *PyroCluster* plug-in in any of the 3D applications that the plug-in is compatible with.

fire F/X using PyroCluster.

Firewire Apple's name for the IEEE-1394 specification. It was developed by Apple in 1986 as a replacement for serial, parallel, SCSI, and to a lesser degree, Ether-net. In the future, computers might have only two interfaces for connecting peripherals: USB for slow devices such as keyboards, mice, and printers, and Firewire for high-speed connectivity to mass storage, cameras, scanners, and even networks. Firewire allows the user to daisy-chain up to 64 devices, with none of the settings or ID concerns of SCSI. The Firewire that is present on most computers and cameras today can transmit data at 100 Mbps (megabits per second). This is equivalent to 12.5MB per second (megabytes per second). (There are 8 bits in a byte, so 100 Mbps divided by 8 yields 12.5 MBps.) Since DV requires only a sustained transfer rate of about 3.6 MBps, 100 megabit Firewire is considered fast.

fireworks Incendiary devices that are designed to provide light effects while burning and moving through space. They are particularly difficult to model.

Fireworks An application by Macromedia used to create, edit, and animate Web graphics using a complete set of bitmap and vector tools. It uses export controls to optimize images, gives them advanced interactivity, and exports them into Macromedia *Dreamweaver* and other HTML editors. The user can launch and edit *Fireworks* graphics from inside *Dreamweaver* or Macromedia *Flash*.

FIR filter A filter that is used to simulate the effects of erosion in computer-generated terrain. A FIR filter converts the sequence x_1, x_2, $x_3 \ldots x_n$ to the sequence y_1, y_2, $y_3 \ldots y_n$ according to the formula:

$$y_i = ky_{i-1} + (1-k)x_i$$

where k is a filtering constant between 0 and 1. Low k means less erosion, and high k means more. Typically, a k of about 0.5 works well.

firmware Computer code that is stored in a computer's ROM or integrated circuit chip.

first in, first out (FIFO) A method of handling data in which the first item to be stored is also the first item to be read out.

first person shooter (FPS) A 3D game genre in which all action is seen from the character's perspective. The player literally looks through the eyes of the character, seeing and hearing what he sees or hears. The point of view is from a person on the street. Examples include: *Castle Wolfenstein 3D*, *Doom*, *Duke Nukem'*, *Quake*, *Dark Forces*, and *Sorcerer*.

first person shooter, vehicle-based These 3D games are much like *first person shooter* games, except the first person vehicle-based shooter has the player in a vehicle that may be a tank, ship, giant robot, or other mobile device. This genre more closely resembles an FPS game than a "racing" genre game, because the player is not simply driving across a finish line. The goals are similar to the FPS: "kill or be killed." Examples include: *Descent*, *Dead Reckoning*, and *Cylindrix*.

fish-eye lens An extremely wide-angle lens characterized by considerable image distortion.

fishpole A long telescoping pole with a supercardioid or hypercardioid microphone attached to one end.

fixed disk A hard disk. The disk and drive are parts of an integrated unit that is permanently installed in the computer. The disk cannot be removed from the drive.

Fixed Side tab A tab in *Wave Generator* that lets the user choose a side to "lock down," which will not be affected by the wave-vertex animation. It is especially useful when creating flowing cloth, like a cape or flag; the user can "lock" the vertices to the pole or object and the animated object will appear to be attached to it.

fixed spacing In typography, a type font in which all of the characters have the same width. In contrast, *proportional spacing* describes a type font where narrow letters such as *i* or *l* use much less space than wide letters such as *m* or *w*.

fixing 1. In photography, the chemical process by which unexposed silver salts are removed from a film or print so that the developed image will remain unchanged for a long period of time. 2. In electrostatic printing, the application of heat to fuse the toner permanently to the paper.

FK See *forward kinematics*.

.fla file An editable *Flash* project file.

Flag A Xenofex plug-in from AlienSkin for *Photoshop*.

flag A black cloth held by a metal frame, used to block light.

flaps Devices that are used to confine a light's effects to a limited area of a scene.

Flare Effects A plug-in for *trueSpace* by Axion Software that allows the user to add a variety of lens flare effects to a *trueSpace* scene.

Flash An application by Macromedia, used to design and deliver low-bandwidth animations, presentations, and Web sites. It offers scripting capabilities and server-side connectivity for creating engaging applications, Web interfaces, and training courses. Once the user has created content, 96 percent of the on-line audience will be able to view it with the Macromedia *Flash Player.*

FlashAmp An application used for manipulating sound files (e.g., setting parameters), including the resolution and scale of amplitude values and optional smoothing of the values. It can be used to lip sync *Flash* animations.

flashing The act of exposing film to light before or after primary exposure to change the tonal distribution.

flatbed plotter A plotter which makes use of a carriage containing a number of pens that moves over a sheet of paper mounted on a flat surface.

flatbed scanner A device that accepts a sheet of written or printed material that is placed on a flat glass plate. The scanner then moves across the sheet, converting the text to digital form for use in a computer.

flat light Shadowless, soft, frontal light.

flat mapping The projection of a map in the same way that a motion picture is projected on a screen, except that the projection is on objects in front of the screen. The back side of the objects shows texture. Also known as *projection* or *planar mapping.*

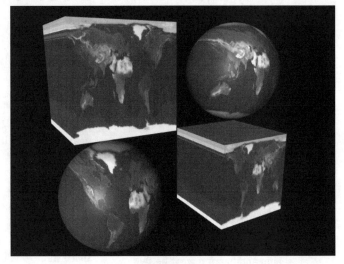

flat mapping.

flats Large wooden "walls," used on a soundstage to construct the set.

flat shading. A technique for producing illumination effects on graphics objects in an image. Each graphics primitive is

flat shading.

divided into a number of polygon surfaces and a single appropriate color is used to fill each polygon.

Flat Squares icon A tool in the *Game Creation System* used for solid-color floor/ceiling polygons.

flatten To convert a hierarchical data structure into a single non-hierarchical list.

flattened display list A display list that has only a single level of hierarchy.

flat tension mask CRT A color cathode ray tube in which the shadow mask is flat rather than curved but is stretched tightly so that it will not warp from heating by the electron beam.

flex area A region that will undergo the largest amount of deformation in an IK/BONES system, e.g,. the arm of a character. If the mesh of the arm is animated in a realistic way through the use of IK/BONES deformation, the polygons in the elbow region will twist and bend, while the polygons in the middle of the forearm will usually undergo very little deformation. The area of polygons comprising the elbow is a flex area. During the modeling process, the modeler needs to pay extra attention to this region of the model and to all other flex areas to ensure problem-free animation. The mesh in and around flex areas needs to be much more highly meshed than mesh in other areas.

flexing a muscle Use of the Magnet and Wave Deformers of *Poser* to represent the flexing of muscles in the human body.

flick When an observer stares at an object for a long time, the bright source appears to move off center and "wander off." This phenomenon is called *drift*. The observer is unaware of this drift

until a quick correction is made to force the eye back to the center. This quick correction is called *flick*.

flicker A perceived rapid variation in the intensity of a displayed image, caused by the refresh rate being too slow for a given observer and set of lighting conditions.

flicker script An attached script that is used to make a *trueSpace* light object vary its intensity randomly throughout a scene's animation. The effect can be useful for simulating animated light coming from a candle flame or fireplace, twinkling Christmas tree lights, and fiery engines on a spaceship.

flight simulation graphics Software that displays a simulation of the images seen when flying an aircraft. It allows the user to interface with the displays by operating various controls as if he were flying the aircraft.

flight simulator A program that simulates the flight of an aircraft and allows the user to gain experience in operating the controls. A number of very complex flight simulators are available for pilots training to fly particular aircraft.

Flight Simulator An inexpensive *flight simulator* developed by Microsoft for use as a home game.

floating An impression that one of two objects that are joined together is floating on the other, caused by light leaks or shadow leaks which occur when creating the image.

floating objects See *buoyancy, simulating*.

flocking behavior The behavior of birds when flying in a flock, particularly the direction of flight, spacing, etc. that they maintain. This behavior is responsible for

189

the direction and pattern of the flock's flight.

flocking behavior.

flocking, linear position The space relative to a *boid*. "Forward" is toward the positive Z-axis, "left" is toward the positive X-axis, and "up" is vertical toward the top of the boid.

flocking motion Flocking motion is accomplished by building a velocity vector during each update cycle that will adjust the boid's local X, Y, and Z orientations to match the needs of the four steering behaviors. These are: 1) *separation*, steer to avoid crowding local flockmates; 2) *alignment*, steer toward the average heading of local flockmates; 3) *cohesion*, steer to move toward the average position of local flockmates; and 4) *avoidance*, steer to avoid running into local obstacles or enemies.

flocking orientation Referred to as "roll, pitch, and yaw," orientation is simply an indication of how a given object is oriented in the local space. *Roll* is rotation around the local Z-axis (the one facing forward and backward). *Pitch* is rotation around the local X-axis (the one running left and right). *Yaw* is rotation around the Y-axis (the one running directly up and down through the boid). Understanding orientation is important be-

cause it is used when making decisions about the boid's position and orientation during movement.

flood filling A technique for filling a connected two-dimensional region with a color or pattern, in which a point is selected within the polygon, and the color or pattern is extended in all directions until the polygon boundary is encountered. Algorithms for flood filling need to be carefully designed to ensure that all parts of peculiarly-shaped polygons are filled. Also known as *seed filling*.

Flood Fill tool A tool in *Paint Shop Pro* and other applications that fills an image with either the current foreground or background color. To fill with the foreground color, left-click; to fill with the background color, right-click. The user can also choose to fill only a selection of the image.

floodlight A light with a wide coverage range, used in illuminating scenes to be photographed.

floor panels, height When creating games, the height and proportion of floor and ceiling panels is important to level design and the credibility of the scene. Many applications, e.g., *Game Creation System*, include tools for creating proper dimensions and proportions for floor, ceiling, and wall panels.

flow layout A window layout procedure used by Java that lays out a number of specified items in a horizontal row (*see figure next page*).

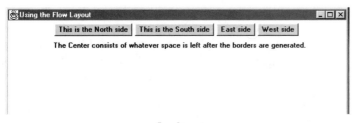

flow layout.

Flow Rollup A menu in *Primal Particles* that lets the user set the rate of particle emission (Rate setting), how long the particles are visible (Lifespan setting), the particle power (Power setting), particle speed (Jitter setting), the direction of emission (XYZ settings), and the speed in each direction.

Floyd-Steinberg filter An algorithm for performing discrete convolution or digital filtering, which is the improving of the appearance of an image by replacing a pixel by some function of that pixel and its neighbors. The Floyd-Steinberg filter is also often used to change color images to images consisting of black, white, and shades of gray.

fluid head tripod A special type of tripod head that is filled with hydraulic fluid that smooths the motion of the camera head.

fluorescence, phosphor The emission of light from certain chemicals when their electrons are excited by an electron beam. The light emission stops when the chemicals are returned to the unexcited state.

fluorescent lights White lights that burn cool. Passing electricity through a gas-filled vacuum tube generates the illumination. Fluorescents come in straight tubular form as well as the compact type (CFL). Perceptively, fluorescent lights are seen as white to pale bluish-white. In reality, however, fluorescent lights emit a limited spectra (mostly green or blue-green) and, when photographed, the environment lit by fluorescent lighting takes on a sickly green cast for the areas far from the light source. The areas that are close to the light source become white because of the phosphorus coating inside the fluorescent tube. The film perceives it as green because the film accurately sees the limited spectra of fluorescent lighting and captures the limited range of the phosphorous white. This is why we perceive fluorescent lighting as white even though it has limited spectral emission. Fluorescent light is deficient in red and magenta colors. The only way to replicate this effect in computer graphics with one dominant light is to again use the 3D light array and make the peripheral light's color greenish and the main central light white.

flush, left, or right alignment In HTML, alignment attributes are used with the paragraph formatting tags, including ALIGN=LEFT, ALIGN=CENTER, and ALIGN=RIGHT. To apply these attributes to a specific paragraph, simply include the desired attribute within the <P> tag, for example:

```
<P ALIGN=RIGHT>
```

This paragraph will be aligned to the right.

```
</P>
```

When there is no alignment attribute in the <P> tag, the paragraph will align to the left, by default.

flux The rate at which light is emitted, usually specified in watts.

Flyaround An option in *Bryce* that allows the user to watch a scene spin in 3D space. It is used to help determine which global camera angles might prove to be interesting when rendering the scene as viewed from different angles.

flyback The relatively fast return of a sweep signal from the end of the sweep to the beginning at the end of each sweep line.

flying logos Moving of a logo across the screen in a unique way—a common use of computer graphics and animation. Also known as *digital video effects (DVE)*.

flying spot scanner A technology in which a document is scanned by a point of light to convert it into electronic signals.

focal distance The distance in front of a camera at which objects are in sharpest focus.

focal length The distance from a lens to the focal plane when the lens is focused at infinity. The focal length of a normal 35-mm camera lens is 50 mm. Lenses having longer focal lengths are known as *telephoto* lenses, and those having shorter focal lengths are known as *wide-angle* lenses. As the focal length of a camera increases, the field of view decreases. Focal length and effect are photography basics. The higher the numbers in the focal length, the narrower the field of view, and the shallower the depth of field. A 15mm lens setting is very wide, and will distort objects and make them seem farther apart

spatially than they really are. For example, consider a camera placed on a road looking down a row of telephone poles. A wide-angle setting will make the poles seem to have a lot of distance between them, and the horizon will seem very far away and less important in the scene, whereas the foreground object will seem bigger and more dominant. A longer focal length will seem to compress the apparent distance between the poles and the items in the scene. The horizon will seem closer, and there will be less dominance attributed to objects relative to the distance from the camera.

focal plane The plane or surface on which a lens focuses to produce a sharp image.

focal point The point at which light rays converge to a point after passing through the lens. The locus of focal points is the *focal plane*.

focus 1. The position at which light rays from a lens converge to produce a sharp image. 2. The process of changing the distance between the lens and the focal plane so that the image on the focal plane becomes as sharp as possible. 3. The controlling of the size of the electron beam in a cathode ray tube so that it is at its minimum when it hits the screen.

focus ring A rotatable ring on the lens of a camera that allows for manual focusing.

focus servo A device in an optical drive that keeps the read/write light beam aligned with the tracks, regardless of imperfections in the disk surface.

fog Partially transparent color used to simulate distance or atmospheric conditions.

fog channel A texture channel that allows for semitransparent shapes. It becomes useful when attempting to create figures of smoke.

fog density The level of light exposure taken on by film due to background radiation, age, and other environmental conditions.

fog, difference between fog and glow Glow lights let lighter areas behind the glow effect to show through, whereas fog lights affect the background uniformly, no matter what the luminosity.

fog, range-based Fog created by rendering the scene without fog applied, and subsequently rendering the scene with an attenuation map, treating the camera position as the "light position." Set the texture matrix to identity, and then scale the matrix by 1 over the light's range. This technique allows per-pixel, perspective-correct range fog. The SRC_ COLOR sent to the frame buffer blending unit is the fog color times fog density. This gives a fog density of zero at the viewer, and at the maximum fog range the density will be one. When rendering the fog pass, set up the alpha blender to perform SRC_COLOR * 1 + DST_COLOR * (1 − SRC_COLOR).

fog water With *Bryce*, a *water effect* can be achieved without water. The user can generate water by using low altitude fog. For example, off the Maine coast in the early morning, there are times when the ocean is subject to large patches of low-level fog, and the water as such is completely obscured. A fantasy of oceans in far away (alien) worlds may include seas of ammonia or other non-water elements that rise and fall with the tides created by more than one moon. In both of these situations, the appreciation of a liquid surface may be enhanced not so much by the constituent components of the sea, as by its actions. Seas that we are familiar with have specific motions, e.g., waves and rising-falling actions. The user can use Fog in *Bryce* to emulate a sea that is either covered with fog, or a non-water liquid.

Foley The process of creating and recording ambient sound effects in real-time while watching the attendant video or film. Foley work is usually performed on a Foley stage equipped with special surfaces and props. Named for Jack Foley, the originator of the technique.

follow-through A law of physics dictates that every action has an equal and opposite reaction. This law must be followed when rendering realistic scenes. If a cannon fires a cannonball, the cannon will roll backwards a short distance. If a car comes to a screeching stop, the car will shimmy from side to side before it comes to rest. The result is more realistic than if the object had simply stopped. Inertia must always be considered.

font A set of characters, letters, and digits of the same type, style and size. When moveable type was common, a font consisted of a certain number of pieces of type for each character, the number depending upon the frequency with which each character was used. (For example, a font contained more "*e*'s" than "*z*'s.") With electronic type fonts, a font refers to only a single occurrence of each character. Examples of commonly used fonts include *Times Roman*, *Geneva*, and *Courier*.

font cache An area of memory where the characters of a currently used type font are stored for easy access.

Font button Clicking the Font button in many applications will trigger a dialog box in which the user can choose the size, style, and font that he wants to use for the text or text object.

font size Font size can be specified in HTML by using the <BASEFONT> tag. Text size varies between 1 (very small) and 7 (very large). The <BASEFONT> tag is placed within the <HEAD> tags and creates a default size for the entire document. It will look similar to the following:

<HEAD>

<BASEFONT SIZE 4>

</HEAD>

It is not necessary to use the <BASE-FONT> tag. If it is not used , the Web browser will default to the text setting in the user's browser. See also *Cascading Style Sheets*.

footage The film or tape produced by filming a video sequence.

footcandle A unit of luminance. Originally the light on a surface per unit area produced by a standard candle. The *footcandle* is now defined as 10.76 lux.

footlambert A unit of luminance (the photometric brightness of a surface). One footlambert is equal to 3,426 nits.

footmouse A mouse that is placed upon the floor and controlled by the ball of the user's foot while the heel remains on the floor.

footprint The solid or patterned cross-section that is to be transferred to a pixel.

footprint, interaction device The work area that a piece of equipment occupies.

footsteps, creating Footsteps, such as made by a character walking through mud or soft soil, can be created in *trueSpace* by using the *DynaWave* plug-in. *DynaWave* creates its own custom objects to be used as effectors, which work when linked to other objects, such as a boat oar or a boat sailing through the water. It also works when linked to a character's feet to create footsteps as the character walks.

foot switch A switch, usually located on the floor near a user's foot, which performs some computer action when stepped upon.

foreground animation See *background, animated*.

foreground/background color 1. Relating to the color of the two planes in a 2D or 3D application. 2. A command in the Display Menu of *Poser* that permits setting of either the foreground or background color of the scene.

foreground planes 1. The front plane in a 3D environment. 2. A technique that can be used in *Bryce*. In a picture or an animation, the way target subjects are framed by other elements often becomes the major part of a composition. This technique is particularly evident in the Disney Studio's work over the years. Often, a black silhouetted foreground acts as a frame for color targets in a picture.

forensic craniofacial reconstruction The science of recreating a person's appearance from a skull.

foreshortened surface area The projection of a surface onto the plane perpendicular to the direction of radiation. Also known as *projected surface area*.

form fill-in A technique for entering computer data in which an entire form is displayed on the screen and the user positions the cursor to boxes on the form and enters data in each.

form follows function A rule, following the design principles of the Bauhaus School, used in developing a user interface to assure that the interface doesn't dictate the capabilities of the entire system.

Formula Function A feature in *Carrara* that allows the user to input mathematical equations which translate into color or grayscale images.

form•Z A full-featured modeling application, developed by AutoDesSy for use in Macintosh and Windows systems. It is especially useful in creating mesh models and architectural designs.

forty-five degree lighting See *Rembrandt lighting*.

forward differencing An iterative method for obtaining a set of points on a surface by evaluating a bicubic function. The *forward difference* is the amount that the function changes when the argument is incremented by a specified step.

forward kinematics (FK) A technique that allows for manipulation of sections of hierarchies by working from the parentmost object down. For instance, in order for a wooden man to bend down to grab a pencil, start with the chest area and rotate it downward. Then, by moving down the hierarchy, rotate the shoulder, then the forearm, and finally the hand. Repeat the process for the other arm. Notice that FK is a process of continually refining a movement. Start with the whole concept and finesse down to the end of the hierarchy. FK is very effective for complex series of movements such as the movements of arms.

forward ray tracing A ray tracing technique in which every light ray is traced in the same direction that it normally travels. Since most light rays never have any effect on the image produced on the screen, some consider forward ray tracing techniques to be very wasteful of computer time and resources.

fountain water An effect that can be created with *trueSpace* using the *Primal Particles* or *CoolPowers* plug-in.

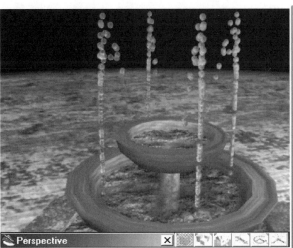

fountain water.

four light studio setup A lighting setup which uses the same three lights (key light, fill light, and back light) as the three light setup but also uses a fourth light called the *grazed background light*, which is used to illuminate a backdrop screen. The grazed background light is placed close to the ground plane and is pointed upward at the background screen at a 45-degree angle.

Fourier transform A formula used to convert a sampled analog signal into its frequency components.

Four Media Company (4MC) A Burbank, California-based company, which developed a process in the early 1970s to make "video to film" transfers. Using an electron beam scanner, the videotape image is recorded by a special 16mm film camera that shoots one frame of red (R), one frame of green (G), and one frame of blue (B) for each frame of 24 fps film. A proprietary process is used to convert the 29.97 video frame rate to 24 fps film.

FOV animations 1. Any animation that uses different FOV (field of view) settings for the camera in any 3D application. 2. In *Bryce*, the larger the camera's FOV setting, the smaller all of the objects in the scene will become. Over time, resizing the FOV in the camera's attributes dialog causes radical distortions near the edge of the visual plane. FOV animations look like zooms with distortion applied.

fovea The part of the retina that is responsible for acute daylight color vision.

foveal vision Vision through the high-resolution center portion of the eye. The total resolution of the human eye is approximately 512 × 512 pixels, but the resolution is not uniform, with the largest number of pixels concentrated close together at the center of the eye

and the remaining pixels distributed more widely around the periphery.

fps See *frames per second*.

FPS See *first person shooter*.

fps display A display in the upper-left portion of the screen that provides a yellow number indicating the frames per second rate of the current animation.

fractal A curve whose Hausdorff-Besicovitch dimension is larger than its Euclidian dimension and which has elements of self-similarity. For example, a curve that consists of a large number of line segments should have the Euclidian dimension of 1, which is a line. If this curve winds around in such a way that it fills all of the space available in a plane, then we would intuitively like to associate it with a dimension of 2, which is the dimension of a plane. Such a curve is a *fractal* and has a Hausdorff-Besicovitch dimension of 2. Mandelbrot claims that just as Euclidian shapes (e.g., circles and squares) are the natural way of describing man-made objects, fractals are the natural way of describing objects that occur in nature, such as mountains and trees.

fractal dimension See *dimension, fractal*.

fractal models Models of natural objects such as trees, mountains, etc. that are created from an assemblage of fractals (*see Figure next page*).

Fractalnoise 1. A process that adds a fractal noise procedural to a selected texture channel in any 3D application. 2. A shader available in *Universe*.

fractal terrain generation, fault formation A way of creating a three-dimensional image that simulates terrain. Starting with an empty height field, we draw a random line through it, and add

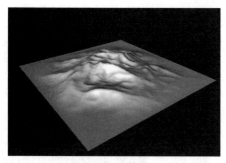

fractal models.

an offset value dHeight to each value on one side of the line. Next, we decrease dHeight, draw a new line, and repeat the process. Continue generating lines and decreasing dHeight until a sufficient level of detail is generated.

fractal terrain generation, midpoint

displacement   See *diamond square algorithm*.

fragmentation When a hard drive has had many files deleted and replaced, it can become fragmented, which can slow its performance. At this point, it may need to be defragmented, or optimized. Frequent storage and deletion of computer graphics on a hard drive is a common cause of fragmentation.

fragmentation, memory When memory in a C or C++ program is allocated using *malloc()* or *new*, memory can become fragmented and result in deteriorated game performance and the possibility of sufficiently large memory blocks becoming unavailable. When an application requests a block of memory, sophisticated operating systems, such as UNIX and Microsoft Windows, employ advanced memory-management systems that can logically rearrange physical chunks of memory to create the requested contiguous memory block. But this rearrange-

ment comes at the cost of CPU cycles that the game could ordinarily have used. With game consoles, where the operating system is usually little more than a tiny set of slimmed-down library functions, there is no such sophisticated memory manager. A solution to these challenges of conventional memory allocation is *frame-based memory*. Frame-based memory eliminates memory fragmentation and is very fast. However, it is not useful as a general-purpose memory allocation system like *malloc()* and *new*. Frame-based memory is best suited for games and level initialization modules. See *frame-based memory*.

Fragment Color A command in the Mr. Nitro section of *Universe* that determines the *color* of fragments at various stages in their lifecycle.

Fragment Shape A command in the Mr. Nitro section of *Universe* that determines the *shape* of fragments. Two options are available: triangles and quadrangles.

Fragment Size A command in the Mr. Nitro section of *Universe* that determines the *size* of fragments.

frame 1. The border of the picture area of a display. 2. One complete film or video picture. Each frame of video contains two fields. Moving images need at least 18 frames per second to appear as full-motion and 24 fps to allow for sync sound. NTSC video plays at 29.97fps and PAL video at 25fps.

frame accuracy The ability for a device, particularly a VTR, to accurately perform edits on a pre-designated frame. Non-frame accurate VTRs may miss the mark by one or more frames.

frame-based memory Frame-based memory works like a stack. At initialization time, the game allocates a single memory block from the operating system, which will be used and managed by the frame memory system. This memory block is allocated only once throughout the lifetime of the game and is released back to the operating system just before the game terminates. From the memory block's pointer, we compute the base and cap memory pointers, optionally aligning them to a memory boundary that fits the specific system the application was designed to run on. The base pointer points to the lowest aligned memory address in the memory block, and the cap pointer points to the next higher-aligned memory address just outside the top of the memory block. The memory block, the base pointer, and the cap pointer remain constant throughout the life of the game. Finally, the lower heap frame and upper heap frame pointers are set equal to the base and cap pointers, respectively. These two pointers change as allocations are made during the course of the game. A call is made to the system, requesting a chunk of memory from one of the two heaps. If the lower heap is specified, the lower heap frame pointer is bumped up by the amount allocated, and its value prior to the modification is returned. The lower heap frame pointer always points to the next available byte of memory. If, on the other hand, the upper heap is specified, the upper heap frame pointer is decreased by the amount allocated, and the new value is returned (because the upper heap frame pointer always points to the last allocated byte of memory). If the two frame pointers cross each other, there is not enough memory to satisfy the request.

frame buffer A hardware device that provides an interface for a frame of computer data to the monitor. It contains memory to store the color of each pixel together with circuitry to manage input to the memory and output in a form that can be accepted by the monitor.

frame buffer synergy The use of image memory in such a way that it may store the output of one program which can be used as the input for another program.

frame-by-frame animation Animation using a series of *keyframes* with no *tweening* that creates a "flipbook." An animation *Flash* file is an example of a frame-by-frame animation.

frame grabber A device that converts a video picture into a digital file.

frame rate 1. In video or film recording, the number of frames per second that are recorded (and then played back). 2. In computer games, especially 3D games, the rate at which frames are created and displayed on the computer screen, just like the frames of a movie. One critical difference, however, is that when a movie's frame rate suddenly drops to half speed, the film itself is playing half speed. In a game, when the frame rate drops, the "world" is still moving at the same speed, but the player is seeing half as many frames. So the action the player is watching is still running at the same speed, but the motion appears choppy.

frames per second (fps) Used to describe the speed at which film and video play. Film plays at 24fps, PAL video at 25fps, and NTSC video at 29.97 fps. Frame speed can seriously affect the quality of video games as it relates to "real-time rendering."

Frax4D/FraxFlame/FraxExplorer A series of *Photoshop* plug-ins from the Corel *KPT* volume. Each can be used to create fractal-based imagery.

free-form An image that is drawn by hand without use of rulers, triangles, or other mechanical devices.

free form model A model of a cube or cylinder that is created by extruding a square or circle. Free form models respond better to the use of a shader than do primitive models.

Free Form Modeler A modeler in *Carrara* that works by an extrusion method that is defined by profiles in all three dimensions.

FreeHand A high-end Macromedia vector-graphics application. Macromedia *Freehand* is a professional solution for designers publishing in print and on the Web, offering sophisticated illustration tools, time-saving productivity features, and integration with the family of Macromedia Web publishing software, including Macromedia *Flash*.

freehand lasso A tool used in 2D applications to select areas for modification.

freeview A simple technique for three-dimensional viewing that places stereo images side by side, left on the left, and right on the right. The viewer must then keep the axes of the eyes parallel as if looking at infinity, while focusing on the display. Initially, this is not easy, and some practice may be necessary.

This display technique is called *freeview*. A restriction is that the images must be placed no farther apart than the spacing of the eyes (and hence they can each be no wider than that space); and, each is limited to using only half the display width. Also known as *parallel viewing*.

freezing f/x An effect of an object freezing that can be created in *trueSpace* using the *Digital Soapbox Fractal Noise* shader.

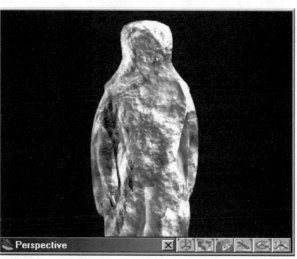

freezing f/x.

Frenet frame A reference frame consisting of a unit length tangent, *T*, to the central axis; a principal normal, *N*; and a binormal, *B*.

frequency 1. The number of recurrences per unit time of a periodic phenomena. 2. An audio signal is made up of different frequencies, or wavelengths, which yield the high (or treble), mid and low (or bass) tones. The human voice resides mostly in the mid-tones.

frequency aliasing An aliasing effect that results from limited sampling of the visible light frequency spectrum. It manifests itself as incorrect colors for objects that are ray traced.

frequency division multiplexing (FDM) A technology that divides the available frequency bandwidth of a transmission line into narrower frequency bands, each of which can be used to transmit an independent voice, conversation, or data stream. This increases the number of transmissions that can be sent simultaneously over a single transmission line.

Fresnel correlator A holographic correlation technique. A defocusing of the correlation plane decreases the shift invariance of the correlators, increasing the number of patterns which can be stored in each correlation operation.

Fresnel effect Edge fall-off in reflections due to attenuation of the reflected beam. This effect is difficult to achieve using standard 3D applications. One useful technique to achieve this is *multipass rendering*.

Fresnel equation An equation that expresses the attenuation of a reflected beam of unpolarized light from a surface as a function of angle of incidence of the light upon the surface, the wavelength of the light, and the properties of the reflecting surface.

Fresnel lens A lens attached to a light that focuses the beam of light. Unlike a conventional lens, which focuses through the curvature of the glass, the Fresnel lens is a flat glass plate that focuses by means of ribs on the glass.

Fresnel term (F_1) The ratio of incident light to reflected light for specular reflection for a smooth surface. When nonmetallic surfaces reflect, the reflectance depends on the angle between incoming

direction and the surface normal. The Fresnel term is used to simulate this dependency by modulating the reflectance. It uses the incoming light's angle and the surface's index of refraction to compute the appropriating weighting. The formula for the Fresnel term is:

$$ F = \frac{(g-k)^2}{2(g+k)^2} \left(1 + \frac{\left[k(g+k)-1 \right]^2}{\left[k(g-k)+1 \right]^2} \right) $$

where:

$$ k = \cos\theta $$

θ is the angle between the incoming direction and the surface normal

$$ g = n_\lambda^2 + k^2 - 1 $$

η_λ is the index of refraction of the surface divided by the index of refraction of the transmitting medium, as a function of wavelength. Since the index of refraction for air is 1, simply supplying the index of refraction is usually sufficient.

When developing games, one typically deals with surfaces and atmospheres that have a constant index of refraction, the only variable in the above equation is k. Thus, the Fresnel term can be written as a function of k, which is a variable in the range [0..1].

fricative phonemes A fricative is the type of consonant that is formed by forcing air through a narrow gap, creating a hissing sound. Typically, air is forced between the tongue and the point of articulation for the particular sound, for example, the "f" in fun, the "v" in victor, and the "z" in zoo. Air turbulence is created by the sounds. Unlike *plosive phonemes*, it is possible to maintain a fricative sound for as long as there is air to blow. The fricatives include: F, V, TH, DH, S, Z, SH, ZH, and H. Fricative consonants are held for a longer duration than any other consonant, e.g., the word "shoe." The "sh" sound lasts longer than the rest of the word, because it is a fricative phoneme. The same applies for the "h" in help and "z" in zoo. When marking the timing sheet for a lip synch animation, it is usually a good idea to mark the fricative phonemes so they are given a higher frame count in the animation.

fringing A line of incorrect color which occurs at the boundary of two colors in a video image. Also called *color edging*.

frisket In publishing, an area of a piece of artwork that is protected from modification. The term comes from the shapes cut out to mask areas from airbrushing.

frontal bone A thick bone that constitutes the forehead structure. It terminates at the brow just above the nose.

frontalis The brow-lifting muscle. The frontalis muscle draws the scalp down and up, wrinkling the forehead skin. It covers the forehead. The frontalis is actually two distinct muscles, one on either side of the head, which makes it

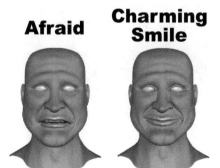

Afraid

Charming Smile

frontalis.

possible to move the eyebrows independently as "Spock" used to do in the original *StarTrek* series. The frontalis is one of the most frequently-used facial muscles. It is a part of nearly every facial expression. Some common expressions that use the frontalis are fear and a charming smile. In these expressions the frontalis muscle is used to pull the forehead skin upward, creating wrinkles.

front clipping plane When a three-dimensional scene is to be transferred to a two-dimensional display, the front clipping plane is a plane that is established in the three-dimensional scene in front of which no objects are projected to the two-dimensional image.

front distance (F) Distance of an object from the *front clipping plane.*

front lighting Placing the key light near the camera or lens axis results in *front lighting*. The actual light placement can be a bit higher than the camera or off to the side. A flattened form and compressed shadows characterize front lighting. Since the light is evenly illuminating the subject and is near the camera, the features of the subject are abstracted and made two-dimensional. Front lighting minimizes a subject's texture and volume. There is no light modeling with front lighting. Front lighting is very unflattering, but certain subjects—namely the elderly and infants—benefit from its flat lighting. In the elderly, front lighting minimizes wrinkles and enlivens the skin. For infants, front lighting matches their relatively flat face. Front lighting is also ideal for thin-faced subjects because it makes their faces look wider.

FrontPage A Web page editing application developed by Microsoft.

frown A facial expression that can be created in *Poser* using the Frown Parameter Dial.

frustrum 1. The part of a solid cone or pyramid that remains when the top is cut off by a plane parallel to the base. 2. The part of a solid between two parallel planes.

frustum of vision The volume within which graphics objects are viewed and processed to form an image. It is bounded by planes that intersect at the viewpoint.

FSM See *finite state machine*.

f-stop The ratio of the focal length to the aperture of a lens. The higher the f-stop is, the smaller the aperture will be. In practical use, the terms f-stop and t-stop are interchangeable and basically mean the same thing. In fact, the two are so interchangeable that users won't find any reference to the latter when working with and learning their favorite 3D applications. For all but professional cinematographers, f-stop will be the most useful term to work with. The f-stop settings include f/1.0, f/1.4, f/2, f2.8, f/4.0, f/5.6, f/8, f/11, f/16, and f/22 to f/32 and so on. Some lenses do not have this f-stop range, however. For example, as the aperture changes from f/8 to f/11, the light is "halved." If the change is reversed from f/11 to f/8, the light is "doubled." So a change of one "stop" means that the aperture was decreased or increased by a factor of two. The larger the f-stop number (f/11–f/32), the smaller the actual diameter of the opening, so less light is allowed into the lens. The smaller the f-stop number (f/1–f/8), the larger the opening and the more light is allowed in. An f-stop is also used to indicate whether a lens is fast or slow. A fast lens is considered faster if it has a maximum aperture greater than f/2.8. A slow lens has a maximum aperture of f/3.5 or higher. The lens with an f/2.8 aperture is considered "faster" than a lens that can open up only to f/3.5. Each change in the exposure represents a "stop." It does not matter if the change occurs in the shutter speed or in the aperture opening. So, in photography, when someone says, "Open up a stop," it means to double the amount of light reaching the film, either by setting the aperture higher (f/8 to f/5.6, for example) or by decreasing the shutter speed (1/250 to 1/125). However, changing both the aperture and the shutter speed by single increments at the same time results in a change to the exposure two stops, meaning the light is either increased 4x or decreased to 1/4, depending on the direction in which the change was made. "Stopping down" a lens means decreasing or cutting the light in half. This could be accomplished by setting the shutter to a higher speed or by shifting the aperture to a higher f-stop number. So, there is an inverse re-

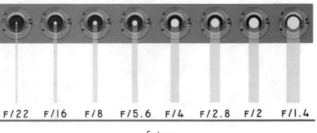

F/22   F/16   F/8   F/5.6   F/4   F/2.8   F/2   F/1.4

f-stop.

lationship between the aperture and the shutter speed; both control the amount of light reaching the film. The f-stop is also known as *relative aperture*. ⊘

FTC (Floor-To-Ceiling) attribute An attribute of the *Game Creation System* used to create barriers in a 3D game. It is used to maximize the frame rate. For maximum performance, this attribute should be set on every solid wall that goes from floor to ceiling.

FTP See *file transfer protocol*.

F(u), Fourier transform of *f* A combination of different harmonically-related frequencies (u) which are equivalent to a complex waveform *f*.

full duplex A data communications method that allows simultaneous transmissions in both directions over a communications link.

Full Figure Morph A capability of *Poser*, composed of all of the separate morphs and deforms that a user develops for a model and subsequently renders as one Full Figure Morph file. Using the Parameter Dial, the figure changes into that selected full-morphed targeted model.

functional design, user interface A document that specifies the detailed functionality of the user-computer interface.

function curves A tool in *trueSpace* that enables the user to toggle the Track Pane into a function curve editor. For any animated property in the Keyframe Editor, the user can adjust the animation by adjusting the curve. Thus, if an object were moving across the screen and then suddenly moved downward and then back upward in the space of only a few frames, one would usually see a curve with a sharp spike. By adjusting the keyframes on either side of the spike, the user could make the movement more gradual and less drastic. Function curves economize animating time.

function key A key on a keyboard that is reserved for activating a specified program function.

function object A function that tells an algorithm when to return a true value. Also known as a *functor*.

functor See *function object*.

fundamental frequency When a signal is represented in the frequency domain as a series of sine waves, the *fundamental frequency* is the lowest frequency signal used in this representation. All of the remaining sine waves that are used are harmonics of the fundamental frequency.

fusing In electrostatic printing, the process of permanently attaching the toner to the paper through the use of heat.

fusion frequency, critical The refresh frequency of a raster image at which the picture stops flickering and fuses into a steady image.

fuzzy landscaping Creating topography in a completely random fashion without regard to the characteristics of the real world.

fuzzy logic Traditional logic works on the idea of "true" and "false"; something is either on or off, zero or one, yes or no, positive or negative. *Fuzzy logic* allows us to work with concepts that are not "crisp"—in other words, things that require an adjective or adverb specifying "to what degree" or "how much." For example, fuzzy logic allows us to mathematically model size concepts such as "pretty big," "awfully small," "medium," "gigantic," and so on.

fuzzy rug A technique for producing an image in which the gray-scale intensity of the image is proportional to height. Also known as a *waterfall*.

fuzzy set A set that has the ability to specify how much (or to what degree) something is in a set. Using a fuzzy set, one can "flex" the separation between "in the set" and "not in the set" to include things like "just a little bit in the set" or "almost entirely in the set." This is done by having the characteristic function return not only zero and one, but also values between zero and one that indicate to what degree the given number is in the set. For a set of tall people, for example, if zero means "not tall" and one means "tall," then 0.5 can mean "sort of tall" (or, "halfway in the set of tall people"), and 0.01 can mean "a little tall" (or, "just barely in the tall set").

F/X Hollywood term for special effects created for motion pictures.

G

G See *geometrical attenuation factor* or *geometry vector*.

gaffer The head electrician on a film set, responsible for directing the set-up of the lights and other electrical equipment.

Gaffer A shading model plug-in from Worley Labs, used in *LightWave* to create soft shadows. It offers a way to control the surface shading and lighting inside *LightWave*. *Gaffer* also comes with Bloom, a tool that creates glows around objects.

Gaffer's Assistant A plug-in for *trueSpace*, developed by Primitive Itch, that allows the user to adjust the settings of grouped lights all at once.

gain The factor by which a signal is increased by an electronic amplifying device.

gain boost A method of electronically increasing the strength, or amplitude, of an audio or video signal, resulting in a higher signal-to-noise ratio. In video, the image becomes brighter, but has more visible noise.

Game Creation System (GCS) A complete system for making 3D action games, from Pie in the Sky Software.

Gamelan A Web site that contains a large collection of Java applets as well as many Java demos and Java information, much of it oriented toward game programming.

game engine The application that runs a game. It can be seen as a logical core that handles the decisions required to power the "game universe." A game engine receives messages in a format that it understands and generates messages that other entities understand. This abstraction means that all hardware aspects of the game device (PC, console, handheld) can be represented by specific units that translate between the hardware and messaging system.

game objects Moveable dynamic entities that are part of a game universe.

game-path planning See *A* algorithm*.

game profiling When the frame rate of a game increases after some change, the only way to find the source of the problem is to "profile" the game. A "real-time" profiler allows the user to monitor any spot or segment of code. It operates by calling for a function at the beginning and at the end of the area to be profiled. Each sample, consisting of a *ProfileBegin* and a *ProfileEnd*, is identified with a unique name that the user chooses. This profiler gives information at the end of each frame, which should be printed to the screen or some other output device. The information consists of the unique name of the sample point, the average minimum and maximum percentages of frame time spent on that sample, the number of times the sample was called per frame, and the relationship of this sample point to other sample points (parent/child). The profiler tries to be smart about samples and keep track of parent/child relationships. For example, if one samples the main loop of the game and the graphics draw routine that is inside the main loop, the parent/child relationship is taken into consideration.

game tree A tree on which the nodes are game states, and children of each node are the positions that are reached from it by one move. A computer player for these games works by considering this game tree as far as it can or wants to into the future from the current game position. It also has an evaluation function that attempts to quantify how good a particular game position is for one player.

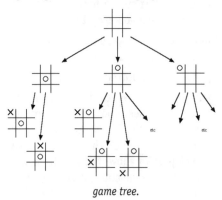

game tree.

game tree, alpha-beta pruning This concept is based on the observation that in some cases, it is clear that further investigation of part of the game tree is pointless. This effectively means we add an extra parameter to the search. This is the best we know the other player can get, based on the parts of the tree previously searched. When our current search returns something that is more advantageous for us (and worse for the other player) than our "current best," we don't

have to search this portion of the game tree any more. Of course, this actually becomes two parameters. One is the best the opposing player has determined so far (called *beta*), and the other is the best we have determined so far (called *alpha*). Alpha is passed to the recursive call for the other player's move, where alpha and beta are swapped. Alpha and beta are effectively a lower and an upper bound on the expected board value.

game tree, move-ordering methods One move-ordering method is "iterated deepening." Instead of straight-away searching at full ply, the programmer searches at a gradually increasing ply, using the results of the previous level of search to "sort" the moves for the next level. The results of the previous level can be stored as a hash table, storing calculated values of board positions. This table hashes board states to board values. It also avoids the recalculation of board values when different sequences of moves produce the same game state. Game-specific heuristics can be used, such as always considering capture moves first in chess. Finally, there is the "killer" heuristic: if a move turned out to be the best in a sibling node in the tree; it should be attempted first.

game tree, negamax algorithm Rather than writing two functions, one that aims to minimize board state, and the other to maximize it, a negation can be inserted to turn this into just one function. Here, the evaluation function must return the quality of the board for the current player, rather than always returning low values, meaning a "good board" for one player and "high" for the other. Board state must therefore include or imply which player goes next.

gamma A measurement of contrast as derived from the distribution curve of a particular film or emulsion. It also denotes the deviation of a display system from a reference signal.

gamma correction A technique that compensates for the nonlinear response of a cathode-ray tube display. The intensity of light emitted by the cathode-ray tube phosphor is proportional to the applied grid voltage raised to the *gamma* power, where *gamma* may range from 2.3 to 2.8, depending upon the cathode-ray tube characteristics. A correction is needed to provide proper contrast to the image. In television signals, this compensation is applied before transmission.

gamut The complete range of colors that can be produced by a display device. This includes luminance and chrominance.

gamut mapping Converting color data designed for a display device with a particular gamut to a new gamut suited for another display device.

Gantt chart A type of bar chart used to plan a project and track the progress and resources used to accomplish the project.

garbage in, garbage out (GIGO) An expression indicating that if the input data are worthless, the output data will be worthless.

garbage matte A special matte used to knock out extraneous objects in a compositing shot. Garbage mattes are usually applied to a blue-screen shot before chroma-keying. They can be used to eliminate props, mic booms, and other objects that can't be eliminated through keying.

garbled The corruption of data.

gate A special type of audio filter that allows only a specific range of frequencies to pass.

Gaussian blur The deliberate introduction of blur into an image through the use of a *Gaussian filter* to produce the effect of a "still" photograph of a moving object. In real life, such blur is not a property of the scene being viewed, but is produced by the motion of the image of the moving object across the film plane during the time while the camera shutter is open.

Gaussian elimination A way to compute the determinant of a matrix by sequences of row operations.

Gaussian filter A filter used for weighing contributions to a pixel in antialiasing. It has the equation $g = 2^{-2x^2}$. The Gaussian $1/2$ and Gaussian $1/\sqrt{2}$ filters use the same equation multiplied by $1/2$ and $1/\sqrt{2}$ respectively.

Gauss-Seidel iteration An iterative method for finding eigenvectors.

gaze direction The direction in which the observer of a ray traced scene is looking.

GCS See *Game Creation System*.

GCS Paint A program (part of the *Game Creation System*) that is used for creating or retouching images for *Game Creation System* games.

GDDM See *graphical data display manager*.

Gel One of the filters in Corel's *KPT*. Use of the filter causes parts of an image to look like gooey gelatin.

gel frame A metal frame that holds lighting gels in front of the light.

gel, lighting Translucent sheets of colored plastic that are placed in front of a light to alter the color of the light or to decrease the brightness. The most common use of lighting gels involves converting tungsten to daylight, or vice versa. Diffusion gels are usually frosty white plastic sheets that make the light source appear softer.

gels Filters for lights used in *Carrara, Bryce, Universe, LightWave, 3ds max,* and other 3D applications. These programs give the user a very easy way to add additional shadows and textures to a scene without having to create additional objects which significantly increase rendering time. Using gels, we can attach an image to a light source and create the effect of the light source shining through the image, thereby projecting it onto the scene.

GEM Designation for paint and drawing programs that are produced by Digital Research Corp. They make use of image storage files having the IMG extension. Such files store monochrome or 16-color images in a run length encoded format.

General Electric *NASA 11* See *NASA 11.*

generalized cylinder The surface that is generated when a two-dimensional contour is swept along a three-dimensional trajectory. See *sweeping.*

generalized ray A light element used in ray tracing that is more sophisticated than a single primitive ray of light, such as a beam or a cone.

generative helix The mathematical expression that creates spiral patterns such as those that occur on pinecones or pineapples.

generator A curve composed of connected straight-line segments that is used to repeatedly replace each straight line segment in a curve to create a self-similar fractal.

Genesis effect The modeling of a small burst of sparks from a region on a planet's surface using an explosion particle system.

GENESYS An animation system.

Genisco SpaceGraph A true 3D display making use of a varifocal mirror. It provides stereopis and head-motion parallax without the need to wear special glasses or headgear.

Genitalia A command in the Figure Menu of *Poser.* Male and female genitalia in *Poser* are very realistic. Since there may be situations where this might be considered inappropriate (when the audience is too young, or it is deemed otherwise inappropriate), it may be necessary to switch this option off.

genlock 1. The capability of a video display device to lock its output to a set of incoming synchronization signals. In television, the display is locked to horizontal and vertical synchronization signals that cause the image to remain stable on the screen. 2. See *alpha map.*

genus of a polyhedron The number of holes that pass through the polyhedron if the polyhedron has a single component.

geodesic A great circle path that gives the shortest distance between two points on the surface of a sphere.

geographic information system (GIS) A system for storage, retrieval, and manipulation of maps and other geographic data.

geoid A hypothetical figure of the earth in which the mean sea level is conceived as extending continuously through all the continents.

geometric aliasing The fact that when a curve is represented by a polygon mesh with sufficient sides so that the resulting image has a satisfactory curved look, the straight lines of the polygon mesh become objectionable when the image is enlarged.

geometrical attenuation factor (G) The proportion by which a microfacet is shielded from incident light.

geometric continuity The manner in which two curve segments join together. If they simply join together, the curve has G^0 *geometric continuity*. If the directions of the two segments' tangent vectors are equal at the point where the segments join, the curve has G^1 *geometric continuity*.

geometric extent See *extent*.

geometric modeling Computational structuring that represents the spatial aspects of objects in a specific application. The study of geometric modeling includes specification methods, procedural modeling, model capture, simulation, visualization, and animation, concentrating on computer representations of surfaces used in computer graphics applications.

geometric normal The surface normal at a particular point on a surface as computed from the geometric characteristics of the surface at that point, as contrasted to the *shading normal*, which the user can set to a different value to modify shading effects.

geometric object A two- or three-dimensional shape.

geometric optics A branch of optics that studies the interaction of light with geometric objects that are much larger than the wavelength of light.

geometric primitive A basic geometric shape that is mathematically defined for treatment by a rendering program.

Geometric Props Basic objects included in *Poser*, including the Ball, Box, Cone, Cylinder, Square, Torus, and a selection of new *Poser* items in the Prop Types folder inside of the Props library.

geometric realism The degree of realism, or resemblance, that a model has to its real-world counterpart. This includes the overall geometric shape of surfaces and the amount of realistic detail that is on the surface. For example, if a storyboard shows a close-up on a helicopter, the digital model of the helicopter should appear authentic. Not only should the surfaces be shaped like those of the original, but small details, such as antenna, rubber glass seals, and distinctive paneling, must be present. If it is apparent that the interior of the helicopter will be seen, even if only briefly, by the camera, then the necessary amount of cockpit and interior detail needs to be built.

geometry The branch of mathematics that studies the relations, properties, and measurement of solids, surfaces, lines, and angles.

geometry engine A chip used for polygon clipping, either by clipping each polygon by as many planes as necessary using a single chip or by using a pipeline of chips, each of which clips the polygon for one plane.

geometry matrix A set of geometric constraints that are used to define a curved surface in a manner similar to the way in which a *geometry vector* defines a curve.

geometry vector (G) A four-element column vector of geometric constraints used to define a curve.

Geomod A modeling system that can model such free-form surfaces as tensor products of nonuniform, rational cubic polynomial curve segments.

geomorphology A science that deals with the land and submarine relief features of the earth's surface.

George Washington University User Interface Management System (GWUIMS) A system of computer controls that uses active values and object-oriented programming concepts to propagate changes among interdependent objects. The visual representations of these changes can be immediately reflected in the display.

geospecific texture A texture derived from aerial or satellite photographs that is mapped onto a terrain model.

Gestalt rules Rules used by graphics designers to describe how a viewer organizes individual visual stimuli into larger overall forms.

ghost images The light that passes through the silver halide layer of a photographic film eventually reaches the "back" of the film. When it does, some of the light is reflected back into the silver halides. This creates what is called *halation*. Halation creates secondary *ghost images* in the film, which are a byproduct of unintentional light and film interaction. Most modern films have an antihalation backing to prevent this from occurring.

ghosting The appearance of a secondary displaced image on a television screen due to reflections of the television signal that arrive at the receiving antenna displaced in time from the primary signal.

Gibbs phenomenon A Fourier transform that suffers from ringing.

Gif_Builder A program that makes it possible to stitch together a sequence of GIF files to create an animated display that is saved as a single GIF file.

GIF (graphics interchange format) A file format developed by CompuServe for compressing and storing graphics image data, and the file extension given to files in this format. GIF files use Lempel-Ziv-Welch (LWZ) compression, a highly-effective method for compressing many kinds of graphics data. The GIF technique reads the screen pixel by pixel rather than on a memory plane-oriented basis, a technique that works well with 256-color modes. GIF files are capable of handling only 256 different colors, which sometimes limits their capability to reproduce full color photographs. However, many photographs and graphics images have a limited number of colors. GIF encoding is somewhat slow, since the speed of encoding is sacrificed for small file size. The LZW technique uses a table of character strings together with a code assigned to each. Instead of storing each character string, only the codes are stored. The table is generated as the data is scanned, the strings being those encountered in the actual data. For decompression, the table can be regenerated from the stored compressed data and used to recreate the original file, so the table need not be saved. If the table gets filled, it is simply discarded and a new table begun for the succeeding data. Many pieces of software are now available that make it possible to combine a series of sequential images into a single GIF file so that they may be played back as an animation.

GIF, transparent Used for Web pages that have a background image that contains a pattern. If the designer were to create an image that is not transparent on the Web page, the image would override the pattern. To avoid this, activate the "transparency" option (e.g., in *Paint Shop Pro*) when creating images. This allows the image to blend with whatever background is used.

GIF Wizard A program for processing GIF images by Raspberry Hill Publishing Inc.

gig An abbreviation for *gigabyte*.

giga One billion. In ordinary mathematics the prefix *giga* denotes that the following quantity is multiplied by 1 billion, but in computer terminology, the prefixes *kilo, mega, giga*, etc. represent successive multiplications by 1024 rather that 1000 so that *giga* is actually 1,073,741,824.

gigabyte 1,073,741,824 bytes of data. Often abbreviated *gig*.

gigaflop One billion floating point operations per second.

GIGO See *garbage in, garbage out*.

gimbal lock With a three-angle (roll, pitch, yaw) system, there are always certain orientations in which there is no simple change to the three values to represent a simple local rotation. This may be seen in the rotation having "pitched up" 90 degrees when the user is trying to specify a local yaw left or right. This is known as *gimbal lock*.

gingerbreadman A fractal curve produced by iterating the following equations:

$$x_{n+1} = 1 - y_n + |x_n|$$

$$y_{n+1} = x_n$$

gingerbreadman.

GIS See *geographic information system*.

GKS See *graphical kernel system*.

Glass 1. One of the distortion filters in *Photoshop* that creates a glass-like overlay for a selected image or image area. 2. One of the *Photoshop* filters that creates a glass-like overlay for an image or image area.

Glass Lens A Corel *KPT* filter that adds a transparent glass sphere to a selected *Photoshop* image.

glass, rendering A glass object can be rendered in a single pass with an environment map applied as a 2D texture, the texture coordinates computed by a sphere-mapping algorithm; a "MODULATE" texturing algorithm and a headlight; or the proper pixel blending and Z testing set up to draw it as a transparent object.

glass settings Settings that are available for rendering glass using the *Material Generator* plug-in for *trueSpace* in *pluSpack*. The settings include Color, Shading, Faceting, Ambient Glow, Shininess, Roughness, and Index of Refraction.

Glidecam A camera-stabilizing mechanism similar to a *Steadicam*.

glInterleavedArrays When using OpenGL, with vertex data already contained in a single structure, *glInterleavedArrays* can be used to submit all the components of the vertex in a single function call. *glInterleavedArrays* is capable of submitting a number of standard interleaved vertex structures ranging from a lightweight position-only vertex, to a heavyweight vertex with position, normal, diffuse color, and texture coordinates. *glInterleavedArrays* submits only a pointer to the vertices to be rendered. Another function such as *glDrawArrays*, *glDrawElements*, or *glArrayElement* must be called to actually render the data.

global illumination The complete accounting of light transfer from the light source to its reflection and dispersion in an environment. It is the accounting of the direct and indirect light distribution in a scene.

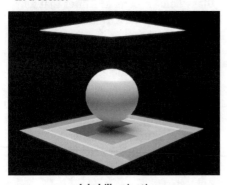

global illumination.

global light The light of a distant, but directional source (e.g., the sun). A global light affects everything in the scene; thus everything is illuminated or casts shadows from it. Applications handle global lights differently. For instance, *Strata StudioPro* gives a small light palette that allows the user to add global lights and then determine where they originate by moving the head of

the "tack" into position. Other applications like *Cinema4D* place this feature within an environment and actually call it "the sun." The user can designate the latitude and longitude of the scene and the time of day. Global lights provide a quick solution to lighting, and are often useful for some outdoor scenes.

global mix shaders A way to mix entire shaders in much the same way that one mixes colors, functions, and subshaders. with a global mix shader, the user can mix two completely different shaders with completely different color, highlight, shininess, bump, and other channels using exactly the same methods used to mix components within individual shader channels.

global object An object that can occur anywhere in a program. The construction and destruction order of global objects is implementation-dependent and is generally impossible to predict in a portable manner.

global parameterizability The characteristic of an implicit curve contained in a proximate interval Y of having at most one point in Y on the curve for any value of the ith parameter.

global resizing A technique used in *Poser* to scale a selected element of a figure (model). This can be done by holding the Shift key down with the Resize tool positioned over the selected element, or by using the Scale Parameter Dial. Either of these operations resizes the selected element in all XYZ directions at the same time.

global transformation matrix A matrix that defines how the components of an object are transformed when it is moved in a geometric space.

globe The professional term for a "light bulb."

Glow A plug-in for *trueSpace* by Axion Software that adds a soft glowing effect, allowing the user to recreate such effects as neon.

glow channel A useful technique for rendering neon lights, photon fire, and other "glowing" apparatuses. Glow channels allow the user to make an object appear with an inner or outer halo, or both. They can be used to make parts of objects glow while others do not. The user can choose what color and intensity to make an object's glow. One drawback of glow channels in most programs is that they are a post-rendering effect; that is, only after the scene is completely rendered and all the reflections and light sources have been calculated does the 3D application return to add the glow effect. This means that glows do not appear in reflective surfaces and they do not actually emit any light.

glow channel.

Glow flag A command in *Universe* that disables the glow characteristics of objects.

glow maps Used to create the illusion of an object casting light. They increase rendering speed and save on modeling time. Glow maps control the location and amount of illumination that a surface emits (rather than reflects). Practical applications of glow maps range from creating the illusion of windows on a building at night to mimicking the reflected glow of a neon sign off a brick wall. When working with either glow maps or glowing objects, it is important to remember that neither casts light of its own.

gl*Pointer **functions** An alternative vertex submission interface used with OpenGL. Similar to *glInterleavedArrays*, pointers to the vertex data are submitted using the *gl*Pointer* functions (e.g., *glVertexPointer*, *glColorPointer*). The submitted vertex data is then rendered using the *glDrawArrays*, *glArrayElement*, or *glDrawElements* functions. The *gl*Pointer* functions also have a uniform stride parameter, similar to *glInterleavedArrays*. The stride specifies the number of bytes from the beginning of one vertex component to the next. When the stride is greater than zero, the operation of the *gl*Pointer* functions is essentially the same as making a single call to *glInterleavedArrays*. When the stride is zero (the data is tightly packed together), the data is referred to as *stream data*. Stream data is very important when using SIMD (Single Instruction Multiple Data) instruction sets like Intel's SSE (Streaming SIMD Instructions) or AMD's 3DNow! instructions to transform, light, and/or clip vertices. If the data are in an interleaved vertex format, the data must be moved piecemeal into and out of the CPU's SIMD registers. With the data in stream format, the CPU can quickly and easily move large amounts of the data into the SIMD registers for processing. Even without taking advantage of the CPU's SIMD instructions for geometry and lighting, a performance boost can be had just by using the *gl*Pointer* functions.

glue operator An operator used to form complex objects by combining primitive objects in a union, with the restriction that the objects must not intersect.

GMSOLID A graphics system that uses multiple representations so that the most efficient representation may be selected for each operation.

gnomonic projection A projection of a sphere onto a plane, accomplished through rays that begin at the center of the sphere. Also known as *central projection*.

gobo A 3D object or model placed in front of a light source that is used to create a pattern in the shadows.

golden hour The hour or so before sunset. It represents the ideal time of day to shoot exteriors. The warm cast of the light is very flattering to human skin tones, and the chance of the scene being overlit is reduced. In addition, the low angle of the sun creates sharp, dark shadows, throwing everything in a scene into sharp relief.

golden mean A proportion that is found to create geometric figures that are pleasing to the eye. It is represented by the following equation:

$$\sigma = \left(\frac{\sqrt{5} + 1}{2} \right)$$

goniometric diagram A distribution plotted in cross-section showing intensity as a function of angular direction around a light's axis in polar coordinates.

Goo One of the filters in Corel's *KPT* volume for *Photoshop* and compatibles. *Goo* is a 2D morphing application that creates both morphed images and animations.

good continuation, visual The fact that given a juncture of lines, the viewer sees as continuous those lines that are smoothly connected.

Gosper curve A self-similar fractal generated by the initiator-generator method, which has a fractal dimension of 1.1292.

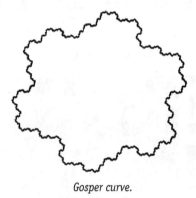

Gosper curve.

Gouraud shading Producing a smooth variation of surface intensity over a triangle or quadrilateral by bilinearly interpolating the intensities from the vertices. Gouraud shading is named for Henri Gouraud, who worked with Louis Daguerre in the early days of photography. Gouraud shading is technically called *intensity interpolation shading*, or *color interpolation shading* because it computes the intensity for each vertex and then distributes the computed intensities across the polygon. By performing this intensity interpolation, it removes the visible boundary between polygons, making them smooth. This

Gouraud shading.

smoothing of the polygon boundary is one of the advantages of using Gouraud shading over *flat shading*, although the disadvantage is that it removes the angular impressions on some models, such as cubes and pyramids. In addition, since the intensity is distributed across

the polygon, it cannot show some specular light reflection situations well. In effect, Gouraud shading "spreads out" the highlights across the polygon.

gradiated filters Filters that feature a grade from dark to light. They can be useful if one needs to take down a bright sky, but wants to keep the area below the horizon line unfiltered.

gradient The smooth blending from one color to another.

gradient function A function available in *Carrara*, used when a smooth transition between colors or other components is desired. If, for example, the user wanted a sphere to blend from blue to yellow, he would create a mix in the color channel with the color blue in the left branch, the color yellow in the right branch and a gradient function as the mixer. One can also use the gradient function in the transparency channel to make an object appear to fade in, or in the reflection channel to simulate a blending from wet to dry (*see Figure next page*).

gradient option An option in *The Games Factory* that will produce a smooth gradient from one color to another.

gradient search The use of variational calculus to determine the lowest energy path required to move an object from one point to another with certain constraints specified.

gradient function.

graftal A class of graphics objects similar to fractals, but generated with a set of rules that permits local modification of properties.

Grain A command in the *Material Generator* (part of *pluSpack*) plug-in for *true-Space* that enables the user to control the direction of the rings in the wood texture.

Grammar-based models A method of describing the structure of certain plants by using parallel graph grammar languages (also known as *graftals*) developed by Lindenmayer.

Gram-Schmidt process A method used to convert a basis to an orthonormal basis.

Granger unit A unit of measurement in *Universe*. Since these units are virtual units, one can use them to reference any unit of measurement. The user can make them millimeters, inches, feet, meters, or miles.

granularity The resolution of an image as limited by pixels in a display, the grains consisting of silver clumps in a photographic film or print, or photoreceptors in the human eye.

graph Numeric data displayed as visual data, using a "grid" method.

Graph A toggle command in the Window Menu of *Poser* that brings the graph into view. This command is also available as Graph Display in the Animation Keyframing window. Clicking the Graph Display button brings up the Graph Display for whatever item is selected in the hierarchy list. Readjusting the display via a splined or linear curve allows the selected element to have whatever priority that is selected animated according to the shape of the curve. The properties include Taper, Scale, Xscale, Yscale, Zscale, Twist, Side-to-Side, and Bend.

graphical data display manager (GDDM) Graphics software for IBM mainframes that accepts scanned data and provides outputs to terminals, plotters, printers, etc.

graphical kernel system (GKS) A graphics software program standard for producing two-dimensional images. GKS provides outputs for line graphics devices such as plotters, or raster graphics devices such as monitors or printers.

graphical languages See *animation, graphical languages*.

graphical user interface (GUI) A computer control system which permits the user to use a pointing device such as a mouse or trackball to position a cursor at one of a number of options shown on a computer screen and then activate a selection device such as a mouse button to cause the computer to perform a desired set of actions.

graphic alphabet A method of thinking about visual elements by considering them as letters of the alphabet.

graphic equalizer A device that is used to slightly modify the sound coming through a microphone to add more bass or treble.

graphics display processors A card that is plugged into a computer, or an integral part of the computer mother board, which contains sufficient dual-port memory to store a computer display image. Each memory location can be accessed by the computer to store part of an image and can also be read to the display at its refresh rate without interfering with computer operation. The card also contains circuitry to properly format the display and furnish sync pulses to it.

graphics interchange format See *GIF*.

graphics mode A display mode in which each pixel can be accessed and colored separately, in contrast to *text mode*, in which only a set of predetermined characters can be displayed.

graphics object One or more geometrical primitives grouped for convenience in rendering.

graphics pipeline A logical model for the computations needed in a raster-display system. It can be implemented in hardware, software, or a combination of both.

graphics subroutine package A collection of software procedures that perform various operations required to create a graphics image.

Graphics Workshop A graphics shareware program.

gravity The use of an implied region around a pre-existing graphics object in two-dimensional graphics so that when a vertex for a new object is created within the *gravity* region, it will be placed at the nearest point on the pre-existing object.

Gravity Direction A command in the Mr. Nito section of *Universe* that enables the user to specify the direction and force of gravity on the generated particles.

Gravity option A feature available in *The Games Factory*. As it suggests, this option selects the effect of gravity. A high setting will have the object fall rapidly, allowing only "short" jumps.

gravity well null In *Bryce*, an object, usually not rendered, that controls a number of moving objects in a scene. A gravity well null can simulate the power of a black hole or a super-magnet, attracting and influencing objects that are linked to it. As a core parent object, its effects can be seen, while the null object itself remains hidden.

gray card A type of card that reflects a known amount of light. Normally this card has a gray side and a white side. The gray side reflects 18% of the light falling on it while the white side reflects 90%.

gray ramp A display showing an ordered progression of shades of gray from black to white.

gray scale The number of shades of gray that can be produced by a graphics system.

grazed light A light that is placed close to the base of the screen near the ground plane to illuminate a background screen or cyclorama. The beam or focus of the grazed light should be set to point upward at a 45° angle.

great arc See *great circle*.

great circle A path along the surface of a sphere where all points on the path are intersections of a plane through the center of the sphere and the sphere's surface. Also known as a *great arc*.

greeking The representation of a page layout using bars, "nonsense text," and boxes to represent groupings of text copy.

green-screen Identical to a *blue-screen*, but used for those occasions where one needs to have blue elements in the foreground.

green spill Identical to a *blue spill*, except that it occurs with a green screen as a backdrop, rather than a blue screen.

grid An array of horizontal and vertical lines used to locate particular objects in a graphics image.

grid bag layout A Java procedure for laying out a sophisticated window. The user may specify the characteristics for a number of components and Java assembles them into a window display.

grid, calculating neighbor states Grids have a natural way of calculating neighbors. The neighbors of (x, y) are (x+1, y), (x+1, y+1), (x, y+1), etc. Most other schemes require that some data structure store the neighbor information for fast lookup, since the neighbor calculations are often expensive.

grid layout A Java procedure for laying out a window. It divides the window into a number of equally-sized rectangles. The contents of each rectangle may then be specified (*See Figure next page*).

grid line distance The distance from a point on a curve that is to be drawn to the nearest pixel that is on a grid line.

grid location A system of letters and numbers assigned to the rows and columns of a grid respectively to permit location of a desired object.

grid map A technique for applying the proper textures or colors to a complex object. First, create a grid with a number in each cell. Then superimpose this grid on the object to be textured. Determine what texture or color to associate with each numbered cell and then make a new grid, replacing the number in each cell replaced with the desired color or texture. When this new grid is mapped to the object, the desired coloring and texturing is achieved.

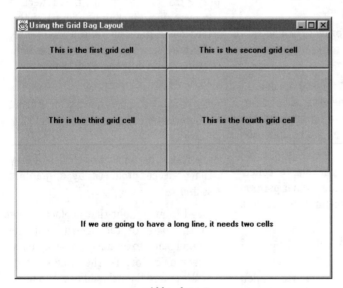

grid bag layout.

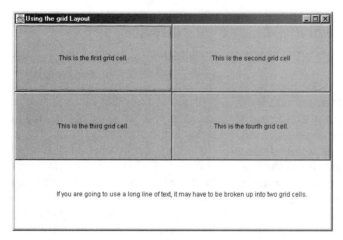

grid layout.

grid snap When making a room with the *Game Creation System*, it is very important that the wall panels are perfectly flush against each other. Gaps (even 1 cm wide) can result in unsightly bright lines between walls. This feature eliminates the gaps. When using grid snap, the walls will naturally line up along the grid without misalignment.

grids, positioning A grid of lines sometimes projected at low intensity onto the work area to help in aligning positions or objects.

Grid tab, Preferences window A tab in the Preferences window of *The Games Factory* that allows the user to create a grid and line up objects to it. When placing active objects on the play area, it is necessary to have all the objects lined up neatly on the screen by using the *Grid tool*.

Grid tool A tool that creates a grid in the *Game Creation System*. The icon looks like a tic-tac-toe board. It sets the grid spacing, usually at 100, 200, or 400. This setting doesn't affect wall-placing grids, but it will affect grids for placing trees and other stand-up objects. It will also set the grid for the editing commands.

grip An area near the edges of a printed page that is reserved for mechanical devices that hold the paper in place during printing and therefore cannot be printed upon.

groove A continuous channel designed into a recording medium to guide the reading device.

ground explosion An effect of an explosion that rises from the ground, created in *trueSpace* by using *PyroCluster*, which provides the power to create volumetric 3D explosions. One of the most powerful features built into the plug-in is its many particle systems, emitter types, and effectors.

ground explosion.

Ground Level A parameter in the Mr. Nitro section of Universe that represents the level at which particles of an explosion stop falling.

ground plane All 3D applications name the ground that models are placed on the ground plane, and it usually has a grid. In *Poser,* the ground plane is a rectangular plane that acts as the recipient for object shadows and also as the base upon which the actors stand or move. *Bryce* has three planar objects, each of which can accept material mapping: Cloud, Water, and Ground Plane. There are only slight differences among these three planes. First, they each load onto the workspace at different heights. Second, they attain their personalities by the materials mapped to their surfaces. Each of these three planes can accept any materials, and each can be moved to any height desired. One can easily map a cloud material, for instance, to a Ground plane, or water to a Cloud plane. All three of these planes are infinite along their x and z axes.

ground shadows Shadows cast on the ground object.

Ground Shadows A command in the Display menu of *Poser* that toggles ground shadows on and off.

Ground Zero A parameter in the Mr. Nitro section of *Universe* that represents the center of the explosion.

group 1. A set of objects in *Carrara* that are linked together so that they may be treated as a single object. 2. Any objects that form a cohesive group in any 3D application. 3. See *autonomous agent.*

Group Info Window A display in *Universe* that allows the user to position and rotate groups by entering coordinates and values.

grouping tool 1. The tool in a 3D application that allows the user to select objects in a scene and group them as one. 2. A tool in *Poser* that allows the user to select any portion of a model or prop for assigning a different texture or for deformations. For instance, one can select any part of a face before a deformation is applied, and have the deformation applied to just that part instead of the whole face. This leads to a higher variety of morph target development. Using the grouping tool to create new texture areas allows the user to colorize *Poser* models in some unique ways, and also allows the application of bitmap labels to props.

Group Material Info Window Materials control the surface characteristics of groups in *Universe* to determine the most fundamental look of the models. The Group Material Info Window (or *Material Editor*) determines these characteristics. It has several tabs that gives the user access to the channels of the material: Geometry, Diffuse, Specular, Ambient, Reflectivity, Transparency, Luminance/Glow, and Transmission. Using the Material Editor's channels, one can determine the color of the object and modify it to be shiny like metal, or dull like clay. It can be transparent or opaque, reflective or nonreflective, with many other options.

group technology The CAD concept that a parameterized primitive defines a family of parts whose members vary in only a few parameters.

growth sequence A characteristic of halftones in which any pixel that is intensified at an intensity level j is also intensified for all levels greater than j.

Guckenheimer's example A Julia set constructed using the following equation:

$$R(z) = (z-2)^2/z^2.$$

GUI See *graphical user interface*.

guide layer In *Flash*, a special *layer* that does not export when the user exports a *Flash* file. This layer is used to help in the registration of various elements of a *Flash* file.

Guides 1. A command in any 2D or 3D application that switches the guides on and off. 2. A command in the Display menu of *Poser* that allows use of any of the optional Display Guides (Ground Plane, Head Lengths, Hip-Shoulder Relationship, Horizon Line, and Vanishing Lines) as posing aids.

guide track An audio track containing the audio from the final edit. It is not part of the final tape or film, but is used as a reference to ensure that edits are correct and in sync.

Gupta-Sproull algorithm A technique for drawing antialiased lines. The algorithm draws three pixel wide lines using *Bresenham's algorithm*. It chooses the proper pixel color by determining the perpendicular distance from the pixel center to the line center, and then using a table lookup.

gutter In publishing, the inside margins between facing pages of a book or magazine, which often include extra space to allow for binding.

GWUIMS See *George Washington University User Interface Management System*.

H

H See *halfway vector*.

Haar wavelets See *wavelets, Haar*.

hackers, online protocols In a game in which a trusted server communicates with a number of players, it is important to prevent hackers from cheating when playing the game. Most protocol hackers are casual; they change bytes in a packet and see what happens. The first line of defense against such attacks is a simple *checksum*. A checksum is a short number produced by combining every byte of the packet. The sender computes the checksum of the packet and sends both the packet and the checksum to the recipient. The recipient takes the packet and recomputes its checksum; if the computed checksum does not match the checksum from the sender, the packet is corrupt and should be rejected. It is important to include the entire packet, including the header, in the checksum computation, so that the recipient can detect changes to the header as well as the payload.

Hadamard matrix An *n* H *n* matrix of elements equal to +1 or −1 and whose rows and columns are mutually orthogonal. Used in applying the *Hadamard transform*.

Hadamard transform A formula used to convert a sampled analog signal into its frequency components. Similar to, but less well known than, the *Fourier transform*.

Hair library A library of hair styles in *Poser*. Hair is a Prop that comes into the scene already parented with the figure's head.

halation 1. The indirect generation of light registration on film through lateral diffusion. 2. The "ghost image" or halo outlines in images. 3. Reflections from outside a cathode-ray tube or within the glass face plate that limit the maximum contrast that may be obtained between neighboring pixels.

half duplex A data communications technique in which transmission can take place in either direction along a line, but in only one direction at a time.

Half-Life A game by Sierra that makes use of flocking algorithms.

half phase filter A filter that uses an even number of samples, thereby producing an output that is situated between two input samples. Compare with *zero phase filter*.

halftone A graphic in which dots are used to represent continuous tones, with large, closely spaced dots representing darker areas and smaller, widely spaced dots representing lighter tones. This permits the printing of photographs on paper using ordinary printing processes, which cannot handle continuous tone images. A halftone can be created from a photograph by re-photographing it through a screen that breaks the picture up into dots. Newspaper halftones use 60 to 80 dots per inch. Magazine halftones use 110 to 200 dots per inch.

halftoning Converting a photograph to a set of dots that can be reproduced by an ordinary printing process. The dot pattern makes a 45 degree angle to the horizontal which is called the *screen angle*. The computer equivalent to halftoning is called *clustered-dot ordered dither*. See *halftone*.

halfway vector (H) A vector whose direction is halfway between the direction of the light source and that of the viewer. It is used in illumination models.

haloed line A line that is part of a group of intersecting lines and which is drawn continuously while the other intersecting lines are drawn with gaps at the intersection points.

Hamilton system An energy-conserving physical assembly.

H and D curve In filming, the amount of light the film is exposed to is directly related to the resulting density of the film. The more light exposed to the film, the denser the negative becomes, and vice versa. When plotted on a graph, this direct correlation between exposure and film density displays a characteristic shape and form. Afterward, the developed film can be inspected using a

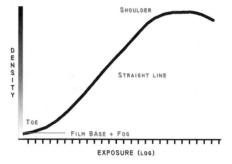

H and D curve.

densitometer, a device that measures the amount of light transmission on a particular area of film. The curve resulting from this test with the densitometer is called an *H and D curve*, for Hurter and Driffeld, who discovered this form of measurement in 1890. It is also called the *density versus log exposure curve*.

handheld The typical handheld microphone used by rock stars, comedians, and wandering talk show hosts. Usually an omnidirectional, dynamic microphone.

handles 1. A programming technique that avoids the dangers of using pointers. An example of a handle is the HANDLE type returned by the CreateFile() call in Win32's file system. A file handle, representing an open file system object, is created through the CreateFile() call, passed to other functions such as ReadFile() and SetFilePointer() for manipulation, and then finally closed off with CloseHandle(). Attempting to call those functions with an invalid or closed handle does not cause a crash; instead, it returns an error code. This method is efficient, safe, and easy to understand. Handles almost always fit into a single CPU register for efficient storage in collections and passing as parameters to functions. They can be easily checked for validity and provide a level of indirection that allows the underlying data organization to change without invalidating any outstanding handles. This has significant advantages over passing around pointers. Handles can also be easily saved to disk, because the data structures they refer to can be reconstructed in the same order on a game restore. This facility allows the handles to be stored directly, with no conversions necessary, because they are already in

223

unique identifier form. 2. Extra footage at the head and tail of each shot to allow the editor room to add dissolves and manipulate the pacing of a scene. 3. Small figures on a display that indicate where the user may place the cursor and then drag and drop to change the size, shape, or orientation of an object.

handling zone The part of an optical disk that can be touched by the disk drive's gripping mechanism.

handshaking The exchange of information at the beginning of a data communications session during which two communicating systems determine the specifications, such as parity, baud rate, speed, etc., which are to be used for the session.

hands, posing and customizing A capability of *Poser* to create detailed hand models. Important hand-associated items are contained in a number of places in *Poser*.

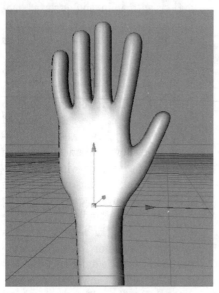

hands, posing and customizing.

hands, posing and customizing.

handwriting recognition Computer software for converting handwritten material into machine-readable text.

hanging microphones Microphones hung from above to record large groups of people or presentations.

hard copy Data, text, or graphics printed on paper rather than residing on a disk or in memory, from which it must be viewed by display on a monitor. Compare with *soft copy*.

hard cut An edit from one shot to another without any transition in between, such as a dissolve.

hard disk A magnetic storage device making use of a disk coated with magnetic material that is an integral part of the disk drive mechanism, in contrast to *floppy disk* where the disk is removable from the drive. Hard disks can have more precise tracking control and thereby store more data in a given area than floppy disks.

hard error An error in data communications, or on a disk, that cannot be corrected with the data correction methods used by the system.

hard hyphen A hyphen that will always appear in the reproduced text. A *soft hyphen* will be printed or displayed only if it comes at the end of a line.

hard light Light from a direct, focused light source.

hard return In word processing, a carriage return that is entered by the user and that causes the succeeding text to move to the beginning of the next line, regardless of whether the current line is full.

hard sectored Describes a floppy disk that has the sector boundaries permanently marked, such as by having holes punched in the disk at the sector boundaries.

hard sound effect A sound that is short, precise, and fairly loud, such as a knock on a door, a burst of applause, or a screech of tires.

hard space A specially designated space character used instead of an ordinary space between two words to make it impossible for a line break to occur between the two words. If the two words occur at the end of a line, they will either both be on the current line or both moved to the next line.

hardware Electronic circuitry designed to perform computer operations.

hardware binding design The determination of how input and output units of meaning are formed from hardware primitives. Also known as *lexical design*.

hardwired Describes a computer option that is permanently set into a computer at the time of installation and cannot easily be changed by switches or software.

harmonic A signal that is an integral multiple of the frequency of a fundamental signal.

Harter-Heightway dragon curve A fractal curve, drawn using the L-systems or initiator-generator technique, which has the appearance of a dragon.

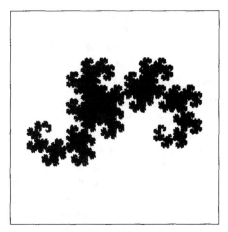

Harter-Heightway dragon curve.

Hash *Animator* A 3D application that uses NURBS and spline modeling for objects, rather than polygons.

hash function A function that is used to map an object into a position in a table, associating a key value with each entry. Ideally, a hash function would not map two objects to the same position, but this is usually impossible. As a compromise, we try to develop a hash function that distributes the objects more or less uniformly. As an example of a hash function, one might choose the sum of the ASCII values of the letter in a string.

hashing function See *hash function*.

hash table A dictionary consisting of an array of numbered keys where all numbers are between 0 and the array length minus one. A value is added to the array by determining the number corresponding to its key (*hash function*) and putting it in that place in the array. A value is looked up by determining the number corresponding to the key and looking in the appropriate cell of the array.

hash total Sum of the data in an information field used to provide a checksum that can be used to determine data accuracy at a later time.

hatchet lighting See *side lighting*.

Hausdorff dimension A dimension greater than the Euclidian dimension which appears to more correctly express the dimensional characteristics of fractal curves. For self-similar fractals where line segments are replaced repeatedly by a generator having N line segments each of which is of length r, where r is a fraction of the line segment being replaced, the Hausdorff dimension is expressed by the equation:

$$D = \frac{\log n}{\log \frac{1}{r}}$$

Also known as the *Hausdorff-Besicovitch dimension*.

Hausdorff distance The distance between two closed bounded subsets of a set.

haze Smoke, dust, or water droplets which obscure visibility by reducing the contrast of objects when interposed between the viewer and the objects.

HDCAM A high-definition recording format by Sony. HDCAM is NTSC/PAL switchable and has an optional 24 fps frame rate. It is aimed at high-end film to digital video uses.

HDTV See *high-definition television*.

head An electronic device designed to read data from a magnetic disk. The head consists of a coil wrapped around a core of magnetic material that contains a small gap. When the gap passes over the magnetized regions of a disk, pulses of magnetic energy occur which are translated into electrical impulses in the coil.

header The beginning of a packet of information, which contains administrative information.

headline In typography, a line of display type at the top of a job. Used to attract the reader's attention.

head-motion parallax See *parallax*.

head-mounted display A display that is mounted on the user's head so that an image appears in front of his eyes. It often includes feedback so that the image changes as the user moves, thereby giving the illusion that the user is walking through the space shown in the display.

head mouse A device that works like a mouse except that it is mounted on the user's head and translates head movements into cursor movements.

Head Parameters A setting in *Poser* that can be used to create faces with different expressions. They include Left/Right Eyebrow Down, Left/Right Eyebrow Up, Open Lips, Smile, Mouth "O," Mouth "F," Mouth "M," Tongue "T," Tongue "L," and more.

headphones In filmmaking, a device that permits hearing audio as it is being recorded and, in addition, blocks out ambient noise from the set.

head thrashing Rapid back and forth movements of a disk head caused by inability of the head positioning mechanism to locate the proper position for the head.

head tracking A specialized display system in which the position of the observer's head is measured and used to control the viewpoint of a scene displayed on a screen.

Hebbian net A single-neurode single layer net that learns, by using input vectors, to modify the weights such that the weights create the best possible linear separation of the inputs and outputs. The net improves if the inputs are orthogonal, and deteriorates when they are not. Also known as a *Hebb net*.

Heckbert's algorithm An algorithm for color quantization using a median-cut technique.

hedgehog A three-dimensional object displayed as a wire frame with associated normal vectors.

Heisenberg's uncertainty principle The principle that the more accurately one measures one quality of an object, the less accurately is it possible to measure its other qualities simultaneously.

Helmholtz-Young theory Hermann von Helmholtz (1821–1894) improved on the color theory advanced by Thomas Young with the Helmholtz-Young theory or the *trichromatic theory*. Helmholtz found that some receptors in the eyes are most sensitive to short wavelengths, whereas others are sensitive to long wavelengths. Helmholtz was also able to derive a sensitivity distribution curve that shows to which colors our eyes are most sensitive. This theory explains the changes of the response of each receptor as the wavelength varies. It explains the ability of the eyes to see color changes as a continuous experience. However, this theory cannot account for the creation of white light from blue and yellow and the fact that the mixture of red and green light looks yellow. It also cannot account for how the receptors are able to respond depending on the wavelength.

Helmholtz-Young theory.

hemi-cube The mapping of a hemisphere onto the surface of a cube.

hemi-cube algorithm An algorithm for calculating radiosity solutions for complex environments.

Henon attractor The attractor produced by the recursive formulas.

herding The group behavior of a number of autonomous agents. See *flocking behavior*.

Hermite polynomial A polynomial used in three-dimensional interpolation.

Hermite polynomial fractal A fractal curve created by iterating a Hermite polynomial equation over the complex plane.

Hermite splines 1. A method of generating a bicubic surface using four control points. The first and third control points are used for interpolation. The second and fourth control points are vectors that determine the tangency of the curve at interpolated points. 2. A method of interpolation between frames in an animation which makes use of the keyframes on either side of the desired position as well as the frames on either side of these keyframes.

Hershey fonts A set of standard character forms, now in the public domain, developed by the U.S. Bureau of Standards.

hertz (Hz) A measure of frequency equal to one cycle per second.

heterogeneous model A model whose elements may have behaviors that differ qualitatively from one another over time.

heterogeneous network A network that connects computers that have different architectures.

heuristic cost An attempt to estimate the true cost from a particular node to the goal when using the A* algorithm. If one always knew the true cost to the goal, A* would beeline a path to the goal without wasting any search time going down the wrong path. But if the heuristic estimate happens to overestimate the true cost, the heuristic becomes "inadmissible," and the algorithm might not find the optimal path (and might find a terrible path). The way to guarantee that the cost is never overestimated is by calculating the geometric distance between the node and the goal. When coding A* for the first time, this is the best thing to do until it is time to optimize. Since the cost will never be more than this distance, the optimal path will always be found.

Hewlett-Packard graphics language (HPGL) A language used to describe a drawing in a form that can be understood and translated directly into drawing actions by a plotter.

hex Short for *hexadecimal*. A numerical system in which 16 digits are used instead of 10. The digits 0 through 9 are used as they would in the decimal system, and the letters A through F are used to represent counts of 10 through 15 in the decimal system. The result is that higher order numbers in the hexadecimal system have a different meaning than in the decimal system. For example, 10 in the hexadecimal system is the same as 16 in the decimal system. In either system we use the convention that we begin counting by using all of the available symbols. When we run out, the next count is represented by the first symbol with a 0 at its right. Thus in the decimal system we can count to 9 with the available symbols. The next count is 10. In the hexadecimal system we can count to F (15 in decimal) and the next count is 10 (16 in decimal).

hexcone color solid A color space used to define colors. It consists of a solid that has a hexagon with red, yellow, green, cyan, blue, and magenta on its vertices, white at its center, and black directly below the center.

HFS See *hierarchical file system*.

hidden line In graphics, a line on a three-dimensional object that cannot be seen when the object is represented two dimensionally.

hidden-line determination See *visible-line determination*.

hidden line removal A software process that produces a wireframe rendering of a three-dimensional object in which lines representing surfaces that would be invisible to the viewer are removed.

hidden page animation An animation technique that requires several pages of display memory, only one of which is displayed at any given time. The background image is stored on a secondary hidden page. To create a new frame, it is transferred to the primary hidden page and the graphics array is drawn on top of it. This page is then displayed; the original display page becomes the primary hidden page, and the process is repeated for the next frame.

hidden surface algorithm An algorithm that determines which surfaces of a three-dimensional object are invisible to the viewer and prevents them from being painted on the screen.

hidden surface problem The problem of determining which surfaces of a three-dimensional object are invisible to a viewer and therefore should not be shown in a two-dimensional mapping of the object.

hidden surface removal The process of applying a *hidden surface algorithm* to identify and remove invisible surfaces.

Hide Figure/Show All Figures Commands in the Figure Menu of *Poser*. When there are so many figures in a scene that it becomes hard to pose the selected one, the user can hide the rest. Selecting the Show All Figures command brings them all into view again.

hierarchical B-spline refinement The adding of additional control points to those initially designated to create a B-spline curve, using a hierarchical data structure. This enables a coarse version of the curve to be drawn using the original control points and the curve then refined using the additional control points when necessary. This significantly reduces the computer time needed to draw the curve when only the coarse version is required.

hierarchical configuration A collection of objects organized into a tree hierarchy with the position and orientation of each object's frame described in the coordinates of its parent.

hierarchical display list An ordered list of display instructions that are saved independently of the main computer so that they can be used to create a display faster and without main-computer intervention.

hierarchical file system (HFS) The file-management system used in DOS which allows a disk to have directories that are divided up into subdirectories, which are divided into sub-subdirectories, etc.

hierarchical menu selection A selection technique in which, when a user selects an action from a menu, a submenu appears allowing choices to refine the initial action. This may be repeated for as many levels as desired.

hierarchical object selection A technique in which, as the user starts to type in the name of a desired object, those object names whose first letters match the ones already typed in are displayed. This enables the user to find the desired object more quickly, particularly when he is uncertain of its spelling.

hierarchical pathfinding A technique that speeds up the pathfinding process. Regardless of which search space representation is used, this technique simplifies that space. Therefore, if the world representation is large, the key is to break up the world hierarchically. Consider a castle. It can be thought of as a single, large building, or as a collection of rooms connected by doors (a large-scale connectivity graph). The pathfinder works in two distinct steps. It first finds the room-to-room path, knowing the starting and ending room. Once that room-to-room path is known, the pathfinder then works on the micro problem of getting from the current room to the next room on the list. Thus, the pathfinder does not need to compute the entire path before it takes the first step. The micro path is figured out on a need-to-know basis as each new room is entered. This method significantly cuts down on the search space and the resulting time necessary to compute the path.

hierarchical structure A series of objects or items divided or classified into ranks or orders.

hierarchy 1. A system of organizing a number of elements into a tree. Each el-

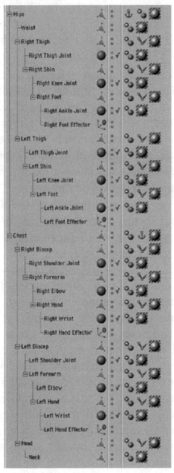

hierarchy.

ement of the hierarchy is known as a *node*. When two nodes are in the hierarchy, the higher one is called the *parent* and the lower one the *child*. A node with no parent is a *root*. A node with no children is a *leaf*. 2. A text file in *Poser* that lists the object files that make up a figure. It has the extension *.phi*. The hierarchy file is then converted by selecting Convert Hier in the *Poser* file menu. The resulting conversion may then be assigned a name and added to the Figure library under New Figures.

hierarchy traversal The traversal of a hierarchy of bounded volumes forming a tree for efficient determination of collision of a ray with an object in ray tracing.

high coherence The characteristic of an image in which adjacent pixels are very likely to be of the same or nearly the same color.

high-definition television (HDTV) A television system having much higher resolution than the former standards. A subgroup of the new DTV digital television broadcast standard that has a 16:9 aspect ratio, a resolution of either 1280x720 or 1920x1080, a frame rate of 23.96, 24, 29.97, 30, 59.95 or 60 fps and either interlaced or progressive scanning.

high density Describes floppy disks that have a greater capacity than the normal capacity of disks of that dimension. For example, normal density $5\frac{1}{4}$-inch floppy disks have a capacity of 360K bytes; high-density $5\frac{1}{4}$-inch floppy disks have a capacity of 1.2 megabytes. Similarly, normal density $3\frac{1}{2}$-inch floppy disks have a capacity of 720K bytes and high-density $3\frac{1}{2}$-inch floppy disks have a capacity of 1.44 megabytes.

highlight A bright region on the surface of an image of a shiny object resulting from a specular reflection from a light source.

highlighting Making the surface of a graphics object brighter to make it stand out from other objects.

high resolution A display or printer image that has a higher number of pixels or dots per inch than normal, producing a better quality image.

Hilbert curve A space-filling fractal curve of the Peano family of curves.

Hilbert curve.

histogram A bar chart or graph that shows the distribution of colors or gray shades in an image.

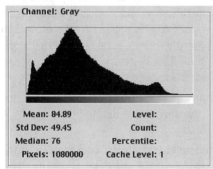

histogram.

Histogram Palette A toggle in *Paint Shop Pro* that displays a histogram of the colors used in an image.

hither A clipping plane that is perpendicular to the line of sight. It is used to remove objects that will not appear in the image because they are behind or too close to the viewpoint.

hits The number of files downloaded in a Web browser from a Web page. The term *hits* is most often confused with actual page views. For example, if a Web page has three images and one sound file on it, and a viewer downloads that page completely into his Web browser, that page would have generated five in that single page view. Three hits count for the images downloaded, one hit counts for the sound file, and one hit counts for the actual HTML file. Hits are actual file downloads in one live session; in this case totalling five.

H & J See *hyphenation and justification*.

HLS color model A three-dimensional model for defining color characteristics in terms of *hue*, *lightness*, and *saturation*. It is based on artists' pigments, with *hue* representing the color of the pigment, *lightness* representing the amount of white included, and *saturation* representing the amount of pigment. This model is easy to use, because it is similar to the way humans intuitively classify color. Also known as the *HSL color model*.

HMI lights High-powered arc lights used to simulate daylight. The lights at a baseball stadium are often HMI lights.

Hobby's polygonal pens A method of drawing wide lines using polygons defined by integer offset vectors.

hogel-vector bandwidth compression A diffraction-specific fringe computation technique that has been implemented and used to generate complex 3D holographic images for interactive real-time display.

hogel-vector decoding The conversion of each hogel vector into a useful fringe in a hogel region. Decoding performs the convolutions through a linear summation of basis fringes using the hogel vector as weighting coefficients. To compute a given hogel, each component of its hogel vector is used to multiply the corresponding basis fringe. The decoded hogel is the accumulation of all the weighted basis fringes. Looking at the array of precomputed basis fringes as a two-dimensional matrix, hogel decoding is an inner product between the basis-fringe matrix and a hogel vector.

Hold and Fetch A plug-in for *trueSpace* from Black Knight Productions that allows the user to freeze a scene at any point. The frozen scene will then be held in memory without overwriting the saved scene.

hollow fill A rendering of graphics objects in which only the pixels adjacent to polygon edges are displayed.

hologram A three-dimensional picture produced by the interference of two laser light beams on a photosensitive plate. The interference is caused by the same beam being split into two beams, one of which is reflected off of an object and onto the plate. The other beam is directed straight at the plate as a reference beam for the first beam to interfere with, thus creating the three-dimensional interference pattern.

hologram, color Full-color holovideo images are produced by computing three separate fringes. Each represents one of the additive primary colors (red, green, and blue) taking into account the three different wavelengths used in a color holovideo display. The three fringes are used to modulate three separate beams of light (one for each primary color).

holography in security One of the fastest growing areas for the use of holograms is in security and product authentication. Holograms are added to driver's licenses, credit and phone cards, for the purposes of tamper proofing, anti-counterfeiting, and customizing ticket protection.

Homesite A Web page editor by Allaire.

homogeneous coordinates A generalization of three-dimensional Euclidian space in which an additional vector is added to the coordinate description. This results in 4×4 transformation matrices which can represent rotation and translation in a single matrix.

homogeneous network A network that connects computers that all have the same architecture.

homogeneous coordinates A positioning system in two dimensions where each point is represented by three parameters, x, y, and W, with W being a multiplier that is applied to the other two coordinates to obtain the actual position. This system is useful in applying matrix transformations to objects.

homogeneous transformation An affine transformation defined by a 4×4 matrix.

homogenization An operation in affine space, where one determines the point at which the line connecting a designated point to the system origin intersects the affine plane.

Hopf bifurcation The behavior of a recursive equation in which a fixed point becomes unstable and gives birth to an invariant circle, which is attractive.

Hopfield net A single-layer network with a number of neurodes equal to the number of inputs X_i. The network is fully connected, meaning that every neurode is connected to every other neurode and the inputs are also the outputs. Thus there is feedback, which is one of the key features of the Hopfield net and the basis for the convergence to the correct result. The Hopfield network is an iterative autoassociative memory. This means that it can take one or more cycles to return the correct result (if at all). The Hopfield network takes an input and then feeds it back. This feedback cycle can occur a number of times before the input vector is returned. Hence, a Hopfield network functional sequence is as follows. First, we determine the weights based on our input vectors that we want to autoassociate, then we input a vector and see what comes out of the activations. If the result is the same as our original input, we are finished; if not, we take the result vector and feed it back through the network.

horizon bitmap In the *Game Creation System*,the Extra Features Editor can be used to enable the game engine to display a horizon bitmap or a sky bitmap in the distance. This option can enable or disable the set horizon. Turning it off can increase performance.

horizon effect A problem that occurs in game design with a fixed-depth search.

horizontal cells Cells in the eye that collect and integrate adjacent photoreceptor signals.

horizontal delay A display feature available on professional video monitors that shows the video signal offset horizontally so as to allow the editor to see and analyze the horizontal sync pulses. See also *vertical delay*.

Horizontal Flip function A manipulation function in *The Games Factory*. The Horizontal Flip function reverses all the images from left to right. This is useful when the user has a character going one way, and he simply wants to turn all the frames to face the other way.

horizontal line resolution The number of vertical lines in the visible portion of the video signal.

horizontal retrace The portion of a video signal during which the scanning electron beam is moved from the end of one scan line to the beginning of the next. Video is usually blanked during horizontal retrace so that retrace lines do not appear on the screen.

horizontal sync The sync pulses in the video signal that regulate the movement and position of the electron beam as it draws each horizontal scan line across the video monitor.

host A processor in a multiprocessor system that manages requests for services, resources, or memory from other processors.

HotLips An extension for *Carrara*, by Autonomous Effects. If an animator wanted a character to speak, he would need to have the character's mouth move synchronously with what it is saying. Conventional animators laboriously determine the exact sequence of phonemes in a sentence, craft a different mouth and tongue position for each phoneme, and then place these positions in the time line to match the audio exactly. Even the shortest utterance can take hours or days to lip sync. *HotLips* can generate an open-and-shut mouth animation exactly synchronized to an audio track.

hot point A point on an object where the cursor can be located in order to click and drag the object to a new location.

Hot Spot In *The Games Factory*, an invisible handle, or anchor, used to drag images around on the screen. It is used as a reference for the X, Y coordinates of an object.

hotspot The area where the beams of several light sources converge.

hot-swapping Replacing a peripheral without shutting off the computer's power.

household lights Ordinary lamps found in a home. Because video requires less light than film, household lighting is often sufficient for recording video. Generally, household lamps are less than 3,200 degrees K and lean more toward the orange side of the spectrum.

HPGL See *Hewlett-Packard graphics language.*

HSB color model. A three-dimensional model for defining color characteristics in terms of *hue*, *saturation*, and *brightness*. It is based on artists' pigments, with *hue* representing the color of the pigment, *saturation* representing the amount of pigment, and *value or brightness* representing the amount of white included. This model is easy to use, be-

cause it is similar to the way humans intuitively classify color. Also known as the *HSV (Hue, Saturation, Value) color model* or the *HVC (Hue, Value, Chroma) color model.*

HSL color model See *HLS color model.*

HSV color model See *HSB color model.*

HTML See *Hypertext Markup Language.*

HTML document A document written in HTML (Hypertext Markup Language) for use by a browser or Web site. The <HTML> tag is the first tag entered into a document to identify it as an *HTML document*. It contains an "on" tag, placed at the beginning of the document, and an "off" tag, placed at the end of the document. Everything else will go in between these tags. The <HTML> tag is placed as follows:

```
<HTML>
</HTML>
```

Hubbard tree An algorithm for developing a Julia set by calculating the external angles.

hue 1. The frequency or wavelength of a color. 2. The property or attribute of color (chroma) as it is perceived and determined by the wavelength of light.

hue, saturation, brightness (HSB) See *HSB color model.*

Huffman encoding A method of compressing data by replacing frequently recurring data strings with shorter codes.

hull A graphics construct that encloses another (usually more complex) graphics construct. For example, straight lines connecting the four control points for a

Bezier curve form a *hull* that encloses the Bezier curve.

Hungarian notation A notation invented by Dr. Charles Simonyi, chief software architect of Microsoft, to help standardize variable naming conventions. The basic premise of Hungarian notation is to preface the variable name with an identifier describing the type of data the variable represents. For instance, an integer variable named *SomeVariable* would instead be named *iSomeVariable*. In addition to variable types, pointers can be represented. A pointer to some class *Foo* might be called *pFooObj*. Prefixes can also be combined to provide more information than a single prefix can provide. For instance, a pointer to an integer would be represented by the prefix *pi*, or a pointer to a pointer would be represented as *pp*. Many contend that such a naming convention is unnecessary in a type-safe language such as C++ and creates more work when changing data types (since it requires changing the variable prefix), but others appreciate the ease and speed with which data types are visually identified.

Hurst exponent A measure of the persistence of statistical phenomena.

Hurter and Driffeld curve See *H and D curve*.

HUTWindows Helsinki University of Technology Window Manager. A windows system that defines objects as self-contained entities, each with its own transition network that is independent of the others.

HVC color model See *HSB color model*.

hybrid parallelism See *parallel rasterization architecture*.

hyperbola A curve that is the locus of a point which moves so that the difference of its undirected distances from two fixed points is constant. It has the equation (*see Figure next page*):

$$\frac{x^2}{a^2} - \frac{y^2}{b^2} = 1$$

hyperbolic cosine fractal A fractal curve produced by iterating the equation:

$$z_n = \cosh(z_{n-1}) + c$$

with $z_0 = 0 + i0$ and c varied over the complex plane.

hyperbolic paraboloid A three-dimensional object whose surface is the locus of all points on the equation:

$$\frac{x^2}{a^2} - \frac{y^2}{b^2} = z$$

hyperbolic sine fractal A fractal curve produced by iterating the equation:

$$z_n = \sinh(z_{n-1}) + c$$

with $z_0 = 0 + i0$ and c varied over the complex plane.

hyperboloid The three-dimensional object produced by rotating a hyperbola around an axis. The *hyperboloid of one sheet* has the equation:

$$\frac{x^2}{a^2} + \frac{y^2}{b^2} - \frac{z^2}{c^2} = 1$$

The *hyperboloid of two sheets* has the equation:

$$\frac{x^2}{a^2} - \frac{y^2}{b^2} - \frac{z^2}{c^2} = 1$$

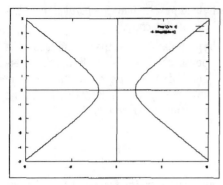

hyperbola.

hypercardioid microphone A microphone that has a highly directional pickup pattern with most of the pick-up coming from the front of the microphone.

hypercube The analog of a cube in a space of greater than three dimensions. In n-space, a hypercube has $2n$ faces and 2^n vertices.

hyperface The face of an n-dimensional solid where n is greater than three.

hyperfocal distance The distance to the nearest object that is in focus when a lens is focused at infinity. If the lens is focused at the hyperfocal distance, everything from half the hyperfocal distance to infinity is in focus.

hyperlattice An n-dimensional lattice, where n is greater than three.

hypermedia A technique for delivering information that provides a large number of interconnections throughout the body of the data so that the user can easily jump from a topic to a related or supplementary topic.

HyperNURBS Generator objects, like all NURBS objects, that create new shapes by using other shapes. Most NURBS ob-jects use spline objects to generate shapes. HyperNURBS are the notable exception. HyperNURBS use polygons or primitives to create new rounded shapes through a subdivision algorithm. This means one can begin with a square and pull facets of faces of it in new directions into lots of new shapes, and then once placed in a HyperNURBS, the square edges become round.

hyper-rectangle A rectilinear region in parameter space.

Hypertext Markup Language (HTML) A computer language used to create Web pages for the World Wide Web (WWW). Essentially, HTML is a text file that is "marked up" with codes often referred to as tags. Tags tell the Web browser how to display Web page elements such as text and images within the Web browser window. HTML reminds Web browsers where to take paragraph breaks, when to change font colors and sizes, where to insert a picture, etc. Without the HTML tags, the Web browser would display the document as a regular text file that doesn't contain any images or formatting.

hypervoxel The equivalent of a voxel in n-dimensional space, where n is greater than three. The HyperVoxel objects in *LightWave* are used to create very realistic clouds and pyrotechnic effects.

hyphenation and justification (H&J) The arrangement of the spacing between words of text so that each line begins and ends evenly at the margins. This includes breaking up words at the appropriate syllable breaks (hyphenation) to avoid wide spaces that might occur if a large word doesn't quite fit on a line.

hypo Short for *sodium hyposulfite*, now known as *sodium thiosulfate*, used in fixers.

hysteresis threshold See *threshold, hysteresis*.

Hz See *hertz*.

I

i The basis of the imaginary number system. *i* equals the square root of -1.

I The in-phase component of a color that is encoded in the *YIQ* color space. The *I* component is the orange-cyan component. See *YIQ color model*.

ICL See *image composition language*.

icon A small image on a computer screen that designates the area in which a mouse cursor is to be placed to activate a particular program.

icons, using with checkboxes Java Swing has a capability that permits a checkbox to consist of an icon rather than a box and associated text. This often makes selection of a desired action easier for the user. For example, suppose an architect wanted to give a customer the choice of a half-dozen kitchen styles. Rather than having six checkboxes with text descriptions, the user could select between six checkboxes, each containing a small picture of a kitchen style. The selected one would then appear as a full screen picture.

icosahedron A 20-sided solid whose faces are triangles.

ID See *identifier*.

I$_{dc\lambda}$ (depth cue color) Color of an object as modified to simulate the change that occurs due to atmospheric attenuation as an object moves farther and farther away from the viewer.

ideal inclusion function A function that provides the tightest bound possible for an object but still permits easier determination of when collisions occur between light rays and the object.

ideal specular illumination The behavior of a perfect specular light.

IDE drives Hard drives that adhere to the IDE interface specification.

identifier (ID) A name for an object.

identity matrix A matrix having 1's on the diagonal and 0's elsewhere. When it multiplies (or is multiplied by) a second matrix, the second matrix is unchanged.

IEEE-1394 A high-speed serial interface that can be used to attach DV cameras, storage devices, printers, or networks to a computer. See *Firewire*.

IES (Illuminating Engineering Society) files Files that provide manufacturer's measured light distribution data for various light sources.

IFF A graphics image file format by Electronic Arts. It was originally used by Amiga and Atari ST personal computers. There are multiple IFF formats, including one for sound files, but the most commonly used is for images. IFF images may also, uncommonly, have the suffix .ILBM, for InterLeaved BitMap, or just .LBM on DOS-based systems.

I-frame In video compression, an intermediate frame between two keyframes.

I-frames store only the data that has changed from the previous frame.

IFS See *iterated function system*.

IGES See *initial graphics exchange specification*.

I_i **(incident radiance)** The radiance of the incident light upon an object.

IK See *inverse kinematics*.

IK tool A tool in *Universe* that moves an entire hierarchy at once. By applying Inverse Kinematics to the chain, the user can work up the hierarchy from the bottom, passing the movements of the lowest child on the chain to the root of the chain.

iLink Sony's name for the IEEE-1394 specification.

illuminance The flux density in lumens per square meter or lux, striking an illuminated surface.

illuminant A light source whose color spectrum is specified. An illuminant light source is needed to assure that comparison of colors is not biased by different light source colors.

illumination 1. The amount of light cast on a subject. 2. The complete description of all light striking a designated point on a selected surface.

illumination model The algorithm or equation used to determine the shading of a particular point or surface. Also known as a *shading model* or *lighting model*.

illumination ray A ray that carries light from a light source to an object.

Illusion A stand-alone pyrotechnic and effects particle system for 2D compositing applications. *Illusion* has also been folded into Discreet *Combustion* effects application.

illusion of form Creating the best lighting for a scene. Spending hours or even days modeling, shading, and arranging a complex scene will become a useless effort if the final composition results are dull due to improper lighting. Setting the lighting correctly will enable the models to utilize the light more effectively. This is extremely important in creating a sense of weight and form. Regardless of what type of scene or mood the designer is creating, the ability to set up the proper lighting configuration will help create a more dynamic composition. The best way to check the scene for balance is to create a sphere that is about the same size as the whole of the primary objects being illuminated. By placing this sphere so that it encompasses the objects of the light's attention, the designer can more clearly observe how light will strike the objects in the scene.

Illustrator, **Adobe** Software from Adobe Systems, Inc., used to paint pictures on a computer screen.

image A representation of a picture or graphic, particularly on a computer screen.

image analysis The identifying and grouping of features in an image into objects and classifying of the objects in order to provide a basis for understanding image content.

image-assembly tree A structure in which each internal node is either an image transformation or a compositing operation, and each leaf node is an image.

image attributes The properties that need to be stored for each pixel to describe an image such as width, height, or color.

image compositing See *compositing, image.*

image composition language (ICL) A language that allows the programmer to declare images as variables. Each image may be described by a composition expression consisting of variables combined by arithmetic, relational, and conditional operations.

image enhancement Improving poorly shot video by modifying the brightness, contrast, saturation, or hue of the footage.

image irradiance The irradiance incident upon a pixel in an image.

Image Lounge A filter package with a variety of plug-ins in one package. In addition to very stylized text, texture, and distortion filters, *Image Lounge* includes fire, clouds, and smoke effects, and special camera effects such as focus racks.

image map An HTML image on a Web page with hyperlinks to other Web pages.

image parallelism See *parallel rasterization architecture.*

image plane The plane or surface on which a focused lens forms a sharp image.

image-precision See *visible-surface determination.*

image processing The class of processing operations that modify a pixel image.

image quality The sharpness, freedom from distortion, and color fidelity of a video image. Two significant factors in determining the image quality produced by a camera are the quality of its lens and the number of chips used to detect the image.

ImageReady A companion application to Adobe *Photoshop* that prepares images for Web display.

image resolution The quality of an image as given by the number of pixels in the horizontal and vertical directions that fill a screen or as the number of dots per inch printed by a printer.

image size Rescaling of images is possible in HTML with the WIDTH and HEIGHT attributes. The image tag permits scaling. By setting WIDTH and HEIGHT, the designer can resize an image. However, resizing images using HTML, rather than scaling them in a paint program, will cause images to appear distorted and jagged. If it is necessary to scale images to a larger or smaller size it is suggested the designer should do so in a paint program first, and then insert them with the correct size attributes in the HTML documents. A more important reason for adding the WIDTH and HEIGHT attributes is that this will allow the image to download faster into the viewer's Web browser. The WIDTH and HEIGHT attributes tell the Web browser how many pixels to set aside for the placement of the image on the Web page. This increases the speed because the Web browser does not have to recalculate the image space as the page is downloaded.

image stabilization See *digital image stabilization.*

Imagine A Windows-only 3D graphics and animation application from Impulse.

imaging model The definition of the abstract behavior of a page-description language on an ideal two-dimensional plane.

imaging system A collection of units used to capture and recreate an image.

At a minimum, such a system should include a scanner or camera, a device for digitizing the analog image and storing it in memory, a computer for processing digital image data, and a display device such as a monitor or printer.

IMG The file extension used to designate a graphics file format for bit-mapped images used by GEM *Paint* and Halo *DPE*.

immediate mode A graphics rendering technique in which each object is rendered immediately upon input rather than being added to a list of objects that are all rendered later.

iMovie An editing software package by Apple, currently bundled with the *iMac DV*, providing most of the tools needed for editing a feature.

implicit equations Equations of the form $f(x,y,z)=0$ that are used to model curves.

implicit surface A surface that consists of the locus of all points satisfying a given equation or set of equations.

Import option An option in *The Games Factory* that allows the user to load up .txt files and place them into a text object from disk, rather than typing them into the window. This allows the creation of text in a word processor where spell-checking and organized storage of the text can be used.

impressions Actual page views downloaded by a user from the Web. This is the typical method used for counting the number of times a banner advertisement has been seen by a visitor. This is also the method used in determining what the cost of a banner ad will be on a particular site.

inbetweening 1. The computation of graphics objects that form intermediate steps between an initial image and a final image. Used especially in animation when the beginning and end frames of a sequence are known but additional frames must be inserted between these to produce the apparent action. 2. A frame produced by inbetweening.

incandescent lights The oldest type of artificial lighting. Incandescent bulbs burn at a lower temperature than other types of lighting, so they give off an orange-yellow light. In most instances, we do not perceive this color to be orange-yellow or even that all the colors are shifted toward the red spectrum. In computer graphics, incandescents are normally simulated using omni lights or point-source lights. A better way to simulate incandescent lighting is to use a 3D light array with the central light slightly whiter than the others. The peripheral lights would need to be yellow-orange, however. The peripheral lights can be made cooler (color shifted toward blue) to emphasize the effect of the warm incandescent lighting. By making the peripheral lights cooler, we enhance perception cues. The main light's intensity would need to be increased by a stop and the peripheral lights decreased by a stop. But in most situations, it is easier to do this with the use of fill-in lights.

inches per second (ips) Measure of speed of a magnetic tape system.

incident light Light coming from a direct source, such as the sun, and falling on an object.

inclusion function A function that bounds an object to permit easier determination of when collisions between light rays and the object occur.

241

inclusion isotony The property that if A and C are subsets of B and D, respectively, then $A \times C$ is a subset of $B \times D$.

incremental backup The process of backing up only files that have been changed since the last backup, rather than all available files.

incremental spacing The ability of a printer to adjust character spacing by very small amounts. Incremental spacing is most commonly used to adjust the size of spaces between words so as to permit justification of a page of text.

independence, linear The characteristic of vectors that are non-zero with no one vector lying within the span of another.

independent script A script that runs directly from the *trueSpace* toolbar's "Run a Script" icon and not attached to any objects in the scene. Generally speaking, an independent script performs its assigned task and is then dismissed. In some cases, independent scripts act a lot like *trueSpace* plug-ins, including dialog boxes and user interaction.

indexed color A number representing an entry in a look-up table that gives a full description of the color. Indexed colors may be changed simply by modifying the look-up table.

index of refraction The ratio of the angle of incidence of light upon a surface to the angle of refraction for light entering a medium from a vacuum. It is also equivalent to the ratio of the speed of light in the medium to the speed of light in a vacuum.

indifferent periodic orbit A periodic orbit for which the absolute value of the eigenvalue is one.

information float The amount of time between the acquisition of data and its availability for use by a user.

infraorbital margin The lower portion of the orbital cavity and the upper portion of the cheekbone. It creates the ridge under the eye. The infraorbital margin is directly responsible for the bags that collect under our eyes when we are tired or when we are older. It supports the excess fluids and tissue to create the bags. One of the common mistakes made in facial animation is to move the infraorbital margin. When the cheeks are raised, the tissue rides up and over the infraorbital margin, collecting under the lower eyelid, forcing it to puff up. Since the muscle tissue cannot move over the infraorbital margin, it collects under it and creates puffy cheeks.

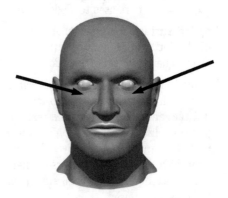

infraorbital margin.

infrared Electromagnetic radiation at frequencies just below that of red light, outside of the visible part of the color spectrum.

inheritance A characteristic of the C and C++ languages in which a derived class can specify a base class from which it inherits various characteristics and routines.

Initial Direction option An option in *The Games Factory* that allows the user to choose one or more directions for an object to move in when the game begins. Having more than one direction selected will result in a random choice being made between the directions that the user has selected.

initial graphics exchange specification (IGES) A standard file format for the storage and interchange of graphics data, published by the U.S. National Institute of Standards and Technology.

initialize To prepare a device for use, such as by loading an operating system into a computer.

initial value problems Initial value problems are simply differential equations with initial conditions. For some equations, an analytic solution can be found and used to calculate the trajectory of a body. In most cases, however, no analytic form exists, and the solution must be integrated numerically.

initiator The initial geometric structure around which a fractal is built in the initiator-generator method of creating fractal curves. It may consist of a single line or several line segments that may be formed into a simple polygon such as a triangle, a square, or a hexagon.

ink jet A printer that produces characters by spraying a fine jet of ink through selected holes onto a sheet of paper.

Inner Blast A capability of the Mr. Nitro section of *Universe*. This is a feature for doing explosions to set two different shockwaves. The Outer Blast will come through and blow away the specified amount of a model, and then the Inner Blast will come though to complete the job.

Inner Border tool A tool in *Universe* that allows the user to create a border inside an existing loop.

in-point The starting point of an edit.

input A signal applied to a finite state machine.

input devices Physical or electronic devices which are capable of reading input information and transferring it to a computer. Examples are mice, trackballs, scanners, keyboards, and modems.

input-indexed color A technique for identifying colors in which the indexed colors are looked up in the table and converted to detailed color information before being stored in a buffer.

INPUT tags Tags used in HTML to specify the kind of input field presented to the user. The input fields used are one-line text fields, radio buttons, check boxes, passwords, images, and buttons. There are a number of attributes for the <INPUT> tag. The most commonly used tags are NAME, MAXLENGTH, SIZE, SRC, VALUE, TYPE, CHECKED, and ALIGN. NAME indicates the name of a particular form field. The NAME attribute is required for most input types. MAXLENGTH indicates the maximum number of characters that can be entered by users in a text field. If this attribute is not set, there is no limit. SIZE specifies the size of the form field in characters. SRC denotes a URL for an image, and is used only with the IMAGE input type. VALUE contains the initial (default) value displayed to viewers. This attribute is required for the radio input type. TYPE defines the type of form field to use, such as a check box, text box, etc. CHECKED indicates that a checkbox or radio button is selected. However, indicating a checkbox or a radio button is selected sets the input field as a checked by default option, meaning that a viewer can change this. ALIGN specifies the vertical alignment of the image on the Web page when an image is used. The alignment can be set at LEFT, RIGHT, CENTER, and JUSTIFY.

insert edit An edit onto videotape which does not replace the control track and allows for the separate editing of video, audio, and timecode.

insert mode In most NLEs, a method of editing in the timeline that allows the placement of a shot between two shots without covering up what is already there. Instead, the second shot (and all the shots following it) move down to accommodate the new shot.

inside-outside function A function whose result differentiates among points that are inside an object, points that are on the surface of the object, and points that are outside the object.

Insight A graphics system, developed by Phoenix Data Systems, that interactively displays volume data sets encoded as octrees.

Inspire 3D (LightWave Jr.) The "light" version of NewTek's *LightWave*. It has features that are useful in deforming *Poser* figures and creating figures and props. It is both Mac and Windows enabled, and reads/writes WaveFront OBJ files, in addition to DXF and 3DS.

Install Maker A program by Clickteam that enables the building of professional installation routines for games.

instance An object that belongs to some class.

instance block A format for storing a set of elements. It begins with a label that uniquely defines the entire block, followed by an interior setting color, followed by the three basic transformations, followed by invocation of the symbol structure.

instance, object hierarchy A geometrically transformed invocation of an object.

instance transformation See *display traversal*.

instancing Instructing the computer to display a copy of an object at a certain place in space; it is not actually keeping track of any more polygons since the instance acts as a placeholder. The computer refers back to the original object for geometry information. Therefore, if the original is altered, then all the instances are instantly changed as well.

instantiation 1. The definition of a graphics object in such a way that it may be used repeatedly at different locations in an image without fully redescribing it each time. 2. When the game universe (or portion closest to the player) needs to be generated for the first time.

integral equation method A technique used in distributed ray tracing which develops a solution to the rendering equation that takes into account all the ways in which light can reach a point.

integral stereograms A form of holography that incorporates conventional motion picture technology and holographic technique to produce the only type of hologram that can represent motion.

intensity cueing The variation of light intensity throughout a scene to simulate depth. The intensity of light from a light source varies as the square of the distance from the source. Thus all objects, near and far, in a sunlit scene, have nearly the same intensity because the square of the 93 million or so miles of the sun from each object in the scene is almost the same. In contrast, for a scene lit by a local light source such as a lamp, far objects should be darker than close objects. This is in accordance with what we see daily and thus gives us the illusion of depth, which would be absent if the scene were produced with constant light intensity. However, the falloff in intensity produced by the square of the distance produces a scene in which the distant objects are too dark, so computer-generated scenes usually make the falloff proportional to distance or to the square root of distance from the light source.

intensity of light The strength of a light source, measured in candelas.

interaction detection, multi-resolution maps for A method for reducing the number of proximity tests that must be performed for games with large numbers of game objects of varying sizes. The cost of testing every object against every other object increases with the square of the number of objects. The simple solution is to divide the "world" into a grid-based map. Each grid square has a linked list of the objects whose centers are located above it. Because the objects are of non-zero size, they may overlap into adjacent map squares. When the time comes to search for all possible collisions between objects, each object has to test only for others after it in the linked list associated with its own map square, and also map squares to the east, southeast, and south. Any collisions to the north and west and with objects earlier in the list are detected when other objects do their check. This enables the user to avoid having to check for the same collision more than once.

interactive video A video program stored on CD-ROM or laser disk that permits a user to manipulate the course of action. Often used as a teaching aid, the program will ask a question of a student and then select the next material to be displayed depending upon whether the student gave the right answer.

Interactors Rollup A menu in the *Primal Particles* plug-in for *trueSpace* that enables the user to define the emitter, a leader (which the particle will flow toward), and a tolerance setting for the emitter, using a percentage of attraction. The user can also define the position of a floor and/or a ceiling, and the type of repulsion of each (gripping, sticky, soft, firm, elastic, bouncy, springy).

interdot distance The reciprocal of *addressability*.

interface 1. The surface defined by the meeting of two different media. 2. The controls and windows used to operate a program.

interface, basic The basic *trueSpace* interface provides one of the most innovative and intuitive ways to create complex computer animations. Through the use of graphical icons rather than text buttons, *trueSpace* squeezes all of its functionality into a set of easy-access toolbars available at the bottom (or top) of the screen. By right-clicking on any of the icons, the user gains access to the advanced features and parameters of the toolset. Every feature with an advanced-parameters dialog box has a red triangle in the upper right-hand corner of the icon. If there is a dark-green triangle in the upper-left corner, that means that by holding down on the icon with the left mouse button, the user will gain access to more tools available under that specific icon menu.

interface, 3D plug-ins panel The 3D plug-ins panel permits access and use of up to eight of the hundreds of plug-ins that are available for *trueSpace*, such as *Primal Particles* or *DynaWave*.

interface, metaballs A technique in *true-Space* that provides a way to create flowing or spraying water, such as water in a glass, or water spouting from a fountain.

interface, Objects Deformation panel Using the Object Deformations in *true-Space*, the user can take those building blocks created with the primitive tools and create some interesting object-based effects, such as an expanding explosion that can be mapped with various shaders to give it a realistic volumetric appearance. The deformations are fully animatable, so the user can change the shapes over time by setting keyframes, and use the deformation tools to alter the object shape. Left-clicking on the Deformation Objects icon will bring up a panel that allows the user to choose a specific axis to deform, and which mode to use in deformation—pull/push, twist, or stretch.

interface, Primitives Menu A menu in *trueSpace* that allows creation of primitive objects such as a sphere, cube, cylinder, cone, torus, or plane.

interface, Shaders Panel A menu in *trueSpace* that allows selection of any of a number of built-in shaders.

interference The wave-like interaction of light that results either in amplification, cancellation, or composite generation of the resultant light wave.

interference fringes Alternating patterns of light and dark created when a single light is passed through two small vertical slits and projected onto a dark chamber's walls. These alternating bands of light are called *interference fringes*. The areas where light overlaps generate a bright line, and areas where the beams of light cancel each other produce a dark line.

interference-pattern hologram An interference pattern is created when two of the same wavelengths of light interfere with each other. This pattern is the hologram in the size and shape of a pixel.

interlace artifact Flicker resulting when adjacent scan lines of an interlaced display are of different colors.

interlaced Describes a display system in which one frame consists of only odd display lines and the next of only even display lines, etc. The persistence of the eye makes it appear as if the full picture is being displayed continuously. This reduces the amount of information required for a given resolution by one-half.

interlaced frame An interlaced frame or image is composed of two fields alternating at 60 fields per second. NTSC television delivers an interlaced frame.

interlaced GIFs Images that, when downloaded, start out blocky and then focus into clear images. Interlaced GIFs are used to give the viewer a rough idea of the type of images that are downloading.

interleaved Describes a system of writing to a hard disk that assigns contiguous sector numbers to noncontiguous sectors on the disk, so that after a sector is written or read, enough space is left on the disk before the next contiguously-numbered sector for the computer to complete processing of the data and be ready to process the next sector.

intermediate cross sections A type of cross section used in *form•Z*, created for the purpose of refining and fine-tuning the curvature of the 3D form.

intermediate print A print made from the final negative for projection or other uses. If it is damaged, a new copy can be made from the original negative.

intermittency The situation in a fractal curve where the orbits of singular values go far away and then return.

internal cost The average cost of solving for the point of intersection of a ray with an object, given that the ray is known to have hit the object's bounding volume.

International Standards Organization (ISO) A group that establishes standards for graphics, image processing, and telecommunications.

internegative (IN) An intermediary step sometimes necessary in film processing. The camera negative is printed and a new negative, the *internegative*, is made (or struck) from that print. The internegative is then used to create more prints.

Internet An extensive computer network that links computers of colleges, universities, government agencies, nonprofit laboratories, and industry. Originally developed and managed by the Defense Advanced Research Project Agency as ARPANET, it is now independently operated. ARPANET began in the 1970s. It assured that DOD computing power was distributed so that it couldn't all be wiped out by a nuclear strike. By 1981 there were 213 computers connected to the Internet. In 1989 the World Wide Web (WWW) was developed by physicists at CEERN (the European Laboratory for Particle Physics) in Switzerland. Around 1993, the Internet was separated from military control and allowed to expand to private companies and individuals. At approximately the same time, Network Solutions took over the task of registering commercial Internet sites with the *.com* domain name.

Internet Explorer A popular Web browser, developed by Microsoft Corporation. In order to offer more control in layout, Internet Explorer incorporates elements that are not always compliant with the HTML standard.

internode In a tree, a segment that is followed by at least one more segment.

interobject communication A technique that is used to control the shapes of objects that are defined by procedures.

interobject reflections Light effects that occur when a surface reflects other surfaces in its environment.

interpenetration An arrangement of two or more graphics objects such that the surfaces of the objects mutually intersect in a way that cannot be specified explicitly.

interPhong shading A modified version of Phong shading, which gives a shading intermediate between faceted shading and Phong shading.

interpolate To determine the value of an intermediate term by averaging or otherwise operating upon neighboring terms that are known.

Interpolation command A command in the *Game Creation System* Paint program that creates a morphing effect between two polygons.

interpolation, frame-rate-dependent-ease-out using floating-point math A method of interpolation that behaves in a frame-rate-dependent manner, so it behaves differently if called at 10 frames per second than it does at, for instance, 20 frames per second. This method should be used only if accuracy is not a prime concern. The concept behind this method is that the user wants to compute a weighted average of the current value and the desired value, with a heavier weight on the current value. This can be done with the following equation:

$$x = \left(x_0 * (weight - 1) + x_f\right) / weight$$

The new x value equals x_0, the original value, multiplied by a weighting factor, added to the final destination x value. The sum is divided by the total weights to properly preserve the scale. The resulting x is used as x_0 for the next pass through the equation. The weight must be a value greater than one to get the expected behavior from this equation. Higher weights make it take longer to reach the desired position. This generates a smooth curve where the value changes rapidly at first, then settles toward the destination value as it approaches, which is called ease-out.

interpolation, frame-rate-dependent-ease-out using integer math A method of interpolation that is very CPU friendly, because it uses no division. This method is more important on console systems or older hardware with limited floating-point support. It works fast but has some restrictions on flexibility, even compared with the previous method. The process of building a weighted average using integer mathematics has some interesting side effects. The rate of change tends to stick at specific levels during the interpolation, and the destination point is unlikely ever to be reached due to round-off errors. The following equation shows the modifications used:

$$x = \left(x_0 * (2^n - 1) + x_f\right) >> n$$

The values for $(2^n - 1)$ and n should be hard coded for speed, which gives a form similar to the following equation:

$$x = \left(x_0 * 7 + x_f\right) >> 3$$

where ">>" represents a shift operator, as in the C language. The computations have some difficulties with round-off which is much less smooth than the floating-point method. Even with the less-than-smooth curve, this method is very useful for larger values. It tends to work well with fixed-point math, where some number of bits in the integer value is defined to be the fractional portion. For instance, a 32-bit number may be thought of as 20 bits for the integer portion and 12 bits for the fractional portion. To convert from the integer representation to the fixed-point representation in that case, divide by 4,096. Increasing the scale in that way allows for much smoother behavior, resulting in a curve more similar to that obtained with the floating point method.

interposition The perception of depth when objects overlap each other, as seen from one perspective. Objects that are superimposed are perceived as having depth, even if they are all situated the same distance from the eye, as long as they overlap.

interposition.

interpositive (IP) An intermediary step sometimes necessary in film processing. The camera negative is printed and this print, called the *interpositive*, is used to create a new negative. The release prints are then struck from that negative.

interrupt A signal sent by a peripheral or some other part of a computer to the processor, causing the processor to suspend its current operation and run a designated service routine.

intersection 1. In constructive solid geometry, the three-dimensional region common to two or more specified objects. 2. In ray tracing, a point that is on a surface and also on a particular ray.

intersection, Boolean See *Boolean intersection*.

InterViews A graphics toolkit.

Intruder A plug-in for *trueSpace* that will render the current view with colors that represent a distance from the viewing plane.

invariant circle A circle in which, if one selects an initial point on the circle and

performs iterations of a recursive equation, all iterated points will also be on it.

inverse color map A map used to translate full RGB colors into a limited set of colors.

inverse Fourier transform A mathematical procedure for transforming a series of harmonically-related sine waves in the frequency domain to a waveform in the spatial domain.

inverse iteration method A method of creating the graphic for a Julia set by computing the backward orbits of points.

inverse kinematics (IK) Complex joint structures that connect groups of objects. Inverse kinematics is used for tasks such as character animation. As a child that has been grouped using IK is moved, the parent objects are also moved according to a variety of preset links and constraints. To assist in IK functions, many programs allow for the definition of constraints and joint limits on an object or bone within an IK structure. Joint limits allow limitation of a limb's range of motion. One can set the knee or object so that it can bend along its x axis at −95 degrees, but may not bend in a positive direction or along any other axis. Joint limits must be defined for each joint, but that causes a bit of overhead. However, once defined, it can make IK functions quite simple. The problem is, there are a lot of rotations in the simple act, such as grabbing a pencil, and often the computer guesses incorrectly how those rotations are to take place. Upper body movement with IK is often frustrating at best. However, IK functions in the lower body where the motion is typically simpler is much easier for an animator. Grab a foot and move it up, and the thigh and shin move into place.

inverse mapping The process of determining the parameters for the explicit representation of a surface that contains a designated point.

inverse-square law A law, formally defined as irradiance (power per unit expressed in watts/meter^2) that is inversely proportional to the square of the distance from the source in the absence of media scattering and absorption. It is the gradual fall off of light or energy from a source as it covers more area.

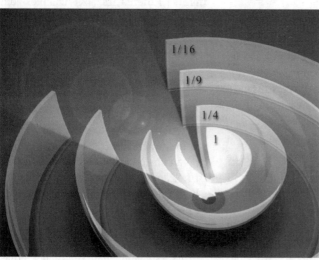

inverse-square law.

inversion A mapping technique that uses a reference circle to map all the points of a plane (except the center point of the reference circle) onto a plane by drawing a line from the center of the circle to the point to be mapped, and then placing the new point on this line so that the product of the distance from the center of the circle to the original point and the distance from the center of the circle to

the new point is equal to the square of the radius of the circle.

invert 1. To reverse a binary number so that all ones become zeroes and all zeroes become ones. 2. To reverse a photographic image so that blacks become white and whites become blacks. Intermediate shades are also reversed. This occurs when an image is produced by projecting light through a negative onto a sheet of light-sensitive paper.

invisible-surface table A table of surfaces that are invisible on a particular scan line.

invisible targets In *Bryce*, objects, lights, or the camera can be linked to a null object to control their movement, rotation, and other animation factors. In addition, a null object can be used as a target for the camera, so that instead of moving the camera itself to create an animation path, the user can move the target.

ion deposition A printing method similar to laser printing. A drum is charged with electrons, the charged portions of the drum attract toner, and paper is then pressed against the drum, picking up the ink.

ips See *inches per second*.

I$_r$ (reflected radiance) The light reflected from a surface per unit of foreshortened area.

IRE units Units of video signal amplitude, where 100 is maximum white, 7.5 is black, and 0 is blanking black.

iris 1. The physical mechanism that can be opened or closed to change the size of the aperture. "Irising down" for example, means to close down the iris (go to a higher f-stop). Synonymous with *aperture*. 2. In the eye, a thin, circular, retractable, variable, shutter-like membrane that is attached to the ciliary body and a small part of the cornea. It controls as well as directs the amount of light entering the eyes.

IRQ Special addressing information used by peripherals attached to a Windows-based computer. Each peripheral must have its own IRQ.

irradiance The light coming onto a surface from other surfaces in the scene, measured by integrating over a hemisphere above the surface.

irradiation Light passing though a film's emulsion creates a primary image by directly interacting with the silver halides; in some areas, it passes directly through the film. In areas where it interacted with the silver halides, the light is reflected indirectly around the film, creating *irradiation*. Irradiation creates a "ghostly edge glow" on the film and tends to soften the perceived captured image. Irradiation, in short, reduces film resolution and edge sharpness. Irradiation is the diffuse spreading of light from the main contact area. In photography, it is hard to avoid irradiation.

ISA slots A type of expansion slot used in Windows-based computers.

ISO See *International Standards Organization*.

ISO-9660 A format for writing CD-ROMs that can be read by either Macintosh or Windows-based computers, and is generally used in producing "hybrid" CD-ROMs.

isometric camera See *camera, isometric*.

isometric projection A perspective projection in which all vertical lines remain vertical. Distances in the x and y directions are usually drawn at a 60-degree angle to the vertical.

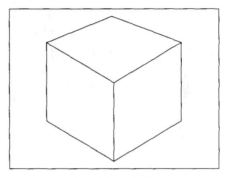

isometric projection.

isosurface A surface along which a field is constant.

isotropic 1. Describes random field in which all points and all directions are statistically equivalent. 2. Describes materials whose refractive indexes are not reliant on the direction of incident light.

iSpace A 3D application from Caligari Corporation, the developers of *trueSpace*, meant specifically for 3D Web page development.

italic In typography, a typeface in which the letters are slanted or cursive.

iterated deepening A move-ordering method in game design that, instead of straight-away searching at full ply, searches at a gradually increasing ply, using the results of the previous level of search to sort the moves for the next level. The results of the previous level can be stored as a *hash table*, storing calculated values of board positions. This table hashes board states to board values. It also helps to avoid recalculating board values when different sequences of moves produce the same game state. Game-specific heuristics can be used, such as always considering capture moves first in chess. Finally, there is the "killer" heuristic; if a move turned out to be the best in a sibling node in the tree, it should be tried before others.

iterated function system (IFS) The repeated application of a contractive affine transformation, starting with any point, until a distinctive pattern is produced. A few carefully-selected contractive affine transformations are sufficient to reproduce a picture having a great deal of detail. Thus the process can be used for image compression.

iteration 1. A single solution of an equation that is to be solved many times. 2. To repeatedly operate upon an equation that uses the current values of one or more variables to determine new values. At each repetition, the new values obtained in the previous iteration are substituted for the old values.

iterator A variable that is used to cause repeated iterations of an algorithm.

iterator, reverse A variable that causes repeated iterations of an algorithm in the reverse direction.

ITU-R 601 See *BT. 601*.

J

Jacobian matrix A matrix used to generate corrections in a rendered image so that the viewpoint correlates with the point at which a reference photograph was taken.

jaggies Artifacts of aliasing. The "stair-stepped" appearance of diagonal lines and curves displayed on a device that has only discrete pixel locations.

JARS See *Java Applet Rating Service*.

Jarvis, Judice, and Nanke filter An algorithm for performing discrete convolution or digital filtering, which is the improving of the appearance of an image by replacing a pixel by some function of that pixel and its neighbors. It is frequently used to change color images to images consisting of black, white, and shades of gray.

Java A compiled and interpreted programming language. When writing a Java program, it is first compiled by the javac compiler. The result is a set of bytecodes that represent a virtual computer—one that does not really exist yet. Then, when the programmer runs a compiled Java program, a Java interpreter designed especially for the machine converts the bytecodes to files the computer can read. ☜

Java Applet Rating Service (JARS) A service that rates the quality of Java Applets.

javac The Java language compiler.

Java 3D A package of 3D graphics classes and methods. This package can provide high-end graphics features on any Java-compatible platform. The Java 3D API makes it possible to describe large virtual worlds that can be rendered very efficiently. The package was developed through the joint efforts of Intel Corporation, Silicon Graphics, Apple Computer, and Sun Microsystems, giving it a wide degree of acceptance across the industry. Java 3D is not part of the Java package, but is available from Sun Microsystems. Running the Java 3D unpacking program incorporates all parts of the Java 3D package into the appropriate directories and subdirectories of a Java installation.

JavaScript A scripting language. JavaScript programs reside within the HTML code on a Web page. These programs run on Web browsers such as Internet Explorer and Netscape Navigator from the HTML document. This means that any JavaScript-enabled Web browser can display JavaScript programs without any additional plug-ins.

JavaScript compatibility JavaScript may display differently on different types of Web browsers. JavaScript code is recognized by and runs in Web browsers developed by different companies. Some of the more advanced features of JavaScript must be scripted specifically for a particular Web browser in order for them to render as intended. Because Netscape created JavaScript, Netscape's Web browser, Netscape Navigator, is considered the native platform for running JavaScript. Microsoft's Internet Explorer runs JavaScript in the same manner as Navigator; however, some of the more advanced JavaScript features may render differently. To ensure that JavaScript is properly rendering in Web browsers, always test Web pages in multiple browsers and versions.

jaw muscles The jaw muscles actually include one major muscle and several smaller supporting muscles. The main muscle is the *masseter*, which is used to clench the teeth and raise the jaw. The masseter is located at the base of the jaw. This muscle plays a major role in any movement where the lower jaw is dropped wide open. "Fear" and "yawning" are two expressions created by the masseter muscle area. In both of these expressions the masseter muscle is used to raise the jaw to the neutral position.

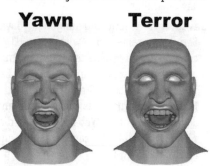

jaw muscles.

jitter 1. Jumping of a display, usually due to poor synchronization. 2. Random displacements in time of a periodic signal from the temporal position that it should occupy.

jitter function A function used to deliberately introduce jitter into a sampling process to reduce aliasing effects.

JKL A way of editing using the J, K, and L keys on computer keyboard specifically programmed to allow for fast shuttling through clips in a non-linear editor.

join surface A surface added to provide continuous transition between two intersecting surfaces in a graphics model. Also known as *blend surface*.

joint 1. The point at which two consecutive segments of a spline curve meet. 2. The point at which one bone connects to another when modeling a skeleton.

joint editing Joint editing in the Joint Parameters Palette is one of the most difficult processes to master in *Poser*, and it can be done only with a lot of trial and error along the way. Each model

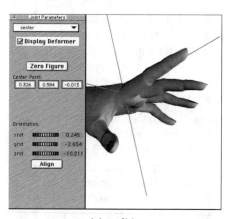

joint editing.

presents different problems when joints are edited. The designer works to minimize the stretching and warping that can occur when bends take place. A joint is a deformation that takes place between two figure elements.

Joint Photographic Experts Group (JPEG) See *JPEG*.

Jordan curve theorem The fact that a simple closed curve partitions the plane into two disjoint regions, a bounded interior and an unbounded exterior, with the curve separating the two. Used to determine whether one is inside or outside a closed curve.

joystick A graphics input device, usually consisting of a vertical rod or handle which can be made to tilt in any direction. When the joystick is tilted, the cursor moves in the tilt direction. Microsoft's *X-Box* has introduced a modern, hand-held design.

joyswitch A variation of the *joystick* that can be moved in any of eight directions, up, down, left, right, and any of the four diagonal directions. Small switches sense the direction in which the joyswitch is moved.

JPEG 1. The Joint Photographic Experts Group. 2. A standard for image compression developed by the Joint Photographic Experts Group. This standard is also sanctioned by the International Standards Organization (ISO) and the Comité Consultatif Internationale de Télégraphique et Téléphonique (CCITT). There are several modes of this standard. The *baseline mode* divides the image into 8 x 8 blocks, each of which is transformed by the Discrete Cosine Transform (DCT). The algorithm then uses a uniform scalar quantizer to quantize the transformed blocks, then zig-zag scans them and entropy codes the results using Huffman coding. A quantization table is used to specify the step size for each of the 64 DCT coefficients. These coefficients for all blocks are coded sep-arately using a predictive technique. JPEG files use the extension ".JPEG."

JPEG 2000 A new image coding specification developed by the Joint Photographic Experts Committee. It is based on the Discrete Wavelet Transform (DWT), scalar quantization, context modeling, arithmetic coding, and post-compression rate allocation. For a given amount of compression, JPEG 2000 results in a better quality picture than the original JPEG.

jukebox A device that holds a number of optical disks and contains one or more optical disk drives. Any disk can be selected for use by a software command.

Julia set A fractal curve set which is a plot representing the result of iterating the equation:

$$z_{n+1} = z_n^2 + c$$

with c held constant and z_0 varied over the complex plane. Also known as the *Julia-Fatou* set. Compare with *Mandelbrot set*.

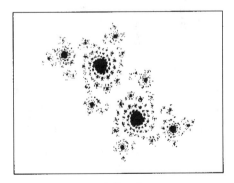

Julia set.

Jump Controls option An option available in *The Games Factory*. Jump controls are used to change the control system for jumps of game objects.

jump cut A sudden switch from one scene to another. The opposite of a seamless edit. Jump cuts are usually avoided because they lack motivation and break up the basic continuity and linear progression of time. Sometimes, however, they are useful to jar the viewer, add energy, or create a special effect.

Jump Strength option Jump Strength selects the jumping power of a character in *The Games Factory*. Changing the gravity will also affect this parameter.

junk data Random data that is transmitted with each packet of information being sent over lines between computers to prevent attackers from being able to determine the packet size and contents.

justification The process of aligning lines of text for printing. *Left justification* makes sure that the left side of every line is lined up. *Right justification* makes sure that the right side of every line is lined up.

just-noticeable color difference Differences in wavelength and saturation which result in the human eye being able to distinguish that two colors are different. Generally, at saturation, most distinguished hues are about 4 nm. apart, although this increases toward the ends of the spectrum. At the middle of the spectrum, about 16 saturation steps can be distinguished, while this increases to about 23 steps at the ends of the spectrum. The human eye can distinguish hundreds of thousands of different colors.

JVC GY-DV500 A full-featured, professional MiniDV camera available for the prosumer market. It looks like a traditional high-end, shoulder-mounted camcorder. In addition to its rugged 11 lb. design, the camera features such high-end features as standard ½" bayonet-mount interchangeable lenses, built-in dual XLR balanced microphone connectors, and built-in genlocking.

K

K Kilo, when used as a prefix. In computing, *kilo* is 1024; in dealing with money, *kilo* is 1000.

k (ambient-reflection coefficient) The amount of ambient light reflected from an object's surface. (Ranges from 0.0 to 1.0).

k (specular-reflection coefficient) The amount of incident light that is specularly reflected from an object's surface. (Ranges from 0.0 to 1.0).

k (transmission coefficient) The transparency of an object. If *k* is 0.0, the object is opaque and transmits no light. If *k* is 1.0, the object is completely transparent and transmits all light that impinges on its surface.

Kantor tree A fractal curve generated by the IFS method.

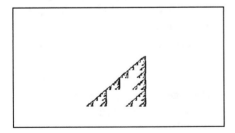

Kantor tree.

Kbyte Kilobyte. 1024 bytes of data.

k_d (diffuse-reflection coefficient) A constant between 0 and 1 that represents the proportion of diffuse light reflected by an object. The value is a characteristic of the material of which the object is made.

kd tree *k*-dimensional tree. A binary subdivision of *k*-dimensional space, one dimension at a time.

Kelvin scale An *absolute temperature scale* used by scientists, similar to Celsius. The Kelvin temperature scale is defined with 0 K as *absolute zero* and each Kelvin having the same magnitude as a Celsius degree, so that a Kelvin temperature is the same as a Celsius temperature with 273 added to it. See *absolute temperature scale* and *absolute zero*.

kermit A protocol for transmitting files from one computer to another across telephone lines.

kerning The use of certain letter pairs that have the space between them minimized to replace the pair of letters in ordinary type.

key 1. A word or phrase that is used to identify the subject matter of a data file. 2. A button on a keyboard that is pushed to transmit alphanumerics or characters. 3. The black primary in color printing.

keyboard An assemblage of systematically-arranged keys by which a machine is operated.

keycode A number on each frame of film, added by the film lab.

key event The event that makes animation logistically feasible. In traditional cel-based animation, a lead artist (also known as a *keyman*) would draw the most important parts of the action, which became known as *keyframes*. The keyframes would then be handed over to hundreds of artists who would draw the frames between the keyframes, a process referred to as *tweening*.

keyframe 1. One of a sequence of images in computer animation from which intermediate images are derived by minor modifications to the *keyframe*. A keyframe is used to tell an object where it is going to start and where it is going to end over the course of several frames. See also *in-betweening*. 2. A frame within a sequence of motion that is most important in defining the mo-  ment or motion sequence. For instance, if a character was hopping over a log, the master animator might draw a keyframe as the character begins his leap, another at the top of the leap, one as the character hits the ground, and another as he straightens up to walk. Then the apprentice comes in and draws all the frames in between these keyframes to flesh out the animation.

keyframe editor 1. The module in any 3D application that allows the user to edit the time constraints and placement of keyframes on the timeline. 2. A feature of *trueSpace*. On the left side is a collapsible tree that allows the user to access and display the entire scene hier-

archy as needed. The animatable properties of the object can be accessed directly and easily. The multi-resolution timeline along the right side of the editor allows easy and direct random access to every keyframe. Numerous keyframe manipulation functions can be accomplished directly in the editor, including cut, copy, paste, delete, move, stretch, repeat, and reverse.

keyframing The creation of frames at key points in an animation to give guid-

keyframing.

ance in filling in the frames between to complete the animation.

keyframe interval When compressing video, the frequency at which a keyframe will occur.

keyframe transform In *form•Z*, the simplest type of animation, which places the least demands on the modeler. Keyframe transform is an animation type in which the model undergoes only geometric transforms. It is important to understand that transforms are relational; that is, if the model does not change its position, orientation, and scale, but the camera does, one still needs to treat the model as if it is transforming. One of the basic principles of animation is that there should always be some kind of movement in the scene. Translation, rotation, and uniform scale are all geometric transforms.

key grip The person who assists the gaffer with lighting and is responsible for coordinating the placement of grip equipment (flags, nets, etc.), special riggings, and the hardware used to move the camera.

key light The primary light source used to illuminate a subject, usually positioned at an angle. This light provides the most illumination and should be the most powerful light in the scene. This is also the light that should do the shadow casting. It is helpful to experiment with the settings of the light, starting at about 75%. While most programs have a default light value of 100%, one may find that this is too bright and will add too much contrast between the shadows and the illuminated area. It is best to start out lower and add light if needed.

key plots Rough sketches to plan how the key and fill lights are going to work to achieve a design.

k_i (intrinsic color) The intrinsic intensity of an object.

kicker 1. A light positioned on the back of the subject, normally opposite the *key light*. It is used mainly for separation. 2. A light modifier that is used to "bounce" light into the dark areas of the subject.

kinematics The science of the positions and velocities of points.

kinescope A method of making a film copy of a videotape by recording the image from a video monitor.

kinetic depth effect The rotating of an object about its central axis to give the illusion of three dimensionality, because the perspective causes nearer portions of the object to move more quickly and in the opposite direction in screen space from more distant portions.

kino-flo tubes Color-corrected fluorescent light tubes used to replace normal fluorescent light tubes when shooting at a location that will have fluorescent lights visible in the shot.

knot A point in parametric space that is part of the definition of a spline curve.

knot, cubic curve A point in parametric space that is part of the definition of a spline curve.

Kochanek-Bartels formulation A method for curve interpolation that provides control over tension, bias, continuity, and approximation.

Koch curve One of a family of curves similar to the *Koch snowflake*, but using different generators.

Koch snowflake A self-similar fractal curve created using the initiator-generator technique. It has an appearance similar to a snowflake.

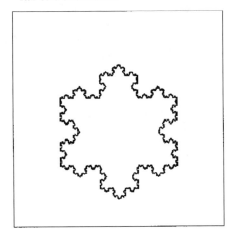

Koch snowflake.

Kolomyjec's organic illusion An early computer-drawn picture created by Kolomyjec.

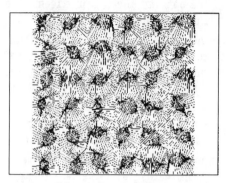

Kolomyjec's organic illusion.

KPT A collection of plug-ins for *Photoshop,* by Corel. Examples of plug-ins from *KPT* packages include *Gradient Designer, 3D Stereo Noise, Gaussian f/x, Blurrr, ShapeShifter, LensFlare, Materializer,* and *SceneBuilder.*

L (vector to light) A vector from the surface of an object being illuminated to the light source.

L* (Pronounced "L-star.") Lightness.

label holography Label type holograms are those that are applied to a previously-produced item. They are usually provided with self-adhesive backing or as hot stamping foil. Label holograms are often used in applications, e.g., advertising pieces, direct mail, promotional products, and point-of-purchase displays.

label, structure element An identifier for an element in the SPHIGS graphics system.

lacunarity A characteristic of fractal texture in which the fractal has gaps that tend to be large or includes large intervals such as disks or balls.

ladder Typeset text having several consecutive lines that end with hyphenated words. This should be avoided for improved appearance.

Ladder option An option available in *The Games Factory* that will treat the backdrop object as a ladder when using a platform-type movement. For those animated objects that have a relevant animation sequence, the animation will automatically be changed when objects are climbing ladders.

Lagrange series A theorem, proved by Lagrange, that states that for any given N points there is a unique (N – 1)th degree polynomial that passes exactly through all the points.

Laguerre fractal curve A fractal curve generated by iterating a Laguerre function over the complex plane.

lambert A unit of luminance.

Lambertian radiosity model A model that uses the radiosity technique to characterize ideal diffuse reflective surfaces.

Lambertian reflection See *diffuse reflection*.

Lambertian shading Shading that has a constant reflection that is independent of the viewer's position.

Lambertian shading.

Lambert's cosine law The rule that the intensity of light reflected from a point on a surface is proportional to the cosine of the angle between a vector from a point to the light source and the surface normal at the point.

Lambert's law of absorption The rule for absorption of light in homogeneous media. It states that

$$I_x = I_0 e^{-(Ax)}$$

where I_x is the intensity of the light after passing through the distance x in the medium, I_0 is the intensity of the light as it enters the medium, and A is the absorption coefficient.

laminate A combination of two materials, both of which must be present on the object. For example, one cannot create two different materials in *Bryce* using just the Materials Lab. The elegant solution incorporates the use of the Advanced Motion Lab. First, select one material, or create one, for frame 1 of an animation (animation length is the animator's choice), and map it to an object. Select or create a second material for the last frame. Then, open the Advanced Motion Lab with the object selected. Find the object in the list, and click on Material. For all of the parameters listed under Material, draw a straight horizontal line midway in the Motion Curve area. This effectively blends the two materials into one for the entire animation. Use this technique to create the following exotic laminates: Double-Wood, Wood-Stone, Double-Stone, Cloud-Stone, Water-Cloud, Water-Stone, Rock-Psychedelic, Mirror-Wood, Cloud-Metal, and more.

LAN See *local area network*.

LANC (Control-L) A device control protocol that is incapable of frame accuracy. It is most commonly found on consumer equipment. See also *RS-422* and *RS-232*.

Lanczos2 sinc function A two-lobed filter function used in antialiasing. It is defined by the following equation:

$$Lanczos2(x) = \begin{cases} \dfrac{\sin(\pi x)}{\pi\,x} \dfrac{\sin\left(\pi\dfrac{x}{2}\right)}{\pi\dfrac{x}{2}}, & |x| < 2 \\[2em] 0 & |x| \geq 2 \end{cases}$$

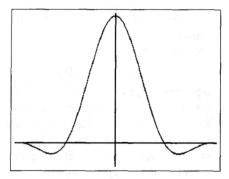

Lanczos2 sinc function.

Lanczos3 sinc function. A three-lobed filter function used in antialiasing. It is defined by the following equation:

$$Lanczos3(x) = \begin{cases} \dfrac{\sin(\pi x)}{\pi\,x} \dfrac{\sin\left(\pi\dfrac{x}{3}\right)}{\pi\dfrac{x}{3}}, & |x| < 3 \\[2em] 0 & |x| \geq 3 \end{cases}$$

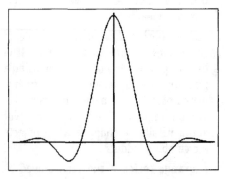

Lanczos3 sinc function.

land and groove A feature manufactured into optical disks during manufacture to identify track locations. The recordable tracks are within the grooves, and the lands separate the grooves from each other.

Landmass A fractal landscape generator that is part of the *CoolPowers* plug-in for *trueSpace*. This plug-in gives the user control over the height, roughness, and overall size of the landscape. It will also allow the user to add noise to the routine, automatically triangulate the object, and generate a simple water plane. This plug-in can be handy for creating an environment for an alien creature.

Landsberg fractal curve A fractal curve constructed by positive mid-point displacements.

landscape Arrangement of type and graphics across the long edge of a page. In a landscape layout, the width of the page exceeds its height. Also known as *comic*. Contrast with a *portrait* layout, in which the height of the page exceeds its width.

landscaping, fault line generation A method of generating terrain in which two points are chosen at random and a line is drawn at a given height between them. Next, two more points are chosen, and again, a line is drawn between them. This is repeated until there are a sufficient number of lines on the screen to simulate terrain.

landscaping, fuzzy The creation of a section of terrain by filling a grid with random values between some stated limits. Smoothing can be applied to make the terrain look more realistic.

language, form The manner in which the meaning of a language is conveyed.

language, meaning The content or message conveyed by the language.

lap-dissolve A way of shifting from one scene to another in a motion picture. The end of one scene is overlapped. At the beginning of the lap-dissolve, the old scene is given full weight and the new scene is given zero weight. As the lap-dissolve progresses, the weight of the old scene is slowly decreased and that of the new scene increased, until at the end of the lap-dissolve, the weight of the old scene is zero and the new scene is full weight.

laser disk An optical disk using the same technology as a CD-ROM, but with a diameter of 12 inches.

laser optical A technique for recording on grooveless disks through the use of a laser-optical-tracking pickup to determine head location.

laser printer A printer that makes use of a beam of light to charge a drum. The charged portions of the drum then pick up toner which is transferred to a sheet of paper and fused permanently by heat.

laser projector A video projector that makes use of three laser beams, one for each primary color, combined into a single beam that is mechanically scanned to provide a raster on a screen.

last in, first out (LIFO) A method of storing data in which the last piece of data to be stored is the first one to be read. Also known as a *stack*.

latency The time required for a single data element to pass from the beginning to the end of a pipeline.

latent image The invisible image captured on film through exposure. It is made visible only after developing.

lateral geniculate nucleus The area of the brain where light signals from the eyes are processed after passing through the retina.

lateral inhibition An effect upon the receptors in the eye. The more light a receptor receives, the more it inhibits the response of the receptors adjacent to it.

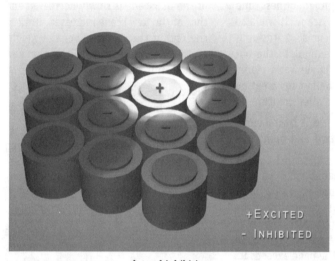

+Excited
- Inhibited

lateral inhibition.

lathe A modeling tool used to create a 3D object out of a 2D shape. The lathe tool is much like a carpenter's lathe, with a 2D template being used to form the profile of an object.

lathing Using a *lathe*. Both straight extrusions and path extrusions work on the idea that the two-dimensional shape is pushed along a third dimension. However, two-dimensional shapes and curves can also be spun around an axis to create a symmetrical three-dimensional shape. Much like a real lathe cuts a profile out of a block of material, lathe extrudes begin with the profile desired and then are spun to create the shape. When

the capabilities of shifting the axis of revolution during the lathe are added, lathes can create very complex shapes. Lathes can be rotated by any amount. Lathing is a powerful tool for working with fairly symmetrical shapes. The basic idea behind lathing is to first create a profile that will be spun to create a three-dimensional shape.

latitude 1. The ability of film to record the range of possible tones in a given scene. 2. Distance measured in degrees north or south of the equator. Lines of equal latitude are circles parallel to the equator.

Lauwerier's Algorithm An algorithm that is used to compute four-digit random numbers. It works in the following way. Select a 4-digit number x. $x => x^2$. Remove the first and last digits of the result until a 4-digit number remains. This is the random number. Repeat, using this new number as x. Not every initial seed x will give a good run of random numbers, so some care is needed in choosing the seed.

lava flows, simulating In nature, volcanic mountain ranges and island systems (like the Pacific Rim's "Ring of Fire") are generated by lava flow. This can be simulated by using a particle system to drop sequences of particles and simulate their flow across a surface composed of previously-dropped particles. Dropping a sufficient number of particles will produce structures that look like the flow patterns of viscous fluid (lava). Start with an empty height field and drop a single particle onto it. Then, drop a second particle on the first and agitate it until it comes to rest (that is, until none of its neighbors is at a lower altitude). Continue dropping particles (varying the drop point periodically) until there is a significant pile. The designer can control the shape of the terrain by controlling how the particle drop point is moved. Keeping the drop point in a single place will create a large peak. Moving the drop point periodically will create chains of multiple small peaks. A less painstaking but equally qualitative method for creating a lava flow is to do it in post-production with Impulse's *Illusion*.

lavalier A small clip-on microphone, usually an omnidirectional condenser.

law of least astonishment A principle used in design of user dialogue with a computer which states that doing what the user considers to be normal in a situation is more important than maintaining absolute consistency.

layback The process of transferring the finished audio back onto the master videotape after *sweetening*.

layer 1. A portion of a graphics image or 3D scene designed so that several layers may be overlaid to produce a complete image or 3D scene. 2. A method in *Carrara* for making it easier to work on a complicated scene by building the scene in layers, keeping visible only the parts of a model that are being worked on at any given time. This lets the user reduce screen clutter and it speeds redraw time.

layer grouping A technique for grouping in *form•Z*. As with the object and color methods, multiple 3DS files are created. Each layer becomes a separate 3DS file. Objects within layers are not joined into a single object. This method is useful if the user wishes to retain objects within export layers as separate entities within *3ds max*.

layering Containing one object as a member of another object. Also known as *composition, containment,* or *embedding*.

layering for depth of field A method for creating depth of field by rendering a scene in layers. Separate the foreground and the background objects into layers and render them separately. In postproduction, apply varying degrees of Gaussian Blur to each layer and then composite them.

lazy evaluation A programming technique for minimizing the calculations needed to handle large data structures. The program assumes that such structures exist, but calculates only necessary parts on demand.

lazy menu See *menu, pull-down*.

LBM A graphics file format used to store bitmap images. It makes use of the IFF file format.

LCD See *liquid crystal display*.

L-cut See *overlapping edit*.

LDS Video Previewer A plug-in for *true-Space* by Leverage Data Systems, Inc. that allows the user to resize the preview window and supports scaling and stretching of the preview. It also supports audio tracks. It possesses a frame counter and an interactive "scrub bar," and it will play any AVI format.

leader 1. An unrecorded portion at the beginning of a roll of magnetic tape that is used solely for threading the tape into the tape recorder/player. The leader is often of a different material than the recordable portion of the tape, and is usually stronger and nonmagnetic. 2. A line of dots or dashes that leads the eye from a displayed topic to associated information such as a page number.

leading 1. *(pronounced "ledding")* The space between lines of a printed text, so-called because this spacing was originally produced in typesetting by inserting strips of lead between the lines of type. 2. *(pronounced "leeding")* Putting space in front of a character who is speaking to someone off-frame.

lead screw A highly accurate screw that is used to position the optical heads of laser disk or CD-ROM drivers to produce spiral recording tracks with uniform spacing.

leaf A node in a hierarchy that has no children.

learning algorithms See *Hebbian net* and *Hopfield net*.

LED See *light-emitting diode*.

Left/Right Brow Down A parameter for setting head shape in *Poser*.

Left/Right Brow Up A parameter for setting head shape in *Poser*.

Legendre fractal curve A fractal curve generated by iterating a Legendre function over the complex plane.

Lempel Ziv Welch (LZW) A lossless algorithm for data or image compression. Used in the *GIF* file format. See *GIF*.

lens 1. Usually a series of separate glass lenses, the lens on a camera is what focuses light onto the focal plane to create an image. Most 3D applications allow the user to create warped glass objects that can act as a lens to be placed in front of the camera, creating limitless rendered image effects. 2. The secondary optical system in the eye. It is located directly behind the iris and changes shape for close and far vision.

lens filters Specially prepared pieces of colored glass housed in a screw-on attachment. Most filters are threaded so that they can be screwed onto other filters in order to stack effects. Filters come in different sizes, so the selection of filters available for a given lens size may vary. Many filters come in different "strengths" whose values are usually measured with a simple number scheme. The higher the number setting, the more the filter will affect the image.

lens flare 1. The starburst pattern that appears when a camera lens is pointed directly at a strong light source. 2. One of the *KPT* filters for *Photoshop* from Corel.

lens flare.

lens flare.

lens flare, simulating Lens flare can be simulated as a 2D overlay on the 3D scene, and the elements of the flare can be rendered along a line intersecting the projected position of the light and the center of the screen. The lens flare effect is rendered with a small collection of textures, one for each style of flare element—circles, rings, hexagons, sunbursts, etc. The grayscale textures are combined with vertex colors to produce subtle coloring. Alpha blending is used to make the effect translucent. Elements are rendered in a variety of sizes. To be truly effective, the lens flare effect must animate convincingly with camera movement. The overall movement of the flare is determined by tracing the line from the projected light position through the center of the screen. Varying the size and translucency of the flare elements produces additional subtlety. This variation is achieved by scaling the size and alpha value of the flare elements based on the distance between the projected light position and the center of the screen. When the light is farther from the center, the elements are smaller and

more transparent, and when the light is closer to the center, they become larger and more opaque.

lenticular film A technique for three-dimensional viewing. A Lenticular film, composed of a set of thin vertical cylindrical lenses (each typically with a width of $1/4$ millimeter), can be placed over the screen, and the two stereo images dissected into vertical stripes and interlaced so that the lenses present each stripe to the appropriate observer's eye. This technique has been used on picture postcards for many years. It has the advantage of not needing the observer to train the eyes or to wear special gear. Its main disadvantages are reduced horizontal resolution and the difficulty of aligning the image stripes with the lenses.

lerp See *linear interpolation.*

letterboxing The process of putting black bars at the top and bottom of the screen to change a 4:3 aspect ratio image to a wider aspect ratio image.

letterspacing In typography, the overall amount of white space between characters of a word.

Level Editor An editor in *The Games Factory* that allows the user to decide which characters, backgrounds, and objects to put in a level and how to animate them. From this screen, one has access to the libraries of all the different objects that are used in a game. This is also where one can create original animated objects, text, and other object types.

leveling Changing the amount of detail used in modeling graphics objects as a function of their distance from the observer so that in the final image, all objects appear to have the same amount of detail. This minimizes the computer time spent on modeling details that will not easily be seen.

level of detail (LOD) Objects and characters are represented in computer graphics as geometric models. Models can be created at different *levels of detail* (LODs), with more polygons and larger textures for the more-detailed models, and fewer polygons and smaller textures for the less-detailed models. This improves rendering performance and visual quality. Drawing fewer polygons when objects are far away from the camera reduces the polygon count of the scene, and so speeds up rendering. Having a more-detailed model for use when an object is close to the camera improves visual quality. If only a single model is used, then there is always a tradeoff between performance and quality—multiple levels of detail help to achieve both. To implement LOD rendering, multiple models are created at different levels of detail, and the model to be rendered is chosen, each frame based on distance from the camera. As a rough rule of thumb, each level of detail should have about twice the number of polygons as the preceding level. The models are created to reduce "popping" as much as possible—when the character or object switches from one level of detail to another, the visible change in geometry (especially at the silhouette edge) and texturing must be minimized. The artist's job is to create models that are as similar as possible when rendered at the scale where the transition will occur. The programmer's job is to determine when to change LODs to achieve the desired performance and quality while minimizing the number of LOD transitions. Note that for objects or characters that stay a relatively constant distance from the camera (such as the hero character in a third-person game), level of detail selection is not necessary.

level surface The set of all points in a volume that have a given scalar value.

lexical design The determination of how input and output units of meaning are actually formed from hardware primitives. Also called *hardware binding design*.

lexicographic sort A sort in alphabetical order with numbers inserted where they would appear if spelled out.

Lexidata Lex A computer whose video system assembles the video stream on the fly from disjoint portions of video memory.

L-grammars Parallel graphic grammar languages used by Lindenmayer to model plants.

Liang-Barsky line-clipping algorithm See *clipping, Liang-Barsky line algorithm*.

library A collection of software routines that is part of a program or language.

LifeForms An application from Credo International that allows the user to create limitless BVH motion files.

life game A game that provides a visual example of the use of cellular automata. The player sets up an array of cells which then are born, grow, decay, or die according to simple rules. The continually changing cell pattern is displayed on the display screen.

LIFO See *last in, first out*.

ligature In typography, a single character that combines two letters that frequently occur together.

light 1. Emissions in the frequency band detectable by the human eye. 2. Brightly colored, having a high color value. 3. Being closer to white than black.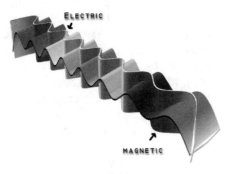

ELECTRIC

MAGNETIC

light.

light and shadow leaks When modeling, it is always desirable to indicate and outline polygon boundaries as well as edges. There should be no overlapping or intersecting planes that do not have their boundaries divided. If the boundaries are not indicated, light or shadow leaks will occur at the intersection. Imagine a long box positioned obliquely in the center of a checkered tile room. The long, rectangular, checkered box forms an angle against the regular tile formation. Now imagine that the checkered tile is the interpolated shading used in radiosity; the position of the rectangular box would divide the exposed tiles in half. Since the shading across the polygon is interpolated, this shading is carried across into the areas unoccluded by the rectangular box, so a *shadow leak* occurs. A *light leak* occurs in the opposite situation of a shadow leak. It forms when an illuminated area crosses an area where there is inadequate meshing to capture the boundary. This is especially evident in polygon-to-polygon boundaries in which there is an exposed, but occluded surface. Light leaks and shadow leaks give the affected polygons a "floating" impression that can be solved by increasing the density of the initial mesh before processing the solution. Of all the radiosity artifacts, light and shadow leaks are the most obvious and offensive.

light buffer A programming technique for efficient computing of shadows. Each point light source is surrounded by a direction cube, and an associated array (which is part of the light buffer) contains a list of all objects visible through that cube. The direction of a light ray is first looked up in the light buffer and only those objects in the proper directional cube are shadow tested.

light controls Methods of controlling lights in *Poser*. It is possible to use as many lights as desired in a scene, including spotlights.

light coordinate system A coordinate system used in rendering shadows. The light coordinate system has its origin at the light source and its Z axis pointing at the blocker object. The Z axis of this coordinate system determines the center line of the perspective projection, while its XY plane defines the orientation of the screen plane on which we project the shadow map. If we transform the blocker object into this light coordinate system we can easily project it onto this plane. To define an arbitrary coordinate system, we need to know the position of the light source's origin and its orientation.

We can describe the orientation of the light coordinate system by the direction of its three axes: X_{light}, Y_{light}, and Z_{light}, all 3D unit vectors in world coordinates.

light-emitting diode (LED) A semiconductor device that emits light when a voltage is applied.

Lightf/x A plug-in for *trueSpace* (part of *CoolPowers*) that creates light arrays or light strips; that is, lights that are arranged in a pattern. The arrangements of multiple lights will result in much smoother shadows than a single light. Lighting is one of the most important steps in creating a good animation. Any tool that aids in creating good lighting is a valuable addition to a tool kit.

Light Info Window A display in *Universe*. It shows the location of the light options: Camera, Parallel, Radial, Ambient, Spot, and Tube lights. *Universe* allows unlimited light sources, determined only by the amount of RAM available.

lighting, ambient See *ambient light*.

lighting, attenuation maps A technique that can be used to implement dynamic point lights with proper quadratic attenuation using multi-texture operations. In addition, the technique can be used for spherical, ellipsoidal, cylindrical, and rectangular lighting or CSG operations, accurate to a per-pixel level, without using the stencil buffer.

lighting, bump mapping for Bump-mapping techniques either calculate or approximate a dot product between the light vector L and the surface normal N in order to calculate diffuse lighting, usually on a per-pixel basis. This functionality is available from several hardware vendors. Specular lighting can be achieved by calculating the dot product between the half-angle vector H and the surface normal N and then raising the result to some power.

lighting, conventional static *Conventional static lighting* is precomputed Gouraud RGB values stored with each vertex and used in a diffuse fashion during rendering. The precomputed RGB values are generated by either a tool or the game's initialization code. In either case, a tool is used to place lights on an object and assign characteristics such as color, intensity, radius, radial fall-off, and light type (omni, directional, spot, etc.). When dealing with static lighting, the lights and all their properties are constant. In addition, their positions are fixed in the object space of the object they are lighting; that is, static lights cannot move relative to the object they are lighting. From the light positions and properties, the effect of each light on each of the object's vertices can easily be computed using any desired lighting equation.

lighting, diffuse lighting factor A term in the omni-light equation that performs another attenuation based on the dot product of the light ray from the omni-light to the vertex being lit and that vertex's normal vector. A *diffuse lighting factor* is a very common way of brightening both vertices that a light ray hits head-on and darkening vertices that a light ray hits more at an angle.

lighting, dramatic *Dramatic lighting* is lighting that helps bring contrast or conflict to the scene, thereby adding dramatic value. One of the keys to dramatic lighting is to rely on cast light from a spot or bulb light to place emphasis on the scene. Because of this, it is a good idea to lower the ambient light setting, which allows more contrast to be added to a scene. The lower the ambient light, the greater the contrast between the background and the lit object, thus increasing its dramatic presence.

lighting gel Translucent pieces of special colored plastic attached to a light source to change the brightness and color of the light.

lighting, low angle Lighting plays a crucial role in achieving and controlling the look of a bump map. In photography, when the photographer wants to accentuate surface texture he tends to lower the light source(s) and "strafe" it across the object.

lighting model The algorithm or equation used to determine the shading of a particular point or surface. Also known as a *shading model* or *illumination model*.

lighting, monochromatic palette Using single-colored lights with different intensities can add dramatic effects to scenes. In addition, the monochromatic palette will help artists understand how lights can be manipulated in *Universe* to create the effects they desire. Choosing the right color for a particular scene can convey a sense of time and space. For example, applying sepia-colored lights to a scene that contained old castles immediately creates a sense of time that reflects the melancholy feeling and mood that might be associated with the genre. Likewise, using deep blue colors would greatly enhance an underwater scene. The possibilities with monochromatic palette are endless and offer the ability to create amazing impact to the final composition. With the power of *Universe*, these effects can be en-

hanced through the use of built-in volumetric options such as Fog, Glow, Light Ray, Smoker, Projection Map, and many more.

lighting, mood-setting More than any other visual element, lighting has the ability to create a sense of mood in a scene. Mood is one of the factors in an image that allows the animator to stir particular emotions in the viewer. There are two primary aspects of lighting that allow the user to do this. A soft, warm light (a light that moves toward the reds, yellows, and browns of the color wheel) usually invokes feelings of heat, calm, and ease. Cool light (light that moves toward the blues and greens of the color wheel), on the other hand, is more apt to invoke a feeling of cold, unease, and harshness. Contrasting colors (those that appear opposite each other on the color wheel) can create a sense of tension, while complementary colors (those that appear close to each other) tend to create a sense of harmony. Shadows are another significant way in which lighting adds to a scene's mood. Dark, high-contrast shadows tend to set a forbidding tone or add a sense of harshness to the scene. Longer, softer shadows can give a scene a more inviting or romantic feel, while minimal shadows or a lack of shadows altogether can create a sense of sterility.

lighting, motif-based static The advantage of conventional static lighting over dynamic lighting is execution speed. There simply are no run-time computations performed; RGB values are retrieved from the vertex structure and plugged directly into the color values for the rendering vertex. However, the drawback is that static lighting produces static results. The RGB values for each vertex are precomputed, stored, and never change from frame to frame. Motif-based static lighting provides a more dynamic look than conventional static lighting at a negligible reduction in performance. The static lights lighting the object are fixed in the object's coordinate space, as is the case with conventional static lighting. However, with motif-based static lighting, we are able to animate the RGB components of the lights in real time. The type of animation is completely up to the designer. Some animations, such as a light switch on the wall of a room that turns on the overhead light, might be under the player's control. Other animations, such as flames, flickering lights with electrical shorts, and blinking lights, might be algorithmically controlled. Furthermore, some lights might have constant RGB values. Each of these animations (including those that are constant) is called a *light motif*.

lighting ratio 1. The ratio of the key light to the fill light. 2. The unit of light contributed by each light in a scene that establishes the tonality.

lighting realism The degree of realism attributed to the appearance of a surface when lit. It is important to understand that a surface that has a high amount of geometric realism will not automatically render realistically when lit, especially when the surface has sharp edges. In the real world there is no such thing as a perfectly sharp edge. Usually, otherwise detailed models will not pass photorealistic scrutiny if they have unbeveled or unrounded edges. It is good practice to add bevel or round to every edge that will be seen by the camera. Adding

bevels to edges is especially critical when modeling surfaces that are perfectly mated to each other. If two adjacent and mated objects, like panels, do not have their edges at the seam beveled, they will shade as a single surface, or at best there will be a hairline seam. For the panels to render realistically, the edges at the seams should have a bevel. The two bevels, one on each edge, will form a V-groove that will catch a shadow at the bottom of the trough and the bevels will generate small subtle highlights. The combination of a bevel highlight and groove shadow creates a subtle yet realistic effect.

lighting, real-time simulations To generate real-time vertex lighting, first transform the normal for each vertex in the object. Then, determine the angle at which the light is facing the vertex normal. Using the facing angle, determine the intensity of the light at that vertex. Repeat for each light illuminating the vertex. Finally, add the ambient light intensity. Real-time lighting using this method requires many computations, which can be reduced dramatically using the interpolation method. In order to "fake" the real-time method, we must set some constraints on our 3D scene: First, determine how many light positions are needed for the interpolation. Then, determine the axis of rotation used to base the interpolation calculation. The vertex color lists represent the lighting on the object at distinct orientations of the figure relative to the lighting in the scene, whether the lighting is one light source or 100. A full 360-degree rotation is required, so one must determine how many vertex color lists will be used. A minimum of three positions is necessary, each located 120 degrees apart. Note that by using more lists, the range of values to be interpolated between is decreased, thereby increasing the accuracy of the faked lighting.

lighting, sun angle and time of day
When lighting an outdoor scene or a scene where the outside can be seen, pay attention to the angle of the sun if the time of day is important. If it is noon, the light should be very close to a point directly above the scene. This will cause very short shadows. If it is later or earlier in the day, the sun should be more angled, creating longer shadows. Also consider the season, as this can change the angle of the sun within the position of a scene.

lighting, transparency rendering To draw a transparent object with 3D hardware, pixel blending, or simply "blending," is often used. Pixel blending is implemented in the last stage of a rendering pipeline, in the pixel renderer after rasterization.

lighting, vertex color interpolation for To generate interpolated vertex lighting, first calculate the facing angle to virtual light source. Then determine which two vertex light sets to interpolate between. Calculate the interpolation percentage, perform the interpolation for each vertex color, and finally, apply an ambient light RGB modifier for each vertex color and clamp the resulting values.

light kit A set of professional lights, light stands, and lighting accessories, usually contained in a heavy-duty carrying case.

light kit, basic The minimum lighting equipment necessary for three-point

lighting. It consists of two 650 watt lights (with Fresnel lenses), two single scrims, two half single scrims, two double scrims, two half double scrims, two sets of barn doors, one 1K or 650W softlight, one egg crate (used to make the softlight more directional), three gel frames, and three light stands.

light maps An approach to calculating lighting that can avoid the triangle tessellation-related artifacts that vertex lighting can have when the size of the triangle is large with respect to the range of a point or spotlight. Light maps require expensive CPU operations to update for dynamic lights and require potentially slow upload to the video card. Still, light maps are a good solution for static lighting and shadows. Light maps are commonly employed to store static lighting data, such as shadows and light calculated through a global illumination solution. Updating light maps at run time for point lights is complicated and costly.

light meter A small, handheld device used to record the illumination at a particular location, usually measured in foot-candles or lux, which can then be translated to f-stops.

light meter, incident Incident light meters can be considered true exposure meters because they are unaffected by directional light sources in a scene. Incident light meters cannot be used to individually "sample" the tones present in a scene. These meters can read only the light falling on a scene. Therefore, these types of light meters must be pointed in the direction of incoming light rather than reading the light reflected off the subject. Incident light meters are mostly hand-held light meters with white diffusers. These diffusers can be either white domes or flat discs. The white domes "average" the amount of light shining on the scene; the flat discs are used to evaluate the individual light's lighting ratio. Most commercial photographers and cinematographers use incident light meters because they can easily measure the various light levels falling on a scene without the subject influencing the reading.

light meter, reflected A reflected light meter reads the light reflected off a scene. This is the type of light meter that is present in most auto-exposure cameras; it assumes a middle gray. Reflected light meters can be used to "inspect" the various tones present in a scene such as the white wall example.

light motif See *lighting, motif-based static*.

lightness The brightness of a color as represented in the CIELAB color space. Also known as *L**.

Lightning 1. An effects modifier found in many 3D applications. 2. One of the *Xenofex* filters for *Photoshop* from Alien-Skin. 3. See *3D Energy*.

Lightning Software See *Wave Generator*.

light pen A pen-like device that detects light pulses from a computer monitor and detects their position on the screen for use by program actions.

lights, camera The camera light is similar to attaching a radial light to the top of a camera. Everywhere the camera goes, the light follows. This is especially useful for exploration-type effects in which the point of an animation is to take a viewer through an old castle, cavern, tunnel, or some other place that needs to be discovered.

light-sensing device An electronic component that produces a voltage proportional to the light that shines on it.

lights, factor setting Many features of lights in *Universe* allow the user to adjust factors. The factor setting determines the degree of fall-off between the inside cone and the outside cone of a light or lighting effect. The default setting of 1.0 produces what appears to be a sharp transition between where the light is at 100% and where it fades out. There really is not a sharp transition; it is an optical illusion, but one that can be eliminated by lowering the factor setting. Dropping a factor down to 0.5 will reduce most of the perceived banding.

lights, false spherical In *Bryce*, *false spherical lights* can be used effectively as suns, and mapped with plain color or more evocative materials for use as background planets. Used for this purpose, they are not usually transparent, though they are fuzzy around the edges. If they are made transparent, they can be used as ghostly lights that can be placed anywhere in the scene.

lights, grouping to objects It may help to place a "real" light at the source of the projected beam object (usually a transparent cone). This enables the designer to use the false light at its maximum effectiveness, while using the real light (usually a spotlight) to cast shadows and offer its contribution to the mix.

lights, material preset In *Bryce* there are two material presets that are very useful to target to spheres, for use as stars or false sun objects (the term "false" is used to distinguish these objects from the *Bryce* Sun).

light source A source of illumination modeled for use in rendering a graphics image.

light source, large A large light source is a light source in which there are almost no dark shadows and the light envelops the object. Large light sources have almost no penumbra and umbra separation, if they generate perceptible shadows at all. Most large light sources have no perceptible shadows because they are so diffused and spread out that they become light and imperceptible. A large light source is diffused, not directional. The orientation of a large light source is difficult to determine because light emanates from all over. The highlights of large light sources tend to spread out and blend together. No light terminator is present in large light sources. An example of a large light source is an overcast, cloudy sky. Other examples include a row of fluorescent lights reflected off a huge ceiling or a series of windows that illuminate the room with filtered and diffuse light that is nondirectional.

lights, parallel The parallel light is best described as an infinitely large wall that emits light. Since the rays of light are coming from a wall, they are parallel to each other, as opposed to lights like radials and spots where the light emits from a single point. They are thus emitted at an angle that intersects at the point of origination. Parallel lights create a lighting effect similar to that of the sun or any large light source. Parallel lights are also spaced an infinite distance away from the scene. The icon for the light can still be seen, but it behaves as if it were placed an infinite distance away from the scene in the opposite direction of the reference point. Since this is the case, parallel lights can be placed anywhere in the scene and the light will always travel in the direction of the reference point.

lights, practical The term *practical lights* refers to all the visible light sources in a scene. Practical lights can be fixed lights such as sconces, chandeliers, and table lamps as well as portable lights such as candles and flashlights. Sometimes a car's headlights or a campfire are used to illuminate a scene.

lights, radial The radial light is synonymous with a real-world light bulb. It is a source of light that radiates in a spherical pattern from the center point. One can adjust the fall-off and intensity of a radial light to simulate various real-world bulb-based lights. Radial lights are useful for many effects, such as casting a light in a spherical pattern.

light tent A conic, white translucent accessory (often referred to as an "umbrella") that covers the whole object with a small hole for the camera lens. The light tent envelopes the whole object and creates light and dark areas depending on the light positions.

light transport The transfer of light through a medium or from one surface to another.

light valve A video projector in which a high-powered lamp produces a beam that is scanned in a raster pattern. The beam passes through an optical device that can use an electronic signal to modulate the intensity of the light that passes through it to the screen.

LightWave One of the first 3D applications on the market to produce high-end graphics and animations for film and broadcast. Originally developed by NewTek for the Amiga system, *LightWave* now addresses Mac, Windows, and Alpha systems. *LightWave* consists of the Modeler and Layout modules.

Lightworks rendering engine A rendering engine that is part of *trueSpace*.

Lightworks shaders A set of shaders that can be used with *trueSpace*.

linear combination A vector resulting from multiplying several vectors by different numerical coefficients and then adding their components together.

linear congruential generator A random-number generator which generates numbers using the following expression:

$$R_{i+1} = \text{mod}(R_i Hs + c, m)$$

where R_{i+1} is the next random number generated, R_i is the seed (or the previous random number), s is a multiplier, c is a constant that is added, and m is the modula number.

linear depth cueing An image in which the color of an object is interpolated between the object color and the background color as a function of distance.

linear editing Editing using linear media (i.e., tape to tape), as opposed to using random access media stored on a computer hard drive. All tape is linear, so linear media can be either digital or analog.

linear expression An expression of the form $F(x,y)=Ax + By + C$.

linear interpolation (lerp) A method of interpolating between quaternion values to obtain smooth animation. Linear interpolation is given as:

$$\text{lerp}(t;q_0,q_1) = (1 - t)q_0 + tq_1 = t(q_1 - q_0) + q_0$$

Linear interpolation does not preserve magnitude, so it is important to normalize the result if it is being used as a rotation. Linear interpolation is fast, but it does not generate smooth animation. This means that the animation speeds up and slows down over the course of the interpolation, even if it is varied at a constant rate. Although this variation in speed might be acceptable for some applications, it is not ideal.

linear-list notations See *animation, linear-list notations*.

linear momentum Newton's first law of motion states that a body remains stationary or maintains a constant velocity unless acted on by an external force. This is also known as the law of conservation of *linear momentum*. The linear momentum vector, p, of a body is calculated by multiplying its velocity, v, by its mass, m:

$$p = mv$$

The rate of change of momentum with respect to time is equal to the sum of all the forces (the net force) on this body:

$$F_{net} = \sum F_i = \frac{dp}{dt} = m\frac{dv}{dt} = ma$$

linear prediction The prediction of the next value in a series of data based on a linear relationship of the behavior of the preceding pieces of data.

LinearSoftFill A procedure used to fill a region whose edge is blurred, often because of antialiasing.

linear spline A line or curve composed of segments that are straight with intermediate control vertices.

line art An image that is composed entirely of line segments, with no shading, dithering, or halftoning. Also known as *line drawing*.

line-art system A technique for creating objects by using the equations that define a sample population and extending them beyond the bounds of the sample population.

line height The space between two paragraphs. Setting a large line height for paragraphs can allow for easier reading of a large body of text.

line of sight The direction in which an observer of a scene is looking.

line-plane intersection in collision detection See *collision detection, line-plane intersection*.

line screen The resolution of the screen used to produce a halftone from a photograph. It is expressed in lines per inch (lpi) and is usually between 53 lpi and 150 lpi.

line segment A short, straight line. A vector.

lines of force An important concept in *form•Z*. When the Smooth Mesh tool processes a cage, the faces of the smooth mesh flow along the segments of the cage. In other words, the segments of the cage define the lines of force along which the smoothed mesh polygons will flow. By carefully arranging the vectors of the cage polygon edges, the user can control the shape of the smooth mesh and the flowlines of its polygons. This enables the user to create meshes that flow along when deforming, and consequently, they will render much more cleanly and deform better than meshes whose polygons are arranged along a single force vector.

line spacing In typography, the distance from baseline to baseline between two lines of type.

line style The characteristic of a line as determined by the solid and broken parts of the line; for example, solid lines, dotted lines, dashed lines, center lines, etc.

line width The thickness of a line drawn on a display.

linguistic interaction task A task in which the user knows the coordinates of a desired position and requires feedback to show when he has moved the cursor to the position designated by these coordinates.

linguistic variables Variables that are used to make a decision using fuzzy logic.

linked material shells In *Bryce*, just as clouds can be mapped to an outer sphere that revolves around a planet object, any object can also have its own outer shell. Shells can be used for clothing on a human figure or for more esoteric looks. For instance, if the user wraps a shell on a human, animal, or robotic figure and maps it with a fuzzy light, it will give the figure a perceptible aura as it moves in the scene.

LINKS-1 A computer built at Osaka University that has an image-parallel architecture that assigns one or more rays to each of a number of separate parallel elements, with the entire database duplicated for each parallel element. This permits accelerated ray tracing techniques.

Link to Parent tool A tool in *Universe* that allows the user to link an object as the child to a selected parent object.

Lipshitz-Holder exponent A term that is introduced into the equation for a multi-fractal to assure that the fractal equation does not diverge to 0 or 4 over the range of iteration.

Lips Out Target Morph A capability of *Poser* to morph the lips of a figure outward or inward.

liquid crystal display (LCD) A display that consists of a thin layer of a special liquid between two glass plates. Application of a voltage through a pair of transparent conductors causes the molecules of the liquid at the affected location to align with the applied field, changing the optical properties of the liquid. A liquid crystal display does not generate light; it must be viewed by reflected light or by backlighting.

liquids, refraction maps for Refraction-mapping of liquids in opaque containers can be achieved by computing refraction, reflection, and Fresnel terms on water simulations.

Lissajous figure A figure formed by two mutually-perpendicular sinusoidal oscillations. Many different patterns can be created by varying the frequency and phase of the two sinusoids. Stable patterns occur when one sinusoid is an exact multiple of the other.

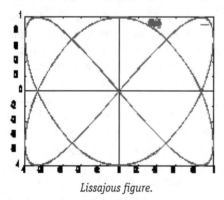

Lissajous figure.

List A capability of the *Stat!* plug-in for *trueSpace*. It gives a list of recognizable objects in the scene.

list priority algorithm An algorithm that assigns priorities to graphics objects in accordance with how they overlap.

LiveSkin A feature of *trueSpace* that allows the user to view changes in a Metaballs object in real time as they are made.

Live Update A capability of the *Superobjects* plug-in for *trueSpace*. It allows the user to view changes as they are created.

Load Morph Target A command in the Object Menu of *Poser* that allows the user to retrieve any saved morph target from storage. Several *Poser* sites on the Web offer free morph target downloads.

local area network (LAN) Computer boards or external boxes, cables, and software used to connect two or more computers so that they have access to one another's resources.

local control, cubic curves B-spline curves consisting of a number of curve segments whose polynomial coefficients depend on just a few control points. Thus moving a control point affects only a small part of the curve.

local light source In rendering a graphics scene, a light source that is near the scene rather than at infinity. For such sources, the light rays do not come from the same direction for every point on an object.

local transformation matrix A matrix used by SPHIGS to change the position or shape of a primitive.

locator In *form•Z*, any object, the points of which are used to precisely define a location in 3D space. In *form•Z*, locators are usually vector lines.

locator logical device A device, such as a tablet, mouse, trackball, or joystick, used to position a cursor.

Lock Actor A command in the Object Menu of *Poser*. Locking can be applied to any part of a model and to any prop. Once locked, that element will not respond to Parameter Dials or other editing tools or alterations until it is unlocked.

Lock Figure A feature in *Poser's* Figure Menu that allows the user to lock an entire figure so that it can no longer be manipulated. It is most useful when working with a scene with multiple figures because it enables the user to work on one selected figure at a time without disturbing the rest.

Lock Hand Parts A command in the Figure Menu of *Poser*. *Poser* hands have articulated fingers and finger/thumb joints. When a figure is being posed, it is sometimes difficult to select a hand without selecting one of the finger/thumb joints. The Lock Hand Parts option can be used to prevent this.

lock height The distance above a digitizing tablet at which the puck or stylus ceases to function.

locking picture The process of formally finalizing the editing of a film, so that the sound editors can start working without having to deal with any changes in timing.

lock link A link in *Carrara* that locks the child to the parent and prevents any movement of the child independent of the parent.

LOD See *level of detail*.

loft A 3D modeling tool that is used to create a 3D shape out of a series of 2D ribs.

lofted surface A surface created by *lofting*.

lofting Determining all of the points on a surface that are defined by a set of cross-section curves through interpolation.

Loft Trajectory In *form•Z*, Loft Trajectory is best described as an imaginary curve (usually open) that follows a natural line of force of the desired object. In many cases, the Loft Trajectory is a straight-line vector bisecting the top profile in two equal halves. Loft Trajectory starts at the extreme front of the model and ends at the extreme rear. It can be a curve, as the target 3D form may be curving and/or twisting on all three axes. Furthermore, it does not have to be a planar curve. If the Loft Trajectory is a curve, the user has the option of bend deforming the profiles to match the curvature of the trajectory curve.

logarithmic space A space in which the coordinate axes are scaled logarithmically.

logarithmic spiral A spiral curve generated by the equation

$$r(\varphi) = r_0 e^{\gamma\varphi}$$

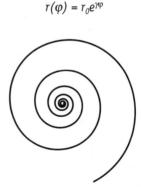

logarithmic spiral.

logging The process of recording the contents of each field tape using timecode,

279

shot names, and descriptions. Logging is the first step in the editing process.

logical A feature supplied by software rather than built-in as part of the unit hardware.

logic-enhanced memory Memory chips that include certain processing capabilities to accelerate the use of memory for particular applications (such as graphics). The disadvantages are reduced memory density and increased cost.

Logic Foundry The producer of a number of shaders for *trueSpace* including an animatable fractal bump shader and *TLF Flame*.

login The process used to gain access to a computer bulletin board or operating system.

logistic parabola An equation that measures the growth of the next generation of a population from the present generation as follows: $x_{n+1} = rx_n(1-x_n)$. When iterated it gives a fractal bifurcation diagram.

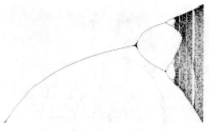

logistic parabola.

logo An artistic emblem that represents a company or product.

longitude Angular measurement from a reference circle orthogonal to the equator. The zero reference is the longitude that passes through Greenwich, England. Lines of equal longitude are circles that pass through both the north and south poles. These circles are called *meridians*.

longitudinal timecode (LTC) A type of SMPTE timecode that is recorded onto the audio track of a videotape.

long shot In film making, a shot that plays out over a long period of time. There are two kinds of long shots. One is an extreme long shot used to depict very expansive areas usually at a great distance. Many early westerns start out with this broad shot of the endless plains with the wagon train crawling across it. This type of shot instantly orients the audience to the vastness of the scene and grabs its attention. Extreme long shots typically work best when done from a high vantage point. The second type, the standard long shot, is used to give the audience an understanding of the area in which the upcoming action is to take place. Long shots give information as to if the action is going to happen in a store, a factory, a house, which room in the house, etc.

long shot.

Look At Object tool A tool in *Universe* that centers the camera on a chosen object. Then, whenever the object is moved, the camera will keep it in view.

This is an effective tool for keeping up with high-action shots.

look-at utilities A means of camera positioning. Basic first-person camera models rely on look-at utilities such as OpenGL's *gluLookAt()*. Given a camera position, view direction, and up vector, this function returns an orientation view matrix. The view matrix is then placed on the OpenGL MODELVIEW matrix stack and concatenated with orientation matrices for each object in the scene as it is rendered.

look-up table color A color obtained from a table of permissible colors that is used to replace several similar colors in a color quantization process.

look-up table (lut) A table used to store image data for displays including animation.

looping The process of re-recording dialogue in a studio. This process is known as *looping* because the actor sometimes watches a continuous loop of the scene that is being re-recorded. Also known as *automatic dialog replacement (ADR)*.

loop interpolation A technique in *Poser* that allows for easier creation of cycling animations.

Loop Pick Filter A tool in *Universe* that can be used to evaluate a topology for rounding. Selecting the Loop Pick Filter and clicking on edges will display the other edges that make up the loop and give clues as to how the faces have been created.

Loop the Movement function A function in *The Games Factory* that will run a defined movement repeatedly.

Lorentz transformation A transformation that mixes space and time together.

lo-res Low resolution. Low-quality reproduction of image or text, often based on the number of dots per inch (dpi).

lossless Describes methods of compressing data or images that permit the data to be restored to its original form without any loss of information.

lossy Describes methods of compressing data or images that result in the loss of some of the original information.

lossy CODEC A codec that reduces image quality when it compresses an image.

lower jaw, human The lower jaw defines the profile of the head and is considered to be a very distinguishing element of the facial structure. The angle of the lower jaw aligns with the corner of the mouth. When viewing from the front, the widest point of the jaw is aligned with the outside edge of the supraorbital margin.

lower thirds See *Chryon*.

Lowface Target Morph A target morph used to control the face shape in *Poser*.

low key The lighting style where there is a dominance of blacks and grays that create a high-contrast scene. There is a high light ratio between the key light and the fill light.

low-pass filtering The process of removing the high frequency part of the spectrum of a signal.

L-systems A language that is used for defining many types of self-similar fractals, including Koch snowflakes and trees.

LTC See *longitudinal timecode*.

luma clamping See *luminance clamping*.

luma key See *luminance key*.

lumen A unit of light measurement that is the power of one candela on one unit of area in one unit of distance.

Lumiere Suite An entry-level video editor developed by Corel.

luminaire 1. A light source in a radiosity model. 2. A lighting industry term for complete light outfits of different designs. This term normally refers to the lamp, reflectors, diffusers, and housing.

luminance 1. The strength (or amplitude) of the grayscale (or brightness) portion of a video signal. 2. The amount of light emitted or reflected by a given area of a subject in a specific direction. 3. The amount of computed light values in a scene.

luminance channel Luminance is sometimes called "light-independent color," which means that an object has its own "inner-light." This differs from a glow texture in that the luminance color is strictly limited to the area the map defines and does not spill out.

luminance clamping The process of clamping (or clipping, or scaling) the luminance value in a video signal. In video that has been luma clamped, luminance values over 235 are eliminated, frequently resulting in video with bright areas that look like solid blobs of white.

luminance-color difference space The color space used to define colors for television broadcasting. It is a three-dimensional space consisting of a *luminance* value Y, which is a weighted value of the three primary color values red (R), green (G), and blue (B) in the form $Y = 0.30R + 0.59G + 0.11B$. The other two dimensions of the space are defined by the $(B - Y)$ and the $(R - Y)$ differences, either of which can produce a good grayscale picture by itself.

Luminance/Glow tab A tab in *Universe* that allows the user to select the luminance and glow characteristics of an object.

luminance key A special key function that will use the luminance values in a layer to determine the transparency of that layer. For example, a luminance key could be set to render the darkest areas of the layer transparent.

luminance meter An instrument for measuring the luminance of light.

luminescence The ability to emit light.

luminosity The emission of light energy per second.

luminous efficiency function The eye's response to light of constant luminance as the dominant wavelength is varied.

lut See *look-up table*.

lux A measure of luminous flux intensity equal to 1 lumen per square meter or 10.76 footcandles.

LZW See *Lempel Ziv Welch*.

M

m Root mean square slope of microfacets used in computing object illumination.

M *mega*. 1. When applied to computer storage, 1,048,576 (= 2^{20}). 2. When applied to money, 1,000,000 (= 10^6).

M2 An analog technique for recording video images.

Mac Slang for the Macintosh computer.

mach band effect A visual illusion caused by the human eye's special sensitivity to edge-like discontinuities. It occurs when a continuously toned surface is rendered with too few intensity steps.

macro command A new command that the user can define as a combination of existing commands.

Macromedia *FreeHand* See *FreeHand*.

magenta A purplish color that is one of the primary colors used in subtractive color imaging processes.

magic energy setup An effect produced in *trueSpace* by using the *Primal Particles* plug-in, in which a pillar appears to be rising from the ground with an energy field around it.

magic wand tool A tool in most 2D image applications that enables the user to select an area of an image based on the color. When the tool is selected, and the user clicks on the image, all pixels with the same color are selected.

magnet and wave deformers Capabilities of *Poser* that can be used to create effects like animated warping of any selected figure element, or to cause wave and ripple effects on any figures or prop.

magnetic ink Ink that can be read by a magnetic scanner. Magnetic ink is commonly used to print identifying numbers on bank checks.

magnetic ink character recognition (MICR) A technique in which a scanning device is used to read characters printed with magnetic ink.

magnetic tape A data storage medium consisting of a thin plastic ribbon coated with a magnetic material such as iron oxide, upon which pulses are magnetically recorded.

magneto-optic A data storage medium similar to magnetic tape or disk, but using a magnetic material with much smaller grains. The material is recorded by heating the grains with a laser to make them susceptible to recording and then impressing data with a write head while the area is still hot.

Magnet tool A tool in *LightWave*'s Modeler that allows the user to push and pull on selected polygons. Most 3D applications have similar tools, though they may be named differently.

magnification factor The screen size of an object relative to its physical size. The magnification factor is simple to compute and is independent of orientation. It can be computed by transforming the object position into view space and then calculating:

$$M = xscale/zview$$

where xscale is the scaling parameter used in the projection equation:

$$xscreen = (xview * xscale) / zview + xcenter$$

magnify 1. To enlarge an image without rotation by scaling the same amount in all coordinates. 2. A tool in 3D applications that allows the user to zoom in on the object or scene.

Magpie A program that enables the user to perform track analysis of a sound track and develop lip-syncing animation.

mailbox A means of avoiding redundant calculations in ray tracing by storing intersection results with each object.

mailto A capability used in HTML to create a link in order to send e-mail. It uses a mailto: protocol as opposed to the http: protocol used for Web addresses. The following example will create an email link:

```
<A HREF="mailto:info@
charlesriver.com">Email Us</A>
```

majority voting A rule used in cellular automata in which a cell assumes a new state that matches the state of the majority of its neighboring cells.

Make Double-sided A command in *Light-Wave's* Modeler that forces selected polygons to be treated as double sided, which is often necessary when rendering both sides of the object (for example, when the inner surface of the object can be seen). Most 3D applications have a similar command.

Make Movie A command found in all 2D/3D applications, although the terms may vary somewhat. The object of this command is to force the application to render out the targeted frames, either as a QuickTime or AVI movie file, or as a sequence of numbered single frames.

management information system (MIS) A software system that provides data needed for management decisions and permits the user to manipulate these data.

manager class A class that provides a single interface to a large collection of related classes, usually a subsystem. Such classes are often designed as singletons because it usually makes sense to have only one manager object per type of subsystem. For example, only one object is needed in order to manage access to audio or graphical user interface subsystems.

Mandelbrot set The fractal curve named for Benoit Mandelbrot. The set is a plot representing the result of iterating the following equation:

$$z_{n+1} = z_n^2 + c$$

with $z_0 = 0 + i0$ and c varied over the complex plane. Compare with *Julia set*.

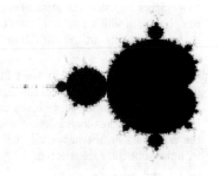

Mandelbrot set.

mandible. The bone that creates the bulk of the lower jaw. The mandible of a female is rounded, while a male mandible is more square.

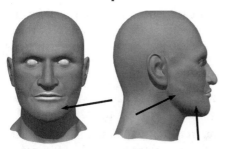

mandible.

Manhattan distance A method of estimating distance that assumes that the sum of the lengths of the three components of a three-dimensional vector is approximately equal to the vector's length.

map 1. An image file that is projected onto the surface of a model when the model is rendered. 2. To project a two-dimensional image onto a surface.

Map Filter A set of check boxes in *Universe*, including the *Interpolate Box* and the *Anti-Aliasing box*. The Interpolate box helps prevent a map from aliasing, but, as a result, can also soften it. The Anti-Aliasing box is another map-filtering option that is used before the final anti-aliasing that occurs during the render. Unchecking this box will sharpen the images.

map, grid-based A method for reducing the number of proximity tests that must be performed for games with large numbers of game objects of varying sizes. The cost of simply testing every object against every other object increases with the square of the number of objects.

map, light coordinate system See *light coordinate system*.

mapping mode Mapping modes vary from one 3D application to another, but the most common are: spherical, cubic, planar, and cylindrical. *LightWave* features a special mapping mode that places the background on the object as a front-faced planar texture, allowing 3D objects to blend with background images.

Mapping Type List A button in *Bryce* that brings up the Mapping Type List for CAB channels. Mapping types are ways that a texture can be placed on the selected object in a scene. They include Object Space, World Space, Parametric, Parametric Scaled, World Top, Spherical, Cylindrical, Reflection Map, Random, Object Top, Cubic, and Object Front.

Mapping Type Name A button in *Bryce* that displays the current mapping type of a CAB channel.

Map Quality A set of edit boxes in *Universe* that allows the user to set the quality of a map. This includes a Blur setting that by default is set at 1.0, but can be reduced to increase map sharpness.

map, shadow A map used in creating realistic shadows in an image. First, set up a perspective projection originating at the light source. This projection projects the blocker object onto a virtual screen plane between the light source and the blocker object, yielding a shadow map.

map, Standard Template Library (STL) A means of handling data. STL maps are perhaps the most complex of the basic containers to use and perhaps the most versatile. The map is essentially a value-pairing container. Two arbitrary types of data are paired as a key/value structure and inserted into the container. Looking up the value via the key then can occur in O(log n) time. Although not quite as efficient as a *hash table*, the difference is often negligible and has the advantage of sorting the data during insertion. This process allows iteration of completely sorted data, which is a beneficial consequence of the method of storage (a balanced binary tree, also known as a *red-black tree*).

maquettes, physical Practical models upon which 3D models can be based.

marble A natural rock-like material that has colored veins running through it. It can be modeled using procedures for modeling turbulence. Marble textures in 3D applications are usually created from procedural (mathematical) algorithms, as opposed to bit-mapped textures.

Marble A filter in the AlienSkin *EyeCandy* collection for *Photoshop* that allows the user to create realistic marble textures.

Marble function A shader function in *Carrara* for creating objects that have the appearance of marble. The Marble function is similar to the Wood function

Marble function.

in the effects it creates, with the most noticeable difference being the way it dithers the edges of the veins instead of blending them smoothly.

marching cubes A technique for rendering solids that uses a lattice in three-dimensional space and determines the intersections of a level surface with the edges of the lattice.

margin In typography, white space surrounding the text area of a page.

marionette, graphical An animated sequence created by recording the motion of a human with lights attached to critical points on his body and then using the resulting film to determine the actions that are to be a part of the final animation.

marker A small graphics object that can be moved on a display without changing size. It is used to identify a location where an action is to take place.

Markov source A source that outputs a one or a zero, with the probability of either being determined by one set of probabilities if the previous output was a one and another set of probabilities if the previous output was a zero.

mask A pattern of bits which are logically ANDed with incoming data to determine which bits will survive to be further acted upon.

Mask One of the modes in *Amorphium Pro* from Electric Image. Using the tools in this mode allows the user to interactively mask-protect parts of a 3D model from modification.

maskable Capable of having some incoming data bits ignored. Thus color data could be *maskable* so that only a single color (red, for example) would be processed.

Mask slider A slider in *Universe* that controls the degree of transparency of an object. When set to full transparency, the object becomes totally invisible and is subtracted from the alpha channel as well.

master The definition of an object in an object hierarchy. Geometrically transformed invocations of the master that appear further down in the hierarchy are called *instances*.

master node list A list of all explored nodes used by the A* path-finding algorithm.

master objects and groups Tools in *Carrara* that allow the user to create an object or group and then make copies (or instances) of it that are tied to the original (or master) in terms of their characteristics. For example, one would probably want to make one wheel of a car a "master group" and then make three more instances to use as the other wheels. Any changes the user makes to the master group would then be made automatically to all four wheels.

master shot A wide shot that contains all the action in a particular scene. Used as the basis for building the scene.

mat An arbitrarily-sized two-dimensional array of real numbers.

material A user-defined substance such as gold, glass, or marble. Generally speaking, materials do not involve a color map, but are created by editing attributes such as specularity and transparency.

material attribute options Channel options that can be altered for a selected texture in any 3D application. When the user needs to alter an object's material in the *Bryce* Advanced Motion Lab, a separate Attribute list becomes available. The user can alter every item in the material's Color, Value, and Optics channel attributes.

material attribute options.

Material Editor See *Group Material Info Window*.

Material Generator A plug-in for *trueSpace* that allows the user to randomize any component of a *trueSpace* procedural texture.

Materializer A filter in the Corel *KPT* collection for *Photoshop* that can be used to create hundreds of tiled variations of an image for use as a Web background page.

material percentage volume New scalar fields that are created on the array of sample points of an object to permit drawing of an object with a textured surface.

material preset lights See *lights, material preset*.

material properties Properties, such as reflectivity, that uniquely describe a particular type of material.

material rectangle 1. The process of applying a decal texture in any 3D application. 2. A capability of *trueSpace* that allows the user to layer additional textures as one would apply a decal. The user can even employ textures with transparency maps, making portions of the surface invisible or allowing underlying textures to show through.

materials reflectivity The reflectivity controls for any selected material in any 3D application that allow the user to control the characteristics and color of the reflections of an object.

matrix A rectangular array of numbers used in mathematical operations such as transformation of objects. Matrices have their own particular mathematical operators. When using C++, a matrix class may be set up and all the usual arithmetic operators (+, −, *, and /) may be overloaded so that they do the proper equivalent operations when operating on matrices.

matrix addressing of display Creating a pattern on a liquid crystal display by applying polarizing voltages to the desired x and y lines of the display grid. At the point where the lines intersect, the

overall voltage is sufficient to polarize the crystals, causing a dark spot to appear.

matrix-based cameras A *vector camera* that uses three vectors to represent its orientation. The U, V, and N vectors are parallel to the X, Y, and Z origin vectors, respectively, if the camera has no rotation and is positioned at (0,0,0). The U vector points to the right, the V vector points up, and the N vector points in the direction that the camera is facing. The camera's 3D screen is created using the camera's U, V, and N vectors, and two field-of-view parameters. The field-of-view parameters are calculated using a user-defined field of view that is then scaled by the aspect ratio.

matrix, basic A matrix that provides information on how to interpret a geometric matrix of control points in order to generate a bicubic patch.

matrix, local-to-world Camera vectors are stored in world space; however, models are typically stored in local space, sometimes called model space. The model is centered around (0,0,0) and is accompanied by a local-to-world matrix. This *local-to-world matrix* defines how the object will rotate and translate in order to end up in its final world space orientation and position.

matrix, state transition A table used in a finite-state machine which shows the relationship between the current state, the input, and the output.

matrix, transpose of A matrix obtained by taking a matrix and interchanging its rows and columns. For example, the transpose of the matrix

$$\begin{vmatrix} a_{11} & a_{12} & \cdots & a_{1n} \\ a_{21} & a_{22} & \cdots & a_{2n} \\ \cdots & \cdots & \cdots & \cdots \\ a_{n1} & a_{n2} & \cdots & a_{nn} \end{vmatrix}$$

is the matrix

$$\begin{vmatrix} a_{11} & a_{21} & \cdots & a_{n1} \\ a_{12} & a_{22} & \cdots & a_{n2} \\ \cdots & \cdots & \cdots & \cdots \\ a_{1n} & a_{2n} & \cdots & a_{nn} \end{vmatrix}$$

matte A special type of mask used to perform composites. Similar to a stencil, a matte makes it possible for the user to cut areas out of one layer of video (or a still) to reveal the layers lying below. For example, if the user wanted to create a composite showing a giant tuna flying behind a building, he would need to use a matte inside a compositing program to knock out the background behind the building layer to reveal the giant flying tuna in the underlying layer.

matte object A graphics object rendered in pure black to provide a space for later insertion of another image.

matte surface A surface that has a dull, rough finish. Matte surfaces are really different reflectors, meaning that they spread out incoming light equally. Since they spread light equally, the surrounding area of a matte object has a higher ambient light level than other objects if the incident light is strong enough.

matte volume A scalar field on volume having a value between one and zero. This value is multiplied by the color/opacity volume to obtain a slice of the original volumetric data.

Max See *3ds max*.

maxilla The upper jawbone, directly under the nose.

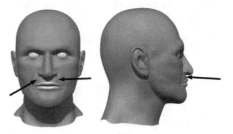

maxilla.

Maximal Key cross-section A cross-section used in *form•Z*. The Maximal Key cross-section is basically a front profile projection of the desired model. Typically, a Profile Loft Assembly has one Maximal cross-section, and it is the largest cross-section in the assembly. With certain 3D forms, especially the ones exhibiting periodic wave function, the Maximal cross-section may be repeated, but these kinds of cases are not common.

Maya A high-end 3D application developed by Alias Wavefront, used for creating special effects and character animation.

maze game A game genre in which the object or player runs around a maze, usually eating or gathering something

matte surface.

while being chased. Typical examples are *Pac Man* and *Ms. Pac Man*.

McCulloch-Pitts nets The first artificial neural networks, created by McCulloch and Pitts in 1943. These neural networks were composed of a number of neurodes and were typically used to compute simple logic functions such as AND, OR, XOR, and combinations of them.

mean time between failures (MTBF) The mean time between two failures of a piece of equipment. A measure of the reliability of the equipment; the higher the *MTBF*, the greater the reliability.

mean time to repair (MTTR) The mean time required to repair an equipment failure. This is a measure of the complexity of the equipment; the higher the *MTTR*, the more complex the equipment.

measure In typography, the length of a typeset line or column width expressed in picas or points.

measure of an interaction device The type of information returned by a logical input device.

mechanical 1. Parts associated with an electronic assembly which perform actions of physical movement. 2. In typography, the completed pasteup for a page.

mechanism The method by which a graphics-application procedure is implemented.

media Plural of *medium*. 1. The material on which data is stored (floppy disk, Zip disk, hard drive, video or audio tape, etc.). 2. The substance used to create visual artifacts (oil paint, watercolors, acrylics, etc.).

Media Cleaner A stand-alone application used to compress video, image, and audio data.

Media Cleaner Pro Non-linear editing software from Media 100 that has a dual stream video option that offers real-time effects and excellent image quality.

Media Composer Sophisticated, non-linear editing software from Avid.

Media Log Software from Avid for logging video shots.

median The middle value of a set of values when they are placed in order.

median-cut algorithm A technique for determining display colors in which a box is fitted around the colors used in an image and is then split along its longer dimension at the median of this dimension. This process continues recursively until 2^m boxes are created. The centroid of each box is then used as the display color for all pixels within that box.

median filtering A filtering technique in which the value of a pixel is set to the median of the values of the neighboring pixels.

MediaPaint A package for developing animated effects that can be overlaid on animation frames. *MediaPaint* offers painting capability and a number of environmental effects. Most 3D applications take a considerable amount of time to render particle and other effects used to simulate nature (fire, clouds, smoke, etc.). With *MediaPaint*, the user can paint these effects on a completed animation. See *Illusion*.

MediaStudio Pro A Windows-only non-linear editing system, developed by Ulead, that offers a collection of post-production editing capabilities. *MediaStudio Pro* is a multimedia component package, consisting of *Video Editor*, *Audio*

Editor, Capture, CG Infinity, and *Video Paint*.

medical imaging The application of image processing and display techniques to electronic data from such medical equipment as tomographs or magnetic resonance scanners.

medium See *media*.

medium light source A regional or localized diffused light source. It is the type of light that is between the harsh, high-contrast quality of a small light source and the soft, almost shadowless quality of a large light source. Medium light sources are always directional as well as diffuse. Highlights generated by medium light sources are soft and diffused. The terminators of a medium light source, however, have light middle tones with less separation between the light and dark areas. There is a subtle gradation between the lighted and the shadowed areas. Examples of medium light sources include window lights, covered overhead ceiling lights, and diffused incandescent lights.

medium shot A transition shot between a long shot and a close-up. Medium shots give the viewer the vital pieces of information of how characters are grouped, what gestures they are using, and for whom those gestures are intended. Medium shots often capture facial expressions and movements of characters within the scene. The most common form of the medium shot is the *two-shot*. The two-shot is the basic scene in which two characters are facing each other while exchanging communication, usually in the form of dialogue. ☞

meg An abbreviation for *megabyte*.

megabyte 1024 kilobytes or 1,048,576 bytes of data. Often abbreviated *meg*.

megaflop One million floating-point operations per second. A megaflop can be used to define relative measures of computer performance.

megahertz (MHz) One million Hertz/cycles per second. A computer that operates at 4 MHz has a clock cycle time of 25 billionths of a second.

Megatek *Sigma* See *Sigma*.

member A named data element that contains part of the state of an instance.

Memorize A command in the *Poser* Edit menu. When using this option on any Element, Figure, Light, or Camera, Restore will return that item to its memorized state.

memory, A* algorithm and The A* algorithm requires a large amount of memory. For each node explored, the algorithm needs to store the following information: a pointer to the parent node; the cost to get to this node; the total cost (cost + heuristic estimate); whether this node is on the Open list; and whether this node is on the Closed list.

memory, corruption of Frame based memory works like a stack. Therefore it is imperative that frames are released in

medium shot.

the order opposite of that in which they were obtained; otherwise memory corruption can occur.

memory dots A means of saving and allowing the recall of various settings and views in *Poser and Bryce.*

memory, flocking and The steering behaviors in flocking say nothing about state information or about a given agent maintaining knowledge of the flock, its environment, where it is headed, etc. Flocking is a stateless algorithm in that no information is maintained from update to update; each boid reevaluates its environment at every update cycle. Not only does this reduce memory requirements that might otherwise be needed to provide a similar behavior using approaches besides flocking, but it also allows the flock to react in real time to changing environmental conditions.

memory, frame-based See *frame-based memory.*

memory, iterative autoassociative See *Hopfield net.*

memory, recognition A computer interface in which visual images are associated with already familiar words and meanings.

memory stomp Some systems always read out to the end of the current sector on a disk. For example, the Sony PlayStation loads data from a CD-ROM in multiples of 2,048 bytes. If the programmer reads data directly into a structure, he "stomps" on whatever is in memory after that structure if it is not a multiple of 2,048 bytes in length. To avoid this *memory stomp,* the programmer needs to have a temporary buffer large enough to hold the data file padded out to a 2K boundary.

Menelaus's theorem A theorem that, given a triangle and three points, each colinear with one side of the triangle determines whether the three points are colinear. Menelaus's theorem is useful in curve and surface generation.

Menger sponge A three-dimensional fractal figure consisting of a cube with a number of square slots removed. It is similar to a *Sierpinski triangle.*

mental protuberance The very tip of the lower jawbone. This bone forms the chin of the human head.

Mentemagica A developer, formerly Quantum Impulse, of a series of plug-ins for *trueSpace* that allow the user to achieve advanced animation and effects. See *DynaWave, SpaceTime Morph,* and *DynaCloth.*

menu A list of available options on a computer screen, together with software that permits selection of one of these options through movement of a cursor by a mouse or keyboard.

menu-driven Describes software in which program options are selected by moving a cursor to select items from menus, rather than by typing in commands.

menu, hierarchical A menu in which the user selects a choice from the menu set that appears at the top of the hierarchy, which causes a menu with a second set of choices to appear. This may continue for as many steps as are necessary.

menu, pie A pie-shaped menu that appears with the center of the pie at the cursor position. As the user moves the cursor from the center toward the desired selection, the target width becomes larger, reducing the chances of an erroneous selection.

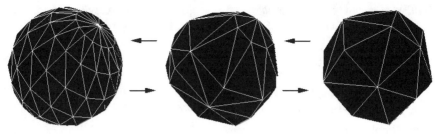

mesh.

menu, pop-up A menu that appears on the screen in response to a user action or because the next program step requires a user response.

menu, pull-down A menu that drops down when the user places the cursor at the top edge of the window, which often has a line of selections.

menu, pull-out A menu that pulls out from the vertical edge of the screen when the cursor is placed at the appropriate area of the screen edge. A mouse click may also be necessary.

Mercator projection A mapping of a sphere onto a plane so that the longitudes are equally spaced. This results in extensive distortion at high latitudes.

Merge/Blend tool A tool in the *Game Creation System* Paint program that allows the user to superimpose another image over a current image.

Merge Image A command in the *Game Creation System* Paint program that allows the user to combine two separate images.

merge polygons A command that merges selected polygons into one where their vertices line up.

meridian A line of longitude.

Mersenne number A number $M_p = 2^p-1$ where p is a prime.

Mersenne prime A *Mersenne number* that is a prime.

mesh A graphics object that is composed entirely of polygons that have common vertices and edges.

mesh density The number of polygons per degree of curvature along each of the three axes. Desired mesh density is dependent upon the requirement of the shot. Some of the factors determining required mesh density are: the closest proximity of the model to the camera, the output resolution, and the deformation of the model. Polygonal silhouetting of the model in the rendered image is a sign of low mesh density.

mesh, view-dependent A view-dependent progressive mesh (VDPM) is able to use triangle counts more effectively, because it has more flexibility in the choice of edge collapse order. This is seldom justified in modern systems because of the large gap in efficiency between the two types of renderers. A VDPM renderer uses fewer triangles for a more visually-pleasing scene, but this thriftiness is drowned out by the increased processor time that must be put into making more level of detail choices, and the data handling involved.

mesh, view-independent A view-independent mesh uses one fixed order for the edge collapses, which can therefore be calculated offline, allowing this tree representation to be discarded.

MeshForge A plug-in for *trueSpace* that permits twisting and tapering of objects.

Mesh Form Modeler A modeler in *Carrara* that has the capability to define extrusion in all three dimensions and allows the editing of individual vertices and polygon faces on the resulting object.

Mesh Simplify A modifier in *3ds max* that optimizes (reduces the polygon count) of selected objects or areas of an object.

message object In game programming, an object that has five fields: a descriptive name, the name of the sender, the name of the receiver, the time at which it should be delivered, and any relevant data. A message provides all the information necessary to pass it to the correct game object at the right time. The receiver of the message gets the message along with all of the information inside it.

message router When a message is sent, it always goes to the *message router*. The router then sends it through the game object and on to the state machine that the game object owns. If a message should be delivered at some time in the future, the router holds the message and sends it at the required delivery time.

metaball 1. A surface similar to a *blob*, but defined by superimposed piecewise quadratic functions rather than exponentials. 2. A method of creating organic shapes. Spheres and elongated spheres are very easy to make in 3D applications. A very complex shape like a nose can be roughed out by making many spheres and arranging them appropriately. Metaballs behave much like balls of mercury in a dish; as they get close together, they begin to influence each other. The closer they are, the more they influence each other until it becomes impossible to tell them apart. 3D applications that use metaballs allow the user to designate how strong this attraction between spheres is. All major 3D applications have a metaball-modeling option. A popular metaball application is *Organica* by Impulse.

metafile A file format for graphics storage and transmission that is machine independent. For an example, see *graphical kernel system*.

metaform A 3D process or tool that is used to deform a selected object or object area, usually by rounding off the polygons by duplication.

metal A shiny, polished object that reflects its environment. Metals also have colored highlights, which are some of the properties that make an object look metallic. Additionally, metals also tend to have dark, shadowed areas, whereas shiny nonmetal objects have some of the diffuse component visible. The size of the specular reflection in metal varies, but the color is always the color of the metal object and not of the light source. This is the main difference between metals and shiny nonmetal objects. Metals often create unwanted reflections. One alternative is to change

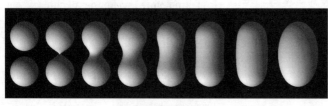

metaballs.

the perspective. Metals obey the law of reflection, so changing the angle of the camera changes the way the light strikes the metal.

metal.

metal-halide lamps HID white lights. These are basically mercury-vapor lamps with metal halides for better spectral emission. This type of light emits full spectra with a slight bias toward the blue. In reality, metal halides come in different color temperatures, but when simulating them in computer graphics, the peripheral lights are set to a slightly bluish-white hue. Metal halides are now used extensively in the industry, so it is important to know how to simulate them in computer graphics to get that industrial-lighting look. Used in conjunction with mercury-vapor lamps, metal halides will make scenes more realistic.

Metallicity Value In *Bryce*, a value that works in conjunction with the Specularity controls to filter light for metallic material.

metallizing A popular means for mass replication of holograms and diffraction gratings. Alternatives such as photopolymers or silver-halide films can be more expensive than metallized em-

bossed materials. The cost of metallized embossed materials has fallen to the point where they are being used for mainstream product packaging such as software packages, food and beverage containers, candy packages, and wrapping paper.

Metal Settings Settings for generating metals using the *Material Generator* plug-in for *trueSpace*. They include: *Color,* which generates a random metal color; *Faceting*, which causes a random faceting to be applied; *Ambient Glow,* which defines the brightness of the object regardless of light sources; and *Roughness,* which defines the surface roughness of the texture.

metamer One of an infinite number of spectra that are perceived as the same color by the human eye.

metameric match Two or more colors that appear identical to the human eye, even though the actual distribution of wavelengths may be different for each color.

metaphor, user interface The use of an icon that shows something the user is familiar with, such as a wastebasket, as an indication of where to click to initiate a desired action.

MetaSynth A sound creation program by U&I Software that can be used to create soundtracks for movies. *MetaSynth* translates graphic images into audio events, allowing the user a wide selection of digitally-sampled instruments and a high degree of intuitive interactivity.

META-Tag Generator A program by WebPromote that helps users generate META tags for Web sites.

MetaTracks A multitrack recorder and composition system by U&I Software for combining layered sound tracks. If the system is MIDI enabled, the user can add Xx, the fully variable MIDI composition system from U&I.

MFLOPS One million floating-point operations per second. See *megaflop*.

MHz See *megahertz*.

mickey A unit of mouse movement. It is usually 1/200th of an inch.

Mickey UIMS An extended Pascal language for the MacIntosh.

MICR See *magnetic ink character recognition*.

microfacet A surface facet assumed for theoretical purposes whose scale is that of the roughness of a surface. Assumed distributions of microfacets are used in some models of surface reflectance.

microfiche A 4" × 6" sheet of film containing a title and highly reduced images of approximately 270 pages of a document that can be read without magnification.

microfilm A roll of 35-mm film on which reduced images of document pages are in recorded sequence.

micromorphing A technique in *Poser* for controlling the shape of figures. When working on a character, the user can make morphs for one area at a time. If the user needs the cheeks to be puffed out, he can make a morph just to move the cheeks. If he needs them rounded more, he can make another morph. This may seem like more work, but by making two separate morphs, one can use the two to make an almost endless combination of cheek smoothness and bulge. Also, these can be used again to make other characters.

microphone A device that converts sound waves to electronic impulses.

microprocessor A computer's central processing unit, designed to work as the controller by accessing a set of encoded instructions when the system is started, using large-scale integrated circuit technology.

Microsoft Internet Explorer See *Internet Explorer*.

MIDI file A file containing sound or music that follows the MIDI (Musical Instrument Digital Interface) format.

midpoint The point halfway between the two ends of a line.

midpoint displacement method A technique for drawing fractal mountains, starting with one or more large triangles and recursively subdivides each triangle into four smaller triangles by drawing lines between the midpoints of the triangle sides. Also known as *midpoint subdivision* or *midpoint recursion*.

MIKE User Interface Management System (UIMS) A system that declares commands and parameters, generates a user interface, and supports direct manipulation of objects.

millilambert A unit of luminance that is equal to 0.3142 nit.

MIMD See *parallelism*.

MiniCD A small CD used for storing data recorded by digital cameras or camcorders. A MiniCD usually holds less than 200 MB of data.

MiniDV Video tape that has the same format as DV, but is in a miniature cartridge.

minify To reduce an image in size (often by a power of 2) by replacing a square group of pixels with a single pixel that has the average color of the group.

Minimal Surfaces A selection of primitive objects for *3ds max,* including Catenoid, Costa Surface, and Helicoid.

Minkowski-Bouligand dimension A dimension greater than the Euclidian dimension which is the proper alternative to the Hausdorff-Besicovitch dimension in expressing the dimensional characteristics of some fractal curves.

minus leading In typography, leading in which the distance from baseline to baseline between two lines of type is less than the type size.

MIPS Millions of instructions per second. A measure of the speed of a computer.

mirror A command in a 3D application that reverses the geometry of a selected object around a coordinate point. Mirroring allows a designer to create half of a form and to create the other half by mirroring. Mirroring is also used to create flipped duplicates, like wings.

mirror image An image in which the original right and left are reversed, but top and bottom remain the same.

mirroring See *mirror.*

MIS See *management information system.*

misconvergence The alignment error of the red, green, and blue guns of a cathode-ray tube measured as a mean distance between centers of color spot pairs.

mise-en-scene The concept that there should be nothing in a scene that is out of place or context. Mise-en-scene means putting in the scene, staging the action, or placing on stage. This is an old theater concept that works well and is a way of establishing the elements in a scene that have a direct influence on how the scene is rendered. In a way, mise-en-scene is composed of generalizations and stereotyped elements about a particular subject or setting as evoked visually. These are things the viewers have come to expect in a scene based on their prior exposure to and experience with a similar situation. For instance, we have certain expectations for different film genres such as westerns, science fiction, romance, and action/adventure films.

Misiurewicz point A value of c on the Mandelbrot set for which the point $z=0$ is pre-periodic but not periodic and is eventually drawn into a circle.

Mitchell filter A filter used in image rescaling.

mitre A method of treating the ends of thick lines that join to create a proper joint.

mix and match imports A method of customizing imported objects in *Bryce* to create fantastic characters. It is based upon the fact that all complex imported objects are saved as a "group" and can be "ungrouped" in *Bryce.* Once an imported object is ungrouped, the user can delete any unwanted parts. One could import a bird, for example, and delete everything but the wings.

mixer A device that accepts outputs from a number of audio devices and mixes them together, allowing the user to control the amplitude of each device.

mix operator A function in *Carrara* that allows the user to mix shader characteristics.

MJPEG A lossy, high-quality CODEC that can deliver full-motion, full-frame video.

MJPEG almost always requires special compression hardware.

M meter A horizontal bar at the bottom of the Level Editor screen of *The Game Creation System*. It shows how much texture RAM has been used.

model A collection of graphics objects that represent a scene or a more complex object.

Modeler One of the two modules in NewTek's *LightWave* and *Inspire 3D*. The second module is Layout.

modeling Activities that construct a graphics data base without any attempt to render the scene.

modem Modulator-demodulator. A device for transmitting and receiving signals over telephone lines. Note that cable modems transfer signals over a non-telephone cable.

Modifier A collection of tools in *3ds max* used to affect or deform a selected object or object area.

Modify Hierarchical Offset A tool in *Universe* that allows the axes of a group of objects to be modified as if they were all one object.

Moebius strip A twisted, curving surface that has only one side. A model can be made by taking a strip of paper, giving one end a 180-degree twist, and then gluing the ends together.

moiré 1. Undesirable global beat patterns in printed material produced by overlaying dot patterns (such as halftone representations of photographs) that have fine detail of approximately the same scale. The resulting pattern shows a tiled array of dots that detracts from the image being halftoned. 2. Deliberate generation of a moiré pattern for creative effect. One can use moirés in *Bryce* to create some very interesting and hypnotic, animated effects. While moirés in a printed graphic are distracting, moirés in an animation can prove quite interesting, resulting in shimmering surface features on the selected object.

molecular modeling The use of computer graphics to model atoms and molecules and determine the interaction of their structures.

mole interaction device A pivoted footrest with integrated switches that is used for controlling a cursor.

monitor A device for displaying computer video output.

monochromatic light Light that contains photons of only a single frequency.

monochromatic triples A set of the three primary colors that are all of the same value, for example (0.6, 0.6, 0.6). Monochromatic triples always produce shades of gray.

monochromic 1. In reference to display cathode-ray tubes, having a single phosphor, thereby producing only a single color display such as white, green, or amber. 2. In reference to light, having a single frequency, as can occur in a laser light beam.

monohedral tiling The repeated use of a single geometric figure (with different orientations, if necessary) to completely fill a plane.

mono mix Mixing all audio down to a single track.

monospacing A spacing technique used by some printers, in which every character occupies the same amount of space regardless of its relative width.

montage.

montage In editing, the process of juxtaposing two shots against each other to arrive at an effect different than each shot would imply on its own.

Monte Carlo solution Use of probabilistic computations to solve the most likely light pathway in a scene.

mood lighting Changing the mood of the subject through lighting. At times, one cannot change the subject's *physical properties*, so the mood must be changed instead. When this situation arises, the only option is a change in lighting.

moon, non-Lambertian surface The characteristic of the moon's surface that causes it to reflect light with relatively uniform intensity, whether reflecting from the center or the sides.

morph 1. To convert one image to another by warping the original image to some intermediate distorted shape and then warping this distorted shape back to the second image over the course of a number of animation frames. 2. A 3D animation feature that lets the user transform the geometry of one model into the geometry of another model, or the details of an image into another image. Some audio packages use a similar process on audio data.

Morph See *WinImages Morph*.

morph grid A feature of *The Games Factory* used to define common points between the two images that the user wants to move. The grid is composed of a number of "elastic bands" that can be stretched to fit various strategic points on the objects that are being morphed.

morphing function A function in *The Games Factory* that allows the user to change one frame into another, allowing for stunning transformations. One can use this function to make a human face morph into a creature, or see a spaceship smoothly change into another spaceship, rather than simply having the images snap from one to the next. This technique is frequently used in Hollywood movies.

morph targets Parameter Dials in *Poser* for modifying figure characteristics. They are created by the use of the Magnet or Wave Deformers or by using

morph.

outside 3D applications, and are saved for future use.

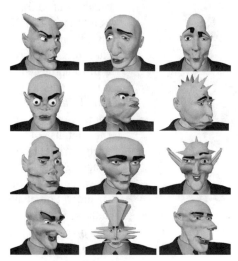

morph targets.

MorphWorld A source of morph targets for use with *Poser*.

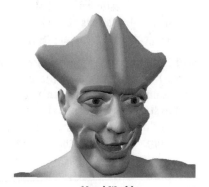

MorphWorld.

motherboard The main printed circuit board of a computer, having the principle circuitry upon it and having connectors for attaching *daughter boards*.

Motif A graphic user interface developed as a proposed standard by the Open Software Foundation.

motion, absolute Motion against a static or neutral background.

motion blur When an object moves quickly, it will look blurrier in a motion picture. Individual frames of video or film should show a certain amount of blur around moving objects. Motion blur is usually the result of average shutter speeds (1/60th to 1/125th of a second). Faster shutter speeds will result in less motion blur; slower shutter speeds will result in more. A lack of motion blur will result in stuttery, stroboscopic motion. Motion blur can also refer to the deliberate blurring of the edges of an object in an image to give the illusion of motion.

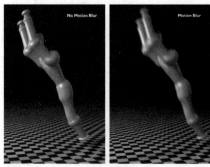

motion blur.

Motion Capture Files BVH motion capture data is an industry-standard motion format. To create ultra-realistic, highly kinetic animation, motion-capture hardware is used every day by scientists and movie-makers alike to record complex human motion through actual photography. Dance, sports, and medical data motions are a few examples of typical usage. Many 3D applications import BVH motion data files and allow the user to apply them to organic figures. The final animation that is generated is remarkably lifelike.

motion facilities Facilities in an editing program that allow the user to move a still image or video clip around on the screen. Useful for creating collages of moving images as well as animated titles and credit rolls.

motion path The path taken by an animated model.

motion, relative Motion against a structured background.

motion wave assignments The central control feature in the *Bryce* Advanced Motion Lab. By clicking on any of the wave thumbnails, that particular wave shape is placed on the screen below. From there, it is possible to move the shape's control points to reshape it, or use the pencil tool that appears when the mouse is over a non-shape area to draw another wave.

motivational lighting When creating computer graphics character lighting setups, it is natural to light the scene first *motivationally*, before lighting the character itself. This means that the feeling or story line of the scene determines the type and color of light. Establishing the key light ensures the ambiance of the scene. It also ensures that the important environmental lighting is present, denoting the setting and the time of the scene. It is often helpful to light motivationally and naturally instead of lighting the character first without regard to the context of the scene or story.

MOTIVE A CADDS tool for analyzing how the layout of a printed circuit board will affect the timing of various signals on it.

mottle Gross variations in the intensity of a printed image that are not intended or desired.

mountains, fractal Realistic images of mountains produced by drawing certain types of fractal curves.

mouse A computer hardware device that the user moves over a surface, causing a ball to roll and moving the cursor on a display.

Mouth, Frown A *Poser* parameter that is used to shape the mouth like a frown.

mouth, human In computer graphics and animation, the mouth is one of the more complicated facial features. It has both an internal and external structure. The mouth itself occupies two-thirds of the space from the tip of the nose to the chin. The corners of the mouth are typically aligned with the center of the ocular cavity. From the side of the head, the corners of the mouth are aligned with the angle of the lower jaw. The lips are a common problem area for 3D models. Artists tend to make them flush, but they are actually angled down. The upper lip overhangs the lower lip slightly, forming a 7.5 degree angle. This is an important consideration because the upper teeth overlap the lower teeth in front, so the upper lip must do the same. Because the interior of the mouth is significantly more complicated than the exterior, it is also one of the major problem areas seen in 3D human heads. One of the common problems is inflated cheek tissue. This causes the cheek tissue to be drawn away from the gums, making the mouth interior look like a balloon. In reality, the cheek tissue should be drawn tightly against the gums.

mouth muscles The mouth muscles include the following: *levator labii superioris* (the sneering muscle), *zygomaticus* *major* (the smiling muscle), *triangularis* (the facial shrug muscle), *depressor labii inferioris* (the lower lip curl muscle), *mentalis* (the pouting muscle), and *orbicularis oris* (the lip tightener muscle). The *levator labii superioris* raises the upper lip beneath the nostrils. It is located around the upper and lower lips. It plays a major role in creating the "disgust" and "disdain" facial expressions. The *zygomaticus major* muscle raises the mouth upward and outward. It is located around the upper and lower lips and attaches just before the ear. It is used for any expression that requires the upper lip to be raised up and out, such as "laughing" and "smiling."

Laughter   Smiling

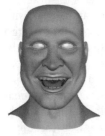 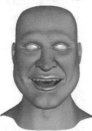

mouth muscles.

The *triangularis* muscle pulls the corner of the mouth downward. It is located around the upper and lower lips and attaches just before the ear and to the mandible. It is a crucial muscle for creating "sadness" or "miserable" demeanors. The *depressor labii inferioris* muscle pulls the lower lip down and out. It is located around the upper and lower lips and attaches to the mandible. It is a crucial muscle for creating expressions like "surprise." The *mentalis* muscle raises and tightens the chin. It is located on either side under the lower lip. This muscle is used to create expressions such as "suppressed sadness" and "fear." The *orbicularis oris* compresses and purses the lips. It circles the mouth. This muscle is used to create expressions such as "disdain" and "repulsion."

move tool A tool in most 2D and 3D applications used to reposition a selected object in a scene or an image element in a framed area.

movies as backgrounds Most 3D applications allow the use of animated data, whether animations or sequenced numbered frames, as background imagery.

moving-points path A hand-drawn path created by the animator and marked to indicate constant time intervals.

MPEG A lossy, high-quality CODEC. MPEG1 is used for the VCD format and MPEG2 is used for DVD format video. Both are suitable for distribution of full-motion, full-frame video.

MPegger An application for MP3 encoding on the Macintosh. It supports both MPEG Layer II and Layer III (MP2 and MP3).

MR scanner Magnetic resonance scanner. A device that measures the magnetic resonance characteristics of spinning atoms to produce images.

MS-DOS The basic operating system used by personal computers.

MTBF See *mean time between failures*.

MTTR See *mean time to repair*.

multifractal Julia set The Julia set of a rational function which has more than two attractors.

multimedia The use of a variety of media in disseminating information. For example, text, audio, graphics, motion pictures, etc., can all be used together to produce an overall effect. The first true multimedia computer was the Commodore *Amiga*.

multipass rendering A way of rendering a final scene as a group of separate movies or images. Each of these individual images contains only one part of the visual information needed for the scene. One may contain all the specular highlights, others may include just reflections, and so on. The power of this lies in the capability to composite them all together in *Photoshop* or *AfterEffects* while still allowing the user full control over each of these characteristic clips.

multipass transformation The moving of an object to another location and/or orientation through several separate transformations that are easier to perform than a single complex transformation, thereby reducing processing time.

multiple basic prop composites In *Poser*, there are two ways to use props in a composite relationship. The first is to simply parent a prop to a hand, as if the hand were holding it. This is good for shields, weapons, and utensils of every kind. For instance, one could use this method to attach a broom to a figure's hands, and then pose the figure to sweep the floor. A sword could be parented to one hand and a shield to the other for a battle scene. The second way to utilize a prop in a composite is to force it to substitute for a body part.

multiple choice games A game genre in which a question is displayed, requesting the player(s) to respond by selecting multiple choice answers (usually 3 or 4). *You Don't Know Jack* and *Jeopardy* are included in this genre, where research-

ing and organizing content may be as difficult as playing the game itself. These games are especially popular online.

multiple instruction multiple data (MIMD) See *parallelism*.

multiple objects, one shader across There are times when the easiest way—or the only way—to model a single object is to create multiple objects and group them. The only problem with this technique is that when it is time to apply a complex shader, the shader will be applied differently to each object in the group, destroying the illusion of the group being a single object.

Multiplex A plug-in for *trueSpace* that is part of *CoolPowers*. *Multiplex* can be used to create multiple copies of an object, applying rotation, translation, and scaling factors to each copy. These objects can be animated, which allows the user to create fantastic shapes that increase over time. There is also an option to animate the original object through a mathematically-calculated path without creating copies. This plug-in could be used to make multiple copies of a spider's leg, for instance.

multi-resolution maps See *interaction detection, multi-resolution maps for*.

multisync monitor A monitor that can automatically synchronize to several horizontal and vertical frequencies so that a number of different resolutions can be produced on the screen.

multitasking Enabling a computer to perform several different tasks at once by dividing time into slices, and allowing the computer to use each "time slice" to work on the task where its services are most urgently needed.

multithreading Most high level computer languages don't allow *multitasking* (the running of several tasks at once). Java, however, allows the user to use *multithreading*. With Java, the user can design several threads, each of which runs in a separate context (although all threads can use some or all of the same variables).

Munsell color system A system using cylindrical coordinates to specify color values. The *hue* of the color is specified as an angle, the *chroma* by radial distance, and the *value* (dark to light) by distance along the *z* axis.

N

n (specular reflection exponent) A reflection characteristic used in the Phong illumination model. It varies from one to several hundred, depending upon the material and the sharpness of the reflection desired.

N Pressing the N key while in the *LightWave* Modeler's Create tab brings up the numeric panel, allowing the user to input data numerically for the selected object.

name set, PHIGS A name shared by a set of primitives in the PHIGS graphics system. It permits the primitives to be organized in various ways to describe a complex object.

NAND 1. A logic function that is the opposite of AND (not AND). For every bit of one of two inputs that is a zero, the corresponding bit of the output is a one. Normally written in all capital letters, although not an acronym, to indicate a logic function. 2. To perform the NAND operation.

Nano Editor A small edit screen window in *Bryce*, useful when quick editing is needed. It appears as an overlay on top of the camera controls.

Nano Options List A command from the left-hand toolbar of *Bryce*. The most useful items in the Nano Options list, other than the view selections, are the three choices for Nano Rendering: Sky Only, Full Scene, and Wireframe.

NAPLPS See *North American presentation level protocol*.

NASA 11 An early flight simulator designed by General Electric.

nasal bone The small bone structure at the top of the nose where it meets the nasion. It is the point where the nasal bone terminates, usually creating a small bump in the nose. The cartilage that forms the tip of the nose is connected to the nasal bone. A common mistake in facial animation is to move the tip of the nose during facial expression. This does not occur in reality because there are no tendons connected to the cartilage because it is a weak structure that is far too flexible. Keep the tip of the nose fixed at all times.

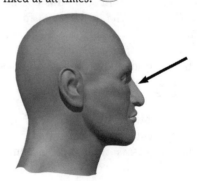

nasal bone.

nasal consonant A nasal consonant is a consonant in which air escapes only through the nose when spoken. For this to happen, the soft palate is lowered to allow air to pass it. At the same time a closure is made in the oral cavity to stop air from escaping through the mouth. There are three nasal sounds in the English language: M, N, and AN.

nasion The point where the frontal bone meets the nasal bone. It is the curvature we see just above the nose.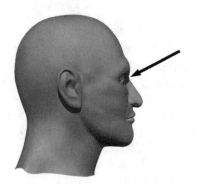

nasion.

National Computer Graphics Association (NCGA) An organization for those interested in computer graphics.

National Television Standards Committee (NTSC) 1. The organization for setting television standards. 2. The standard for color television in the United States, Japan, and parts of South America. It uses a frame rate of 29.97 fps and 525 horizontal scan lines.

natural cubic spline A C^0, C^1, or C^2 continuous cubic polynomial that interpolates (passes through) the control points.

natural language dialogue A way of controlling computers by typed or spoken everyday English.

Natural Scene Designer (NSD) A 3D graphics and animation application from Natural Graphics for both Macintosh and Windows platforms. *NSD* is used to create environmental images and animations, with controls for clouds, terrain, and other natural objects and phenomena. Natural Graphics also markets a wide array of data files that represent geographical data in the United States.

natural wipes See *clearing frame and natural wipes.*

navigational mesh For most game environments, one can predict where objects can and cannot move. From that information, a simple set of geometry can be created to define this area as a "walkable" surface area. One way to visualize this area is to imagine a room within a typical 3D environment. If the characters are humanoid and the planet hosting the game has gravity, one can assume the game objects will spend most of their time on the floor of this room. Think of this geometry as a sort of polygonal carpet, or *navigation mesh*. It represents the area around which objects can move within the environment.

NCGA See *National Computer Graphics Association.*

ND See *neutral density.*

near letter quality (NLQ) Output from a printer that is almost as good as typewriter output.

Necker cube illusion A two-dimensional drawing of a three dimensional cube in which both the hidden and the visible edges of the cube are drawn. The viewer decides which face of the cube is at the front, since the drawing by itself offers no clues.

negamax variation on minimax algorithm In game programming, when faced with writing two functions, one that aims to minimize board state and the other to maximize it, the method of inserting a negation and turning the two into just one function. Now the evaluation function must return the quality of the board for the current player, rather than always returning low values, meaning a good board for one player and high for the other. Board state must therefore include or imply which player goes next. The most efficient system for this function is to have the board/game state put forward and reversed by a function within the algorithm and for the evaluation function to be calculated incrementally rather than calculated from scratch every time it is called.

negative A photographic image in which the tone values are reversed. Black tones are white on the negative, white tones are black, etc. When light is projected through a negative onto photosensitive film or paper, a positive image is produced.

negative cutter The person who physically cuts the film negative to conform to the final cut.

negative light A light source whose color is defined in negative numbers. Negative light is an artificial construct used when rendering a scene to make an object surface darker without modifying all the existing light sources.

negative orientation A basis that does not have the same orientation as the standard basis.

Nendo A polymesh modeler that can import and output both 3DS and OBJ files. *Nendo* is mainly a polygon mesh modeler, using its own primitives as a start, and is intended less as a 3DS or OBJ customization application. *Nendo* also features a full 3D painting module. The 3DS

models it creates load very quickly into *Poser* and *Bryce*.

neon light A light consisting of a glass tube filled with neon gas, which varies in color.

nested face A polygon that is coplanar with another polygon, from which it inherits attributes.

nesting A hierarchical file structure. It may consist of directories, subdirectories, sub-subdirectories, etc.

nesting feature A feature of an editor that permits the placement of one edited sequence inside another. That sequence can, in turn, be nested inside yet another, and so forth.

net A large screen used to decrease the strength of the light falling on the subject, usually used for exterior shoots.

Netscape Navigator A Web browser created by Netscape in 1995. When introduced, Netscape Navigator's main advantage was speed and the ability to support Java applets, JavaScript, and display graphics. The most significant feature for Web designers was the Netscape HTML extensions. Netscape HTML extensions are HTML-like elements that Netscape Navigator can recognize in Web pages when displaying them. Netscape included these HTML elements to offer more control over the layout and design of Web pages, more than the HTML standard allows. This can pose a problem for a viewer not using Netscape Navigator to view certain Web sites.

Net Toob A tool that enables the user to display animations at larger than saved sizes on a Windows system. *Net Toob* allows the user to play animations at normal, double, and full-screen sizes, at speeds ranging from 10 to 400%. *Net*

Toob can also be used to save AVI, Quick-Time, or MPEG animations as screen savers.

network Two or more computers, electronically connected so that they may share one another's resources.

neural net A software technique for finding solutions based on highly parallel, distributed, probabilistic models that differ from the usual way a computer program solves problems. Instead, they model a network of cells that can find, ascertain, or correlate possible solutions to a problem in a more biological way based on the human brain by first solving the problem in little pieces, and later putting the result together. Neural nets can be used for such things as environmental scanning and classification, memory, behavior control, and response mapping.

Environmental scanning and classification: A neural net can be fed with information that could be interpreted as vision or auditory information. This information can then be used to select an output response or teach the net. These responses can be learned in real time and updated to optimize the response.

Memory: A neural net can be used by game creatures as a form of memory. The neural net can learn a set of responses through experience; then when a new experience occurs, the net can respond with something that is the best guess at what should be done.

Behavioral control: The output of a neural net can be used to control the actions of a game creature. The inputs can be various variables in the game engine. The net can then control the behavior of the creature.

Response mapping: Neural nets are good at "association," which is the mapping of one space to another. Association may be classified in one of two forms: autoassociation, which is the mapping of an input with itself, and heteroassociation, which is the mapping of an input with something else. Response mapping uses a neural net at the back end or output to create another layer of indirection in the control or behavior of an object. Basically, we might have a number of control variables, but we have crisp responses for only a number of certain combinations with which we can teach the net. However, using a neural net on the output, we can obtain other responses that are in the same ballpark as our well-defined ones.

neural net, plasticity The capability of a neural net to accept new information while remaining stable and able to recall previously stored information correctly.

neural net, temporal considerations Compared to a digital computer, the human brain is relatively slow. In fact, our brains have cycle times in the millisecond range, whereas digital computers have cycle times in the nanosecond and, soon, subnanosecond range. This means that in the brain signals take time to travel from neuron to neuron. This fact is also modeled by artificial neurons in the sense that we perform the computations layer by layer and transmit the results sequentially. This model helps to better model the time lag involved in the signal transmission in biological systems such as humans.

neurode A software version of a *neuron*.

neuron A biological device that is a component of the human brain. The average brain has 10^{11} neurons. There are three main parts to the neuron: *dendrites*, which are responsible for collecting incoming signals; *somas*, which are responsible for the main processing and summation of signals; and *axons*, which are responsible for transmitting signals to other dendrites. The dendrites collect the signals received from other neurons, then the soma performs a summation of sorts and, based on the result, causes the axon to fire and transmit the signal. The firing is contingent upon a number of factors, but we can model it as a transfer function that processes the summed inputs and then creates an output if the properties of the transfer function are met. In addition, the output is non-linear in real neurons—that is, signals aren't digital, they are analog. In fact, neurons are constantly receiving and sending signals, and the real model of them is frequency dependent and must be analyzed in the S-domain (the frequency domain). The real transfer function of a simple biological neuron has been derived.

neutral density (ND) A lens filter or lighting gel that tones down brightness without changing the color temperature.

neutral lighting condition, setup The purpose of neutral lighting condition is to enable rendered or real-time shaded visual evaluation of mesh quality from all angles. Neutral lighting setup emulates natural lighting of an object suspended in space being illuminated by one or two indirect light sources, by placement of Phong light sources—usually one or two spotlights, and a number of low-intensity Omni/Radial light sources, with only one of the spotlights being a shadow-casting light. The model

is illuminated in a way that allows evaluation of geometry from all angles without having any part of geometry not illuminated or being washed out by the light sources. Neutral lighting can be effectively set up in *form•Z* or in the animation environment. The most important condition of neutral lighting is that there is no dramatic effect that is created by the light placement. Dramatic lighting takes attention away from the model, and may obscure imperfections. While dramatic lighting plays an important role in image composition and storytelling, it interferes with the model evaluation process. Shadows pose a special problem, as they should be used to add depth and a sense of proportion. However, dark shadows can darken shadowed geometry to a point that problems in those areas would be obscured. Lights and shadows need to be defined in a way so that shadows do not darken the geometry by more than 50%. This is accomplished through a clever placement of key shadow-casting spotlights and nonshadow casting fill lights.

Newell-Newell-Sancha algorithm See *depth-sort algorithm*.

Newell's method A way of computing the plane equation of an arbitrary 3-D polygon.

Newton-Euler equations Equations that describe the basic principles of motion of rigid bodies in the real world.

Newton-Raphson iteration See *Newton's method*.

Newton's method A method for solving an equation that begins by making a guess z_0 as to a root of the equation and then iterating the following equation:

$$z_{n+1} = z_n - \frac{f(z_n)}{f'(z_n)}$$

At each iteration the result comes closer to the actual value of a root.

Newton's method fractal A fractal created by mapping the solution of an equation by Newton's method for every starting point within the complex plane.

nibble Four binary bits, or half a byte. Sometimes spelled *nybble*.

Nicholl-Lee-Nicholl algorithm See *Clipping, Nicholl-Lee-Nicholl line algorithm*.

nit A unit of luminance. The photometric brightness of a surface equal to a candela per square meter or to 0.2919 footlamberts.

NLDV See *non-linear digital video*.

NLE See *non-linear editing system*.

NLQ See *near letter quality*.

N2MP3 Professional A state-of-the-art solution designed to handle encoding needs, such as putting music on the Web, recording audio onto a Mac, or converting a CD collection into MP3.

node 1. A connection point on a network. 2. An entry in a hierarchy.

noise A signal whose amplitude varies randomly with time.

noise-based modeling The summing of band-limited noise to make texture maps that model wave trains.

noise-based texture mapping The use of noise functions to create the textures that appear on the faces of objects.

noise, 1/f A completely random amplitude signal whose power is inverse to frequency. Also known as *pink noise*.

noise function A function that has statistical invariance under rigid motions

and band limiting in the frequency domain. It is used in generating textures.

Noise f/x A *Photoshop* filter in the Corel *KPT* collection that adds pixelated noise to an image. A variation of this filter is called *Noize*.

nolid An Archimedean solid with fourteen faces, each consisting of squares or triangles. Also known as a *cuboctahedron*.

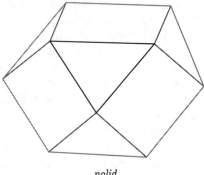

nolid.

Noll box A device used for recording three-dimensional hand movements. It consists of a cubic box with 12-inch sides, within which a knob can be freely moved. The knob is connected to slider mechanisms linked to potentiometers.

nominative information Information that names different types of things.

non-destructive editing Any form of editing (either video or audio) that leaves the original source material unaltered.

non-dialog ADR Automatic dialog replacement used to replace badly-recorded sound when dialog is not required in the replacement.

nonexterior rule Using a polyline and a point that is distant from it, any point that can be connected to the seed point by a path that does not intersect the polyline is outside the polyline.

non-impact printer A printer that uses a technique that does not require mechanical devices to strike the paper.

non-interfaced Describes a display in which each line is written in sequence and all lines are refreshed for each vertical scan.

non-linear digital video (NLDV) Using an editing program to edit a sequence of animations. Editing in 3D is usually done in software that allows for placing clips (both movies and sound) together to produce one cohesive story. Adobe's *Premiere*, Apple's *Final Cut Pro*, *iMovie*, or *QuickTime Pro* are all consumer-level editing packages.

non-linear editing system (NLE) A digital editing system that uses a software interface and digitized audio and video stored on a hard drive which allows for random access, non-linearity, and non-destructive editing.

nonlinear mapping Transformation of an image from one surface to another with variations in scale or rotation that change the shape of the final image.

nonlocality tension A parameter used in *interPhong shading* to help determine whether the shading should be closer to *faceted* or *Phong shading*.

nonplanar polys A polygon with more than three vertices that have been twisted out of alignment. Nonplanar poly anomalies include difficulty in applying textures and the display of holes when the non-alignment gets too severe. The best fix is to tesselate the polys, thereby dividing them into triangular polys.

nonspectral color A color that cannot be defined by a dominant wavelength.

nonuniform Having subdivisions that are not equally spaced.

nonuniform rational B-spline (NURBS) A mathematical description of a curved surface in which the surface is specified as a ratio of two polynomials for each region of the spline.

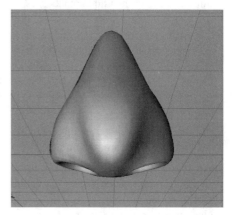

nonuniform rational B-spline.

NOR 1. A logic function that is the opposite of OR (not OR). For every bit where either one of two inputs is a one, the corresponding bit of the output is a zero. Normally written in all capital letters, although not an acronym, to indicate a logic function. 2. To perform the NOR operation.

normal 1. Perpendicular to a surface. 2. A unit vector that is perpendicular to a surface at a designated point. 3. In modeling and animation programs there are two types of normals, face normals and vertex normals. Face normals control the direction of the face, which determines whether or not a face will be shaded when it is visible to the digital camera. A face with a flipped normal will appear as a hole in the surface where that face is supposed to be. Most professional 3D animation applications have utilities and features that can fix inverted normals. Vertex normals determine the smoothness between faces that share that point with which the seams are shaded. Vertex normals are adjusted via smoothing attributes. Problem vertex normals manifest themselves through various shading anomalies, especially random darkening or lightening of the surface. Vertex normals and shading anomalies often occur when the renderer encounters a complex polygon and attempts to decompose it into either quadrangles or triangles. When modeling, it is best to stay away from complex polygons, and manually decompose complex polygons into four- or three-point faces.

normalized Scaled to a designated range or value. A *normalized* vector is a vector that is scaled so that its length is one. Also known as a *unit vector*.

normal vector interpolation shading See *Phong illumination*.

North American presentation level protocol (NAPLPS) A standard object-oriented graphics ASCII-character file format.

nose, human The nose divides the facial mass down the middle, and its length covers half the vertical distance of the facial mass. The length of the nose from the bridge (nasion) to the tip is the same distance as the tip of the nose to the bottom of the chin (mental protuberance). The base of the nose is the same width as the eye. The upper nasal mass is divided in the middle where the *nasal bone* terminates, thus creating the bulge. The last measurement for the nose is the bridge between the eyes, which is one eye width across.

notch A special type of audio filter that can eliminate a specific, defined frequency of sound.

notches, in scan conversion Artifacts left in a thick curve when it is scanned using an antialiasing technique.

NTSC See *National Television Standards Committee*.

NTSC encoder An electronic circuit that converts an RGB video signal and associated sync signals to an NTSC-compatible composite video signal.

NTSC legal Refers to colors that fit within the NTSC guidelines for broadcast television. A vectorscope is used to determine if an image is within the NTSC legal color boundaries.

NTSC monitor See *NTSC/PAL monitor*.

NTSC/PAL monitor The monitor attached to a camera, video deck, or NTSC outputs of a video-digitizing system. Used to display the video that is being edited.

Nugraf Rendering System A 3D rendering system, from Okino Computer Graphics, that can render images from a wide array of 3D scene file formats.

null object A non-rendering, representational object that serves multiple purposes. A null object is any object in a scene that has power over other objects or facets of an animation without itself having to be rendered. Null objects are usually invisible and vital for certain animation actions and effects. Also known as a *dummy object*.

number of angles option An option in *The Games Factory* that sets the number of angles for an object to bounce in. Setting it to 32 will result in the smoothest, most realistic effect. Setting it to 8 will result in an object that can move only left, right, up, down, and diagonally in-between, and would not suit an object that is supposed to bounce like a ball.

number of directions radio button A set of radio buttons in the Animation Editor of *The Games Factory*. The user can select the total number of different directions or animations by clicking one of the buttons. The higher the number of different directions, the smoother the turning effect will be. This is particularly useful for race-car movement.

Number of Frames option An option in *The Games Factory* that allows the user to select how many frames will be between the original image and the grown or shrunken final image. The higher the number, the smoother the effect will be.

Number of Splines A control in *Universe* that allows the user to set the number of splines used in a NURBS rendition.

Number of Steps A setting in *Universe* that determines how many steps will be used in creating a rotation.

NURBS See *nonuniform rational B-spline*.

nybble See *nibble*.

Nyquist limit The highest frequency in an electronic signal that may be reliably sampled for a given sampling rate. The theoretical limit is one-half the sampling rate.

Nystagmus movements Movements of the eye in which stimulation of the peripheral vision generates an impulse to turn the head if the stimulus interests the person.

O

object 1. A primitive graphics geometric figure. 2. A collection of related data that may be operated upon by a particular set of functions.

object adjacency A technique that uses an *adjacency table* to record the chances (probability) of two objects being located next to each other. The dimensions of the table are arbitrary. For example, in order to store letter pairs, it must be 26×26 bytes, or 28×28 bytes to include the possibility of a space preceding or following the letter. The 0th and 27th byte will be used to store occasions where a letter may be preceded (it begins a word) or followed by a space character (it is at the end of a word). To represent combinations of words (phrases), we would need a table that is large enough to accommodate the total number of words (to which we assign n) in the sample, plus two that we use to determine whether the nth word may begin or end a phrase. We can also assume that we need an additional z number of bytes to store the words themselves, since we are referring to each by way of a number. This template can also be applied to shadow picture representations of objects. We simply ensure that we construct a grid as large as the largest object of the type that we are examining.

Object Array A plug-in for *trueSpace* that allows the user to create simple matrices of an object. One can specify the distance between copies, the rotational difference, and also the rotational or movement "acceleration."

object attribute options Using the *Bryce* Advanced Motion Lab Motion Curves "in the Motion Graph," the user can alter the selected object's position, rotation, scale, shear, origin, or material by selecting that attribute in the Object/Item list.

object buffer A ray-tracing technique that first renders an image by storing the object number of the nearest intersected object for each ray in a frame buffer. For each pixel, the color of the object at the intersection is then determined.

object deformation Using a selection of modification tools to deform a selected object.

Object Deformation Panel A *trueSpace* menu that allows the user to select options for using deformation tools to alter the shape of objects.

object file A data set created by a compiler from language source code that relates to a 3D object construct, which must be linked before it can be executed. Object files have OBJ as their file name extension.

object hypothesis The way a viewer interprets an object when ambiguous information is displayed.

object/item selection options A part of the *Bryce* Advanced Motion Lab. Three categories are listed: Selected Objects, Sky, and Sun. Object options are included for every animated object in a scene, including the camera and any lights. The parameters of a selected item must be animated, so that the way the animation unfolds can be modified in the Advanced Motion Lab. If an object's position, for instance, is not animated over time but its rotation is, then the user can customize its animated rotation only in the Advanced Motion Lab. All animated attributes can be reconfigured in the Advanced Motion Lab.

object library The folder in any selected 3D application that is used to store object geometry for use in scenes.

Object Library A plug-in for *trueSpace* that provides a complete visual solution for managing an object collection. Groups of objects are stored in an *Object Library* file along with their thumbnails. This allows the user to visually browse objects. The plug-in is designed to grab a thumbnail from one of *trueSpace's* secondary view windows and resize it automatically.

object memory manager, basic The job of a resource manager is to create resources on demand, hand them out to anyone who asks, and then eventually delete them. Handing out those resources as simple pointers is easy and convenient, but not very safe. Pointers can "dangle"; one part of the system can tell the resource manager to delete a resource, which then immediately invalidates all other outstanding pointers. Another problem is that the underlying data organization cannot change with pointers. Any reallocation of buffers immediately invalidates all outstanding pointers. This becomes especially impor-

tant when saving an application to disk. Pointers cannot be saved to disk, because the next time the game is loaded, system memory will probably be configured differently, or the user could even be on a completely different machine. The pointers must be converted into a form that can be restored, which will probably be an offset or a unique identifier of some sort. This can require a lot of work to support in client code. Rather than using pointers or attempting to write some kind of super-intelligent, overly-complicated "smart pointer," we can add one layer of abstraction and use handles instead, putting the burden on the manager class. Handles are a programming concept that APIs have been using with great success for decades. An example of a handle is the HANDLE type returned by the CreateFile() call in Win32's file system. A file handle, representing an open file system object, is created through the CreateFile() call, passed to other functions such as ReadFile() and SetFilePointer() for manipulation, and then finally closed off with CloseHandle(). Attempting to call those functions with an invalid or closed handle does not cause a crash; instead, it returns an error code. This method is efficient, safe, and easy to understand.

object-oriented 1. Graphics operations that deal directly with primitive geometric figures rather than bit-mapped representations. 2. See *object-oriented programming*.

object-oriented programming (OOP) A programming technique that takes functions, and the data those functions operate on, and places them in separate, independent structures that float inside a larger house program. This structure is

315

the "object." The main program can, at any time, call upon the object to perform its function. The data created can then be served up to the main program, or even to other objects, which have their own specific functions. C++ is an example of an object-oriented programming language.

object-precision See *visible-surface determination*.

objects and backdrops All games can be reduced to a collection of interacting *objects*, which are set against a *backdrop*. Generally speaking, backdrops are static, and objects are dynamic. This difference is applicable in both programming terms and logical terms. The backdrop is usually created and instantiated at a specific time and does not change during its lifetime; after which, it is destroyed. Objects can be created and destroyed at will, and may change during their lifetimes. Backdrops can contain objects and objects can be used to represent parts of the backdrop that might change. Objects, however, cannot contain backdrops.

object snap A technique in the *Game Creation System* that snaps new objects to existing walls, rather than to a fixed grid.

object space The particular coordinate system that is used to define a graphics object.

Object Won't Show Up On Radar attribute An attribute in the *Game Creation System* that controls whether enemies can walk through walls or not. This feature is used when constructing door frames that enemy characters are able to walk and fire through.

.obj file A file format for describing objects to be drawn using plain text. It was designed to create and edit models in *Alias WaveFront*, but is used by many other programs. If the first character is a pound sign (#) the line is a comment and the rest of the line is ignored. Any blank lines are also ignored. The file is read by a tool and parsed from top to bottom just as it would be read by a person.

Observable class A class in Java that is watched by at least one other class (called an *Observer class*). When there is a change in the *Observable class*, this is reported to all *Observer classes* that are watching it, so that they may take any updating actions that are needed.

Observer class A Java class that watches an *Observable class*. See *Observable class*.

occlusion See *occultation*.

occlusion culling A technique for culling unwanted geometry from the field of view. This is an extension of field of view culling, in that it helps reduce unnecessary processing time associated with rendering a mesh (i.e., transformation, lighting, and rasterization). The occlusion provides a culling method that will work on arbitrary and dynamic geometry data. This means the mesh data does not have to contain any information about the potentially visible data set. Occlusion culling also is not limited to indoor scenes and can be used to mark anywhere in the mesh data that could be blocked from a field of view.

occlusion mask A pattern of bits that consists of selected samples from an array covering a pixel. An occlusion mask is used in antialiasing to determine how much of a pixel is on a specified surface.

occultation The part of graphics image processing that deals with the phenomenon that objects nearer to an observer cover those that are farther away. Also called *occlusion*.

ocean water 1. An environmental object that can be created in most 3D applications, and also emulated in many 2D compositing applications. 2. A phenomenon that can be modeled in *trueSpace* by careful selection of realistic color, transparency, reflectance, bump mapping, and vertex animation.

OCR See *optical character recognition*.

octahedron. An eight-sided solid.

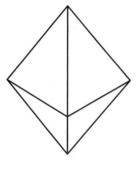

octahedron.

octal A number system to the base eight. Octal numbers can be converted to binary by writing each octal digit as a pattern of three bits.

octant One of eight divisions of a plane produced by drawing lines starting with the x axis and then at 45-degree angles around the circle.

octet An eight-bit byte.

octree A tree-like subdivision of three-dimensional space created by recursively subdividing a cube into eight equal sized smaller cubes, down to the smallest size cubes desired. At the lowest level of subdivision, the elements are known as *voxels*. For any particular subdivision cube,

it is possible to stop the subdivision process without going further. Thus an *octree* could be created where subdivision stopped when each subdivided cube contained precisely one primitive graphics object.

odd-parity rule, polygons A rule that states that to determine whether a region lies inside or outside of a polygon, one can select a test point inside the region and draw a line extending infinitely in any direction as long as it does not pass through any vertices. If the line intersects the polygon an odd number of times, the region is within the polygon.

O_{dl} (object diffuse color) A term of the illumination equation that represents the wavelength-dependent diffuse color of an object.

OEM See *original equipment manufacturer*.

off-line 1. Not presently available for use by the computer system. 2. Operations on data that are performed apart from the computer system in which it is to be used.

off-line clip An off-line clip is one that has been logged but does not have any audio or video media attached to it, whether that is because it has not been captured yet or because the media has been deleted.

off-line editing Working in a draft mode with the intention to eventually take the project to a better resolution and possibly, better videotape format, in order to do a final pass that will improve its look, quality and polish.

OIS See *optical image stabilization*.

omnidirectional microphone A microphone that picks up sounds from all directions.

omnifont A character recognition system that can recognize any font without having to relearn its characteristics.

omni-light A point light that radiates light in all directions. The intensity of the light rays diminishes (attenuates) the farther the vertex is from the omni-light's position.

Omnimax film format An extremely wide screen format that requires a non-geometric projection.

one-light print A film print created from the film negative that uses a single, constant, optimized light setting (i.e., one light) for the red, green, and blue lights used to create the print.

one-sided surface A surface that is rendered when one side faces the observer and omitted when the other side faces the observer.

onion-skinning In some animation programs, displaying semi-opaque overlays of previous frames. These "onion-skin" frames can be used as a reference for drawing or retouching the current frame.

on-line editing The creation of the final master videotape, whatever the means or format involved, usually conformed from the original production footage using an EDL.

OOP See *object-oriented programming*.

opacity The degree to which an object prevents light from passing through it.

opacity versus transparency Because the standard Z-buffer technique simply overwrites a pixel if it belongs to a surface that is closer to the viewer than the one already drawn, it is capable of drawing only perfectly opaque surfaces. To draw a transparent surface, instead of overwriting the pixel color in the frame buffer with the incoming (source) color, the two colors must be blended.

opaque operator An operator that only acts upon the *a-channel* of an object's color.

open Describes a graphics object that has a surface which may be viewed from either side, depending upon the viewpoint.

open fill In Java, a method of filling an arc with color. Since an arc is not a closed figure, some assumption has to be made as to how it will be filled. If an *open fill* is used, Java fills the arc as if a chord were drawn between the ends of the arc, but Java does not actually draw the chord.

OpenGL An application program interface (API) developed by Silicon Graphics for defining 2D and 3D graphic images.

Open Lips A control in *Poser* used for controlling the shape of the mouth.

Open Mouth See *Open Lips*.

Open Software Foundation (OSF) A foundation that develops software and specifications that are available for unlimited use without any licenses or fees.

open system A computer system in which the details of system architecture, input and output hardware, and software interfaces are made available to outside developers.

operating system The low-level program that controls the communication between all of the subsystems (storage, memory, video, peripherals, etc.) in a computer, e.g., MAC OSX, Windows, Linux, etc.

optical character recognition (OCR) Use of a combination of software with a scanner to capture and recognize text characters on a printed page and convert them into machine-readable data.

optical disk A storage device that is written to and read by a laser light beam. Some optical disks are known as WORM (write once read many) disks because a given part of the surface can be written only once and is then not erasable. However, it can be read as many times as desired.

optical holographic correlators Holographic correlators store images which can be compared in real-time to input images. Due to selectivity in holography, many such correlations can be carried out in parallel.

optical image stabilization (OIS) A special optical apparatus in a camera that attempts to compensate for shaking and vibrating by altering the camera's optical properties on-the-fly to compensate for camera movement. Because OIS doesn't alter the image data, there is no image degradation.

optical modulation and processing A process of holographic display. Information about the desired 3D scene passes from electronic bits to photons by modulating light with a computed holographic fringe using spatial light modulators (SLMs).

optical printer A device in which a background image and a matte are placed and the background projected on a new piece of film with a hole where the matte is in each frame.

optical scanner A device that scans pages of human-readable text and converts them to machine-readable digital data.

opticals Special effects that are traditionally added by an "optical" department. Usually, these effects are added through a separate optical printing pass. Lightning bolts, light flares, glows, and halos are all traditional optical effects that can now performed through roto-scoping, or with the application of custom filters.

optical soundtracks A soundtrack recorded on movie film alongside the images.

optical storage The storing of data on laser or CD-ROM disks.

optical viewfinder The eyepiece on a camera that one looks through to frame a shot, as opposed to the flip-out LCD viewfinder present on some cameras.

optic chasm The area where the optic nerves cross in an "x" shape. Each visual field is split so that each side of the brain "sees" half of each visual field. This means that perceived visual files are cut in half, with the right visual field from both eyes going to the right side of the brain and the left visual field from both eyes going to the left side of the brain. This structure ensures that each brain hemisphere has it own visual field representation. In the event of brain injury to one hemisphere, the other hemisphere will still be able to process visual signals from each eye.

optic nerve The bundle of biological wire that directly transmits the visual signals from the retina to the brain for processing (*See figure next page*).

optics A branch of physics that studies the behavior of light.

Optics The bottom third of the Color/Value/Optics palette in *Bryce*. Like the Color and Value settings, Optics elements can take their data from either a palette color or from one or more of the four texture channels. The Optics

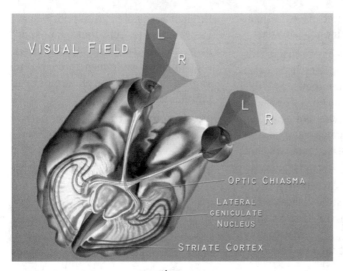

optic nerve.

controls address Transparency, Reflection, and Refraction.

optics, reflection In *Bryce*, a completely reflective object is a mirror. Most metals are at least partially reflective, and metals like chrome are almost mirrors. Polished wood can be very reflective, ranging up to a maximum of 75%. Still water can also be reflective as a mirror, so in some cases a mirror can be used as a substitute for water. This slider controls the amount of reflectivity an object possesses.

optics, refraction indexing An index that indicates the mass of a material as compared to that of a vacuum. The refraction index of a vacuum is 1.0000, so all other materials have a higher refraction index than 1.0. The more massive a substance is, or dense, the higher its refraction index number. "Clear, clean air" has a refraction index number close to 1.0, but the more hazing and particulate the air gets, the more its refraction index number rises. By comparison, the refraction controls in *Bryce* go from 0 to 300. 100 is air and 150 is water. This effectively moves the decimal point over two positions from the standard calculations. For example, a standard refraction index of 1.00 is represented by a *Bryce* number of 100.

optimization The modification of a software package to make it as efficient as possible. An optimize tool is used in many 3D applications to reduce the number of polygons for a selected object.

OR 1. A logic function in which for every bit of any of two or more inputs that is a one, the corresponding bit of the output is a one. Normally written in all capital letters, although not an acronym, to indicate a logic function. 2. To perform the OR operation.

orbit The path of a point when a transformation is recursively applied.

order for lofting When using a lofting technique to create a 3D form from 2D shapes, it is important that the shapes be selected in the order in which they were created.

ordered dithering A technique for reducing high-precision, two-dimensional information to lower precision, while retaining as much information as possible through the use of positional information.

ordinal information, coding Information that is ordered and has a greater than and less than relation.

ordinate The vertical or y component of a two-dimensional coordinate system. The horizontal or x component is the *abscissa*.

Organica A metaball modeling program. Metaballs are modeling elements that stretch out to each other when brought into proximity, so creating very organic-looking components is extremely intuitive. The main item that differentiates *Organica* from other Metaball modeling utilities is that it includes a large library of metaball primitive shapes in addition to spheres.

orientation The relative direction of text or images on a printed page. If the text is oriented horizontally, this is called *landscape* orientation. If the text is oriented vertically, it is called *portrait* orientation. These terms originated from the way in which landscape and portrait pictures are usually oriented in photographs.

orientation of a basis The relationship of the basis to a standard basis. If their orientations are the same, the basis is said to be *positively oriented*. It the orientations are different, the basis is said to be *negatively oriented*.

Origami A filter in the AlienSkin *Xenofex* collection for *Photoshop*. By using this filter, the targeted image area is transformed into what appears to be a series of overlapping folds.

original equipment manufacturer (OEM) The original maker of equipment marketed by and under the name of another vender.

orphan A word or short line of text ending a paragraph which is carried over to the beginning of the next page.

orthochromatic A type of early film emulsion that is sensitive to a wider range of light spectrum but is blind in the red region.

orthogonal Describes two lines with a dot product of zero. They then form a right angle with each other.

orthographic projection A projection from three dimensions to two dimensions that does not make any provision for perspective, so that object sizes do not change regardless of their distance from the observer. With these projections, parallel lines in the model do not converge on a vanishing point as they do in perspective; instead they remain parallel, or at right angles to the projection plane. This is very unlike the world as we observe it.

orthonormal basis A set of normalized vectors that are orthogonal to each other.

OS2 IBM operating system for personal computers.

OSF See *Open Software Foundation*.

O_{sl} (object specular color) A term of the illumination equation that represents the wavelength-dependent specular color of an object.

Oslo algorithm, cubic curves An algorithm that inserts any number of knots into a B-spline curve in a single set of computations.

Ostwald color-order system A system of ordering colors that is similar to the artist's model, wherein a *tint* results from adding white to a pure pigment, a *shade* results from adding black to a

321

pure pigment, and a *tone* results from adding both black and white pigments to a pure pigment.

outcode, clipping A method of clipping in which a region is assigned a four bit *outcode* whose value aids in determining whether the region should be clipped or not.

overexposure.

Outer Bevel A filter in the AlienSkin *EyeCandy* collection from AlienSkin for *Photoshop*. This filter creates a 3D beveled frame around selected image content.

outline font A type font in which the characters are formed by curves rather that being bit-mapped. This permits scaling of the type to any desired size and also permits character rotation.

out-point The end point of an edit.

output device A device such, as a monitor or printer, that presents computer information to the outside world.

output state The state that results when an input is applied to a finite-state machine.

overcoat A layer of transparent plastic that protects optical recording media from damage by dust and scratches.

overcutting The use of too many unmotivated cutaways in a scene.

overexposure Shooting video or film with too much light or the wrong camera settings, resulting in a whitish, washed-out, faded-looking image.

Overhauser spline See *Catmull-Rom spline*.

overhead Transmitted or stored data that are not part of the actual text. Overhead is used for control, addressing, error checking and recovery, etc.

overlapping edit An edit in which the picture ends before or after the sound ends. Also known as an *L-cut* or a *split-edit*.

overlay 1. A graphics image that is superimposed on another graphics image. 2. A portion of a computer program that is loaded into memory only when a kernel program calls for its execution.

overlay planes Additional memory planes that permit storage of an overlay image so that it may be displayed temporarily without destroying the underlying main image.

overlit situation A situation in which there is so much natural light that it is impossible to develop enough contrast between the key and fill lights, resulting in lack of sculpting.

overloaded function In C++, a function, such as +, that is redefined for a different class of object. Also known as an *overload operator*.

oversampling Reducing aliasing artifacts by computing the color of a number of sample points within a pixel and taking a weighted average of the samples as the pixel color. When a computer renders, it essentially takes colored bits of information and arranges them so that the whole looks like a cohesive image. Figures consist of small pixels that can be thought of as tiles. In this way, bit-mapped figures are similar to Byzantine mosaics. The computer is the artisan placing mosaic tiles together to make the image. Oversampling determines how large the tiles are in the mosaic. The larger the tiles, the faster the artisan computer can fill in the spaces. The smaller the tiles, the tighter the detail, but the longer it takes the artisan to fill the spaces. Use oversampling when close-up detail is important, but use it sparingly overall—it is a time hole and can take unnecessarily long to render. Also called *supersampling*.

overscan A part of a displayed image that cannot be seen because the display scan extends beyond the borders of the display device. All video formats scan larger images than they need to compensate for the fact that not all monitors and televisions display images at exactly the same size. To keep the action and titles within the visible area, one should pay attention to the action and title-safe areas of the screen.

Oxygen A graphics board that renders high-quality images and animations.

Ozone 3D A plug-in from E-on Software that allows *LightWave* access to the myriad sky and cloud effects used by *Vue D'Esprit*. See *Vue D'Esprit*.

P

pack To compress data.

packet A group of bits consisting of control information, data, and error correction bits, packaged together for transmission purposes.

packet exchange (PEX) A message communication service used in the Xerox Network Systems (XNS) architecture.

Pac-Man One of the original interactive computer games.

page description language A specialized computer language that describes the appearance of a printed page. A page description language typically includes descriptions of the type fonts used, instructions for margins, spacing, other layout information, and the text and graphics to appear on the page. Printers or electronic typesetters designed to work with a page description language include a processor that converts the language to an actual page layout, which is then printed.

PageMaker A page composition application from Adobe.

page mode A memory-addressing mode in which a row is selected once and then remains in effect, thereby requiring only column addressing (one operation instead of two) until another row address is required. For group data, this halves the memory access time.

page printer A printer that prints an entire page at a time instead of printing character by character or line by line.

paint An operation in graphics-creating software in which the mouse is used to create a line on the screen as it is moved. The user may select the characteristics (such as width and texture) of the "brush" that is used to *paint*.

Paint An interactive vector- and object-oriented painting and animation system. *Paint* allows the user to paint and animate paint strokes, geometry, text, and effects, and it is compatible with plug-ins designed for *Photoshop* and *3ds max*.

Paintbox A plug-in for *trueSpace* (part of *CoolPowers*) that presents a textual list of the colors in a scene, allowing the user to locate a color by name. *Paintbox commands include* Colors, which allows the user to select the color group, and List, which allows users to click on any of the colors to make it the currently selected material. *Paintbox* uses the existing material, only changing the color, so that the user can see how different colors affect the material.

paintbrush tool A tool in *Paint Shop Pro*, *Photoshop*, and similar applications that enables the user to paint images. Through the menu controls, one can select different paintbrushes and different sizes. It is also used to "touch up" a current image.

Painter A bitmap painting application with brushes and other image-enhancing options. For textures, one of its most useful tools is its Image Hose, a utility that allows the user to spray sizable images. The Image Hose has a large collection of nozzle libraries to select from. It offers an almost unlimited number and variety of painting effects which can be used, among other things, to paint on Poser templates.

Painter 3D A three-dimensional painting program that features the painting and texturing options of *Painter*.

painter's algorithm A method of solving the problem of hidden surfaces by rendering objects in the reverse order of their distance from the observer (farther objects first; closer objects last). All surfaces are rendered; those that are hidden in the final picture are simply painted over.

Paint Image icon An icon in *Universe* that allows the user to select a previously-imported background image to use as a background template with a clearly delineated bleed area. This function is used for building and test-rendering a scene.

paint program A computer program that creates raster images in color by using the mouse to draw lines and create simple geometric figures directly on the screen. The final image is stored in a file in bit-mapped form.

Paint Shop Pro A 2D painting program by JASC.

PAL See *phase alternate line* and *programmable array logic*.

pale A color with such low color saturation it appears almost white.

palette The colors that may be displayed at any one time by a computer monitor.

Colors are limited primarily by the amount of memory in the video adapter board that is used to store video information. Typically, color modes allow 16 colors to be displayed out of 64 available and 256 to be displayed out of 16 million available.

palette animation A method of simulating animation in which the palette of colors used for the scene is changed from one frame to the next to give the appearance of motion.

PAL monitor See *NTSC/PAL monitor*.

Palo Alto Research Center (PARC) A research center for Xerox Corp., which has made significant contributions to the development of graphics user interfaces (GUIs).

pan To change the image that is being viewed by rotating the camera around its horizontal or vertical axis.

pancake window An optical device that is placed in front of the cathode-ray tube in flight simulators to make the displayed image appear more distant.

panchromatic A type of film emulsion that is sensitive to the visible spectrum from red to violets, although it is still dominated by its blue-green sensitivity.

panic key A feature of *The Games Factory*. When the user presses the panic key it will take him back to the Windows screen, leaving the game to run in the background. The panic key turns off the sound and minimizes the display.

panning a scene Creating an animated pan of a scene by altering the camera pan settings in a 3D application. Pans can be horizontal or vertical. There are two types of panning operations: *general* and *targeted*. In general panning, the user provides the audience with a feel for the panoramic environment on an incremental basis. With targeted panning, the object is to pan to an object of interest, like a special feature in the foreground on the left, or a vehicle traversing the scene.

panoramic vista techniques One can develop sweeping scenes of large areas (e.g., a desert with surrounding mountains) that can be translated to Web panoramas for use on a home page with the display help of Apple's QuickTime VR technology, by using a panorama option in a 3D application.

Pantone matching system (PMS) A method of describing colors in which each color is assigned a number. Pantone provides books of "color guides," with corresponding numbers for ease of reference.

pan-zoom movie An animation technique in which several small low-resolution frames of an animation are placed in a rectangular array. The camera *pans* to center on one of these frames and then *zooms* so that the image fills the whole screen. The process is repeated for several frames and the result stored in the single image to give the effect of continuity.

parabola A curve that is the locus of a point that moves in such a way that its undirected distances from a fixed point and a fixed line are equal. Its equation is $y = ax^2 + bx + c$.

parabolic microphone A special type of microphone that can be used to record sounds from great distances.

parallax The apparent displacement or difference in apparent direction of an object when seen from two different viewpoints not on a straight line from the object.

parallel Transmission of bits over a set of parallel wires with one wire devoted to each bit that is to be transmitted simultaneously. Commonly used to send the 8 bits that make up one ASCII character simultaneously to a printer.

parallel connected stripes (PCS) A hierarchical data structure used to store graphics object data.

parallelism The division of a computation so that portions can be processed independently by separate processors.

parallel light projection The type of light needed for projecting window lights, or for creating pseudo-slide shows and movies within scenes. The illuminated area is often in the shape of a square.

parallel light sources A light source that mimics the parallel beams of light cast by a distant light source such as the sun.

parallelogram rule A rule for the addition of vectors. Given two vectors **v** and **w**, the vectors are placed with their starting points at the origin and two more lines drawn from the end points of the vectors, each parallel to the other vector, resulting in a parallelogram. A vector drawn from the origin to the intersection of these two new lines is the vector sum of the original vectors.

parallel port An interface port on the computer that has the necessary handshaking flags for the utilization of standard parallel-addressing circuitry. Parallel port connects are typically used to connect with printers and other devices, although many more modern computers substitute the USB port for these connections.

parallel projection A technique for converting a three-dimensional scene into two dimensions. A projection plane is placed in front of the scene and parallel to its coordinate system. A center of projection is selected by projecting a line from the center of the scene through the center of the projection plane and selecting a point on this line somewhere in front of the projection plane. Each line or surface of the scene is then projected on the projection screen by drawing a line from it to the center of projection and marking where this line intersects the projection screen.

parallel rasterization architecture A way in which the pixels of an image may be partitioned to improve rendering speed. Types of parallel rasterization architecture include *image-parallel*, in which the scan line algorithm calculates the image pixel by pixel, rather than by individual primitives; *object-parallel*, in which multiple primitives are processed in parallel so that the final pixels may be calculated more quickly; and *hybrid-parallel*, in which the image-parallel and object-parallel techniques are used in combination.

parameter dials Settings in *Poser* that can be used to set the characteristics of a scene. Parameter setting names differ, depending upon the object, figure element, camera, or light selected. A human, for instance, has different parameters than a quadruped, so the settings that need to be adjusted are named accordingly.

parameter track A track that stores various parameter values, which vary by object. A parameter of a primitive torus might be the diameter of the ring. The parameters of a light source could include its brightness, the width of the angle it entails, and its color. The para-

meters of a camera could include its focal length or depth of field. Deformation animations are created with parameter tracks. When altering any of these characteristics, the animation takes place within parameters.

parametric The equation for a curve or surface that is defined in terms of intermediate variables rather than directly in terms of coordinate values.

parametric bivariate polynomial surface patches The definition of points on a three-dimensional curve by using three polynomials in a parameter t, one for each of x, y, and z.

Parametric Heads A plug-in for *3ds max*, created and marketed by Digimation, used to create a series of heads of different racial and gender types. Also known as *Head Designer*.

parametric mapping A technique in many 3D applications for mapping a texture to the surface of an object. When animating the vertices or the shape of an object, parametric mapping will keep the map aligned with the surface of the object in the best possible way.

parametric representation, in line clipping Representing a line to be clipped by parametric equations in t and then finding the values of t where the line intersects the lines that represent the clipping bounds. The actual x and y values for clipping the line can then be calculated only when a t intersection occurs.

parametric velocity The tangent vector to a curve.

paraxial ray In ray tracing, one of a bundle of rays surrounding a central *axial ray*.

PARC See *Palo Alto Research Center*.

parcel A collection of primitive graphics objects that have been preprocessed so that they can be rendered efficiently with any desired viewpoint.

parent A node in a hierarchy that is higher than another node.

parent object A single object that contains several objects that have been selected, grouped, and listed together. The objects contained within this parent group are called *children*. All changes made to the parent object are inherited by all the children. Usually, these children can still be altered separately without affecting the whole. The details of grouping vary from application to application. Some applications allow the user to simply select several figures and group them. Others require that one object be a parent while the other objects become the children. Some require the creation of a "null" object, or an object that has no geometry to act as the parent for the other objects in the group hierarchy. Also known as a *parent group*.

parietal bone The bone comprising the side of the head. It is a smooth curved surface that extends outward until it lines up with the back of the jawbone.

parity An additional bit that is added to a block of data for error detection. For odd parity, the number of bits in the block (including the parity bit) that are 1's is odd; for even parity, the number of bits in the block (including the parity bit) that are 1's is even. If the number is not odd or even, as required for the type parity, the computer knows that the block contains an error, but does not know which bit is in error.

parity rule See *even-odd rule*.

partial kd tree Partial *k*-dimensional tree. A binary subdivision of *k*-dimensional space, one dimension at a time, in which empty subdivisions are not represented.

particle deposition See *lava flows, simulating*.

particle emitter A construction shape that generates objects according to the settings defined by the user. Often, particle emitters allow for variety of speeds and sizes of the particles emitted. Some programs (like *Cinema4D XL* and *3ds max*) allow the user to place any shape as the particle to be emitted. Particle emitters can work well for the creation of a variety of special effects, including smoke, water fountains, and the spurting of blood.

particle group A group of points or models created in a 3D or 2D application that can be used to create special effects such as fire, fog, smoke, sparks, or water. Particle groups are usually animated by one global set of parameters or behaviors.

particles rollup A menu in a 3D application that enables the user to select the particle type from a series of predefined particle primitives, and to select an object of the user's own creation.

particle system A computer graphics technique, originated by W. Reeves, which represents irregular objects, such as smoke, clouds, or water, as a collection of particles that are varying in time. Stochastic processes are used to create, move, and remove particles to control the overall shape and texture of the object.

Particlz A plug-in for *trueSpace* with four emission styles: explosion, Gaussian, pulsed, and uniform. Particles can also be generated from an area with control over velocity, emission, etc. There are settings for gravity, vortexes, magnets, and winds. Particles can also be assigned to an animation path and given a life-span and elasticity functions.

Particulator A plug-in (part of *CoolPowers*) for *trueSpace* that works as a scatter tool. It will copy one object over the entire surface of the currently selected object with a certain amount of noise so that the result is not overly uniform. Potential uses for this technique include creating quills on a porcupine or covering the parts of a scorpion with small sensory hairs, such as those that occur in nature. *3ds max* includes similar plug-ins.

partitioned frame buffer See *parallel rasterization architecture.*

partitioning Subdividing a space into a number of smaller spaces or cells.

partitions Logical divisions in a hard drive that make the drive appear to be more than a single drive.

Paste Into Background A command in the Display Menu of *Poser* that creates a snapshot of every item in the scene and pastes a replica onto the background. This is not a keyframe option, so the background holds for the entire sequence. Using this feature, it's very easy to create a non-moving background group of figures, a crowd, or even a more abstracted background design.

patch 1. A small, simple curved surface that is combined with other patches to create a complex surface. 2. A mathematically-defined surface usually composed of two or more curves. 3. An object with a surface or solidity that is defined by intersecting spline curves. 4. A correction inserted in a software program to correct an error without extensive rewriting of the program.

patch bay A rack of video and audio input and output connectors that makes it easier to reconfigure the hardware in an editing system.

patch cracking Cracking that occurs when a surface is subdivided into patches and then the patches are redrawn to approximate the original surface. It occurs because the edges of adjacent patches are not identically described due to computer round-off errors. See *cracking*.

patch visibility index A number associated with a vertex that measures the potential occlusion.

path An open or closed curve or line that can be used as a modeling template or as a vector path for animated objects.

path creation, basic The standard paths that result from the movement of an object in space over time in a 3D application.

path extrude A command used by many 3D applications (*LightWave, 3ds max,* and others) that allows the user to extrude a shape along a selected path to create a 3D form.

Path option An option in *The Games Factory* that allows the user to select a track on which the object moves, make the object loop or play just once, regulate the speed of the movement, and, most importantly, test the movement.

path pauses In game programming, every time the character enters a new room, a new local path must be computed. Since this obviously takes time, the character appears to pause as he enters each doorway. The search itself cannot be increased, but the new path request can be anticipated and computed before needed. This simple trick maintains the character's fluid motion throughout the path.

path, ribbon See *ribbon path*.

path, smooth Paths computed by A* are usually riddled with sharp turns. Even if the programmer employs a technique to make straighter paths, sharp turns still have the potential to make characters look like robots. By applying rotational dampening to turns, the programmer can partially mask them, but they will swing wide on every sharp corner. A more effective method is to create an algorithm that makes paths (a series of points in space) *smooth*. Using a Catmull-Rom spline, the user can create a curve that handles all the control points in the original path (unlike a Bézier curve, which is smoother but does not go through the control points). It is usually better to go directly through the points, because A* deemed them clear and free of obstacles. The Catmull-Rom formula requires four input points and gives back a smooth curve between the second and third points. To get the points between the first and second input points, give the function the first point twice, then the second and third. To get the points between the third and fourth, give the function the second and third, and double up on the fourth. Each time the Catmull-Rom formula is used, it gives a point roughly u% between the second and third inputs, where u is a number passed through.

path tracing Following the path of a ray backwards from the eye.

patrolling In game programming, the repetition of a sequence of places as a pattern. By employing the state machine movement queue, each "patrol" spot can be placed on the queue. However, when a state machine reaches its goal, it needs to put itself on the back end of the queue in order to maintain the cycle.

pattern designing When creating a solution to a common programming problem, most developers refer to a similar problem that they have solved previously and then extrapolate the new solution from the old. Design patterns are about formalizing these general software solutions to give a common frame of reference when discussing everyday engineering tasks.

pattern filling See *filling, pattern*.

pattern mapping Applying a pattern to the surface of an object so that it will not have an unrealistically smooth surface.

pattern mask A matrix of threshold values that is used to determine which of two adjacent output grayscale values will be assigned to a pixel.

pattern matching A technique for optical character reading. The software contains a template of each possible character. When the scanner reads a character, it compares the character with the templates until a match is found. It then reports the resulting ASCII equivalent.

Pattern option An option in *The Games Factory* used to change color. The Pattern option uses a crosshatch to grade the colors from one to another rather than smoothly fading the color.

pattern recognition interaction technique A technique in which a user makes a sequence of movements with a device, such as a mouse, and the pattern recognition software automatically compares this with a set of defined patterns and selects the proper action that matches a pattern.

Pause function A function in *The Games Factory* that stops an object at its current position for a pause that is defined in seconds.

payload The part of an information packet that follows the *header*. It contains the actual data to be communicated.

PCB See *printed circuit board*.

PCL See *printer control language*.

PCM See *pulse code modulation*.

PCS See *parallel connected stripes*.

P-curve A parametric representation of the motion (or other attribute) of an object or group of objects in a scene.

PCX A file format using run-length encoding to store bit-mapped graphics in compressed form. Originated by Z-Soft Corp and first used in the *PC Paintbrush* program.

Peano curve A space-filling fractal curve obtained by repeatedly replacing the middle third of each line segment by a pattern of six line segments that are each one-third of the length of the original line segment, causing a square to be formed at the left and right of the middle third of the original line segment.

pedestal To raise a camera up or down.

pedestal level The voltage level of a video signal that completely suppresses the electron beam of the cathode-ray tube during blanking. Also known as *blanking level*.

pel See *pixel*.

pen-based computer A computer system that makes use of an electronic pen or stylus to provide data input.

pencil A narrow beam of rays used in ray tracing.

penetron A type of color cathode-ray tube in which layers of red and green phosphors are applied to the interior of the faceplate in such a way that the color of the display depends upon the amount that the electron beam penetrates the phosphor layers, which in turn depends upon the electron beam's accelerating voltage. It provides simpler and higher resolution displays than color-mask tubes, but cannot produce shades of blue. Also known as a *beam penetration display*.

pen plotter A plotter in which one or more pens are electronically moved to trace the data on a sheet of paper.

pen polygon A figure in which opposite sides are parallel and, if the polygon is translated so that one vertex of an edge lies at the origin, the line containing the opposite edge must pass through a point with integer coordinates.

Penrose tiling The tiling of a plane with only two different tiles.

pen, sonic A device that emits periodic sounds, which are tracked by three orthogonal strip microphones to determine the pen location.

Pen tool A tool in *The Games Factory* that is used to either draw one pixel at a time or to draw a freehand line. To create a grainy effect, use this tool with several different colors and go over the drawing area very quickly. Doing this over a gray background with brown, black, and white will give the effect of a brown, stone tile.

penumbra That portion of a shadow where part, but not all, of an extended light source is occluded by a shadowing object.

perceived intensity of light The psychological sensation of light brightness, as opposed to the actual, physical quantity of light intensity.

perception range A constraint on boids in flocking algorithms that restricts how far a flockmate can "look" around its environment to detect other flockmates, potential obstacles, or enemies. The larger this range, the more organized and coherent the flocks and the better they are at avoiding enemies and obstacles. Making this range smaller results in more erratic flocks, groups of boids splitting off more often when confronted by obstacles or enemies, etc.

perceptually uniform color space A color space in which two colors that are equally distant from the viewer are perceived as being equally distant.

Peridot A system for creating user-interface software.

period doubling A phenomenon in fractal attractors in which, at a certain critical value, the attractor splits in two.

periodic orbit The path followed by a point when a set of values is calculated using a recursion equation.

periodic plane tessellation The complete tiling of a plane by repetition of the same shape. In some cases, the term *periodic plane tessellation* is also used as a command that transforms all polygons into three-sided polygons, which are better when distorting the object because they tend to remain planar.

peripheral Any device connected externally to the computer.

peripheral vision Vision from the edges of the eye, where distribution of rods exceeds that of cones. It is characterized by lower resolution, less color perception, higher sensitivity to motion, and higher sensitivity to light.

Perlin noise function A function that varies randomly between −1 and +1 throughout three-dimensional space with an autocorrelation distance of about 1 in every direction. Also known as the *random noise function*.

Perlin Noise A fractal shader for *trueSpace* that allows the user to create rocky mountains, realistic water, and many other interesting effects.

persistence The capability of a cathode-ray tube phosphor to continue to emit light for a time after the exciting stream of electrons is removed. Phosphors that have long persistence glow for a long time after the beam is removed. This reduces objectionable flicker but causes blurring of fast moving data. Phosphors with short persistence glow for only a very short time after the beam is removed. They are capable of displaying fast-moving action without blur, but need to be refreshed more often to avoid flicker.

persistence of vision The illusion of movement created by rapidly-changing still images.

Person icon An icon in the *Game Creation System* for placing enemies selected from a library.

perspective The apparent reduction in size of objects in proportion to their distance from the observer when viewed in three-dimensional space. Also known as an *orthographic view*.

perspective foreshortening The visual effect of a perspective projection. Perspective foreshortening results in images that appear lifelike, but such a projection cannot be used to determine the actual shape and size of objects.

perspective matching Matching a virtual camera's FOV, aspect ratio, height, and placement to that of a photograph.

perspective projection The mathematical transformation of three-dimensional objects into two dimensions by dividing the x and y lengths of the object by z (the distance from the observer) to give the illusion of depth.

PET (positron emission tomography) scanner An electronic device that produces the images of inner body parts for medical purposes.

PEX See *PHIGS extension to X* and *packet exchange*.

PGL A file extension used to designate the Hewlett-Packard graphics language format.

phantom vertices, cubic curves A technique for interpolating endpoints of cubic curves.

Pharaoh's breastplate. A fractal curve produced through the use of inversion.

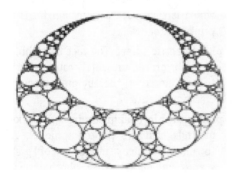

Pharaoh's breastplate.

phase alternate line (PAL) The standard for color television in many countries. It has a frame rate of 25 fps and 625 horizontal scan lines, resulting in somewhat higher quality video than NTSC.

phase change recording An optical data recording technique in which data are recorded by causing a laser beam to strike the recording medium and cause it to crystallize. The medium is read by reading it with a laser beam that reflects only from the crystallized areas.

phase space A space in which all of the characteristics of a dynamical system at an instant in time are collapsed into a single point. As time is varied, the picture shows the complete behavior of the system over a time interval.

phi file See *hierarchy*.

PHIGS An acronym for *programmers' hierarchical interface for graphics systems*, a software interface standard for graphics that includes data structures for high-level three-dimensional applications.

PHIGS+ An extension to the original PHIGS specification that includes more extensive lighting models.

PHIGS extension to X (PEX) A protocol for a three-dimensional extension to X11 based on PHIGS+.

phoneme The smallest speech sound that distinguishes one spoken word from another. The difference between "tooth" and "truth" is one phoneme (the "r" sound) even though the spelling is quite different. As another example, in the word "foot", the "oo" sound would be represented by the "UH" phoneme. The phonetic spelling of the word would be "F-UH-T." Phonemes are the backbone of speech and therefore paramount to the success of lip synch. The only way (and even trained phonologists do this) to work out which phoneme should be used is for the person doing it to mouth it. There are 40 phonemes in the American English language (*see Figure next page*).

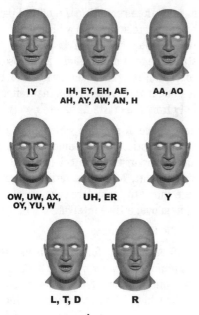

IY   IH, EY, EH, AE,   AA, AO
AH, AY, AW, AN, H

OW, UW, AX,   UH, ER   Y
OY, YU, W

L, T, D   R

phoneme.

phoneme, visual A mouth position that represents the sounds of speech. These are the building blocks for lip synch animation. When creating 3D character lip synch, start by modeling the phonemes. There are sixteen visual phonemes.

Phong evaluation See *raytrace evaluation.*

Phong illumination A technique for rendering the highlights that appear on glossy surfaces by taking the cosine of

Phong illumination.

the angle between the incident light on the surface and the viewing direction vector and raising it to a predetermined power. The diffused light is then increased by this factor. Originated by Phong Bui Tong in 1975. Also known as *Phong shading* or *normal vector interpolation shading.*

phono connector See *RCA connector.*

phosphor A chemical substance, such as that used on the back of a cathode-ray tube face, that emits light when struck by a beam of electrons.

phosphorescence The light given off by the return of the relatively more stable excited electrons to their unexcited state after electron beam exitation is removed.

phot A unit of illuminance equal to 0.0001 lux.

photochromic A compound that becomes dark when exposed to light.

photocomposition Using photographic means to produce characters and graphics on a light-sensitive paper or film, which is then used as a master for the printing process.

photoelectric effect The fact that shining light on certain metals causes them to emit electrons, thereby producing an electric current.

photographic backgrounds 1. Backgrounds that are photographic. 2. A technique for increasing realism of *Poser* scenes by adding stock photographs. Backgrounds photographed with a digital camera can be added to scenes.

photography The process or act of making and recording visual images using a light-sensitive media.

photo-inversion The transformation of a grayscale computer graphics image by replacing each pixel with its grayscale opposite. In photography, this process creates a positive print from a negative.

photomapping The mapping of a photographic image onto a surface.

photometer A device that measures luminance and reports the results in units weighted to match the spectral intensity of the human visual system.

photometric Relating to light measurements weighted for the properties of the human visual system.

photon An imaginary particle of light. It is the single unit of light illumination. It is also a "packet" of light energy with zero mass.

photo-optic memory An optical data storage technique in which a laser is used to record data on light-sensitive film.

Photo-Paint A program by Corel, used for photo editing and painting. *Photo-Paint* allows the user to enhance images with lenses, masks, and other photo-editing features. It creates diverse painting effects with artistic media tools.

photopic Relating to vision principally by the cones of the human eye, characterized by bright light and color sensitivity.

photopic luminous efficiency function A function of the wavelength of light that specifies the relative sensitivity of the human visual system under high brightness conditions.

photoplotter A high-accuracy, high-definition plotter that plots with a beam of light on photosensitive material.

photorealistic rendering Techniques for rendering an image so that it appears as realistic as a photograph.

photoresist A smooth glass plate that is treated with photo-sensitive coating 1.5 microns thick. The photoresist is sensitive only to certain wavelengths of light. Through the use of fiber optics, the computer is set to start exposing the photoresist pixel by pixel. The interference pattern is created by the lasers as it is exposed into the photoresist.

photosensitive receptor cells See *rods* and *cones*.

photosensor A light-sensitive reading device employed in optical scanners.

Photoshop A graphics editing program developed by Adobe.

phototypesetter A device that uses photographic means to produce character images on a light-sensitive paper or film to create a master for use in a printing process.

physics engine Software that contains a real-time physics simulation that provides, among other things, an accurate collision-detection algorithm.

pi 1. In typography, jumbled type that needs to be sorted into the proper bins of a type case before reuse. 2. In mathematics, π, the ratio of the circumference of a circle to its diameter.

PIC A file extension designating a compressed bitmap image format compatible with the *PC Paint Plus* painting program.

pica A unit of measurement used in typography and desktop publishing. One pica is equal to 12 points or $\frac{1}{6}$ inch.

pi character In typography, a nonalphanumeric symbol, such as a smiling face, that has the same size as a letter or number. Type fonts consisting entirely of *pi characters* are available. Using such a font, each letter or number of a standard keyboard will cause an associated *pi character* to be printed. Also known as a *dingbat* or *wingding*.

pick aperture The area on a computer screen in which the cursor must be placed to select a desired action.

pick correlation The determination by a computer application of which screen button, icon, or other object was selected when the user pushed the locator button (e.g., clicking the mouse button).

pick-highlight cycle The modification of a particular object's color or appearance on the display to indicate that it has been selected by the cursor.

pick identifier See *picking*.

picking Moving a cursor on a display to a particular area in order to select an application that the computer is to perform. The software must first identify the cursor location coordinates, and then compare them with a table of location areas versus numbers called the *pick identifiers*. Finally, the program will perform a set of functions identified with the selected number.

pick-up An additional scene that is shot after the first rough cut of a movie is made.

PICT A file extension used to designate object-oriented graphics files compatible with many Macintosh graphics programs.

picture maps See *bit-mapped texture*.

Picture Tube tool A tool in *Paint Shop Pro* that uses tubes to paint on an image. Tubes are built from images arranged in a grid. These images usually share a common theme and appear randomly on the image each time the user clicks on the image. "Coins" is an example of a picture tube provided in *Paint Shop Pro*.

piecewise continuous polynomial A method of representing a curve by a parametric polynomial.

pie chart A graph in which a circle represents the whole and is divided into proportionally sized segments, each representing the part of the whole having some characteristic.

pie fill A term used in Java to denote a method of filling an arc with color. Since an arc is not a closed figure, some assumption has to be made as to how it will be filled. If a *pie fill* is used, Java actually draws a straight line from each end of the arc to the center of the underlying circle or ellipse and then fills the resulting closed figure with color.

pimple An objectionable artifact that occurs when using scan lines of insufficient pixel resolution to create letters.

pinch roller A rubber wheel that presses a magnetic tape against the capstan with constant pressure to assure that the tape speed remains constant during reading and writing.

pincushioning Distortion of the image on a video screen in which the middle of the top, bottom, and sides of the display are pushed in.

ping-ponging The infinite exchange of energy between two patches that face each other when calculating radiosity by approximation using patches or meshing. If two patches are facing each other, the light will bounce back and forth forever.

pinhole camera The simplest form of camera, consisting of a box with a pinhole in the center of one wall and a sheet of film on the inside of the other wall. As long as the pinhole is small enough, it acts as a good-quality lens of very small aperture.

pink noise A completely random amplitude signal whose power is inverse to frequency. Also known as *1/f noise*.

pipelining The partitioning of a computation into stages that can be executed sequentially in separate processing elements. This reduces total processing time when a number of similar computations are involved.

pistol-grip tripod A tripod with a head that is controlled by a single pistol-grip mechanism. Such heads can be freely rotated around all axes simultaneously, making it very difficult to perform a smooth motion along a single axis.

pit A laser-created indentation in an optical disk that represents a bit of data.

pitch 1. The number of characters per inch in a line of text, measured horizontally. This number is meaningful only for fixed spacing fonts, since proportional fonts have a different *pitch* for every character. 2. The angular displacement of an object about the *x* axis in the *x-y* plane. 3. The distance between the centers of RGB phosphor triads on a cathode ray tube screen.

pixblt See *bitblt*.

pixel Short for *picture element*. A single element of a discrete display. Also known as a *pel*.

pixel aspect ratio The ratio of the horizontal length of a pixel to the vertical length of the pixel. Computer monitors have square pixels. However, pixels are rectangular in some video formats. In order to work with such formats on a computer monitor, software that corrects the picture on the monitor is required.

pixelation An effect created when a texture map with insufficient resolution is mapped onto a surface.

pixellization A video effect in which an image is divided into a grid containing

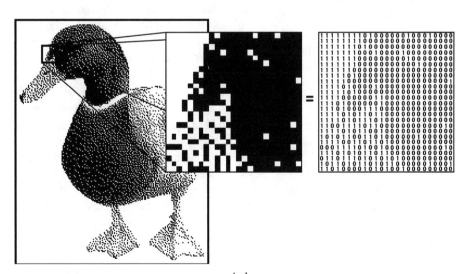

pixel.

337

squares that are treated as oversized pixels, with each assigned a color derived from the original image color in the area.

Pixels 3D A 3D graphics and animation application for Macintosh systems.

pixel-stream editor A device whose input and output are each a stream of pixels. The user specifies the actions that the device performs on the pixels.

pixmap 1. Memory that serves to store the values for pixels that make up a display. 2. In the X Window system, a two-dimensional array of graphics data in which each pixel of a display has its color represented by at least one bit.

Pixrect A two-dimensional graphics program by Sun Microsystems for Sun workstations.

Pixwin A program used in the implementation of the Sun-Windows window system.

PKUNZIP A program for decompressing files that have been compressed with *PKZIP*. Such files have the extension *.ZIP*.

PKZIP A popular program for compressing computer files using the *Lempel Ziv Welch* compression algorithm. Files compressed with this program have the extension *.ZIP*.

PLA See *point-level animation.*

placement The positioning of titles over video.

Place mode In the *Game Creation System,* a technique for changing an "anchor point" after selecting a wall.

planar 1. Contained within a plane. 2. Having two dimensions.

planar cubic curve A curve defined by a cubic equation and confined to a plane.

planar geometric projection Projection onto a plane using a straight projector.

planar mapping A method of mapping that projects a 2D image in a flat or planar manner onto the surface of a 3D object.

plane A two-dimensional surface of infinite extent.

plane equations Equations that define lines, points, or curves on a plane.

plane of light When lighting, it is important to establish a *plane of light*. That is, the scene is mentally broken down into layers or groups of subjects that have separation and distinctiveness. In theater, the upstage and downstage normally create this separation, where the levels of illumination for the foreground and background are different. This does not mean that one layer is always brighter than the others; it means only that the planes of light are established as required by the story line or scene.

plane-parallel copy A method of generating a display in which the pixel color information is stored on a number of memory planes and is transferred to the display from all planes simultaneously. This is a fast method of display generation, but may require special hardware.

plane-serial copy A method of generating a display in which the pixel color information is stored on a number of memory planes and is transferred to the display one plane at a time. Plane-serial copy is relatively slow and results in a display that looks strange during the time when all planes have not fully been transferred.

Plant Studio A Windows program for creating plants.

plasma display A flat display screen consisting of a gas sandwiched between two glass plates. A grid of horizontal and vertical wires associated with the display causes the gas to glow at the intersection of the particular pair of horizontal and vertical wires that are activated by application of a voltage.

Plastiform A tool in *trueSpace* that allows the user to deform objects. It can create new polygons where it deforms the mesh, allowing the programmer to add subtle little details.

platform A rectangular area in the 3D world that senses the presence of a player. One of the most common uses of a platform is to *raise* the player when he steps on one. Another function is to use the platform as a trigger for a teleport device to another level. In fact, this is how most level-switches are implemented with *Game Creation System*. The rectangular platforms are, by default, not drawn; they are completely invisible. Usually, they are placed right in front of tunnels or staircases. When the player walks up to the staircase, the game switches levels as if he had traversed the staircase.

player object A backdrop object that moves and changes. It is called a *player object* because it can contain other types of objects, both real and backdrop. It is persistent; its lifetime ends when the play session ends. In multiplayer games,

this is also the case; once the player object is destroyed, the object can no longer have an effect on the game universe. The player object's position is a special type of master seed. It changes constantly, but is also completely predictable. That is, there is a limit within which the player can move in the game universe, a discrete number of coordinates that the player can inhabit. Even in an infinite universe, the player's position can be uniquely identified in a coordinate system.

Play Movie File A command in the *Poser* Animation Menu that permits the user to play AVI or QuickTime movies inside of *Poser*. Play Movie File is useful when previewing an animation just rendered, and also for previewing an animation the user is considering for use as a background.

Plop Rendering A rendering feature unique to *Bryce*, used especially for the creation of a single figure.

plosive phonemes Phonemes that involve the same restriction of the speech canal as fricatives, but the speech organs are

Plop Rendering.

substantially less tense during the articulation of a spirant. Rather than friction, a resonant sound is produced at the point of articulation. The plosives in the English language are: P, B, T, D, K, and G. Plosives are commonly referred to as the "drop consonants" in lip sync. These sounds are uttered quickly and abruptly, meaning they are quite often passed over by the visual phonemes. Not all consonants need to be reflected with visual phonemes, particularly if they are plosive.

plot 1. To create an image by drawing straight line segments. 2. A constrained sequence of events that may or may not follow a pattern. The most abstract meaning that can be attached to the term *plot* is the main theme, or story line behind a game. Usually, we take the plot to be a series of two or more connected events. They are usually, but not always, connected by the actions of the player with relation to the game universe. The player may have a direct or indirect influence on the plot of a game. Action games generally have a very simple plot, comprised mainly of a journey through a maze or similar, shooting anything that moves. Real-time strategy or simulation-style games may have a plot that is more intricate and based on an indirect relationship between the player and game universe.

Plot3D 1. A program developed by NASA for displaying scientific data in graphics form. *Plot3D* is often used to display fluid dynamics data. 2. The file format used for storing *Plot3D* graphics images.

plots and event chains Plots can be defined as containing a sequence of event chains, linked by specific events or sequences of events. The seed is used to start a plot, and from this plot, events can be chained, the outcome of each one providing information for generating the next event. Each generated event may give rise to another plot. It is important to note that event chains can be predicted only up to a point, because the player has an unpredictable effect on each chain. The plots, however, are entirely predictable, since they are triggered by specific events or event chains. The sequencing of the plots depends on the event chains, so even if the plots are pregenerated, there is the very real possibility that they might be executed in an order different from what was originally intended by the designer.

plot sequencing and game rules All games have a set of allowed actions, or *rules*. The rules of a game universe should apply equally to the player, objects, and characters that the player might encounter. If something shoots the player's character, and it becomes injured, the player reasonably expects that if he shoots something, then it will become injured also. This simple sequence of events is a very small example of a plot in an action game. The rules are that both parties have a loaded gun, and that they can see each other well enough to aim and fire the weapon. Once fired, they reasonably expect the projectile to hit the opponent and cause damage. There are, however, a number of possible ways in which the expected outcome of the plot can be altered. Either party could run out of ammunition. One party could have a more powerful gun. Either of them could be endowed with an armor-plated suit or supernatural reactions to dodge the projectile. These plot twists could themselves be the results of other plots that have chained together to produce the new plot. Some of these "other" plots could be totally independent of the player's actions, and take place at a designated time. The plot is the application of game rules on the objects that inhabit the universe. We usually determine the game rules at the time of designing the game. In special cases, we can allow game rules to evolve naturally of their own accord, but this is usually a result of the convergence of predetermined plot lines. Plots start with an event, be it predetermined or evolutionary. The flow of the plot is dictated by the game rules. In addition, a plot can be a sequence of predetermined events, chained together by the application of game rules at separate intervals.

plot, pregenerated A plot in which each object has a distinct set of properties that are fixed at design time, and vary within a set of values that are also fixed at design time. Pregenerated plots are controlled by the positioning of game objects within the portion of the universe they inhabit, with a given set of properties that define their behavior. Consider a simple example. In the game of *Pac-Man*, the plot is simple. The little yellow creature that represents the player should travel around the maze, eating dots and avoiding ghosts. There is one ghost in each corner of the maze. Also in the corner of each maze is a special pill that, when eaten, allows the yellow creature to eat the ghosts. The plot manifests itself in a sequence of controlled events in which the ghosts move around the maze in a certain pattern (which is predefined) for a certain length of time. After a while, they begin to converge on the player, with just enough intelligence to trap an unwary

player, at which point the player is eaten. Therefore, the plot is entirely pregenerated; that is, there is nothing the player can do to alter the plot. It is controlled—and the player is also, if unwittingly, controlled—by the behavior pattern of the ghosts, which is also predetermined. Even if a pregenerated sequence of seeds is used to control the plot, variations are possible by combining them with the outcomes of events in which the player has had an effect. Subsequent detail can therefore be generated using this interaction as a seed.

plotter A device that creates images by drawing lines on paper with a series of color pens.

plug-in A piece of software that can be added to a host application to perform a special function. Plug-in filters enhance the capabilities of the application they are folded into. There are hundreds of plug-in filters available for both 2D and 3D applications, each one offering distinct image enhancement and modification capabilities.

pluSpack A collection of plug-ins for *trueSpace*, by Caligari.

PM See *progressive mesh*.

PMS See *pantone matching system*.

PNG See *Portable Network Graphics*.

point 1. A unit of measurement in typography or desktop publishing. One point is $1/72$ of an inch. 2. A location in space specified by a set of coordinate values.

point and shoot interface A graphics user interface (GUI) featuring icons that are selected by moving a cursor on the display with a mouse.

pointcloud rendering The rendering of an object as a series of points at critical places in the form. Pointcloud rendering allows one to see the back of the object as well as the front.

pointing device A piece of hardware used to move the position of a cursor on the display screen in order to input position data to a computer. Examples include *mice* and *track balls*.

point-in-triangle test Any method for determining whether a point lies within a triangle or not.

point-level animation (PLA) A function of some 3D applications that allows the user to make alterations of a model from the point level or the level of the model where polygons meet. The ability to animate these movements allows for detailed facial expressions.

point level deformation See *vertex level deformation*.

point light source A light source that radiates from a single point in space.

point-on-line test Any method for determining whether a given point is on a specified line.

points, adding Addition of points to modify geometry in a 3D application.

point sampling The process of determining pixel color by sampling a point on the image that is within the pixel bounds.

point size In typography, the size of type measured from the top of the ascender to the bottom of the descender, such as:

point size (10 point, Times Roman)

point size (14 point, Times Roman)

point size (20 point, Times Roman)

polarization The selective transmission of light based on its orientation. When light is reflected or refracted, its orientation and alignment change.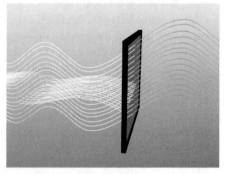

polarization.

polarizer A lens filter which polarizes the light coming into the lens. Can be used to increase saturation and to eliminate reflections in glass or water.

Polaroid Mirage photopolymer hologram A hologram similar to an *embossed hologram*, but produced in a manner similar to that of a film reproduction system. The finished product is created by exposing an emulsion on plastic film and then developing it. These holograms are extremely realistic in color tone and dimension. They do not have a shiny, mirrored back; they can be produced clear, with a black or other colored background.

polling 1. A technique for data transfer on a computer network in which a network server interrogates the other computers periodically to determine when one of them has data ready to transfer. 2. Describes software that polls all objects in a graphics image to determine their reaction to some event.

poly-count The number of polygons used by the computer to model an object.

When dealing with polygon-based objects, it is important to keep the number of polygons as low as possible, thus conserving computer memory and rendering time. Use no more than 512 triangles for spheres or cylinders unless they will be taking up 60% of the image at resolutions greater than 640 × 480. Cubes

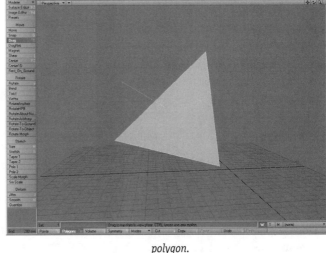

polygon.

and rectilinear objects should be kept under 256 vertices as well. Areas where there is bending usually have as much as two or three times the polygon count as non-bending areas. A single 1024-triangle-based object with just default mapping and lighting requires almost 1MB of memory to handle. ☞

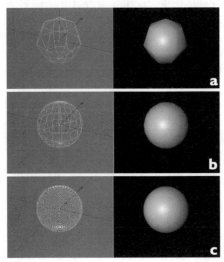

poly-count.

polygon A two-dimensional figure described by three or more points, consisting of an ordered set of vertices connected in sequence by sides that do not intersect, forming a closed surface. A polygon may be tessellated into triangles. See *concave polygon* and *convex polygon*.

polygonal pens A method of drawing wide lines using polygons defined by integer offset vectors.

polygonal topology In *form•Z*, the arrangement and shape of faces within the mesh. Polygons should be arranged along curves of force within the model. Polygonal shape refers to the shape and point count of polygons. Meshes with regular rectangular grid patterns composed of four-point rectangular polygons result in the most cleanly rendered images. In general, it is best to avoid polygons with aspect ratios greater than 5:1. Very long rectangles and triangles, known as *slivers*, can cause shading anomalies. Incorrect mesh topology and

343

slivered faces are a sign of poor modeling technique.

polygon, area of Given a polygon in a plane with vertices $v_1, \ldots, v_n$, $(v_n=v_1)$, and $v_i=(x_i, y_i)$ for each I, its area is:

$$\alpha = \frac{1}{2} \sum_{i=1}^{n-1} x_i y_{i+1} - x_{i+1} y_i$$

polygon clipping See *clipping, polygon*.

polygon count See *poly-count*.

polygon creation Drawing a polygon by specifying a starting point and a series of line segments, the last of which terminates at the starting point.

Polygon Draw A tool in *trueSpace* that allows the user to draw polygons.

polygon floor In a 3D game world, the floor polygons are specifically marked and used directly as the search space. This *polygonal floor* is identical to the rendered geometry, thus being arbitrarily simple or complex.

polygon, generalized A graphics figure, not necessarily coplanar, consisting of an ordered set of vertices connected in sequence by sides that may intersect forming a closed surface. It may not be possible to tessellate a *generalized polygon* into triangles.

polygon mesh A collection of edges, vertices, and polygons connected such that each edge is shared at most by two polygons.

polygon modeling Creating shells of 3D shapes by organizing 2D polygons (usually squares or triangles) in digital space. Polygon models are the least taxing on a computer's processor. Because of this, most low- to mid-range 3D applications rely heavily or solely on polygon modeling.

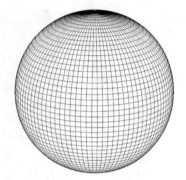

polygon modeling.

polygon overlap An algorithm for determining whether a polygon lies within a cube. This is a fast method for testing whether a triangle intersects a *voxel*. This algorithm can also be expanded for testing whether a triangle intersects a world-aligned cube of any size. It is necessary to determine what translation and scale will transform the cube into a voxel. Then, that transform is performed on each triangle. Each transformed triangle is then tested for intersection with a voxel.

Polygon Reduction A tool in *trueSpace* that creates a duplicate of an object with only 60% of the polygons that made up the original object.

polygon table A table of data used in scan conversion that contains the coefficients of the plane equation, shading or color information, and an in-out Boolean flag for each polygon that is part of the image that is being scan converted.

polyhedron A closed three-dimensional object composed of polygons, where each edge of a polygon is shared with another polygon and each vertex is shared by two or more polygons.

polyline A set of contiguous straight line segments that approximates a curve.

Polyline tool A tool available in *Carrara* that allows the user to draw a set of contiguous line segments. This straight line representation is a quick way to rough out a cross section to which the necessary curves can be applied later.

polymarker A graphics object that is defined by a marker and a list of marker locations.

polymorphism A characteristic of object-oriented programming in which a given name may refer to an object of any one of a number of related classes that may respond to a given operation in different ways.

polyocular techniques Techniques for viewing three-dimensional images by creating an image of solid appearance that is viewable by any number of eyes, and by extension, by several people at once. Various methods have been tried to do this. One is *volume scanning*. A display screen can be driven mechanically to scan a volume, preferably faster than the critical flicker frequency of the eye. For example, a cathode ray tube can be constructed so that the screen oscillates or rotates inside the vacuum. Alternatively, a semi-transparent screen on which a scannable laser beam shines can be arranged to scan out a volume.

popping The visible change in geometry (especially at the silhouette edge) and texturing when a character or object switches from one level of detail to another.

popularity algorithm A method of quantizing colors in which the new, limited range of colors consists of the *K* colors most frequently occurring in the image.

port A computer channel that interfaces with an input or output device.

Portable Network Graphics (PNG) A file format for raster images. PNG supports 24-bit and 48-bit color depth, palettes up to 256 colors, two different types of transparency, highly efficient lossless compression, and patent-free and open source code.

portrait Orientation of a page such that the page height exceeds the page width. Contrast with *landscape* orientation, in which the width of the page exceeds its height.

Poseable Clothes A feature of *Poser* found in the Figures/Clothing Male and Clothing Female libraries. Poseable Clothes are composed of articulated parts, just like a figure. After importing a clothes selection to the scene, position the clothes over the figure, lining them up on all axes. The clothes will snap into place over the figure, just like hair.

Poser An application from CuriousLabs for storyboarding, visualization, and animating 3D articulated figures and props. With *Poser*, the user can create 3D figures, props, and sets that can be posed and manipulated to create complex choreographies and scenes. Because the user can move the camera and characters in true 3D space, it is possible to view a scene from different angles to block character and camera position as well as choreography. If the set designers have been designing or modeling in a 3D package, the user can import their set models into *Poser* to visualize the scene.

Poser Objects A plug-in for *3ds max* from CuriousLabs that allows *3ds max* users to import *Poser* scene files, including animated figures.

Poser Props Modeler's Guild A group that collects models for use with *Poser*.

345

All renders are 200 × 150 pixels. Renders use the supplied backdrop. All renders must be in .JPG format.

position track In animation, a separate track that keeps track of the position of an object. Whenever an object is moved within digital space, its position track is altered. Also known as a *move track*.

positive A photographic film or print that accurately represents the original tone value (that is, original blacks are black in the print and original whites are white). Contrast with *negative*.

positive orientation A basis that has the same orientation as the standard basis.

postconcatenation A modification of transformation matrices that permits the transformation process to be performed much faster on a computer.

postconditions Changes that occur to state variables when a command is executed.

posterization Reducing the number of colors or shades of gray in an image so that boundaries between different colors or shades of gray are obvious, with no blending effects. Used to give an artistic effect.

post-filtering Filtering that is performed after point sampling.

post house See *post-production facility*.

post-production Effects that are added to an animation after it has been completely drawn.

post-production facility A service bureau that provides editing and other post-production facilities and services. Also known as a *post house*.

post-rendering effects Effects that rendering engines can perform after the image is finished rendering. Post-rendering effects are essential effects drawn on the final render after it has been calculated. For instance, *glow* is a post-rendering effect. That is why a glowing light bulb does not show up in a reflection. By the time the 3D application applies the post-rendering effect, all reflections and lighting concerns have already been addressed. Despite their limitations, post-rendering effects add some nice touches to figures or animations. The following are some post-rendering effects and examples of their use.

Depth of field: We may not consciously notice it, but our eyes are not able to have everything within our site in focus all the time. We can focus on an object sitting atop a computer monitor, but the wall 10 feet behind it is actually out of focus. Cameras (both still and video) work the same way. We can have a focal point, but there can be objects in front and behind that focal point that we can see but are out of focus.

Motion blur: This occurs because the shutter of a camera (still or video) opens and closes too slowly to capture pristine shots of fast movement. When the shutter is open, fast-moving objects cover too much ground, leaving a smeared or blurred image. 3D applications do not have that problem, since they record each frame as though motion were frozen in time, but it is possible for a 3D application to simulate the effect of motion blur. They do this by rendering movement within a single frame, then shifting the movement in previous and subsequent frames and rendering those frames. They then composite the frames before and after the original frame into a blurred image. This gives a nice illusion of blur due to slow camera shutter speed. This helps make 3D animations look much less sterile.

Lens effects: Lens flares attempt to emulate the effect lights have as they are bent through a camera lens.

PostScript A language, developed by Adobe Systems, that represents fonts, text, and graphics in a form that a printer can understand and use to produce a printed page.

potentially visible A graphics object that may be partially or completely occluded and therefore requires further processing.

potentiometer A variable resistor consisting of a resistance element and a pointer that may be moved along the element, often in a circular path.

POWER IRIS A computing system using multiple instruction multiple data (MIMD) interleaved memory.

practical light A light source that is both part of the scenery and a source of light for the camera.

preamplifier 1. A small amplifier included inside a microphone to increase signal amplitude before any noise or hum can be introduced. 2. A small amplifier inserted between the microphone and amplifier when the amplifier lacks a microphone-level input.

preconditions Conditions on state variables that must be satisfied for a command to be invoked.

predictability When using pseudorandom numbers, the fact that two runs with the same set of starting values produce identical sequences of numbers.

prediction-correction coding An image data file compression technique that makes a prediction based on past history to estimate the current value of a datum and then generates a correction term to correct any error.

prefiltering Filtering before sampling.

prefiltering, glossy A technique that uses the Phong bidirectional reflectance distribution function (BRDF) to apply appropriate blurring to environment maps. Each texel of the filtered environment map is produced by finding its corresponding unit vector (used as the outgoing direction) and computing the color at that texel with the following integral:

$$pref(o) = s \cdot c \cdot \int_{\Omega} p(o \cdot i)^{\frac{1}{r}} \cdot orig(i) \cdot d\omega(i)$$

where:

orig is the original texture map.

pref is the prefiltered texture map.

r is the roughness parameter (reciprocal of the Phong exponent).

s is the coefficient of specularity.

practical light.

c is the Phong correction factor, $(r+1) / \pi$.

i and o are the incoming and outgoing directions (respectively).

$p(x)$ is a function that returns x if x >= 0 and returns 0 otherwise.

Ω is the domain of the integral, the unit sphere.

$d\omega(i)$ is the measure of the solid angle in the direction of i.

pregenerated sequence A sequence of numbers that is generated while developing a game program and is stored to provide seeds for selecting random numbers used in creating game actions. One benefit of pregenerating a fixed set of numbers is that we can avoid repetition within the sequence. We can simply remove any duplicates and regenerate a series of replacements.

premastering The process whereby data files are converted into a compact disc format for producing CD-ROMs. A 288-byte error correction block is added to every 2048-byte user block.

Premiere The original QuickTime editing program, developed by Adobe Systems, used in video editing to produce broadcast-quality movies for video, film, multimedia, and the Web.

preparatory movement A movement in an animation that occurs just prior to a major action. Before an actor participates in an action, there is usually some hint about what is to occur. Think of a tiger about to leap on its prey. The tiger's body tenses, it goes into an anticipatory crouch, and the powerful spring of its muscles readies for the jump. Preparatory motions create more realistic animations. Compared to actions like leaping, preparatory motions take up to three or four times (and sometimes more) as long as the action will take. The keyframes are spaced widely apart, leading to slower and smoother motion overall. It is this preparatory movement that lends an air of anticipation and suspense to an animation.

preroll The process of rewinding the videotape to a cue point several seconds prior to the in-point so that playback of the tape is stabilized and up to full speed when the tape reaches the in-point.

preview/playback screen A part of the *Bryce* Advanced Motion Lab that allows the user to preview any adjustments that have been made to the animation. The VCR controls below are the same as those in the Animation palette, the Terrain Editor, and the Materials Lab.

Prewitt operators A pair of 3×3 matrices used to sharpen the edges of objects in an image.

Primal Particles A plug-in for *trueSpace* that creates complicated particle effects through an intuitive interface.

Primal Particles **and explosions F/X** See *explosions F/X*.

Primal Particles **and fire F/X** See *fire F/X using Primal Particles*.

Primal Particles **and shockwave F/X** See *shockwave F/X*.

primary colors Fundamental colors (red, green, and blue) that create a *secondary color* when mixed. These hues are said to be "pure colors." (*see Figure next page.*)

primary light See *key light*.

prime lens A lens with fixed-focal length. It usually produces a sharper image than does a zoom lens.

primitive A graphics object for which processing is included in a graphics or rendering program. Primitives may be rendered directly or combined to create more complex graphics objects.

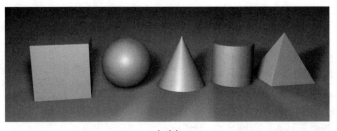

primitives.

primitive instancing The definition by a modeling system of a set of primitive three-dimensional solid objects that are relevant to the application area.

primitives menu A menu of selections in most 3D applications that contains basic objects used for modeling. The standard primitives include the sphere, cube, cone, cylinder, and torus.

Primitives Plus A plug-in for *trueSpace*. Options include Shape Used, Noise Scale, Falloff and Direction, Detail Level, and Random Seed.

printed circuit board (PCB) A plastic board coated with copper on one or both sides. The copper coating is etched to create a pattern of wire connections. Holes are then drilled for mounting electronic components to the board.

printer control language (PCL) A common page description language for laser printers developed by Hewlett-Packard.

Print Screen A computer command that saves an image of the data on the monitor display screen, which may then be printed.

print spooler A memory buffer devoted to the printer and the software needed to transfer data being printed to this memory. This frees up the computer for other use while the printer loads and prints directly from the memory buffer.

prioritization The sorting of graphics objects according to their closeness to the observer.

priority, display The order in which images of objects are posted to the display, thereby determining which images overlap others.

priority ordered Describes graphics objects listed in order from near to far for occlusion processing, which takes place during rendering of a graphics image.

priority queue Similar to a queue, with one important difference: all inserted elements are immediately sorted in descending order based on a comparison using the < (less than) operator. Because of the sorting functionality, an additional third parameter is offered in the constructor, allowing one to override the default < operator with his own function. This ability is useful if the programmer is inserting pointers to objects instead of passing in the objects by value. Avoiding sorting the queue based on the value of the pointers requires writing a functor class that calls the < operator after first de-referencing the pointers.

prism A special optical construct (usually a single piece of glass) that can split light into its component parts.

procedural materials Material textures in a 3D application created from mathematical formulae (algorithms).

procedural surface A graphics surface that is implicitly defined for modeling by specifying the equation of a curve or solid, by giving the expression for sweeping such a curve or solid through space, or by Boolean intersections of simpler solids using constructive solid geometry.

procedural texturing Mathematically calculated fractal images that are generated by a shader in *trueSpace* at render time, and can be used to surface anything from water to rock. Procedural texturing provides an unlimited resolution, untiling texture with fully keyframeable parameters for detail, noise, velocity (speed of movement), and color.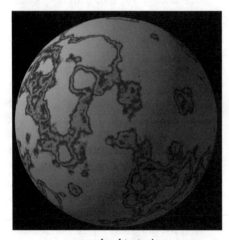

procedural texturing.

process color printing The production of a full-color image on paper by combining two or more subtractive color inks. The colors used for full-color reproduction are cyan, magenta, yellow, and black.

process separation The creation of the four negatives used to generate the cyan, magenta, yellow, and black subtractive color images in process color printing.

production board A hardbacked set of spreadsheets designed specifically for organizing film production.

production designer The designer who is responsible for the look of the entire production. He supervises the set decorators, costumes, and other visual artists.

production strip A removable color-coded paper strip that fits into the spreadsheet layout of the production board and allows for easy reorganization.

profile In *form•Z*, the closed curve of an object, seen from the orthogonal side and orthogonal top view. There are a number of ways to derive a profile curve. One way is to use scanned plan drawings of the target object as underlays. The plans should contain side and top elevations. Simply sketch a polyline around the desired shape and convert to C-Curve. Use C-Curve controls to match as closely as possible the curvature of the C-Curve to the curvature of the elevation drawing. Be sure to include enough control points in the source polyline to handle the curvature changes.

profile lofting In *form•Z*, a technique for deriving complex single-object solids or surface mesh objects. Profile lofting works best for objects whose silhouettes, when viewed from orthogonal views, do not self intersect. The shape of any curvilinear solid or surface can be broken down into four basic construction components: two profiles (one side profile and one top profile), any number of cross-sections, and a general loft trajectory.

profiling Monitoring a spot or segment of code to find the "hot spots" in source code. Anyone (other programmers, producers, designers, artists, and testers) can view this information on screen. This information makes profiling an accessible tool that ultimately helps fine-tune code and find bugs. The profiler gives the following important data: the unique name of the sample point; the average, minimum, and maximum percentages of frame time spent on that sample; the number of times the sample was called per frame; and the relationship of this sample point to other sample points (parent/child).

programmable array logic (PAL) An integrated circuit that contains an array of logic gates that can be permanently programmed for a particular purpose.

programmable read-only memory (PROM) Digital memory in which data can be stored permanently by one write operation. Data can be read many times, but cannot be rewritten.

progressive mesh (PM) A triangle-based mesh that is able to vary its level of detail in real-time, gaining or losing a couple of triangles at a time, while preserving its original shape as much as possible. It can be drawn at any detail level between the conventional mesh from which it was created and a lowest detail "base mesh" as defined by the detail reduction heuristic, which may be as small as no polygons at all. Typically, these meshes are rendered at lower detail in the distance, so that more system resources are available to draw higher-resolution meshes in the foreground. The global detail level of the graphics engine can also be based on the power of the computer it is running on.

progressive refinement Rendering a coarse version of a picture first and then improving upon it during idle computer cycles, rather than initially rendering a picture in its final form.

progressive scan A type of video display in which each horizontal line is scanned consecutively from top to bottom, resulting in a full frame of video without the need for fields.

projection The mapping of the surface of a three-dimensional object onto another, differently shaped surface, or vice versa.

projection implementation, parallel The process of transforming a scene that is defined in world-coordinate positions to canonical view volume.

projection implementation, perspective The process of transforming a scene that is defined in world-coordinate positions to perspective-projection canonical view volume.

projection mapping See *flat mapping*.

projection matrix A matrix that transforms a three-dimensional object to a two-dimensional image on a projection plane perpendicular to the z axis.

projection plane A plane upon which rays emanating from a three-dimensional scene are projected to give a two-dimensional image.

projection reference point (PRP) A point that defines the center and direction of projection.

projection textures The application of a texture to an object where the value of the texture function is constant along certain parallel lines in the object volume.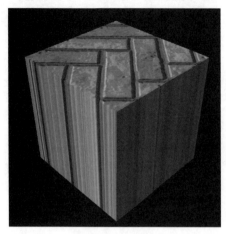

projection textures.

projector A straight projection ray emanating from a center of projection, passing through a point in an object, and intersecting a *projection plane*.

Projector One of the *Photoshop* filters from the Corel *KPT* collection, used to transform an image into a perspective image.

PROM See *programmable read-only memory*.

ProMist A high contrast filter that can be used to reduce contrast to achieve more of a film look to a scene.

prop 1. Short for *property*, any object on a set that is used by the actors (e.g., a knife), as opposed to set dressing and scenery that provide a backdrop for the action. 2. Any element in a *Poser* scene that is not a part of any *Poser* figure. A prop can be a sphere that acts as a ball, or a staircase that the figure navigates.

propagated light Light that arrives at a surface and is then transmitted again in some way.

prop morphing *Poser* allows the use of deformations on props, just as they are used on figure elements. Use any of *Poser*'s Grouping and Morph Target Deformation Tools to augment the shape of any prop.

ProTools Professional audio editing hardware, manufactured by DigiDesign, that provides multichannel, high-quality digital recording with real-time effects and editing.

prototile A small, geometric figure used repeatedly to fill a plane.

ProVTR A capture utility by Pipeline.

proximity search A search in which two words can be specified together with the maximum number of words that may occur between them and every occurrence that meets this specification is detected.

proximity testing 1. A method of reducing a color image to fourteen colors by finding the face of a cuboctahedron that is nearest to the coordinates of the point in three-dimensional space that defines the original color. 2. A method of testing objects in games against each other to determine how close they are to each other.

proxy A placeholder. A proxy is often used in editing programs to take the place of video that has yet to be shot, or that has yet to be digitized at the highest quality.

proxy modeling enhancements In *Poser*, a model can be a temporary proxy for other figure types, simply by selecting that figure from the Figure Height item on the Figure menu. Alternate Figure

Height types include Baby, Toddler, Child, Juvenile, Adolescent, Ideal Adult, Fashion Model, and Heroic Model. All that is adjusted is the proportions of the figures' anatomical geometry. Otherwise, all costuming remains intact. Selecting a Business figure for instance, and then selecting the Baby Figure Height, will result in a baby that is attired in a business suit.

proxy server A server that stores information from other servers. Instead of allowing users to access other servers, it distributes outside Web sites from its own server.

PRP See *projection reference point.*

pruning, structure network The elimination of a part of a structure network that does not need to be examined because it is outside the clipping limits of the view volume.

pseudocoloring Use of a color table to assign colors other than the natural object colors to an image.

pseudorandom number A number generated by an algorithm that produces a series of numbers that have all of the characteristics of random numbers, except that the set is periodic with a very large period. All such algorithms must have an initial value which provides input to the calculations. At the end of each iteration, the resulting value is used as the initial value for the next iteration. The original value is called the *seed*, because it is the value from which all subsequent values are "grown." By keeping the seed constant each time, we retain a scientific approach in evaluating the differences between algorithms.

pseudorealism, rendering See *photorealistic rendering*.

Psychedelic function A function in *Carrara* that simulates waves and swirls of differing levels and blends. Using this function, the user can generate smooth blends from color to color or function to function, or any combination of the above. The Psychedelic function is often used as a mixer in the Color channel and/or all by itself in the Bump channel. It can also create a hypnotic effect.

Psychedelic function.

puck An input device similar to a mouse but with a number of additional special-purpose pushbuttons. It is used in creating computer graphics.

Puddle A filter from AlienSkin's *Eye-Candy* collection for *Photoshop* that causes gelatinous-like blobs to appear over selected portions of the image.

Pulfrich effect A technique that can be used to create a 3D illusion. This depends on the fact that the eye requires longer to process dim images than bright ones. The Pulfrich effect is most effective when viewed with glasses having one dark lens. Colored lenses alter the color perception of the picture. Genuine

353

Pulfrich glasses do not require colored lenses, therefore allowing perfect, unaltered program color. Furthermore, if animation is created of a scene rotating about a vertical axis, and the appropriate eye is covered with a dark filter, the scene will appear in 3D. If the left eye is the one darkened then the scene must be rotating clockwise at about 40 degrees per second for the effect to occur.

pull focus A technique used to change focal lengths during a large camera or subject move, such as a dolly. The camera assistant literally moves the lens to compensate for the camera/subject movement so that the subject remains in focus throughout the shot. Also known as *pulling*.

pull-up To shorten the pauses in a scene to pick up the pace.

pulse code modulation (PCM) The modulation of a carrier with pulses whose presence at a given position represents the existence of a one in a binary number. The series of binary numbers often represents samples of an analog signal.

pulse function A function that is used to perform low-pass filtering in the frequency domain.

pupil The opening in the eye left by the iris.

pure 1. Appearing saturated in color. 2. A monochromatic (single-frequency) color, as produced by a laser beam.

purity The degree to which a uniformly-colored region is correctly displayed, particularly on a shadow-mask cathode-ray tube.

Purkinje effect The change in color perception for low light levels as the eye adjusts from day (scoptic) vision (using primarily the cones as receptors) to night (photopic) vision (using primarily the rods as receptors). Reds and oranges appear to lose brightness relative to blues and greens.

Puzzle One of the filters from the Alien-Skin *Xenofex* collection for *Photoshop* that breaks an image into puzzle pieces.

puzzle games A game genre in which pieces fall from above and must be lined up before they hit bottom; or, the player must have to fit them all together in the most efficient manner. The goal is to eliminate open spaces between the pieces. The pieces become more complex and fall faster as the game progresses. *Tetris*, and *Dr. Mario* are examples of puzzle games.

pyramid A solid having five faces; a square base and four triangle sides.

PyroCluster A plug-in for *trueSpace* for creating advanced pyrotechnic effects.

PyroCluster.

Q

Q The green-to-magenta component of a color represented in the YIQ color coordinate space. It is the *quadrature* component in a composite color television signal.

QBF The message, *The quick brown fox jumped over the lazy dog*. It is used for testing printers and displays.

QE See *quality engineering*.

QTVR QuickTime Virtual Reality. A QuickTime format that wraps a scene using either cylindrical or cubic mapping, so that by interacting with the image, the user feels as if he is standing at the center of a 3D space.

quad See *quadrilateral*.

quad, concave A quad in which it is possible to draw a line between two vertices that does not pass entirely through the quad.

quad, convex A quad in which every line segment connecting two vertices is entirely within the quad.

quad, generalized Any quad, including ones that are self-intersecting or non-planar.

quadrant In two-dimensional geometry, one of the four quarters into which the plane is divided by the orthogonal *x* and *y* axes of the Cartesian coordinate system.

quadrant lighting See *Rembrandt lighting*.

quadratic blending The interpolation between two colors by using the function $N(t) = (1 - t)^2 N_1 + t^2 N_2$.

quadratic interpolation The use of quadratic functions as blending functions in creating a Bezier curve.

quadratic polynomials Polynomial equations used to define conic surfaces.

quadratic spline A piecewise function that interpolates a given set of points. Given a set of points (x1,y1), (x2,y2), ..., (xn,yn) where each x is greater than the previous x, a qaudratic spline consists of n−1 degree 2 (i.e., quadratic) functions f1, f2, ..., f[n−1] which interpolate the points. Each function f[i] represents the interval from x[i] to x[i+1]. The values of the function f[i] at the endpoints x[i] and x[i+1] are exactly y[i] and y[i+1] respectively. Furthermore, at a point x[i], the derivative of the function f[i] and the derivative of the function f[i−1] (on the previous interval) have the same value, making the derivative of the overall spline continuous. Compare to the more often used *cubic spline*.

quadratic surface equation The general implicit equation for a quadric surface. When expressed as a 4 × 4 matrix it is said to be in the quadric form.

quadric Koch curve One of the Koch family of fractal curves generated by the initiator-generator technique. Quadric Koch curves have a square as the initiator and have a generator that is made up of line segments that meet at 90-degree angles.

quadric surface A curved surface that is the locus of all points that satisfy a second-degree polynomial equation having three variables. Depending upon the coefficients of the various terms of the equation, the quadric surface may be a sphere, a paraboloid, an ellipsoid, a cone, a hyperboloid, or a hyperbolic paraboloid.

quadrilateral A graphics figure that is defined by four vertices connected by line segments. Also known as a *quad*.

quadrilateral mesh See *polygon mesh*.

quad tessellation The subdivision of a quad into two triangles.

quadtree The organization of two-dimensional space into a tree by starting with a square that encompasses all of the desired space and then recursively subdividing squares into four smaller squares until the lowest desired level of detail is reached.

quality engineering (QE) The processes whereby the quality of a designed and/or manufactured product is assured.

quantization coefficient A coefficient that is applied to blocks of data in the JPEG file compression algorithm to reduce high frequency information and thereby increase image compression.

quantization technique A method for reducing a large number of colors to the limited number available for a particular display mode. Such techniques include *uniform quantization*, use of the *popularity algorithm*, *median cut*, and *octree quantization*.

quantization transform A one-to-one pixel transformation used to modify or enhance an image.

quantized noise A digitally-sampled noise signal that is almost identical to the original analog noise signal.

quantizing The process of measuring an analog signal to determine its amplitude at sample points with a sampling rate chosen for the equipment. The measured amplitude of each sample is then converted to a digital code to produce *pulse code modulation*.

quantum mechanics The theory that energy is emitted in packets or quanta.

quarter ellipse algorithm An algorithm that draws a quarter of an ellipse (a curve that spans $\pi/2$ radians of elliptical arc) by performing an affine transformation of a quarter circle.

quartic roots The roots of a fourth-degree equation. Such an equation can be used to represent a large number of different solids.

quartic surface A curved surface that is the locus of all points that satisfy a third-degree polynomial equation having three variables. Depending upon the coefficients of the various terms of the equation, various geometric objects may be obtained. The torus is an example of an object with a quartic surface.

quartz halogen lamp A type of tungsten light in a sealed casing that emits a bright to medium soft light.

quaternion An alternative mathematical entity used by 3D graphics programmers to represent rotations. The use of quaternions has advantages over rotation matrices in many situations, because quaternions require less storage space, concatenation of quaternions requires fewer arithmetic operations, and quaternions are more easily interpolated for producing smooth animation. A quaternion is represented by a set of four numbers, one of which is a scalar, and the other three represent the three-dimensional components of a three-dimensional vector that has a coordinate system represented by three mutually orthogonal unit vectors *i, j,* and *k*. Quaternions extend the concept of a square root of –1 to have three square roots of –1, being i, j, and k:

$$i * i = -1$$
$$j * j = -1$$
$$k * k = -1$$

Multiplication of pairs of these elements together behaves much like the cross products of the usual three axes in 3D space:

$$i * j = -j * i = k$$
$$j * k = -k * j = i$$
$$k * i = -i * k = j$$

This means that quaternions are defined in terms of a real number and an i, j, and k term. Because i, j, and k behave like axes, quaternions are sometimes written as a vector (here **v**) and a scalar (**s**) or as a vector of their four terms.

$$q = w + x\,i + y\,j + z\,k$$

$q = [s\ v]$ where s = w and v = [x y z]

$q = [x\ y\ z\ w]$ note scalar "w" at the end

Transformations in three-dimensional space can be implemented with quaternions without any singularities occurring. See also *quaternions, camera control.*

quaternion calculus The following are some calculus functions of quaternions: Let $q = \cos(\theta) + v\sin(\theta)$ be a unit quaternion (v is a three-dimensional unit vector).

Euler's identity for complex numbers applies to quaternions:

$$q = \cos(\theta) + v\sin(\theta) = \exp(v\theta)$$

From this identity, we can define the power function for quaternions:

$$q^t = [\cos(\theta) + v\sin(\theta)]^t = \exp(vt\theta) = \cos(t\theta) + v\sin(t\theta)$$

We can also express the logarithm of a quaternion using this identity:

$$\log(q) = \log(\exp(v\theta)) = v\theta$$

We can express the derivative of q^t as:

$$(q^t)' = q^t\log(q)$$

Applying the chain rule, we can express the derivative of $q^{f(t)}$:

$$(q^{f(t)})' = f'(t)q^{f(t)}\log(q)$$

Applying the chain rule for functions of two independent variables, we can express the derivative of $q(t)^{f(t)}$ (t omitted for clarity):

$$(q^f)' = f'q^f\log(q) + q'fq^{f-1}$$

quaternion interpolation A mathematical interpolation technique that produces inbetween motions that are more predictable between poses, but can cause strange discontinuities when graphing individual rotation parameters. The interpolation happens by using all three rotation channels at once, instead of simply interpolating each one individually (which is the default).

quaternions, camera control Quaternions have become an integral part of game programming and play an important role in camera-orientation techniques. There are many benefits to using quaternions to internally represent orientations. The three-parameter representation of Euler angles requires trigonometry and nine-parameter orthogonal matrices. Quaternions, on the other hand, require only four parameters and are less computationally expensive. When it comes to view interpolation, the Euler angle implementation is inherently buggy. If one wishes to rotate the object 90 degrees in the Y-axis (yaw = $\pi/2$), this operation rotates the X-axis onto the negative Z-axis, because each rotation is computed separately. Hence, the result of a rotation in the X-axis by an angle θ is the same as rotating $-\theta$ in the Z-axis. In other words, the camera will roll when a change in the yaw is applied. This parametric singularity is called *gimbal lock*. Because of this lock, interpolating through these singularities produces strange and most likely unwanted results. Quaternions, on the other hand, do not have this problem, and can be interpolated quite easily. By representing camera orientation with quaternions, one can perform smooth interpolations between two viewpoints.

queue A number of tasks arranged in a line waiting for processing.

QuickDirt A plug-in for *3ds max* that creates a noisy texture that emulates dirt or grime for a selected object.

QuickDraw A graphics package for the Apple computer.

QuickTime A software architecture for displaying and manipulating time-based data (such as video and audio) on a computer.

QuickTime Animation codec A compressor for reducing the size of animated sequences.

quiz games A game genre in which questions are displayed in multiple choice format, with three or four answers. Examples of this genre include *You Don't Know Jack*, *Who Wants to Be a Millionaire*, and *Jeopardy*.

QWERTY keyboard The standard keyboard, named for the arrangement of the left side of the first row of letters.

R

Racial Morphs In Poser, a series of pre-crafted morphs that affect those areas of a face normally associated with racial features. Each feature involved can also be reconfigured to create a unique personal look within each racial group.

racing game A game genre that centers around the concept of driving at accelerated speeds around different tracks. Originally, 2D racing games were made with a scrolling road and the sprite of the car moving over the surface. With the increased popularity of the color *Gameboy*, these games are becoming more popular. Examples of racing games include *Wipeout*, *Destruction Derby*, *Mario Kart*, and *South Park Derby*.

rack focus A camera shot in which the focus is set on an object in the background, then the focus is pulled, or "racked," to an object in the foreground (or vice-versa).

radial acceleration The acceleration of a track on a rotating disk toward or away from the center of rotation. Radial acceleration occurs when a track is not perfectly centered.

radial light 1. A light that casts illumination in all directions from its center. 2. One of four types of light used in *Bryce*. The radial light is represented by the spherical light icon in the Create toolbar. Radial lights are useful for illuminating everything in a scene equally from a single light source. Radial lights also throw illumination on the ground plane, which no other light does. Illumination from radial lights is represented by a circular patch on the objects that receive the light. 3. In *Universe* a radial light is synonymous with a real-world lightbulb. It is a source of light that radiates in a spherical pattern from the center point. One can adjust the fall-off and intensity of a radial light to simulate various real-world bulb-based lights.

radial sort method A technique for generating images in which the database contains world coordinates for all surfaces of the model, and the computer program determines which surfaces are visible or hidden, depending upon the viewing angle.

radiance The radiant intensity per unit of foreshortened surface area, measured in watts per steradian times square meters.

radiant intensity The flux radiated into a unit solid angle in a particular direction, measured in watts per steradian.

radiation The transfer or release of energy through particle emission. All objects emit some form of radiation.

radiation, reflected *Reflected radiation* (such as blacktop or metal giving off heat) is the type of radiation that is reflected off objects and is indirectly distributed. Radiation from objects that are not self-burning or undergoing a chemical reaction is considered reflected radiation.

radiation, thermal *Thermal radiation is* the type of radiation that depends on the temperature of the object emitting it. This means that any radiation given off by an object is generated from that object itself. Sunlight and light from burning objects are examples of thermal radiation.

radio button interaction technique An interaction technique patterned after the tuning buttons on car radios.

radio cut An edit of a scene based on dialogue only, disregarding the picture.

radio-frequency interference (RFI) Electrical noise or unwanted spurious emissions at radio frequencies that interfere with normal transmissions.

radiometer An instrument used to measure light intensity or radiance, in actual physical units independent of the human eye's sensitivity to various wavelengths or levels of intensity.

radiosity 1. In computer graphics, an algorithm for rendering graphics scenes by computing the balancing of light energy coming toward and going away from every point on a surface. Radiosity is a powerful and photorealistic rendering engine. Radiosity analyzes a scene and treats every object and surface as a po-

radiosity.

tential light source. This allows incoming light to bounce off surfaces and change characteristics as it goes. This detailed manner of handling light makes radiosity a very sophisticated rendering method. One drawback is that calculating extra bounces of light is extremely time intensive. It is not unusual for a radiosity rendering to take from 4 to 100 times longer than a raytracing render. 2. The rate of energy leaving a surface per unit time and unit area.

RAID See *redundant array of inexpensive or independent disks*.

RailBevel A command in *LightWave's* Modeler that creates a bevel on a selected object based upon a rail or curve in a background layer.

rainbows A rainbow generator in *Bryce* that functions in accordance with the laws of optics. The sun must be positioned in the opposite direction from the viewer of the rainbow. If a rainbow is in the west, the sun must be in the east.

RAMDAC See *random access memory digital-to-analog converter*.

rand function A function available in many computer language libraries that generates random numbers. It has low precision (many implementations have only 15 bits) and therefore not suitable when high precision is required.

random access memory digital-to-analog converter (RAMDAC) A digital-to-analog converter that, instead of providing a linear conversion, compensates for color or gamma correction through the use of a built-in table contained in RAM.

random dither A method of creating dot patterns that permits printing of a photographic image with a device that can print only in black or white. Similar to *halftoning*.

random fractal A fractal curve that is generated using a stochastic process.

random iteration algorithm A technique for rendering pictures of attractors of an iterated function system by starting with a point and randomly performing one of a set of contractive affine transformations.

random noise function See *Perlin noise function*.

random numbers Numbers selected from a range, usually from 0 to some maximum value. The computer performs a mathematical algorithm to generate the "random" selections. A good random number algorithm should meet the following characteristics: 1. When numbers of random numbers are selected, the probability of selecting each number within the range must be the same. This can easily be determined by methods of probability. 2. When numerous random numbers are selected, there must be no discernible pattern of the numbers. Thus, an algorithm that provided numbers 1 through n and then repeated this process as many times as necessary would meet the first condition, but obviously does not meet the second condition. Unfortunately, although patterns are very discernible to the human eye, they are very difficult to analyze mathematically. Random numbers are essential in creating games that have an indeterminate outcome, whether used for simple tasks, like shuffling a deck of cards, or to create unique worlds or universes.

random patrol option An option in the *Game Creation System* that sets enemy behavior. The enemy walks about at random, and then chases the player when finally observed.

random scan display A display in which each vector or character is drawn by direct deflection, so that the electron beam is used to trace the actual line or character shape on the screen at the appropriate location. This is in contrast to a *raster scan*, where the beam scans the CRT face in an orderly fashion and is illuminated at those points where a picture element is to be other than black. *Random scan* is faster as long as no complex colored backgrounds are required.

range contrast The ratio of the brightest area of a display to the dimmest area.

raptor A dinosaur model available in *Poser* (*see Figure next page*).

raster The arrangement of pixels as a two-dimensional array or grid in a display monitor.

raster coordinates The coordinate system that defines the location of pixels

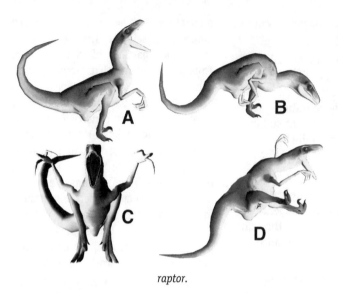

raptor.

rasterize To convert a picture into pixel-sized elements for display on a raster display.

raster lines A set of horizontal lines, each made up of a row of pixels, which defines a display image.

raster operation (ROP) Any logical operation (e.g., AND, OR, NOT, NOR, XOR, etc.) that is performed on the bit planes of a frame buffer in the course of performing block moves, fades, etc., of video data. Also known as *raster-op*.

raster rotation The rotation of a digitized graphics raster by an arbitrary angle.

on a raster display. By convention, the coordinate (0,0) is at the top left-hand corner of the display.

raster display A computer display in which the screen is scanned in an orderly fashion from left to right for each line and then from top to bottom for the frame to produce a rectangular array of pixels. The scanning technique is known as *raster scan* and is the most common method of creating a computer or television display.

raster graphic An image file format that contains the color information for each pixel. Raster graphics' file sizes are relatively large.

raster image processor (RIP) The part of a graphics reproducing printer that reads bitmap instructions and translates them into actions of the print mechanism.

rastering The sharp transitions between adjacent pixels due to high-frequency components that are beyond the sampling range.

raster scan A technique used to create a computer or television display, in which the electron beams of a cathode-ray tube are scanned across the face of the tube in an orderly fashion, beginning at the top left corner, traveling from left to right with a slight downward motion, moving back to the left edge at the next lower line level when the right edge is reached and proceeding thus until the last scan line is drawn, at which point the beam jumps back to the top left corner. At any point on the scanning path the beams may be activated to produce a spot of light of the desired color on the screen.

raster shearing The rotation of a raster through the use of shear matrices.

raster space The coordinate system used to identify the location of pixels when displaying an image on a monitor.

raster text Textual characters defined by patterns of pixels that are applied to a monitor image during raster scan.

ratio information Information (such as temperature, height, weight, or quantity) in which there are varying distances between categories.

ray casting See *ray tracing.*

ray collision test, octrees for The octree can be used for culling in collision detection. Consider the simple case of a ray collision test. Two points define a collision ray: a start and an end point. The collision test begins by finding the leaf node of the octree that the start point lies within. The segment is broken into a subsegment at each cube face it intersects. The new subsegment is tested against all the geometry and objects within its node. The next subsegment starts at the end point of the previous subsegment, in the node that neighbors the cube face that it intersected. This traversal through neighbors continues, colliding with the geometry and objects at every node until the original end point is reached. Several other collision tests such as axis-aligned box and sphere tests also work very well when using the octree.

ray depth See *transparency recursion.*

Ray Dream Studio A 3D application, now superseded by *Carrara,* developed by Eovia Software and marketed by Meta-Creations.

ray, eye A ray from the center of projection through the center of a pixel into the scene.

RayFX toolset A toolset that can create soft shadows from single light instances. RayFX toolset does not negate the principle and logic behind the use of a light array. In fact, it enhances the effect of a light array setup since a few lights would perform the function of many.

ray-object intersection In ray tracing, the intersection of the backward ray that passes from the eye to the screen with some object in the scene. This is the fundamental operation in any ray tracing algorithm.

ray rejection test In ray tracing, a test that rejects all eye rays that do not intersect with objects in the scene.

raytrace evaluation A means of evaluating meshes created in *form•Z.* Raytrace evaluation is intended to back up the results of the hidden line evaluation. Raytraced evaluation is usually performed after hidden line evaluation, and usually shows no undesirable mesh qualities. Raytrace evaluation has two purposes. The first is to confirm findings of the hidden line evaluation, and the second is to locate any shading anomalies and mesh problems that hidden line failed to pick up. Also known as *Phong evaluation.*

ray tracing The creation of a realistic image by tracing light rays. In *forward ray tracing,* all rays of light illuminating a scene are traced from the light source

ray tracing.

ray tracing.

to the object they intersect; if there are reflections or refractions the tracing continues until the ray leaves the scene. In *backward ray tracing,* rays are traced from the observer to the display screen back to the scene objects and light source. The result is that all reflections and shadows appear in the image without being specifically described in the scene description. Also known as *ray casting.*

ray tracing, bi-directional Backward and forward ray tracing can be combined to generate realistic light transfer phenomena, especially in the simulation of focused specularity. This process of combining backward and forward ray tracing, called *bidirectional ray tracing,* traces from the eye as well as the light source. Most raytracers are not bidirectional.

RCA connector A small, single prong connector most commonly used to carry composite video and unbalanced audio signals. Also known as a *phono connector.*

RCTC (Rewriteable Consumer Time Code) A timecode developed for use with consumer Hi8 video equipment.

reaction phase The portion of a game in which any effects on objects not di-

rectly affected by the action phase are generated.

reaction shot A shot of a person in a scene as he reacts to the dialogue or action of the scene.

real estate distribution The assignment of input data to whichever window on a display currently contains the cursor.

realistic rendering Producing images that include the lighting, coloring, shadows, reflections, etc., of a real-world scene.

RealMedia A special streaming video and audio architecture created by RealNetworks, Inc.

real time Describes the process of accepting incoming data immediately displaying them as fast as the data occur in the real world. A function, such as playback or recording, that occurs in real time, does not require additional rendering or any acceleration of the process, such as 4x (quadruple speed) recording.

real-time editing Editing occurs in *real time,* without having to be calculated or rendered before they can be seen.

real-time strategy game A game genre in which a quick response to opponents' moves is important. The faster player is able to make many moves in a short period of time. These games are similar to *simulation games,* since the player usually oversees a large battle or war, as well as the building of towns and outposts. *Populous, Syndicate, Warcraft,* and *Command and Conquer* are examples of real-time strategy games.

receiver objects, shadow maps When rendering objects that are in shadow, there are many different ways to draw the object receiving the shadow. If there is no other texture on the receiver object, we can draw it in one pass, applying a black-on-white shadow map as a texture and using the light source to illuminate the object. This is called *single pass rendering*. If a receiver already has a texture on it and the hardware does not support multitexturing, we need multiple passes. This is called *multipass rendering with subtractive blending*. These two are the most common methods of drawing the object receiving the shadow.

receptive fields Portions of the eye that detect orientation, accutance, and line. They respond to vertical, horizontal, and specific orientations of visual stimuli, which are governed mainly by light and dark tonally-contrasting stimuli. The light and dark stimuli excite and inhibit the cells in the receptive field; these stimuli need to be located in a specific place in the visual field and they do respond to a single point of light. They also respond to a series of aligned lights in a particular area of the receptive field. The complex receptive fields have a larger receptive field than the simple cells. They are called complex because they do not blindly respond to contrasting tones that are oriented in a specific way, and they never respond to a single point source of light.

reconstruction The attempt to rebuild a replica of an original signal from sampled data.

Recording Rollup A menu in the *Primal Particles* plug-in for *trueSpace* that allows the user to set the length of the particle animation in keyframes (Frames setting). The user has the option to record the particle animation in the forward or reverse (Direction setting) direction. Using the Reverse setting reverses

the direction of the particle animation so they flow toward the emitter rather than away. The user can also set the starting frame for the particles if he wants them to start at a specific frame (*trueSpace* Start Frame and *Primal Particles* Start Frame settings).

recording zone The portion of a disk upon which data can be recorded.

rectangle and filled rectangle tools Tools available in *The Games Factory*, *Universe*, and other programs that allow the user to draw rectangles and squares more easily than by trying to construct them out of four separate lines.

RectArray script An independent script in *tsxPython* that is used in *trueSpace*. It is loaded and run by the user, and is then dismissed once it has accomplished its task. RectArray is used to make a number of copies of an object and place them in a rectangular array using user-defined spacing between rows, columns, and levels.

rectilinear domain A domain composed of Cartesian products of intervals of R.

recto In typography, the right-hand page of a book or magazine. The left-hand page is called *verso*.

recursive computation A mathematical process involving an equation that finds a new value for a variable when the current value is known. The new value is then inserted in the equation and the equation is solved again to obtain the next value in the series. This process is repeated as often as desired (*See Figure on next page*).

recursive subdivision, curves and surfaces A process of drawing a curve or surface by recursively dividing the curve and finding intermediate points until

recursive computation.

the control points are sufficiently close to the curve itself.

redo command A command that reinstates the last action canceled by the *undo command*.

Reduce Degree tool A tool in *Universe* that reduces the number of NURBS control vertices and control hulls used to represent a surface.

reduced instruction set computer (RISC) A computer that uses a microprocessor with fewer and faster instructions. Many instructions that are usually built into the microprocessor must be computed by software in the RISC microprocessor. The RISC is faster than the usual microprocessor system.

Reduce Points. Reduce Polygons A command in *LightWave* that allows the user to reduce the selected points or polygons on a selected object or object area. Other 3D applications offer similar commands.

redundant array of inexpensive or independent disks (RAID) A group of disk drives connected by software, increasing speed of access and allowing all data to be written twice, so that if a single drive fails, no data will be permanently lost.

ReelMotion A plug-in for *LightWave* and *3ds max* that permits generation of animated sequences.

Reels The collection of animations contained in the ArtBeats *ReelMotion* volumes, collections of photographic effects and images.

re-entrant polygon clipping An algorithm used for clipping a polygon to a convex polygonal clipping region. The input polygon is successively clipped to each edge of the clipping region until all edges have been applied. Also known as the *Sutherland-Hodgeman algorithm*.

reference geoid A standard model for the shape of the earth. The simplest form is a sphere having the mean equatorial radius of the earth.

reference model A collection of rules for determining the semantics of a graphics system.

reference port The hardware system that serves as a standard for the design and testing of a piece of software.

refinement, curves A process for improving the fidelity of a curve by adding an arbitrary number of control points to the curve's nonuniform B-spline representation.

refinement procedure A procedure used to create the image of an object in more detail.

reflectance The ratio of light reflected from the surface of an object to the light incident upon the surface. Reflectance is a key factor in making realistic water.

Reflectance A control in the Shaders panel of *trueSpace*. It allows the user to choose from predetermined settings such as Chrome, Glass, Metal, Mirror, or Phong.

reflectance map An image, often computed as a projection on a cube, used to reduce computation in rendering of reflecting surfaces. It is produced by first computing each point of an image as a function of the direction from the center point of the object and then referencing the image to the directions of reflected rays from the surface of the object. Also known as an *environment map*.

reflected light Light from an illumination source that is reflected back to the viewer from the surface of some object.

reflecting materials 1. Textures (procedural or bit-mapped) that are used in the reflection channel of an object. 2. A characteristic of materials that can be created with the *Poser* Surface Materials window.

reflection The return of a portion of the illumination that impinges on the surface of an object. ⬮

Reflection Bias A check box in *Universe* that allows the user to control the color of reflections.

reflection channel 1. A channel that allows an object to reflect other objects or environments around it. See *reflection map*.

reflection, diffuse The even reflection of light, regardless of the direction from which it came.

reflection, directional diffuse A reflection that is a combination of biased diffuse reflection (directional) and specular reflection.

reflection hologram Display holograms that are lit from the front. They can be hung on walls and illuminated simply with a clear high-intensity bulb. Reflection holograms can range from jewelry size, which can be made into pendants, key chains and paper weights, up to four to five feet, which are ideal for educational or display purposes.

reflection, law of The law of reflection states that the angle of the reflection equals the angle of the incidence as relative to the surface's normal, a line perpendicular to the reflecting surface at the point of incidence. This means

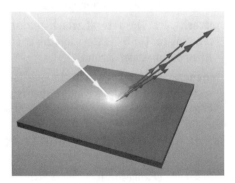

reflection.

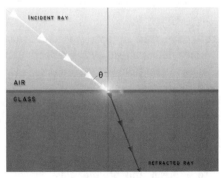

reflection, law of.

367

that the reflected light's angle is the same as the incoming light's angle.

reflection map An image mapped onto a surface to simulate the mirror-like reflections of other objects in the scene. Reflection maps allow the user to define which parts of an object will be reflective, and which areas will be matte. Unless a surface is perfectly reflective, its color will be evident in its reflections. As a result, a shader will give the user richer, more realistic reflections if the user copies its color into the reflection channel.

reflection recursion A setting that determines how many times an object is reflected. If two mirrors were placed facing each other, in theory, the reflections would reflect forever. 3D applications attempt to keep rendering times low by limiting the number of times the render attempts to draw the reflected image. Also known as *reflection depth*.

reflection, specular Focused reflection that is determined by the direction of the incoming light.

reflections, Torrance-Sparrow-Cooke illumination model See *Blinn shading*.

reflective light Light coming from an indirect source, such as a bounce card, the sky (but not the sun), etc. See also *incident light*.

reflective read An optical medium from which data are read by the reflection of a laser beam from the medium.

reflector A shiny board or fabric used to redirect a bright light source.

reflex camera A camera in which a mirror is interposed between the lens and the film to divert the incoming image to a prism and ground glass viewing

screen for use as a view finder. When the shutter-release button is pressed, the mirror first withdraws and then the shutter is opened.

refraction The bending of light rays when they pass through the boundary between two dissimilar materials. The *index of refraction* is a measure of this bending and is equivalent to the ratio of the speed of light in the two mediums.

refraction.

refresh 1. To reactivate the phosphor of a cathode-ray screen by repeatedly positioning the electron gun at the same point. This causes the phosphor to glow continually instead of fading after the beam is removed. 2. To recharge cells of a dynamic memory so that data stored in them do not dissipate and get lost.

refresh rate The rate at which refresh takes place. For U.S. television this is 60 Hz or 60 times per second.

regeneration strategy A technique for restoring a portion of a window that has been overlapped when it becomes visible again.

Regen tool A tool in *Universe* that regenerates a rendered image after the user has made changes to it.

region of interest (ROI) A portion of an image that is selected for further examination or processing.

registration The alignment or degree of alignment of two or more images that are to overlay. For example, in color printing, the red, green, yellow, and black ink images must register exactly to produce a quality color picture.

regularized Boolean set operations Operations of Boolean algebra that are defined in such a way that operations on solids always yield solids.

relative address The address of a datum in computer memory with respect to some reference address already stored in the computer. The sum of the reference address and the *relative address* should be the *absolute address* of the datum. Compare with *absolute address*.

relative index of refraction A measure of the amount of light that is refracted when a light ray passes through the surface of two dissimilar materials.

relaxation techniques Techniques in which an object that is required to meet certain constraints is moved so that the constraints become closer to being satisfied.

release print A print of a film that is sent to a theater for projection.

Rembrandt lighting The placement of a key light to the side of the camera with the light focused on the subject. The position of the key light in Rembrandt lighting is normally elevated above and placed to the side of the subject in portraiture. This placement illuminates three-quarters of the subject's surface. Rembrandt lighting is derived from the position of the sun in late morning or late afternoon, when it is above and to the side of the subject. The light at this position is flattering in the way it models the subject into a three-dimensional form. The contours and form of the face are revealed. This is the classic position of key light in painting and photography. Also known as *¾ lighting, quadrant lighting,* or *45-degree lighting*.

remote procedure call (RPC) A software function that is used while a computer is running another program, enabling it to run a subprogram on another computer in the same network.

render The computer process of taking the three-dimensional model with its accompanying textures and lights, and turning that into a two-dimensional image composed of an array of pixel colors. In simplest terms, when a computer "renders" it paints all the information thus far created.

render.

Render An icon in *trueSpace* that allows the user to select such options as raytracing and antialiasing.

renderfarm A group of computers used to render a single animation. Each computer in the series renders every x number of frames.

Render Info window A window in *Universe* that shows the characteristics that are being used to render an image and gives the user an opportunity to modify them.

rendering controls 1. Controls in a GUI that target rendering options. 2. A grouped array of five button controls in *Bryce* for single picture rendering. Rendering an animation is controlled by selecting the Render Animation command from the File menu. From left to right, the rendering controls are: Texture toggle, Fast Preview toggle, Render, Resume Render, and Clear and Render.

rendering equation An equation that expresses the transfer of light from one point to another in terms of the intensity of the light emitted from the first point to the second, together with the intensity of light emitted from all other points that reaches the first point and is reflected from it to the second point.

rendering style The style in which an image is rendered to produce a specific media look. Examples of rendering styles

rendering style.

include: silhouette, outline, wireframe, hidden line, lit wireframe, flat shaded, flat lined, cartoon, cartoon with lines, smooth shaded, smooth lined, and texture shaded. ◁◦

RenderMan 1. A high-level program for rendering of realistic graphics scenes, developed by Pixar, Inc. 2. A proposed standard for interfacing to rendering programs.

Render Resolution In *trueSpace*, the resolution of the mesh when the user renders an object, or converts it to a polyhedron. Acceptable values range from 20 to 250.

re-origination counterfeit technique An advanced counterfeit technique that creates a hologram "from scratch" and requires a skilled staff and comprehensive laboratory facilities.

repaint To replace the current screen image with a new image having the same characteristics. This usually is needed when operations on the screen image have caused some of the original image information to be lost.

repelling periodic orbit A periodic orbit for which the absolute value of the eigenvalue is greater than one.

Report Render Time An option in *Bryce* and other 3D applications that gives the user an idea of which rendering times may be excessive. This option is useful for test renderings.

request mode An operating mode in which the application program requests input from a device and requires the user to perform an action with the device (called a *trigger*) before the graphics program returns control along with the device measure.

residency mask A bit vector in which each bit is assigned to a cell within partitioned object space. A residency mask is used to determine which objects in a scene are intersected by a particular ray.

residual The perpendicular distance from a point to a curve. The curve can be described as the set of all points on the Euclidian plane where the residual is zero.

Resistance property A property of the *Game Creation System* that presets the amount of damage the enemy can sustain before succumbing.

Resize Zoom option An option in *The Games Factory* that allows the user to automatically create several frames of animation that will gradually shrink or grow in relation to the first frame.

resizing See *axial resizing* and *global resizing*.

resolution A measure of the quality of an image. For halftones, this is expressed in lines per inch. For printed material from computer printers, it is usually expressed in dots per inch (e.g., 300 dpi). For a computer display, resolution is expressed in terms of the number of pixels in the horizontal and vertical directions.

resource Something that is limited and so must be allocated carefully, such as display screen space, computer memory, or hardware-limited table space.

resource manager Software that controls the operations of resource objects.

resource objects Objects that are able to automatically load, discard, and reload their data based upon usage patterns.

response time See *latency*.

Rest On Ground A command in *Light-Wave* that causes a selected object to be placed relative to the ground plane. Other 3D applications offer similar commands.

Restore 1. A command that returns any modified condition back to its original state. 2. A command in the Display Menu of *Poser*. Although the UNDO option erases the last operation performed, using Restore allows the user to return any Element, Figure, Light, or Camera (or All) to its original state with one click.

retained mode A graphics processing technique in which a datum is stored for later rendering as part of a group, rather than rendering each datum as it is input. Contrast with *immediate mode*.

retained-mode graphics See *SPHIGS*.

RETAS Pro A 2.5D digital animation production system that includes digital drawing, pencil test, line trace, ink and paint, compositing, and special effects.

retina The part of the eye where light is converted to an electrochemical signal that the brain understands. It is both a light receptor and a signal processor. The retina is the soft, semitransparent, purplish light-gathering membrane of the eye. This is the innermost layer of the eye. It is composed of ten distinctive layers that detect and process light. The most important layer is known as Jacob's membrane, which contains the rods and the cones (*see Figure next page*).

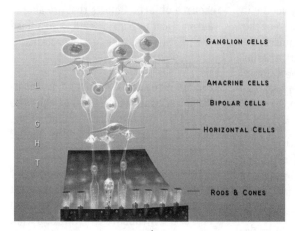

retina.

Retinal Bloom A filter from the Digi-Effects *Web Euphoria* collection for *Photoshop* that creates bright areas on a selected image.

Retouch tool A tool in *Paint Shop Pro* that lets the user modify areas of an image. The controls allow the user to lighten, darken, soften, and much more.

retrace The portion of a video signal during which the scanning electron beam is moved from the end of one scan line to the beginning of the next (*horizontal retrace*) or from the end of one field to the beginning of the next (*vertical retrace*). Video is usually blanked during retrace so that retrace lines do not appear on the screen.

retrieval The recovery of objects from a database and the display of them upon a screen.

retrieval key A word or phrase that gives a clue to the contents of a document and is used in searching for documents related to some particular subject.

retro games Classic computer games now available for modern PCs.

retroreflectivity The fraction of light that is returned from a collimated light source for a particular object at a specified angle of incidence and along the line of incidence.

Reverse At End Function A function in *The Games Factory*. This function simply reverses an object's movement and sends it back along the original path. This function is effective for a guard patrolling the grounds.

reverse engineering The analysis of a computer program so as to be able to duplicate or modify it without the original developer's permission. The hardest problem to address when attempting to stop such protocol tampering, is that the client contains the entire encryption algorithm, which can always be reverse engineered. Some steps one can take to make reverse engineering harder are as follows: Remove all symbols and debugging information from any code released to the public; do not isolate buffer encryption and decryption in their own functions; instead, combine these with some other network code; compute "magic numbers" (such as initialization seeds) at run time instead of placing their values directly in the executable; include a good encryption scheme in every version of the client, even early betas. If any client version lacks encryption, a user can record a stream of unencrypted packets from one client and then use knowledge of the packet payload to help break the encryption in a later version. Remember that the goal is to make cheating prohibitively expensive, not impossible.

reverse video Replacing an original background color with the color of a character and vice versa. Reverse video is used to highlight a particular line of a display, often one that has been selected by the cursor.

Reverse Z button A button in *Universe* that reverses the direction of the Z axis of the model.

revision bar A vertical line in the margin of a revised text that indicates the part of a document that has been revised.

Revolve tool A tool in *Universe* that allows the user to create a solid by revolving a profile around an axis.

rewritable Media on which data may be erased and rewritten. All magnetic disks are rewritable, but optical disks usually are not.

RFI See *radio frequency interference.*

RGB The primary colors which are combined at various intensities in an *additive* color system to produce all intermediate shades.

RGB color space The range of colors that can be displayed and recorded by a computer.

RGB color space.

RGB monitor A color monitor that accepts separate red, green, and blue video signals rather than composite video.

RGB video Red, green, and blue video signals transmitted separately over individual wires. To drive a monitor, a separate synchronization signal is also required.

rhombic dodecahedron A twelve-sided solid whose faces are rhombuses.

rhombus An equilateral parallelogram whose angles are oblique.

rhythm and pacing The changing of action from periods of calm to intense action to create suspense and engage the audience in the story.

ribbon A twisted three-dimensional curve used in modeling molecular structures.

ribbon cable A flat cable composed of a number of wires arranged in a horizontal plane and held in this position by plastic bonding.

ribbon path A new way of editing paths that is unique to *Bryce*. Unlike standard paths, which are not things, but only the result of the action of things, ribbon paths are full-fledged objects. As an object, one can edit a ribbon path directly, without selecting any object(s) assigned to it.

RIFF A general attribute-value database system having a flexible format useful for storing image information.

right justification A method of setting text type in which each line ends evenly at the right margin and any excessive space is between the left margin and the beginning of the line.

right reading Normal reproduction of an image from left to right.

Right Side View A control for *Universe Modeler* that allows the user to view the right side, which is actually the left side of the object itself.

rigid bodies Objects in which every element of matter is unable to translate or rotate with respect to every other element of matter within that body.

rim lighting Lighting that places the main light behind and slightly offset from the subject to create the effect of light caressing the subject. Since the key light comes from the back, the light creates an edge highlight that shows the contour of the subject while the opposite side is shadowed. Rim lights are generally positioned at the same level as the subject and are set to be stronger than the key light. Rim lighting is used for drawing attention to a profile or shape of a subject. It enhances the shape of the head, neck, and shoulders in portraiture. Hollywood portrait photographers first popularized this lighting technique.

ring A planar object bounded on the outside and inside by concentric circles.

ringing Additional high frequency signal components that are passed when a signal is passed through a filter. Also known as *Gibbs phenomenon*.

ring light array A light array generally composed of 12 to 16 lights arranged in a circular shape around a central main light. The ring arrangement can be horizontal, vertical, or even oblique. Each half of the ring can have its own color.

RIP See *raster image processor*.

Ripple Any command or plug-in in a 2D or 3D application that causes a ripple to appear on an image or texture or that influences the geometry in a similar fashion.

ripple edit To extend the beginning or ending shots of a scene.

RippleRain An application, from Kerlin Softworks, that is used to create both raindrops and water ripples for use in 3D applications.

RISC See *reduced instruction set computers*.

risorius/platysma The lower lip stretching muscle. This muscle is a unique facial muscle because it is primarily a neck muscle, although it does draw the lower lip downward and outward. It covers the neck, mandible, and parts of the mouth. The risorius/platysma is one of the most frequently used facial muscles. It is a part of nearly every facial expression. Some common expressions that use the risorius/platysma are "terrified" and "crying."

RLE See *run length encoding*.

RLL Run length limited. See *run length encoding*.

robust Describes software or algorithm capable of handling unusual cases without failure.

rock A virtual rock object created in a 3D application. Two tricks are used to create realistic-looking rocks in *Carrara*. The first is to create a realistic model. The second is to create a realistic shader. The Marble and Spots functions are the keys to creating an effective Rock shader.

rods One of the two types of photosensitive receptor cells in the eye. These cells primarily provide contrast perception, which is useful in low-light situations, pattern recognition, and discrimination. Rods are also used for motion detection and analysis, as well as night vision. These cells collectively function like an ultrasensitive black-and-white contrast and motion detector. Rods are uniformly distributed in the retina and are the

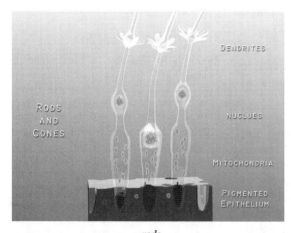

rods

most abundant type of photosensitive cell. The other type of photosensitive receptor cells are *cones*. ⌀

ROI See *region of interest*.

role-playing game (RPG) A game genre that emulates traditional pen-and-paper games, where characters have numerous characteristics (e.g., health, intelligence, strength, and other skills), and players simulate adventure. Examples include *Wizardry*, *Ultima*, *NetHack*, *Dungeon Hack*, *Might and Magic*, and *Daggerfall*.

roll Rotation around the local Z-axis (facing backward and forward).

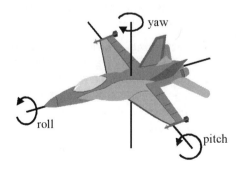

roll.

rolling-ball algorithm A technique for mouse-driven three-dimensional orientation control.

rolling edit To extend the ending shot and tighten the beginning shot of the next scene simultaneously.

rollover sound A sound effect that plays any time a user places his cursor over a button.

ROM Read-only memory. Memory that stores data permanently. The data can be read as often as desired, but the memory cannot be written to.

room tone The sound of the room in which a scene is recorded. During a shoot, the sound recorder will record roughly a minute's worth of the quieted location to create an "empty" sound with the right atmosphere. This sound will be used by the sound editor to correct audio problems.

root 1. A node in a hierarchy that has no parent. 2. A solution of an equation. 3. The first in a chain of bones.

ROP See *raster operation*.

roping An aliasing effect in which a line appears to change in color, brightness, or width to produce a pattern suggestive of a braided rope.

Rotating Speed A control in *The Games Factory* that sets the rate of turn. A high value will allow tight corners to be turned; a low value reduces the cornering ability.

rotation The turning of an object around a specified axis. ⌀

rotation angle A command that allows the user to specify the amount of rotation for an object.

rotation arc A function that returns a quaternion q, where $q*v_0==v_1$ where v_0 and v_1 are two given vectors.

rotation matrix A matrix that is used to multiply a vector, causing a rotation of the vector.

rotation track In animation, a separate track that keeps track of the movement of a rotating object. When a ball bounces down a hall, there is an up/down/forward motion (position), a scale change (stretch and squash), and in addition, the ball is rotating. Rotation tracks are very important to believable movements.

Roth diagram A diagram used in ray tracing models in which constructive solid geometry is used to represent the path of a ray including regions inside and outside the composite model.

Rothstein code A binary sequence that describes a line whose slope is q/p.

rotoscoping The process of painting over existing frames of video or film. In digital video production, rotoscoping is used for everything from painting in special effects, to painting custom-made mattes for compositing.

rough cut An early edit of a project, as opposed to the final cut.

roughness The property of the surface of an object that causes scattering of the light that reflects from it. A smooth surface causes little scattering and appears like a mirror; a rough surface causes a great deal of scattering.

Rounding tool A tool in *Universe* that allows the user to round the edges of an object.

route sheet A description of each scene of an animation and the people responsible for the various aspects of producing the scene.

RPC See *remote procedure call*.

RPG See *role-playing game*.

RS-170A An IEEE standard for composite video that is the same as NTSC composite video.

RS-232 An IEEE standard for serial interfaces such as those between computers and printers, terminals, modems, mice, etc. Now superseded by RS-488.

RS-422 A serial device control protocol that allows for computers to control video decks and other hardware. RS-422 is the standard for professional equipment, uses SMPTE timecode and is capable of frame accuracy.

RT11 A floppy disk format used by high-end linear on-line editing equipment to store EDLs.

rubber-banding A technique for scaling the size of an object in a computer drawing by selecting a reference point on the object and then using the cursor to move another point away from or closer to the first point selected. All of the other points on the object except the selected point move, preserving the shape of the object.

RubberSpaceWarp A plug-in for *3ds max* from RubberFlex that allows the user to deform selected objects as if they were made out of rubber.

rubber-stamping Replicating a two-dimensional object on a graphics display by selecting a point on it with the cursor and then dragging that point to a new location where another copy of the object is placed.

runarounds In typography, lines of irregular length that are used to surround an irregularly shaped figure.

Runge-Kutta method A numerical method for solving differential equations. It employs the recurrence formula:

$$y_{i+1} = y_i + \sum_{j=1}^{n} \alpha_j K_j$$

to calculate successive values of the dependent value y of the differential equation:

$$\frac{dy}{dx} = y' = f(x, y)$$

where

$$k_j = hf\left(x_i + p_{j-1}, y_i + \sum_{l=1}^{j-1} q_{j-1,l} k_l\right)$$

$$(j = 1, 2, \ldots, n)$$

and by definition

$$p_0 = 0 \ \text{ and } \ \sum_{l=1}^{j-1} q_{j-1,l} k_l = 0 \ \text{ for } \ j = 1$$

run length encoding (RLE) A method of data compression in which strings of like bytes are encoded into two bytes, one a number of repetitions and the other the repeated byte value. Also known as *run length limited (RLL)*.

rust f/x Creating a texture that looks like rust. This is accomplished by applying a procedural noise or a noisy texture to either or both the textures' bump and specular channels.

S

saccade The long-range action of the eye as it moves from one object to another across the visual field. Visual input is suppressed during saccade and for a short time afterward.

SAG Acronym for the Screen Actors' Guild.

SAGE See *Systolic Array Graphics Engine.*

sample and hold A video display technique in which samples in a frame buffer are translated to a continuous video signal by reading the value of each pixel from the buffer and holding it for the duration of the pixel.

sampled data theory The mathematical discipline that deals with taking discrete samples of continuous information. It explains that, when sampling a continuous piece of data (such as a straight line) at discrete intervals, we not only lose some of the information about the line, but also introduce new and unwanted information at multiples of the sampling frequency.

sample mode A method of interaction handling in which a single device is sampled and its output immediately returned. The user can select one of several devices. However, the system does not recognize additional user selections while it is processing one selection so that if several selections are made quickly, some of them may be lost.

sample point In antialiasing, one of several locations within a pixel for which

color or *z*-distance is computed. The results obtained for all sample points are averaged to determine the pixel color.

Samples box A box in *Universe* that allows the user to select the sampling rate for texture maps.

sampling 1. The process of converting an analog representation (such as a continuously variable voltage or a mathematical equation) into discrete (usually digital) values by measuring the value at the corresponding discrete points in time. 2. The way *Universe* obtains information to create the pixels that one sees in a final image. The renderer must decide which color to make a pixel in the render based on the information from all of the colors in the area of the scene that is being represented by that one pixel.

sampling ratio The human eye is more sensitive to differences in light and dark (luminance) than to differences in color (chrominance). When a digital camera samples an image, the degree to which it samples each primary color is called the color *sampling ratio*. A fully uncompressed video signal (also known as *RGB color*) has a color sampling ratio of 4:4:4. The first number stands for the luma signal (abbreviated *y*), and the second two numbers stand for the color difference components (*Cb* and *Cr*) which together add up to the full chroma signal. A color sampling ratio of 4:4:4 means that for every pixel, four samples each are taken for the luma signal and the two parts of the chroma signal. A color sampling ratio of 4:2:2 means that for every 4 luma samples, there are 2 color difference complete samples. This results in the loss of half the color detail. Because this is color detail that the human eye cannot perceive, it is recommended to discard for the sake of saving storage space. 4:2:2 is the color sampling ratio of D1 video and ITU-BR 601. DV formats use 4:1:1 color sampling, which is an amount of color reduction that is considered visible to the viewer. However, one should check to see if the amount of degradation is acceptable. Because PAL video handles color differently, a color sampling ratio of 4:2:0 in PAL is equivalent to 4:1:1 in NTSC.

sampling theorem A theorem that states that a continuous signal can be reconstructed perfectly from its samples if it is appropriately band-limited before sampling.

San Marco dragon A fractal Julia set whose constant term is the real number 3. It is called the *San Marco dragon* because it resembles the skyline of the basilica in Venice, including its reflection in a flooded square.

Sanson-Flamsteed sinusoidal projection A mapping of a sphere onto a plane that uses the central meridian as the axis of constant spacing. This technique can produce a map that preserves area.

sans serif In typography, those typefaces that do not have filleted decorations (*tails*) at the edges and ends of the letters and which usually do not have variations in stroke width. Examples are *Gothic* and *Helvetica* typefaces. Compare with *serif*.

This is a "sans serif" typeface.

This is a "serif" typeface.

Sasquatch A plug-in for *LightWave*, from Worley Labs, that allows the user to create a variety of hair effects for any selected 3D model.

satellite One of a collection of computers whose main controlling and storage system is a central server.

saturated color The technical term for bright, bold colors is *saturated*. For example, a true red is saturated, while pink and maroon are *desaturated* reds.

saturation The amount that a color is composed of the pure color. High saturation colors consist of the color frequency band to a high degree. Low saturation colors contain a great deal of white and therefore appear as pastels.

saturation.

Saturn's rings 1. The colored rings of light surrounding the planet Saturn. 2. Rings of colored light that appear in human vision, often as a result of glaucoma.

scalar Represented by a single number or dimension. Compare with *vector*, which is a representation by a set of numbers that describe a multi-dimensional space.

scalar field A collection of numbers, one associated with each point in a volume.

scale 1. The ratio of the size of units in a drawing or model to the size of the units in the actual object that is being pictured. 2. A multiplier for changing the size of an object representation.

Scale tool A tool in *Universe* that allows the user to create a copy of an object that is scaled differently from the original object.

scale track In animation, a separate track that keeps track of the size of an object that grows or shrinks. The size or scale of each object within an animation can be animated with techniques such as "stretch" and "squash."

scaling Changing the size of characters or graphics.

scallop shell A fractal Julia set having as its constant term the real number 1.

scalp and neck muscles, frontalis See *frontalis*.

scalp and neck muscles, risorius/ platysma See *risorius/platysma*.

scan To convert pictures or printed pages of text into computer-readable code, such as ASCII characters or bitmaps.

scan conversion The process of converting an image into scan lines that can be displayed on a raster scan monitor.

scan converter A device that converts one video format (consisting of a particular horizontal and vertical resolution) to another. In addition to modifying the video to fit the new scanned structure, synchronization signals must be provided.

scan head The part of a scanner that optically senses text or graphics as it moves across a page.

scan line 1. A horizontal line of a raster display. Synchronous with the scanning of the display beam, the video for the scan line must vary to represent the colors of each of the pixels in the line. 2. A row of pixels.

Scan Line Access Memory (SLAM) A memory chip specially designed for rasterizing general two-dimensional primitives.

scan line algorithm A technique for rendering an image in which the image is rendered one scan line at a time, rather than on an object-by-object basis.

scanner Hardware used to scan analogue data, so that it can be saved in a digital form.

scan rate The rate (in samples per second) at which a scanner samples an image.

scattering The dispersal of light in many directions when it is reflected from a point on a surface.

scattering.

Scefo **(Scene Format)** A program for generating animations. It includes linear-list notation, groups, object hierarchy, abstractions of changes (actions), and some higher-level programming language constructs.

SceneBuilder One of the *Photoshop* filters from the Corel *KPT* collection. *SceneBuilder* allows the user to create 3D scenes inside of *Photoshop* with 3DS and other object format models.

scene description The specification of a scene in terms of objects, light sources, and viewing devices as an initial step in rendering the scene.

scene radiance The radiance emitted by an entire scene.

Scheduling A program from Movie Magic that can import properly-formatted screenplays and automatically create breakdown sheets and production strips. The user can print these strips and place them in special plastic sleeves for placement on a board.

schematic capture The use of a CAD system to construct a schematic diagram using a set of symbols included in the software and allowing the user to select symbols and interconnect them with lines representing wires.

Schroeder stairway illusion A drawing of a stairway that can be seen as a right side up stairway or an upside down stairway depending upon how the eye interprets it.

Schumacher algorithm An algorithm for creating a priority list of clusters of convex polygons, using a plane tree structure.

scientific visualization The creation of computer graphics images that show the relationships among incoming data.

scissoring A technique for clipping an image at the boundaries of a screen, using hardware tailored for that purpose.

sclera The white, thick, opaque, fibrous tissue that forms and holds the spherical shape of the eyes. It forms the outer layer of the eyes. It is thicker in the back than in the front. The front areas are covered with thin conjunctiva, which make the eye shiny.

scoptic Achromatic vision in dim light using the rods in the eye. Compare to *photopic*.

screen 1. The display surface of a cathode-ray tube or other display device. 2. A grid of fine wires through which an image is photographed to break it into dots and produce a halftone.

screen angles Angles at which halftone screens are oriented with respect to the image to avoid moiré patterns. When creating four-color separation negatives, the commonly used angles are 45 degrees for black, 75 degrees for magenta, 90 degrees for yellow, and 105 degrees for cyan.

screen capture To transfer the contents of a display screen to a computer file.

screen coordinates The coordinate system used to define the position of a pixel on the display screen.

screen correction shot A shot of a blue-screen or green-screen stage that has no actors in it, used by compositing software to help create the matte.

screen door transparency A graphics technique in which surfaces are rendered by a pattern instead of solid color, so that occluded objects are partially visible.

screen dump To transfer the contents of a display screen to a printer.

screen extent The size of the rectangle enclosing an image to be displayed.

screen font Data designed to display a type font on the display screen that is a close match in size and style for a similar font that is to be used by the printer. This gives a display that looks very much like the final printed product.

ScreenForge A screenwriting program.

screen size The *diagonal* of the rectangle within which an image may be displayed on a screen. This measure became common when round display tubes were used, when it corresponded to the useful diameter of the cathode-ray tube.

screenwriting software A program that permits the user to write screenplays in standard screenplay format.

scrim A lighting accessory used to tone down the brightness of a light. Single scrims dim the light by 1/2 f-stop and double scrims dim the light by a full f-stop. Half scrims are a half-moon shape to allow for further manipulation of the light.

script A way to define behavior outside of the code. Scripts are useful for defining sequential steps that need to occur in a game, or game events that need to be triggered.

scripted cameras Scripted cameras are a crucial part of many games, from cinematic scenes in role-playing games to helicopter fly-throughs of a golf course. Most games that use this camera technique use an animation package to script the camera, then import the animation into their game engines.

Script Manager tsxPython scripts within *trueSpace* are accessed through the Script Manager. Users can load, execute, edit, and save tsxPython scripts, as well as attach scripts to *trueSpace* scenes and objects.

Scriptwriter A program from Screenplay Systems for writing scripts in standard screenplay format.

scroll bars Rectangular regions bordering a window which, when accessed by the cursor, control the scrolling of the window contents.

scrolling The movement of an entire image up or down on the display screen, so that new material appears at the top or bottom of the screen and old material is dropped off at the bottom or top.

scroll rate The rate at which an image moves in a fixed window when scrolling.

scrubbing A feature of many non-linear editing systems that lets the user "scrub" through the audio, which means that as the user slowly scrolls through a clip, the audio plays back in slow motion along with the video. This helps the user find a particular sound, such as a pause in a line of dialogue or the beat in a piece of music.

SCSI Small computer system interface. An industry standard for interfacing peripheral devices to a personal computer. It includes definitions for both hardware and software. When using SCSI devices, each device on the SCSI chain must have its own unique SCSI ID. A SCSI port can support up to seven devices.

sculptured surface A free-form surface, that is, one that cannot be represented by a simple mathematical equation.

SDI See *Serial Digital Interface*.

SDTV See *Standard Definition Television*.

S-dynamics A system for producing animations on a computer.

search algorithm See *A* algorithm*.

search engine A method that enables Web users to access millions of topics, Web pages, or Web sites by typing "key words." Search engines are made up of three major elements. First, a *spider*, sometimes referred to as a "crawler," visits a Web page, reads it, determines its usefulness, and then follows links to other pages within the site, searching for appropriate information. Everything the spider reads is delivered to the second part of a search engine, the *index*. The index is a database containing a duplicate of every Web page that the spider reads. *Search engine software* is the third element of a search engine. This is the software that examines the millions of pages recorded in the index to find matches to a search criterion entered by a user and ranks the Web pages in an order of what it considers most relevant. The term "search engine" is often used broadly to describe both search engines and directories. However, they are not the same. Search engines, such as Alta Vista, create their listings without human intervention. Search engines crawl the Web, read the HTML files and then index the Web pages automatically. The method used to design the content of Web pages can affect how they are listed. Web page titles, body content and other Web page elements all play a role. Directories such as Yahoo depend on human intervention for their listings. Either a short description to the directory for an entire site is submitted, or the directory editors write them for sites they review. The Web page text has no effect on a listing. Methods for improving a listing with a search engine have nothing to do with improving a listing in a directory. The only exception is how the site is graded by a directory editor. If a site provides useful content, it will be more likely to be indexed. Note that a human is grading and indexing the Web site.

SECAM Séquentiel couleur avec memoire. The color television standard used by many countries. Because of the lack of equipment designed for this particular system, pictures are usually recorded and stored using the PAL system and encoded in the SECAM format just prior to transmission.

seclites Secondary light sources.

secondary colors The colors that result when the primary colors (red, blue, and yellow) are mixed. These colors are green, violet, and orange.

secondary light See *fill light*.

section plane A plane used to mark the position at which an object is cut to provide a cutaway view.

section space A clipping volume that is defined by a collection of planes defined in world coordinates.

sector The smallest addressable unit on a magnetic or optical disk. Usually contains 512 bytes.

sectoring The construction of multiple nonoverlapping view volumes that radiate out from a light source when the light source's view volume cannot encompass all objects in a scene.

Secure Sockets Layer (SSL) A method of encryption on the Web that protects communications with a server, so credit card orders can be taken securely and hackers cannot access a clients' information.

security holograms Holograms belong to a class of images known as Diffractive Optical Variable Image Devices (DOVIDs) and are used as a method of protection against counterfeiting. Highly valued for security, DOVIDs can be produced only by using specialized, technologically advanced equipment. They cannot be replicated by color copiers, computer-scanning equipment, or by standard printing techniques, analog or digital. This is because they are governed by different physical properties (holograms diffract light, whereas print reflects it).

seed An arbitrary number used to begin the generation sequence when using an algorithm to generate a series of pseudo-random numbers.

seed filling See *flood filling*.

seeding from the universe Just as the user interacts with the game universe to set up values for the various objects, the objects themselves can provide input into their generation. In other words, even before the player is allowed to have an effect on the universe, the universe can be generated. This commonly occurs only once in a given game session, although it may happen more than once if the player performs an action that causes the immediate portion of the game universe to become irrelevant. For example, players could transport themselves from one planet to another using some form of hyperspace or teleport device.

segment 1. A portion of a curve or straight line. 2. In the GKS standard, a set of logically-related primitives, such as lines, polygons, or character strings, and their attributes. 3. A section of memory that may be switched in or out of working memory by a memory manager.

segment bunching A problem that must be dealt with when triangulating meshes. Segment bunching occurs when four or more segments share a common point and the angle between the segments is small. In many cases, this bunching creates a smoothing problem for the *3ds max* Scanline Renderer resulting in a darkening of the area.

Selected Polygons A tool in *Universe* that allows the user to select desired polygons from those that make up the face of an object.

selective focus Selective focus is based on people's instinctive reaction to be drawn to the brightest area of a scene. When in the 3D environment, the artist has complete control over the lights so it makes sense to exploit this power to show the audience where to look, as well as where not to look when hiding shortcomings in the scene.

selector An electronic device that switches between inputs or outputs as dictated by a control signal.

self-affine Describes a function that has more than one scaling factor.

self-intersection The property of a curve or surface that intersects itself.

self-luminous object An object, such as a light bulb, that emits light rather than reflecting it.

self-occlusion The property of an object, in which light cast from a point behind the object's surface does not illuminate it.

self-similarity A property of a geometric figure in which the overall shape of the figure is duplicated at smaller and smaller scales as the figure is enlarged. See also *fractal*.

semantic design See *functional design, user interface*.

sensitivity A measure of the amplitude of a signal needed to record data on a magnetic or optical disk or an image on a film.

Sentry Then Hunt option In the *Game Creation System*, an option where the enemy stands still until he sees the player, then chases after the player in attack mode.

separating plane tree A data structure consisting of objects separated by mathematical planes in such a way as to facilitate placing the objects in the occlusion order of priority.

separation A rule for flocking behavior that requires steering to avoid crowding local flockmates.

separation plane method A technique for rendering images that makes use of an imaginary plane between objects. This method can be used with the results of a hidden surface algorithm to determine which object is nearest the viewpoint and permits drawing of the farthest object first.

sequence In filmmaking, an assembly of shots edited together.

sequence container See *deque*.

serial A data communications method in which each data bit is transmitted sequentially.

Serial Digital Interface (SDI) The professional digital video standard I/O protocol with a data rate of either 270Mbps or 360Mbps. See also *Firewire*.

serialization 1. Processing of data sent serially from a source in the same order that it was received. 2. A technique that revolves around the reference coordinates of a given object in a game universe to determine what properties it should have. An object's position at the time that it is to be instantiated is used to give it a set of properties that dictate its appearance and behavior within the game universe. If the properties of an object are defined by its position in the game universe, then it also follows that the same object in a different position will have different properties—it will appear and behave in a different way. This is one of the reasons why backdrop objects do not move, and one of the reasons why infinite game universes are possible.

serif A class of typefaces having small filleted decorations at the ends of strokes and horizontal strokes that are thinner than vertical strokes. Compare with *sans serif*.

This is a "serif" typeface.

This is a "sans serif" typeface.

serpentine raster pattern A raster scan in which odd scanlines are traversed left-to-right and even lines traversed right-to-left.

server The computer in a network that controls all requests from other computers for data access.

Set Elevation icon An icon in the *Game Creation System* for moving walls up and down.

Set Figure Parent 1. Parenting an element in a hierarchical chain. 2. A command in the Figure menu of *Poser*. Any element in the scene may become the parent of another element. Parent actions set the movement, rotation, and sizing actions of the child. This is handy when developing a walk cycle and assigning it to one figure, when exactly the same choreography needs to be emulated by another figure(s), or when a child figure is to emulate the parent's behavior.

set lights Lights that open up the background set. They are the ambient lighting of the set. When the background is a 2D image or painted muslin, the light illuminating it is called *backdrop light*. Set lights, however, are not regularly used in computer graphics, since the use of radiosity to "fake" fill lights serves the same purpose. They light up the dark areas of the room to suggest interobject reflection. Furthermore, when using 3D dual-light arrays, it is possible to attenuate the set's shadow areas from the key light's position. So, in computer graphics, a set light may not be that practical.

Set Wall Lighting by Angle attribute An attribute of the *Game Creation System*. It is possible to enhance the 3D look of a level with this feature. Walls with a north/south orientation are shaded differently than walls with an east/west orientation.

shade The resultant color from the addition of black to a pure hue. ◁

shade.

shader A graphics subroutine that computes the effects of illumination upon a visible surface and thereby determines the pixel colors. ◁

shading The assignment of shades of color to the surfaces of a graphics object to represent the visual effects of light sources upon the object. See *Phong illumination*.

shading model The algorithm or equation that computes the effects of light upon a surface and determines the shade

of color to be used for a particular point or surface. Also known as an *illumination model* or *lighting model*.

Shading tab A tab in the Group Info window of *Universe* that allows the user to select the type of shading for rendering an object.

shadow An area in which there is partial or total absence of illumination due to an obstruction between the light source and the area of illumination. Shadows are a significant way in which lighting adds to a scene's mood. Dark, high-contrast shadows tend to set a forbidding tone or add a sense of harshness to the scene. Longer, softer shadows can give a scene a more inviting or romantic feel, while minimal shadows or a lack of shadows altogether can create a sense of sterility. To get an idea of just how much impact shadows can have on a scene, study a favorite movie and notice how shadows are used to set or enhance the mood in each scene. The effect is usually more dramatic in older movies from the 1940s and 1950s.

Shadow A *Photoshop* filter from Andromeda Software that allows the user to create 3D perspective shadows from 2D image areas.

shadow algorithm An algorithm or equation used to determine if a point or surface is in the shadow of an object and if so, what its color should be.

shadow, butterfly See *butterfly lighting*.

shadow, color and See *constancy, color*.

Shadow Cone A setting in the Properties tab of *Universe* that allows the user to determine the shadow buffer area around an object.

shadow depth map A technique for determining the shadows in a scene by performing z-buffer scan conversion and visibility determination of the scene from the perspective of a light source, and then storing only the depth information in a 2D array.

shadow, film exposure and A basic rule of photography is "expose for the shadows, develop for the highlights." We expose for the shadows because no amount of film processing is able to give details on the shadow areas if these areas did not receive adequate exposure. This is true because the photochemistry does not affect the shadow areas very much. In other words, the development process cannot create shadow details if there were not enough light to reveal the details of those areas to start with. However, the highlights can be controlled through development because the developer affects these areas a great deal. The exposure of the film affects the number of silver halide crystals that are converted into metallic silver, but it is the development that affects the extent of metallic conversion that occurs. In short, development controls how much physical and chemical change would occur on the exposed silver halide crystals.

shadow leaks See *light and shadow leaks*.

shadow map An array having a member for each direction that a ray travels from the viewpoint in rendering a scene, with each member containing the distance to the first object encountered by the ray. Used to test if object surfaces are illuminated or in shadow.

shadow map, animated *Poser* can be used to create content for an alpha channel to act as a shadow map in a post-editing application (such as Adobe's *After Effects*). An alpha channel contains only gray scale data, and can be either in black and white or in 256 shades that range from black to white. Pure white prints itself on the channel that the alpha is placed above, while pure black acts like a drop-out mask. The grays in between act as different levels of transparency, so that the blacker the gray is, the more opaque it is.

shadow mask A perforated metal plate that is positioned between the electron gun and the phosphor of a cathode-ray tube in such a manner that the beam from each electron gun passes through the proper hole to activate a phosphor dot of the corresponding color.

shadow position Depth is based, in part, on the shadow that objects cast on their surroundings. Since our eyes are sensitive to contrast change, we "read" spatial orientation based on an object's shadow. This is basically depth perception through illumination position and shadow orientation extraction. The position of the shadow is also used for eval-

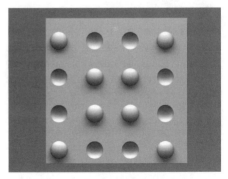

shadow position.

uation of texture, material density, and composition. Shadows are also used for light position analysis, even if the light source itself is not visible. This means that by looking at shadows around an object, we can determine the form, shape, and composition of the object.

shadow rays Additional rays shooting from the pixel toward each light source. In ray tracing, shadow rays are used for determining shadows. If the rays are obstructed before reaching the light source, there is no light from that direction. Alternatively, if the shadow ray passes through without obstruction, that particular pixel reflects that light.

shadow rings An undesired artifact that can occur when using shadow maps. Also called *contrast banding*.

shadow theorem The random shift dynamical system orbit on the overlapping attractor *A* is the shadow of a deterministic orbit on *Ă*.

shaft culling A method of computing a list of potential occluders for a given source-receiver pair. The source is totally visible when the list is empty. If an object in the list cuts the shaft, the source is totally occluded. In other cases, shadow rays are traced to determine the shadow characteristics.

Shapes tool A tool in *Paint Shop Pro* that allows the user to insert preset shapes into an image. The user can either draw outlined shapes or filled shapes such as rectangles, squares, ellipses, and circles.

sharpening 1. An image processing technique that enhances edges and fine details of the image. 2. In a video camera, a special algorithm that is applied to the video image to increase focus. With too much sharpening, strange artifacts will appear in the image.

sharpening filter A filter used to enhance the differences between the pixels that make up an image, thereby causing an edge-sharpening effect.

Shatter One of the filters from AlienSkin's *Xenofex* collection for *Photoshop*, used to break an image into shattered elements.

shear A coordinate transformation that involves changing the angles between axes.

shear matrix A 2×2 matrix, with a diagonal of all 1s and a determinant of 1, used in raster rotation.

sheeting A process used in producing holograms. Sheeting involves slitting and trimming the roll. The roll is then cut into sheets for the printing phase. This process can also involve optical sheeting and slitting where eyemarks are used to sheet to a specific place on each roll.

shine through See *textures, shine through*.

shockwave F/X The effect of a leading cloud, which rises off of the ground, and a trailing cloud, which stays closer to the ground. The effect can be created using *Primal Particles, wfmm glow*, and *wfmm motrails* (*see Figure next page*).

shoot 'em up games A genre of 2D games in which the players are in a spaceship and shoot objects or enemies before the opponents return fire with missiles, alien ships, etc. Examples of this genre include *Space Invaders, Asteroids, Sinistar, Space Battle*, and the original *Spacewar*.

shooting ratio The ratio of the length of footage shot to the length of the final film. For example, a project with a 5:1

shockwave F/X.

ratio would have shot five hours of footage for a one-hour long final project.

shore lines as boundary conditions See *water simulation, boundary conditions.*

short lighting The placement of the key light toward the far side of a three-quarters turned face. Short lighting illuminates the narrow, far cheek area of the face. It is ideal for round or broad-faced individuals, because it makes the face look slimmer by shadowing its broad side. By lighting the narrow, short side, we emphasize the outline of the face, and by darkening the broad side of the face, we form an illuminated narrow triangle on the lighted side.

shotgun A very directional microphone that is often affixed to the front of the camera or to a boom or fishpole.

shot list A list of the shots a director plans to shoot on a particular day of filming or taping. Usually a shot list is derived by carefully reviewing the script, the storyboard, and blocking the scene with the actors in rehearsals.

Show/Clear Background Footage A command in the Display menu of *Poser* that allows the user to show or clear the background after loading background movie footage.

Show/Clear Background Picture A command in the Display menu of *Poser* allows the user to show or clear the background after loading a background image.

Showmehideu A plug-in for *trueSpace* designed to speed up screen refresh. It can be valuable when working on a large, complex scene. It works by hiding all except the currently selected object.

shrinking raster A method of measuring resolution of a cathode-ray tube. A number of equally-spaced parallel lines that alternate between black and white are displayed and the interline spacing is uniformly decreased by reducing the size of the raster until the lines just begin to merge together to produce a uniform field of gray. This merging occurs when interline spacing is equal to the diameter at which the intensity of a spot on the CRT is 60 percent of the intensity at the center of the spot. Resolution is measured by dividing the overall raster vertical dimension by the number of lines in the raster at this point.

Shrink tool A tool in *The Games Factory* that removes any unnecessary transparent border areas from the image, reducing its size. This is useful for saving memory and will speed up the game by removing overly-large images, trimming them to the minimum required.

shuffle generator A table of numbers used to jitter a function so that any spatial patterns resulting from sampling are removed.

shutter The part of a camera that opens and closes to control how long the focal plane is exposed to light. There is no physical shutter in a video camera; instead the camera's CCD samples light for an appropriate length of time, and then shuts off.

shuttered glasses A tool for three-dimensional viewing. The left and right images are displayed alternately at a rate faster than the critical flicker frequency of the eye (about 20 per second). The observer needs to wear special *shuttered glasses* with lenses that alternately blacken out each eye in synchronism with the display. The images with this technique can now use the whole screen and be in full color, but the eyewear requirement remains.

shutter speed The speed of the rotation of the shutter inside the lens, measured in rotations per second.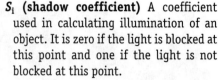

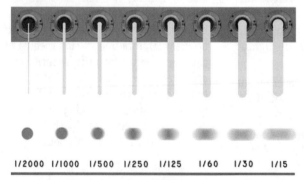

shutter speed.

S_i **(shadow coefficient)** A coefficient used in calculating illumination of an object. It is zero if the light is blocked at this point and one if the light is not blocked at this point.

side lighting The placement of the key light 90 degrees to the side of the subject. Side lighting emphasizes the texture of the subject. It also reveals the form and shape of the subject. In side lighting, one side of the subject is completely illuminated while the other side is completely dark. By nature, side lighting is high-contrast hard lighting. Side lighting is also called *hatchet lighting* because it divides or separates the face into two areas, the light zone and the dark zone.

sides A dialogue-only version of a script, used to make readings easier for actors.

side scroller A game genre in which the hero runs along platforms, jumping from one to the next, while trying not to fall into canyons, lava pits, or get hit by projectiles. *Prince of Persia* is an example of a side scroller.

Siegel disk A fractal curve that is a complement of a Julia set using the iterated equation:

$$z_{n+1} = az_n + z^2.$$

Sierpinski triangle A fractal curve that can be created by starting with a filled-in equilateral triangle and removing that triangle by connecting the mid-points of the sides. This leaves four filled-in equilateral triangles for which the same process is repeated, and the procedure then continues for as long as desired.

Sierpinski triangle.

Sierra error diffusion filter An algorithm for performing discrete convolution or digital filtering, which is the improvement of the appearance of an image by replacing a pixel with a function of that pixel and its neighbors. It is frequently used to change color images to images consisting of black, white, and shades of gray.

SIGGRAPH 1. The Special Interest Group for Graphics of the Association for Computer Machinery. One of the major organizations for computer graphics professionals. 2. An annual conference for computer professionals held in late July or early August, sponsored by SIGGRAPH.

Sigma A high-end graphics workstation by Megatek.

signal, continuous A signal defined at a continuum of positions in space.

signal, discrete A signal that is defined by a set of discrete points in space.

signal frequency spectrum A signal that is defined in the frequency domain, as, for example, by the sum of a set of sine waves having different frequencies and amplitudes.

signal-to-noise ratio (SNR) The ratio of signal power to unwanted noise power in an analog electronic signal. This is usually expressed in *decibels*, which are 10 times the logarithm of the ratio.

signature analysis The comparison of a function computed from the outputs of a digital circuit with a previously-stored value to determine whether the circuit is functioning properly.

Sign Language One of the collections in the *Poser* Hand Poses library. It includes all of the hand positions for the alphabet in the international sign language.

silhouette edge 1. An edge obtained by tracing the outer boundary of the two-dimensional representation of a graphics object. It separates all of the pixels dedicated to the object from the rest of an image. 2. An edge of a patch that is not a real edge of an object, but appears as an edge when a three-dimensional object is projected as two dimensions.

Silicon Graphics See *OpenGL*.

Silicon Valley A portion of the Santa Clara Valley of California starting approximately 50 miles south of San Francisco, called *Silicon Valley* because of the large number of companies in the area that specialize in the design and development of transistors and integrated circuits composed of silicon.

silver A common precious metal, many of whose salts are light sensitive. These salts are used as the light-sensitive emulsion for photographic film and printing paper.

silver halide A compound of silver that is photosensitive and used in film emulsions. It turns black in the presence of light.

Simbiont A shader for *trueSpace, LightWave, and 3ds max* that permits procedurally-generated textures from *DarkTree* to be used directly in the targeted 3D application.

SIMD Single-instruction multiple data. See *parallelism*.

similarity, visual A rule of visual organization that states that two visual stimuli with a common property are seen as belonging together.

simplices A set of primitive shapes that includes triangles, tetrahedra, etc.

simploids A set of shapes that includes both simplices and boxes (such as squares, cubes, etc.).

simulation The representation of a real life situation, a mathematical algorithm, or an electronic circuit by a software model so that the *simulation* can be run with various parameters to determine how the real case will behave.

simulation game A game genre in which the player builds a simulation of a town, world, or ant colony, making decisions and managing resources. Often called "God Games" because the player has the role of God in the game world. Examples of this genre include *Sim City, Sim Earth,* and *Sim Ant.*

sine fractal A fractal curve produced by iterating the following equation:

$$z_n = \sin\!\left(z_{n-1}\right) + c$$

with $z_0 = 0 + i0$ and c varied over the complex plane.

sine function The function $\dfrac{\sin x}{x}$

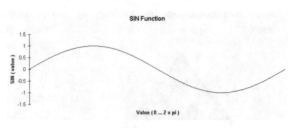

sine function.

single-chip A camera that uses a single CCD to gather all three (red, green, and blue) of the signals that will be used to create a full-color image.

single-field resolution Some low-resolution CODECs cut down the size of the captured video files by discarding one field for each frame of video. The resulting single-field video plays fairly well but contains half the information of two-field video.

single group grouping A method of grouping objects in *form•Z.* Single group grouping is the only grouping method that creates a single 3DS file with multiple objects in it. All other 3DS export grouping methods create multiple 3DS files. The single group method is the recommended way of exporting geometry via the 3DS format.

single instruction multiple data (SIMD) See *parallelism*.

single lens reflex (SLR) camera A camera in which the photographer looks through the lens directly at the subject, through a separate viewfinder. A 35mm still camera with removable lenses is typically an SLR.

singleton An object that has only one instance in a system at any time.

sink 1. In typography, extra white space at the top of a published page that is used to emphasize the body text. 2. A heavy piece of metal, often finned, that is used to draw heat away from a heat-producing electronic component. Also known as a *heat sink*.

sinusoid A curve produced by plotting the sine or cosine function.

site map A page within a Web site that offers a map of all the Web pages pertaining to the site. Typically, this is an outline of hyperlinks to the other Web pages and remote sites.

sixty-cycle tone (60 Hz tone) Used as an audio reference to calibrate the audio levels on editing equipment and speakers. Typically, the 60 Hz tone should fall at 0dB on a VU.

sketchpad An input device that consists of a rectangular drawing area and an attached stylus. The motions of the stylus are transferred to the computer by electronic means.

skew To slant a selected character or graphics object.

skew transform A geometric transformation that changes the angle between the coordinate axes, resulting in a change in the shape of all figures being transformed.

skinning A way of converting a skeleton to a human figure. The artist creates a single skin model. He then duplicates this skin, scales it down fractionally, and proceeds to cut this smaller skin up into even smaller bits (body parts), which are used as bones. As each bone is created, it is given the same name as the skin with a number appended to it, so it can easily be recognized as a bone by the program.

Skin tool A tool used in *form•Z* and *Universe* to create skin surfaces on figures.

Skip Frames A toggle control in *Poser* that allows the user to play an entire animation sequence or the keyframes only.

skitter A coordinate system placed on the surface of an object to define possible directions of movement.

sky dome A reference to the whole sky.

SkyEffects One of the *Photoshop* filters in the Corel *KPT* collection that allows the user to create sky and cloud data for an image.

Sky&Fog A three-tabbed environmental attributes dialog in *Bryce*. The tabs are named Sun & Moon, Cloud Cover, and Atmosphere.

skylight The ambient light from the sky, which consists of the reflected light of the sun. On a cloudy day there is no sunlight but there is still skylight.

sky memory dots In *Bryce*, a stack of memory dots for storing sky designs, located at the very right hand of the Sky and Fog toolbar.

sky options A part of the Advanced Motion Lab of *Bryce*. Sky options are keyframed when nothing else is selected in a scene. There are thirty-four sky attributes that can be animation-customized in the Advanced Motion Lab by applying or creating a motion graph or assigning multiple keyframes from the Sky&Fog palette.

SkyPaint A special application that allows the user to paint on panorama files. Panoramas are interactive visualizations that allow the user to view an image as if it were mapped on a cylinder or sphere, with the viewpoint in the center of the scene. Once a panorama is stitched together (*Bryce* has a cylindrical panorama renderer), it can be posted to the Web or used on a CD for viewers to interactively navigate.

sky stack trip An effect that can be created with *Bryce*. This animation is similar to the effect at the end of Stanley Kubrick's *2001: A Space Odyssey*, when the spacecraft moves through a series of infinite planes. The difference is, this effect moves the object vertically through the planes.

SkyTracer A *LightWave* rendering option that allows the user to configure sky and clouds for use as a background and/or a texture component.

SLAM See *Scan Line Access Memory*.

slating When recording the sound separately from the video or film, the process of holding a slate in front of the camera. On the slate are written the scene and take numbers. The top of the slate can be clapped to produce a distinct sound that will be used for syncing the audio and video.

slerp See *spherical linear interpolation*.

slew rate 1. The rate of change of the output of a servo system as it changes to lock in on a new input signal. 2. The rate at which a display system pans through an image file.

slice To apply section-plane clipping to an object space.

slide edit To edit a sequence of three shots by sliding the middle shot back or forward in time. The beginning and ending shots are lengthened or shortened as necessary so that the total time for the three shots remains the same.

Slider link A link in *Carrara* that allows the user to constrain movement on each of the X, Y, and Z axes. Similar commands exist in most 3D applications.

slide-show effects A sequential collection of images on a single GIF file.

slip edit To edit the footage contained in the middle of three shots so that it starts at a different place without affecting the shots surrounding it or the duration of the sequence.

sliver When creating a mesh, a triangle whose width is less than $\frac{1}{6}$ of its length. There are three primary reasons for avoiding slivered triangles: a) possible shading anomalies are caused by incorrect smooth shading of slivers; b) slivered triangles prevent clean deformation of the mesh by causing shading anomalies during deformation, even though the mesh renders cleanly when it is not deforming; c) slivered triangles can cause problems when special effects are applied to the mesh.

sliver polygon A polygon whose area is so thin that its interior does not contain a distinct span for each scan line.

slow-in/slow-out Achieving smooth initiation and termination of changes in an animation.

slow-motion A shot that plays at a slower speed than full-motion film or video. Usually described as a percentage of full motion.

slow reveal A moving shot, often a pan or dolly, that slowly allows the viewer to see the total action of the scene; often used in "crime scenes," in which the camera pans slowly across the room to reveal a body on the floor.

SLR See *single lens reflex camera*.

slugline The first line of a scene in a screenplay that identifies, in upper-case letters, whether the scene is interior or exterior, the location, and the time of day.

Smale's horseshoe map A physical system characterized by having a strange attractor.

small computer system interface See *SCSI*.

small light source A distant, unobstructed, bright light source. Small light sources have hard-edged, dark shadows with a very bright highlight. The penumbra generated by a small light source blends with the umbra. A small light source is always directional, and it always indicates the orientation of the light source. The sun on a clear, cloudless day functions as a small light source. A distant, bright, focused spotlight also functions as a small light source, as does a bright torch in a dark cave. If one can tell the direction from which the light is coming and if the shadows it casts are hard edged and dark, it is a small light source.

Smart Clip A movie clip with parameters unique to each instance. In addition, Smart Clips can include a custom user interface to populate the parameters.

SMD See *surface mount device*.

smearing Modifying the color of a pixel with a function of adjacent pixel colors to smooth out violent discontinuities in a picture.

Smile A control used to create facial expressions in *Poser*. It adds a smile at positive values, and a "droopy" look at negative values. The Smile and Frown parameters are not opposites. Each de-

forms very different muscle groups on the face.

smoke See *drifting smoke effect*.

Smooth Image tool A special effect in the *Game Creation System* used to smooth all the pixels in an image and apply the tool to the edges of the image. Other effects include negative image, *grainy glass*, and double image. The pixel wraparound feature is especially useful when working on wall panels.

smoothing The reduction of noise effects in an image by spreading of the noise over a larger area.

Smooth Mesh tool A tool in *form•Z* that takes a low-count polygonal mesh and, based on user-defined variables, generates a smooth mesh, a more complex and much more polygonally-heavy mesh. The resulting shape of the smooth mesh can have subtle detail that would be very hard or even impossible to achieve with more conventional tools. Using smooth meshing it is possible to create a limb of a character complete with muscle ripples and having an appearance of an underlying bone structure.

Smoothmove A plug-in for *trueSpace* that allows the user to create a 360 degree spherical panorama from a variety of camera positions. It can also be used with real photos or other computer graphics programs.

smooth pursuit A type of eye movement in which the eye tracks an object that is moving at slow to moderate speed. The eye follows the object in a smooth manner, ignoring all other stimuli.

smooth shading The shading of a graphics surface by continuously varying the color tones over the surface in accordance with the way the surface is illuminated. This is the most difficult shading technique. *Phong shading* and *Gouraud shading* are simplified techniques for accomplishing an approximation of *smooth shading* while reducing the computer computations required.

SMPTE See *Society of Motion Picture and Television Engineers*.

SMPTE timecode The professional industry standard set by the Society of Motion Picture and Television Engineers (SMPTE). Most professional equipment can read SMPTE timecode, so in order to work with existing professional equipment, SMPTE timecode must be used.

SMT See *surface mount technology*.

snap 1. In a CAD system, a process in which the cursor is automatically moved to the nearest point on an existing line or grid. 2. A command in any 2D or 3D application that "snaps" a selected point to another point on the object or to the grid.

Snell's law A law that expresses the relationship that governs the refraction of light. The law states that the sine of the incident angle of light to a surface of an object is equal to the refractive index of the material multiplied by the sine of the refracted angle. The relationship between the angle of incidence θ_i and the angle of refraction θ_t is given by the following equation:

$$\frac{\sin \theta_i}{\sin \theta_t} = \frac{\eta_{t\lambda}}{\eta_{i\lambda}}$$

where $\eta_{i\lambda}$ and $\eta_{t\lambda}$ are the indices of refraction of the materials through which the light passes.

snow The image produced by the display of noise on a video screen.

snowflake halls A self-similar fractal curve created using the initiator-generator technique. It uses an eleven segment generator with two different length line segments.

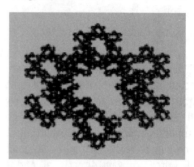

snowflake halls.

snowflake, Koch See *Koch snowflake*.

SNR See *signal-to-noise ratio*.

snub figure A solid formed by surrounding the edges of each of a regular solid's faces with equilateral triangles.

Sobel operators A pair of 3×3 matrices used to sharpen the edges of objects in an image.

Society of Motion Picture and Television Engineers (SMPTE) The professional organization for engineers working in motion pictures or television.

Soddy's formula A formula for the radius of a circle inscribed in the curvilinear triangle formed by three tangent circles. The formula is:

$$\frac{1}{r} = \frac{1}{a} + \frac{1}{b} + \frac{1}{c} + 2\sqrt{\frac{1}{b} + \frac{1}{ac} + \frac{1}{ab}}$$

where a, b, and c are the radii of the tangent circles and r is the radius of the inscribed circle.

sodium vapor lights High-pressure or low-pressure lights that cast an orange-yellow or pinkish hue if not phosphorized. This type of light emits mostly reds and yellows and lacks blue-green to blue spectra. These lights are very bright-light sources that are used in streetlights and in illuminating huge public spaces. They usually have a color temperature of about 2,100 degrees Kelvin, resulting in yellow-orange illumination.

softbox A cubic or rhomboid-shaped light box with a reflective inner surface and a diffusing material in front. It generates a large area of even illumination, which, when reflected by shiny objects, also creates an outline.

soft copy A copy of digital data on a storage medium that cannot be read with the human eye, such as a floppy or hard disk, an optical disk, or a magnetic tape. Compare with *hard copy*.

SoftDV The DV CODEC provided by Media100 for their EditDV line of video editing products.

SoftImage High-end graphics and animation software.

soft light Light from a diffuse, often indirect, light source.

solid angle The angle at the apex of a cone.

solid modeling The rendering of a scene, described in terms of graphics primitives

by converting to two dimensions and directly computing surface colors. Solid modeling uses constructive solid geometry techniques.

solid modeling.

solid texture A texture pattern that is defined in three-dimensional space so that volumes cut out of the object will reveal the proper internal texture pattern.

Sonic Foundry A developer of a range of audio and multimedia applications.

sonic tablet A digitizing table composed of a surface having strip microphones along a horizontal and vertical edge. A stylus is used to mark the desired position. Ultrasound pulses from the stylus are picked up by the microphones and the time delay of the signals used to determine the selected position.

Sorenson compressor A lossy QuickTime CODEC.

sorting, bucket A device used to simplify scan-line algorithms, in which primitives are transformed into screen space and

397

then sorted into buckets according to the first scan line in which each appears.

sort mode The edits in a list can be sorted in several different ways, depending on the needs of a project and the requirements of the on-line facility. *A-mode* is the most common and easiest to understand. A-mode EDLs are sorted in terms of master record-in. In other words, edits will be performed in a linear manner, from start to finish. This is the simplest and most intuitive way, but often *C-mode* is a better choice. C-mode EDLs are sorted by source tape number, then by master record-in. With C-mode, the on-line editor starts with the lowest tape number and sets the video levels for that source tape. Then all the shots from that reel are edited onto the master. The same procedure is followed for the next source tape and so on. If there are 20 source reels and 650 video edits in a list, A-mode, the on-line editor, will have to set the video levels up to 650 times; with C-mode, as little as 20 times. Other sort modes include *B*, *D*, and *E modes*, which are rarely used for long format projects.

Sound Replacer An application that replaces sounds already in a mix.

Sound Studio A digital audio recording and editing application for the Macintosh. It allows the user to take full advantage of the Mac's built-in sound recording and playback capabilities, as well as digitize a collection of vinyl and tapes, do live recording of audio, and edit new and pre-existing digital audio.

source monitor The monitor or window that displays the unedited source footage, as opposed to the destination (or record) monitor, which plays the edited sequence.

source objects Objects are used as base shapes for the creation of other shapes. A cross-section for an extruded object is a source object. The extruded solid of a surface is a derivative.

SpaceTime Morph An animatable morph target plug-in for *trueSpace*, developed by Mentemagica, used primarily for facial animation, but with many other uses.

spaghetti model Storage of spatial data in the form of a list of *(x,y)* coordinates without any other information.

span A set of pixels that comprise the portion of a scan line between edges of a convex polygon.

spatial Pertaining to three-dimensional space.

spatial integration A characteristic of the human eye; when a small area is viewed from a sufficiently long distance, the eye averages out the fine detail within the smaller area, and records only the overall intensity of the area.

spatial occupancy enumeration A special case of cell decomposition in which a solid is decomposed into identical cells arranged in a fixed regular grid.

spatial partitioning The breaking down of a large problem into several smaller ones by assigning objects or their projections to spatially-coherent groups during preprocessing.

spatial partitioning representations Decomposing a solid into a group of nonintersecting adjoining solids that are more primitive than the original solid.

spatial summation The integration of small objects into a larger collective perception, even if the small details on their own are independent. Spatial summation is the "summation" of adjacent areas into one. It is the fusing of small stimuli into a larger sensation.

spatial summation.

Spawning Props A feature of *Poser* that permits creating new props by cutting away sections of any props targeted.

SP-DIF Sony/Phillips Digital Interface, a digital audio format used for consumer equipment.

SPEC Benchmark Suite See *System Performance Evaluation Cooperative Benchmark Suite.*

special effect In cinema, computer graphics, and game development, a visual effect produced by using animated images to represent explosions, fires, tornadoes, and other dramatic visual elements. Also known as *F/X*.

special orthogonal matrix A 2 × 2 matrix whose vectors have the following characteristics: each is a unit vector, each is perpendicular to the other (their dot product is zero), and the determinant of the matrix is one. This matrix is especially useful in performing rotations.

speckle A non-additive noise effect resulting when local interference patterns are produced by monochromatic (laser) light reflecting from surfaces whose roughness is of the same order as the light wavelength.

spectral energy distribution The amount of energy present at each wavelength for a light source or light reflected from an object.

spectral-response functions The response of the cones in a human retina to light of various wavelengths.

spectral sampling Taking a large number of samples across the visible spectrum of a light source or light reflected from an object to determine its proper color.

spectrophotometer An instrument used to measure the light intensity for a selected narrow frequency band.

spectroradiometer A device that measures both the spectral energy distribution and the tristimulus values of light.

spectrum, visible The range of wavelengths of electromagnetic emission that can be seen by the human eye. It ranges from 400 to 700 nanometers.

specular 1. A focused light reflection, normally bright and blinding. 2. A highly-directional quality of reflected light (*See Figure next page*).

399

specular.

specular channel A channel that defines whether an object has highlights. Usually, the specular channel allows the user to define how large the highlight is, how bright it is, and often the color of the highlight.

specular color The color indicated by the spectral channel in a texture.

Specular Color A color control in *Bryce*. Objects that are shiny have *specularity*, or a hot spot that appears when a light shines on them. Specular color is the color of the hot spot. The amount of a set color applied to the hot spot is determined by the slider next to specular color.

Specular Halo Color A color control in *Bryce*. The specular halo is the blurred edge around the specular hot spot. A hard, shiny, metal material has a small hot spot with not a lot of halo. A buffed metal, or a plastic, has a larger halo. Some substances have more halo and little or no hot spot, like buffed wood. Other materials, like fabrics, have neither.

specularity value The value indicated in a spectral channel. In *Bryce*, the specularity element is based upon either a color palette assignment or a texture in one or more of the ABCD texture channels. The specularity value slider will determine how strong its presence will be in the material. The slider settings should be high for metals and plastics, medium to medium-high for woods and metallic liquids, and off for softer materials like fabrics.

specular reflection The reflection of light from a mirror-like or very shiny object.

specular reflection exponent (n) Reflection characteristic used in the Phong illumination model. It varies from one to several hundred, depending upon the material and the sharpness of the reflection desired.

speech recognition See *voice recognition*.

speech synthesizer See *voice synthesizer*.

Speed A setting in the Mr. Nitro section of *Universe* that determines how fast the shockwave passes through a scene.

Speed Razor A popular Windows-based editing package that offers real-time, dual stream playback and, when combined with the right hardware, uncompressed D1 NTSC or PAL video in the Video for Windows AVI format. *Speed Razor* offers a full-range of professional tools including RS-422 deck control, SMPTE timecode support, low and high resolutions, and EDLs. *Speed Razor* has several editing tools: multiple levels of Undo, keyboard shortcuts, storyboard editing, up to 20 tracks of real-time audio mixing, and field-rendering for effects and transitions.

sphere The locus in three dimensions of all points equidistant from a given center point.

Sphereglo A color and transparency shader for creating geometry-based explosions.

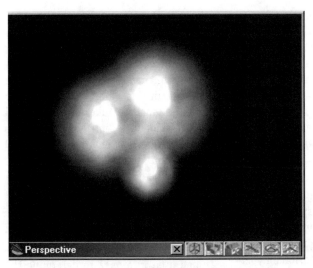

Sphereglo.

flect around the normal at the point of contact. Whatever this reflected ray hits should be seen reflected at the point of contact on the sphere. Since it is not computationally feasible to perform one-bounce ray tracing for every point on a sphere, we instead create a texture map that contains the necessary environmental information. This map is called a *spherical reflection map*, or a *sphere map*.

sphere map A single *texture map* that contains a full 360-degree view of the environment surrounding a point in space. Creating a sphere map requires two assumptions. First, no matter the size and shape of the object being mapped, it is assumed to reflect the surrounding environment like a sphere. This concept is important because, logically, a point on a character's hand should reflect something different than a point on a character's foot with the same normal. With sphere mapping, these two points reflect exactly the same thing because they have the same normal. Second, the reflective sphere is assumed to be infinitely small. This means that all rays from the point of the eye in the scene to any point on the infinitely-small sphere are parallel to each other. Given these limitations, the sphere-mapping method operates on basic laws of reflection. Take, for instance, a ray from the eye point in a scene to a point on the reflective sphere. This ray should hit the sphere and re-

Sphere of Attraction tool A tool available in *Carrara* that allows the user to modify the form of a mesh.

spherical cubic interpolation (squad) *Slerp* produces smooth animations, but it always follows a great arc connecting two quaternions. Just as using straight lines to connect a series of points, using slerp to interpolate through a series of quaternions produces a jagged path. In practice, this means that animations change directions abruptly at the control points. To smoothly interpolate through a series of quaternions, use splines. The basis for spline interpolation is spherical cubic interpolation, or *squad*:

$$squad(t;p,q,a,b) =$$
$$slerp(2t(1-t);slerp(t;p,q),slerp(t;a,b))$$

The animation from p to q does not follow the great arc connecting p and q but curves toward the arc connecting a and b. It is common for *slerp* implementations to invert one of the input quaternions when the angle between the two

401

exceeds 90 degrees. Although it is true that q and –q represent the same rotation, *slerp(t;p,q)* does not produce the same result as *slerp(t;p,–q)*. Since the control points a and b are chosen to work with p and q, not –p or –q, it is best not to invert the input quaternions in the version of *slerp* used with *squad*. See *spherical linear interpolation*.

spherical linear interpolation (slerp) A method of interpolating between two quaternions by following the shortest path between them on a sphere. Just as three-dimensional unit vectors define points on a sphere, unit quaternions define points on a four-dimensional hypersphere. Smooth animation is achieved by interpolating values along the great arc connecting the two. Spherical linear interpolation (slerp) is given as:

$$slerp(t;q_0,q_1) = [q_0 sin(\theta(1-t))+q_1 sin(\theta t)]/sin(\theta)$$

where θ is the angle between q_0 and q_1. We can find θ by treating q_0 and q_1 as four-dimensional vectors and calculating the dot product:

$$q_0 \bullet q_1 = x_0 x_1 + y_0 y_1 + z_0 z_1 + w_0 w_1 = cos(\theta)$$

See *spherical cubic interpolation*.

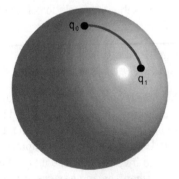

spherical linear interpolation.

spherical mapping A map of the world stretches and distorts the countries near the poles to make a flat representation; thus, Antarctica and the northern European countries seem larger. Only after one examines a globe of the world do those landmasses take on their actual sizes. A globe has "pinched" poles. This is how *spherical mapping* works; the 3D application "pinches" the poles of the map as it wraps around an object. Spherical mapping can also work effectively on nonspherical objects.

spherical mesh density determination technique A simple but effective technique used in *form•Z* to determine the average mesh density for a curvilinear model.

spherical product surface The surface generated using two curves whose x and y components are defined by parametric equations. Each point on the surface is defined by taking the product of the x coordinates of the two curves as the x coordinate and the product of the y coordinates of the two curves as the y coordinate. A sphere is obtained if the two curves are circles.

SpheroidDesigner One of the *Photoshop* filters from Corel's *KPT* collection, used to create an infinite range of textured spheres on the selected image.

SPHIGS Simple Programmer's Hierarchical Interactive Graphics System. A package of routines for performing graphics tasks.

spikes A tool in a 3D application that allows the user to transform selected polygons into spiked elements.

spindle The center part of a disk drive which is located at the axis of rotation and provides the force that causes the disk to rotate.

spin rate The speed at which a hard drive spins, measured in revolutions per minute.

spin-up The time between the application of power to a disk drive until the disk has accelerated to the normal operating speed.

splash A splash can be created by instantaneously displacing one or several z-values at a particular location. As the solution progresses, waves radiate from this location. This concept illustrates another advantage over explicitly evaluating the general solution: if any discontinuity in z(t) occurs, new values for A_{mn} must be computed with a discrete Fourier transform.

spline A mathematically defined curve that provides a smooth path from one point to another with a shape controlled by a number of control points. See *B-spline*.

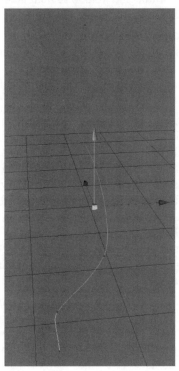

spline.

spline interpolation Let $\{q_n, a_n, b_n\}_{(n=0\rightarrow N-1)}$ be sequences of N quaternions. Let $S_n(t) =$ squad$(t; q_n, q_{n+1}, a_n, b_{n+1})$ To generate a sequence of smooth interpolations, $\{a_n, b_n\}$ is given as:

$$a_n = b_n = q_n exp[-(log(q_n^{-1}q_{n-1}) + log(q_n^{-1}q_{n+1}))/4]$$

spline tessellation A part of the tessellation tab in *Universe* that allows the user to set the number of splines in the U and V directions.

split complementary colors A color combination using three colors of any hue and the two colors adjacent to its complementary color, such as yellow with lavender and magenta, or red with apple-green and cyan.

split edit See *overlapping edit*.

split face lighting See *side lighting*.

split-track dialogue Dialogue that is spread across several separate tracks, rather than mixed onto a single track. Usually, split track dialogue has one track dedicated to each actor, or, if the dialogue is checkerboarded, two tracks dedicated to each actor.

spotlight 1. A light that concentrates its beam over a very narrow conical area. 2. One of four types of light used in *Bryce*. Spotlights are the second most common lights that are chosen, with radial lights being first. Spotlights are used for two main purposes. The first is to target a specific element in a scene, perhaps by moving across it to reveal it in steps. The second use for selecting the spotlight is to emulate a variety of light sources. 3. A type of light used in *Universe*. Spot-

spotlight.

lights produce a focused beam of light and are useful for things like flashlights, searchlights, headlights, and any other light where tightly-focused control is desired. 💿

spot meter A type of light meter that measures reflective light rather than incident light.

Spots function A *Carrara* function that creates random splotches—a type of visual noise. These splotches can be small enough to create a random noise effect, or large enough to create noticeable patterns. This makes them perfect for

Spots function.

use in the color and bump channels. Other 3D applications offer similar shaders.

spotting Watching a locked-picture edit of a project with the intent of identifying all of the sound effect and music cues that will be needed.

spraying A feature of a software painting program (e.g., *Painter*) that simulates the action of a spray gun.

sprite A small, moveable graphics pattern on a display, often used in video game animation.

squad See *spherical cubic interpolation*.

square spotlight One of four types of light used in *Bryce*, especially well-suited for global illumination. This light casts a squarish illumination that tends to smear and be somewhat rounded. Its best use is for general scene illumination from a specific direction, such as a light streaming through a window to light all of the objects in its direction.

square wave A continuous waveform that is characterized by almost instantaneous transitions from −1 to +1 and +1 to −1 and has equal portions of the wave form at the −1 and +1 levels.

squash and stretch One of the traditional rules of animation, in which the physical properties of an object are shown by distortions in shape. For example, a rubber ball might be shown as elongating as it approaches the floor, flattening out when it hits the floor, and elongating again as it rebounds. In contrast, the reactions of a ball of putty would be shown in a completely different way.

Squashnstretch A plug-in for *trueSpace* that makes it easier to *squash and stretch* objects automatically. Other 3D applications offer similar deformation modifiers.

srand A function in the C language that sets the seed for the random number generator.

SREE-D An acceleration technology built into *Poser*. This built-in high-speed 3D renderer allows real-time performance, eliminating the need for platform- or operating system-specific 3D software. Faster redraw of 3D models on screen allows for more realistic, shadowed previews, easier positioning of models, faster playback of keyframed animation, and higher-resolution models with much more physical detail. In computer graphics and animation, this increase in speed results in a more natural creative approach by the 3D artist.

SRGB A color space which, while not completely device independent, is based on a calibrated colorimetric and is well suited to use with color monitors and printers. This color space is quite similar to the way in which colors have been defined in the color television industry for years.

SRGP Simple Raster Graphics Package. A device-independent graphics package using raster capabilities.

SSL See *Secure Sockets Layer*.

stacks The C++ Standard Template library (STL) stack class provides three primary members—push(), pop(), and top()—for adding and removing elements from the container. These member functions, respectively, push an element on the stack, pop it off the stack, or retrieve the top element. To check the current state of the stack, size() and empty() are provided.

Stage The large, white rectangle in the middle of the *Flash* work space where a file is created. The image that appears

"on Stage" is what the user will see when he plays a *Flash* file.

staging See *animation, staging of*.

staircasing The representation of a straight line in a graphics image as a jagged staircase-like pattern, as a result of aliasing effects.

Standalone Deformations Panel A menu for *trueSpace* that can create a warping effect on an object, such as stretching it out or squishing it down, without needing to animate the actual geometry.

Stand and Shoot option An option in the *Game Creation System* in which the enemy stands still. If he sees the player, he will remain in his current position and will shoot.

standard affine plane A plane in affine space where points are triples of the form:

$$\begin{bmatrix} \alpha \\ b \\ 0 \end{bmatrix}$$

standard affine, 3-space A 3-space in affine space where points are of the form:

$$\begin{bmatrix} \alpha \\ b \\ c \\ 1 \end{bmatrix}$$

Standard Definition Television (SDTV) A subgroup of the DTV digital television broadcast standard designed to replace the current NTSC standard.

standard graphics pipeline See *graphics pipeline*.

standardized object An object defined at the origin and aligned mainly with the principle axes.

standard key cross-section A cross-section used in *form•Z*. A key cross-section is a user-defined 2D shape, usually a planar closed curve that defines the shape of the 3D form at the location along the loft trajectory where it is placed. A key cross-section is placed along the loft trajectory and is aligned to both profile shapes. With respect to profile shapes, a key cross-section is placed at apex points of maximal curvature for each of the profiles. The position at which a key cross-section is placed is called an "apex maximal," and it is a point on a curve where the degree of curvature is the greatest.

Standard Shape A plug-in for *Universe* that provides several shape options, such as toruses, tubes, and hemispheres. All of the parameters for *Standard Shape* are animatable.

Standard Template Library (STL) A library for the C++ language. The STL is a collection of container (collections of data) classes, ranging from vectors to balanced binary trees. In addition to the basic containers, the STL provides an assortment of algorithms that can operate on those basic containers.

Star One of the Photoshop filters from AlienSkin's *EyeCandy* collection, used to create n-sided stars and bursts.

Stat! A plug-in for *trueSpace*. The original purpose of this plug-in was to keep track of the three main scene statistics: vertices, polygons, and lights. It has been expanded to give a list of all recognizable objects so that the user can see which polyhedron is responsible for the majority of the scene's polygons.

state machine A simple AI concept that delivers power with very little complexity. A game object has a different *state* for each main segment of behavior it exhibits. The goal is to break down a game object's behavior into these logical states. In a baseball game, for example, the pitcher might have the states Ready-ForWindup, Windup, WaitForHit, InterceptBall, CoverBase, etc. It could be useful if, during a baseball game, the programmer could simply display on-screen the current and past states of all nine players on the field. Alternatively, if the programmer came across a bug, he could dump to a file all the past state information along with what caused each state transition. For example, if a right fielder never responded to the ball being hit, the programmer could see why he was not in the right state to listen for that event. So state machines not only break behavior into manageable units, but they also provide instant access to the mindset or thoughts of AI objects.

statement A single line of code in a script.

state patterns Almost every game programmer has had to deal with the problem of keeping track of constantly shifting game states in real time. States usually start out as simple enumerations, and behavior is implemented based on switching between states in a switch . . . case structure. Problems can develop, however, when the number of states starts growing larger and functionality must be shared in a greater number of these states. A cut-and-paste problem can quickly ensue, wherein the programmer tries to find all the states that share code and make sure that any changes to one state occur in all of them. A more elegant object-oriented solution is to simply use objects to represent logical states. The advantages of using objects are that states are better encapsulated; states can logically share code in their base classes; and new states can easily be derived from existing ones using inheritance. These advantages reduce the typical problem of having to cut and paste code between discrete states.

state transition The change in a finite state machine from the current state to an output state (which becomes the new current state) when an input is applied.

state-transition diagram A sequence-specification method for a user-interface management system.

state transition function The function in a finite state machine that defines which state will be the *output state* given a *current state* and a particular *input*.

state variable A variable that is used to encode the user-interface state of a system.

static graphics Graphics with no animation or interactivity. The computer-image equivalent of a photograph or a painting.

Steadicam A special camera mount that provides hydraulic, gimbaled support for a camera. Steadicam allows steady, fluid motion of the camera.

steering behaviors A set of three simple rules that determine the behavior of flocks. They are: separation, steering to avoid crowding local flockmates; alignment, steering toward the average heading of local flockmates; and cohesion, steering to move toward the average position of local flockmates.

stencil A method of storing color data in frame buffers, in which the ones in an incoming bit pattern cause the corresponding pixels in the frame buffer to be overwritten and the zeroes cause the corresponding pixels to remain unchanged.

step size property A property in the *Game Creation System* that determines walking speeds of the enemy by adjusting the distance traveled in each walking step.

steradian (sr) The solid angle of a cone whose apex is at a sphere's center that intercepts an area equal to the square of the sphere's radius r.

stereo A three-dimensional picture produced by creating two separate images, one for each eye, and viewed from its viewpoint. On cathode-ray tubes, the images may be side by side, viewed through an optical combining device; or an image in red may be superimposed on an image in blue and the result viewed through glasses, one having a red lens and the other a blue lens. Other techniques make use of different polarizations for the two images.

stereogram An image that combines two separate views to create one perception of a 3D object, often hidden within a picture. Usually the picture is composed of a series of dots. In order to see the "hidden" image, the viewer must "stare" at the picture until the image begins to take shape.

stereographic map A map of a sphere onto a plane, where the point of projection is at the tangent point's opposite pole. It is both conformal and circle preserving.

stereopsis The interpretation of the two slightly displaced images from the eyes as being three-dimensional. Also known as *stereo vision*.

Stevenson-Arce error diffusion filter An algorithm for performing discrete convolution or digital filtering, which is the improvement of the appearance of an image by replacing a pixel with a function of that pixel and its neighbors. The Stevenson-Arce error diffusion filter is frequently used to change color images to images consisting of black, white, and shades of gray.

sticky plane problem A small object, depending on its location, may be stored in an octree node with a very large bounding volume. This happens when an object straddles the boundary plane between two large nodes. This creates "sticky" areas in the partitioning hierarchy, keeping small objects high in the tree hierarchy and reducing the effectiveness of the partitioning.

stilb A unit of luminance equal to 1/1000 nit.

stimulus-response (S-R) compatibility The principle that system responses to user actions must be in the same direction or orientation and that the magnitude of the responses to such actions must be proportional to the actions.

stipple A pattern of dots or short dashes, often used to fill a background.

stitching Stitching operates on a continuous mesh attached to a bone structure. In rigid-body animation, a polygon is transformed by one matrix representing the bone to which that polygon is attached. With stitching, each vertex in a polygon can be transformed by a different matrix representing the bone to which the individual vertex is attached. Polygons can be created that "stitch" multiple bones together by attaching different vertices in the polygon to different bones. When the bones are manipulated, this polygon should fill the gap in rigid-body animation.

Stitch tool A tool in *form•Z* that stitches together meshed surfaces. If the result is topologically a solid, that result will be treated as a solid by *form•Z* and reported as such in the Query tool. This feature allows the user to migrate the object from solid to meshed surface and back again with relative ease.

STL See *Standard Template Library*.

stochastic sampling An antialiasing technique that computes a sequence of images. For each pixel, a different sample point is used in each of the images. The final pixel color is the average for that pixel in each of the images. In computation, only a single frame needs to be stored, containing the average value for each pixel up to that point in the computation. Each new set of values is averaged into the value contained in the frame.

storage Non-volatile storage that is used for long-term holding of programs and data. Storage is usually magnetic or optical.

storage media The physical material upon which data are recorded such as magnetic disks, optical disks, or magnetic tape.

storyboard editing A method of editing using thumbnails of each shot and organizing them in a bin, prior to drag-and-drop editing them into a sequence (*see Figure next page*).

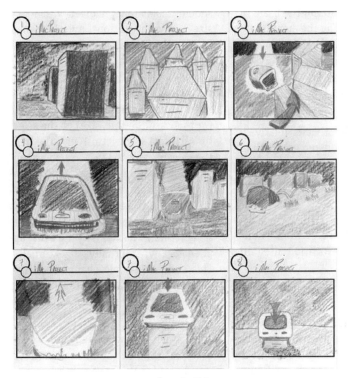

storyboard editing.

ples of this genre include *Breach*, *Paladin*, *Empire*, *Civilization*, *Stellar Conflict*, and *Master of Orion*.

streaking An error in displaying or computing an image that causes objects to extend horizontally beyond their actual boundaries.

streaming video Video that is downloaded, on-demand, iteratively to the viewer's computer.

stretching Changing the shape of graphics objects by altering the scale in one axis direction and decreasing it in the orthogonal axis direction.

string A series of characters.

strip A mesh of triangles or quads that is only one triangle or quad wide.

strip light A diffuse, narrow light source.

strobing The stuttery motion caused by fast shutter speeds. Strobing appears because of a lack of motion blur.

stroke A short, straight line segment used as part of a vector graphics image.

stroke device An input device, such as a mouse or digitizing tablet, that provides a sequence of point coordinate sets.

stroke display A type of cathode-ray tube display in which lines and characters are drawn by directly moving the electron beam to trace out the desired

strange attractor A set of values on which many orbits of a dynamical set of equations tend to land.

strategy game A game genre in which players each make their decisions and the game progresses after each person has taken his turn. This genre requires considerable strategic thought and planning to go into a game, much like chess. In real-time strategy games, such as *Populous*, *Syndicate*, *Command and Conquer*, and *Warcraft*, it is important for players to make moves quickly. Fast players can make many moves in a short period of time. These games are similar to *simulation games*, since the player is usually overseeing a large battle or war and the building of towns and outposts. Resource management is important. Exam-

shape rather than scanning the beam in a raster and illuminating the appropriate points in the raster scan. Also known as a *stroker* or *calligraphic display*.

stroke text Text characters that are defined in terms of lines, making it easy to scale text size.

strong Describes color that is relatively high in color saturation and color value.

structure In PHIGS, a sequence of elements, such as primitives, transformation matrices, etc. that are used to define a coherent geometric object.

structure network referral A nonstandard structure execution used in PHIGS.

structure text Text that is to be scaled, rotated, put into perspective, etc.

Stucki error diffusion filter An algorithm for performing discrete convolution or digital filtering, which improves the appearance of an image by replacing a pixel by some function of that pixel and its neighbors. The Stucki error diffusion filter is frequently used to change color images to images consisting of black, white, and shades of gray.

StudioArtist A 2D image application, developed by Synthetik Software for the Macintosh, that allows the user to create effects for graphics and QuickTime movies.

Studio Pro A 3D graphics and animation application from Strata, with a collection of modeling and deformation tools.

style sheet, syntax of A style sheet in HTML is made up of a selector and a declaration. A selector is the actual HTML tag such as <H1>, <P>, etc., which the declaration will be affecting. The declaration determines how the selector should display (e.g., in green with a 14pt size and with the font style Verdana). Each declaration is made up of a property, a colon and then the property's value (e.g., font-size: 12pt). The following syntax example offers only a declaration which changes one property value (in this case the font size) of the selector <H1>: H1 {font-size: 14pt}. The H1 is the selector and the "{ }" symbols contain a declaration. The declaration identifies the property font size that will be affected by the value, which is 14pt. The syntax of declarations follows the same format, whether they are being applied locally, internally, or externally. This syntax example changes multiple declarations of the selector <H1>: H1 {font-size: 14; color: green; font-family: Verdana}.

stylus A pen-like instrument used with a graphics tablet to obtain position information for input to a computer.

subatomic primitive A graphics primitive that is at a level below a primitive object, such as the definition of a portion of a scan line.

subdivision The recursive division of a line, curve, or surface into smaller and smaller segments.

subpixel A subdivision of a pixel used to render one part of the pixel separately, so that the results from several subdivisions can be combined in a weighted fashion to obtain an antialiased value for the pixel.

subscript A character that is reduced in size and printed below the baseline for a line of text characters.

subspace, affine or linear A *linear subspace* is a subset of a vector space where, if any vectors **v** and **w** are in the subspace, so are **v** + **w** and av, where a is any real number. An *affine subspace* S is a subset of a vector space where the set S' = {u − v|u,v in S} is a linear subspace of the vector space.

subtraction, Boolean Boolean subtraction (A minus B) subtracts one shape's geometry from another. Imagine "magic" shapes that can be inserted into any shape. These magic shapes would surround parts of the shape into which they were inserted. When these magic shapes are told to disappear, they take with them any polygons that may be within them. Boolean subtraction allows for the creation of shapes that would be very difficult to create any other way.

subtractive color model The color model used for mixing paints and inks, where the pigments absorb some colors and reflect others. The basic colors are cyan, magenta, and yellow. Black is also often used to produce a richer picture. When two or more layers of different colored ink are superimposed, the apparent color is the reflected color, which is what remains after each layer of ink has absorbed its characteristic part of the light spectrum.

subtractive color model.

succolarity The property of a fractal curve that has filaments that nearly fill space. The term *succolarity* was coined by Benoit Mandelbrot in 1977.

summed area table A table whose value at pixel *(x,y)* is the sum of all the values in the source image in the rectangle whose corners are *(0,0)* and *(x,y)*. A summed area table is used for box filtering an image.

sun guns Lights that are mounted on the camera. The are great for run and gun photography, but do not do well when carefully crafted lighting is the goal.

sun options Using the *Bryce* Advanced Motion Lab and Motion Wave, one can alter the sun's color, intensity, disc and halo colors, and direction.

sunShine A plug-in for *trueSpace* that allows the user to add a realistic sun to any scene.

super See *superimpose*.

superattractive periodic orbit A periodic orbit for which the absolute value of the eigenvalue is equal to zero.

superblack A level below that of black in a composite video signal, used for synchronizing color information.

supercardioid microphone A very narrow cardioid microphone pick-up pattern that is very directional.

supercase In typography, a set of characters that are neither upper nor lowercase. On a keyboard, they are accessed by first hitting a key designated for a *supershift* code.

superciliary arch The portion of the human face that overhangs the ocular cavity, providing protection for the eyes and shade from the sun. The superciliary arch on a male is large and pronounced.

411

superconic An extension of the conic curve in which the terms of the conic equation are raised to an arbitrary power to vary the shape and smoothness of the curve.

superimpose To place a partially-transparent image or text over another image, so that portions of both images appear in the final composite image. Also known as *super*.

superimposed geometric shapes Shapes that are created by using adjacency techniques to randomly add together randomly-selected shapes. This technique by itself is best suited to abstract objects.

Superobjects A plug-in for *trueSpace* that creates superquadratic objects, both supertoroids and superellipsoids. These rounded objects can be used in a variety of situations.

superposition, principle of The fact that the intensity of an image containing two non-overlapping primitives is the sum of the intensities of the two primitives.

superquadric An extension of quadric surfaces formed by computing the spherical product surface of two superconics.

superred See *CIE color space*.

supergreen See *CIE color space*.

superblue See *CIE color space*.

supersampling The rendering of several sample points within a single pixel, so that the resulting values can be combined in a weighted fashion to produce antialiasing.

superscript A character that is reduced in size and printed above the baseline for a line of text characters.

supertwist A liquid crystal display (LCD) device in which the crystals are twisted to provide a wider viewing angle and greater contrast than an ordinary LCD.

Super VGA (SVGA) A display graphics interface standard that complies fully with the characteristics of the IBM Video Graphics Array (VGA) and also offers a number of advanced video modes not often supported by IBM.

superwhite A high-intensity white that is 10 percent higher in voltage than white signals obtained from normal images. Superwhite can be used to display a cursor that does not disappear when it is moved to the white area of a display.

supplementary light An incidental or situational light. These lights are placed depending on the script and the scene. *Practical* lights, a type of supplementary light, are the visible light sources in the frame. *Eye* lights, or *catch* lights, are the little specular reflections and soft illumination of the eye area. These lights perform an important but subtle task of imparting realism to the scene. Practical lights are necessary in scenes where there are visible lights. Eye lights are subtle but effective ways of making characters come alive. By attaching an eye light or focused key light to each eye with a null object, one can attain a realistic reflection on the eye throughout the positioning and animation of characters. Supplementary lights are often overlooked in computer graphics.

support of filter The circular base of a cone, produced by a weighting function that has its maximum at the center of a pixel and decreases linearly with increasing distance from the center.

supraorbital margin One of the most distinct bone masses of the face. It creates the ridge above the eyes. The supraorbital lies directly under the eyebrows, hanging over the eyes like an awning, blocking the sunlight from directly hitting the eyes. When animating character facial expressions, the skin moves over the supraorbital margin. A common mistake is to actually move the supraorbital margin on the model, which tends to make the effect unrealistic. A more effective approach is to move the physical tissue on the upper portion of the supraorbital margin, keeping the lower portion locked in place.

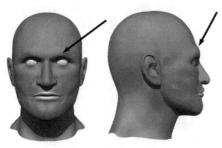

supraorbital margin.

surface blending The process of building a third surface to blend two separate surfaces. Depending on the achieved continuity, the three surfaces will either shade with seams, or will shade as one continuous, complex surface. The latter is usually the desired result and can be difficult to achieve, depending on the situation. The smoothness with which the surfaces shade is dependent on the achieved continuity between the two base surfaces and the blend surface. Specifically, it is the achieved continuity at blended edges that defines the smoothness of the rendered surface. With regard to surface modeling, there are three basic types of mathematical continuity: Positional (C0), Tangential (C1), and Curvature (C2).

surface geometry The means by which a surface is modeled. This may be polygonal, patch, NURBS, or a combination of all three.

surface mapping The projection of a two-dimensional image or pattern from the plane on which it was defined onto a curved or flat surface.

surface, matte See *matte surface.*

surface modeling 1. A technique for representing solid objects on a two-dimensional display. 2. The definition, formation, and representation of 3D objects without regard to their volume or solidity.

surface mount device (SMD) An electronic component that is designed to mount on the surface of a printed circuit board without drilling any mounting holes.

surface mount technology (SMT) The technology by which SMDs are soldered to printed circuit boards.

surface normal A unit vector at a specified point on a graphics surface that is perpendicular to a plane, which is tangent to the surface at that point.

surface of revolution A three-dimensional solid that is defined as the locus of all points on a curve that is swept around a central axis.

SurfaceSuite Pro An application that enables the user to create seamless textures that wrap around objects.

surface table A table containing all the surfaces of a polygon.

surround sound Sound that emulates reality by being reproduced at the same points in space, surrounding the listener.

413

Dolby digital is a typical implementation of surround sound, employing five audio channels, each with its own speaker.

Sutherland-Hodgeman algorithm An algorithm used for clipping a polygon to a convex polygonal clipping region. The input polygon is successively clipped to each edge of the clipping region until all edges have been applied. Also known as *re-entrant polygon clipping*.

SVGA See *Super VGA*.

S-Video connector A proprietary cable that is used to carry the Y/C video signal.

swabbing Converting an image file from one format to another.

swarming See *flocking behavior*.

swash character In typography, an alternate to a standard alphabetic character that has a curved flourish extending over or under adjacent characters.

sweeping 1. The generation of a three-dimensional surface by "sweeping" a two-dimensional curve over a trajectory. 2. Scanning a cathode-ray tube face with an electron beam to produce a raster scan.

sweetening The process of polishing the audio on a project by adding effects, equalizing, and fine-tuning edits.

swept contour A three-dimensional shape produced by translating a contour along a straight line or by rotating it about an axis.

.swf file A *Flash* file meant only for distribution. It can be watched, but not edited.

swimming An instability of a video image that makes portions of the image move in an undulating pattern. Swimming is particularly likely to occur in interlaced scanned images.

Swing classes A set of graphical user interface (GUI) classes for use with Java. Swing classes provide a more polished look than the standard AWT component set, and are written completely in Java so that there is no change in the appearance of the graphics when moving from one platform to another. Swing is targeted toward form-based applications, but has many other applications.

swizzle To reverse the order of bits in a byte from left-to-right to right-to-left.

symbol A graphic, movie clip, or button that is stored in the *Flash* Library. A symbol is especially useful because no matter how many instances of a symbol are used, it only has to download once, and changes made to the master symbol are immediately reflected in all instances already used.

symbolic link A tag that dictates how data are to be routed indirectly to a file rather than having the data sent directly.

symmetrical half object In *form•Z*, symmetrical objects are a type of working object for surfaces that are symmetrical across one or more axes. These objects are first built as a half. To obtain the entire surface, the *symmetrical half object* is mirrored across the axis of symmetry and the two halves are stitched to form a complete surface.

sync 1. Short for *synchronization*, the electronic pulses used to coordinate the operation of several interconnected pieces of video hardware. 2. The electronic pulses used to regulate the playback of the videotape in the VTR. See also *sync sound*.

synchronous A data stream that is timed by a master clock.

sync sound Recording sound and video that are synchronized together, whether onto the same tape or by two or more separate recording devices.

System Performance Evaluation Cooperative (SPEC) Benchmark Suite A set of software routines designed to test the speed of various aspects of computer performance. The SPEC Benchmark Suite is a quasi-standard agreed to by a group of companies that are leaders in computer system design.

Systolic Array Graphics Engine (SAGE) A system using a scan line virtual-buffer approach implemented by a one-dimensional array of pixel processors in VSLI chips.

T

T (refraction vector) A unit vector in the direction of light refraction.

tablet A device used to input the position of a stylus or puck to a computer. Most tablets make use of an embedded grid of wires carrying electrical signals. The stylus picks up these signals, the strength of which determines position. A resistive tablet uses a battery-powered stylus that emits high-frequency radio signals. The tablet picks up these signals and uses them to calculate stylus position. A sonic tablet uses microphones at the edges of the digitizing area, which pick up sound bursts from the stylus and use the delay between when the sound is emitted and when it arrives at the microphone to calculate position.

tactile continuity The use of familiar hand motions to control the actions of a computer program.

TAE-Plus Transportable Application Executive. A *style guide* (a written codification of many of the elements of user-interface format) developed by NASA.

tagged image file format (TIFF) A flexible format for storing monochrome or color graphics images in the form of bitmaps. The three-letter extension is TIF for Windows systems.

Takagi fractal curve A fractal curve constructed by positive midpoint displacements.

tangent space A space that lies tangent to the surface of a sphere. Points on the sphere are located by a 3×3 coordinate system using the surface normal as the +Z axis.

tangent vector A vector that is the limiting position of a secant of a curve through a fixed point and a variable point on the curve as the variable point approaches the fixed point.

tape drive A device that transports magnetic tape past a head that reads or writes data.

Tape Mouse function A function used for animation in *The Games Factory*. It allows the user to set a very complex path movement.

Taper tool A tool for adjusting object shapes in *Poser*.

Taylor series A power series that defines a given function. The formula is

$$f(x) = \sum_{n=0}^{\infty} \frac{f^{(n)}(a)(x - a)^n}{n!}$$

This is a convenient way to generate such functions as the sine and cosine. The series can be terminated at any desired point depending upon the accuracy that is desired. However, there can be a continuity problem for certain points in the function.

TBC See *time base corrector*.

Tchebychev fractal curve A fractal produced by iterating one of the Tchebychev family of orthogonal polynomials over the complex plane.

TCP/IP Transmission control protocol/ Internet protocol. A set of protocols developed for the U.S. Defense Department, used to link computers of dissimilar architectures across networks.

telecine The process of transferring film to videotape.

teleconferencing Conducting a conference among two or more parties at different locations by means of closed-circuit television. The video is often compressed to fit the bandwidth limitations of telephone circuits.

telephoto lens A lens with a very narrow field of view and, therefore, a long focal length. Telephoto lenses magnify objects in their field of view.

teletex Encoded text hidden in a broadcast video signal for decoding and display on specially-equipped television receivers. Teletex is used for transmission of closed-caption information for deaf viewers.

television An electronics signal that consists of horizontal and vertical synchronization signals and video levels for successive frames of a moving picture. At the receiving end, the synchronization signals are used to synchronize the raster sweep of a cathode-ray tube and the video is displayed as pictures on the CRT screen.

temperature, absolute zero See *absolute zero*.

temperature, color In lighting, the color of light is not indicated in terms of red, yellow, or blue; instead, it is specified as a *color temperature*. The unit of measurement used in color temperature is the Kelvin. See *Kelvin scale*.

temperature, Kelvin scale See *Kelvin scale*.

temperature, Wein's law Wein's law states that the wavelength of the peak radiance decreases linearly as the temperature increases. The hotter the object gets, the bluer the radiation it emits. Visible light is also a form of heat that we see. Imagine a totally black ball that radiates and absorbs light perfectly. If we started to heat this light, it would start to give off color in stages as it gets hotter. This means that the color it would give off would start from infrared to the reds, orange, and yellows until it reached the blue and ultraviolet light and beyond.

template 1. A gauge, pattern, or mold used as a guide to the form of a desired object. 2. A capability of C++ to define a function that works similarly for all variable types.

template matching In image processing, detection of an image by convoluting the image with a template that consists of an array containing the feature searched for and thresholding the output.

template procedure A procedure that generates a sequence of elements that defines a standard building block and is designed to be used repetitively.

temporal Varying with time, such as the change in frame images for an animation sequence.

temporal aliasing An undesirable strobing effect in an animation sequence that results from abrupt changes in the scene from one frame to the next.

temporal modeling in neural nets
Human brains are fairly slow compared to a digital computer. In fact, our brains have cycle times in the millisecond range, whereas digital computers have cycle times in the nanosecond range. This means that signals take time to travel from neuron to neuron. This fact is also modeled by artificial neurons in the sense that we perform the computations layer by layer and transmit the results sequentially. This helps to better model the time lag involved in the signal transmission in biological systems such as humans.

temporal ridge The part of a human face that runs along the outer side of the upper skull. It is not very pronounced, but it is responsible for creating the square-shaped appearance of the upper skull.

temporal ridge.

temporary object In *form•Z*, an object that is created to assist in the creation of other objects. Temporary objects can be copies of existing geometry and are usually expendable. The most frequent use of temporary objects is to test the result of trimming or Booleans prior to accepting the object and continuing the modeling process.

tension The relative amount of curvature near the control points of a curve or surface whose shape is controlled by control points such as a Bezier or B-spline curve.

tension parameter, B-splines A parameter b_2, which is used to define the shape of a B-spline curve.

tensor product A mathematical matrix function used to generate a curved surface from two orthogonal sets of splines.

tent filter A filter whose frequency response is in the shape of a triangle.

terabyte 1,024 gigabytes, or 1,099,511, 627,776 bytes of data.

teraflop One trillion (10^{12}) floating point computer operations per second.

terminate and stay resident (TSR) The action of exiting a software program so that the program remains in computer memory ready to be accessed instantly whenever desired.

termination The last device in a SCSI chain must have a *terminator*, which is a connector containing a resistor that terminates the chain. Bad termination can result in the entire SCSI chain malfunctioning.

terrain map In *form•Z*, a sketch that serves as a plan for the terrain model. After completion of the sketch, scan (if drawn) or export as a bitmap out of *form•Z* and bring it into any compatible image-editing application. Once there, paint a gray scale map using the sketch bitmap as a background. The displacement map is painted to have the darkest pixels representing the lowest terrain elevation and the whitest pixels representing the highest elevations. The elevation differential between the low-

terrain map.

tertiary colors Colors that result from mixing of the adjacent secondary colors. ☞

tessellate To subdivide a surface into a number of simpler figures. For example, a quadrangular polygon can be divided into a number of triangular polygons.

test fringing A thin, white fringe that may appear around text, depending on text size and background color.

test suite A set of inputs that is applied to a software system in testing together with the results expected from these inputs.

tetrad color A cross of four hues, composed of a primary, secondary and tertiary color. ☞

tetrahedron A regular solid having four faces.

est and highest displacement is defined in the Displace tool options.

terrain modeling 3D applications often provide what are referred to as fractal landscape generators. Fractal landscapes often contain details in shapes that would take long periods to model using any other method. Most provide for the generation of landscapes through gray scale figures. Using a drawing program, or even using satellite photographs, one can create an image that designates valleys as black and mountain tops as white. The brighter the region, the taller it will appear in 3D form, and vice versa for dark regions. Upon import, the 3D application will take this two-dimensional color image and convert it into a three-dimensional object. Other ways to build digital terrains include DTM (Digital Terrain Map) or DTED (Digital Terrain Elevation Data) as provided by the USGS (United States Geological Survey).

Terrain Model tool In *form•Z*, a tool that uses prebuilt and preselected contour lines and a site closed surface to generate a terrain mesh based on user settings.

Terrazo A *Photoshop* plug-in from Xaos, used to create user-controlled tiled images.

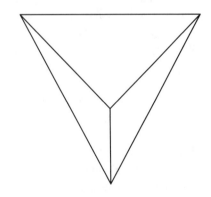

tetrahedron.

T$_E$X A comprehensive typesetting software system, developed by the American Mathematical Society, that contains

419

extensive capabilities for the writing of mathematical equations.

texel A set of data that describes a three-dimensional texture pattern, including surface and lighting model data.

text based The storage of data in the form of character codes rather than graphics techniques.

text file A data file that consists entirely of character codes such as *ASCII* or *EBCDIC*.

textless master A videotape master that has no titles or any other text in it, used for creating foreign-language versions.

text mode A display mode in which only a set of predetermined characters can be displayed as contrasted to graphics mode, in which each pixel can be accessed and colored separately.

Text tool A tool in *Paint Shop Pro* that enables the user to enter text onto an image. The user can choose from several fonts and sizes. When the tool is activated, click anywhere on the image, and the Text tool dialog box appears, allowing the user to enter text and adjust the settings.

textual Consisting entirely of text, with no graphics data.

texture The properties of a surface that result in changes in the color at different points on the surface, such as wood grain or marble textures.

texture coordinate generation Mapping textures at run time can produce interesting results. Developers use *texture coordinate generation* to perform animation, lighting, reflection, refraction, and bump mapping. The most common method of texture coordinate genera-

tion is that of transforming data (position, normals, texture coordinates) by a matrix to yield a set of texture coordinates.

Texture Info Window Filter A tab in the Texture Info window of *Universe* that allows the user to specify filters to blur or sharpen textures.

texture lists A feature of *Bryce* that allows the user to access and import procedural textures. There are five texture lists one can access, each with dozens of items not found or displayed in the Materials Presets library. The lists include Basic, Bump, Clouds, Rocks, Sand, Psychedelic, and User.

texture map An image that is mapped to a surface to specify its texture. Also known as a *decal*.

texture map.

texture mapping organization In *form•Z*, the breakdown of a model's surfaces in order to facilitate quick and effective texture mapping. It is a measure of how effectively a model can be textured in a given animation package. For example, a fuselage of an aircraft is textured with either planar or cylindrical projections running along the length of the aircraft. Wings are best mapped with planar projections applied from the top. If the model has wings and fuselage joined into a single object, then effectively texture mapping it becomes a difficult task. A model must be adapted to the animation environment in which it is going to be used.

texture maps as masks Using *Carrara*, if a designer uses a mix operator with a grayscale or black-and-white texture map as the mix function, the texture map will act as a mask for the two mix functions. Since a texture map can be a movie, this technique opens up a whole range of possibilities when used in animations.

textures, bump mapping for See *bump mapping*.

Texture space A three-dimensional space with a texture value assigned to each point in it. The texture of a solid surface can be determined by obtaining the surface's texture values in the corresponding points of texture space.

Textureshop A plug-in created by *Alien-Skin Software* for *Virtus* for use with all 2D and 3D applications. The resultant textures can be used to simulate skin and scale textures for organic forms.

textures, projection of A technique most often used to simulate lighting effects such as spotlights or shadows. The result of texture projection is fairly straightforward. A texture is projected onto some geometry from some point in space. For example, we can define a spotlight at some point in a scene and project a texture (e.g., a light circle) onto the geometry, creating the illusion of a spotlight.

textures, shine through A problem encountered when using textures. When we project a texture onto a sphere, for instance, the texture appears on both the front and back sides of the sphere as it relates to the light. This is because vertices on both the front and back of the sphere project into the correct texture space. There are ways to remedy this problem. One is to perform a dot product between the vertex normal and the light normal to determine whether the vertex is back facing. If the vertex is back facing, set the texture coordinate out of the range of 0 to 1. Second, the output of the standard lighting equation can be used to determine whether a vertex is back facing. Place a parallel light at the location of the texture projector. If the color output from this parallel light for a vertex is black, the vertex is back facing, because the only way for this vertex to become black is if the associated normal is facing away from the light.

textures, sphere map See *sphere map*.

texturing When modeling within a 3D application, the gray or white object that the application shows is simply a collection of colorless polygons. Texturing is similar to a veneer that is placed over the top of the polygons to make the polygons look like a recognizable object with a tactile surface. Some textures actually make changes to the polygons they are laid over (such as displacement maps).

TGA A file format for 24-bit color images in uncompressed form, originally developed for Truevision's TARGA video adapter boards.

Thaw A plug-in for *3ds max* from Effect-Ware that causes a target object to appear as if it were made of melting ice. *Cinema 4DXL* features a similar modifier called *Melt*.

thermal dye transfer printing A system of high-quality color printing in which dyes are selectively transferred from a plastic medium to paper.

ThermoClay A plug-in for *trueSpace* used for mesh-smoothing. It uses a proprietary Bi-Cubic Spline Interpolation to transform a polygonal object into a smooth organic object.

thickness The distance between a primitive's boundaries perpendicular to its tangent.

third-person 3D games A game genre in which the player experiences the action through a character on the screen. It enables the player to see the movements, acrobatics, and struggles against opponents that would be missed in a first-person perspective. Examples of this genre include *Tomb Raider*, *Dark Vengeance*, *Deathtrap Dungeon*, and *Fighting Force*.

ThOr A plug-in that permits lightning generation and animation.

threads Separate tasks that run concurrently under Java.

three-chip A camera that uses three separate CCDs to gather separate red, green, and blue data.

three-light studio setup A way of setting up studio lights to provide adequate lighting of a scene. The three lights are the *key light*, the *fill light*, and the *back* or *rim light*.

three-point editing A method of editing in which each edit is performed using an "in" and an "out" point on both the source footage and the edited sequence. Once the editor enters three of the four in and out points, the NLE or edit controller will automatically calculate the fourth in or out point.

three-point lighting The standard way to light a person using a strong, directed key light, a diffuse, less intense fill light and a strong backlight.

threshold A predetermined level of signal amplitude above which the signal is considered to represent a one and below which it represents a zero.

threshold dithering A method of digitizing an image using a dithering matrix to vary the threshold between black and white, thereby reducing the amount of aliasing.

threshold, hysteresis A method of determining a threshold that uses an upper and a lower threshold and remembers the previous output value. The output does not change if the input is between the upper and lower thresholds:

$$output(t) = \begin{cases} 1 \text{ if input} >= T_{high} \\ 0 \text{ if input} < T_{low} \\ output(t-1) \text{ otherwise} \end{cases}$$

thresholding Highlighting the points of an image that are at or near a particular value.

throughput A measure of the speed at which data can be moved through a computer or storage system.

thumbnail A small copy of a picture that is used for previewing.

thumbwheel A positioning device that consists of a wheel-like knob partially exposed through a slot in a panel, where it can be rotated by the thumb.

tick marks Small orthogonal lines drawn at intervals across the axes of a graph to indicate distance.

TIDY A utility for modifying and correcting HTML code. It is often used to read markup generated by specialized HTML editors and conversion tools, and it can help to identify "accessibility" issues.

TIFF See *tagged image file format*.

tile effect A raster graphic used as the fill color in any shape that is drawn.

tiling Constructing a large graphics image by repeating a small graphics image until the available display space is filled.

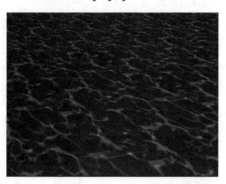

tiling.

tilt To rotate a camera up and down around its horizontal axis.

tilted ellipse An ellipse whose *length* and *height* axes are not parallel to the *x* and *y* axes, respectively. Some graphics packages do not allow drawing of such ellipses without complicated workarounds.

time base corrector (TBC) An electronic device used to correct video signal instability during videotape playback. Most modern professional VTRs have internal TBCs.

timecode A numbering system encoded in the video tape itself. It measures time in the following format: hh:mm:ss:ff, where h = hours, m = minutes, s = seconds and f = frames.

time delay, input The result of the user activating a command and then moving the cursor before the computer pro-

cesses the command. This may result, for example, in drawing an object at a place other than where the user intended.

timeline A chronological display of an edited sequence in a non-linear editing system. It is essentially a visual representation of time and what is occurring within specified time periods.

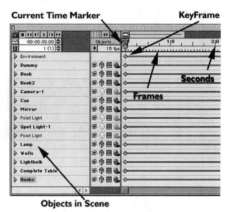

timeline.

time-of-day seeding A function that returns the number of time units since the current session was started. Such functions come with the same reservations as using the time of day; it will never be the same time of day for a given point in the game on separate occasions. However, this type of function works well to calculate game-time, since it is a simpler value to deal with, measured in milliseconds or seconds. Time of day as defined by the ANSI C library is measured in milliseconds, making the values extremely large when calculations to retrieve game-time are concerned.

Timmer's method A method of implicit curve approximation where intersections of the implicit curve with a predetermined grid are determined first, and then the curve inside each grid cell is

423

traced to determine how to connect the intersections.

tint, color The result of adding white pigment to a pure pigment, thereby decreasing the original color's saturation.

tint fill An algorithm for coloring a primitive in which the border of a region to be filled is determined not by the point at which another color is detected, but by the point at which the original color has faded to zero.

tint.

tintype The collodion wet-plate process yielding both a negative and a positive. When the dried collodion plate was contact printed, it gave a positive image. However, when the negative was backed with a black or dark material, the negative became a positive image. Metal-based collodions were called *tintypes*, which used cheap tin plates instead of enameled iron. The advent of the Civil War saw the widespread use of tintypes and their popularity by war photographers, including Mathew Brady.

Titan A graphics workstation, developed by Ardent, that combines general-purpose processing with high-speed 3D graphics. It is particularly applicable to scientific and engineering applications.

title safe A guide similar to the *action safe* area, but slightly smaller. To ensure that titles are visible on any monitor, al-ways make certain that they fall within the "title safe" area.

TLF Flame A shader plug-in for *trueSpace* used to create animated flames on geometry. *TLF Flame* allows the user to save rendering time by using a simple plane to create torches and other pyrotechnic effects, rather than creating thousands of particles to achieve a similar effect.

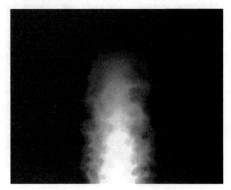

TLF Flame.

token A bit pattern used for identification of a specific action rather than as a binary number.

tone A hue with the addition of gray. Tone results from the addition of black and white to a pure color.

tone.

tone mapping The distribution or plotting of computed luminance values on a display device. Radiosity computes the luminance in a scene, and, since it is physically based, it uses real-world units. Consequently, the range of its calculations is very high (in the high dynamic range). If displayed, the extent of the calculated luminance in radiosity would exceed the capability of current display devices (monitors and video cards). Therefore, in order for the luminance to be "visible," it must be "mapped" to the limited range of the display device.

toolkit A set of utility programs, usually furnished along with a main program to perform special infrequently-used applications not included in the main program.

top-down model A model that is designed by first modeling the overall structure and then filling in the details.

top lighting The key light position above the subject. It can be placed above and to the side, but the overall direction of the light must come from overhead. This type of key light is evident during midday, when the sun is at its zenith and shines directly down. Top lighting forms deep shadows on the subject while making the illuminated side featureless.

topological model A model of three-dimensional data, particularly of geographical surfaces, containing all of the information necessary to examine relationships between various surfaces.

topology The set of geometric properties related to connectivity, particularly the definition of nodes and their interconnection and constraints on pathways around interconnected networks.

torque When a force acts to change angular momentum, it causes *torque*. The time derivative of the angular momentum is equal to the net torque on the body:

$$N_{net} = \sum N_i = \frac{dL}{dt} = r \times \frac{dp}{dt} = r \times F$$

where the angular momentum vector **L** is defined as the cross product of the position vector **r** and the linear momentum vector **p**. The vector **L** is therefore orthogonal to both **r** and **p**.

Torrance-Sparrow reflectivity model A physically-based model of a reflecting surface in which the surface is assumed to be an isotropic collection of planar microscopic facets, each of which is a perfectly smooth reflector. See also *Blinn shading.*

torus A doughnut-shaped, three-dimensional object. It is the locus of all points on a circle swept around a larger orthogonal circle.

torus, Fichter-Hunt The surface swept out by two series-connected rotational linkages.

Total Annihilation A game that uses data-driven methodology so that new units can be released on a weekly basis over the Web, providing unlimited gaming possibilities.

total internal reflection The situation where the characteristics of a medium interface are such that a ray of light is completely reflected from the media junction with none of it being transmitted.

touch screen A display screen designed so that a desired position on the screen may be selected and the cursor moved to that position simply by touching the screen at that point.

Trace A common command in 2D vector-drawing applications that allows the user to transform a pixelated image into a vectorgraphics drawing. Macromedia *Flash* is an example of an application that incorporates full-featured tracing capabilities.

track The path on magnetic or optical media that is followed by the head in recording or reading data.

track analysis See *breakdown*.

trackball A caged ball whose upper surface is rotated to position a cursor on a display screen. It is essentially a mouse turned upside down.

trackball, virtual A software routine that permits the user to use a mouse to rotate an object as if it were a trackball. The old and new mouse positions (2D [X, Y]) are converted into rays (3D) that point from the viewpoint into the window. Next, we determine where these rays would intersect a sphere around the object the user is manipulating. If a ray does not intersect the sphere, the closest point on the silhouette of the sphere is used. The sphere is rotated so that the point of intersection from the old mouse ray coincides with the point of intersection from the new mouse ray. This is achieved by passing these two points (using the center of the sphere as the origin of the coordinate system) as input to a function called *RotationArc()*. This returns a quaternion that is used to adjust the object's orientation.

tracking servo A feedback mechanism that senses variations in track position in recording media caused by minor defects, and makes corrections in the head position so it is kept centered on the track.

transcoder A device that changes the video signal from one format to another, such as from component to composite or from analog to digital.

transcoding The process of changing from one digital video format to another.

transduction The transfer of photonic energy into signals that the brain can understand.

transfer mode The type of calculation that will be used to determine how layers that are stacked on top of one another will combine.

transformation A function that is applied to the points of a coordinate system to redefine their position. This can be used to change to a different coordinate system or to change the size, shape, or position of an object by rotation, scaling, or translation.

transformation matrix A 4×4 matrix used to specify a transformation.

transition An effect that creates a bridge from one shot to another. The most often-used transition is the *cross-dissolve*. Others include various wipes and pushes, page turns, and white flashes.

transitional walk In *Poser* a walk assigned from the Walk Designer that targets fewer frames than the total number in a sequence. The extra frames can be at the start, end, or both the start and end of an animation. This necessitates checking the Transition From at Path Start and/or Transition To at Path End (*see Figure next page*).

translation The changing of the position of an object through a combination of linear motions, each parallel to one of the coordinate axes.

translucent Partially transparent. The color of an image viewed through a translucent material is usually less pure and the shapes are often blurred.

transmission The conduction or conveying of light through a medium.

transmission coefficient The fraction of the intensity of light remaining after

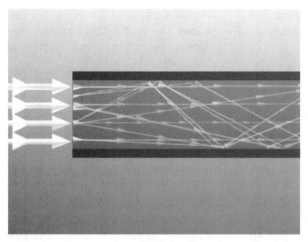

transmission.

traveling a unit distance through a volume.

transmission control protocol/Internet protocol See *TCP/IP*.

transmission hologram An image that is hit with light from behind the image. They are illuminated with a laser, or arc lamp specifically designed for holographic viewing, or a high-intensity white light. They can range in size from a few square inches to 4 × 8 feet, and can produce images of great depth and projection.

transparency map A procedural or bitmap texture applied to the trans-

transparency map.

parency channel of a material. Any element in a *Poser* scene can accept a transparency map simply by selecting the element and then selecting the map in the Surface Material window. The user can create transparency maps in any 2D bitmap application, saving them in any format that *Poser* can import. ◉

transparency recursion Describes the number of times a computer will "see" through a transparent object. The computer needs to set a limit on this, otherwise in some instances it might continue to calculate this effect infinitely in an endless loop. Fewer transparency recursions keep rendering times to a minimum, so this setting is often by default set to a low value. Usually this need not be altered, but if the user has many transparent objects, he may want to selectively adjust this. Also known as *ray depth*.

Transparency shader A feature of *true-Space* that gives the user control of the amount of transparency of an object.

transparent 1. Capable of being seen through. 2. Software or hardware that is automatically invoked and performs its function without the user being aware that it is there.

traveling matte A *matte* that changes over time to follow the action of a moving element. Traveling mattes are used to composite a moving element into a scene. In the digital world, an animated alpha channel serves the same function as a traveling matte.

427

traversal The process of sequentially addressing and processing the elements of a display list.

traversal coherence The coherence of pixels when an image is scanned.

Tree Professional A high-end 3D application from Onyx Software that generates foliage. It comes with a library of hundreds of tree forms and rendered 2D graphics. The pre-rendered graphics can be used when it is necessary to place groups of trees in the background or write to 2D picture planes. A separate module called *Tree Storm* acts as a plug-in for several professional 3D applications, allowing the user to run *TreeProfessional* from that application's internal geometry creator.

tree-structured directories A familiar name for a hierarchical file system. The file management system used in DOS allows a disk to have directories that are divided up into subdirectories that are divided into subsubdirectories, etc.

tremor In a darkened room with a lighted cigarette as a light source, the light appears as if it is hovering, and any attempts to make it stationary will fail. The perception of movement is illusory. In addition, if we fixate on it, the image appears to vibrate. This phenomenon, called *tremor*, is due to the imperceptible tugging of the eye muscles.

triad colors Any three colors that are balanced and equidistant from each other on the color wheel. ⬯

triangulate 1. To locate a distant point by taking two separated bearings and computing the triangle geometry. 2. To divide a polygon into triangles to simplify rendering.

Triangulate tool In *form•Z*, a tool that allows the user detailed control over face shapes and polygonal topology of the model.

triboluminescence Light generated when certain minerals are rubbed together, such as rubbing one quartz crystal against another or rubbing corundum (aluminum oxide) against a metal.

trichromatic 1. Sensitivity to three primary colors. 2. Relating to or referring to three colors.

trichromic The representation of colors as levels of the red, green, and blue (RGB) primary colors.

trigger A pulse used to initiate an event.

trigonometric functions A function (such as *sine, cosine, tangent, cotangent, secant,* or *cosecant*) that is expressed as the ratio of a pair of sides of a right triangle. Most computer languages include a library of trigonometric functions, but often in game programming it is more efficient to create new approximations of these functions using truncated infinite series.

trim curve A curve that is used to mark the boundary of a surface.

trim marks Marks on an uncut document that show where it is to be cut to fit the proper size of a final document.

trimming curves Spline curves defined in (s,t) parameter space rather than the (x,y,z) space on a bicubic surface. They are used when it is desired to draw only a portion of a bicubic surface.

trim mode The process of adjusting or fine-tuning an existing edit in a non-linear editor.

trim object In *form•Z*, a source object that is used as a cutting object. Open surfaces (lines and curves), closed surfaces, meshed surfaces, and solids can all be trim objects.

Trinitron A type of color cathode-ray tube, by Sony, that uses in-line electron guns to illuminate phosphors that are laid down in stripes on the screen surface rather than as clumps of dots, as in conventional color CRT design.

tripod A three-legged device for holding a camera in a steady position.

Tripod A tool in *Bryce* that simulates a camera attached to a tripod. It locates the camera so that it is securely fastened to a tripod, allowing the user to view the scene from that vantage point by using the trackball to rotate (but not move) the camera in 3D space.

tristimulus values The *X, Y,* and *Z* coordinates of a color value in the CIE color space.

trivial acceptance When clipping, the acceptance of a line that is completely within the clipping region.

trivial rejection When clipping, the rejection of a line that is totally outside the clipping region.

trompe l'oeil An oil painting or mural that is so realistic that it is easily mistaken for the real object.

trueSpace A 3D graphics and animation application from Caligari.

trueSpace Python See *tsxPython*.

truncate To end a number after a certain number of digits, ignoring any digits that may come afterward. A number may be truncated at any point *after* the decimal point without a change in value. If truncated to the left of the decimal point, the fact that the last digit shown is *not* a units digit must be indicated.

trU-V An application used to create textures for 3D objects that show no seams or stretches once an object is rendered and animated. *trU-V* creates a polymap, a stretched-out gridded map that addresses the selected polygonal object, that is then used as a painting reference. It is used in conjunction with other graphics applications such as *LightWave* or *3ds max*.

Try Movement parameter A parameter in *The Games Factory* that tests movement on the screen.

TSR See *terminate and stay resident*.

T-Stop Transmission stop. The measurement of the actual light transmission across the lens and aperture opening.

tSX Builder A program that enables the user to write 3D plug-ins for *trueSpace*.

tsxPython A version of the Python programming language that can be used for creating scripts to be used in *trueSpace*.

tsxPython, attached script A script for *trueSpace* that is an integral part of a *trueSpace* object. The script will remain attached until it is removed from the object, or another script is assigned to that object. There can be only one script attached to a *trueSpace* object at any given time. If a *trueSpace* object is saved as a .COB file, the script is saved along with it. Attached scripts can be assigned to any *trueSpace* object, including meshes, lights, cameras, and even the scenes themselves.

tsxPython, independent script Independent scripts are run directly from the *trueSpace* toolbar's "Run a Script" icon and are not attached to any objects in the scene. An independent script performs its assigned task and is then dismissed.

tube light A light similar to a stretched-out radial light. Tube lights are useful when a long field of uninterrupted light is needed. Fluorescent tubes are a use for tube lights, but another use is a scene that has a long row of light sources, for example, a corridor. Instead of having every single one of those light sources illuminating a scene, one long tube light could be stretched down the corridor to simulate the effect of many lights with one.

tubular light array A light array arranged as a main central light, situated on the invisible central axis of the light cylinder, with the peripherals on the sides arranged in a ring.

tungsten light Light from an incandescent source, such as a household light bulb.

TurboSilver An early high-end 3D art and animation application for the Amiga computer.

turbulence Departure from a smooth flow. Effects of turbulence, such as the characteristic color patterns of marble, are difficult to model but can be modeled using turbulence functions.

Turbulence One of the *Photoshop* filters in the Corel *KPT* collection that distorts selected images or image areas into turbulent designs.

turning vertex A vertex that is generated by an edge when it enters a corner region.

turnkey system A video editing system that is preconfigured and assembled, and that provides everything needed for the user to start editing.

TV standards Standards for various TV systems. They include:

Standard	NTSC	PAL	HDTV	Film
Frame rate	29.97	25	24 or 30	24
Fields	2 fields	2 fields	No fields	No fields
Vertical res.	525	625	1080	N/A
Scanning method	Interlaced	Interlaced	Progressive	N/A
Aspect ratio	1.33:1	1.33:1	16:9 or 1.78:1	1.33:1

tweak To use an operator that moves existing vertices, edges, or faces.

tweening 1. Short for *inbetweening*. The computation of graphics objects that form intermediate steps between an initial image and a final image. Used especially in animation when the beginning and end frames of a sequence are known but additional frames must be inserted between these to produce the apparent action. 2. A frame produced by inbetweening.

twin dragon A fractal curve drawn using the L-systems or initiator-generator technique which has the appearance of a dragon. It is a variation of the *Harter-Heightway dragon curve* in which the dragon is drawn a second time in the

twin dragon.

reverse direction on the initial starting line. The two curves fit together perfectly.

twist and taper Tools that are used to shape geometric figures. A "twisted" shape is simply an extruded shape that has been rotated along the *central* axis of extrusion, while a "tapered" shape can be scaled along the axis of extrusion.

twisted pair A type of cable consisting of two wires twisted together, usually without sheathing, to reduce noise pickup. Twisted pairs are used for telephone lines and for interconnecting computer networks.

two-and-a-half dimensions A two-dimensional graphic in which a three-dimensional effect is produced by assigning an occlusion priority to overlapping objects.

TwoBitArray class See *BitArray2D class*.

Two Horns Target Morph A target morph for *Poser* that creates two horns on the sides of the head.

two-pass transformation See *multipass transformation*.

two-shot A basic scene in which two characters face each other while ex-

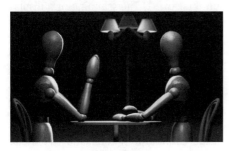

two-shot.

changing communication, usually in the form of dialogue.

typeahead A program capability that can begin executing a command while the user is concurrently entering information with an input device.

typeface See *character, typeface*.

type font A set of characters, letters, and digits of the same type style and size. When moveable type was common, a font consisted of a certain number of pieces of type for each character, the number depending upon the frequency with which each character was used. (For example, a font contained more *e*'s than *z*'s.) With electronic type fonts, a font refers to only a single occurrence of each character. Sample type fonts include *Times Roman* and *Courier*.

Type Manager Software from Adobe Systems that defines typefaces using Bezier curves and various hints that enable a printer to produce PostScript type fonts of various sizes and rotations on the fly without jagged edges.

type style 1. In line drawing, the type of line, whether solid, dotted, dashed, center line, etc. 2. In typography, a variation of a basic typeface, such as italic, bold, etc.

typography, digital A specialized field concerned with the problems of creating typefaces using digital techniques.

U

UberNurbs A set of tools in *Universe* that allow the user to create organic shapes by pushing and pulling a mesh.

UberNurbs Edit Cage tool A tool in *Universe* that allows the user to pull on the edges and vertices of a mesh.

UIMS See *User Interface Management System.*

Ulead An international developer of a range of other multimedia applications and *Photoshop* plug-ins.

ultimate display A proposed display standard in which the display would produce images and other sensory input that the user could not distinguish from real objects.

UltraATA A type of hard drive interface. Not as fast as SCSI, but fast enough for Digital Video.

ultrafiche A form of microfiche that can hold 1000 document pages per sheet, in contrast to normal microfiche, which holds 270 pages per sheet.

ultraviolet Electromagnetic radiation at frequencies just beyond that of violet light, outside of the visible part of the color spectrum.

umbra The completely occluded area of a shadow that has no illumination.

uncompressed video Video that has not had any compression applied to it either by the camera or by a computer.

undercolor removal The replacement of equal amounts of cyan, magenta, and yellow ink by black in the four color printing process. This gives richer blacks than could be produced by a mixture of the three colors alone and also speeds up drying time by reducing the amounts of colored inks.

under lighting The placement of the key light *below* the subject. It is usually pointed upward toward the subject, illuminating the bottom areas of the subject. It produces a strange shadow formation, because light sources seldom come from below. Psychologically, under lighting produces an eerie, mysterious, and sinister feeling. It is often used to suggest a villainous and evil disposition. It is also used to imply alien, otherworldly creatures and environments. Also known as *down lighting.*

underscan 1. The scanning of a display screen so that the scan does not cover the entire screen face, leaving a border around the edges. 2. A display feature available on professional video monitors that allows the viewer to see the complete video signal, including the sync pulses.

undo command A command that helps correct user errors by returning the system to its state prior to the issuance of the last previous command. Often a number of previous system states are stored so that the user can use the undo command to eliminate the effect of more than one previous command. See *redo command*.

unidirectional microphone A microphone that picks up sounds primarily from the direction in which it is pointed.

uniform Having equally-spaced subdivisions.

uniformly shaped B-spline curves A curve similar to the B-spline curve, but with two additional parameters, b_1 and b_2, to provide additional control over the shape of the curve.

uniform nonrational B-spline curves See *B-spline*.

Uniform Resource Locator (URL) The address of a document on the Web or Internet. Its structure is made up of four parts, including protocols, host name, folder name, and file name. A typical URL is:

http://www.charlesriver.com/titles/
   compgrdictionary.html

where *http:* is the protocol, *www .charlesriver.com* is the host name, *titles* is the folder name, and *compgrdictionary .html* is the file name.

unimodular transform A matrix with integral weights and a unit determinant that relates equivalent lattices.

uninterruptable power supply (UPS) An interface between the power outlet, computer, and peripherals that supplies a limited amount of current if the power should fail, providing enough time to save files and shut the system down.

union In constructive solid geometry, a region in space that is within at least one of two or more specified objects.

universal product code (UPC) A standard bar code applied to the packages of retail products. A reader for this code can convert it into pulses that are read by a computer. It is used to keep track of inventory, sales, etc.

Universal Serial Bus (USB) A standard for attaching serial devices such as keyboards, disk drives, and some types of storage.

Universe A 3D graphics package by Electric Image, formerly called *ElectricImage*. In *Universe*, each final geometry object requires its own texture mapping and material definition.

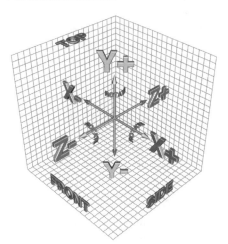

Universe.

UNIX A multiuser/multitasking computer operating system originally developed and trademarked by AT&T. It is available in versions that work with many different computer architectures.

Unlink from Parent A tool in *Universe* that unlinks a child object from its parent object.

unpredictable series When generating a series of random numbers, a series of numbers in which the next number cannot be guessed from examination of the previous *n* iterations.

Unreal A game that makes use of flocking algorithms.

Unwrapper A plug-in for *trueSpace* that allows the user to render an image of a mesh's UV space. This is useful for creating precision texture maps which can then be brought back into *trueSpace* and mapped onto the object. It also functions as a visualization aid for UV mappings. This feature is also contained in most professional 3D applications, although it may be listed under different names.

unzip To decompress a file that has been compressed with the *PKZIP* compression program, by using the *PKUNZIP* program.

UPC See *universal product code*.

update rate The rate at which a new image is displayed on a monitor screen. Contrast to *refresh rate*, which is the rate at which an image is redrawn on the screen regardless of whether it is the same or a new image.

update, screen See *display traversal*.

uplift A geological process that forms mountain ranges like the Rockies, Sierras, and Himalayas. Lateral pressure from the movement of tectonic plates causes the surface of the Earth to wrinkle like fabric, pushing up mountain ranges. This process can be simulated for computer graphics with a recursive midpoint displacement algorithm, also known as the *plasma fractal* or the *diamond-square algorithm*.

UPS See *uninterruptible power supply*.

up state Normally a button's default state, which occurs when the user has not clicked or passed over the button with the mouse.

UQUM See *use quick update methods*.

URL See *Uniform Resource Locator*.

USB See *Universal Serial Bus*.

Use Channel: Alpha Only An option in the Filter tab of *Universe* that allows the user to work on the alpha channel without affecting the RGB channel.

Use Channel: RGB Only An option in the Filter tab of *Universe* that allows the user to work on the RGB channel without affecting the alpha channel.

Use Contour Heights An option in *form•Z* that uses the heights of contour lines to generate terrain. The Use Contour Heights option allows the use of nonplanar contour lines. This is a significant advantage over the Contour Interval method, as it allows the creation of more topographically complex terrain. In certain cases, the user does not need to have as many contours as he would in the At Height Interval method.

use quick update methods (UQUM) A command in the PHIGS system that initiates fast erase and repaint techniques that may have minor imperfections. When such imperfections have accumulated to the point where the image is severely degraded, it must be completely regenerated.

user interface The means by which the user addresses the capabilities of a program. Also called *Graphical User Interface (GUI)*.

User Interface Management System (UIMS) A means for interface designers to develop, test, and modify their interface concepts in a cost-saving environment.

user's model See *conceptual design*.

Utah Raster Toolkit A software system that includes a number of improvements on the run-length encoding compression technique to achieve a large amount of file compression.

UV filter A filter that can be attached to the front of a lens to filter excess ultraviolet light and protect the lens from scratching and breaking.

UVMapper A utility for texture mapping WaveFront OBJ 3D models. It can be used to create texture map templates for models that are already fully texture mapped. This template can then be brought into a 2D paint program such as *Photoshop* or *Paint Shop Pro*, painted on, and then applied to the model in a 3D rendering program such as *Poser* or *Bryce*. If the model has no texture map (UV) coordinates, the user can generate texture map coordinates using *UVMapper*.

UV mapping Most textures have two-dimensional coordinates, x and y. These coordinates define the texture's horizontal and vertical positions. Many 3D applications use U and V instead of x and y to refer to textures when they are defining horizontal and vertical positions. In most cases, two coordinates would be sufficient, but 3D has three dimensions and some textures have emerged that are 3D shaders. In order to fix a texture in three-dimensional space, a third coordinate W is added. Many mapping methods treat the object as if it were a simple shape (a cube for cubic, cylinder for cylindrical, etc.); UV mapping recognizes more complex shapes and attempts to wrap itself around the various contours of the shape. Another advantage of UV mapping is the ability to stamp out "crawling" textures. Often, when using other mapping methods, the texture will appear to crawl along the surface of the object as it is animated through distortion methods (deformation lattices, inverse kinematics, etc).

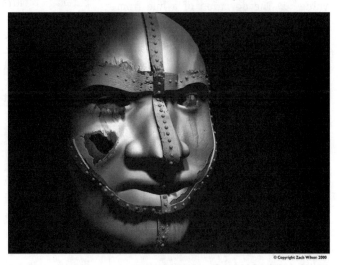

© Copyright Zach Wilson 2000

UV mapping.

UVN coordinate system A coordinate system used in ray tracing that is based on the viewing plane.

V

V (direction to viewpoint) A vector from a point on an object to the viewpoint of the image.

vacuum tubes Used by video cameras to convert light into electronic signals, before the invention of the CCD.

valuator device A computer device that inputs absolute numbers rather than relative data (as produced by a trackball or mouse).

value 1. The deviation of a hue from white or black which indicates how light or dark an object or material is. Also known as *lightness*. 2. A property of a color that is proportional to the brightness of the light impinging on the colored object.

value.

value component The component in a channel setting for a texture (any channel that accepts grayscale data) that places a slider or percentage indicator in the current channel that can be adjusted from 0 (solid black) to 100 (all white) with various shades of gray in between.

value discretization The rounding off of an actual value to an approximation represented by the closest digital value that can be achieved with the number of bits allowed to store that value.

vanishing point The distance at which all projections converge to a single point when drawing a scene in perspective.

vaporware Software whose availability has been announced or demonstrated, but is not currently available to customers, often because it contains too many bugs for commercial use.

variable-length record A record in a database that may vary in length depending upon the data stored in it. Reading variable-length records requires more sophisticated software than is needed to read fixed-length records.

variational calculus A technique used to compute the path of an object over time. It begins by selecting an arbitrary path. The path is then modified slightly by changing the values of a few of its points. If the new path is closer to satisfying the beginning and ending conditions with a lower energy expenditure, the process is repeated with the new path. If the new path is farther away, the process is repeated with the old path, using the opposite of the original perturbations.

variation-diminishing property A property of all spline curves that have the convex-hull property in which each time a new set of control points is calculated for the curve, they are no farther from the curve than the original control points and usually are closer.

varifocal mirror A device used to produce three-dimensional images. A flexible mirror vibrates mechanically to vary its focal length. At the same time, an image is reflected from the mirror, which is changed in synchronism to display the image that should appear at a coordinated distance. This results in an image that appears to be truly three-dimensional.

VCD See *video compact disc.*

VDM See *virtual device metafile.*

VDPM See *mesh, view-dependent.*

vec An arbitrarily-sized one-dimensional array of real numbers.

vector A line defined by its direction and speed.

vector camera A generalized form of the matrix-based camera found in many traditional graphics engines. Matrices are often difficult to read, due to the fact that they typically hold several operations concatenated together. The vector camera uses only simple vectors to describe its orientation, position, field of view, and aspect ratio. This format allows for some interesting optimizations to the overall graphics pipeline. The vector camera uses the same information found in matrix-based cameras. The world-to-camera matrix (view matrix) is broken down into four vectors. Three

vectors represent the three axes that define the camera's orientation, and one vector represents the camera's position in the world coordinate space. In total, this provides six degrees of freedom. In some graphics engines, it may be necessary to invert the view matrix to be compatible with the vector camera.

vector cross-hatching Cross-hatching of a primitive using a coordinate system based upon the primitive itself. This is purely geometric and therefore, rotates with rotation of the primitive.

vector display A monitor that displays images using vectored line segments rather than pixel-by-pixel writing.

vector dither A technique that uses a dither matrix that is not fixed in screen space, but instead is oriented along the length of a line.

vector generator A device that converts digital coordinates representing the beginning and end points of lines into suitable analog voltages.

vector graphic A file that contains all the calculations to redraw an image on-screen. A vector graphic's file size remains small, and the image can be scaled to any size without any degradation to image quality. For example, *Flash* .swf files are saved as vector graphics.

vectorgraphic displays Displays, usually of the flat-panel type, which are characterized by having individually-addressable pixels.

vectorization The translation of a bit-mapped image into an image defined by vectors.

vector quantization An image compression technique in which the image is encoded as a sequence of addresses to a table of small blocks of pixels that are relatively close representations of blocks of pixels in the original image. This technique is known as *vector quantization* because each block of pixels represents the components of a vector and attempts to find vectors that are close together.

vectorscope A special monitor for calibrating the hue, or color information, in a video signal.

vector space A space consisting of a set of elements, called *vectors*, where addition and multiplication by a constant can occur.

Vectorworks A 2D/3D vector graphics application from Nemetschek. For direct rendering of *Vectorworks* drawings, the *Renderworks* plug-in may be appropriate.

vergence When one holds his index finger about 14 inches from his face and slowly brings it closer until his eyes can no longer focus on it clearly, there is, at that point, a perceptible image disparity. The eyes looking at an object 300 feet away, however, do not detect a discernible disparity. This is because each image on the retina is almost identical, and there are no eye muscle strains. As the image gets closer, however, the eyes begin to experience image disparity as well as eye strain. This experience generates the sixth eye movement, which is called *vergence*. To gauge distance, the brain strains the eye muscles.

verification suite A set of tests developed to verify that a program meets all of its specifications. Use of the verification suite is essential to ensure that program modifications do not introduce secondary bugs.

verso In typography, the left-hand page of a book or magazine. The right-hand page is known as the *recto*.

vertex A point which marks the intersection of two or more edges of a polygon or other graphics object.

vertex collapse Deciding which edge of a mesh is least significant and removing this edge by making the two vertex positions at its ends equal. This edge collapse operation typically makes two triangles sharing the edge redundant. Detail is put back into the mesh by reversing these collapses through vertex splits.

vertex level deformation A technique, available in many 3D applications, that enables the programmer to see the vertexes where polygons meet to pull and push those points. It simulates "virtual clay." Many programs show the vertex points as Bezier handles or spline points. This assists in creating smooth deformations so the programmer can "pull" those points out to make a rounder face.

vertex normal A normal vector at a vertex of a graphics object. Rather than being normal to one of the intersecting surfaces, it is normal to the average of the surface normals of all of the intersecting surfaces.

Vertex Paint A modifier in *3ds max* that allows the user to paint the selected vertices of an object different hues.

vertical banding Bright vertical smears that can occur in some video cameras when the camera is pointed at a very bright source.

vertical blanking interval The period during which a video image goes blank as the electron beam returns from scanning one field of interlaced video to start scanning the next field. This "empty" space in the video signal is sometimes used to store VITC time code, closed-captioning, and other information.

vertical delay A display feature available on professional video monitors that shows the video signal offset vertically, allowing the editor to see and analyze the vertical sync pulses. See also *horizontal delay*.

Vertical Flip function A manipulation function in *The Games Factory* that turns all images upside-down. This is useful when the user has created several new directions from the original animation, and some of the sequences are positioned incorrectly. It can also be used to make a character walk on the ceiling.

vertical line resolution The number of horizontal lines in a frame of video.

vertical recording A magnetic disk recording technique that records pulses into the media rather than across it. This permits a higher density of stored data.

vertical resolution 1. The number of scan lines that are visible on a monitor display screen. 2. The number of horizontal lines that can be reproduced by a video camera and monitor combination.

vertical retrace The portion of a video signal during which the scanning electron beam is moved from the end of one field to the beginning of the next. Video is usually blanked during vertical retrace so that retrace lines do not appear on the screen.

vertical scan frequency The rate, in hertz, at which the display image frame is refreshed.

vertical sync The sync pulses in a video signal that control the field-by-field

scanning of each frame of interlaced video.

vertices, data format When storing vertices to be used to generate triangles, a common technique is to form a vertex list by defining three vertices for each triangle. When the triangles are part of a triangle mesh, however, space can be saved by forming a *triangle* strip or a face vertex index list, in which three vertices need to be defined for the first triangle, but only one for each additional triangle.

vertices, interleaved data See *glInterleavedArrays*.

vertices, projected depth value See *depth value of a vertex*.

vertices, rendering performance General recommendations for increasing vertex submission and rendering performance follow: 1. When using indexed data, care should be taken to co-locate all the vertices for a single triangle as near to one another as possible. If the vertices required for a triangle are too far apart in the array, it may cause the graphics adapter to continually re-process subparts of the array as it jumps around. 2. Presorting vertex data by material, shader, and texture settings can help increase the number of vertices that can be submitted and/or rendered in a single function call. 3. Keep the amount of information submitted per vertex as lean as possible. Do not include extra information that is used only occasionally. This must be balanced with continually-changing vertex formats. For example, do not submit a vertex with additional color information if that information is rarely used. 4. There is a balance between submitting too little data and too much data. Most array functions require at least 10–50 vertices to be submitted to overcome the function overhead. On the upper end of the scale, no more than 32KB–64KB of data of vertex data should be submitted. These amounts vary by graphics adapter. 5. Spending too much time grouping a large amount of vertex data together into a single buffer (if it is not a driver-allocated buffer) can present more problems than it solves on the CPU. These problems include cache issues, letting the graphics card stall, and overwhelming the function with too much data.

vertices, strided and streamed data See *gl*Pointer functions*.

VertiLectric A plug-in that allows animators who use *LightWave* or *trueSpace* to create highly-realistic lightning and organic effects. This program is also useful for creating organic objects such as trees, veins, coral, etc.

very large scale integration (VLSI) A technique for placing thousands of active elements on an integrated circuit chip.

VESA See *Video Electronics Standards Association*.

vesicular film A film similar to diazo film that uses diazo salts. It is used to make copies of microfilm originals.

VGA See *Video Graphics Array*.

VGA monitor A computer monitor that operates on the VGA standard.

VHD *Very high density*.

VHS Video home system. A format for recording television signals on half-inch tape cassettes.

video A sequence of electronic signals that can be transformed into animated images for viewing on a display screen.

video camera A camera that can accept a light image and convert it into a television signal.

video codec Electronic circuitry for converting an analog video signal into digital code.

video compact disc (VCD) A format for storing 70 minutes of full-frame, full-motion, MPEG1-compressed video on a normal compact disc or recordable compact disc.

video digitizer A device that converts a video picture into a digital file. Also known as a *frame grabber*.

videodisk A read-only optical disk that holds up to two hours of analog video data and permits instant access to any of the data on the disk.

Video Electronics Standards Association (VESA) A body that sets video standards.

video fields See *fields, video*.

Video for Windows A software architecture for displaying and manipulating time-based data (such as video and audio) on a computer.

video game A computer game in which the action takes place through an animated video display.

Video Graphics Array (VGA) A video display graphics standard that is capable of 640 pixel × 480 pixel × 16 color and 320 pixel × 200 pixel × 256 color displays.

VideoLook A plug-in from the DigiEffects *Web Euphoria* collection that superimposes a rastered video look on a selected image.

video look-up table See *look-up table*.

video mixing The combination of two images by mixing their video signals.

video mode A selection of screen resolutions and available display colors from a PC graphics adapter card.

video multiplexer A device that loads data from several banks of memory into a shift register in parallel and then shifts it out serially at video rates.

video random access memory (VRAM) A type of random access memory (RAM) that can read out all pixels on a scan line in a single memory cycle, thereby increasing the speed and efficiency of memory refresh. Each address can be accessed individually by the computer, but the memory can be treated as a shift register for reading data to the display device.

VideoShop A software package from Strata that allows the user to apply any of 35 image effects to footage, including warping, blurring, and a number of other options. One can create edited movies by combining any number of clips together. *VideoShop* features an enhanced audio-editing module.

video signal An analog signal representing the brightness of an optical image.

videotex A display that is a combination of text and simple, locally rendered graphics. A videotex is produced by a low bandwidth stream of encoded drawing commands, permitting transmission over low bandwidth devices such as phone lines.

vid2flash An application, by Javakitty Media, that adds video to a Web site or banner ad. By encoding video into the .swf media format, the user can stream media to any platform without the need for Media Player software.

View as Tile command A command in the *Game Creation System*. A common problem with artwork repeated or stacked in a 3D world is that distracting patterns appear. Edges look harsh and ill fitting. This command gives the user a preview of what the image will look like when it is placed side by side or stacked one on top of another in a 3D world. It is especially useful when creating walls, fences, or foliage.

view dependence The inability to view a scene without recalculating to generate a new perspective. Ray tracing is an example of a view-dependent solution.

view-dependent progressive mesh (VDPM) See *mesh, view-dependent*.

view frustum The volume of space containing everything that is visible in a three-dimensional scene. The view frustum is shaped like a pyramid whose apex lies at the camera position. It has this shape because it represents the exact volume that would be visible to a camera that is looking through a rectangular window—the computer screen.

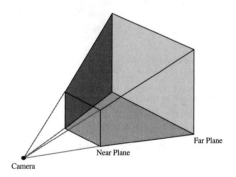

view frustum.

view independence The ability to view a scene without recalculating to generate a new perspective. Since radiosity is view-independent (scene information is stored in the geometry), all that needs to be done when a new view is needed is reorient the polygons, find the normals, and a new display will be generated. So, with radiosity it is possible to generate an interactive walk-through using the existing solution.

viewing angle The perspective from which a scene is shot. Choosing the right viewing angle is an essential part of making a scene more interesting and dynamic. The viewing angle does much more for the scene than simply give the viewer a sense of being above or below it. Used properly, the viewing angle can add a sense of excitement and interest. See *eye-level view*, *bird's- eye view*, and *worm's-eye view*.

viewing coordinates A coordinate system that is centered at the viewpoint of a scene.

viewing geometry The geometry involved in viewing a scene from an observer's viewpoint with a display screen interposed between the viewer and the scene.

view mapping matrix A matrix, created using the view volume specifications and the three-dimensional viewport specification, that is used to transform points in the viewing reference coordinate (VRC) system into normalized projection coordinates.

view orientation matrix A combination of the view reference point, the view plane normal, and the view up vector, used to transform positions represented in world coordinates into positions represented in the viewing reference coordinate (VRC) system.

view plane The plane upon which a three-dimensional image is projected to convert it to two dimensions.

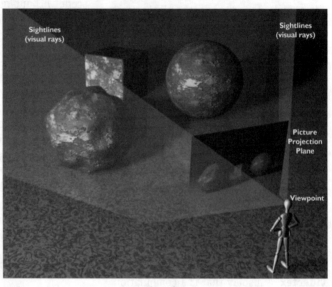

view plane.

view plane normal (VPN) A vector normal to the view plane that helps define the view plane.

viewpoint The coordinates of a point from which a camera or the human eye views a scene.

viewport A rectangular region of screen coordinates onto which the world-coordinate window is to be mapped.

view reference point (VRP) A point on the view plane that is used to help define the view plane.

view up vector (VUP) A vector that defines the *v-axis* on the view plane.

view volume A view of the world that is specified by a projection onto a projection plane and a viewport on the view surface.

virgin object In *form•Z*, a *direct derivative* that will be edited later. Examples of virgin objects include C-MESH surfaces, extrusions, sweeps, and a Boolean operand.

virtual buffer A buffer used with parallel rasterization to compute the image for one of a number of uniformly-sized regions of a display screen.

virtual device metafile (VDM) An ANSI/ISO standard used to establish formats for direct communication of graphics primitives from computers to display devices, printers, and plotters. Also known as *computer graphics interface*.

virtual memory A process by which disk space can be used as a substitute for RAM.

virtual processor An image processing system in which a number of parallel processors are used, one dedicated to each object that is to be part of the final image.

virtual reality (VR) A simulation of real experience that includes stereo vision, with the observed scene coordinated with head movement of the observer; stereo sound; and the ability to control certain parts of the display through the movements of the hand within a special glove.

visibility algorithm In scene-rendering graphics, a method for determining whether a point is visible from the observer's viewpoint.

visibility, in geometric model A capability for grouping objects and then making them visible or invisible as desired. For example, all objects that are electrical outlets, light fixtures, etc., could be grouped in a category called *electric* and then the user could choose whether these objects would or would not be displayed in an image.

visibility, points of A means of partitioning space. Not all techniques divide the space into regions; some identify locations directly. Points of visibility are concerned mainly with obstacle avoidance. Place a search location just a little beyond each convex vertex of each obstacle, just far enough away to avoid collision with the obstacles. The shortest path around obstacles typically passes near these vertices, as though a rubber band connected the start and goal locations. One could possibly extend this method to consider terrain cost by adding these points to those derived from convex uniform polygons.

visibility test A test that determines whether any two points on a mesh can see each other. This can be used to smooth a path between two points. Each time we arrive at a waypoint in our path, we look ahead to the next few waypoints on the list. By creating a line of motion from our current position to each of these waypoints, we can quickly test to determine if the waypoints are "visible." To do this, we test the path against each cell between our current position and the waypoint, using a test function. If the function returns a solid-wall intersection, we know the waypoint is not visible from our current position. Conversely, if we reach the waypoint without such an intersection, we know the point is visible to us. By searching for the farthest visible waypoint up the chain, we can skip over some of the meandering waypoints and smooth out our path.

visible light A light that appears in a scene as part of the rendering. See also *volumetric lighting*.

visible-line determination A technique for determining which lines in an image represent objects concealed by other objects and therefore need not be shown. Also known as *hidden line removal*.

visible-line determination, Appel's algorithm An algorithm for determining the visibility of a line. It defines the quantitative invisibility of a point on a line as the number of front-facing polygons that obscure that point. When a line goes behind a front-facing polygon, the quantitative invisibility of all points from there on is incremented by one until the line passes out from the polygon, at which point all points on the line have the quantitative visibility incremented by one. After this process is completed for a line, the only parts of the line that are visible and therefore should be drawn in the image are those whose quantitative invisibility is zero.

visible-line determination, Roberts's algorithm An algorithm for determining the visibility of a line. It uses a parametric representation of the projector from the eye to a point on the line being tested. A linear-programming approach is used to determine those values of the line equation that cause the projector to pass through a polyhedron, thereby making those portions of the line invisible.

visible spectrum The bandwidth of wavelengths at which electronic emissions can be seen by the human eye. The visible spectrum includes the range of wavelengths from 400 nanometers (red) to 700 nanometers (violet).

visible-surface determination A technique for determining which surfaces of a three-dimensional object cannot be seen because they are behind other objects. Also known as *hidden surface removal*.

VistaPro A 3D application used to create environmental scenes with terrain objects and sky components.

visual acuity The maximum resolution of the human eye. This occurs at the center of the eye; resolution falls off toward the edges. A human's visual acuity is about 1 milliradian.

visual computing Software methods for creating and displaying graphics images.

visual field A collective regional visual area, which is either stimulated aggressively or is inhibited by a direct or indirect pathway or light source.

visualization The creation of computer graphics images that display data for human interpretation. Visualization is particularly useful for multidimensional scientific data.

visual phonemes See *phonemes, visual*.

visual ray theory An early (now disproved) theory of vision by Pythagoras of Samos (582–500 BC). He thought of light as something emitted by the eyes that shines on the objects that we see. He saw light as "antennas" or "tentacles" that reach out to the objects we see.

VITC (Vertical Interval Time Code) Time code that is encoded in the vertical blanking interval of the video signal.

VLSI See *very large scale integration*.

voice recognition The computer application of pattern recognition to the waveforms produced by the spoken word, using the results to institute various program actions.

voice synthesizers Devices that create waveforms that approximate actual spoken words.

voicing The creation of voiced phonemes in computer animation. If the vocal cords vibrate during articulation, the sound is called *voiced*. The vocal cords vibrate under the pressure of the air being forced through them by the lungs. Technically, only consonants are classified as voiced or voiceless, because when a vowel is spoken, the vocal tract is wide open and the vocal chords are vibrating. The important thing to consider about voicing is that voiced phonemes are more likely to be represented visually. For example, vowels are always voiced phonemes, so they are accentuated with visual phonemes. Voicing is important when creating lip-sync animation.

volcano In nature, a mountain, mountain range, or island system (like the Pacific Rim's "Ring of Fire") that is generated by lava flow. Volcanoes can be modeled in a computer graphics image using a particle system technique borrowed from the field of molecular beam epitaxy.

volume label A name (up to 11 characters in MS-DOS) that may be assigned to a floppy or hard disk.

volume rendering The production of an image that shows the spatial relationships of a three-dimensional data set.

volumetric lighting Lighting that makes use of intense light sources like the sun or a theatre spotlight. The light is so in-tense that it actually illuminates the dust in the air. When volumetric qualities are activated in a light and the shadows are set to "hard," the result is the look of an actor on the stage. The location is defined strictly through lighting conventions—no added geometry is needed. Also known as *visible light*.

volumetrics See *animatics*.

von Koch snowflake See *Koch snowflake*.

Voronoi diagram A structure used to map colors in the RGB color space.

Vortex Tiling One of the *Photoshop* plug-ins from the Corel *KPT* collection. *Vortex Tiling* creates an image that converges on a selected point in the original image.

voxel One of an array of equal-sized cubes that comprise a discretely-defined three-dimensional space.

VPN See *view plane normal*.

VRAM See *video random access memory*.

VRP See *view reference point*.

VST A file format for storing a color graphics image. It is an extension of the TGA format.

Vue D'Esprit A high-end environmental scene creation application from E-On Software that allows the user to create scenes with terrains, atmospheres, water, trees, and other flora.

VU Meter The meter that measures volume on a sound-recording device. VU meters help gauge whether recordings are at acceptable audio levels.

VUP See *view up vector*.

VX-1000 Released in 1995 by Sony, one of the first high-quality, MiniDV cameras. Used on many films, including *The Cruise*, *The Saltmen of Tibet*, *Bamboozled*, *Windhorse*, and *The Idiots*.

W

WAC window See *wide area collimating window.*

wagon wheel illusion An example of temporal aliasing, in which wheels of a moving wagon appear to be going backwards in a motion picture.

WaitEvent A subroutine that causes the computer to wait until a user input is received.

walk cycle A description of the completed character's appendage movements during a walk or run.

Walk Designer A *Poser* tool that enables the user to create animated figures that walk realistically.

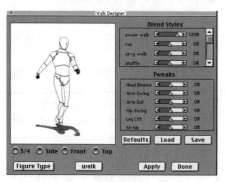

Walk Designer.

walkthrough A virtual reality interaction that allows the viewer to interactively walk through a scene or 3D construct.

wall bumping See *collision detection.*

wallpaper A background pattern, often the tiling of a small geometric pattern.

warm cast The yellow to yellow-orange coloration of a scene or image. It separates sunlight, fire, and candlelight situations.

Warn lighting controls A system of lighting controls that model the directional of lights used by photographers. Unlike the Phong model, which uses only a point light source having an intensity and position, the Warn model uses as a light source a point source that reflects from a hypothetical specular reflecting surface.

Warnock's algorithm A solution of the *hidden surface problem* by recursively subdividing the image area until a single polygon is found to be occluding all other polygons residing in each subdivision.

warping 1. The two-dimensional mapping of an image to produce an image for display. 2. The distortion of an image to create an unusual effect. This technique stretches an image in some areas and compresses it in others. It is accomplished by remapping the pixels of the image using affine transformations that are determined by the relation of each original pixel to some established control points. Warping is often used in association with animation, slowly distorting an image from its original shape to the final shape over a period of time (*see Figure next page*).

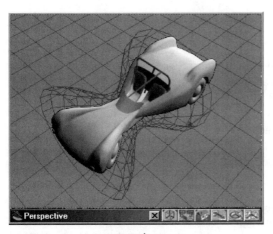

warping.

wash out Increasing the intensity of highlights so that much of the color is lost into white. Washing out, together with darkening shadows, creates a light intensity similar to the sun at high noon.

waterfall 1. A technique for producing an image where the gray scale intensity of the image is proportional to its height. Also known as a *fuzzy rug*. 2. Simulation of a waterfall in *Bryce*. Waterfall simulations are valued effects in computer graphics. This water effect is usually added in a post-production phase of the animation by another application (e.g., Adobe *After Effects* or *Illusion*).

water, fountain See *fountain water*.

water, ocean See *ocean water*.

water simulation, alpha blending for transparency When drawing water, a technique used to give the appearance of transparency. In order to draw alpha-blended triangles properly, however, one must draw the ones farthest from the viewer first, without the help of the Z-buffer. Furthermore, double blending occurs whenever one triangle is visible through another.

water simulation, boundary conditions In nature, bodies of water are usually not square. Rivers, lakes, and oceans have irregular shorelines of varying slope, and islands might exist within these bodies of water. If the bank is very steep or vertical, waves reflect off the shoreline with very little energy loss, whereas if the bank is gently sloped, a wave might have a very weak reflection or none at all. If the waves do not come in straight, they reflect off at an angle. These effects can be simulated by scaling the z^{n+1} value by a local damping coefficient, $d_{i,j}$. A coefficient of 1 allows free movement of the height value without any energy loss, whereas a coefficient of 0 restricts all movement of the water at that location. If these coefficients are distributed and scaled according to the terrain features, waves react to the shoreline more naturally. For example, if the bank is steep, the damping coefficients should make a quick transition from 1 (water) to 0 (land). On the other hand, if the bank is gently sloped, the damping coefficients should make a gradual transition from 1 to 0. In practice, it is usually better to use damping coefficients that are slightly less than 1 in wet cells to produce a little energy loss. Otherwise, wave motion continues indefinitely.

water simulation, buoyant objects Objects float on water because their overall density is less than that of the surrounding water. The force of buoyancy on an object is equal to the weight of the water displaced by that object. This force is actually in the direction of the pressure gradient, but in most cases,

447

the direction normal to the water surface is appropriate. If the shape of the hull of an object is approximated as a set of discrete points, normals, and area patches, the force of buoyancy can be calculated by performing a volume integral over the submerged portion. The volume of water displaced by a section of the hull is:

$$\Delta V_k = \Delta A_k \left(z_{water} - p_{k,z} \right) \hat{n}_{k,z}$$

where z_{water} is the bilinearly-interpolated water height at p_k. Bilinear interpolation is recommended, since other methods might produce primary or first order discontinuities. It is also probably an efficient interpolation method for a regular grid. The buoyant force at this position is:

$$F_k = p\Delta V_k \hat{n}_{water}$$

and the torque is simply:

$$N_k = r_k \times F_k$$

where r_k is the vector from the center of mass to p_k. The total force and torque are calculated by summing the contributions from each hull vertex. Remember also that only the submerged portions contribute to the buoyancy.

water simulation, particulate matter in Modeling the particulate matter present in the water is an important visual cue that can easily be added to a water model. In fact, the distance that the refracted ray travels through the medium in a container is computed as a by-product of the intersection test when the boundaries of water in a container are tested. Using this term, it is possible to blend in a "water color" at the vertices in much the same way that terrain engines and flight simulators blend in a fog color to simulate atmospheric effects. It should be noted that only the refractive term is affected by particulate matter in the water.

water simulation, splashes Splashes can be created by instantaneously displacing one or several z-values at a particular location in a water model. As the solution progresses, waves radiate from this location. This concept illustrates another advantage over explicitly evaluating the general solution; if any discontinuity in $z(t)$ occurs, new values for A_{mn} must be computed with a discrete Fourier transform.

wattage A measurement of electrical power. A light's intensity is measured in wattage.

wave A periodic disturbance that travels through a medium. It has a frequency and amplitude.

Wave deformer Wave is a *Poser* deformer. It attaches itself to any object or figure element selected in the scene, and appears as a wavy object. The Wave deformer has a list of parameters associated with it that the user can modify to create different effects.

wave equation An equation that expresses the motion of waves in water. A water surface can be thought of as a tightly-stretched elastic membrane in which gravity can be ignored. As infinitesimal sections are displaced, their direct neighbors exert linear "spring" forces (surface tension) to minimize the space between them. Since horizontal forces are equalized, particles move in only the z-direction. The vertical position with respect to time and space can be described with the partial differential equation:

$$\frac{\partial^2 z}{\partial t^2} = c^2 \left(\frac{\partial^2 z}{\partial x^2} + \frac{\partial^2 z}{\partial y^2} \right)$$

where c is the speed at which waves travel across the surface.

waveform monitor A special monitor for calibrating the brightness, or luminance, of a video signal. Waveform monitors are used to set the proper white and black levels.

Wavefront OBJ A graphics file format that has no limit on the number of polygons that can be stored. *form•Z* has a built-in Wavefront OBJ export/import capability.

Wave Generator A program that can help achieve complicated vertex animation simulating wave movement. By changing a few parameters, one can create a flowing cape, or ripples on the surface of a pond. In addition, one can use *Wave Generator* to randomize the vertex locations of a *Primal Particles* Emitter object, making the emission of particles appear more random.

wavelength Light, as observed, has a dual nature. It can be manifest as a wave or a particle. Waves are displacements of undulated disturbance. The spaces between the undulations of equal displacement are called the *wavelengths*. The wavelength is the distance between two crests, which are commonly denoted with the Greek letter λ. The height of a crest or trough is called amplitude, as denoted by the letter A.

wavelet A set of mathematical functions that may be used to divide data into different frequency components and then analyze each component with a resolution matched to its scale. For analyzing signals that have discontinuities or sharp spikes, wavelets do a better job than using Fourier series. In addition, some wavelets can be represented by sparse matrices and are therefore ideal for data compression. The process involves sacrificing values to lose the least information possible. By thus minimizing error, we obtain very impressive results. For example, an image of a few hundred kilobytes can be compressed to only a few kilobytes with very little perceptible loss. Areas of little detail are highly compressed, while those of greater details are less compressed. Visually, then, the loss of information is barely perceptible.

wavelets, Haar A type of wavelet that is especially suited to compressing discrete values such as scalar vectors.

Wave Type tab An interface tab in *Wave-Generator* that lets the user specify the type of wave vertex animation he wants to create, from which he can select many wave types.

Weber's law The fact that a just-noticeable increase in sensation depends on the ratio of the increase to the original stimulus.

Webisode A single episode, preview, or other presentation from a Web site using streaming media.

Web resolution The resolution required for graphics on the Web, typically 72 dpi.

wedge, filling Filling for the special case of a wedge that consists of two bounding lines starting from a central point and ending at different points on the arc of a circle or ellipse. First, the rays that define the starting and ending angles with the curve boundary must be computed and used as limit values for the decision variable. Then incremental algorithms, modified to select only internal pixels may be applied.

weight In typography, the thickness of strokes of a character in proportion to the height of the typeface. The weight determines whether a font is classified as light, regular, bold, etc.

weight, center of motion In the human body, the central point around which most general motion takes place, creating balance. The center of motion resides about halfway between our navel and crotch. We turn around this point. When we walk, our appendages all move at different speeds. However, our center of motion unites these movements.

Weiler-Atherton algorithm A solution of the *hidden surface problem* by subdividing the image area along polygon boundaries until in each subdivision a single polygon is found to be occluding all other polygons that are in that subdivision.

Wein's law A law that states that the wavelength of the peak radiance decreases linearly as the temperature increases. The hotter the object gets, the bluer the radiation it emits.

weld To convert vertices that are in close proximity to a common set of coordinates to eliminate cracking. The assumption is that these vertices are close enough so that the differences in their coordinates are due to computer roundoff or accuracy errors and that they are actually all the same vertex.

wheel of reincarnation A name given to the dilemma of assigning functions to special-purpose hardware to improve speed or running them on general-purpose hardware to decrease cost.

white balance Describes a camera that has been calibrated to correctly display white. Once it is calibrated for white, other colors should display properly.

white level The peak level of the luminance (or grayscale) of a video signal (i.e., the brightest part of the image), usually set at 100 IRE.

whitening filter A filter used to increase the white content of a colored area.

white noise Noise whose power is constant across the frequency spectrum.

white space In typography, the amount of blank space left on a page to give it a pleasing appearance.

Whitted's method A technique for deriving refraction formulas.

WID See *window identifier*.

wide angle lens A lens with a very wide field of view and, therefore, a short focal length.

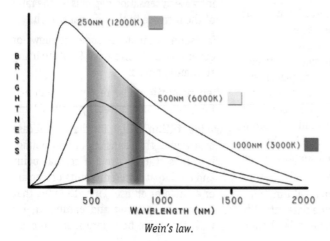

Wein's law.

Typically, the smaller the focal length of the lens (measured in millimeters), the wider the angle.

wide area collimating window (WAC window) An assembly consisting of a beam splitter and a curved mirror that is used to enlarge the image on a cathode-ray tube.

widescreen A video format in which the width of the image significantly exceeds its height. Standard NTSC or PAL video uses an aspect ratio of 4:3. Most film features are shot in a wider-screen aspect ratio. Some cameras include an option for shooting in a 16:9 aspect ratio. However, these modes are not actually any wider. Rather, they are just cropped 4:3 images.

widget An operator interaction technique such as dialogue boxes, file-selection boxes, fixed menus, pop-up menus, choice-buttons, etc.

WID RAM See *window identifier random access memory*.

width scans A method of antialiasing that involves drawing a line normal to the curve and then computing an intensity for every sufficiently-close point along this line.

width table A table stored in a word processor or other publishing software that lists all of the characters in a font and their widths.

Wiggledy A plug-in (part of *CoolPowers*) for *trueSpace* that works by taking a selected polyhedron and randomly modifying each vertex according to the amount of spikiness specified by the user. This plug-in can be used to create things like rocks and boulders.

wild sounds Non-sync sounds recorded by hand "in the wild" using a portable recording system.

winding rule A method for determining whether a point is inside or outside a polygon by summing the angles with respect to the point.

Windmill Fraser Multimedia Developer of shaders for *trueSpace*, including *wfmm reflects*, a reflectance shader, and *sphereglo*, a color and transparency shader for creating geometry-based explosions.

window A method of displaying a document on a computer screen so that elements appear as graphics and features are available to the user as on-screen choices.

window event An input or program action that requires a change in the appearance of a window on the computer screen.

window identifier random access memory (WID RAM) A table of color modes or window identifiers used to decode WID values on output.

window identifier (WID) An attribute stored with each pixel of an image which may be used to identify the associated window or color mode.

Windows An operating system, developed by Microsoft, that is known for its multi-screen graphical user interface.

window-to-viewport mapping A technique in which a rectangular region is specified in world coordinates and is then transformed to a corresponding region in screen coordinates called the *viewport*.

windscreen A covering for a microphone that cuts out the sound of wind or particularly breathy voices.

winged-edge data structure A technique for describing the faces and vertices of a solid that simplifies computations, such as determining whether the faces make up a valid solid.

WinImages Morph A Windows-only image and animation effects application from BlackBelt Systems that features more 2D and 3D effects.

wireframe modeling A graphics modeling technique in which graphics objects are represented by an array of polygons and only the edges of the polygons are drawn.

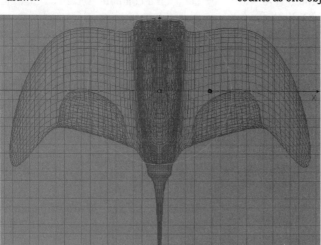

wireframe modeling.

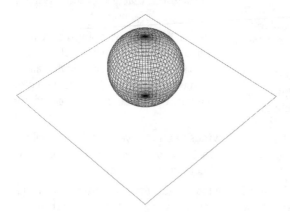

wireframe modeling.

wire printer A dot matrix printer that uses a column of wire hammers to strike a ribbon and produce ink dots on a sheet of paper.

W meter A meter at the bottom of the Level Editor in the *Game Creation System* that measures the number of objects that have been placed in the 3D world. Any object placed into a 3D world, whether it is a small key or a large wall, counts as one object. Adding an enemy, a platform, or a solid-color floor panel also counts as one object.

wobulator A technique for widening the raster line of a cathode-ray tube display by modulating the deflection in an orthogonal direction at a much higher rate than the line scan frequency.

world coordinates A coordinate system used to define the three-dimensional space in which a scene occurs.

World Info Window A menu in *Universe* that allows the user to view and modify the characteristics of his world.

worldwide type designation system (WTDS) A universal system for designating the phosphors used on the face of cathode-ray tubes.

Worley Labs A developer of high-end plug-in collections for *LightWave*, including *Sasquatch*.

WORM See *write once read many*.

worm's-eye view A viewing angle of a scene from a position on the ground plane looking upward.

WPM A file extension denoting an object-oriented graphics file compatible with the Microsoft Windows system.

write once read many (WORM) An optical storage device having a medium on which data can be written only once, but may be read as often as desired.

WTDS See *worldwide type designation system*.

Wu's algorithm An algorithm used to perform color quantization.

WYSIWYG (pronounced wiz-ee-wig) An acronym for "what you see is what you get." A display for a word processing or publishing program that uses graphics to represent the size and shape of text characters as closely as possible so that the displayed page will be nearly identical to the corresponding printed page.

X

X3H3 The American National Standards Committee concerned with graphics specifications.

x axis The horizontal axis of a two-dimensional (x,y) Cartesian coordinate system. Increasing positive values of x move to the right.

XDR External data representation. A technique for sharing data over a network among different computers.

Xenofex A collection of *Photoshop* plug-ins from AlienSkin Software.

Xfrog A high-end (Windows only) application from GreenWorks that allows the user to create all of the components for trees, flowers, and plants in general.

XGA See *Extended Graphics Adapter*.

x-height A method of measuring type size by measuring the height of a lowercase x in a given type font.

XHTML (EXtensible HyperText Markup Language) A Web standard, similar to HTML 4, but stricter, cleaner, and defined as an application of XML.

XLR connectors Three-pronged, balanced audio connectors for connecting microphones and other recording equipment.

X-on/X-off A technique for serial transmission of data to a device that cannot accept data as fast as the transmission rate. When the receiving device has accepted all the information that it can store and process, it sends an *X-off* character to the transmitter, which then pauses. When the receiver is ready to accept more data, it sends an *X-on* character to the transmitter which then begins sending data again.

XOR The exclusive OR logic function. When two inputs are alike, a zero is output; when they are different, a one is output. Normally written in all capital letters, though not an acronym, to indicate a logical function.

XT The designation of the IBM PC/XT personal computer, the first IBM personal computer to have a hard disk. It also applied to clones having similar characteristics, including the Intel 8088 microprocessor.

X terminal A display device for receiving input, displaying text and graphics, and transmitting keyboard output from an X Window System.

X Window System A window operating system developed at the Massachusetts Institute of Technology for use in networked UNIX applications. It is now also available for PCs and the Linux operating system and is widely used as an industry standard.

Xx A fully variable MIDI composition system by U&I.

x-y plotter A plotter that plots using Cartesian coordinates.

xyY space A three-dimensional space for defining colors based on the CIE system. The x component is the chromacity and the y component is the luminance. The z component need not be defined, since in this system the sum of the x, y, and z components is one.

XYZ space See *CIE color space*.

Y

Y The luminance component of a color video signal encoded in the YIQ color space.

Yamenko shaders A collection of shaders, including *Yamenko Phong* and *Yameko Noise*. *Yamenko Phong* is a reflectance shader with settings for Fresnel attenuation, allowing the user to achieve realistic edge highlights. *Yamenko Noise* is a fractal noise shader available in all four shader components; used for uneven surface reflections, e.g., a dirty window.

yaw Periodic angular displacement of a vehicle about the vertical axis in the plane of the longitudinal and lateral axes.

y axis The vertical axis of a two-dimensional (x,y) Cartesian coordinate system. Normally, increasing positive values of y move upward, but in most computer graphics displays, the origin is at the top left corner of the screen and increasing positive values of y move downward.

YCbCr color system A color system in which the luminance component (Y) contains the high-frequency grayscale information to which the eye is most sensitive, while the two chrominance components (Cb and Cr) contain high-frequency color information to which the eye is much less sensitive. Consequently, much of the Cb and Cr information can be discarded in compressing without the eye seeing much difference.

Y/C video Video with separate luma (Y) and chroma (C) video signals. Also known as *S-video* (short for separate video). See also *component video* and *composite video*.

yellow One of the four subtractive process colors (*CMYK*) that are used in four-color printing.

Yellowbook A CD-ROM data standard, used mostly in the recording of audio CDs.

yes option An option for controlling background objects in the *Game Creation System* used to detect a collision with an active object. The user should usually test for a collision with a background object, and insert the appropriate stop action.

YIQ color model The three-dimensional space for defining colors used by U.S. commercial television. The three orthogonal axes are Y, the luminance or brightness component; I, the in-phase signal, which is orange-cyan; and Q, the quadrature signal, which is green-magenta. The space is designed so that the Y signal by itself produces an acceptable black and white picture. The *YIQ* color space is related to the *RGB* color space as follows:

$$\begin{bmatrix} Y \\ I \\ Q \end{bmatrix} = \begin{bmatrix} 0.299 & 0.587 & 0.114 \\ 0.596 & -0.275 & -0.321 \\ 0.212 & -0.528 & 0.311 \end{bmatrix} \begin{bmatrix} R \\ G \\ B \end{bmatrix}$$

YMCK See *CMYK*.

yon 1. A clipping plane perpendicular to the line of sight that is used to eliminate rendering of objects that are too distant to be of interest in a scene. 2. The distance from the viewpoint to the *yon* clipping plane along the line of sight.

YUV color space The range of colors that can be displayed and recorded on digital video. YUV separates the luminance and chrominance signals into Y (luminance) at full bandwidth and UV (Chrominance) at half-bandwidth.

Z

z When rendering a graphics image, the distance perpendicular to the display (image) plane from an object to a plane parallel to the display plane through the viewpoint.

Zapf dingbats A font of *dingbats* (non-alphanumeric symbols) created by typeface designer Hermann Zapf.

z axis The depth axis in a three-dimensional (x,y,z) Cartesian coordinate system.

ZaxWerks Vector Lathe A plug-in for *Universe* that allows the user to model solid objects by rotating a profile around an axis.

Z-Brush A multi-platform 3D modeling and animation application that features intuitive tool usage to create 3D forms as if using a 3D brush on a 2D surface.

z-buffer 1. A two-dimensional array made up of a grid of points on a sea-level plane, each containing the value of the height (z) at that point. 2. An option in the *Game Creation System* for placing floors and ceiling panels at varying heights.

z-buffer algorithm An algorithm, developed by Catmull, that makes use of a frame buffer (in which pixel colors are stored) and a z-buffer with the same number of entries, each of which represents a pixel distance from the back of the clipping plane. The z-buffer is initialized to zero, representing the z value at the back of the plane and the frame buffer is initialized to the selected background color. Each point (x, y) in each buffer represents a width and height. For each pixel, a comparison is made to all objects that have a component at that (x, y) point. If the object's z location is larger than that of the current *z-buffer* value for that pixel (the object is closer than previously-examined objects) the new z value is inserted into the proper member of the *z-buffer* and the object color is inserted into the corresponding member of the frame buffer. At the end of this process, each frame buffer member contains the color of the nearest object at that location.

z compression problem Because of the finite precision of the *z-buffer*, two points that would have different integer z values if close to the view plane may transform to the same z value if they are farther back. This can have a serious effect on the intersections and depth-ordering of distant objects in the final display.

zebra Special lines that can be displayed in a viewfinder, indicating areas of overexposure in an image.

zero phase filter A filter that uses an odd number of samples, thereby producing an output that is situated at the same location as the middle input sample. Compare with *half phase filter*.

zero-sum game A game in which a move that creates an advantage for one player causes an equal disadvantage for the opponent.

zip To compress a file using the *PKZIP* program.

Zip An Iomega drive with removable media, often used for backup of hard drive data.

zone system A photographic system of film exposure and development used to arrive at a particular set of tones when printing. It is the precise control of the highlights and the shadows as captured on film and rendered on paper. This process will also allow the user to make rendering evaluations based on graphic and tonal relationships for computer graphics lighting. There are 11 zones numbered from 0 to 10. *Zone X* is the whitest white possible, devoid of any discernible texture. *Zone IX* is slightly darker than Zone X but still has no texture. *Zone VIII* is grayer than Zone IX and has texture, mainly where highlight patterns and formations are rendered. *Zone VII* renders the textured highlight with detail. It renders the crisp details of snow and sand. *Zone VI* renders skin tones, fabric patterns, and concrete texture. *Zone V*, middle gray, represents what the reflected light meter assumes the scene to be when reading. *Zone IV* renders the visible but dark shadows such as those in tree bark and dark stones. This is a medium dark-gray tone with details. *Zone III* renders the darkest shadows with visible details and texture. It renders a dark gray with detail. *Zone II* is

very dark but still retains discernible texture and detail. *Zone I* is one step away from total black. It is slightly lighter than full black. *Zone 0* is the blackest zone. It has no visible texture or detail of any kind.

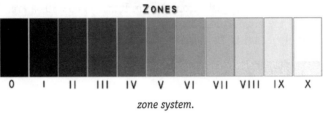

ZONES

0 I II III IV V VI VII VIII IX X

zone system.

zoom 1. To enlarge a portion of an image so that it fills the entire screen. 2. To act, process, or change in apparent magnification of an object on display.

zoom pyramid A sequence of digital images starting with a high-resolution image and continuing with lower-resolution images, each of which has one-half the resolution of the previous image. A zoom pyramid requires only one-third more storage than the high-resolution image and permits the display of an image of any desired resolution, either directly or through interpolation.

zygomatic bone The cheekbone that lies directly under the infraorbital margin. The zygomatic bone is obscured by the infraorbital margin from the front view but is visible on the outer edge where it protrudes from the face, creating the cheekbone. When smiling, the tissue

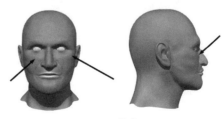

zygomatic bone.

collects in front of the zygomatic bone, which pushes it outward to create the "puffy" cheeks. ⬭

zygomaticus major The facial muscle that raises the mouth upward and outward. It is located around the upper and lower lips and attaches just before the ear. It is used for any expression that requires the upper lip to be raised up and out, such as smiling and laughing. In both of these expressions the zygomaticus major muscle is used to raise the upper lip, pulling it outward in the process. Also known as the *smiling muscle*.

Zygote Media Group The former name of Daz 3D, a creator of high-end 3D computer models and texture maps for use in the entertainment industry.